MODERN FRENCH PAINTERS

by the same author

*

DUTCH PAINTING

ENGLISH PAINTING

AN OUTLINE OF ENGLISH PAINTING

THE MODERN MOVEMENT IN ART

THE STUDY OF ART

JOHN RUSKIN

R. H. "WILENSKI"

"MODERN FRENCH PAINTERS"

ARCOURT, BRACE AND COMPANY, NEW YORK

This book is dedicated

to

S. S.

PRINTED IN GREAT BRITAIN

1949

PREFACE TO THE 1944 EDITION

In this new edition eight colour plates have been added. I have written a note about each in the List of Illustrations (pp. xi-xii). All the original monochrome illustrations have been retained and the full text of the original edition is reprinted.

The original edition was finished a week or two before the Germans again launched destructive war on Europe. The reader must therefore now add for the time being the words 'up to September 1939' to most of the locations of pictures (except of course those described as in Great Britain or America).

When the war is over the French people will be faced with terribly difficult problems of reconstruction. In my first preface I wrote: 'In the period covered by my book the French authoritarian civilization of the Second Empire was replaced by the Liberal Democratic civilization which still exists today.' As I write now a heavy blow has been dealt that liberal democracy by the German invader and by those elements of reaction in France which, as this book incidentally records, have obstructed the noble social efforts of the Third Republic all through its history. As I see things there is much danger, at any rate for the artists, in the present talk of post-war entirely new beginnings and post-war slates wiped wholly clean. Much of that talk is reaction in disguise. For the artists no such clean sweeping is surely possible or desirable. The continuation of the freedom enjoyed under the Third Republic—with the present misfortunes looked on as an interruption—is all the artists really need.

The link-up point for the artists might well be the decade which followed the last war. In that decade, creative artists in France were not subjected to political interference with their work. In the later years of the period covered by my survey conditions changed. Totalitarians spread the doctrine of 'Art for the sake of Authoritarian Government' (which they called 'Art for the State's sake' or 'Art as Public Service'); creative art experiment, independent critical comment, and the doctrine of Art for Art's sake were methodically discredited by that doctrine as aspects of the free thought and free expression which the totalitarians were resolved to destroy; this propaganda seeped into the Parisian art schools as it seeped into art schools in Great Britain; and when I wrote the last sentence in my first Preface the most idealist and productive decade of my lifetime had been dubbed 'The Cocktail Twenties' by the conscious and unconscious agents of Dr. Goebbels, and a whole generation of young artists had been persuaded that aesthetic art is decadent art and that the artist concentrating in the studio on the expression of his personal will is an anti-social nuisance and a selfish pretentious fool.

v

My hope is that there will be no link up with the period of this demoralizing propaganda designed to break the artist's spirit and then to exploit him for political ends. The first essential, as I see things, is re-establishment of the conditions which obtained in France in the twenties—the conditions which encouraged the creative artist to concern himself wholly and confidently with art as such. In those conditions the story here told of creative art flowering within the Third Republic will go on.

London, February, 1944.

PREFACE TO THE 1945 EDITION

In this edition I have corrected some errors of detail, made some additions to the list of works in Appendix I and made good some omissions in the Index.

For 'National Gallery, Millbank' and 'National Gallery, Millbank (Tate Gallery)' please read 'Tate Gallery' throughout, that being now the official title of the Gallery.

London, October, 1944

PREFACE TO THE 1946 EDITION

In this edition I have put right the spelling of *Folies Bergère*, made some other minor corrections and brought the locations of some pictures up to date.

If owners or others will inform me of the present locations of pictures which have changed hands during the war years I shall be greatly obliged to them.

London, December, 1945.

PREFACE TO THE 1947 EDITION

Some further changes in the locations of pictures (kindly communicated to me in answer to the above request) are noted in this edition. Rousseau *La bohémienne endormie* (Plate 42), Dérain *Fenêtre sur le parc* (Plate 66), and Picasso *Chien et poulet* (Plate 79 a) are all now in New York: Museum of Modern Art. Renoir *La danse à la campagne* (sometimes called Le bal à Bougival) is now in Boston: Museum of Fine Arts.

CONTENTS

CONTENTS

CONTENTS

ILLUSTRATIONS: COLOUR PLATES

Pl. A. DEGAS: *Miss Lola au Cirque Fernando*, 1879 *facing page* 36
London. National Gallery, Millbank (Tate Gallery)

Miss Lola, as portrayed by Degas, recalls the angels and putti which float, illuminated, in baroque cupolas; she also recalls Watteau's visions of the Italian Comedy, and Goya's etching, *A Circus Queen*. At the same time she heralds the images of music hall and circus performers set down by Seurat, Lautrec, Rouault, Picasso, Sickert and so many others since 1879 when Degas sent this picture to the Fourth Impressionist Exhibition. (Cf. Pls. C, E, 22*a*, 28*b*, 39*a*, 53*b*, 57*b*, 59, 90*a*, 93.)

Pl. B. CÉZANNE: *Baigneuses devant la tente*, c. 1885 *facing page* 74
Oslo. W. Halvorsen

All the leaders of the Cubist-Classical Renaissance made compositions with nude figures. (Cf. Pls. 19*a*, 19*b*, 41 and 63.) This picture already shows the principles on which Cézanne eventually constructed *Les grandes baigneuses* (Pl. 49). The blond atmosphere of *Baigneuses devant la tente* suggests that it was painted in the north, probably at Vernon where Cézanne worked in 1885. The picture was in Vollard's 1895 exhibition which laid the foundation of Cézanne's fame. (Cf. pp. 150 and 346.)

Pl. C. SEURAT: *Sketch for Chahut*, 1889 *facing page* 106
London. Samuel Courtauld, Esq.

Composition sketch for the final painting (Pl. 28*b*). Seurat evidently felt that the half circle of light spots in the sketch inadequately balanced the rhythms of the main group; in the final painting he therefore added a fifth light and repeated this on the shoe-bows; he also reversed the angle of the conductor's baton, and lightened the hands of the flautist and the face and coat of the man at the bottom on the right. The sketch (which is relatively less wide than the final painting) is about the size of this plate. The subject is the Can-Can quadrille at the Moulin Rouge.

Pl. D. THE DOUANIER ROUSSEAU: *L'octroi*, c. 1897 *facing page* 158
London. Samuel Courtauld, Esq.

The Douanier Rousseau is one of the heroes of this book. He has the direct original vision and the simple original imagination of the primitive artist. *L'octroi* shows the type of suburban toll-house in which he himself served for a number of years. It was probably painted about the same time as *La banlieue* (Pl. 43*a*) and *La carrière* (Pl. 43*b*) and his surrealist achievement *La bohémienne endormie* (Pl. 42).

xi

Pl. E.   PICASSO: *Jeune homme et cheval*, 1905   *facing page* 200
London. National Gallery, Millbank (Tate Gallery)

This gouache belongs to the *saltimbanque* series ('Blue' and 'Pink' periods) discussed on pp. 199 and 200. Its romantic charm and Tanagra aesthetic make Degas' *Miss Lola* (Pl. A) seem mainly drama and Lautrec's *Au Cirque Fernando* (Pl. 22*a*) seem mainly illustration. A few months later Picasso rejected all his works of these periods as 'merely sentiment' and began the infinitely various experiments which became a central influence in European painting for three decades.

Pl. F.   RENOIR: *Femme nouant son soulier, c.* 1916   *facing page* 248
London. Samuel Courtauld, Esq.

In my judgment the paintings of Renoir's last 'Red' period are the finest achievements of his long career. This example, placed here in its chronological position, shows the continued creative energy of an artist who, aged seventy-five and crippled with rheumatism, still contributed to contemporary research.

Pl. G.   MATISSE: *Arbre près de l'étang de Trivaux*, 1916   *facing page* 262
London. National Gallery, Millbank (Tate Gallery)

It would, of course, have been more obvious to have illustrated Matisse's talents by one of his multi-coloured decorative pieces. But I have chosen this one which, standing between his 'Fauve' and decorative pictures on the one hand and his calligraphic genre interiors on the other, shows, I think, the essence of his art. (N.B.—In the Tate Gallery this picture is wrongly titled *La forêt*.)

Pl. H.   CHAGALL: *Poète allongé*, 1915   *facing page* 278
London. National Gallery, Millbank (Tate Gallery)

Since this book was first published the Tate Gallery has acquired this delicate painting described here on p. 261. The subject is partly the last moment of daylight when the lilac sky is about to go cold-grey and partly the poet who is about to awaken from his day-dreaming and go indoors for his supper. For Chagall's surrealism and *Le marchand de bestiaux* (Pl. 67) see pp. 207, 208.

MONOCHROME ILLUSTRATIONS

xiii

ACT I: 1884–1891

ACT II: 1892–1903

MONOCHROME ILLUSTRATIONS

INTERLUDE AND ACT IV: 1914 TO THE PRESENT DAY

PREFACE FOR THE GENERAL READER

*Paris est en Europe la ville occidentale par excellence. Vers elle
émigrent non seulement les hommes mais les choses . . . choses curi-
euses . . . idées . . . états d'âme . . . créations . . . créations
d'artistes réelles ou pensées. . . .*   Chirico

J'ai horreur de me copier.   Picasso

Je ne cherche pas, je trouve.   Picasso

*C'est avec beaucoup de petites histoires que se fait en fin de compte
la grande, la vraie. . . .*   Robert Rey

This book is an attempt to tell the story of modern French painting as developed by
the Impressionists and subsequent adventurers in the last seventy-five years in Paris.
The story begins, properly speaking, with the foundation of the *Salon des Indépendants* in 1884; but it is preceded by a Prologue starting in 1863 when Napoleon III
created the *Salon des Refusés* where Manet's *Déjeuner sur l'herbe* (now an object of
respectful veneration in the Louvre) was described as an affront to decency and the
work of a vulgar self-advertiser or a man afflicted with disquieting taints; and it
continues to the present day—though it does not end there, because the stream of
modern French painting is still flowing and there must be, as the phrase goes, 'as
good fish in the water as ever came out of it'.

    Some of the facts of the matter are pretty widely known. The names of the lead-
ing artists, the most dramatic episodes in their lives, and some of their works are
familiar to everyone who reads books on art and visits picture galleries and
museums. Who has not heard of Impressionism, Cubism, Surrealism? Who does
not know that Renoir painted *Le Moulin de la Galette* and Seurat *Un dimanche d'été à
la Grande Jatte* and The Douanier Rousseau *La bohémienne endormie*? Who does not
know that Van Gogh cut off his ear, that Gauguin pasted bills in Paris for five francs
a day and 'went native' in Tahiti, that The Douanier gave fiddle lessons to tradesmen's children for the money he required to buy his colours, and that Cézanne, at
all times immune from money troubles, inherited a third of a million francs at the
age of forty-seven? Who has not heard of Picasso and Matisse? But many of the
facts of the matter are nevertheless not known because most of the literature on
the subject consists of appreciative comment or art criticism on the one hand and
of dramatized biography on the other. Few, if any, attempts have been made to tell

the story simply as a series of actions by men who lived in certain conditions at a certain date in a certain place. But the time is ripe for plain historical telling of the story; and I have therefore tried to tell it in that way.

As the reader will soon discover, I really offer him four or five books in one. The first book comprises the *Introductions* to the *Prologue* and the four *Acts* into which my text is divided; in these introductions I have described in general critical terms the main developments of modern French painting, decade by decade, as I understand them; and readers who choose to do so can read the series consecutively as a single essay in criticism. The second book comprises the sections headed '*How it happened*' in which I have tried to provide, historically, a kind of Parisian diary recording year by year the outstanding pictures by the original artists and some plays, musical compositions, ballets, exhibitions and so forth, the contacts of these artists with one another and with certain novelists, musicians and dramatists, and to some extent the political happenings which excited the artists or affected their careers. The third book titled '*The Masters' Lives*' comprises biographical notes on the most creative of the deceased artists (Manet being omitted because, properly speaking, the book does not start till after his death); I have divided these biographical notes into the periods covered by the Prologue and the several Acts and attached them to the appropriate sections in order to stress the varying historical importance of each artist in the different decades; but each man's whole biography can, of course, be read as a consecutive story by any reader who chooses to do so. In *Appendices* I offer some *Bibliographical and Catalogue Notes* for students, some lists showing the present distribution of some pictures exhibited without success by certain artists in their lifetime, and a summary of an entertaining play by The Douanier Rousseau. The *Illustrations*, which are chronologically arranged, are designed to tell my story, to some extent, without the text.

The sections headed '*How it happened*' have cost me much labour, because writers on art—and more especially French writers on art—have a singular complex against dates and facts and indices. But I venture to hope that the labour may be judged to have been worth while because, although those sections are little more than an indication of the lines on which a cross-view of this kind might eventually be written, they nevertheless reveal, I submit, the overlapping of the generations, the moments when certain creative ideas appeared in the Parisian art world, and a social pattern in which distinctive parts were played by *civilization* (i.e. local government concerned with social services), creative *culture* (free thought and creative action by curious and original spirits), the *dilettanti* (persons of moderate means, education and taste who 'patronize' art and talk a lot about it and occasionally buy pictures), the *rich collectors* and *museums* (the only owners capable of preserving works in a permanent way), and the *dealers* (the international art trade which is concerned with pictures as objects in commerce).

In the period covered by my book the French authoritarian civilization of the Second Empire was replaced by the Liberal Democratic civilization which still exists in France today. In '*How it happened*' we see this French Liberal Democratic civilization continuously protecting creative culture against political attacks by extremists on the Right and on the Left, and allowing it ever more liberty to choose its own problems and solve them in its own way; and we see there too that French civilization has thus made Paris the intellectual and artistic centre of the modern world. This French civilization realized that all civilizations have need of creative culture, which includes creative artists, because local social conditions can never be rendered static (even by the most brutally tyrannical civilization) and the necessary adjustments to changing conditions can only be made with continuous help from free and original thought. But it has also realized that no civilization can harness culture for its own immediate and local purposes, and that culture cannot create to order or confine its curiosity to fields deemed appropriate by a local civilization —(since culture's field of vision is not a locality but life itself, and its field of service is not a city or a national or a racial group but humanity as such); French civilization, for its own immediate and local purposes, has accordingly used other artists— artists of the type which I described in *The Modern Movement in Art* as *derivative popular artists* (i.e. artists who work outside the field of creative culture because they are concerned to establish contact with the familiar experience of some particular type or group of spectators); it has used these other artists—these cultural vulgarizors—to dilute, or otherwise adapt, for its purposes, the contributions of original culture which are always incomprehensible by the masses at the time of their first appearance and which are rarely suitable, in their initial form, for direct local, temporary or material social service; and, esteeming it rightly within the function of governing civilizors to make the civilizees 'feel good' about their local art, the French civilizors have always officially supported these cultural vulgarizors because large numbers of the civilizees can readily understand their productions.

I am not concerned in this book with these officially supported derivative-popular cultural vulgarizors who have been far more numerous than our original artists all through our period. But the reader must remember that these vulgarizors, organized in official art institutions and official exhibiting societies, have been all the time influential as active enemies of our original artists whose works they pillaged; that many of them were famous in their lifetime (though the reputations of such artists habitually die with them); and that, by flattering the average well-to-do French bourgeois civilizees they were always able to extract a good deal of money from their pockets. And it is also important to remember that the French Liberal Democratic civilization has hardly ever officially bought pictures by any of the original artists we are concerned with, or willingly admitted gifts of them to the State museums in the artists' lifetime.[1] As a result of these conditions the original artists in Paris had all the liberty and protection they required for their creative efforts; they set themselves their own problems and solved them by their signal powers; and they put the results of their researches on the table for all the world to use as it might please; but they had to look to the dilettanti and to dealers and to some extent to rich collectors and American museums for material support.

The dilettanti, as I show in '*How it happened*', always tend to discover creative artists when they have arrived at middle age and to use their appreciation of those artists as a rod with which to bludgeon the younger original men. There

[1] Cf. below, pp. 149–155.

have, nevertheless, been some dilettanti who helped our artists in their early days when they most required assistance, and I have made a point of recording as many such cases as I could. Rich collectors, museums and dealers tend to buy pictures by artists who are dead; and, as everyone knows, the exchange values in the international art trade of works by the original nineteenth century French masters have rapidly risen in the twentieth century; but the reader will find here few records of 'sensational' or 'romantic' increases in such exchange values because I am wholly concerned with the attitudes, motives and procedures of the artists who created the pictures and I am not at all concerned with the profits made by the international art trade. I have, however, recorded the encouragement, in recent years, of some living French creative artists by some rich American collectors and by the New York University Museum of Living Art and the New York Museum of Modern Art and some other American museums; and I have also recorded some actions by dealers who gave, or are giving, financial assistance to artists in their lifetime— assistance which has enabled those artists to continue their creative work, and is not the less valuable if the motive behind it is the dealer's conviction that the artist's pictures will eventually appeal to rich collectors and museums and thus bring him eventually much profit.

The life stories of some of our artists have frequently been presented as a kind of martyrology. But to present them thus is a romantic, if not indeed a ghoulish, perversion of the facts. Thanks to independent incomes or to actions by contemporary dilettanti and dealers, none of these artists had in fact material difficulties greater than those encountered daily by thousands of wage earners who live from week to week. Manet, Degas, Cézanne and Lautrec were men with private fortunes; Van Gogh was supported by his brother; Gauguin was only in great financial difficulties for two or three periods each lasting a few weeks or months; Pissarro, Renoir, Monet and Sisley after a few lean years were helped by dealers till success came to them in various degrees when they were between forty and fifty; and both Matisse and Picasso after brief struggles were discovered by dealers and collectors who were eager to secure their works. There were, of course, original artists in this period who had no private fortunes, who were unable to sell their pictures, and whom nobody at any time was willing to finance; but the names and works of those artists are unknown to us because in this period, as in others, they had to turn to other occupations (where they were perhaps successful) or else they died; and in this connection we must remember that the four unschooled men of the people whose works I chronicle—The Douanier Rousseau, Bombois, Bauchant and Vivin—all earned their living in other ways for a great many years.

The pattern of French life, as indicated by 'How it happened', includes the parts played at various times by professional art critics. There can, I think, be no doubt that the test of a critic is his ability to understand the original art of his own generation; because, if he cannot understand the creative activity of men with whom he has the best opportunities of contact, he is not likely to understand the analogous activities of men, now dead, who produced other forms of original art in other times and places. The critics whose works survive as criticism are the men who began by surveying contemporary production, which was there in its entirety before them, and who proved themselves able to distinguish the original artists from the cultural vulgarizors and the hack practitioners. The critics who began at the other end, the critics, that is, who have attempted to judge the art of their own generation by standards extracted from the fragmentary remains of the art of past ages preserved in museums, have always failed to understand contemporary original production and failed likewise to distinguish original from popular and hack productions in the past. For my own part I know that the value of my art-critical, as distinguished from my art-historical, work depends on the extent to which I may in fact have understood the work of the original artists of my own generation—the work, that is to say, of the men born between 1880 and 1895, the men who appeared as artists in the period between 1900 and the German Invasion of 1914. I have studied that art since the days when I worked in the Parisian art schools between 1907 and 1909 (and frequented the then very small and most modest Café du Dôme on the Boulevard Montparnasse); I like to think that I have learned progressively to understand it; and I have certainly become progressively more enthusiastic in my admiration of its achievements. I have grown older in the intervening years—but so have the artists; and though I have sometimes found it difficult to follow their later productions—(particularly some of the later productions of the always astonishing Picasso)—I rarely find myself very puzzled for long by any of their pictures or completely out of sympathy with their attitudes and procedures. This being so, I offer with some confidence my comments on Fauvism, Cubism, Futurism, Purism, Functionalism, Surrealism and Dada. But my comments on the works by the succeeding generation I offer with some diffidence, because a critic, who is an enthusiast for the original art of his own generation, is always at a disadvantage when called on to understand the art of generations following his own. To understand the works of these new generations the critic has to make adjustments in his standards and explore new ways of thought; and eventually, of course, he is faced by a generation removed from him by the barriers that separate the fire, vitality and confidence of adventurous youth from the complacent knowledge of timid, cold and sedentary old age. In this book I am called on to understand the art which I title Neo-Surrealism to distinguish it from the Surrealism of Chagall, Chirico, Picasso and some others in the nineteen-twenties. And here I find myself in presence of artists who have cast aside those aesthetic and formal pre-occupations which meant almost everything to the original artists of my generation, artists who seem to prefer direction from a civilization to freedom in culture's own domain, artists who no longer abominate the photographic image but work with images resembling coloured photographs and coloured cinematographic 'stills', artists who make the subject-matter the dominant factor and select a subject-matter which I, personally, cannot contemplate without discomfort and distaste. In these circumstances, as an art historian, I have allowed these Neo-Surrealist artists to speak as far as might be for themselves, merely adding what seem to me to be historical precedents for their attitudes and procedures; I have indicated in 'How it happened' the chronological accompaniments of their efforts in other fields—Pirandello's plays, for example, and James Joyce's Ulysses; and, as a critic, I have named, in the Introduction to Act IV, those who appear to me to be the original artists, and made it clear that, though I personally dislike the central characters of their productions, I realize that Freudian concepts were bound to be explored as new material by some original artists in the nineteen-twenties, and that the terrible and ignoble sadisms which have disfigured life in the totalitarian countries of Europe in the nineteen-thirties may consciously or unconsciously be symbolized in certain aspects of Neo-Surrealist productions.[1]

Looking back on the whole period covered by this book the peak decades from my standpoint were the 'eighties, the first decade of the twentieth century, and above all the nineteen-twenties when the mind and conscience of the world was more truly liberal, international and idealistic than at any moment in my lifetime. In the *Introduction* to *Act IV* I have discussed the *Associationist* ideas which ruled in the nineteen-twenties and produced such fine results in aesthetic and architectural art. Here I need only add a despairing hope that the forces now engaged everywhere, for their own ends, in vilification of that decade, will fail to do more than temporarily obscure the high idealism which it served.[2]

[1] Cf. pp. 281-284.   [2] Cf. pp. 267, 271-273, 315-317.

London, August, 1939.

PREFACE FOR STUDENTS

The ideal historical treatment of my subject would be, of course, a comparative chronology in three or four columns. But since this book is primarily intended for the general reader, I have written the historical sections, '*How it happened*,' as, to some extent, a narrative which the student can use as a chronology with the aid of the General Index at the end.

The sources of my information are (*a*) my knowledge, as far as it goes, of the pictures, books, plays, ballets, etc., referred to; (*b*) some of the existing books on the subject; and (*c*) the contemporary French and English press. As regards the first, I have referred only to pictures which I have seen or of which I had reproductions before me at the time of writing; no other pictures are referred to in the text or included in the lists in Appendix I. As regards the second, I have used the standard biographies of the artists, and I have named those books, and others which I have drawn upon, in Appendix I. As regards the third, I have had the assistance of Mr. Felix Crosse whose services I detail in the following acknowledgment.

ACKNOWLEDGMENT TO MR. CROSSE

I have had great help, particularly in the earlier portions of this book, from Mr. Felix Crosse, who worked for me at the British Museum and in the London Library and brought me extracts from books and newspapers and many of the countless dates I asked for, and who also placed at my disposal his extensive knowledge of French political history in the nineteenth century. I am very particularly indebted to his assistance.

OTHER ACKNOWLEDGMENTS

I have also been much helped by many other people. They include Mr. Beaumont Newhall of the New York Museum of Modern Art and Mr. Freeman Lewis with Messrs. Reynal and Hitchcock, who have procured for me a great deal of information from American museums and collectors; the directors and secretaries of many American museums; Mr. Walt Kuhn, who has sent me information about the Armory Exhibition of 1913; many American collectors (especially Mr. Sam Lewisohn, Mr. Carter Harrison, Mr. Stephen C. Clark and Mr. Preston Harrison) and some English collectors, including Sir Kenneth Clark, who have sent me photographs or catalogues; M. Félix Fénéon, who gave me some valuable information about the attitude of the French intelligentsia to the Anarchists in the 'nineties; Mr. John Palmer author of *Studies in the Contemporary Theatre*, Mr. Carl Wildman Assistant Lecturer in French in the University of Manchester, and Mr. Rollo Myers (translator of M. Cocteau's *Coq et Arlequin*), who helped me to find the dates of some theatrical productions and ballets with which our artists were connected; M. Vizzavona of Paris who lent me reproductions of all his photographs for study; Mr. Willard Morgan of New York who sent me photographs and catalogues; Mme Paul Guillaume and Mme Leray, M. Georges Wildenstein, M. Paul Rosenberg, MM. Durand-Ruel, M. Kahnweiler, M. Bignou, M. Henri Bing, MM. Bernheim Jeune and Messrs. J. Seligmann of Paris, and Messrs. Reid & Lefevre, Messrs. Tooth, Messrs. Brown and Phillips, Mrs. Marchant, and Mr. Zwemmer of London and others who provided photographs and information. I am also much indebted to Mr. Alfred Cracknell of London, who has made me some splendid photographs, to Mr. Godfray Sellick who has made the General Index, and to helpful secretaries at various stages.

DRAMATIS PERSONAE

The following are among the painters whose works are discussed in this book.[1]

REALISM AND IMPRESSIONISM

Edouard Manet	1832–1883
Camille Pissarro	1830–1903
Edgar Degas	1834–1917
Paul Cézanne	1839–1906
Claude Monet	1840–1926
Alfred Sisley	1840–1899
Auguste Renoir	1841–1919
Berthe Morisot	1840–1895
Paul Gauguin	1848–1903
Vincent van Gogh	1853–1890
Henri de Toulouse-Lautrec	1864–1901
Pierre Bonnard	Born 1867
Jean Edouard Vuillard	Born 1868
Pablo Picasso	Born 1881
Albert Marquet	Born 1875
Maurice Utrillo	Born 1883

SYMBOLISM AND SYNTHETISM

Paul Gauguin	1848–1903
Vincent van Gogh	1853–1890
Emile Bernard	Born 1868
Paul Sérusier	1863–1927

THE MODERN CLASSICAL RENAISSANCE

Paul Cézanne	1839–1906
Georges Seurat	1859–1891
Auguste Renoir	1841–1919
The Douanier Rousseau	1844–1910
Paul Gauguin	1848–1903

[1]When an artist has played a part in more than one movement his name is repeated.

DRAMATIS PERSONAE

Vincent Van Gogh	1853–1890
H. de Toulouse-Lautrec	1864–1901
Emile Bernard	Born 1868
Maurice Denis	Born 1870
Paul Sérusier	1863–1927
Henri Matisse	Born 1869
Amédée Modigliani	1884–1920
Gino Severini	Born 1883

FAUVISM

Henri Matisse	Born 1869
Maurice de Vlaminck	Born 1876
André Derain	Born 1880
Georges Rouault	Born 1871
Othon Friesz	Born 1879
Raoul Dufy	Born 1879
Kees Van Dongen	Born 1877
Albert Marquet	Born 1875

FUTURISM

Gino Severini	Born 1883
Robert Delaunay	Born 1882
Marcel Duchamp	Born 1887

RHYTHMIC DECORATION

Henri Matisse	Born 1869
Raoul Dufy	Born 1879
Amédée Modigliani	1884–1920
Georges Rouault	Born 1871
Pablo Picasso	Born 1881

CUBISM, FUNCTIONALISM, AND STYLE MÉCANIQUE

Paul Cézanne	Born 1839
Pablo Picasso	Born 1881
Georges Braque	Born 1881
Juan Gris	1887–1922
André Derain	Born 1880
Amédée Ozenfant	Born 1886
C. E. Jeanneret (Le Corbusier)	Born 1888
Fernand Léger	Born 1881
Jean Metzinger	Born 1883
André Lhote	Born 1885
R. de la Fresnaye	1885–1925

DRAMATIS PERSONAE

EXPRESSIONISM

Vincent van Gogh	1853–1890
Georges Rouault	Born 1871
Pablo Picasso	Born 1881
Amédée Modigliani	1884–1920
Maurice de Vlaminck	Born 1876
Haim Soutine	Born 1894

SURREALISM

Odilon Redon	1840–1916
James Ensor	Born 1860
The Douanier Rousseau	1844–1910
Marc Chagall	Born 1887
Giorgio de Chirico	Born 1888
Pablo Picasso	Born 1881
Francis Picabia	Born 1879
Joan Miro	Born 1893
Pierre Roy	Born 1880
Jean Lurçat	Born 1892

DADA

Paul Klee	Born 1879
Marcel Duchamp	Born 1887
Francis Picabia	Born 1879
Max Ernst	Born 1891

NEO-SURREALISM

Max Ernst	Born 1891
Salvador Dali	Born 1904
Pablo Picasso	Born 1881

UNSCHOOLED PAINTERS

The Douanier Rousseau	1844–1910
Camille Bombois	Born 1883
André Bauchant	Born 1873
Louis Vivin	1861–1936

PROLOGUE

1863-1883

From the *Salon des Refusés* to the death of Manet

PROLOGUE: 1863-1883

From the *Salon des Refusés* to the death of Manet

INTRODUCTION

I begin this book with the *Portrait de Victorine Meurend* (Pl. 1) which Manet painted at the age of thirty in 1862. The picture was Manet's first experiment in his personal handling of oil paint which is known in the studios as *peinture claire* and is now specifically associated with his name. Manet's aim in his *peinture claire* (developed in *La femme au perroquet* (Pl. 4) of 1866, perfected in *La prune* (Pl. 10) of 1878 and used with final virtuosity in his last exhibition picture *Un bar aux Folies Bergères*[1] in 1881) was to achieve a high-keyed picture by direct statement of the light passages in 'fat' flowing pigment and subsequent painting of the half-tones and darks into this light pigment while it was still wet. In Manet's hands this method—the exact opposite of academic practice which worked not downwards from the light passages but upwards from the dark ones—was a technical procedure invented to express his personal aesthetic and his personal pleasure in the power of oil paint to provide an equivalent of surfaces suffused with light. But this technical procedure was only one aspect of Manet's achievements. In other aspects he was a champion of the Realist and of the Impressionist movements.

The *Realist Movement* which had begun at the end of the 'forties was a development of the Romantic Movement of the 'thirties and 'forties. The Romantics had thought of art as in the first place a record of emotional excitement in the artist and secondly—but only secondly—as a record of the particular fragments of life which had aroused in him that particular excitement; and they had proved in their paintings and novels and in a poem like Baudelaire's *Une charogne*—(as Rembrandt had proved in *Carcass of an ox* two centuries before)—that an exceptionally sensitive, passionate or intelligent artist can charm, move or interest us even though the fragments of life he is concerned with are not charming, or moving or interesting in themselves. The Realists went further and declared that *all* fragments of life are charming or moving or interesting in themselves and all equally suitable as material for art; that the artist must try to record fragments of life as impersonally as possible in the scientific spirit, because the fragments recorded are more important than the state of mind or the emotional condition of the artist; and that the artist must restrict himself to records of his actual experience in contemporary life, because all forms of 'imaginative art' are really nothing but mendacious non-

[1] London. National Gallery (Courtauld Collection).

3

sense. Before the period of this Prologue these realist doctrines had already produced, in the field of letters, the social documentations in novels by Balzac and
George Sand, the acceptance of the *petite bourgeoisie* as material for art in Flaubert's
Madame Bovary of 1857 and the use of hospital data as material in Jules and Edmond
de Goncourt's *Sœur Philomène* of 1861; and in painting they had been responsible
for Courbet's two huge pictures *Un enterrement à Ornans*[1] of 1849 and *L'atelier du
peintre*[1] of 1855. By 1863 Courbet was no longer concerned to make pioneer
realist gestures in his pictures because he had canalised his desire to be realist,
defiant and actual by concerning himself with socialist politics; and as an artist he
was now comparatively suave and academic in his methods. The torch had passed
to Manet whose exhibition pictures in the 'sixties—*Le déjeuner sur l'herbe*,[1] *Olympia*[1]
and so forth—were all, in one sense, realist gestures which defied the canons not
only of academic but also of romantic art.

But Manet in these exhibition pictures was not only a champion of the realist
doctrines. He was also concerned to challenge the Old Masters; *Le déjeuner sur
l'herbe* of 1863 is a realist version of Giorgione's *Concert Champêtre* with the composition taken from a sixteenth century engraving after Raphael; the *Matador mort*[2]
of 1864 is a challenge to the unknown Spanish seventeenth century painter of
Orlando Muerto (now in the London National Gallery but then in Paris); *Olympia* of
1863 is a realist version of the recumbent Venus motif which had inspired Giorgione, Titian and Velasquez; *Les musiciens ambulants*[3] of 1862, *Le philosophe*[4] of 1865
and *Les bulles de savon*[5] of 1868 are challenges to Ribera and Murillo; *Le balcon*[1] of
1869 is a challenge to Goya. The traditional characters in these pictures are evident
to all to-day. But in the 'sixties they were looked on as purely realist and therefore as purely revolutionary pictures.

Art historians habitually suggest that Manet became a convert to Impressionism
towards the end of his career. But in point of fact he made his first contributions to
that movement concurrently with his traditional and realist exhibition pictures
and with his experiments in *peinture claire*. He began to paint Impressionist records
of race-course scenes, marines and ports quite early in the 'sixties: in 1864 he saw
the fight between the North and South American ships, the *Kearsage* and the
Alabama, off Cherbourg harbour and painted a picture of the scene from Impressionist sketches;[6] in 1867 he painted an Impressionist view of the grounds of
the *Exposition Universelle*[7] of that year; and he had become an Impressionist master
when he painted *Le bateau de Folkestone* (Pl. 5B) in 1869.

To understand the *Impressionist Movement* we must remember that it began with
Manet's pictures of the type of *Le bateau de Folkestone* (Pl. 5B) and that all Manet's
pictures of this type are within the Realist doctrines as defined above; for the
scenes depicted in all these pictures are scenes of everyday contemporary life,
there is no Romantic parade of the artist's emotion, and the artist has been at
pains to persuade us that he has declined all imaginative excursions. But Im-

[1] Paris. Louvre.　　　　　　　　　　　　　[2] Philadelphia. J. Widener.
[3] New York. Mr. and Mrs. Chester Dale.　　[4] Chicago. Art Institute.
[5] New York. Adolph Lewisohn.　　　　　　[6] Philadelphia. John J. Johnson.
[7] Oslo: National Gallery.

1. MANET
Victorine Meurend, 1862
Boston. Robert Treat Paine 2nd, Esq.

2. BOUDIN
Trouville : L'embarcadère, 1863
Scotland. A. T. Reid, Esq.

pressionism, though within the realist theory, was also a development of and a contribution to that theory with several features of its own. The first contribution of Impressionism to the realist theory was the attachment of high value to an effect of *accident* in the subject and disposal of the picture. The Impressionist painter is always concerned to persuade us that his subject is his visual impression of a scene accidentally encountered, and that he has made it a point of honour to accept everything as it chanced to appear at the particular moment when he happened to be there. This doctrine, the first article of faith in the Impressionist creed, was rarely in fact carried out as completely as theory demanded or as might be supposed from the pictures. In practice the pioneer Impressionists were always unconsciously guided by their personal feeling for design, and that feeling in turn was conditioned by the influence of compositions produced by the camera (then still a new toy) and by the compositions in Japanese prints which were popular in Paris from the middle of the 'fifties (as I show in 'How it happened'). But though the doctrine was thus unconsciously violated in these ways it nevertheless determined the special character of the Impressionist pictures within the Realist Movement; and we see it at work not only in Manet's *Le bateau de Folkestone* (Pl. 5B) but also in Monet's *Le pont neuf* (Pl. 5A), in Pissarro's *La route de Versailles à Louveciennes* (Pl. 8A), Renoir's *Canotiers à Chatou* (Pl. 6A), Sisley's *Effet de neige* (Pl. 8B), Degas' *Voiture aux courses* (Pl. 9A) and *Femme à sa toilette* (Pl. 13), and in Renoir's elaborate *Le Moulin de la Galette* (Pl. 9B). This first article of the Impressionist creed led, moreover, inevitably to a second. For once it was held that the picture must be a record of the scene as it appeared at the moment when the artist chanced to be there, it was only logical to hold that all pictures of outdoor scenes must be begun and finished on the spot—(a drastic innovation at that time, since outdoor subjects had hitherto been habitually painted in the studio from notes and sketches). And this again led to a third doctrine that the actual handling of the pigment must be evidently spontaneous and rapid—a frank confession that when the artist sat down to paint he worked as rapidly as possible in order to record as much as possible while there; and thus all Impressionist pictures are stamped quite frankly and deliberately with the spontaneous character of sketches.

From the outset of the Impressionist movement we can observe certain differences in the attitudes and procedures of the individual artists. Degas, for example, subscribed to the realist-impressionist doctrine that the scene must be depicted— or look as though it had been depicted—without arrangement by the artist. In practice of course he composed deliberately, and he was more influenced than the others were by compositions derived from photographs; but in theory the basis of the composition in all his works of the 'sixties and 'seventies and early 'eighties is the doctrine that the scene is recorded as it chanced to appear at the moment when he happened to be there. But Degas was never happy with the doctrine that an outdoor scene must be painted on the spot; he detested the discomforts of painting out-of-doors—('*la peinture*,' he said, '*ce n'est pas du sport*')—and in practice he painted all his race-course and other outdoor scenes and his occasional landscapes in his studio.[1] There were also differences from the outset between the

[1] Cf. below, p. 52.

influence of photographs on the procedures of Degas, Manet, Monet and Renoir. Degas was influenced as stated by the composition in photographs; but his actual language of representation was not essentially the camera's language which is restricted to records of light, reflections of light, obstructions to light and cast shadows. Manet, however, in pictures like *Le bateau de Folkestone* used a language of representation which was fundamentally photographic—or to put it in studio terms, Manet painted in these pictures 'by the tone values', i.e. he imitated the tonal effects of phenomena at a particular moment in a particular light. In photographic tone-painting the artist half closes his eyes in order to eliminate the effects of local colour as far as possible, and he attempts to see the objects before him— as the camera has always seen them and as television also now sees them—as a pattern made up of degrees of light. In pictures thus painted the colour always tends to be a series of graduations of tinted greys—pink greys and yellow greys for the light passages and blue greys and buff greys graduated to black in the shadows, because any attempt to stress the local colours in any part of the picture generally results in a passage which 'jumps' as the phrase goes 'out of tone'. In Manet's hands these greys have a subtle coral and oyster quality rendered lively by suddenly contrasted darks. But to understand the later developments of modern painting— which were partly a reaction against photographic painting 'by the tone values'— we must begin by realising that Manet's Impressionist pictures are properly called photographic. Manet followed, or rather created, the Impressionist doctrine that a picture must be frankly stamped with the spontaneous character of a sketch, and his photographic representations are therefore, compared with the camera's representations, extremely incomplete; but, setting aside of course the incidence of the oyster and coral tinting, the difference between Manet's representational language in his Impressionist pictures like *Le bateau de Folkestone* (Pl. 5B), and the camera's language, is really a difference not of kind but of degree. Manet launched one kind of Impressionism in the early 'sixties with pictures like *Le bateau de Folkestone*; this photographic Impressionism was first imitated by Claude Monet in a number of pictures including *Le pont neuf* (Pl. 5A) painted between 1870 and 1873—(and as I write, in 1939, it is still being imitated by thousands of painters in Europe, America and the British Dominions). Renoir launched another and quite different type of Impressionism in pictures like *Canotiers à Chatou* (Pl. 6A) at the end of the 'sixties. The prelude to this contribution by Renoir was a chance meeting with the Barbizon painter Diaz in Fontainebleau forest; Renoir was painting in an old smock of a type used by the *ouvriers* in the china factory where he worked in his youth; this garment caused curious trippers to surround his easel and stare and giggle; Diaz appeared, drove the crowd away, and said, looking at Renoir's picture: 'It is not bad, but why the devil do you paint so black?' This corresponded to Renoir's own desires at the moment; for he saw sunlight as rose and citron and the shadows in sunlight as violet and blue; and thereafter he used these colours in his landscapes to the amazement of Sisley, who generally painted with him, and told him he was '*fou*'. Renoir's first personal contribution was thus the rainbow palette which we habitually associate with the whole Impressionist school, and the first works, in which the colours of the spectrum predominate, were his first

Impressionist pictures of people boating on the river or stopping for refreshment at a riverside restaurant La Grenouillère which he began about 1869 and continued in the 'seventies. Monochrome reproduction cannot, of course, stress the essential differences between this type of Impressionist picture by Renoir—*Canotiers à Chatou* (Pl. 6A) for example—and Manet's photographic 'tone-value' Impressionism in *Le bateau de Folkestone* (Pl. 5B). In theory Renoir's picture is the same as Manet's; it is Realist in the sense that it depicts a scene of contemporary life and it is specifically Impressionist in the sense that it purports to record the scene, as it appeared at the moment, without previous planning or subsequent composition. But Renoir's language of representation in his pictures of this type was never photographic, it was never tonal sketching, never the language of the camera; Renoir never aimed primarily at imitating the tonal effects of phenomena in a particular light but always at creating an equivalent for the animation of a scene by sunlight. Though he never used the spectrum palette scientifically (as it was used later by Seurat and his school) he began from 1869 onwards to use rainbow colouring in an instinctive way as a symbol for sunlight; and, since he was never primarily concerned with tone, he was never impelled to half close his eyes against local colours which, on the contrary, he habitually exploited as factors contributing to the gaiety of the picture. In the middle and later 'seventies he sometimes merged the local colours in the general scheme of his rainbow colouring, but he never suppressed them dogmatically—there are salmon pinks and cerulean blues in *Le Moulin de la Galette* (Pl. 9B) for example—and he never repressed them to a gamut of tinted greys.

To his first contribution—the rainbow palette—Renoir added a second contribution in this same first series of Impressionist pictures. This second contribution was the use of what painters refer to as 'broken colour'—the application, that is, of pigment in small strokes of different tints which merge at a distance—as distinguished from the application of tints mixed up on the palette. This procedure of broken colour had already been used by a number of painters; it had been used by Watteau (in whose work Renoir especially delighted and whom he emulated when he was over seventy in the splendid picture *Les grandes laveuses* (Pl. 71A); it had been used in his later work with charming delicacy by Gainsborough; it had been used by Velasquez in the pink and silver of the Infanta's dress,[1] and by Goya in the gold and silver of the Queen's dress in *The Family of King Charles IV*[1]; and it had been used in certain works by Delacroix. But it had not been used by the Realist school in the 'sixties; Courbet, a coarse colourist, never attempted it; and Manet in these early years mixed all his oyster and coral tints on his palette. The Impressionists thus owed the introduction of broken colour to Renoir, who used it charmingly with a light and vibrant touch, as a means auxiliary to the rainbow palette, to suggest the vivacity and movement of sunlight as distinguished from the still light from a grey sky which was admirably rendered by Corot and by Boudin (Pl. 2) and which dominates Manet's Impressionism of the 'sixties and also the early pictures by Pissarro and Monet. Pissarro was the first to imitate Renoir's double contribution as we see in *La Route de Versailles à Louveciennes* (Pl. 8A) of 1870.

[1] Madrid. Prado.

Monet became a follower of Renoir and adopted his rainbow palette and broken colour about 1872, and in 1873 he painted in Renoir's manner a bird's-eye view of a Parisian street scene in sunlight *Le Boulevard des Capucines*,[1] and thus launched a new type of picture (which Pissarro imitated in a series of bird's-eye views of street scenes between 1892 and 1900). Sisley also was soon converted to Renoir's innovations; and in the later 'seventies Manet himself began to fuse Renoir's spectrum colouring with his own *peinture claire* in pictures like *Les paveurs de la rue de Berne*[2] of 1878.

Renoir was personal in yet another manner at this period. He was the most essentially French of the Impressionist painters; he was not fundamentally attracted by any art except French art; the drama in Spanish painting, which appealed so much to Manet, meant little to him; and alone of the Impressionists he resisted the craze for '*japonaiseries*' from its beginning. In this period, when he was a young man, he was frankly an admirer of everything pretty—pretty women, pretty children, pretty flowers, pictures by Watteau, Fragonard and Boucher and French eighteenth century tapestries and sculpture. As an Impressionist he worked within the Realist Movement and always painted contemporary subjects; but he was not happy with the Realist doctrine that *all* fragments of life are charming, moving or interesting, and all equally suitable as material for art, and as he was not happy with the doctrine he ignored it. He chose pretty models and painted them in pretty clothes, with flowers on their hats and in their hands; and he posed them in pleasant arbours between sunlight and shade—as in *La balançoire*[3] and *Sur la terrasse* (Pl. 12). When we look at his *Le Moulin de la Galette* (Pl. 9B) we have the impression that all the girls who danced there were as pretty as girls can be—and it is not till we look at Lautrec's *Au bal du Moulin de la Galette* (Pl. 32B), painted some thirteen years later, that we begin to wonder if they really were. In pictures like *Le Moulin de la Galette* and *Sur la terrasse* Renoir made no resistance to the femininity of the models he selected; he was so essentially French that he was not afraid of it and so essentially an artist that he transformed it to art from the moment the canvas received the first rainbow touches from his brush. In 1881, after a tour in Italy where he had contact with the Venetian solution of this problem and with the art of Raphael, he began to tire of Impressionism and to develop a feeling for larger forms; and he then dropped the rainbow technique and painted with more attention to line and with tints prepared on the palette. We see the new technique and the new method of sublimation in the lovely picture *La baigneuse blonde* (Pl. 16). Degas' attitude when painting women in this period was, of course, entirely different. Fundamentally snobbish, neurotic and pessimist, Degas seems to say to us: 'These creatures, commonly mistaken by men for seductive sirens, are in fact just miserable plebeian puppets performing characteristic gestures in the sordid occupations by which they earn their living; but the gestures make intriguing patterns enhanced by accidents of light and setting, and those patterns and those accidents are worth recording—so here goes!' On occasion Degas painted dancers who seem to us at first glance to be pretty girls; but the effect of

---

[1] Moscow. Museum of Modern Western Art.
[2] London. Samuel Courtauld.   [3] Paris. Louvre.

prettiness—as in the popular *Danseuse sur la scène*[1]—is mainly due to the light, the clothes, the gesture and the setting; and as the 'seventies advanced he shows a marked preference for plebeian and ungainly models like the woman who posed for the Realist-Impressionist pastel *Femme à sa toilette* (Pl. 13).

Manet, Renoir and Degas, the three masters of the Realist-Impressionist Movement, were helped by realist and impressionist theories and doctrines; but since they were masters they were less dependent upon the theories and doctrines than were the secondary figures Monet, Pissarro and Sisley. For the theories and doctrines of a movement, though always largely created by the masters, are always above all of service to the secondary and the minor figures who accept direction from them and base their procedures on the masters' works. The secondary figures in the Impressionist movement, Monet, Pissarro and Sisley, made nevertheless in the 'seventies a contribution of their own. That contribution was made exclusively in their landscapes, and it was largely the result of the realist-impressionist doctrine which instructed the artists to paint out-of-doors—or from windows as the next best thing. For working thus the artists became, like farmers or sailors, eminently sensitive to the changes of the season and the weather, and it can be said with truth of Monet, Pissarro and Sisley—(as it cannot be said with truth of Manet, Renoir and Degas)—that they continued and developed the art created by Turner's atmospheric landscapes and Constable's landscape sketches. Any really representative collection of works by Monet, Pissarro and Sisley in this period will always be not so much a series of landscape views as a series of records of effects of weather in spring, summer, autumn and winter, and it is for this reason that I have chosen the rain picture *Le pont neuf* (Pl. 5A) by Monet, the sunlit summer scenes *Les falaises de Pourville* (Pl. 15B) by Monet and *La route de Versailles à Louveciennes* (Pl. 8A) by Pissarro, and the *Effet de neige* (Pl. 8B) by Sisley, to represent their art. These three artists had made their whole contribution by 1883 when this Prologue ends; their later works—(notwithstanding Pissarro's connection with Seurat)—were really the same in character as their works in this period; as secondary figures they lacked the continuous creative impulse which had carried Manet from the *Matador mort* to *Le bateau de Folkestone* and *La prune* and thence to the *Bar aux Folies Bergères*, which carried Degas from his early academic 'history' pictures to *Voiture aux courses* and *Femme à sa toilette* and to a later development, which I shall chronicle, in the 'eighties, and which enabled Renoir to keep pace with contemporary efforts not only in the 'seventies and 'eighties but also, as I shall show, in the first decades of the new century when he was old and partly paralysed and worked in a wheeled chair with a brush strapped to his contracted right hand.

And Cézanne? What was his contribution in the 'sixties and 'seventies? Where does he stand in relation to the Realist-Impressionist Movement and in relation to these masters and the secondary figures? Cézanne from the outset was a solitary worker—though he was intimate with Pissarro, Renoir and Monet, and had contact also with the others. He began as a romantic who knew Baudelaire's *Une charogne* by heart and was excited by Wagner's music. Under the influence of his friend Zola he became a realist in the early 'sixties and his first enthusiasms were

[1] Paris. Louvre.

9

for Courbet and Manet. But warmer-blooded and more deeply passionate than Courbet or Manet—(he is said to have had some negro blood in his veins)—he handled paint, in his youth, with sensuality and richness. In *L'oncle Dominique* (Pl. 3), painted in the middle 'sixties, he has applied some passages with a palette-knife (a trick borrowed from Courbet) and he has rejoiced in the rich chord of the sitter's southern skin and the brown-black hair. But he has not only enjoyed the handling of the copious pigment and the warmth of the personality before him; he has also observed the formal effects of the colour-shapes; he has perceived the moustache and beard as a dark brown circle enclosing a pink one and balanced in a particular way with the shapes of creamy white and brick red made by the collar and tie. Already in the 'sixties Cézanne was thus less concerned to paint a realist portrait than to handle oil paint in a particular way and to record his personal experience of related forms and colours; and in his portraits of this period we perceive a dualism in his reactions—a warm deep sympathy with the spirit of the sitter as a human being and an aesthetic concern with colour and form as such. This dualism which appears in *L'oncle Dominique* is still more conspicuous in the *Achille Emperaire*,[1] (a study of a crippled dwarf seated in a high-backed, chintz-covered chair with his shrunken legs supported on a stool)—the outstanding masterpiece among Cézanne's portraits in the 'sixties. As a result of this dualism he found it a relief, from the outset, to turn to landscape and still life painting where the human element was not there to disturb him; and here too in this period his work was much influenced by romantic and realist ideals. He also found it a relief to turn to compositions with nude or dressed figures which he painted without models—sometimes with the aid of photographs or prints. I reproduce one such composition *Conversation* (Pl. 7) of 1870–1871 which was evidently painted without models (though the figures are said to be portraits of his sisters and two friends).

In the 'seventies Cézanne passed through what is known as his Impressionist phase. But properly speaking Cézanne was never an Impressionist. In the early 'seventies he was in frequent contact with Pissarro, and in his company and under his influence he tried his hand at Impressionist methods; but at bottom he never accepted the Impressionist doctrines; he was never content to stamp his pictures with the character of sketches; and he was never willing to sacrifice local colours in a photographic tonal record. The celebrated picture *La maison de Zola à Medan*[2] painted in 1880, for example, a rich green landscape 'accidented', as the French say, with the red roofs of the houses half hidden by the trees, is only Impressionist in the sense that it purports to record a scene without imaginative excursions or deliberate composition; but there is nothing here of Manet's photographic tonal sketching and no shower here of rainbow sunlight as in Renoir's Impressionism; and the picture bears really less resemblance to Impressionist landscapes than to Cézanne's own *La route tournante* (Pl. 15A) painted in 1881–1882 when his personal attitude to landscape is already clear. In *La route tournante* we have the work of an artist who is more alive to the *structure* of the scene depicted than Manet or Renoir and the other Impressionists were alive to it. Cézanne's per-

[1] Paris. Lecomte Collection. [2] London. Messrs. Reid & Lefevre.

ception of the scene, warmed by his sensation in perceiving it, was fundamentally a grasp of the formal relations of the individual forms and colours; at bottom *La route tournante* is an architectural statement, a record of Cézanne's feeling that the scene is affective because the tree forms and house forms are dovetailed together in a three-dimensional formal pattern poised on the curve created by the road. We can see the difference between Cézanne's art in 1881–2 and Impressionist painting if we compare *La route tournante* with Monet's *Les falaises de Pourville* (Pl. 15B) which dates from the same time. Monet's picture records the artist's concern with light and atmosphere and weather; the spectrum coloured edge of cliff that constitutes the foreground is there to emphasise the summer haze upon the sea from which the white spots of the sailing boats sing out in a pattern that is deliberately haphazard. Monet's picture is admittedly complete and successful within its special limitations. But Cézanne in *La route tournante* was trying to do something new and much more difficult; and in so doing he was already laying foundations that he and others were to build on in the next decade.

Two other artists of historical importance to our story appeared at this period— Gustave Moreau and Odilon Redon. Both are most properly described as painters of ideas and mental images as distinguished from painters of visual experience. Gustave Moreau sent his works to the *Salon* in the 'seventies and I reproduce his *L'apparition* (Pl. 11A) which was a 'picture of the year' in 1876. Trained as an academic artist and exclusively concerned with the dramatic illustration of his imaginative experience Moreau was quite unaffected by the Realist and Impressionist movements, and the leading Impressionists detested his pictures—(Renoir said that he put jewels on his figures to impress the Jew Ephrussi, editor of the *Gazette des Beaux Arts*, and Degas said that he was the kind of person who would put gold watch chains on the Olympian gods). But Moreau was nevertheless a man of unusual intelligence who twenty years later proved himself an inspiring teacher of Georges Rouault and Henri Matisse. Odilon Redon appeared as the creator of imaginative lithographs in 1880 after some years' exercise as a painter, sculptor and etcher. Redon like Moreau was unaffected by Realist and Impressionist doctrines and we shall find him in contact with the artists who reacted against those doctrines in the period next to be considered; the nearest equivalent to William Blake that France has yet produced, Redon was concerned to record the images of his mind's eye; and as those images were closely related to dream images he ranks as a pioneer worker in the field we now habitually refer to as Surrealism. I reproduce his *Gnome* (Pl. 11B) from a series of lithographs called *Dans le rêve* which he published in 1879.

It is common knowledge in our day that Manet fought an uphill battle single handed in the 'sixties (when Cézanne had not begun to exhibit and the Impressionists had scarcely appeared) and that Manet and the Impressionists and Cézanne were bitterly attacked in the 'seventies. To understand the opposition we must remember that in the 'sixties our artists lived in Second Empire Paris. In 'How it happened' I try to visualise them in that setting. When we get to 1870 and 1871 we have a general upheaval only comparable with the conditions caused by the German invasion of 1914. In 1870 and 1871 the writers and artists were lost sight of in the prevailing turmoil, and in 'How it happened' I try, by recording their individual fortunes, to show the turmoil from their point of view. From 1872 to 1883 our artists witnessed the birth struggles of the Liberal French Republic as we know it; in this period their persistent enemies were the academic artists of the official *Salon* and the critics who upheld those artists, but on certain occasions they were also attacked in Right Wing political propaganda which frightened the dealers and collectors by describing Realism and Impressionism as socially subversive doctrines. In 1883, when Manet died, French Liberalism had conquered; and with that conquest and Manet's last pictures our Prologue ends.

3. CÉZANNE
L'oncle Dominique, c. 1866
New York. Museum of Modern Art (Bliss)

4. MANET
La femme au perroquet, 1866
New York. Metropolitan Museum

PROLOGUE: HOW IT HAPPENED

SCENE I: 1863-1867

From the *Salon des Refusés* to the *Exposition Universelle*

In the spring of 1863 the Emperor Napoleon III paid a surprise and incognito visit to the *Salon des Beaux Arts* which was not yet open to the public though the pictures were hung. He went round the exhibition and then asked to see the works rejected by the Jury. He was taken to a gallery where hundreds of pictures were stacked face inwards against the walls; porters were ordered to parade some before him; becoming impatient he turned some round himself; when he had seen a score or so he pronounced the rejected pictures 'quite as good' as those exhibited; and he asked the Administration of the Beaux Arts to revise the verdicts. The Administration replied that the number of would-be artists had greatly increased in recent years and it was essential to dam the stream against this flood of individualities ('*mettre une digue devant tant d'individualités*') and thus discourage these *êtres déclassés* who might otherwise become '*un danger sérieux pour la société*'. Thereupon the Emperor gave a categoric order that all the rejected pictures should be shown in the Palais de l'Industrie in rooms adjacent to the official *Salon*; the Beaux Arts obeyed; and the artists were invited to leave their pictures for a *Salon des Refusés*. The Emperor had been moved to this action because numerous protests against the Jury's rejections had appeared in the press and some artists with influence had persuaded friends at Court to bring the matter to his notice. Rumour had it that both the Emperor and Empress were glad of this chance to snub the pretentious de Niewe-kerke, lover of the Princesse Mathilde, who lived, as Surintendant of the Beaux Arts and Director of the Imperial Museums, in a suite of seventeen rooms on the first floor of the Louvre and was *ex officio* responsible for the *Salon*.

This *Salon des Refusés*, the first landmark in our story, brings a number of our artists on the scene—Edouard Manet and Camille Pissarro as exhibitors; Claude Monet, Auguste Renoir, Alfred Sisley, Jean-Frédéric Bazille and Paul Cézanne, all still students, among the visitors. Manet at this time was thirty-one. His father, a magistrate, had died the year before and left him enough money to secure his independence. Tall, elegant, wearing the fashionable full beard, and lunching frequently at the fashionable rendez-vous the Café Tortoni, Manet was essentially the urban gentleman-artist as distinguished from provincial and bohemian types. He married in this year a Dutch pianist Suzanne Leenhoff; and his friend the poet Baudelaire wrote on the occasion: 'Manet had just told me the most astonishing news. He leaves tonight for Holland, whence he will bring back a *wife*. His excuses are that the lady is handsome, good-natured and an admirable musician. *Tant de trésors dans une seule personne n'est-ce pas monstrueux?*' Baudelaire at this time was forty-two, and had just published his essay *C. G. Le peintre de la vie moderne* on Constantin Guys, the witty illustrator of Second Empire life. Manet had been before the public since 1861 when his *Chanteur espagnol (Le guitarrero)*[1] and *Les parents de l'artiste*[2] had been shown at the *Salon*. His pictures in the *Salon des Refusés* were *Victorine en costume d'espada*,[3] *Jeune homme en costume de majo*[3] and the celebrated *Déjeuner sur l'herbe*.[4] Earlier in the year he had had a one-man show in the gallery of a dealer named Martinet, which included *Lola de Valence*[4], *Musique aux Tuileries*,[5] *Musiciens ambulants (Le vieux musicien)*[6] and *La chanteuse des rues*;[7] the press had bitterly attacked these pictures and one visitor was so enraged by the *Musique aux Tuileries* that he tried to destroy it with his stick. Pissarro's pictures in the *Salon des Refusés* were landscapes which attracted no attention from the public or the critics. Pissarro at this time, though quite unknown, was already thirty-three—two years older than Manet. Son of a Creole mother and a French Jewish father who owned an iron-mongery business at Saint Thomas in the Danish West Indies, he was born in 1830, and he was sent as a boy to school near Paris. Recalled to his father's business, he was restless and discontented because he was eager to paint ('In Saint Thomas', he wrote later, 'I was in a well-paid job, but I couldn't stick it'). Actually he stuck it for six years; and then, at the age of twenty-five, he ran away to Venezuela with an artist friend. Faced with the *fait accompli*, his father had accepted his vocation and financed his return to Paris, where he had worked obscurely since 1855. At the time of the *Salon des Refusés* he was not acquainted with Manet, Monet, Renoir, Sisley or Bazille; but he knew Cézanne whom he had met at an informal art school called the *Académie Suisse* where there was no tuition but always a model and artists dropped in to draw from the figure as they pleased. Cézanne in 1863 was twenty-four and a student in Paris on an allowance provided by his father, a prosperous banker of Aix-en-Provence. His chief friend at this time was Emile Zola, who had been at school with him at Aix and was now twenty-three and a clerk at the Librairie Hachette in Paris after working for two years as a clerk at the docks.

The Emperor and Empress paid a formal visit to the *Salon des Refusés* and were shocked by Manet's *Le Déjeuner sur l'herbe* (then titled *Le bain*). The Empress pretended not to see it; the Emperor examined it in silence and then said: '*Ce tableau offense la pudeur.*' The critics and the public both followed the Imperial lead; and Manet was widely spoken of as a seeker for notoriety who had painted a scandalous picture of a naked woman in a wood with two dressed men. From the standpoint of the artists this scandal caused by *Le Déjeuner sur l'herbe* was nothing less than a disaster—because it enabled the Beaux Arts academicians, who had told the Emperor that the rejected pictures were the work of dangerous 'individualities' and subversive *déclassés*, to say in the event, 'We warned you, sir, and this is the

[1] New York. W. Church Osborn.
[2] Paris. M. et Mme Ernest Rouart.
[3] New York. Metropolitan Museum.
[4] Paris. Louvre.
[5] London. National Gallery, Millbank.
[6] New York. Mr. and Mrs. Chester Dale.
[7] Boston. Mrs. Montgomery Sears.

result.' Thus the *Salon des Refusés* was never repeated and individual artists with creative talent had to wait twenty years before the *Salon des Indépendants* gave them the same freedom to exhibit.

Manet's pictures, misjudged by the Emperor and Empress, the general public and most of the critics, were understood and appreciated by the four young men, Monet, Renoir, Sisley and Bazille, whom I have named among the visitors to the *Salon des Refusés*. Monet and Sisley were twenty-three when they saw this exhibition and Manet's show at Martinet's gallery. Renoir and Bazille were twenty-two. All four were students in an art school run by an academic artist, Marc-Gabriel Gleyre. Monet, son of a grocer of Le Havre, had come to Paris at the age of seventeen on money saved from the sale of caricatures; he had worked in various art schools, done two years' military service, and returned to Le Havre where he met J. B. Jongkind (born 1819) and Eugène Boudin (born 1824), marine and plage painters; Jongkind and Boudin often painted together and they allowed the youth Monet to paint with them; and impressed with his talent they had persuaded his parents to finance his return for a further period of study in Paris. Auguste Renoir was the son of a tailor of Limoges; he had worked as a boy as a painter's apprentice in a china factory and later in a factory of portable devotional pictures used by mission-aries; he had aspired all the time to be an independent artist and by 1862 he had saved enough money to pay for some tuition in the *Académie Gleyre*. Frédéric Bazille and Alfred Sisley were both at this time monied amateurs. Bazille's father was a well-to-do gentleman of Montpellier. Sisley's father was an Englishman, established in Paris, who conducted a profitable business with South America, and had sent his son to England at the age of eighteen to study business methods; but Sisley, like Pissarro, detested business and wanted to be a painter, and his father eventually put up the money for his studies in Paris.

After seeing the *Salon des Refusés* and Manet's exhibition at Martinet's gallery, Monet, Renoir, Sisley and Bazille decided that they had had enough of Gleyre's uninspiring academic teaching; and in July of this year, 1863, they left together. Bazille, as the '*copain*' with most money, hired a studio in Paris and invited Renoir to share it. Monet and Sisley who wanted to specialise in landscape, took lodgings in the then still rural suburbs. Monet sometimes dropped in at the *Académie Suisse* to draw from the figure; there he met Pissarro, made friends with him, and took him round to Bazille's studio. Pissarro then introduced Cézanne. And thus the group, later known as the Impressionists, began. All these young artists looked upon Pissarro—ten years their senior, married and already an exhibitor—as their informal leader; but there was as yet no plan for a formal group; the members of the circle were just friends who all hoped to attract attention in the *Salon* year by year and to sell their pictures, meanwhile, to dealers for such sums as they could get. Pissarro was kind, deeply respectful of creative effort, but also experienced and cautious; Monet was tough, provincial, obstinate, ambitious and strong-willed; Renoir was easy-going, delicately good-looking, happy-go-lucky, fond of the girls, and gay. None of these artists were yet acquainted with Manet, whom they worshipped from afar, and none had yet heard the name of Degas. But Manet and Degas were acquainted—as Manet had accosted Degas one day in the Louvre when he was copying the *Infanta* by Velasquez and said to him, '*Quel toupet! Mon gaillard*, you'll be lucky if you can copy that.'

Degas, whose early life I record, with those of Renoir and Cézanne, in the section headed 'The Masters' Lives',[1] was twenty-nine in 1863 and he had already painted *Jeunes Spartiates s'exerçant à la lutte*[2] and a number of family portraits, and made plans for a series of 'history' pictures to be exhibited at the *Salon*. Plentifully supplied with money from his father, a rich banker, he had no need to hurry to exhibit and he had not yet sent any pictures to the Salon, or become a member of any artistic 'set'.

There were of course a number of artistic 'sets' in Second Empire Paris. One such foregathered in the house of M. Tiburce Morisot, Advisory Councillor at the Cour de Comptes and Secretary-General of the Crédit Foncier, who had studied painting and practised as an architect in earlier life. Tiburce Morisot was a rich man with a country house between Pontoise and Auvers and a town house with a studio on the heights of the Trocadéro. He had three daughters, Berthe, Edna and Yves. Berthe Morisot, who was twenty-two in 1863, had a genuine artistic talent. Both Berthe and Edna had worked under various masters including Corot who was now approaching seventy and who allowed Berthe to sign her early pictures *Elève de Corot*. M. and Mme Morisot entertained painters and musicians in their Paris house, and their guests, besides Corot, included Alfred Stevens (a Belgian academic painter of fashionably dressed women), Carolus Duran (late a successful portrait painter), and the musician Rossini, aged sixty-six, who doubtless wore one of the wigs which terrified Jean Cocteau's mother.[3]

In 1864 we thus have nine of our artists on the scene—Manet with an independent income, Degas and Cézanne with allowances from their banker fathers, Sisley, Bazille and Berthe Morisot also well supplied with money from rich parents, Pissarro helped with a little money from his mother who had come to live in Paris, and Renoir and Monet with nothing but the money they could earn.

In 1865 Zola who had just published *La confession de Claude* and who was working as journalist and reviewer, was introduced by Cézanne to the habitués of Bazille's studio. In 1866 the group accepted as newcomers Armand Guillaumin, whom Cézanne had met at the *Académie Suisse*, and Antoine Guillemet who knew Manet and took Cézanne and Zola to his studio. About the same time Monet was taken to Manet's studio by a sculptor and critic named Zacharie Astruc who had just sat to Manet for his portrait; and the other members of the group met Manet at the *Café Guerbois* on the Avenue de Clichy where Manet habitually went in the evenings.

The Parisian cafés have rendered great service to our artists. On the neutral ground of the café, the artist is nobody's host and nobody's guest; he comes and goes as he pleases, wears what he pleases, and drinks, if he pleases, no more than

---

[1] cf. p. 51 ss.   [2] London. National Gallery, Millbank.

[3] Rossini used to stay with Cocteau's grandparents. '*Rossini terrifiait ma mère*,' Cocteau tells us. '*Mon grand-père la poussait le matin dans sa chambre à coucher porteuse d'un panier d'œufs. Sur le piano elle apercevait une suite de perruques destinées à l'œuf monumental qui émergeait des couvertures et des édredons. Ces perruques, en haut des supports allaient de la chevelure courte à la chevelure longue. Le maître les portait les unes après les autres, jusqu'à la visite fictive du coiffeur.*' (Jean Cocteau: *Portraits-Souvenir*.)

a single cup of coffee or a single glass of beer in an evening that begins at sunset and ends only when the last visitor is willing to leave and allow the waiters to stack the chairs and tables and sleepily close the doors. Conversation at artists' meetings in cafés like the Café Guerbois in the 'sixties, and in others (which I shall refer to later) in succeeding decades, was uninhibited. Here creative painters met creative writers and musicians and exchanged ideas and aspirations and pooled experience of their enemies—the academic artists, the collectors of 'Old Masters', the slim dealers and agents, and so forth. In these meetings, where all the company were bound by the freemasonry of creative, as distinguished from commercial, enterprise, the beginner had equal rights with the already famous or notorious artists; at the Café Guerbois, in the years between the *Salon des Refusés* and the Franco-Prussian War, Pissarro, Cézanne and the younger men from Bazille's studio sat on equal terms with Manet and Degas; and by their side there were writers like Zola, the novelist and critic Edmond Duranty, the journalist and critic Théodore Duret, and the poet and critic Catulle Mendès. The habitués at these meetings were nevertheless divided, inevitably, into several groups and *cliques*. Of the artists we are concerned with Monet and Renoir were intimates— both being sons of the people and forcibly concerned to earn their living, and neither was ever intimate with Manet or Degas, both members of the monied middle class and in personal sympathy—though their politics were opposed (Manet being a Liberal Republican who wore fashionable clothes and Degas a Royalist and reactionary who affected the fashions of some years back). Bazille, Sisley and Pissarro were links between these fundamentally hostile though outwardly friendly groups. Degas made friends especially with Duranty and discussed with him the doctrines which led him, before the end of this period, to abandon the composition of academic 'history' pictures which chiefly occupied him in the opening years. Cézanne, who had a horror of discussions, was always ill at ease in this company which assembled to argue and exchange ideas, and he went accordingly less often than the others. Zola, who was liked by Manet and disliked by Renoir and Degas, was always more or less at loggerheads with Duranty who thought little of his writing and took his cue in this, as in other matters, from Degas. Nothing comparable with these café meetings existed anywhere outside Paris in the 'sixties. English artists and writers, for example, had no such opportunities to assemble informally on neutral ground. And it is tempting to speculate on what might have happened if Ruskin, who was often in Paris in the 'sixties, had wandered one night from the Hôtel Meurice (his 'luxuriously small and luxuriously quiet cell'), and found himself outside the Café Guerbois and gone in. As it was, Ruskin knew nothing of these reunions, and to the end of his life he never mentioned the name of any of the artists we are concerned with, in any of his letters, lectures or books.

There was much talk at the Café Guerbois of the realist doctrines as they appeared in Manet's pictures, in Jules and Edmond de Goncourt's servant girl novel *Germinie Lacerteux* (published in 1865) and their play *Henriette Maréchal* which was hissed off the stage of the Comédie Française the same year. The poets discussed were Baudelaire (who was now paralysed in Brussels), the Parnassians

(Théodore de Banville, Leconte de Lisle, J. M. Hérédia, François Coppée, Sully Prudhomme, Catulle Mendès) and a new man Paul Verlaine (now twenty-two and a clerk at the Hôtel de Ville) who had just written *Poèmes saturniens* and who appeared in 1866 in the Parnassian anthology *Le Parnasse contemporain*. Parnassian poems would seem at first glance to have little in common with the realist paintings and novels of this time. But there was a connecting link. For the Parnassians held the doctrine that the artist's emotions must not be paraded in his productions and that, avoiding romantic self-confessions, he must write as far as might be in a detached impersonal and objective way.

In the 'sixties all the painters in the Café Guerbois group submitted their pictures to the official *Salon* year by year. The jury of this *Salon*, elected each year by the artist members of the Institute, was composed for the most part of academic painters and sculptors, who favoured the numerous academic artists whose names no longer survive, and also some half-and-half artists like Fantin-Latour (who painted photographic flower pieces and portraits and drew lithographs illustrating Wagner's operas) and Puvis de Chavannes who painted semi-classical mural decorations. In the *Salon* of 1864 Fantin had a group picture *Hommage à Delacroix*[1] showing Manet, Whistler, the engraver Bracquemond, Alphonse Legros (who later settled in England), Edmond Duranty, Baudelaire, Fantin himself and some others grouped round a portrait of Delacroix (who had died in 1863); Whistler had proposed to Fantin that Rossetti should be included in this group—because he had such a decorative head; but nothing came of the suggestion; and indeed Rossetti had no place in this company, for he wrote this year on a visit to Paris: 'The new French school is simple putrescence and decomposition. There is a man named Manet (to whose studio I was taken by Fantin) whose pictures are for the most part mere scrawls and who seems to be one of the lights of the school. Courbet the head of it is not much better.' In these years 1864–1867 the artists we are concerned with were more often accepted by the *Salon* than might have been expected; Cézanne's works were indeed rejected every year; and all the artists suffered from caprices of the jury and from its especially academic constitution in 1867; but they all had pictures hung in certain *Salons*. Manet's *Le Christ aux Anges*[2] and *Une course de taureaux* (from which the *Matador mort* was subsequently cut) were shown in 1864, and his *Olympia* and *Le Christ insulté par les soldats*[3] were shown in 1865; his *Acteur tragique*[4] and *Le fifre*[5] were rejected in 1866; in 1867, the year of an *Exposition Universelle*, he did not submit as he had erected a Pavilion at his own expense in the Exhibition grounds and hung a large number of his pictures there. Pissarro's landscapes were accepted every year except 1867. Monet's *Camille*[6] was accepted in 1866, but his *L'été: Femmes dans un jardin*[6] was rejected in 1867. Sisley's landscapes were accepted in 1866 and rejected in 1867. Renoir's *Esmeralda*[7] was shown in 1864, his *Soirée d'été*[6] in 1865, and his *Diane chasseresse*[8]

[1] Paris. Louvre.
[2] New York. Metropolitan Museum.
[3] Chicago. Art Institute (James Deering Collection).
[4] New York. George Vanderbilt.
[5] Paris. Louvre.
[6] German Collection.
[7] Destroyed.
[8] New York. Private Collection.

5A. MONET
Le Pont Neuf, 1870
Headington. Sir Michael Sadler
5B. MANET
Le bateau de Folkestone, 1869
Winterthur. M. O. Reinhardt

6A. RENOIR
Canotiers à Chatou, 1872
New York. Adolph Lewisohn, Esq.
6B. RENOIR
La femme d'Algers, 1870
New York. Chester Dale, Esq.

was rejected in 1867. Berthe Morisot's pictures were accepted every year and pictures by her sister Edna, who was merely an amateur and gave up painting when she married in 1866, were hung that year (when works by Cézanne and Manet, as stated, were rejected). Degas appeared for the first time in 1865 with the large academic composition *Les malheurs de la ville d'Orléans*;[1] his *Scène de steeplechase*[2] was accepted in 1866, his *Deux sœurs*[3] in 1867. Most of these pictures passed unnoticed in these *Salons*; but Manet's works attracted attention and roused controversy almost every year; the academic painters and their supporting critics attacked *Le Christ aux Anges* and *Le Christ insulté par les soldats* as impious and the *Olympia* as an indecent demonstration of Realist theories, and the public complained—as they had complained of Courbet in the 'fifties—that Manet selected models who were physically ugly and offensively plebeian.

Zola appeared as an art critic at the beginning of 1866 when he reviewed *Du principe de l'art et sa destination sociale* by the socialist Proudhon (who had died in 1865). In this book Proudhon expressed the view that artists must contribute direct service to a Socialist State, and he praised Courbet (who had been his friend and a follower of his ideas) as a socialist painter who had painted sturdy proletarian figures and suffering unfortunates and attacked the priests in an anti-clerical picture *Le retour de la conférence*. Zola replied that though Courbet was an admirable realist painter he must be judged 'absolutely' as an artist and not relatively as a cog in a socialist machine; that art is individualism; and that the artist's originality alone can give life to a work of art (*l'œuvre ne vit que par l'originalité*). Zola thus proclaimed his personal Liberalism at the start of his career; but his praise of Courbet was not well received at the Café Guerbois firstly because Courbet, as noted, had become less vigorous and uncompromising as an artist in recent years, and secondly because he had offended Manet by describing his *Olympia* as a playing card (*une dame de pique*). Later in 1866 Zola obtained a regular column on a paper called *L'Evénement*, and there he defended the works of his painter friends in a series of articles on the 1866 *Salon* (republished as *Mon Salon*). As Manet's pictures *L'Acteur tragique* and *Le fifre* and Cézanne's pictures had been rejected, Zola dedicated his articles to Cézanne and defied the Jury by declaring that Manet would ultimately triumph and crush *les médiocrités timides qui l'entourent*. Of Monet, Zola wrote: '*Voilà un homme dans la foule des eunuques*'; of Pissarro: '*Merci: Monsieur, votre paysage m'a reposé une bonne demi-heure lors de mon voyage dans le grand désert du Salon*'; and (retrieving his error) he now attacked Courbet and his *Femme au perroquet* with the *mot qui tue*, the bitterest of Realist reproaches: '*Courbet a fait du joli*'. The *Salon* artists and their supporters were furious with these articles and especially with the passages in praise of Manet, and they complained so loudly to the proprietor of the paper that he stopped the series and caused it to be completed by a writer with less realist views. But Manet himself and the others were delighted; Cézanne showed his satisfaction in a picture called *Le père de l'artiste lisant L'Evénement*[4]; and Renoir recorded the articles in a picture

[1] Paris. Luxembourg.
[2] Perhaps the picture titled *Courses de gentlemen*, now in the Louvre.
[3] Paris. J. Laroche.   [4] Paris. Lecomte collection.

called *Le cabaret de la mère Anthony*,[1] where Sisley is shown with *L'Evénement* on his knee.

In 1867 Manet rewarded Zola for these articles by lending him money and by painting his portrait where we see him seated at a desk with a Japanese screen behind his chair and a Japanese print on the wall—(evidence of the craze for Japanese bibelots, fans, kimonos and so forth, launched by the de Goncourts and Baudelaire in the 'fifties, and first recorded in Whistler's *Princesse du pays de la porcelaine* exhibited in the *Salon* of 1865).[2] Zola was twenty-seven when he sat to Manet for this portrait and he now published the short novel *Thérèse Raquin* and his first play *Les mystères de Marseilles* which was produced without success at Marseilles where Cézanne sat beside him at the *première*.

In this year 1867 Georges Clémenceau, aged twenty-six, was teaching French in New York; Karl Marx, aged forty-nine, published *Das Kapital Vol. I*; Pierre Bonnard was born at Fontenay-aux-Roses; Mme Chrysostome Seurat walked in the Allée de Mexico of the new Parc des Buttes-Chaumont with Georges Seurat who was eight; Henri de Toulouse-Lautrec, aged three, was photographed in a kilt on the terrace of one of his father's estates; Gauguin, aged nineteen, was a sailor in the merchant marine; Sarah Bernhardt, aged twenty-two, scored her first success, as Cordelia, at the Odéon; the de Goncourts published *Manette Salomon*; Baudelaire died paralysed at the age of forty-six; and Ingres died of a chill at the age of eighty-seven.

All these events took place in the setting of Second Empire Paris which Baron Haussmann, in vast building operations, was then converting to the city that we know—the city designed like a series of cakes cut into slices, the sides of the slices converging to strategic centres to be occupied, if need be, by police or troops. And these events took place beneath a dictatorial regime that looked on all 'individualities' as *êtres déclassés* and a menace to the State. In these years 1863–1867 none of the artists we are concerned with knew any politicians or took any part in political affairs. From the standpoint of the Government they were negligible units from whom in fact there was nothing to be feared. But the dictatorial emperor had real and formidable opponents. On the Right he had the Royalists (Legitimists and Orleanists) who included the veteran historian and politician Adolphe Thiers, now approaching seventy; and on the Left he had the Liberals and Republicans. He had, moreover, his difficulties abroad. His imposition of the Archduke

---

[1] This picture (Stockholm: National Gallery) was painted at Marlotte on the outskirts of Fontainebleau forest. The inn was much frequented by writers and artists and its walls were covered with caricatures, including one of Murger drawn by Renoir which occurs in the background of this picture. Murger (whose *Scènes de la vie de Bohème* published as a serial in *Le Corsaire* in the 'forties, and performed as a play in 1849, was published in book form in 1851) had been a habitué of Marlotte and had written his last book there two years before he died in 1861.

[2] Manet's portrait of Zola is now in the Louvre. According to Paul Lafond the taste for 'japonaiseries' was launched in Paris in 1856 by the engraver Bracquemond who was a friend of Degas and who showed him a set of colour-prints by Hokusai; and Japanese colour prints were obtainable in Paris from 1862 when one Soye, who had been in the East, began to sell them in a shop called *La porte Chinoise* (P. Lafond: *Degas*. vol. i., p. 36). The de Goncourts ascribe the introduction to themselves and Baudelaire.

Maximilian on the Mexicans had been a failure. The French troops in Mexico (who included The Douanier Rousseau, aged twenty-one, as a regimental flautist) were exposed to guerilla warfare, and also to threats of hostile action by the United States whose sympathies were with the Mexicans; and in 1866 the Emperor withdrew his troops from Mexico, leaving the Archduke Maximilian to whatever his fate might be. At the same time the Germans slaughtered the Austrians at Sadowa, and Bismarck united Germany by the Treaty of Nicolsbourg, which Thiers described as the greatest disaster which France had suffered for four hundred years. In 1867 the Mexicans shot the Archduke Maximilian, and Manet was forbidden to exhibit the pictures which, with the aid of prints and photographs, he painted of the scene.[1] The *Exposition Universelle* of that year was made the occasion of glittering fêtes and ceremonies which masked the Emperor's embarrassments; Kings and Emperors were magnificently received; there were gala performances and balls and receptions at Versailles; and all the world said that, whatever the facts might be about the Emperor's position, he had at any rate stage-managed a most brilliant show.

[1] Sections of Manet's large painting of the subject are now in the London National Gallery (cf. p. 192). Another version is in a German collection and sketches are owned by the Copenhagen and Boston Museums. Manet lithographed the subject, and the exhibition of this lithograph was also forbidden.

PROLOGUE: HOW IT HAPPENED

SCENE II: 1868-September 1870

Last years of the Empire

In the last three *Salons* of the Empire the artists we are concerned with again had varying treatment. Cézanne's works as before were rejected every year. But Manet appeared with *La femme au perroquet* (Pl. 4) and *Portrait de Zola*[1] in 1868, *Le déjeuner*[2] and *Le balcon*[1] in 1869, and *Eva Gonzalez*[3] and *La leçon de musique*[4] in 1870. Pissarro's large landscape *Ermitage à Pontoise*[5] and Monet's large marine *La jetée du Havre*[5] were both hung in 1868. Renoir's *Lise*[2] appeared in 1868, his *Baigneuse au griffon*[2] and *Femme d'Algers* (Pl. 6B) in 1870. Bazille's *Vue de village*[1] was accepted in 1869, but his group picture showing himself (painted by Manet) with Monet, Manet, Renoir and other friends in his studio (*Mon atelier*)[1] was rejected in 1870. Berthe Morisot (who became Manet's pupil in 1868 and posed to him for *Le balcon* and a number of other pictures) had her work accepted every year. Degas was represented by *Mdlle Fiocre dans le ballet de La Source*[6] in 1868, by *La femme aux mains jointes (Mme G.)*[7] in 1869 and by *Mme Camus en rose*[8] in 1870. But none of these paintings were examples of the new Impressionist art; they were all exhibition pictures which the artists had specially painted for the *Salons*, pictures designed to attract attention and demonstrate competence in the disordered competition of large mixed displays. For our artists did not send their original pictures—the Impressionist pictures where they made creative efforts—to these shows. Thus Renoir, for example, sent *La femme d'Algers* (Pl. 6B) to the *Salon*; but he did not send his early Impressionist pictures—the riverside scenes like *Canotiers à Chatou* (Pl. 6A)—for such works at this time were kept in the artists' studios where they were only seen by the artists' friends.

In the field of letters the year 1868 saw the publication of the first part of the horrible nightmare fantasia *Les Chants de Maldoror* by Isadore Ducasse, who called himself the Comte de Lautréamont. Born at Montevideo, Lautréamont had recently arrived in Paris and he was twenty-two when a publisher named Lacroix took the risk of putting these prose-poems into print. There is no denying the imaginative fertility and the literary genius that went to the making of this terribly affective

[1] Paris. Louvre.
[2] German collection.
[3] London. National Gallery, Millbank.
[4] Chicago. Art Institute.
[5] London. Reid & Lefevre.
[6] New York. Metropolitan Museum.
[7] Boston. Mrs. Gardner.
[8] London. H. Coleman.

work; but it is also impossible to deny that the book in many places is sadistic and obscene. I record the publication because Neo-Surrealist writers and painters from 1924 onwards have often cited it as, technically at any rate, a pioneer achievement; and I must state here, as I explain more fully later, that Surrealist art, properly so called, is not in essence obscene or sadistic and that the works of Redon, Ensor, Chirico and Chagall, whom I refer to later as pioneer Surrealists, are neither one nor the other in any aspect or degree.[1]

In 1869 Lautréamont's publisher Lacroix commissioned Zola to start the realist Rougon-Macquart series of novels—Zola undertaking to deliver a book a year for a retaining fee of 500 francs a month. In this year also Verlaine published *Fêtes galantes*; Henri Matisse was born at Le Cateau; Vincent Van Gogh, aged sixteen, began to earn his living as an assistant in the Goupil Gallery at The Hague; Gauguin, aged twenty-one, was transferred from the merchant service to the navy; Wagner, aged fifty-six, became intimate with Nietzsche, aged twenty-five, who had just been elected Professor of Classical Philology at Bâle; Verdi, aged fifty-six, was commissioned by the Khedive of Egypt to write an opera (*Aïda*) to celebrate the opening of the Suez Canal; and Georges Clémenceau returned from America and resolved to enter politics by means of the coming municipal elections.

The political conditions from 1868 till the Franco-Prussian war can be briefly summarised as follows. In 1868 observers commented on '*le ferment secret qui gonfle sourdement la masse*'; and the Emperor agreed to some Liberal concessions including the right of public assembly and a measure of freedom for the press. As a result Republicanism at once became articulate; Tenot, editor of *Le Siècle*, published *Paris pendant le coup d'état*, an attack on the Emperor; Théodore Duret and Zola were outspokenly Republican in *La Tribune*; Delescluze (a proscrit of 1851) was frankly Revolutionary in *Réveil*; Henri Rochefort, who now became prominent as an audacious Republican journalist, was witty and scurrilous in *La Lanterne*, which he launched with a leader beginning: '*La France contient, dit l'Almanach impérial, trente six millions de sujets sans compter les sujets de mécontentement*'—an opening which achieved a sale of a hundred thousand copies. The Emperor, alarmed, made plans for replying by his own pen and projected a novel exhibiting the benefits of the Imperial régime; but on second thoughts he had proceedings started against sixty-four papers, including *La Lanterne* and *Réveil*, instead. *La Lanterne* was suppressed in August and Rochefort fled to Belgium; the editor of *Réveil* was defended by Léon Gambetta, a lawyer aged forty who specialised in political cases and had contributed Republican articles to various papers. In 1869 the opposition had Jules Simon, Jules Ferry and Gambetta as recruits in the Corps Législatif; and hard pressed the Emperor issued an amnesty for political offenders and a *Senatus-consulte* which gave the Corps Législatif the right of initiative and the right to discuss and vote the details of the budget. Rochefort, protected by this amnesty, returned to Paris and founded a new opposition paper *La Marseillaise*. In January 1870 the Emperor's cousin Prince Pierre Bonaparte was described (with justification) as a disreputable person by Rochefort and another journalist named Paschal Grousset in *La Marseillaise*, and the Prince challenged

[1] Cf. Index under Surrealism and Neo-Surrealism.

both writers to duels; Victor Noir, one of Grousset's seconds, called at the Prince's house at Auteuil, quarrelled with him, struck him, and was shot dead by him; Rochefort commented: 'I was a fool to have treated a Bonaparte as anything but an assassin', and was promptly imprisoned; Noir's funeral was made an occasion for anti-Imperial demonstrations; the Prince, tried in March, was acquitted on the ground that he had fired in self-defence. This affair was a serious blow to the Imperial prestige. And the Emperor decided on the bold stroke of a plebiscite to test his position. The affirmative asked for was 'The people approve the Liberal Reforms which the Emperor has made in the Constitution since 1860'. Industrial labour and the middle classes in Paris voted mainly against him; the peasants voted solidly for him; seventeen per cent. of the army, which polled separately, voted against him; and in the end he won with 7,350,000 votes against 1,538,000.

On July 19 the Franco-Prussian War began. On September 2 the Emperor raised the white flag at Sedan; the Germans demanded unconditional surrender; and the Emperor gave up 90,000 men and went himself to Wilhelmshöhe as a prisoner of war. When the Empress heard the news she went, escorted by the Austrian and Italian ambassadors, to her American dentist; and a few days later she was a refugee in England.

The artists and writers we are concerned with were variously affected by the war. Manet, aged thirty-eight, and Degas, aged thirty-six, were both in the artillery of the National Guard in Paris. Manet's commander was the genre and history painter, J. L. E. Meissonier, and tradition has it that Meissonier left sketches about and was much chagrined that Manet ignored them. The company in which Degas served was commanded by the painter Henri Rouart who had been at school with him and who now became and remained his intimate friend. Pissarro, aged forty, was living, at the outbreak, in a little house at Louveciennes where he had just painted his wife and daughter in the front garden(Pl. 8A); when the Germans advanced towards Paris he abandoned all his pictures and went to Sydenham on the outskirts of London where his married sister was living. Monet, aged thirty, fled from his house at Argenteuil to Holland and thence to England where he joined Pissarro. Cézanne, aged thirty-one, received a calling-up notice at Aix, but evaded service by retiring to L'Estaque a few miles away where he was not disturbed though his presence there was known. Renoir, aged twenty-nine, had the offer of a commission in the cavalry but preferred to serve in the ranks; as his physique was frail he was employed in auxiliary service and does not appear to have taken part in any fighting. Bazille had a commission and was killed. The sculptor Auguste Rodin, aged thirty and still unknown, was in the National Guard. Odilon Redon, also aged thirty and also still unknown, saw fighting in a battle near Tours and was invalided out. The Douanier Rousseau, aged twenty-six, was in the army with the rank of sergeant. Gauguin, aged twenty-two, was a minor officer on the *Jérome Napoléon*, commanded by Prince Jerome Napoleon himself. Corot, aged seventy-four, remained for a time with his sister at Ville d'Avray and then returned to his studio in Paris where he painted *La femme à la perle*[1] and sent a packet of bank notes to the mayor of his district with a note: '*Monsieur le maire, je consacre l'argent ci-*

[1] Paris. Louvre.

joint à la confection de canons pour chasser les Prussiens des bois de Ville d'Avray'. Catulle Mendès, aged twenty-seven, was in the National Guard. Jules de Goncourt died in June and Edmond de Goncourt continued the famous 'Diary' undisturbed. Zola, who was in Marseilles, was also not disturbed. Verlaine was arrested in August for shouting *Vive la République* in the Café de Madrid. At the same time the poet Rimbaud, aged sixteen (not yet known to Verlaine), fled from his home at Charleville near Sedan and arrived at the Gare de l'Est in Paris where he was at once arrested because he had no ticket and had nothing on him but a notebook full of unintelligible verses which the police suspected to be code. On the day the Empress fled, Victor Hugo arrived from Guernsey viâ Brussels and was received in Paris by Clémenceau the new Mayor of Montmartre; Hugo's carriage was escorted to the Hôtel de Ville by a cheering crowd; and the poet, aged sixty-eight, clasped hands with six thousand of his admirers before retiring to his bed.

PROLOGUE: HOW IT HAPPENED

SCENE III: October 1870-1873

First years of the Third Republic

When the Emperor surrendered and the Empress fled the Third Republic was proclaimed. A Government of National Defence was established with Gambetta, Jules Favre and Jules Simon under General Trochu as Governor of Paris; and Thiers was sent on a diplomatic tour to plead the French cause in London, Vienna, St. Petersburg and Florence. The Germans blocked the French Army of the Rhine in Metz, and demanded Alsace and Lorraine as a condition preliminary to an armistice. As their demand was refused they marched on Paris and they began to besiege it on September 19. Gambetta flew to Tours in a balloon and organized new armies. Manet and Degas mounted guard on the fortifications (and went on free evenings to the *Club des Folies Bergère* where they heard political orations). Daumier, aged sixty-two, made drawings for Hugo's *Châtiments*; a new gun, publicly baptized 'Victor Hugo', was blessed by the poet:

> *La lutte nous attend, viens, ô mon fils étrange,*
> *Doublons-nous l'un pour l'autre et faisons un échange,*
> *Et mets, ô noir vengeur, combattant souverain,*
> *Ton bronze dans mon cœur, mon âme en ton airain.*

and Sarah Bernhardt, aged twenty-five, recited *Châtiments* to excited crowds who threw coins into the Prussian helmets which she held out to receive them. But food shortage soon began. On October 10 de Goncourt entered in his Diary: 'I have just applied for my meat ration permit' and on October 25 Manet wrote to his wife who had gone to the Pyrenees: 'We are reduced to 75 grammes of meat; only children and sick people now have milk.' On December 2 Manet fought in the sortie to Champigny where the French lost 10,000 men. 'I have just seen German prisoners for the first time,' he wrote to Mme Manet, 'they are mostly very young, like our militia; they are well treated and seem quite glad to be captured and thus out of the war. We eat horse flesh when we can get it—cats, dogs, and rats are now sold in the butchers' shops.' In the last week of December Victor Hugo noted: '*Hier j'ai mangé du rat.*' On Christmas Day Bismarck and Moltke eat copious Christmas dinners; the inhabitants of Paris eat their dogs and rats; Manet painted *Effet de neige à Montrouge*;[1] and Cosima Wagner was awakened by the 'Siegfried Idyll'.

[1] New York. Miss Davies.

On January 5, 1871, the Germans began to bombard the starving city. The Parisian *gamins*, undaunted, sold fresh fallen shrapnel as 'hot chestnuts' in the streets; and Anatole France, aged twenty-seven, bought some of these 'chestnuts' at a franc a piece. On January 15 Manet wrote to his wife: 'There are no cabs because all the horses have been eaten; there is no gas; the bombardment continues by day and by night and the St. Germain quarter is seriously damaged.' Three days later Ruskin wrote to the *Daily Telegraph* to remind the world that Notre Dame, 'absolutely unreplaceable as a pure and lovely source of art instruction by any future energy or ingenuity', was in hourly danger of destruction; and on the same day Wilhelm I of Prussia was proclaimed German Emperor in the Galerie des Glaces at Versailles. On January 19 three thousand National Guardsmen were killed in a futile and desperate sortie—while Thiers, instructed by the Government, was secretly discussing an armistice with Bismarck. On January 22 sections of the National Guard revolted in protest at the sortie which had been, they said, a treacherous attempt to scare them to accept the armistice. A week later the armistice was signed. And Manet wrote to his wife: '*C'est fini . . . Il n'y avait plus moyen d'y tenir . . . on mourait de faim . . . nous sommes tous maigres comme des clous.*'

The war ended on February 1. Three weeks later the ex-Emperor, released from Wilhelmshöhe, established himself in Chislehurst in a house called Camden Place. By the terms of the armistice the French had agreed to elect a National Assembly to discuss the peace terms. This Assembly was now established at Bordeaux, and Thiers, aged seventy-two, was acting Prime Minister. By the peace terms, as all the world knows, France was forced to surrender Alsace and Lorraine, to pay an indemnity of five milliard francs, and to submit to a forty-eight hour occupation of Paris. The Parisians were furious at this climax to their sufferings. Victor Hugo as a Deputy of Paris and Gambetta as Deputy for Strasbourg resigned from the Assembly in protest; Hugo went to Brussels and Gambetta went to Spain. On March 1 twenty-eight thousand Germans marched through Paris and parked their guns on the Place de la Concorde. Every shop was shut, every blind drawn. In the streets the Germans saw only the irrepressible *gamins* who jeered their hate. The officers, to show their *Kultur*, inspected the pictures in the Louvre.

From the signing of the armistice at the end of January it again became possible for the inhabitants to leave the city and for visitors to arrive. Degas and Manet both left in February. Degas went to his friends the Valpinçons at Château Menil-Hubert, where he painted *Mlle Valpinçon enfant*[1]; Manet joined his wife in the Pyrenees where he painted *Oloron-Sainte-Marie*,[2] and he then went to Arcachon where he painted *Le bassin d'Arcachon*[3] and a bicycling picture *Le vélocipède*.[4] At the same time Zola, Cézanne and Renoir returned to Paris, and Rimbaud, now seventeen, resolved on a second adventure in the city. This time Rimbaud had sold his watch to buy a ticket and he had a girl as his companion; the two young things arrived on February 25 and slept on a seat on the Boulevards; the next day Rimbaud

[1] Paris. Georges Wildenstein et Cie.   [2] Paris. Hector Brame.
[3] Bâle. Rudolf Stoechelin.   [4] Formerly in the Moreau-Nelaton Collection.

27

sent the girl to some people she knew in a suburb; he then went to the studio of the cartoonist André Gill—probably with an introduction from Gill's pupil, the draughtsman Forain, who was then eighteen. Gill's studio had a rabbit painted on the door and was known accordingly as *Le lapin à Gill* (and the house became later a noted Montmartre café, known as the *Lapin agile*, frequented by Picasso and his friends). When Rimbaud arrived at the *Lapin à Gill* the owner was out; so Rimbaud went to sleep on the sofa; when Gill came in he gave him ten francs and sent him about his business; Rimbaud faced Paris as best he could for the next few days and then went back, on foot, to Charleville, begging his way from farm to farm and posing as a hunted *franc-tireur*.

In March when the German parade was over the Parisians hoped that they might at length be able to resume their normal lives. But the next months brought them desperate troubles, another siege and hideous slaughter in the streets. And we must recall these happenings because the memory of them was deep in the minds of all our artists in the next decades. France at this moment was nominally a Republic. But this new Republic had as yet no constitutional form; and there were many who feared that the National Assembly at Bordeaux would impose a Monarchist Restoration. The Assembly in fact had 400 Royalists, 100 Republicans, 30 Bonapartists, and 20 Socialists; the Royalists had this large majority because the Assembly had been elected in a moment of panic when the country as a whole thought that the Republican Party would refuse the German Peace Terms and continue the war. Well-informed Parisians in March 1871 foresaw a conflict between the Provisional Government under Thiers and this Royalist Assembly on the one hand, and Left Wing elements among the Republican National Guardsmen on the other; and all who could afford to do so left the city as Manet and Degas had done—Berthe Morisot, for example, was taken by her parents to stay with Puvis de Chavannes at Saint-Germain. In February and March Paris was thus depleted of a hundred thousand ordinary well-to-do bourgeois; and the Provisional Government faced a suspicious population of ardently Republican artisans, small shopkeepers, proletariat, and National Guardsmen. Thiers increased the fears of these elements by provocative actions as soon as the Germans had left Paris. He drafted thirty thousand troops into the city, lifted a moratorium in force since the beginning of the siege (which threatened thousands of small traders with ruin) and tried to disarm the National Guard (having first abolished their wages). The National Guard resisted and the populace supported their resistance. Thiers withdrew his thirty thousand soldiers to the rest of the army under Marshal MacMahon at Versailles. A week later the city held municipal elections and invested the government of Paris in a new body called the *Conseil Général de la Commune de Paris*—now generally referred to as *The Commune*.

In these circumstances the banking and business powers made it plain to Thiers that they would not subscribe to loans for the German Indemnity until the Government of the country was master in Paris. And on April 2 Thiers ordered the Versaillais army under Marshal MacMahon to begin a second siege of the city. On April 7 Thiers ordered bombardment, and the suburb of Neuilly was entirely destroyed, the inhabitants—quite neutral in the conflict—being forced to huddle in their cellars where some eventually went mad. The Commune resisted the Versaillais siege for seven weeks and during their brief period of rule, in terrible conditions, they found time to institute a *Fédération des Artistes*. Courbet and Eugène Pottier (a decorative artist who wrote the words of the song called *L'Internationale*) were joint Presidents of this *Fédération des Artistes*, which began activities on April 13 by electing, among others, Corot, Millet, Manet, Daumier, André Gill (Rimbaud's unwilling host) and the sculptor Dalou as members. Some of the artists elected were not in Paris. But Corot, Daumier, Gill, Dalou and Manet were there—Manet having returned at the beginning of the month. The *Fédération des Artistes* guaranteed the artists complete freedom from State interference on all questions relating to the style of their productions; it resolved to replace the Ecole des Beaux Arts by technical schools; and it announced its intention of safeguarding the contents of the national museums and employing artists on public commissions. A few days after the issue of this programme Courbet was elected to the Communal Council and the Education Commission; Gill was made Director of the Luxembourg Museum; Dalou was charged with the protection of the treasures in the Louvre; and Verlaine was elected to the Bureau de la Presse. At the beginning of May the Communards made hysterical gestures against Right Wing symbols; the Colonne Vendôme was pulled down and Courbet was photographed shaking hands with the destroyers; Thiers' house was burned; and Verlaine told de Goncourt (probably to 'pull his leg') that he had quashed a proposal to set fire to Notre Dame. In these hectic days Manet drew two lithographs, *Barricade* and *Guerre civile*; Renoir secured a safe conduct to Louveciennes; Zola left the city by procuring a Prussian passport; and Seurat, aged twelve, escaped with his parents from the Boulevard Magenta to a retreat at Fontainebleau.

When the Versaillais entered Paris on May 21, the *semaine sanglante* began. The Communards, men and women, fought behind the famous barricades. André Antoine (founder, later, of a realist movement in the theatre) saw countless horrors as a boy of thirteen running about the streets. Marcel Proust's mother, seven months with child, learned that her husband, a distinguished doctor, had been wounded by a random shot while returning from a hospital to their home at Auteuil; and Georges Rouault's mother bore him in a cellar on May 27, while the *bataille des rues* was raging overhead. By May 28 the Versaillais had killed some seventeen thousand Parisians and taken some thirty-six thousand prisoners whom they cruelly ill-treated; and the Thiers Government was master in a Paris where the Hôtel de Ville, the Palais de Justice, the Tuileries, the Cour de Comptes, the Louvre and the Palais Royal had been wholly or partially destroyed by the Versaillais bombardment and by fires started (in some cases for strategic reasons) by the defenders. A week after the *semaine sanglante*, de Goncourt walked on the Boulevard des Italiens and noted with satisfaction: '*Ce soir, pour la première fois on commence à avoir peine à se frayer un chemin entre la badauderie des hommes et la prostitution des femmes.*' But others suffered agonies in the short White Terror that followed. Courts martial dealt out savage vengeance on Communard prisoners and others denounced by informers, thousands being sentenced to imprisonment, penal servitude on galleys, exile, deportation, or death. Courbet, sentenced to six months' imprisonment and the reconstruction of the Colonne Vendôme at his own expense, escaped to Switzerland; the sculptor Dalou fled to London; Verlaine went into hiding; Julien Tanguy, a colour grinder—later painted by Van Gogh (Pl. 24B)—was sentenced to two years in the galleys and four years' banishment from Paris. Rimbaud (who said later that he had fought with the Communards behind the barricades) was in fact at Charleville writing anti-Thiers poems and *Bateau ivre*. On July 4 Zola wrote in a letter to Cézanne: 'I now find myself quietly at home again in the Batignolles quarter as if I had just awakened from a bad dream. My little garden-house is the same as ever, my garden is untouched; not a stick of furniture, not a plant has been damaged and I could almost believe that the two sieges were bad jokes invented to scare children.' On July 10 Marcel Proust was born.

The artists we are concerned with now resumed their normal life. Cézanne established himself in Paris with Hortense Fiquet, about to be the mother of his son; his studio easels held *Conversation* (Pl. 7) and *La pendule noire*.[1] Renoir took a studio in the rue Notre Dame des Champs and painted *Le Capitain Darras*[2]—the portrait of an officer he had served under in the war. Degas returned from Menil-Hubert and painted *Trois Camarades*[3]—a group of three former companions in the National Guard; Berthe Morisot returned from Saint-Germain and painted *Mme Pontillon*[4]; Pissarro and Monet returned from London—Pissarro with *La route de Sydenham*,[5] *La tour de Sydenham* and *Le Crystal Palace*.[6] The Douanier Rousseau, demobilized from the army, and Gauguin, demobilized from the navy, sought employment in Paris. Manet was often seen at the meetings of the National Assembly now sitting at Versailles; he was there to make sketches for a portrait of Gambetta who had returned from Spain; Gambetta posed for him several times in his Paris studio; but dissatisfied with the picture Manet destroyed it in a rage, saying: '*Encore un dont le portrait sera fait par Bonnat*' (which was in fact to be the case).[7] In the autumn Manet sold twenty-two pictures to the dealer Durand-Ruel, who had met Pissarro and Monet in London and had been convinced by them that the artists who had foregathered at the Café Guerbois were the coming men. The price paid was 35,000 francs.

In the autumn, also, Rimbaud arrived once more from Charleville. He had sent his poems to Verlaine who had answered: '*Venez, chère grande âme, on vous attend, on vous désire.*' On his arrival Verlaine introduced him to the Parnassian poets and to Mallarmé who had just been transferred from the provinces to teach English in a lycée in Paris. Rimbaud then introduced Verlaine to the draughtsman Forain, and Verlaine took Rimbaud to the studio of Fantin-Latour where, in the spring of 1872, they posed together among the group of poets represented in Fantin's *Un coin de table*.[8] Rimbaud only gave Fantin one sitting for his portrait in this picture

[1] Hollywood. Edward G. Robinson. [2] German Collection.
[3] Paris. M. Jeantaud. [4] Paris. Louvre.
[5] Bâle. Baron Robert von Hirsch. (This picture is sometimes referred to as *Après midi d'été*.)
[6] London. Messrs. Reid & Lefevre.
[7] Léon Bonnat painted Gambetta's portrait in 1880. The portrait belongs to M. Joseph Reinach.
[8] Paris. Louvre.

7. CÉZANNE
Conversation, 1871
Paris. J. Bernheim Jeune

8A. PISSARRO
La route de Versailles à Louveciennes, 1870

8B. SISLEY
Effet de neige, 1874

which represents him at the age of eighteen when he had just written the sonnet
Voyelles:

> *A noir, E blanc, I rouge, U vert, O bleu, voyelles,*
> *Je dirai quelque jour vos naissances latentes . . .*

In the summer of 1872 he persuaded Verlaine, who was twenty years his senior,
to go with him to Belgium; later in the year the two poets were in London where
Rimbaud wrote *Illuminations* and Verlaine wrote *Romances sans paroles*, while, in
Paris, Mme Mauté, Verlaine's mother-in-law, formerly a pupil of Chopin, was
giving piano lessons to Claude Debussy who was then aged ten, Catulle Mendès was
publishing Zola's *La Curée* in his paper *La République des Lettres*, and Zola's *Thérèse
Raquin* was produced and failed as a play.

In 1872 our artists were rather scattered and unsettled. Manet painted race-
course scenes and pictures of Berthe Morisot and then went to Holland where he
saw Franz Hals' pictures and projected *Le bon bock*.[1] Degas began his *Ecole de danse*
studies in the old Opera in the rue le Peletier and then went with his brother to
New Orleans where his family had a branch of their bank. Renoir painted *Parisiennes habillées en Algériennes*[2] (an Impressionist version of Delacroix's *Femmes
Algériennes*[3]) and the sunlit Impressionist river scene *Canotiers à Chatou* (Pl. 6A).
Pissarro painted the sunlit *Entrée de village*[3] at Pontoise where he was now established, as his old house at Louveciennes was uninhabitable—the Germans having
used it as a meat store and destroyed the majority of his pictures. Cézanne went to
live at Auvers and painted the first of his so-called Impressionist pictures with
Pissarro at the neighbouring Pontoise. Monet and Sisley moved cautiously towards
the rainbow palette.

In 1873 our artists decided to launch the Impressionist movement by a joint
exhibition in the following year. The plans were made at the Nouvelle Athènes café
which Manet and the painters and writers who surrounded him were now frequenting as they had formerly frequented the Café Guerbois. A joint exhibition
was evidently called for because the *Salon* jury of 1873 had rejected pictures by
Pissarro, Monet, Renoir, Cézanne and Sisley, and the plan was doubtless encouraged by Durand-Ruel who was now buying and laying down Impressionist
pictures in his gallery in the rue le Peletier (where they narrowly escaped destruction when the old Opera House across the street was burned down this year). The
joint exhibition was to demonstrate the Realist doctrines on the one hand, and
Impressionism on the other; and the pictures produced by these artists this year
all fall within that double scheme. Cézanne painted *La maison du pendu*[3] while
working with Pissarro at Auvers; Monet painted one of his last pictures influenced by Manet *Mlle Bonnet* and the first Impressionist bird's-eye view of a street
scene in rainbow colours *Boulevard des Capucines*;[4] Renoir painted *L'allée cavalière
du Bois de Boulogne*[5] and sunlit river scenes; and Degas produced a series of pictures
of contemporary life—*Place de la Concorde*,[5] *A la Bourse*[3] and *Voiture aux courses*
(Pl.9A); Manet, who intended, at this time, to contribute to the exhibition, painted

[1] Philadelphia. C. S. Tyson.   [2] Tokio. Baron Matsukata.
[3] Paris. Louvre.   [4] Moscow. Museum of Modern Western Art.
[5] German Collection.

the Impressionist *Bal masqué à l'Opéra*,[1] and the sketches *Polichinelle*[2] and *La dame aux éventails*.[3] Meanwhile he had sent *Le bon bock*[4] to the *Salon* and scored his first—and only—popular success; the public liked this picture of a cheery fat man with his pipe and his glass of beer; and the picture was so much talked of that an enterprising actor reproduced it as a *tableau vivant* in a music-hall Revue. The model for Manet's *La dame aux éventails* was an intelligent demi-mondaine named Nina de Callias who had a *salon* frequented by Degas, Renoir, Forain, Mallarmé, Catulle Mendès, and Cézanne. Nina de Callias was then living with the poet Charles Cros. Manet's picture shows her in Spanish costume on a sofa against a wall half covered with Japanese fans—a mode which had begun, as noted, in the 'fifties and which increased in this decade.[5] It was in Nina's *salon* that Mallarmé first met Manet, and thereafter he formed the habit of calling at his studio on his way home from the lycée where he taught. None of our artists had yet heard of Gauguin, then twenty-five and working as a stockbroker, or of Van Gogh, then twenty and a salesman in the Goupil Gallery in London, or of The Douanier Rousseau, then twenty-eight and a minor Customs official in an *octroi* station on the outskirts of Paris, or of George Moore aged twenty-one who had just arrived in Paris as a monied art student with academic tastes. But there was much talk at the Nouvelle Athènes of Zola's *Le Ventre de Paris* which was attacked for its realism by Anatole France who had just published *Poèmes dorés* at the age of twenty-nine, and of Verlaine's condemnation to two years' imprisonment for shooting at Rimbaud in Brussels.

The ex-Emperor died at Chislehurst on January 9, 1873; and the Republic was now assailed by the Royalists who coalesced and agreed to work for the restoration of the Legitimist Comte de Chambord—the Orleanist Comte de Paris standing down in his favour. The Republicans were divided into Liberals led by Gambetta, Jules Grevy, Jules Simon and Jules Ferry, and those who followed Thiers in desiring a Conservative Republic with himself at the head. In May Thiers was driven out and the Royalists made the Royalist Marshal MacMahon the acting President and the Royalist Duc de Broglie the acting Prime Minister. This Royalist Government—(MacMahon's wife said: '*Nous ne sommes ici que pour tenir la place*')—forbade anti-Monarchist activities, retired officials with Republican sentiments, removed Republican emblems from official buildings and documents, and restricted the sale of Republican papers in the streets. For his outspoken Republican writings Rochefort and another journalist named Olivier Pain were deported to a penal settlement in Noumea. In August and September plans were made for a Royalist *coup d'état*; the Comte de Chambord was to come from his retreat at Fröhsdorf in October and enter Paris with an imposing escort and procession. But the plot collapsed because the Comte refused to use the tricolor flag and insisted on the white flag of the old kings of France. Meanwhile the Germans had been paid the whole of their indemnity by a series of loans successfully launched by Thiers. And before 1873 was out the last German soldier had left France.

[1] New York. Havemayer Collection.　　[2] Paris. M. Lecomte.
[3] Paris. Louvre.　　[4] Philadelphia. C. S. Tyson.
[5] Cf. above, p. 20.

PROLOGUE: HOW IT HAPPENED

SCENE IV: 1874-1878

From the *First Impressionist Exhibition* to the *Exposition Universelle*

At the beginning of 1874 Manet discussed the question of the proposed Impressionist exhibition with Fantin-Latour, and on Fantin's advice he decided to abstain from it. This defection was a grave blow to the Impressionist group because it deprived their posters of the one name already known to any considerable section of the public. Manet however was loyal to his friends in his own fashion. After the popular success of *Le bon bock* in the *Salon* of the previous year he might have continued to win applause there with similar genre subjects and become a recognized pillar of the *Salon* as a painter of genial types; but he declined the temptation and sent this year to the *Salon* his *Chemin de fer*[1] (painted the year before) and a lithograph of his *Polichinelle*[2] which were accepted, and two Impressionist sketches —*Bal masqué à l'Opéra*[1] and *Hirondelles*[3]—which the jury refused. Mallarmé and the critic Burty attacked the *Salon* jury for these rejections and Théodore de Banville wrote an unforgettable couplet on *Polichinelle*:

> *Féroce et rose, avec du feu dans la prunelle,*
> *Effronté, saoul, divin, c'est lui, Polichinelle.*

The *First Impressionist Exhibition* was therefore organized without Manet and it opened in April 1874 in a set of studios on the Boulevard des Capucines formerly occupied by Baudelaire's friend the photographer Nadar. The exhibitors were Pissarro, Monet, Renoir, Cézanne, Sisley, Guillaumin and Berthe Morisot; Degas and three friends introduced by him—Henri Rouart, the engraver Bracquemond, the Italian de Nittis; Eugène Boudin, representing an older generation, and a number of others making thirty altogether. Degas himself sent ten works including *Voiture aux courses* (Pl. 9A) and his latest dance and laundress compositions; Renoir sent among other things *La loge*[4] and *La petite danseuse*[5]; Cézanne *La maison du pendu*,[6] *Paysage à Auvers* and *Une moderne Olympia* (catalogued as lent by Dr. Gachet);[7] Berthe Morisot twelve paintings including *Le berceau*,[8] *Cache-cache* and

[1] New York. Havemayer Collection.
[2] Paris. M. Lecomte.
[3] Paris. Mme Hecht.
[4] London. Samuel Courtauld.
[5] Philadelphia. J. Widener.
[6] Paris. Louvre.
[7] Auvers. Paul Gachet.
[8] Paris. Mme Forget.

Sur la falaise;[6] Pissarro landscapes painted in the region of Pontoise; Monet landscapes and genre pictures including *Impression: Soleil levant*—which gave the group its name, as a journalist in derision called the whole exhibition 'Impression-iste'. The public paid a franc for admission and went in considerable numbers; most of the visitors laughed at the pictures; many of the press comments were unsympathetic—one critic declaring that Cézanne must surely be afflicted with delirium tremens. But de Goncourt noted in his Diary that Degas of all the artists of his acquaintance was the one best able to catch '*dans la copie de la vie moderne, l'âme de cette vie*'; Count Doria bought Cézanne's *La maison du pendu*; Count Camondo appeared and began his collection; the singer Faure came and talked of the pictures he already owned by Manet and Degas; Victor Choquet, an official in the Customs, made the acquaintance of Renoir and Cézanne and began to collect their pictures; Hoschedé, founder of the shops known as *Au Gagne-Petit* and of the magazine *L'Art et la Mode*, and already a patron of Manet, went to the exhibition and began to concern himself with Manet's friends; Durand-Ruel acquired more pictures for his stocks, and another dealer acquired Renoir's *La loge*; Duret, Duranty, Georges Rivière and Burty were helpful critics; Zola brought Charpentier who had now become his publisher and Mme Charpentier who had just started a literary, artistic and Republican salon; and Pissarro brought a new acquaintance, the stockbroker Gauguin, and suggested to him that it would surely be a good investment to buy some Impressionist pictures. The exhibition from the standpoint of the organizers was thus a considerable success. It put the movement as the phrase goes 'on the map' and it attracted collectors, dealers and supporters for the artists.

In this year 1874 a young American Mary Cassatt had a picture accepted by the *Salon* and made the acquaintance of Degas who took her as his pupil. Whistler (in London) painted *Miss Alexander* and *Thomas Carlyle*. The American portrait painter John Singer Sargent, aged eighteen, came to Paris from his birthplace Florence and entered the studio of Carolus Duran; Berthe Morisot married Manet's brother Eugène Manet; Cézanne painted *Portrait de Choquet*;[1] Pissarro painted *Portrait de Cézanne*; Renoir painted *La promenade*[2] *La source*[3] and *La serre*;[4] Jean François Millet, aged sixty, died at Barbizon; Van Gogh, aged twenty-one, paid his first visit to Paris and worked in the Goupil Gallery; and the journalists Rochefort and Olivier Pain escaped in a rowing boat from the penal settlement at Noumea in circumstances recorded later in a picture by Manet.[5] In the field of letters Zola was now intimate with Flaubert, Daudet, de Goncourt and Tour-guenief; and Mallarmé, in the intervals of schoolmastering, was editing a fashion paper, *La Dernière Mode*.[7]

[1] Cambridge. Victor Rothschild.
[2] Paris. Paul Rosenberg
[3] Merion. Barnes Foundation.
[4] Scotland. D. W. T. Cargill.
[5] Cf. pp. 46 and 91.
[6] Paris. Gabriel Thomas.

[7] Mallarmé printed his translation of Tennyson's *Mariana* in this magazine and also poems by the Parnassians including de Banville and Catulle Mendès. He is said to have contributed fashion notes under the pseudonym of 'Marasquin'. In one issue 'Marasquin' described the following '*costume sporting pour dames*' of his own design: '*Pantalon breton fermé et froncé au genou par un élas-tique; bottes molles en peau de daim naturelle. Jupe courte en drap bleu marin avec garnitures de tresses de soie; elle est montée derrière à la ceinture par des plis à la religieuse, mais reste plate devant. Veste en drap*

9A. DEGAS
Voiture aux courses, 1873
Boston. Museum of Fine Arts

9B. RENOIR
Le Moulin de la Galette, 1876
Paris. Louvre

10. MANET
La prune, 1878
New York. Arthur Sachs, Esq.

On January 5, 1875, Garnier's Opera House (in the construction of which Baedeker says 'there is hardly a variety of marble or costly stone that has not been used') was opened with pomp and ceremony; a Peruvian paid £700 for a box; the region round the Opera was illuminated, and the Lord Mayor of London and the Sheriffs, specially invited, arrived in coaches preceded by trumpeters and were loudly cheered by the crowd; the programme included selections from *La Juive*, *Guillaume Tell*, *Les Huguenots* and several interludes of ballet. Later in the year Corot died at the age of seventy-nine; Tanguy opened a shop to sell colours, Japanese prints and pictures; Van Gogh, still a salesman in the Goupil Gallery on the Boulevard Montmartre and reading Erckmann-Chatrian, Longfellow, George Eliot, Keats, Bulwer Lytton, Renan, Michelet, and the Bible, became obsessed with the idea that he must devote his spirit to religion; Gauguin, assisted by Pissarro and encouraged by Emile Schuffenecker (an amateur artist and a colleague in his stockbroker's office) began to buy pictures by the Impressionists and to paint and sculpt; the sculptor Rodin made his début at the *Salon* with *L'homme au nez cassé*; Mallarmé published his translation of Poe's *The Raven* with Manet's illustrations; Zola, Paul Alexis and a third Aixois, Numa Coste, who had just inherited a hundred thousand francs, founded a new review *L'Art Libre* to defend the Impressionists and especially Cézanne; Verlaine, released from prison where he had written *Parallèlement* and *Sagesse*, went to Stuttgart to join Rimbaud (who had gone there to learn German), quarrelled again with him and then went to Lincolnshire as French teacher at the Stickney Grammar School, stopping on the way '*dans le brouillard rose et jaune et sale des Sohos, avec des* indeeds *et des* all rights *et des* haos'; and Maurice Ravel was born, son of a Franco-Swiss father and a Basque mother.

There was no Impressionist exhibition in 1875 but Manet carried the fight into the enemy's camp by showing *Argenteuil*[1] (an Impressionist boating picture with large figures) in the *Salon*, where its bright colouring made the visitors blink and enraged the academic artists. The Impressionists' names were meanwhile kept before the public in various auction sales at the Hôtel Drouot. Works by Pissarro made reasonable prices in several of the sales; one landscape was sold for 580 frs. and another for 950 frs. (figures to be trebled at least to obtain the equivalent in present money); referring to the latter Pissarro wrote: '*Un monsieur a dit que c'était étonnant pour un paysage pur.*' Monet, Renoir, Sisley and Berthe Morisot were less successful; seventy of their paintings put up at the Hôtel Drouot made a total (including withdrawn pictures) of 10,350 frs.; George Moore, not yet acquainted with Degas or Manet and still an admirer of *Salon* painting, attended this sale, elegantly dressed, his yellow hair and beard immaculately barbered, and giggled at the pictures. The relatively small total made at this sale was of no consequence to Berthe Morisot who had a private income and whose husband Eugène Manet also

bleu marin croisée et boutonnée sur un gilet en pareil; le parement de cette veste, des poches et de la manche, en soie. Un chapeau tyrolien de feutre gris naturel avec le velours bleu marin et ailes de fantaisie . . .' A fashion note by de Goncourt in his Diary of this year reads: 'All the Parisian brunettes are now consumed by a passion to become blondes and they all dye their hair with potassium dissolved in water to achieve that result.'

[1] Tournai. Musée des Beaux-Arts.

had means; it was a set back but not a disaster for Renoir who could always make money by painting portraits and was now a favourite with Durand-Ruel; but it was gravely embarrassing for Sisley whose father had been ruined in 1870, and for Monet whose parents had always been poor, especially as neither could or would paint portraits and neither seems to have been supported to the same extent as Renoir by Durand-Ruel. Manet, informed of Monet's situation, wrote to Duret: 'I went to see Monet yesterday. I found him wretched and completely on the rocks. He asked me to find him someone who would choose ten or twenty pictures at 100 francs apiece. Will you join me in doing this—each of us buying to the extent of 500 francs? It would of course be understood that nobody—least of all Monet—must know that we are the buyers. I thought first of approaching a dealer or a collector, but I think I should be refused. *Il faut malheureusement s'y connaître comme nous pour faire, malgré la répugnance qu'on pourrait avoir, une excellente affaire, et en même temps, rendre service à un homme de talent. . . .*' It seems to be uncertain whether Duret agreed to this plan or not. But help for Monet and Sisley—and later for Renoir and Pissarro—was now forthcoming in the person of Eugène Murer who had been at school with Guillaumin and was now the keeper of a *crêmerie* on the Boulevard Voltaire; Murer delighted in brightly coloured pictures and hoped one day to retire from the pastry cook business and take to painting himself; meanwhile he gave generous credit for meals to Guillaumin's friends, taking an occasional picture in lieu of settlement; his *crêmerie* became a meeting place for the poor members of the Impressionist group, and also for poor writers and musicians; Tanguy frequently lunched there; and it was possibly thus that Tanguy first met Monet, Sisley and Renoir whom he supplied with colours in the same sort of way that Murer supplied them with food.

In 1876 Verlaine was a schoolmaster at Bournemouth, Van Gogh was a schoolmaster at Ramsgate, and Mallarmé, who now published *L'après-midi d'un faune*, was a schoolmaster in Paris. Maurice de Vlaminck was born, and Diaz died. Forain, aged twenty-four, began to draw for *Le Scapin* and other papers; Anatole France published *Les noces Corinthiennes*; Jules Laforgue (born in Montevideo in 1860) came from Tarbes to Paris; Daudet published '*Jack*'; Zola's *L'assommoir* (begun as a serial in *Le Bien Public*, and stopped by a frightened editor) was published by Catulle Mendès in *La République des Lettres*; Victor Hugo, aged seventy-two, took his seat as Senator at the instance of Clémenceau who was now in the Chamber as a Deputy for Paris; Hugo's *Hernani*, revived at the Comédie Française (with Mounet Sully and Sarah Bernhardt), was applauded by a claque which included André Antoine, now eighteen and working in the day time as a clerk in Hachette's shop; Hugo began an imposing salon frequented by Gambetta, Clémenceau, Rochefort, de Goncourt, Flaubert, Daudet, Mallarmé, Leconte de Lisle, Mendès, Ernest Renan, Gill, Dalou, Rodin, and countless others; Ruskin was miserably despondent at the Hôtel Meurice and still not disposed to inquire about French art or letters; and the Bayreuth Festspielhaus was opened in the presence of the German Emperor, Liszt (just reconciled with Wagner) and Nietzsche (who was soon to attack him).

The *Salon* jury incensed at the growing interest in the realists and the Impres-

Plate (A) DEGAS
Miss Lola au Cirque Fernando, 1879
London, National Gallery, Millbank (Tate Gallery)
(cf. page xi)

sionists among collectors, critics and dealers revenged themselves on Manet this year by rejecting *Le linge*[1] and *L'artiste*[2]—the first the celebrated picture of a woman at the wash tub in a garden with her child, the second a portrait of the engraver Marcellin Desboutin (who had also sat for Degas for *L'absinthe* which shows him and an actress called Ellen Andrée at a table of the Nouvelle Athènes). This jury admitted a woodland scene by Gauguin whose name was unknown to them and whom they did not associate with the group. The picture in this 1876 *Salon* which attracted most attention was Gustave Moreau's *L'apparition* (Pl. 11A).

In this same year 1876 the *Second Impressionist Exhibition* took place in Durand-Ruel's gallery. The number of exhibitors had fallen from thirty to nineteen—because the leading artists decided that the minor figures in the first exhibition had done them harm. Cézanne and Guillaumin abstained. The most notable newcomer was Gustave Caillebotte, aged twenty-eight, a rich naval architect and a painter of contemporary subjects, who was intensely keen on Impressionist art. To this exhibition Degas sent *L'absinthe*[3] (catalogued as *Dans un café*), *Petites paysannes se lavant à la mer* (probably the picture now known as *Femmes se peignant sur la plage*[4]), several studies of laundresses, some theatre and *école de danse* scenes, a *Modiste*, some portraits and *Le bureau de coton*[5] (painted in 1872)—twenty-four works in all; Renoir sent *La fillette attentive*[6] and seventeen other pictures; Pissarro and Monet each sent eighteen works; Sisley sent eight and Berthe Morisot seventeen; Caillebotte's contribution was *Les raboteurs de parquet*.[3] There is no evidence that the public was in any way hostile to these pictures—though many visitors were doubtless disconcerted by the bright colours in the Impressionist landscapes. Real hostility was only shown by the critics who admired the *Salon* painters and more particularly by Albert Wolff who wrote of 'flinging paint haphazard on to canvas'—as English academic critics had written of Turner n 1842, and as Ruskin was to write of Whistler in 1878. But the movement now had its own supporting critics. Castagnary described the landscapes by Monet, Pissarro and Sisley as 'true and pulsating with life'; and Duranty published a brochure '*La nouvelle peinture à propos du groupe d'artistes qui exposent dans les Galeries Durand-Ruel*' which especially explained and defended the standpoint of his friend Degas (who is said to have had a hand in its composition).

All things considered it will thus be seen that at the end of 1876 Degas and the Impressionists had every cause to be well content with the progress of their movement and every cause to look to the future with assurance. In the four or five years since normal life had again been possible in Paris they had acquired support from a growing phalanx of collectors, critics and dealers, and in the three years since they had appeared in group formation they had attracted the respectful attention of numerous Parisian art lovers. It was true that they sold their pictures for relatively modest sums—which meant that Monet, Sisley, Renoir, and Pissarro

[1] Painted 1874. Exhibited Messrs. Reid & Lefevre Galleries 1937.

[2] German Collection. Painted 1875.

[3] Paris. Louvre.   [4] Paris. M. Guillaume Lerolle.   [5] Pau. Museum.

[6] Paris. Bernheim Jeune. The sitter for this picture Mlle Legrand was the daughter of a former assistant at Durand-Ruel's who had just opened a shop of his own in the rue Laffitte where he showed Impressionist pictures.

(whose family was steadily increasing) were always more or less hard up; but none of these artists could complain that they were victimized by organized opposition or rudely treated by anyone—except by the academic painters and their supporting critics.

But all this changed for the worse in 1877. And to understand the change we must look at the political conditions which brought the change about. In 1874, after the failure of the Royalist plot of 1873, the Liberal Republicans had climbed swiftly to the saddle. In 1875 they won the battle of the Constitution; the Third Republic was given the form we know; MacMahon was re-elected the first constitutional President for seven years; and the Prime Minister at the moment became the first constitutional Prime Minister responsible to two legislative bodies, the Chamber of Deputies (elected by universal male adult suffrage) and the Senate (elected by a special electoral college); on paper the appointment of future ministers was to be the task of the President; and future Presidents were to be elected by the two Chambers sitting as a National Assembly for that purpose. But the Royalists, who still had the President MacMahon and many rich men and Right Extremists as their supporters, were resolved to attempt yet another fight; they hoped that the middle classes would rally round them if they were frightened by propaganda pretending that there was no distinction between a Liberal Republican Government and Red Terror or as they put it *Le Spectre Rouge*; in 1876 they worked secretly and enlisted the Bonapartists as allies; and in the spring of 1877 they induced MacMahon to begin an open conflict with the Liberal Prime Minister Jules Simon who resigned. MacMahon then formed the famous *Ministère du Seize Mai* with the Royalist de Broglie as Prime Minister; and before the June elections to the Chamber the Royalists, the Bonapartists and the Right extremists together began an intensive campaign of corruption, intimidation and propaganda, calling upon the country to choose between themselves 'The Party of Order' and the Republican '*Spectre Rouge*'. They wrote and spoke openly of a coming Restoration and they promised to make of the Republicans '*une patée dont les chiens eux-mêmes ne voudront pas*'. On the other side Victor Hugo republished his *Histoire d'un crime* (the *Coup d'état* of 1851) with a new preface: '*Ce livre est plus qu'actuel, il est urgent*'; and Gambetta made violent speeches describing the Restoration campaign as a manoeuvre engineered by the Church. In this crisis the aged Thiers stood by the Republicans and supported Gambetta; the country refused to be stampeded to a Restoration; the Republicans were returned with a majority and de Broglie resigned. In September Thiers died (at the age of eighty) and the Archbishop of Paris refused to sanction a memorial service at the Eglise de la Madeleine because the deceased had allied himself with the Church's enemy Gambetta. But the Liberals had the country behind them; and in December MacMahon was obliged to accept a Liberal Republican Prime Minister and a Liberal President of the Chamber.

Manet and the Impressionists were victimized by this so-called 'Party of Order's' propaganda of this year and they heard themselves referred to as producers of 'Gambettist' and 'Communard' art, as aiders and abettors of the *Spectre rouge*, as degenerates who revealed their taints in pictures like *Olympia* and the

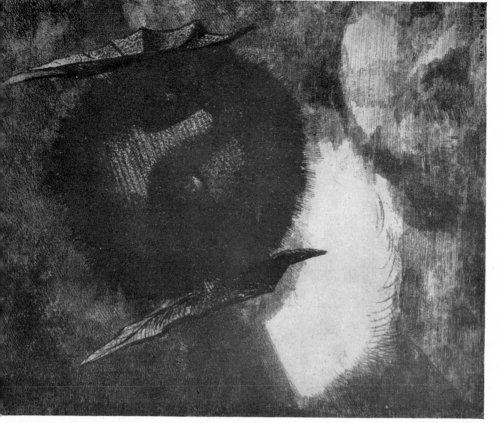

11B. ODILON REDON
Gnome, c. 1880
Lithograph

11A. MOREAU
L'apparition, 1876
Paris. Louvre

12. RENOIR
Sur la terrasse, 1881
Chicago. Art Institute

Déjeuner sur l'herbe, as associates of Zola whose *L'assommoir* (just published in book form) was patently indecent, and as imbeciles whose pictures painted in disordered spots and dashes were only admired and only dealt in and collected by people with unhealthy tastes. It is clear from the press of the period that all through 1877 half France and all Europe expected a Right Wing *coup d'état* followed by a White Terror like Thiers' White Terror which had followed the Commune six years before; and that all the snobs and hedgers in Paris took steps to put themselves on what they expected to be the winning side. Thus in Mme Charpentier's Republican salon the weathercock society women, who had always spent their evenings in the smoke room round Gambetta, now suddenly abandoned their former idol and left him in a corner all alone.[1] And in the same way collectors and dealers now began to fight shy of the Impressionists' pictures. In point of fact, Manet was a Liberal Republican, essentially bourgeois, who kept clear of the socialist theories which had proved so disastrous for Courbet (who died in misery this year); Degas was a Royalist; Cézanne was a staunch Catholic who detested Gambetta and all anti-clericals; Renoir, though he met Gambetta frequently at Mme Charpentier's Republican salon, took no interest in politics; Pissarro and Monet and Sisley were wholly concerned with painting pictures that would render sun-light and with trying to make ends meet. But as nobody at this time knew much about these artists the insinuations spread by the 'Party of Order's' propagandists were believed.

With these facts in mind we can understand what happened when the *Third Impressionist Exhibition* opened in April 1877 in the midst of MacMahon's momentary success which led to the *Ministère du seize Mai*, and what happened in June when the Impressionists held an auction of their pictures in the midst of the propaganda campaign for the election.

The *Third Impressionist Exhibition* was larger than the others and arranged in a series of five or six rooms in a building on the rue le Peletier. It contained scores of pictures which are looked on to-day as masterpieces by millions of art lovers in Europe and America. The first room was given to Monet, Renoir and Caillebotte; the second had landscapes by Monet, Pissarro, Sisley, Guillaumin and some others, rural subjects by Pissarro, Monet's *Les dindons blancs*[2] and Renoir's *La balançoire*;[3] the third, which was the largest, had Renoir's *Le Moulin de la Galette* (Pl. 9B), a large landscape by Pissarro, a group of paintings by Berthe Morisot, and sixteen paintings by Cézanne—including *Portrait de Choquet*,[4] *Scène fantastique*, *Le vase rococo*,[5] *Baigneurs au repos* and various landscapes and still life studies; and in other rooms were works by Berthe Morisot and twenty-two paintings, pastels and drawings by Degas—including *Danseuse au bouquet saluant sur la scène*,[3] *Un café; Boulevard Montmartre*,[3] *Répétition d'un ballet sur la scène*,[3] a number of *café concert* and

[1] This was related by Renoir, who witnessed it, to Vollard. In reporting Renoir's account, Vollard refers to Gambetta as *Président du Conseil*, assuming the date to be January, 1882. But that date is impossible because Renoir was then in Marseilles on his way back from Palermo where he had painted Wagner on January 15. De Goncourt tells us that Gambetta was frequenting this salon in 1877, and it was in this year and the next two that Renoir frequented it.

[2] Paris. Princess Edmond de Polignac.   [3] Paris. Louvre.
[4] Cambridge. Lord Rothschild.   [5] New York. Mr. and Mrs. Chester Dale.

école de danse scenes, several studies of women at their toilet and some portraits. The public went in much the same numbers as before; but they now included elements who were obviously hostile in a political way and who were grossly offensive to Caillebotte, Choquet, Duret and Georges Rivière who offered them a paper called *L'Impressioniste* which Rivière was editing as a kind of commentary on the pictures.

In June, when Renoir, Pissarro and Caillebotte put up forty-five pictures at the Hôtel Drouot, the sale room was invaded by mysterious groups whose conduct was so outrageous that it can only be explained as organized political attack; as each picture appeared it was greeted with loud jeers and cat-calls, and amid the clamour a picture by Renoir (who, we must remember, had just exhibited *Le Moulin de la Galette*) was sold for 45 frs., and Pissarro (whose pictures had sold for 580 frs. and 950 frs., as noted, in 1875) saw his pictures knocked down at prices between 100 frs. and 200 frs.

As a result of these conditions the artists now suffered a still worse blow. Their chief supporter among the dealers, Durand-Ruel, seized with panic, resolved to show no more Impressionist pictures till the wind changed, and hung his gallery with works by Corot and the Barbizon painters, Rousseau and Millet, who were safely dead and could not be accused of aiding and abetting the *Spectre Rouge*.

In the next year, 1878, the Liberal Republicans made firm their position, but Manet and the Impressionists continued to suffer from the campaign of calumny of the previous year. It was in vain that Duret published his pamphlet *Les peintres Impressionistes* with biographical accounts to show the artists' respectability and with a pointed reference to 'the wide spread prejudice which has represented these artists as social vagabonds (*dévoyés*) and the admirers of their pictures as people with unhealthy tastes (*goûts malsains*)'; the harm had been done; collectors still fought shy of these suspect artists, the *Salon* refused all the pictures submitted by Manet, and the slaughter of Impressionist pictures at auction sales went on. In June Hoschedé (already referred to as of *Gagne-Petit* fame and proprietor of *L'Art et la Mode*) decided to unload his Impressionist pictures; at this sale at the Hôtel Drouot pictures by Pissarro and the others were sold for nominal sums and Manet's *La femme au perroquet* (Pl. 4) was knocked down for 700 frs.[1]

In these circumstances the Impressionists decided to postpone their Fourth Impressionist Exhibition projected for this year; and the members of the group who had no private incomes were exceedingly hard hit. In July Monet took Manet a bundle of his pictures and besought him to try and sell them; in August Sisley implored Duret to find someone who would pay him 500 francs a month for six months and take thirty pictures in exchange. Only a few true friends were conspicuously loyal. The singer Faure tried to stop the rot at the Hôtel Drouot by putting up Manet's *Le bon bock*, *Le bal de l'Opéra* and *Polichinelle* and publicly buying in the first at 10,000 frs., the second at 6,000 frs., and selling the third, a small picture, for 2,000 frs. (and Manet rewarded him by letting him have *Le déjeuner sur*

[1] When Durand-Ruel bought twenty-two pictures by Manet seven years earlier (in 1871) he paid an average price of 1500 frs. apiece. *La femme au perroquet* was among them. Hedosché bought it from Durand-Ruel for 2000 frs.

l'herbe and some copies of 'Old Masters' for 2,600 frs.); Charpentier gave Renoir a handsome commission to paint a large portrait group of his wife and children to hang in his house and be seen by the now numerous and increasingly powerful frequenters of Mme Charpentier's salon; Caillebotte, Gauguin and Mary Cassatt, as well-disposed amateurs with money, bought some pictures by Pissarro, Renoir, Sisley and Monet; an eccentric named de Bellio, who lunched every day at the Café Riche and believed in the Impressionists, bought any picture the artists brought him for 200 francs without troubling himself to look at it; and Murer and Tanguy took pictures by Pissarro, Monet and Sisley in exchange for food and colours supplied to them on credit. The eclipse of the Impressionist movement in 1878 was especially unlucky for the artists because there was again an *Exposition Universelle* in this year for which the Palais du Champ de Mars and the Palais du Trocadéro (demolished for the 1937 Exposition) were built and this Exposition brought many art-loving foreigners to Paris. As it was, those visitors either heard nothing of these artists or heard them spoken of as suspect eccentrics or 'reds' or failures.

In this year 1878 Monet painted his first Vetheuil pictures; and Manet painted *La prune* (Pl. 10); Cézanne, threatened with loss of his allowance because his father had found out his liaison with Hortense Fiquet, asked Zola to find him a salaried post in Paris, and Zola who had just bought his country house at Medan, sent Hortense a monthly sum till Cézanne's allowance was renewed; Seurat, aged nineteen, entered the Ecole des Beaux-Arts; Van Gogh, aged twenty-five, became a lay preacher in the Borinage; Debussy, aged sixteen, was taken to London where he heard Sullivan's *H.M.S. Pinafore*; Whistler, aged forty-four, won a farthing damages for libel from Ruskin, aged fifty-nine, who had just recovered from his first attack of madness; Daubigny died at sixty-one; George Moore published *Flowers of Passion*; and André Antoine, now a clerk in the Gas Company, saw *Un drame sous Philippe II* by Porto Riche at the Odéon.

PROLOGUE: HOW IT HAPPENED

SCENE V: 1879-1883

From the *Fourth Impressionist Exhibition* to the death of Manet

---

In 1879 the remaining fears of a Right Wing *coup d'état* were dissipated; MacMahon resigned the Presidency and the Liberal Jules Grévy was elected to succeed him; the Liberal Waddington became Prime Minister; the Liberal Jules Ferry became Minister of Education and Fine Arts, and Sadi Carnot became Minister of Public Works; Gambetta was President of the Chamber where Clémenceau sat as a Left Wing Deputy. The two Chambers were now moved from Versailles to Paris; a general amnesty for all political offenders since the Commune was ordained; and the *Marseillaise* was officially adopted as the national anthem. In July Jules Ferry secured the first reading of an Education Bill excluding army officers, magistrates and clergy from the Education Council and forbidding members of religious congregations to teach in schools until they had applied for, and been granted, authorization to do so; and this started the fight for secular education which continued for twenty-five years.

In these more favourable conditions the Impressionists decided to hold their *Fourth Impressionist Exhibition* postponed from the year before. Renoir who had been promised, through Charpentier's influence, a good place in the *Salon* for his portrait group *Mme Charpentier et ses enfants*,[1] deserted his former colleagues. Sisley, Berthe Morisot and Cézanne also declined to exhibit—Cézanne writing a lame excuse to Pissarro that he would find it difficult to arrange for transport of his pictures from Melun where he was staying. Degas stood by Pissarro and Monet on condition that the word 'Impressionist' was not used in the title of the exhibition (which in fact was advertised as *Exposition des Indépendants* as in 1874); and he sent five painted fans and twenty pictures including *Miss Lola au Cirque Fernando*,[2] *Blanchisseuses portant du linge en ville*,[3] *Danseuse posant chez un photographe* and other *danseuse* pictures, a *Chanteuse de café*, the *Portrait de Duranty*,[4] the *Portraits à la Bourse*[5] (containing portraits of the Vicomte Lepic and the banker Ernest May) and *Portraits d'amis sur la scène*[6] and finally the portrait of the art critic Diego Martelli. To compensate to some extent for the defections Degas introduced as newcomers his American pupil Mary Cassatt and his friend Forain who was now

[1] New York. Metropolitan Museum.   [2] Plate A.
[3] Then owned by M. Coquelin (cadet). [4] Scotland. Sir William Burrell.
[5] Paris. Louvre.   [6] Rhode Island. School of Design.

42

13 . DEGAS

Femme à sa toilette, c. 1880

Paris. Georges Wildenstein

14. RENOIR
Portrait de Wagner, 1882
Paris. M. Alfred Cortot

drawing for the Royalist paper *Le Monde Parisien*. Forain's contributions included a water colour *Cabinet particulier* and *Coulisses de l'Opéra*. This Exhibition was visited by fifteen thousand people; there were no abnormal demonstrations and the press comments were reasonable; at the end Degas wrote to the engraver Bracquemond who had exhibited: '*L'Exposition est fermée. Dépêchez-vous. Il y a 439 fr. 5c. à toucher par personne.* . . .'

The 1879 *Salon* had *Dans la serre*[1] and *En bateau*[2] by Manet; *La loge aux Italiens*[3] by Eva Gonzalez (much assisted doubtless by Manet); *Mlle Samary*[4] and *Mme Charpentier et ses enfants*[2] by Renoir; *Victor Hugo* by Bonnat, *Sarah Bernhardt* by Bastien-Lepage; and as the popular picture of the year *Un asile pour la vieillesse* by Herkomer. J.-K. Huysmans, aged thirty-one, made his reputation as an art critic with articles on this *Salon* in *Le Voltaire*; he described the *Salon* as far less interesting because less modern than the *Fourth Impressionist Exhibition*; and he scolded the hanging committee for placing Renoir's *Mlle Samary* in a bad position. When the *Salon* was over Manet offered his services to the Préfet de la Seine as decorator of the new Hôtel de Ville; he proposed a series of panels titled '*Le Ventre de Paris: la vie publique et commerciale de nos jours*'—with individual panels titled *Paris-Halles, Paris-Chemins de fer, Paris-Pont, Paris-Souterrain, Paris-Courses-et-Jardins*; the proposal was not considered and Manet painted instead the restaurant scene *Chez le père Lathuille*,[5] the café-concert scene *La serveuse de bocks*,[6] and three sketches of George Moore whom he had just met at the Nouvelle Athènes and enrolled as a disciple.[7]

Zola's publisher Charpentier was now more than ever active as a supporter of the Impressionists and especially of Renoir; he had started a review *La vie moderne* to help them and opened a gallery in its offices where he organized exhibitions of their works. Zola himself on the other hand, defending his own procedures as a realist novelist and influenced by Flaubert (who wrote him this year that he could make nothing of Manet's painting), had now come to the conclusion that Manet and the Impressionists were shirking their duties as realist artists. He expounded this notion in the St. Petersburg *Messager d'Europe* to which he contributed as Paris correspondent (through the good offices of Tourguenief): '*Pour être un homme de talent il faut qu'un homme réalise ce qui vit en lui. Tous ces artistes-là sont trop facilement satisfaits. Ils dédaignent à tort la solidité des œuvres longuement méditées: ils n'étudient pas la nature avec la passion des vrais créateurs.*' Quotations from this article were published in the *Revue politique et littéraire* and in the *Figaro*, and Zola in dismay wrote Manet that they were mistranslated and republished his *Salon* articles of the 'sixties to remind him and the others of services rendered. For the rest, this was a time of great success for Zola; his *Nana* appearing in *Le Voltaire* was

[1] German collection. [2] New York. Metropolitan Museum. (Painted 1874.)
[3] Paris. Louvre. [4] Moscow. Museum of Modern Western Art.
[5] Tournai. Museum.
[6] London. National Gallery, Millbank. (Another version belongs to Baron Matsukata at Tokio.)
[7] One of these sketches *George Moore au café* belongs to M. Albert S. Henraux in Paris. Another is in a German collection. The third, a pastel, is in the Metropolitan Museum, New York.

widely discussed; *L'assommoir* produced as a play ran for three hundred nights; at a dinner and costume ball given to celebrate the *première* George Moore appeared as Manet's *Le buveur d'absinthe*[1]; and Cézanne came from Aix to see a performance—having first written to Zola to make sure that he would not have to pay for his ticket.

In this year 1879 Daumier died at the age of seventy-one; he had been almost blind since 1877 and living, on a small pension provided by the State, in a cottage given him by Corot; he had never exhibited his paintings which were then unknown to collectors and stored to the number of two hundred in his cottage.[2] In this year also Odilon Redon, aged thirty-nine, published his first set of lithographs called *Dans le Rêve*, from which I reproduce the print called *Gnome* (Pl. 11B); Pierre Loti, aged thirty-five, published his first novel *Aziyadé*; Catulle Mendès published *La vie et la mort d'un clown*; Verlaine, dismissed from the Catholic College, was farming with one of the pupils; Othon Friesz and Raoul Dufy were born at Le Havre and Paul Klee was born at Berne. Toulouse-Lautrec, aged fifteen, painted *Artilleur sellant son cheval*;[3] and Seurat, aged twenty, read Chevreul's *De la loi du contraste simultané des couleurs et de l'assortiment des objets coloriés* in the library of the Ecole des Beaux-Arts.

The *Fifth Impressionist Exhibition* took place in 1880. Degas and Caillebotte quarrelled about the announcements; Caillebotte wanted posters mentioning only the most 'drawing' names; Degas wanted all the names or none; Caillebotte, powerful in his dual role of collector and exhibitor, had his way. Cézanne, Renoir, Monet and Sisley abstained from this show and the Committee were reduced to inviting Raffaelli—whom they looked on as a follower—and Gauguin—whom they looked on as collector and amateur painter—to join them. Gauguin and Pissarro sent landscapes; Caillebotte *Au café* and some bourgeois interiors with figures; Berthe Morisot *Jeune femme au bal*[4]; Mary Cassatt *Le Thé*; Forain *Maison close* and *La promenade du voyou à la campagne* (illustrating a poem by Verlaine); Bracquemond *Portrait d'Edmond de Goncourt*; and Degas several *école de danse* scenes, *La loge au théâtre*,[5] the *Portrait de Duranty* already exhibited last year, and *Jeunes Spartiates s'exerçant à la lutte* (painted in 1860 and catalogued as *Petites filles spartiates provoquant des garçons*)[6]. Huysmans wrote at length on this exhibition which he tells us was well received by the public. He himself approved of the show because, apart from Berthe Morisot's contributions which he described as *ébauches morbides*, and the relatively pedestrian works by Pissarro, the majority of the pictures were realist works by Degas, Caillebotte and Forain whom he especially admired; he made no mention of Gauguin's exhibits, which struck him (he stated later) as 'une dilution des œuvres encore incertaines de Pissarro'.

Manet now had a one-man show in Charpentier's *La vie moderne* gallery and

[1] Copenhagen. Ny Carlsberg Museum. (Painted in 1859–1860.)
[2] '*Très peu de ces œuvres furent acquises à des prix modestes par des amis de Daumier. Un grand nombre fut en quelque sorte raflé à sa veuve pour une vile somme par une association de marchands peu scrupuleux.*' Arsène Alexandre in Bénézit. *Dictionnaire des peintres* (1924).
[3] Albi. Musée Lautrec.   [4] Paris. Luxembourg.
[5] Washington. Corcoran Gallery of Art (Clark Collection).
[6] London. National Gallery, Millbank.

painted his *Portrait de Clémenceau*.[1] At the same time Bonnat painted Gambetta, thus fulfilling Manet's prophecy of 1871.[2] After the Manet exhibition *La vie moderne* gallery had a successful one-man show by Claude Monet, and then a show of ostrich eggs painted by, among others, Manet, Forain and the satirical engraver and draughtsman Félicien Rops. Degas, secure in his financial independence, referred scornfully to the *'réclame effrénée'* of the *Vie Moderne* exhibitions—partly, no doubt, because he disapproved of Charpentier as a Liberal and as Zola's publisher, and partly, may be, because he had not been invited to paint an egg.

In this year 1880 André Derain was born at Chatou and Pierre Roy was born at Nantes. André Antoine and Georges Seurat were doing military service. Gauguin bought Cézanne's *Compotier, verre et pommes*[3] for his collection. Marcel Proust had his first attack of asthma at the age of nine; Manet took hydropathic treatment for incipient paralysis at the age of forty-eight; Duranty died at forty-seven; and Flaubert died at fifty-nine. Courbet's *L'atelier du peintre*,[4] included in a Retrospective Exhibition of his works, was described by Huysmans as *'une terrifiante ânerie imaginée par un homme sans éducation et peinte par un vieux manœuvre'*. Pierre Loti published *Rarahu*, and Mallarmé *Les dieux antiques*. Zola published *Les soirées de Medan* (short stories by realist writers including de Maupassant's *Boule de suif*) and *Nana* in book form which sold sixty-five thousand copies in the first four weeks; Zola spent his now ample income on bric-a-brac for his Paris house and his villa at Medan; he spent no money on pictures by the Impressionists, and he put the pictures which Cézanne had given him in the 'sixties[5] in an attic out of sight; and his friendship with those artists, already frayed by his article in the St. Petersburg paper, began from this period to wear thin.

The *Sixth Impressionist Exhibition* took place in 1881 and was well received. It had mainly the same exhibitors as the Fifth—except that Monet and Guillaumin now returned, and Caillebotte joined Renoir and Cézanne as abstainers. Gauguin was represented by landscapes, a *Nature morte* (flowers on a chair in a sunlit garden) and *Etude de nu : femme raccommodant sa chemise*,[6] and he also sent a carved and coloured wooden figure *Dame en promenade* and a coloured plaster relief *Chanteuse*. Mary Cassatt sent pictures of women and children, interiors and garden scenes (referred to by Degas in a letter as *'beaucoup plus ferme et plus noble que ce qu'elle a fait l'année passée'*); and Degas himself sent portraits, a *Blanchisseuse*, a drawing titled *Physionomie de criminel* and the celebrated wax statue with real clothes *Petite danseuse de quatorze ans*.[4] Huysmans, in a detailed notice of this exhibition, declared that Pissarro was now a master and Mary Cassatt comparable with Dickens and Millais; he described Gauguin's polychrome carving as *gothiquement moderne* and wrote famous passages on his *Etude de nu* and on Degas' *Petite danseuse de quatorze ans*.[7]

---

[1] Paris. Louvre. This picture was given by Mme Manet to Clémenceau in 1883. Clémenceau disliked it and it was acquired in 1896 by Mrs. Havemayer of New York. who presented it to the Louvre in 1927. Clémenceau also disliked his bust by Rodin (cf. p. 232).

[2] Cf. p. 30. [3] Paris. Lecomte Collection. [4] Paris. Louvre.
[5] Cf. below, p. 57. [6] Copenhagen. Ny Carlsberg Museum.

[7] For the passage on Gauguin's picture, cf. p. 66. On Degas' wax figure Huysmans wrote: *'Devant cette statue de cire le public, très ahuri et comme gêné, se sauve. La terrible réalité de cette statuette lui produit un évident malaise. . . . De même que certaines Madones maquillées et vêtues de robes, de même*

45

The *Salon* now reorganized itself as the *Société des Artistes Français* with an annual jury elected by the exhibitors of the previous year. But visitors to the Society's succeeding exhibitions saw no evidences of the change, and the *Salon* was still generally called, and still remained, the *Salon*. Its exhibits this year included *Le pauvre pêcheur*[1] by Puvis de Chavannes; *En route pour le temple de Ceres* by Alma Tadema; illustrated albums by Kate Greenaway and Walter Crane; *Mlle Irène Cahen*[2] and other portraits by Renoir; and Manet's *Portrait de Rochefort*[3] and *Portrait de Pertuiset, chasseur de lions*.[4] Manet had been in touch with Rochefort (returned with Olivier Pain to Paris) since the end of the previous year when he began to make sketches for *L'évasion de Rochefort et d'Olivier Pain de Nouméa*;[5] Desboutin (who referred to them as 'Robinson-Rochefort' and 'Olivier Pain-Vendredi') had brought them to his studio and Manet had persuaded them to sit for individual portraits and also to give him details of the size and colour of the boat they had escaped in and so forth. The portrait of the lion hunter Pertuiset, who is shown kneeling in a soi-disant forest with a rifle in his hand, was in fact painted in the garden of a restaurant on the Boulevard de Clichy; for this picture Manet received a medal at the *Salon*. In the course of the year he painted the popular picture *Le printemps*,[6] the *Portrait d'Henry Bernstein enfant*,[7] some sketches in the garden of the house at Versailles where he was living and the greater part of *Le Bar aux Folies Bergère*.[8] At the same time Charpentier's *La Vie Moderne* gallery arranged a show of Odilon Redon's Surrealist *Dans le rêve* lithographs (including *Gnome* (Pl. 11B), of which Huysmans wrote: '*C'est le cauchemar transporté dans l'art. Mêlez dans un milieu macabre de somnambulesques figures ayant une vague parenté avec celles de Gustave Moreau, tournées à l'effroi, et peut-être vous ferez-vous une idée du bizarre talent de ce singulier artiste.*'

In this year 1881 Pablo Picasso was born at Malaga, and Fernand Léger was born in Paris; André Gill went mad; and Carlyle, Dostoievsky and Moussorgsky died. Anatole France published *Le crime de Silvestre Bonnard*, Pierre Loti *Le roman d'un Spahi*; Jules Laforgue wrote articles on Dürer and other German artists in

que ce Christ de la cathédrale de Burgos dont les cheveux sont de vrais cheveux, les épines de vraies épines, la draperie une véritable étoffe, la danseuse de M. Degas a de vraies jupes, de vrais rubans, un vrai corsage, de vrais cheveux. La tête peinte, un peu renversée, le menton en l'air, entr'ouvrant la bouche dans la face maladive et bise, tirée et vieille avant l'âge, les mains ramenées derrière le dos et jointes, la gorge plate moulée par un blanc corsage dont l'étoffe est pétrie de cire, les jambes en place pour la lutte, d'admirables jambes rompues aux exercices, nerveuses et tordues, surmontées comme d'un pavillon par la mousseline des jupes, le cou raide, cerclé d'un ruban porreau, les cheveux retombant sur l'épaule et arborant, dans le chignon orné d'un ruban pareil à celui du cou, de réels crins, elle est cette danseuse qui s'anime sous le regard et semble prête à quitter son socle. . . . Cette statuette est la seule tentative vraiment moderne que je connaisse dans la sculpture.'

Paul Mantz writing in *Le Temps* described the statue as *presque effrayante* and enlarged on '*L'instructive laideur d'un visage où tous les vices impriment leur détestables promesses*'—which was hard on a model of fourteen. Degas, Mantz added, was destined for '*une petite place dans l'histoire des arts cruels*'.

[1] Paris. Luxembourg.   [2] Paris. M. Reinach.
[3] German Collection.   [4] Abbazia (Italy). Mme T. Durieux.
[5] Paris. Mme Hecht.
[6] New York. Metropolitan Museum. (Mrs. Payne Bingham.)
[7] Paris. M. Henry Bernstein.   [8] London. National Gallery. (Courtauld Collection.)

15A. CÉZANNE
La route tournante, c. 1882
Boston. John T. Spaulding, Esq.
15B. MONET
Les falaises de Pourville, 1882
Exhibited London, Tooth's Galleries, 1936

16. RENOIR
La baigneuse blonde, 1882
London. Sir Kenneth Clark

Ephrussi's *Gazette des Beaux-Arts* and then went to Berlin as lector to the Empress Augusta; Joséphin Péladan, aged twenty-two, began his career with an essay on Rembrandt; George Moore, after his exciting contacts with Parisian artists, returned to Ireland and wrote *Pagan Poems*; Emile Schuffenecker, Gauguin's colleague in his stockbroking office, resigned his post to become a painter; Rodolphe Salis opened the *Chat Noir* cabaret (fitted up in 'Ye Olde Louis XIII' style) in Montmartre; de Goncourt, visiting the actress Mlle Samary in her dressing room, found the walls hung with drawings by Forain and the ceiling covered with Japanese fans; and Verlaine's *Sagesse* was issued by the *Société Générale de Libraire Catholique*.

The *Seventh Impressionist Exhibition* took place in 1882. Cézanne, Degas and Degas' followers Forain and Mary Cassatt abstained; but Renoir returned and exhibited with Pissarro, Monet, Sisley, Guillaumin, Caillebotte, Berthe Morisot and Gauguin. Renoir's pictures—twenty in all—included *Le déjeuner des Canotiers*,[1] *La femme à l'éventail*,[2] and some heads and figures in Algerian costumes (records of a visit to Algiers on his way back from Palermo where he had painted the *Portrait de Wagner* (Pl. 14) in January). Pissarro sent landscapes including *La route de Pontoise à Auvers*, *Vue de la prison de Pontoise* and some peasant pictures; Monet sent *Les falaises de Pourville* (Pl. 15B), some Vetheuil scenes and *Les coquelicots*;[3] Caillebotte's chief exhibit was *La partie de bésigue*; Gauguin sent landscapes, *La voiture d'enfants*,[4] *Intérieur d'atelier*, and some sketches of his children. Apart from the centre piece, Renoir's *Le déjeuner des Canotiers*, this exhibition was mainly a landscape show which was quietly accepted by the public and the critics and by the growing number of dilettanti who now admired and collected Impressionist pictures.

The outstanding pictures at the 1882 *Salon* were Manet's *Bar aux Folies Bergère* and Whistler's *Lady Meux*. Degas referred to both in a letter to Henri Rouart; of the first he wrote: '*Manet bête et fin, carte à jouer sans impression, trompe l'œil espagnole, peintre . . .*'; of the second '*Un Whistler étonnant, raffiné à l'excès, mais d'une trempe . . .*' John Singer Sargent's *Danse Espagnole* was a favourite picture with the crowd.

In this year 1882 Georges Braque was born at Argenteuil; Van Gogh, aged twenty-nine, was living miserably with a harlot at the Hague; Oscar Wilde, aged twenty-six, was touring the American cities lecturing on Aesthetic; Odilon Redon published his lithographs *A Edgar Poe*; Jules Laforgue wrote *Complaintes* and parts of *Moralités légendaires* in Berlin; Rimbaud, aged twenty-eight, was at Aden, and planning to explore Abyssinia; Verlaine, aged thirty-eight, lionised at the Café François Premier on the Boulevard Saint Michel, wrote *Les poètes maudits* (with the essay on Rimbaud that made him famous and the essay on himself—*Le pauvre Lélian*); Pierre Loti published *Le mariage de Loti*, and Zola *Pot-Bouille*; Becque's *Les Corbeaux* was performed at the Comédie Française; and Victor Hugo's eightieth birthday was celebrated in fêtes and processions where fifty thousand children paraded before his window and the railways delivered forty truckloads of floral gifts. In the summer Manet took a villa at Rueil where he painted sunlit Impression-

[1] Washington. Phillips Memorial Gallery.   [2] Paris. J. Laroche.
[3] Paris. Louvre.   [4] Copenhagen. Ny Carlsberg Museum.

ist sketches and some still life studies and pastel heads; his illness was now increasingly distressing and he had to take to a wheeled chair; when Albert Wolff wrote to congratulate him on the success of the *Bar aux Folies Bergère* in the *Salon* he replied: 'Thank you for your kind remarks. But I confess I should be glad to read in my lifetime the fine article that you will devote to me—as soon as I am dead.'

In 1883, the last year of our Prologue, Seurat's drawing *Portrait du peintre Aman Jean* (Pl. 17A) was shown in the *Salon* and discovered by the critic Roger Marx, who wrote of it in *Le progrès artistique*: 'I was so much struck by this portrait that I searched for further exhibits by M. Seurat in the other sections; the search was vain; but a drawing of this merit is surely not the work of an artist of ordinary talent.' Seurat at this time was twenty-four and this was his first exhibit.

In 1883 also Gauguin, aged thirty-five, abandoned his stockbroking business and became a professional instead of an amateur painter; Van Gogh, aged thirty, was painting his first pictures at Drenthe in Holland and making drawings which he hoped, naively enough, to sell as 'Views of Picturesque Holland' to illustrated papers in London and New York; Toulouse-Lautrec, aged nineteen, was attending the art school of an academic painter Fernand Cormon; the exhibiting Society *Les XX* was founded in Brussels with the Englishman James Ensor (who was then twenty-three and had just painted the Surrealist *Masques Scandalisées*) as its most adventurous member; Maurice Utrillo, son of an obscure artist named Boissy and Suzanne Valadon (friend and model of Renoir and Degas) was born in Paris; Gino Severini was born at Cortona; Jean Metzinger was born at Nantes; Wagner died in Venice at the age of seventy-one and Karl Marx died in London at sixty-five. Pierre Loti published *Mon frère Yves*; Paul Bourget, aged thirty-three, published *Essais de psychologie contemporains* and Gabriele d'Annunzio, aged twenty, published *Intermezzo di rime*. Zola published *Au bonheur des dames* describing conditions in department stores like the *Printemps* (whereYvette Guilbert, aged sixteen, had just been engaged as an apprentice). Nietzsche began *Zarathustra*; the Swedish novelist, playwright and painter August Strindberg, aged thirty-four, was in Paris with his first wife and her dog which he passionately detested; Anatole France, aged thirty-nine, met Mme de Caillavet and began to frequent her *salon* where Alexandre Dumas *fils* and the novelist-playwright Henri Rivière (then in Cochin-China) had hitherto been the outstanding 'lions'; Eric Satie, aged seventeen, began his musical studies at the Paris Conservatoire; and Oscar Wilde, aged twenty-seven, 'wrapped in a monkish robe with a large cowl' in imitation of Balzac, wrote *The Duchess of Padua* at the Hôtel Voltaire on the Quai Voltaire. In March Ruskin, aged sixty-four, received a complimentary copy of *L'éducation de l'artiste* from the French art historian Ernest Chesneau; he replied before reading it: 'I expect much from the book on the artist's education. But they're very like pigs as far as I know them; all I can say is, I hope that flogging won't be abolished in any schools instituted for them by modern enlightenment.' In April Ruskin sent Chesneau some examples of his own drawing (plates from *Modern Painters*) and wrote in the covering letter: 'If you will give five minutes' glance with a lens you will see at once through what sort of work I have been led to such scrupulosity or fastidiousness in execution as makes me angry at those fast sketches of the modern French school.'

The Impressionists held no joint exhibition in 1883. But Durand-Ruel staged a series of one-man shows on the first floor of an empty house on the Boulevard de la Madeleine which he rented for the purpose; he began with a Monet exhibition in March; and followed with Renoir, Pissarro and Sisley in April, May and June. The Monet, Sisley and Renoir shows were successful, and a number of pictures were sold; Renoir's show contained among other things *Le Moulin de la Galette* (Pl. 9B), *La baigneuse blonde* (Pl. 16), *Portrait de Wagner* (Pl. 14), and two pictures painted from Suzanne Valadon and Mme Renoir—*La danse à la campagne*[1] and *La danse à la ville*.[1] The Pissarro show was relatively a failure—doubtless because collectors found it cautious and monotonous after Renoir's varied display. After the exhibition Pissarro went to Rouen where he found Gauguin embarked on his new career; 'I have worked for thirty years', he told him, 'and here I am, on the rocks, at fifty-three'; but in point of fact, his most difficult period was now past, and the year before he had written to Duret: '*Je ne roule pas sur l'or, mais je jouis du fruit d'une vente modeste et régulière*', and if he still had financial worries it was mainly because his family was large.

Degas, like the others, had a contract to deliver pictures to Durand-Ruel; but he would not consent to a one-man show in the temporary gallery on the Boulevard de la Madeleine, and Durand-Ruel showed his work to likely customers in his own gallery, in the impressive intimacy of a private room. In a letter to a friend at this moment Degas refers to the café-concert singer Thérésa: '*Allez vite entendre Thérésa à l'Alcazar, rue Faubourg Poissonnière. C'est près du Conservatoire et c'est mieux. . . . C'est le moment d'entendre cette admirable artiste. Elle ouvre sa grande bouche et il en sort la voix la plus grossièrement, la plus délicatement, la plus spirituellement tendre qu'il soit. Et l'âme et le goût, où peut-on trouver du meilleur? C'est admirable.*' Thérésa at this time had already been popular for a number of years and her vogue was almost done; Degas made several pastels and lithographs depicting her; in one, *La chanson du chien*,[2] she is seen imitating the action of a begging dog.

In March of this year Degas wrote to the sculptor Bartholomé: 'Manet is done for. That doctor Hureau de Villeneuve seems to have poisoned him with ergot of rye. Some of the newspapers have already been at pains to announce his approaching end. I hope they've been read to him as he has no idea of his condition. His foot is gangrenous.' At the beginning of April Manet submitted to the amputation of his foot; but this did not save him, and he died on April 30, at fifty-one. Monet, Zola, Alfred Stevens, Theodore Duret and Fantin-Latour were pall bearers at his funeral. On May 1 Albert Wolff published in the *Figaro* the obituary notice that Manet had foreseen; Manet's place in art history, he said, would be based more on what he wished to do than on what he had done; but a few of his works—such as *Le bon bock* and *L'enfant à l'épée*—'*conçues en dehors de toute préoccupation revolutionnaire*' would live. Manet left numerous unsold sketches, pastels, etc., and about a hundred unsold pictures including *Le vieux musicien*, *Le balcon*, *Olympia*, *Le linge*, *Nana*, *Jésus insulté par les soldats*, *L'éxécution de l'Empereur Maximilien*, *Chez le pèr*

[1] Boston. Museum of Fine Arts. [2] New York. Horace Havemeyer.

Lathuille and *Bar aux Folies Bergères* which passed to his widow; Victorine Meurend, his favourite model from 1862 to 1874, was now destitute and wrote to Mme Manet for assistance; Mme Manet's reply, if any, is not, I believe, preserved.

While our artists fared thus in 1880–1883 they witnessed, among others, the following political events. In 1880 the *Quatorze Juillet* was fixed for an annual *Fête Nationale* and Jules Ferry fell after his success in establishing a French Protectorate in Tunis and his campaign to make primary education free, compulsory and secular for both sexes. In 1881 Gambetta became Prime Minister and resolved to balance the imminent Austro-German-Italian Triple Alliance by understandings with England and Russia. Gambetta's Cabinet contained Antonin Proust (a life-long friend of Manet) as Minister of Fine Arts, and Proust at once named Manet for the *Légion d'honneur*; Jules Grévy, President of the Republic, resisted the nomination but gave way when Gambetta wrote to him: '*Monsieur le Président, c'est à vos ministres qu'il appartient de conférer des croix. Nous vous demandons par déférence votre signature; mais vous n'avez pas le droit de discuter nos choix.*' In 1881 also the Panama Canal Company was formed with Ferdinand de Lesseps, engineer of the Suez Canal, as a dominant figure; and Catholics and conservatives of all classes rushed to invest their savings in the *Union Générale des Banques*—an enterprise which assured them that if they bought its shares all Jewish and foreign bankers would be ruined. In 1882 the *Union Générale des Banques* went bankrupt and hundreds of the investors lost their money; the Gambetta Ministry fell; Paul Déroulède and other Right Wing extremists founded the militant *Ligue des Patriotes*; forty-seven socialists, including the Russian exile Prince Kropotkin, were imprisoned after bombs, placed by three anarchists, had exploded in the Théâtre Bellecour and in the recruiting offices at Lyons; and Gambetta shot himself by accident while cleaning his revolver, at the age of forty-four. In 1883 Jules Ferry, again Prime Minister, pressed on with his programme for secular education at home and colonial expansion abroad; and France now acquired her territories in the Congo and Cochin-China.

At this moment when our Prologue ends, the Liberal Republicans were thus the real masters of the country. They had nothing to fear from the Extreme Left as the Communists were neither numerous nor organized and the Anarchists were not yet a serious nuisance; they had nothing to fear from the Extreme Right as Déroulède's *Ligue des Patriotes* was also not yet a nuisance; and they had nothing to fear from the Royalists (the Comte de Chambord died this year) or from the Bonapartists (whose Pretender was now the Duc d'Aumale as the Prince Imperial had been killed while fighting in the British Army against the Zulus). Their triumph was recognized even by their enemies and Degas wrote gloomily: '*Tâchons de nous cramponner à cette terre—toute républicaine qu'elle soit.*'

PROLOGUE: THE MASTERS' LIVES

EDGAR DEGAS[1] (i)

To the age of forty-nine (1834–1883)

In 1863 Edgar Degas was twenty-nine. Born in Paris on June 19, 1834, and christened Hilaire-Germain-Edgar De Gas (he himself being the first of his family to write the name Degas), he came of a rich French family who owned a banking business in Naples and was connected by marriage with noble Italian families. His father, a man of parts and an amateur of pictures, lived at Naples until his marriage with a French Creole lady from New Orleans; he then established a branch of his bank in Paris and moved there. Edgar was educated in Paris and then studied law. Before he was twenty he had decided to become an artist and he entered the Ecole des Beaux-Arts where he worked with one Louis Lamothe, a pupil and keen admirer of Ingres. His portrait of his younger brother, *René De Gas*, one of his earliest surviving pictures, was probably painted in 1855 when he was twenty-one. In 1856 he went to Naples, where his sister and other members of his family were living. Thence he went to other Italian cities, settling eventually for three years in Rome. In Italy he copied frescoes and drawings by fifteenth and sixteenth century artists including many by or ascribed to Leonardo da Vinci and his school; he continued this habit of copying old master drawings for many years and in Paris he copied, among other things, some drawings ascribed to Clouet in the Louvre. Several pictures painted in Italy survive; they include two full length studies of Italian peasant women, a number of family portraits, several self-portraits, and *Jeunes Spartiates s'exerçant à la lutte*, originally titled *Petites filles spartiates provoquant des garçons*.[2]

He returned to Paris at the age of twenty-seven in 1861 and worked on a series of 'history pictures' for the *Salon*. Three of these, *La fille de Jephté*, *Sémiramis élévant les murs de Babylone*, and *Les malheurs de la ville d'Orléans*, were still in his studio when he died; plans and drawings for them had probably been made in Italy. While working on these pictures he copied often in the Louvre, where he met Manet as related.[3] In the years which followed he was gradually converted by the Realist

---

[1] For the present distribution of the pictures mentioned and of others painted by Degas in these years cf. my Bibliographical and Catalogue Notes in Appendix I.

[2] This picture I imagine was considerably redrawn and repainted before Degas sent it to the Fifth Impressionist Exhibition in 1880.

[3] Cf. above, p. 16.

Movement and he painted his first race course subject *Course de gentlemen : avant le départ* in 1862.[1] In 1865, when he was thirty-one, he made the acquaintance of Ingres who was eighty-five. He met him at the Château de Menil-Hubert owned by mutual friends, the Valpinçons who had several of Ingres' pictures. After the first meeting Ingres invited him to his studio in Paris and said: '*Faites des lignes et des lignes, d'après la nature ou de mémoire, et vous deviendrez un bon artiste.*' Between 1862 and 1870 he drew and painted a number of portraits of his friends and his family including *Le duc et la duchesse de Morbilli* (representing one of his sisters and her husband), *La femme aux mains jointes : Mme G. . .* (an actress named Mme Gaujelin) and *Baron Jules Finot* showing Finot (a minor artist now forgotten) seated in a studio with a large painting of a dance in a Japanese tea house on the wall and beneath it a small portrait by Lucas Cranach. The first of his stage scenes, *Mlle Fiocre dans le ballet de La Source* was shown, as noted, in the *Salon* of 1868. *L'Orchestre* painted in that year marks the beginning of his studies from the stalls. In the summer of 1869 he produced some landscapes and coast scenes. But landscape painting made little appeal to him; he disliked the inconvenience of working out of doors; and his rare landscapes were all produced from notes and from memory indoors; the same applies to his race course pictures for which he used a wooden figure of a horse, saying, 'How could I turn real horses round to get the light upon them as I want it ?'[2]

In 1870 he served, as I have chronicled, in the artillery of the National Guard. He was not wounded; but he often said, later, that the damp of the quarters he occupied on service had affected his eyes which he began to complain about soon after. He left Paris early in 1871 and went to Menil-Hubert; there, while the Versaillais were fighting the Communards, he painted two pictures of the Valpinçon children: *Henri Valpinçon enfant* (showing the boy in his baby-carriage, his nurse seated at the side) and the *Mlle Valpinçon enfant* (Hortense Valpinçon, leaning on a table covered with an embroidered cloth and holding an apple in her hand) already referred to. At the end of 1871 he returned to Paris where he painted the group of three former companions in the National Guard, *Trois camarades*, already referred to, and also *Le Grand Rabbin Astruc et le Général Mellinet* (a double portrait of a Rabbi and a General who had worked with him in an ambulance corps with which he had been connected).[3]

At the beginning of 1872 he was established in Montmartre making studies of dancers in training at the old Opera House in the rue Le Peletier, and working on *Musiciens à l'orchestre*. In this picture his interest, which had been centred on the individual musicians in *L'orchestre* of 1868, was transferred beyond their heads to the stage. In the autumn he was visited by his brother René from New Orleans (where René and a third brother Achille had a branch of the family bank in which Degas himself may have had an interest, as he also had interests in various family properties in Naples). When René's visit ended Degas went to see him off at the

[1] Degas is known to have repainted this picture to some extent about 1880; but he left the original date, 1862, unaltered.

[2] Cf. above, p. 5.

[3] Degas' anti-Semitism, to which I refer later, did not become virulent till the time of the Affaire Dreyfus.

Gare Saint-Lazare, and as the train started he jumped in and travelled with him to Le Havre; at Le Havre he lingered on the boat with him—and travelled to New Orleans. He stayed in New Orleans about six months and painted a number of family portraits without any special relish—'*Des portraits de famille*' he wrote in a letter '*il faut les faire assez au goût de la famille, dans les lumières impossibles, très dérangé, avec des modèles pleins d'affection mais un peu sans gêne et vous prenant bien moins au sérieux parce que vous êtes leur neveu ou leur cousin.*' These portraits included *La femme à la potiche* and *Jeune femme arrangeant un bouquet*, both painted from his cousin, René's wife, who was blind; and *Le bureau de Coton* showing his uncle, René's father-in-law, in the office of the cotton business which he owned, surrounded by his associates and employés. One of his pleasures in New Orleans was to watch the women—'*les jolies femmes de sang pur et les jolies quarteronnes et les négresses si bien plantées*'; of the Creole women, he wrote to his friend Henri Rouart: '*elles sont presque toutes jolies, et beaucoup ont même dans leurs charmes cette pointe de laideur sans laquelle point de salut.*' For the rest he was restless and nervous, 'beginning works that would take ten years to finish and leaving them after ten minutes', anxious to get back to France and toying with a vision of a home with wife and children (which was never in fact to be fulfilled).

Back in Paris in the summer of 1873 he resumed his contacts with the writers and painters who were then deserting the Café Guerbois for the Nouvelle Athènes. He also saw something of the singer Faure who had met him at Manet's studio and commissioned a picture. But he reserved his intimacy, as he reserved it all his life, for his chosen personal friends who included, in the 'seventies, the Vicomte Lepic, the Valpinçons at Menil-Hubert, Duranty, Henri Rouart, the engraver Bracquemond and Mary Cassatt. The Vicomte Lepic posed to him for several pictures: *Place de la Concorde—Vicomte Lepic et ses enfants; Voiture aux courses* (Pl. 9A); and a double portrait showing the Vicomte with Marcellin Desboutin who was teaching him engraving. His friendship with Duranty is recorded in four works produced before 1880 when Duranty died: *Intérieur (le viol)* which illustrates a scene from Duranty's novel *Combats de Françoise Duquesnoy; Le journal* (a ballet dancer reading a newspaper by a studio stove) inscribed '*A mon ami Duranty*', and two versions of the *Portrait de Duranty* where the writer sits at his library table meditating, his finger on his cheek. Mary Cassatt he wittily depicted leaning on her umbrella studying the pictures in the Louvre.

In the years 1873–1883 he produced a large proportion of his most famous paintings and pastels. These include race course, music hall, circus, and café scenes, as well as the studies of the Opera *corps de ballet* in training and performing on the stage; and in the second half of the period they include one or two *plage* scenes, some studies of women in *maisons closes*, of milliners and their customers, and of laundresses at work, and many of nude women at their toilet. When the old Opera House in the rue Le Peletier was burned down the dance school seems to have been lodged somewhere on two floors connected by an iron spiral staircase; there in rooms with long french windows Degas studied the little dance girls being dressed by their mothers, sitting on benches waiting for their turn, leaning over the rails that protected the winding stairs, coming down the stairs to take their lessons, and training their muscles at *la barre*. He only made notes and sketches on the spot; the actual works were all produced in his studio where he had provided himself with a spiral staircase and ballet clothes and shoes and so forth for the dancers who came to him to pose.

In this period he modelled frequently in wax (the realist *Petite danseuse de quatorze ans*, a wax figure with real clothes, already referred to, dates from 1880). He also paid much attention to and experimented in etching, engraving, aquatinting and lithography. In 1880 he projected a publication of prints to be called *Le jour et la nuit* to which he and Pissarro, Mary Cassatt and others of the Impressionist group were regularly to contribute; the publication was to be financed by the banker Ernest May and Caillebotte; but though many of the plates were prepared by the artists the publication never in fact appeared. He was keenly interested in photography and, like Manet, he used photographs as aids in many of his works There were also moments when he tried his hand at verses and sent them for revision to Mallarmé (whom he had met as chronicled at the *salon* of Nina de Callias). One poem entitled *Danseuse*, known to have been thus revised by Mallarmé, reads:

> Elle danse en mourant, comme autour d'un roseau,
> D'une flûte, où le vent triste de Weber joue;
> Le ruban de ses pas s'entortille et se noue,
> Son corps s'affaisse et tombe en un geste d'oiseau.
>
> Sifflent les violons. Fraîche du bleu de l'eau,
> Silvana vient, et là, curieuse s'ébroue;
> Le bonheur de revivre et l'amour pur se joue,
> Sur ses yeux, sur ses seins, sur tout l'être nouveau,
>
> Et ses pieds de satin brodent, comme l'aiguille,
> Des dessins de plaisir. La capricante fille
> Use mes pauvres yeux à la suivre peinant.
>
> Mais d'un signe toujours cesse le beau mystère:
> Elle retire trop les jambes en sautant:
> C'est un saut de grenouille aux mares de Cythère.

Another of his poems begins:

> Danse, gamin ailé, sur les gazons de bois,
> N'aime rien que ça, danseuse pour la vie.
> Ton bras mince placé dans la ligne choisie,
> Equilibre, balance et ton vol et ton poids. . . .[1]

From the beginning of the 'seventies he ceased entirely to submit to the *Salon*; and throughout this period his works could only be seen in the galleries of his dealer and agent Durand-Ruel, in the houses of the collectors Faure, Henri

---

[1] These and other poems by Degas are printed in Paul Lafond's *Degas* (cf. below, Appendix I).

Rouart, Ernest May, Count Camondo, Caillebotte and some others, and at the various Impressionist Exhibitions to which he contributed.[1]

Degas was the first of the Impressionist group (excluding, of course, Manet who never officially adhered) to achieve a reputation and success. From the time of the First Impressionist Exhibition he was recognized as a brilliant and highly original artist by a considerable number of intelligent art lovers. He had first Duranty and then Huysmans as literary champions; in the troubles of 1877 he was known by all who knew him to be on what was expected to be the winning side; he had no money embarrassments—as he had private means and profitable arrangements with Durand-Ruel; and his health in this period was good. But he was always moody and neurasthenic. In 1874 when he was forty, he struck de Goncourt, who visited his studio, as an 'esprit bien inquiet' and 'un maladif, un névrosé, un ophthalmique à un point qu'il craint de perdre la vue'—though at this time and for decades afterwards there was really little the matter with his eyes; and his letters of the 'seventies show him frequently depressed and, still in the prime of life, lamenting the imminent coming of old age. With friends who humoured him he was wittily querulous; engaged in work or some enterprise that roused his interest he could act with energy; and he amused de Goncourt by performing the steps danced by the ballet dancers in his pictures; but at bottom he was profoundly neurotic and hypochondriac. In 1873 at thirty-nine he had already written: 'Je n'en finis pas de mes achèvements de tableaux, pastels, etc. Que c'est long, et que mes dernières bonnes années s'en vont dans le médiocre! Je pleure bien souvent sur ma pauvre vie', and his neuroses and his hypochondria became ever more apparent as the years advanced. One characteristic was a craving when he had painted pictures to get them back. He would borrow a picture on the plea that he wanted to retouch it and the owner thereafter never saw it again. He was amused and discomfited when Henri Rouart, who had suffered in this manner, eventually chained and padlocked his remaining favourites to the walls. In 1874, having sold some pictures to Durand-Ruel, he was seized with a desire to get them back and he therefore persuaded the singer Faure to buy them and return them to him, promising in exchange to paint him two theatre scenes, a race course and a laundress picture; his correspondence in this period refers repeatedly to these four pictures which he is always promising to send the next day; two of them Danseuses roses and L'Orchestre de Robert le Diable were in fact delivered in 1876; but the other two were still undelivered in 1883. But though his neurasthenia was thus apparent it was not yet severe enough to impede his work; and all through this period he was relatively industrious and at the height of his powers.

[1] Cf. 'How it happened', above, under 1874, 1876, 1877, 1879, 1880 and 1881, and below, Appendix I.

PROLOGUE: THE MASTERS' LIVES

PAUL CÉZANNE[1] (i)

To the age of forty-four (1839–1883)

Paul Cézanne, who was twenty-four in 1863, was born at Aix-en-Provence on January 19, 1839. His father was a prosperous hat-maker who became a still more prosperous banker from 1848 onwards. His mother, who is said to have had some negro blood, was the daughter of an Aixois cabinet-maker and a girl from Marseilles. By 1859, Cézanne *père* had a town house in Aix and a country property of thirty-seven acres called Le Jas de Bouffan just outside the town. Le Jas de Bouffan, which figures in so many of Cézanne's pictures, comprised a house approached by an avenue of chestnut trees, a garden, a vineyard, and a farm. Cézanne was educated at an Aixois school where Emile Zola one year his junior was also a pupil. On *jours de fête*, when the students of this school marched in procession with a band, Cézanne played the cornet, and Zola the clarinet. While still at school Cézanne began to draw and when he was nineteen he attended evening classes at an art school attached to the Aix Museum. In 1859 and 1860 he studied law; in his free time he drew and painted, wandered in the Aix Museum, and wrote verses. Letters from Zola who had gone to Paris made him long to join him and study in the art schools there. But Cézanne *père* refused his support till the spring of 1861 when he went with him to Paris to arrange for a trial period of art study. In April 1861 Cézanne *père* returned to Aix and Cézanne remained in Paris for about six months, with an adequate allowance from his father. A photograph of the period shows him with short clipped hair, broad high forehead, small shaven chin, drooping moustache and dark negroid eyes with conspicuous whites.[2] He took rooms near Zola on the left bank in the region of the Panthéon and began to paint his portrait; in the mornings he attended the Académie Suisse; in the afternoons he worked in a friend's studio, or studied and copied in the Louvre. Zola found him moody and obstinate: 'To convince him of anything' he wrote to a mutual friend 'is like trying to persuade the towers of Notre-Dame to dance a quadrille. . . . He has a horror of arguments, firstly because talking is tiring and secondly because he might have to change his opinion if his opponent were right. . . . Here he is, thrown into life, bringing to it certain ideas, unwilling to change them

---

[1] The present distribution of a hundred and thirty pictures painted by Cézanne in these years is given in Venturi's Catalogue (cf. below, Appendix I).

[2] Reproduced by Mack: *Paul Cézanne* (cf. Appendix I).

except on his own judgment; at the same time remaining the kindest fellow in the world, always agreeing with you in speech, because of his dislike of arguments, but thinking his own thoughts unmoved. . . . He has frequent spells of discouragement. In spite of the rather exaggerated contempt he pretends to feel for glory, I can see that he would like to make a success. When his work turns out badly, he talks of returning to Aix and becoming a clerk in some business . . . he has been twice on the point of leaving . . . he may go at any minute.'[1] Cézanne in fact went back to Aix, discouraged, in September; and he worked in his father's bank till the autumn of the following year when he finally decided that he could only be happy as a painter and returned to Paris with an increased allowance.

He passed the whole of 1863 in Paris where he saw Manet's exhibition and the *Salon des Refusés* as noted. From 1864 to the outbreak of war he spent part of each year in Paris and part at Aix and at Le Jas de Bouffan where a room on the top floor was made into his studio. In these years he painted a series of panels in the drawing-room at Le Jas de Bouffan, a number of landscapes round Aix and at l'Estaque, a series of portraits of his father, his sister, his mother's brother known as Uncle Dominique and various friends, including Achille Emperaire, Paul Alexis and Zola. In Paris and at Aix he also painted his first still life pictures and a number of compositions. Early in this period he met Pissarro, Bazille, Renoir, Monet, Guillaumin, Guillemet, Sisley and Manet and he went occasionally to the Café Guerbois as already related. In 1866 two pictures which he sent to the *Salon* were rejected and he wrote a protest to de Niewekerke demanding a second *Salon des Refusés*; but the letter was without effect. In the summer of that year he went to Bennecourt with Zola and other friends; and Zola wrote to a mutual friend: 'Cézanne . . . is becoming more and more firmly fixed in the eccentric course into which his nature forces him. I have great hopes for him. At the same time we expect that he will be rejected for the next ten years. . . .' Cezanne on his side was much attached to Zola and by 1870 or thereabouts he had given him nine pictures.[2]

When the war broke out, Cézanne ignored the summons to the army as related and worked peaceably at l'Estaque till some time in 1871 when he returned to Paris. Hortense Fiquet, whom he subsequently married, was then living with him, and his son Paul was born in Paris on January 4, 1872. Shortly after, he established himself at Auvers near Pontoise where he worked with Pissarro and made Dr. Gachet's acquaintance. He remained in that region until the end of 1873 painting numerous landscapes including *La maison du pendu*[3] and *Auvers: Maison du Dr. Gachet*.[4] In the spring of 1874 he returned to Paris and sent three pictures to the First Impressionist Exhibition (where he sold *La maison du pendu* to Count Doria) as related. He then went to Aix leaving Hortense and his

[1] Translation by Mack.

[2] *Femme en manteau gris, Le village des pêcheurs à l'Estaque* (Paris: J. V. Pellerin), *Le poêle dans l'atelier* (London: Mrs. Chester Beatty), *La pendule noire* (Hollywood: Edward G. Robinson), *Portrait d'un homme barbu* (Paris: Lecomte), *L'enlèvement* (London: J. Maynard Keynes), *Une lecture chez Zola* (Paris: J. V. Pellerin), *Paul Alexis lisant à Zola* (Paris: Georges Wildenstein et Cie), and a small still life.

[3] Paris. Louvre.   [4] Chicago. M. A. Ryerson.

son in Paris. At Aix he spoke of his liaison to his mother but kept the secret from his father. He returned to Paris in the autumn and wrote in confident mood to his mother: '*Pissarro a bonne opinion de moi, qui ai très bonne opinion de moi-même. Je commence à me trouver plus fort que tous ceux qui m'entourent. . . . J'ai à travailler tou-iours—non pas pour arriver au fini, qui fait l'admiration des imbéciles. Cette chose que vulgairement on apprécie tant, n'est que le fait d'un métier d'ouvrier et rend toute œuvre qui en résulte inartistique et commune. Je ne dois chercher à compléter que pour le plaisir de faire plus vrai et plus savant. Et croyez bien qu'il y a toujours une heure où l'on s'impose et on a des admirateurs bien plus fervents, plus convaincus que ceux qui ne sont flattés que par une vaine apparence.*' This confidence was characteristic. Cézanne painted in a number of different ways at different periods and he pursued a number of objectives; those objectives were immensely difficult to attain, and he never expected to attain them easily or soon; but he never doubted his power to attain them eventually. He valued everything he did; and he quietly stored, in his studios in Paris, Aix, and Le Jas de Bouffan, many scores of finished and unfinished pictures from the very beginning of his long career.

He spent 1875 and 1876 at Aix and in the environs with occasional visits to Paris. He submitted works to the *Salon* in both years; and they were both times rejected. In July 1876 he wrote to Pissarro from l'Estaque, 'I have begun two small studies with the sea in them for Monsieur Choquet, who had suggested them to me. They are like playing-cards. Red roofs against the blue sea. . . . The sun-light here is so intense that it seems to me objects stand out in silhouette not only in black or white, but in blue, in red, in brown, in violet. I may be mistaken, but it seems to me the antithesis of modelling. . . .' He abstained from the Second Impressionist Exhibition in 1876 and said that he did so because the Exhibition was held in a dealer's gallery, i.e. Durand-Ruel's—(the facts being doubtless that Durand-Ruel was not buying his pictures as he was buying those by his friends, because he did not understand or like them and lacked faith in Cézanne's future as an artist, and that Cézanne, knowing this, declined to show his pictures where they were evidently not desired). He returned to the Third Impressionist Ex-hibition with sixteen pictures in 1877 because it was organized by the artists themselves, and the Hanging Committee (Renoir, Monet, Pissarro and Caille-botte) promised to give his pictures good positions, which in the event they did. He went to Paris for this occasion and had contacts with Desboutin, Forain, Georges Rivière and Choquet. In the next year or two he ceded the *Achille Emperaire*[1] and some other pictures to the colourman Tanguy in settlement of outstanding colour bills—partly because, with Hortense and his child to provide for, his allowance was now less adequate for his needs and partly because he was always stingy with his money. In 1878 he installed Hortense and the child in lodgings at Marseilles and himself went back to Aix hoping to persuade his father to increase his allowance. But as Cézanne *père* had opened some of his letters and suspected his secret, he was threatened with no allowance instead of the desired increase. In these circumstances he asked Zola to find him a salaried post in Paris and to lend him money, and Zola came to the rescue by lending him a monthly sum

[1] Paris. Lecomte.

sent directly to Hortense.[1] At the end of the year Cézanne wrote to Zola: 'I am at l'Estaque with my mother; I think papa has been casting his eye on a pretty maid we have at Aix'; and soon after this Cézanne *père* produced the increased allowance, having already in fact, unbeknown to him, settled a third of his fortune upon him in order to circumvent death duties. In 1879 Cézanne moved north to Melun near Fontainebleau and it was probably at this moment that he painted the still life *Compotier, verre et pommes*[2] acquired by Gauguin for his collection. In June he visited Zola at Medan. In 1880 he took a new studio in Paris in the Plaisance quarter behind Montparnasse and saw the Fifth Impressionist Exhibition; in August he stayed with Zola and painted *La maison de Zola à Medan*,[3] which Gauguin also bought. In 1881 he passed some months at Pontoise working again with Pissarro; in the summer he went again to Medan where he was embarrassed by Zola's prosperity and himself embarrassed Zola by sitting in his shirt sleeves at a party where the guests and their ladies were in evening dress. He spent the first half of 1882 in Paris, the second at Aix; and in 1883 he established himself for some time at l'Estaque with Hortense and his son.

He was now forty-four and completely independent, since the securities from which he drew his allowance had been registered in his name. But compared with Degas, Renoir, Monet, Sisley and Pissarro he still had no repute as an artist; the genuine admirers of his paintings could still be counted on the fingers of one hand; and though he had had a picture in the *Salon* of 1882 it passed unnoticed and had only been admitted *pour la charité* at the instance of his old friend Guillemet who had now become an academic and prosperous artist.[4]

[1] Cf. above, p. 41.   [2] Paris. Lecomte.   [3] London. Messrs. Reid & Lefevre.
[4] Guillemet was on the *Salon* jury for the year and had the right to introduce a picture by a pupil '*pour la charité*'. Cézanne's picture (which cannot be identified) was therefore catalogued as by *Cézanne (Paul) élève de M. Guillemet* presumably with Cézanne's consent.

PROLOGUE: THE MASTERS' LIVES

AUGUSTE RENOIR [1] (i)

To the age of forty-two (1841–1883)

Pierre-Auguste Renoir, who was twenty-two in 1863, was born at Limoges on February 25, 1841. Son of an artisan (some biographers say a tailor), he was apprenticed at fourteen as a painter's assistant in a china manufactory in Paris. In the dinner hour he went to the Louvre or bought a sandwich in the region of Les Halles and munched it gazing at Goujon's Fontaine des Innocents; in the evenings he was often invited to the studio of a sculptor who worked in the factory and had noticed his unusual talents. The china factory was far from prosperous; it was in vain that the *patron* stamped a forged Sèvres mark on exported pieces in the hope of deceiving the barbarians; the public had acquired a taste for machine decoration and declined to pay more for hand-painted wares. In 1858 the factory closed down. Renoir, now seventeen, painted fans, did other odd jobs, and then again found regular employment in a business which sold devotional pictures to missionaries who took them, rolled up, in their luggage and then hung them in improvised churches. As a painter on porcelain and a painter of fans he had been mainly concerned with figures imitating the works of Watteau, Lancret and Boucher and with Louis XV floral *motifs*; as a painter of devotional subjects he turned to Italian paintings and engravings and pictures by Vouet, Poussin and Le Sueur. The 'Adoration of the Magi' (with cloud background) and 'Saint Vincent de Paul' (with architectural background) were the subjects most frequently demanded. He produced these paintings with facility and speed; and as he was paid on piece work he soon began to save money. By the time he was twenty-one he felt rich enough to leave this factory and enter Gleyre's Academy where, as related, he found Monet, Sisley and Bazille. Gleyre disapproved of his studies: 'You seem to take painting as a pleasure', he said to him one day. 'Quite true', Renoir answered, 'if painting were not a pleasure to me I should certainly not do it.' He left Gleyre's Academy with Monet, Sisley and Bazille in 1863 after seeing Manet's show at Martinet's gallery, and the *Salon des Refusés*; and thereafter he shared Bazille's studio where the group of artists later known as the Impressionists foregathered. From 1864 to the war he was mainly concerned to make a reputation by pictures in the *Salon*; and as noted the *Salon* accepted *Esmeralda* in 1864, *Soirée d'été* in 1865, *Lise* in 1868, and

[1] For the present distribution of the pictures mentioned and of others painted by Renoir in these years cf. my Bibliographical and Catalogue Notes in Appendix I.

Baigneuse au griffon and *La femme d'Algers* (Pl. 6B) in 1870. He destroyed the *Esmeralda* which had been painted with bitumen after the meeting with Diaz which I have already chronicled.[1] In 1869 he went frequently to Louveciennes where Pissarro had just established himself and where his own parents lived. The orchard picture *Le poirier d'Angleterre* is a record of these visits. I have recorded his war service and his luck in escaping from Paris before the Versaillais siege. When Paris was calm again he took a studio in the rue Notre Dame des Champs where he put himself in funds by doing decorative work for Prince Bibesco and painting portraits—*Le Capitaine Darras, Mme Darras, Mme Maitre*. In September he went to Celle-St.-Cloud where he painted the garden picture *La famille Henriot*. We know his appearance at this time from Fantin-Latour's *L'atelier des Batignolles*[2]; he is shown there with delicate features, light beard and moustache, wearing a caped ulster and small soft hat.

From 1872 to 1876 he had to fight a stiffish battle against the *Salon* artists and their supporting critics who treated his rainbow palette and broken touch as monstrous affronts to the academic tradition. His work was also not appreciated by sections of the dilettanti who preferred the more vigorous work by Manet and the more realist paintings by Degas; and Manet himself thought nothing of him as an artist, saying in 1874 to Monet, when he and Renoir were painting together in Monet's garden, '*Ah ce malheureux, c'est exécrable ce qu'il fait. Il n'arrivera jamais à rien.*' The political attacks which caused panic among the dealers and dilettanti in 1877 and 1878 were a serious set-back, as related. But Renoir thereafter rapidly won through. In 1872 to 1878 he had first the support of Durand-Ruel who began to buy in 1872 (and continued to do so—even I fancy in 1877 and 1878 when he stored his Impressionist pictures); Choquet and Caillebotte were helpful from 1874 onwards; the Charpentiers from 1876.

Throughout he was also helped by his equable temperament and an engaging gaiety which brought him friends. Amiable and easy going, he took pleasure in the company of gay impecunious young men and pretty girls in boating parties on the river and at dancing places like the Moulin de la Galette; and he invited his friends to his Montmartre studio which had a garden where the young men and the pretty girls posed to him in the sunlight and shadow that appear in *La balançoire, Le Moulin de la Galette* (Pl. 9B) and similar pictures of this time. He was never depressed and querulous like Degas—because he was never in any degree a neurasthenic.

As already stated, he was always able to make some money by painting portraits which his sitters liked. Sometimes he could do this and at the same time give full play to his personal artistic sense—that was the case, for example, when he painted portraits for Choquet who delighted in the lightness of his touch and in his colouring. But in the dark years, 1877 and 1878, he resolved to secure his position by attracting customers with deeper purses than Choquet; and knowing that customers with deep purses would certainly demand approximations to the prevailing *Salon* styles in portraits, he set himself to evolve a compromise that would please them. To train himself for this he painted substantial studies from his

[1] Cf. above, p. 6.   [2] Paris. Luxembourg.

favourite models—*La jeune fille au chat*, *Femme cousant au bouquet*, *La tasse de chocolat*; and by 1878 he was equipped for the full length portrait *Mlle Samary* and the portrait group *Mme Charpentier et ses enfants*. With the success of these pictures in the *Salon* of 1879 a career as a portrait painter of rich people was at his feet; but he declined the temptation and only accepted a few well paid commissions which provided the money he required. After the *Salon* of 1879 he went on the proceeds of the Charpentier group to Algiers. On his return he was approached by a wealthy family named Bérard who had seen his picture *La petite danseuse* at a friend's house and desired to have their children painted in a series of portraits. The Bérards had a country property called Wargemont at Berneval near Dieppe. He at once began this series and becoming friends with the Bérards he went repeatedly to stay with them. *Paysage à Wargemont*, *La Fête de Pan*, and *Pêcheuses de moules*—the last named painted from sketches made on Berneval beach—record the earliest of these visits. He continued occasional portrait painting—with his other work—to the end of the period. A little puffed up perhaps by the new feeling of security thus acquired he abandoned his colleagues in the Impressionist Exhibitions of 1879, 1880 and 1881; but he returned to them with *Le déjeuner des canotiers* and nineteen other paintings in 1882.

On the money made from his portrait painting in 1879 he married, and in 1881 he spent the summer at Guernsey, and then went to Italy for the remainder of the year. In Italy he began with Venice and travelled down through Rome to Naples. From Venice he wrote to Mme Charpentier: 'Here I am swallowing down my Italy. Now I can up and say when I am asked, "Yes, Sir, I have seen the Raphaels, and in Venice I have seen the great etc., etc." But what in fact have I seen in Venice? I will tell you. Nothing that you cannot see better by taking a boat to the quai des Orfèvres or opposite the Tuileries; nothing that you cannot see better in the Louvre; Veronese you can certainly see better there. I must except Tiepolo hitherto unknown to me—but it's a big price to pay to come here just for that. No, it's not true; it's all very fine—when the weather's fine, as they say. La Laguna; San Marco; splendid. Doges' Palace—more splendid still. But I prefer St. Germain l'Auxerrois.' In Venice he painted *Gondole sur le Grand Canal* and some other Venetian landscapes, and in Naples he painted some landscapes and *La baigneuse blonde* (Pl. 16).[1] At the beginning of January 1882 Wagner was at Palermo and Renoir went there from Naples to ask him to sit for his portrait; Wagner, sixty-nine, tortured by erysipelas, and engaged on the final scoring of *Parsifal*, was difficult to handle; he told Renoir that he had never permitted anyone to paint him 'from life'; but he sat on January 15—the day he finished *Parsifal*—for twenty minutes or half an hour; then he said that he was tired and went away—and that was the last that Renoir saw of him. I reproduce the portrait (Pl. 14).[2]

Renoir's health to this point appears to have been normal. But he now experienced the first symptoms of the rheumatic gout or arthritis (which eventually

[1] The picture which I reproduce as Pl. 16 is from a replica which Renoir painted in Paris next year.

[2] The picture which I reproduce is from this painting made by Renoir at Palermo. There is a replica made later which is more like the official portraits and photographs of Wagner.

crippled him) after a cold caught in Marseilles on his way back from Palermo at the age of forty-one. On doctor's advice he paid a second visit to Algiers in the hope of curing it before returning to Paris to prepare his pictures for the Seventh Impressionist Exhibition. In 1883 he still had his studio with garden in Montmartre and there, in the spring, he painted *La danse à la campagne* and *La danse à la ville* for the one-man show of his works which Durand-Ruel staged in April. The show contained some seventy paintings and represented his achievements since the war. It included *Le déjeuner des canotiers, La loge, La liseuse, La bucheronne, La fillette au faucon, Les rosiers à Wargemont, Venise, Claude Monet, Mlle Irène Cahen, Le Moulin de la Galette, La baigneuse blonde* and *Portrait de Wagner.* This exhibition converted all the hesitants and established his position. Prosperity was assured to him if he sedulously repeated his Impressionist paintings. But he declined the temptation and resolved to explore the Classical attitude and play his part in the new movement that I shall chronicle in Act I.

PROLOGUE: THE MASTERS' LIVES

PAUL GAUGUIN[1] (i)

To the age of thirty-four (1848–1883)

Paul Gauguin, fourteen in 1863, was born in Paris on June 7, 1848. His father Clovis Gauguin was a journalist from Orléans, his mother was a Creole. His father was not successful as a journalist; three years after Paul's birth he decided to try his luck in Lima where his wife had influential relations; and he died on the journey. Paul arrived safely with his mother. In his later years Gauguin wrote charming passages about his mother—('*ce que ma mère était jolie quand elle mettait son costume de Liménienne, la mantille de soie couvrant le visage et ne laissant voir qu'un seul œil: cet œil si doux, si impératif, si pur et caressant!*')—and also about his grandmother, Flora Tristan, a noted socialist in her day. He has also recorded some images of his Lima days: a little negress spreading a carpet, a Chinese boy ironing, a madman chained on a roof terrace. In 1855 when he was seven his mother returned to France to collect an inheritance from her husband's father and sent Gauguin to school in Orléans. Of his school days he only tells us that he ran away carrying a handkerchief filled with sand on the end of a stick above his shoulder— emulating the picture of a tramp which had impressed him. At the end of his schooldays he sat for the entrance examination to the navy, and failed. In 1865 at the age of seventeen he entered the merchant marine as a navigating cadet to be trained as an officer in that service. On his first journey to Rio de Janeiro, he had with him an introduction from a chance acquaintance to Madame Aimée, an actress then performing in one of Offenbach's operas at Rio; he used the introduction as soon as he arrived; and Madame Aimée, '*tout à fait jolie malgré ses trente ans*', proved kind and amorous. Three years later he entered the navy. During the 1870 war he served on the cruiser *Jérôme-Napoléon* as related. In 1871 at the age of twenty-three, he left the navy. His mother who had been living at St. Cloud was now dead. When he reached St. Cloud he found that her house and most of the contents had been destroyed by the German bombardment. He thus found himself without property and, apparently, with little money and he set to work at once to find employment in Paris. Up to this date he had never, it would seem, either drawn or painted or taken any interest in painting. But he tells us that he carved dagger handles with a pen knife as a boy and his early images included Peruvian pottery and silver collected by his mother.

[1] For the present distribution of pictures mentioned and of others painted by Gauguin in these years cf. my Bibliographical and Catalogue Notes in Appendix I.

At the beginning of 1872 he found employment in the stockbroking business of one Bertin in the rue Laffitte. He was quick to master speculative finance and he soon added to his stipend by speculations of his own. By the end of 1873, when he was twenty-five, he was already making considerable money, and he then married a Copenhagen girl from a bourgeois Lutheran family whom he met by chance in a restaurant. He made friends with a colleague in his office, Emile Schuffenecker, an amateur painter, and he was thus induced to take an interest in art. In 1874 he looked in at Durand-Ruel's gallery where he met Pissarro, who took him to the First Impressionist Exhibition. Soon after this he began to buy Impressionist pictures; and encouraged by Schuffenecker and assisted by Pissarro he also began to paint and sculpt. In 1875 he often drew from the model at the *Académie Colarossi* in the evenings; and on Sundays and other free times he carved and modelled in the studio of his landlord who chanced to be a mason and carver. In 1876 he had a woodland landscape, which attracted no attention, in the *Salon*.

In 1877 he took a new house with a studio and began to escape from domesticity by spending long evenings at the Nouvelle Athènes where he gradually found his level in the company of painters, authors and artists. He had little in common with Monet and Renoir, both simple men who had not yet travelled and were still comparatively unacquainted with affairs; he was always embarrassed by the taciturn Cézanne; but he enjoyed the society of Manet, Degas and Pissarro who had all crossed the ocean and had other points of contact with his experience—since Pissarro and Degas had Creole mothers, Pissarro had been in business, and both Manet and Degas had revenues from property and stocks and shares. Moreover, since he was himself neurotic, he felt at home with the occasional persecution mania that sometimes descended upon Manet, with the querulous neurasthenia of Degas, and with the Jewish disquietude that underlay Pissarro's broad sympathies and understanding. Manet, Degas and Pissarro in their turn were touched and intrigued by this heavy-eyed, hawk-nosed giant who had sailed all the seas and was now occupied with gambling on the Stock Exchange, collecting Impressionist pictures and trying to sculpt and paint. Gauguin showed his work to Manet saying humbly '*Je ne suis qu'un amateur*' and Manet answered '*Mais non, il n'y a d'amateurs que ceux qui font de la mauvaise peinture*'. But it was of course as a monied amateur that the Nouvelle Athènes company received him, and his new friends did not invite him to exhibit at the Third or Fourth Impressionist Exhibitions of 1877 and 1879.

By 1880 he was more seriously treated—largely, doubtless, because he was spending more money as a collector; and when Cézanne, Renoir, Monet and Sisley declined to exhibit at the Fifth Impressionist Exhibition the Committee included him with other newcomers admitted to fill to some extent the gaps. The Impressionist landscapes which he contributed attracted, however, no particular attention and Huysmans made no mention of them in his famous article on this show. But Huysmans made amends the following year when Gauguin sent *Etude de nu : femme raccommodant sa chemise*, *Nature morte* (flowers on a chair in a sunlit garden), several landscapes, *Dame en promenade*, a carved and coloured wooden figure and *Chanteuse* (a coloured plaster relief) to the Sixth Impressionist Exhibition. On that occasion Huysmans described his carving as '*gothiquement moderne*', and his land-scapes as influenced by Pissarro, but he wrote as follows of the *Etude de nu*: '*M. Gauguin se présente avec une toile bien à lui, une toile qui révèle un incontestable tempéra-ment de peintre moderne. C'est une fille de nos jours, et une fille qui ne pose pas pour la galerie, qui n'est ni lascive ni minaudière, qui s'occupe tout bonnement à repriser ses nippes. . . . Je suis heureux d'acclamer un peintre qui ait éprouvé, ainsi que moi, l'impérieux dégoût des mannequins, aux seins mesurés et roses, aux ventres courts et durs, des mannequins posés par un soi-disant bon goût, dessinés suivant des recettes apprises dans la copie des plâtres. . . . Parmi les peintres contemporains qui ont travaillé le nu, aucun n'a encore donné une note aussi véhémente dans le réel.*' Gauguin's contributions to the Seventh Impressionist Exhibition in 1882—*La voiture d'enfants, Intérieur d'atelier,* landscapes and sketches of his children—made no appeal to Huysmans; but they were favourably received by the artists at the Nouvelle Athènes.

His stockbroking affairs had meanwhile continued to prosper. He had made not only his requirements but enough to spend a sum calculated at £600 in present money on his collection which then included Manet's *Vue en Hollande*[1] and *Femme assise dans un jardin*[2] (also known as *Le tricot*); Cézanne's *La maison de Zola à Medan*[3] and *Compotier, verre et pommes*;[4] various pictures by Pissarro, Renoir, Monet, Guillau-min and Sisley; drawings by Daumier and a picture by the sporting painter John Lewis Brown. This collection was hung in the comfortable house which he occupied with his wife and five children. From that house he now longed more and more to escape. His triple desire was to shed his status of monied amateur, to paint fine pictures, and to be accepted as an artist among the artists he admired. His colleague, Emile Schuffenecker—who had never been invited to show his work at the Impressionist Exhibitions or been praised by Huysmans—had left Bertin's office to paint all day; and he now resolved to do the same.

He took the plunge at the age of thirty-five in January 1883. He resigned from Bertin's office, gave up his house, sold his property, stored his collection and went with his wife and children to Rouen. There he was soon joined by Pissarro who introduced him to Dr. Gachet and helped and encouraged him while pre-tending horror at his imprudence. He remained in Rouen and the region for eight months which brought disillusions. He painted landscapes, many of which would seem to have disappeared. Dealers to whom he tried to sell these pictures were complimentary but bought nothing. His wife, who disapproved of what seemed to be a fantastic adventure, now urged him to come with her to Copenhagen where, she assured him, her Danish relatives would find him some occupation less hazardous than art; and at this moment a chance acquaintance, who was manufacturing a new type of sunblind or awning, told Gauguin that there was money to be made by interesting the Danish railways in these productions and offered him the Danish agency. Persuaded by his wife Gauguin in his discourage-ment accepted; and at the end of the year he went with his wife and children to Copenhagen—as a traveller in sunblinds—until his wife's relations could find him more lucrative employment.

[1] This picture was later acquired by Alexander Cassatt, Philadelphia.
[2] German Collection.   [3] London. Reid & Lefevre.   [4] Paris. Lecomte.

PROLOGUE: THE MASTERS' LIVES

GEORGES SEURAT[1] (i)

To the age of twenty-four (1859–1883)

Georges Seurat, born on December 2, 1859, has appeared in our story as a child of eight walking with his mother in the Parc des Buttes-Chaumont, and as a child of twelve in refuge with his parents at Fontainebleau while the Versaillais were bombarding Paris. His mother seems to have been a placid Parisian *bourgeoise*; but his father, a bailiff, led a curious life; he was rarely seen in the Boulevard de Magenta apartment where his wife and family lived, as he passed most of his days at La Villette, where he had his office, and spent most of his nights in a villa at Raincy where he collected devotional pictures and had a private oratory. Seurat was thirteen when his parents returned to Paris after the Versaillais siege, and he then returned to school. His school days over he showed an aptitude for drawing, and as his parents were in easy circumstances, they sent him, at seventeen, to take drawing lessons from a sculptor named Justin Lequien. At Lequien's classes he met Aman Jean aged sixteen who was to remain all his life a friend; and Lequien set both youths to copy lithographed rows of noses and eyes and ears. At nineteen, in 1878, Seurat was admitted to the Ecole des Beaux-Arts, and Aman Jean was also admitted. At the Beaux-Arts their teacher was a naturalised German Charles-Ernest-Rodolphe-Heinrich-Salem Lehmann, a pupil of Ingres and so fierce an opponent of the Romantic and Impressionist movements that he founded a prize '*destiné à encourager la défense de la tradition académique*'. Thus guided Seurat acquired a reverence for Ingres, and he took from the outset a keen interest in the theory of composition, working assiduously in the Beaux-Arts library. In 1879 his parents made him an allowance and he took a studio with Aman Jean while continuing to draw and paint from the model at the Beaux-Arts. With Aman Jean he read the authors of the time—(the de Goncourts were among his literary heroes)—and applied himself to geometric theory. In 1880 he did one year's military service at Brest. He returned to his studio in 1881 and resumed his studies, exploring the action of light on form in a series of drawings in charcoal and crayon. He now found Delacroix deeply interesting as designer and colourist; and he studied in particular his paintings in the Eglise Saint Sulpice—*Héliodore chassé du temple, La lutte de Jacob avec l'ange* and *L'archange Saint-Michel terrassant le démon*. He also discovered Delacroix's writings, copied passages from them, and made analyses of

[1] For Bibliographical Notes cf. Appendix I.

the colour relations in his pictures—commenting at the end '*C'est l'application la plus stricte des principes scientifiques vus à travers une personnalité*'. Among contemporary artists he seems to have been chiefly attracted by Puvis de Chavannes, then aged fifty-seven, who gave him some help and encouragement. In 1882, when he was twenty-three, he began to paint from his drawings and to make the drawings more deliberate and complex. The drawing *Portrait du peintre Aman Jean* (Pl. 17A), produced at the beginning of 1883, was exhibited in the *Salon* where the critic Roger Marx discovered it as related[1]; another drawing *La brodeuse*[2] (a portrait of his mother), also submitted, was refused. Seurat now took a studio of his own and throughout 1883 he made *croquetons*[3] at Asnières on the river for his first large composition, *Baignade*, which was almost completed by December.

[1] Cf. above, p. 48.   [2] New York. Museum of Modern Art. (Bliss.)
[3] Cf. p. 74.

17B. VAN GOGH
Paysan hollandais, 1884
Paris. Bernheim Jeune

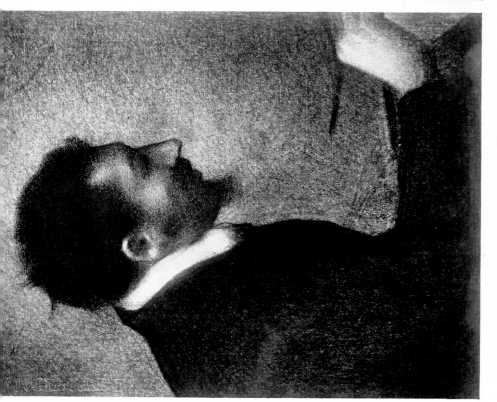

17A. SEURAT
Portrait du peintre Aman-Jean, 1883
New York. Stephen C. Clark, Esq.

18. SEURAT

ACT I

1884-1891

From the First *Salon des Indépendants* to the death of Seurat

ACT I

1884-1891

From the First *Salon des Indépendants* to the death of Seurat

INTRODUCTION

With the triumph of French Liberalism, life in Paris, as it affected our artists, assumed a pattern maintained with minor changes to this day. In that pattern I seem to perceive a place held by Civilization (i.e. Government concerned with social services), a place held by Dilettantism (i.e. art patronage by people of means, education and taste, for their personal pleasure) and a place held by Culture (original action by creative spirits). In the period 1884–1891 French civilization provided the *Salon* as an official social service, and the *Salon* pictures—mainly popular works corresponding to the average man's familiar experience—were sufficient and satisfactory for the once-a-year-art-inspecting Parisian public[1]; dilettantism in this period was disposed to patronize Realist and Impressionist painting, Realist novels, Realist plays, and Realist songs in cabarets and music halls; and culture in this period created a new Classical Renaissance in painting which neither Civilization nor Dilettantism could then understand.

The dilettanti who patronized Realism and Impressionism in this period were a serious nuisance to the culture of the time, for they were opposed to the original artistic attitudes of the 'eighties because those attitudes were not the Realist and Impressionist attitudes which had been original in the preceding decades and which they had recently learned to appreciate. Gauguin said later that his chief enemies were the admirers of Impressionist pictures; and in so saying he was right; but he might have added that the conquests made by the realist doctrines in the 'fifties, 'sixties and 'seventies were also obstructions. In 'How it happened' I give the history of Antoine's realist productions at the *Théâtre Libre* which he founded in 1887; and I give that history in some detail because it demonstrates not only Antoine's heroic spirit but also the camaraderie of artists in Paris which enabled him to do what he did without resources of his own or wealthy backers. But it must not be forgotten that the art which Antoine fought for was realist art and that a public had been won for such art by Courbet in the 'fifties, by the de Goncourts in the 'sixties, and by Zola, Daudet and de Maupassant in the 'seventies and first

---

[1] Cf. above, pp. xx and xxi.

71

years of the 'eighties; in the Paris theatre itself spade work had already been done by the productions of de Goncourt's *Henriette Maréchal* in 1865, Zola's *Thérèse Raquin* in 1872 and *L'assommoir* in 1879, by Becque's *Les corbeaux* in 1882, and Becque's *La Parisienne* and Daudet's *Sapho* in 1885. Antoine was helped, moreover, by the success of the *Chat Noir* cabaret (founded as noted in 1881) and that of the new cabaret *Le Mirliton* founded in 1885 by Aristide Bruant who launched a vogue for half-realist, half-romantic and half-sentimental songs extolling and dramatizing the adventures and miseries of *pierreuses* and *apaches* in the Parisian underworld. It is inspiring to watch Antoine fighting. But we must not forget that the theatre which would appropriately have been founded in 1887—and indeed at the beginning of the 'eighties—was not a Realist theatre like Antoine's *Théâtre Libre* but a Classical 'Symbolist' theatre like Paul Fort's *Théâtre d'Art* (actually founded in 1890); and that Daudet's *Sapho* published in 1884 and Zola's novels of the 'eighties were the aftermath of realist originality in previous decades.

It is also important, I think, to remember that two significant publications, *Le vice suprême* by Joséphin Péladan and Huysmans' fantasia *A rebours*, both appeared at the outset of this period in 1884. Péladan's book, designed as the first volume of a series called *La décadence latine*, propounded the thesis that salvation for the Western world could only be achieved by the Magic of the East occultly contained in the doctrines of the Catholic Church. Péladan (whom we shall meet in 'How it happened' as the organizer of *Rose-Croix* 'mystic' concerts and exhibitions of *Rose-Croix* 'mystic' paintings) sensed Culture's discontent with Realism and Impressionism at this moment and he perceived one attitude which the reaction might adopt. Huysmans, on the other hand, foresaw the growth of the attitude that we now habitually call Aesthetic; and by pushing that attitude to its extreme conclusion in a moving caricature he pointed its dangers at the start. In *A rebours* Huysmans draws the portrait of a fantastic wealthy neurotic dilettante, 'Des Esseintes', said to have been modelled in part on Comte Robert de Montesquiou (whom Boldini and Whistler actually painted and who served later as model for certain aspects of Proust's 'M. de Charlus'). 'Des Esseintes', after exploring all natural and some vicious pleasures and inventing a hundred fantastic settings for them (including a black banquet—*caviar, boudins fumés de Francfort, gibier sauce noire, coulis de truffes* and so forth, washed down by '*des porter et des stout*' and served by *belles négresses* in a black velvet room), attempts to refine his exhausted sensibilities to the final point in a solitary retreat; there he toys aesthetically with rare stones, strange flowers, perfumes, and mingled drinks (he installed what we should now describe as an experimental cocktail bar), and the colour-scheme of one room was completed by a live tortoise inlaid with rubies, emeralds and pearls. *A rebours*, for which the term 'decadent' was coined by the critics, had a far reaching influence. With the French Symbolist and Rose-Croix Movements of the 'eighties (that I shall discuss below) it formed the basis of the English Aesthetic Movement of the 'nineties and pre-war nineteen hundreds. It inspired Beardsley's drawings and all the 'decadent' posing of the period in England; and it had a truly sinister effect on Oscar Wilde (who took it seriously and 'lifted' whole passages from it). In another aspect it foreshadowed the Surrealist exploration of disquietudes; and thus quite appropriately the only living artists whose works 'Des Esseintes' is described as admitting to his sanctum were Gustave Moreau and Odilon Redon. And in yet another aspect its glorification of the power of machines—it foreshadowed the Futurist Movement, for it contains a passage describing the locomotives '*La Crampton, une admirable blonde*' and '*L'Engerth, une monumentale et sombre brune*' which links Ruskin's description of a locomotive's 'glittering cylinders' and 'fine ribbed rods' and 'complex anatomy of active steel' (*Cestus of Aglaia*, 1865) with Marinetti's attitude in 1909. But, though *A rebours* was thus in many ways prophetic, Huysmans was nevertheless not conscious of the central direction in which French culture in the 'eighties was beginning to advance; he did not realize that immediate revolt against Realism and Impressionism would be based on the classical doctrine that Architecture is the Mother of the Arts.

In the eight years 1884–1891, when this revolt against Realism and Impressionism was achieved, Monet and Sisley, who continued to paint Impressionist pictures and to win more and more appreciation from the dilettanti, disappear from the creative scene. The artists who constructed the Modern Classical Renaissance in these years were Seurat, Renoir, Cézanne, Gauguin, The Douanier Rousseau, and to some extent Degas, Van Gogh and Toulouse-Lautrec. I begin my illustrations with the *Portrait du peintre Aman Jean* (Pl. 17A) which Seurat drew in 1883 and Van Gogh's *Paysan Hollandais* (Pl. 17B) painted in 1884 which form as it were a bridge from the illustrations in my Prologue to the illustrations in this Act. Van Gogh had just turned thirty when he painted *Paysan Hollandais* at Neunen in Holland; he had been an artist for about three years, and he was not yet familiar with French Impressionist painting or acquainted with any of the Parisian artists who later became his friends. *Paysan Hollandais*, typical of his work at this moment when he was making studies for the large group *Les mangeurs de pommes de terre*,[1] is sombre in colour; the head is slashed on to the canvas in rapid brush strokes expressing the painter's eagerness to transfer his vision instantly and completely into paint; the artist is so impatient that he bounds upstairs as it were three steps at a time, leaping from shadow to high light with no intermediate bridge passages; the result arrests attention and holds it for a moment, but it is too unconsidered, uncontrolled and disordered to hold attention for long. Seurat's *Portrait du peintre Aman Jean* (Pl. 17A), already referred to,[2] has qualities of the opposite kind; Seurat was twenty-four when he made this drawing and already a controlled personality with infinite patience, who advanced with deliberation, constructing his drawing step by step on a previously determined plan. At first glance, compared with Van Gogh's picture, Seurat's drawing seems tame, timid, and photographic; but as we study it, as we follow, say, the plane that recedes from the cheek bone to the beard we realize that this artist's feeling for form is in fact much greater than Van Gogh's; and Seurat's feeling for and grasp of phenomenal and pictorial form became ever greater as the period advanced.

It is difficult to exaggerate the significance of Seurat's contribution to the history of modern art. Coming immediately after the Impressionists he took, as they did, scenes of contemporary life and landscapes as the subjects of his pictures;

[1] Laren. V. W. van Gogh.   [2] Cf. above, pp. 48 and 68.

and the scenes he selected were much the same as theirs—boating and bathing parties by the river, popular resorts of pleasure, the theatre, the circus, and so on. But whereas all the Impressionist presentations of such scenes, from Manet's *Le bateau de Folkestone* (Pl. 5B) to Renoir's *Le Moulin de la Galette* (Pl. 9B), were deliberately stamped with the spontaneous character of sketches, Seurat took the view that this character was only suitable for minor and quite small preliminary notes, done on the spot as memoranda, of the type habitually referred to as *pochades* but which he himself called *croquetons*; and that the major work of art must have the opposite character and be stamped with the serenity and stability that only the architecturally ordered composition can achieve. It was thus his custom, having selected a subject, to begin work by many visits to the scene where he made Impressionist '*croquetons*' which he took back to his studio; he then worked out the formal relations of all the lines and tones and colours, leaving nothing to chance, accepting no accidents, and declining spontaneous splutters of all kinds. The subject of his first picture *Baignade*[1] is much the same as that of Renoir's *Canotiers à Chatou* (Pl. 6A) and the essential character of the Classical Renaissance which Seurat launched when he planned and painted this picture at the age of twenty-four must be apparent to everyone who studies the two plates. Seurat used Renoir's rainbow palette much more exclusively and scientifically than the Impressionists had done. He restricted himself to the colours of the spectrum and juxtaposed spots of spectrum colours on a scientific system which worked out with the aid of scientific books. At the same time he studied the formal relations of different types of lines and curves and solids; and there too he worked out a system which he embodied in his pictures and drawings. As he applied his pigments in little dots his pictures were described in his day as 'Pointillism' (and referred to by hostile critics as *Petit-point*). But this 'Pointillism', imitated by Seurat's followers, was only an incident in his procedures as a whole which he himself described as 'Divisionism' and which his friend Signac thus defined: 'Divisionism is a method of securing the utmost luminosity, colour, and harmony by (a) the use of all the colours of the spectrum and all degrees of those colours without any mixing, (b) the separation of local colours from the colour of the light, reflections, etc., (c) the balance of these factors and the establishment of these relations in accordance with laws of contrast, tone and radiation, and (d) the use of a technique of dots of a size determined by the size of the picture.' The system further contained the doctrine that the lines (directions and angles), the chiaroscuro, and the colours could and should be so disposed and mutually related as to express the emotional idea behind the picture—slow ascending lines and cool colours and medium tones expressing calm and content, swifter and more animated ascending lines and warmer colours expressing gaiety, and the opposite lines and tones and colours expressing the opposite moods. In Seurat's hands this system was justified by the results. His pictures are great works of art because they are architectural compositions providing an ordered microcosm of a selected aspect of the visible world. His *Un dimanche d'été à la Grande Jatte* (Pl. 18) is a calm synthesis of a chaotic contemporary scene; the artist's vision of a crowd

[1] London. National Gallery, Millbank.

of *petits bourgeois* on the *Grande Jatte* island on a Sunday afternoon is here exterior-ised in a three dimensional design where a hundred intricacies are ordered with consummate skill. I reproduce also his later compositions *Poseuses* (Pl. 19A) where a corner of *Un dimanche d'été à la Grande Jatte* standing in his studio forms part of the composition and *Chahut* (Pl. 28B) where the rhythm of high kicking expressed in 'Divisionist' principles is the central motif.

With Seurat's *Poseuses* I reproduce Renoir's great composition known as *Les grandes baigneuses* (Pl. 19B) which was painted between 1885 and 1887. Early in the 'eighties Renoir swung away from the realist-impressionist to the classical standpoint. Abandoning the 'sketch' character of his Impressionist pictures and his personal light vibrant touch, and even (as Seurat himself never did) the spectrum palette, he concentrated on the linear structure of his pictures, and on serenity and architectural order in the composition; and in his language of repre-sentation he concentrated on deliberately considered contours. We get the first results of this new manner in *Les parapluies*[1], painted about 1880, and we see the character of the change if we compare *Les grandes baigneuses* (Pl. 19B) with *Le Moulin de la Galette* (Pl. 9B). Thus Renoir was converted by that mysterious force, a new creative attitude, which always seems at any given moment to capture the keener minds and the more sensitive spirits. We note the same influence in certain works by Degas at this period; in the fine pastel *Danseuses roses* (Pl. 29) for example, drawn at the end of the 'eighties or early in the 'nineties, Degas was more concerned with the rhythm of concerted dancing (as Seurat was concerned with it in *Chahut* (Pl. 28B)) than with the realist recording of contemporary life as in *Voiture aux courses* (Pl. 9A) or with effects of accidental light and casual composition as in *Femme dans une chambre à sa toilette* (Pl. 13). And when we turn to Pissarro we find him an avowed disciple of Seurat at this time; '*Je ne rougis pas*', Pissarro said later, '*d'avoir été conquis par sa méthode; je rougis seulement de n'avoir pas réalisé un certain nombre de mes tableaux.*'

Renoir owed something at this period to his contacts with Cézanne who had now worked through his so-called Impressionist manner; and Cézanne himself contributed as much as Seurat in these years. Cézanne's aim, foreshadowed in *La route tournante* (Pl. 15A), was now more than ever to make his picture a microcosm of his experience of the architecture of the scenes which moved him to paint them; and by architecture he meant not only form but also colour, and by colour he meant local colour intensified or modified to suggest an equivalent of pervading light, without any attempts at imitating passing effects of light and shade. The minor Impressionists, Pissarro, Monet and Sisley, who followed Turner, had invented a term 'atmospheric perspective', meaning thereby not only the suggest-ing of recession by progressive diminishing, from foreground to distance, of the strength of the contrasts between lights and shades (the progression which the camera renders by strong contrasts of black and white in the foreground and variations of grey in the distance) but also the suggesting of recession by pro-gressive increasing, from foreground to distance, of the extent to which local colours are modified by light. From the end of the 'seventies Cézanne declined the use of this 'atmospheric perspective' which he looked upon as a purely photo-

[1] London. National Gallery.

graphic procedure. He left it aside because he was not concerned to imitate the appearance of a scene in terms of transitory effects of light but to record his personal sensations in contact with the permanent characters of the scene itself. Cézanne's refusal to use atmospheric perspective was one of the things that made the understanding of his pictures extremely difficult for people taught by the Impressionists to expect and admire such perspective in landscapes. The dilettanti of this period, for example, could not realize that the distant hills in Cézanne's pictures were made definite in form and seemed locked to the foreground not because Cézanne did not know how to make them appear hazy and distant but because he wanted to use them as part of a dovetailed pictorial construction, and not as an agent for suggesting distance; and they also did not realize that what Cézanne was after was something much more difficult than the photographic Impressionist painting which they assumed he was too incompetent to achieve. In point of fact Cézanne arrived at great command of his own method in this period 1884–1891. But he did not do so at a single leap; he conquered the difficulties one by one, and went forward with his efforts slowly step by step. Thus *Le golfe de Marseille, vu de l'Estaque* (Pl. 20B), painted about 1884, is one of a series of studies where he has wrestled with the task of recording formal relations between the village forms that constitute the foreground and the hill forms that bound the bay; the problem here was to make the water join (not separate) the component parts in a lateral composition; and though he changed this and that in picture after picture of this subject the separate parts did not always come together as a perfectly dovetailed whole. By 1885, when he painted *Le verger* (Pl. 21), he had evolved a diagonal composition to join foreground to background with a great arch joining the two parts and with, as it were, sign-posts leading the spectator from point to point on the earth beneath; and thereafter he often used this structure in his landscapes, notably in the several versions of *La montagne Sainte-Victoire au grand pin*[1] and of *Marronniers et ferme au Jas de Bouffan*[2], all of 1885–1887 (and finally in *Le lac d'Annecy*[3] of 1897). He worked very slowly at his pictures and though he never used Seurat's scientific Divisionist technique he applied his paint, as Seurat did, in very deliberate small touches, each touch being carefully considered in relation to the others. I reproduce his landscape sketch *La montagne Sainte-Victoire: Environs de Gardanne* (Pl. 20A) which shows his procedure when commencing a landscape; taking certain points in the foreground, the dip at the side of the road and the hill that rises at its turn, he states their character and position in relation to the points in the second plane (the shrub and tree), which are indicated in relation to the third plane (the green and brown earth and the houses with their red-violet roofs) which in their turn are stated in relation to the blue hills and mountains behind; every touch of colour, every line is thus a factor in the structure of the picture; and the white spaces in the reproduction, which represent *bare canvas*, are the parts of the structure which had not yet been

[1] London. National Gallery (Courtauld Collection), and Washington, Phillips Memorial Gallery.

[2] Moscow. Museum of Modern Western Art, and Rhode Island, School of Design.

[3] London. National Gallery (Courtauld Collection).

19A. SEURAT
Poseuses, 1887–8
Merion. Barnes Foundation

19B. RENOIR
Les grandes baigneuses, 1885–7
Philadelphia. C. S. Tyson, Esq.

20A. CÉZANNE
La Sainte Victoire: environs de Gardanne, c. 1885
New York. Marie Harriman Gallery
20B. CÉZANNE
Le golfe de Marseille vu de L'Estaque, c. 1884
New York. Metropolitan Museum

decided upon—or as Cézanne himself always said 'realized'—in relation to the others. Cézanne's sketches are thus always complete as far as they go because they are statements of the features of the scene that indicate its main structure as he perceived it; and his finished pictures only differ from his sketches by the fact that the intermediate structures have been 'realized' and dovetailed in. Cézanne proceeded in the same way when he was painting the figures which we call his 'portraits' or 'genre' figures—though the terms 'portrait' and 'genre', in the ordinary senses, are really not applicable to these paintings; content with the quietest attitudes and the simplest accessories he built up a formal structure touch by touch, working first from one centre and then from another, each group of touches being governed both by their mutual relations and by their combined relation to the structure as a whole; in many of these figure pictures there are the same spaces of blank canvas that we find in the landscapes—we see them, for example, in *Paysan assis* (Pl. 24A)—and these blanks, as in his landscapes, are passages not yet 'realized' in relation to their immediate neighbours and the ensemble of the picture.

Gauguin, now a professional artist, was mainly influenced by the Impressionists for the first three years of this period. But somewhere in 1886–1887 he too was converted to the new ideas. In his case, as in all others, the first step was to leave the shore where the painter's business is thought of as primarily the descriptive representation of phenomena and to cross to the opposite shore where it is thought of as primarily the creation of an ordered harmony analogous to architecture or to music; that Rubicon crossed, the next step was to use representation, no longer an end in itself, as a means in the creation of this pictorial architecture or music. In some of his works produced at Pont Aven in 1886–1887, and in Martinique in 1887, Gauguin had already reached the stage of using representation as a means and not an end, and in 1888–9 he painted with relatively flat spaces of colour and frank outlines in deliberate patterns influenced by Japanese prints and by the aesthetic of stained glass workers which he studied with Emile Bernard who had contacts with him at this time. When he first exhibited his pictures of 1886–1887 in the Café Volpini exhibition (which I chronicle in 'How it happened') Gauguin described his work as 'Synthetist-Symbolic'. This cacophonic label was intended to describe two aspects of his attitude which characterize his paintings from 1887 for some years. By 'Synthesis' Gauguin meant simply the recording of form in symbolic line and colour as distinguished from the imitative procedures prescribed in realist and Impressionist doctrines; in other words he meant nothing more or less by the term than the replacement of naturalistic by conventional, i.e. classical, procedures; Gauguin thus had no need of a special term like Synthesis to describe his particular contribution to the Classical Renaissance; and in point of fact he did not use the term except in this one case. By 'Symbolist' in this label *Synthetist-Symbolic* Gauguin meant Symbolist in the sense that the word was used at that time and for some time later by the French Symbolist writers and poets; he used the term, that is, to indicate that certain characters in his pictures were intended to record mental images and ideas as distinguished from visual experience. This aspect of his attitude continued as I have said for some years after 1887. But Gauguin did not call himself a Symbolist after 1889 because by that time the term had been appropriated by his painter followers and associates and he left it contemptuously to them.[1]

I reproduce four pictures by Gauguin in this period—*Vision après le sermon: Lutte de Jacob avec l'ange* (Pl. 22B), *Arlésiennes se rendant à l'église* (Pl. 23A), *Jésus au Jardin des Oliviers* (Pl. 26), and *Mlle Loulou* (Pl. 30). The first, *Vision après le sermon: Lutte de Jacob avec l'ange*, which is dated 188[8] with an indistinct fourth figure was painted I think certainly in 1888 at Pont Aven before Gauguin went to Arles, and it was possibly worked on also in 1889; the white caps of the peasants are silhouetted against a bright scarlet ground, the angel has a blue robe and yellow wings, and Jacob's robe is olive green. In this picture we see Gauguin as Synthetist, i.e. as contributor to the Classical Renaissance launched by Seurat, and also as Symbolist in the literary sense; the aesthetic here is the aesthetic of stained glass workers in the sense that the artist has created a pattern of rich flat colour spaces clearly separated from one another and defined by enclosing lines; and these enclosing lines have a semi-Oriental rhythm which Gauguin extracted from Japanese prints and which hereafter he was to simplify and ennoble and make characteristically his own. At the same time this picture shows Gauguin as a Symbolist, in the literary sense, for the wrestling is depicted in a form which Gauguin thought the peasants in the foreground might have imaged it after listening to a sermon on the subject by the village priest; and there are deliberate distortions in the drawing to convey the character of this literary idea. I have discussed various types of distortion in painting (religious distortion, romantic distortion, architectural distortion and fashionable distortion) in *The Modern Movement in Art*. Here I need only remind the reader that all these distortions are essentially different in kind, the first being there to give intensity to a religious emotion, the second to stress the unusual emotive character in some fragment of life which has thrilled the artist, the third to force all the constituents of a formal structure to the service of the structure as a whole (as in Cézanne's *Les grandes baigneuses* (Pl. 49)) and the fourth to render a figure emotive by reference to the factors which fashion regards as emotive at the time. Gauguin's distortions in *Vision après le sermon: Lutte de Jacob avec l'ange* are of course religious distortions resembling in character the distortions used by the Byzantine devotional artists, the Gothic glass workers and El Greco. In *Arlésiennes se rendant à l'église* (Pl. 23A), painted when Gauguin was with Van Gogh at Arles, there is no literary symbolism and there are no religious distortions, for here we have a classical picture where the forms are distorted for the purpose of a pattern; the flowing semi-Oriental rhythm of *Vision après le sermon: Lutte de Jacob avec l'ange* gives place in this picture to graver, more static treatment which I cannot recall in any other picture known to me by Gauguin; and I cannot resist the suspicion that Gauguin was here recalling some early pictures by The Douanier Rousseau seen at his rooms or in the *Salon des Indépendants*—pictures resembling the *Portrait de Pierre Loti*[2] (Pl. 23B). The noble and expressive *Jésus au*

---

[1] Gauguin's *Portrait de l'artiste en style symboliste* (London: Reid & Lefevre) of 1889 is a satirical portrait of himself as leader of the Symbolists. In a similar spirit Chirico has portrayed himself as *Le peintre de chevaux* (cf. p. 309).

[2] Cf. below, pp. 80, 81, 82, 90, 110, and 120.

Jardin des Oliviers (Pl. 26) is one of a series of religious pictures including *Le Calvaire*[1] and *Le Christ jaune*[2] which Gauguin painted at Le Pouldu in 1889–1890 after the dreadful experience of his sojourn with Van Gogh; in these pictures we again have religious distortions and literary symbolism expressed in the aesthetic of the Gothic glass painters; in *Jésus au Jardin des Oliviers* for example the tree is purple, the sky is a deep night blue, the hair and beard of Jesus are a fiery luminous —and, possibly in Gauguin's mind, a symbolic—scarlet; and the drawing is distorted to give intensity to the religious emotion of the subject. In *Mlle Loulou* (Pl. 30), painted in 1890, Gauguin has developed the semi-Oriental calligraphy of *Vision après le sermon: Lutte de Jacob avec l'ange*; he is now a master of the flowing line and liquid rhythm which were later to make music of many pictures by Matisse; and indeed in all his pictures of 1888–1890 Gauguin was a pioneer who liberated line and colour to some extent from representational duty and an early explorer of that rhythmic abstraction which was to characterize one aspect of twentieth-century art. In 'How it happened' I give the history of the 'Symbolist' and 'Rose-Croix' and 'Nabi' movements which were largely the work of Gauguin's followers and associates in the early 'nineties; here I need only chronicle that all these movements were echoes of Gauguin's Brittany pictures of 1888–1890; and that Gauguin himself developed other and still richer aspects of his genius, that were beyond the ken of minor painters, when he went to Tahiti in 1891.

Van Gogh appeared as an artist in Paris at the beginning of 1886; and in that year and the next, as I relate in 'How it happened', he met Lautrec, Pissarro and Gauguin and discovered Japanese prints—experiences which produced first a series of Impressionist pictures including *La guinguette*[3] and *Restaurant de la Sirène à Joinville*[3] and then the famous portrait *Le père Tanguy*[4] (Pl. 24B). After painting this portrait he went to Arles where he worked alone for eight months producing local landscapes, townscapes and café scenes, the interiors *Ma chambre à coucher*,[5] *Café de nuit*[6] and *La chaise à la pipe*,[7] *Le facteur Roulin*[8] (three-quarter length), and other portraits, and the celebrated flower piece *Les tournesols*.[9] In essence these pictures are Romantic-Realism. Van Gogh a neurotic frustrated Northerner was thrilled by Southern France. As spring turned into summer and summer to early autumn he flung his excitement on his canvas with an ever more vibrating hand. In the townscapes painted in the spring the touch is sharp, angular and relatively severe; in the *Champ de blé* (Pl. 25B) painted in late August or September the touch is swirling to record his passionate delight in the richness of the growth around him; and the little-known picture *La nuit étoilée*[10] painted in September 1888 records his sensation of night sky literally ablaze with stars, reflected with

---

[1] Brussels. Musée Royal.   [2] Paris. Paul Rosenberg.   [3] Paris. Louvre.

[4] There is another version of this picture in the Musée Rodin, Paris.

[5] Versions of this belong to V. W. Van Gogh in Laren, Holland, and the Chicago Art Institute (Birch-Bartlett Collection).

[6] New York. Stephen C. Clark.   [7] London. National Gallery, Millbank.

[8] Boston. Robert Treat Paine.

[9] Laren. G. W. van Gogh. Other versions are in London, National Gallery, Millbank, in the Tokio Museum, and in a German collection.

[10] Paris. M. F. Moch.

the bridge lights, in the river. At Arles, up to the autumn of 1888, when Gauguin joined him, he made no real efforts to control his instincts, to subdue his exuberance, or to co-ordinate his records in stable designs. We have but to compare Seurat's harbour scene *Le Crotoy—Aval* (Pl. 25A) with the *Champ de blé* (Pl. 25B) to see the difference between the classical attitude and Van Gogh's disordered expressionist approach. But in November of this year when he was working under Gauguin's influence and advice and watching Gauguin painting, and himself painting from drawings made by Gauguin, he tried for a time to control his passions and to discipline his hand. *L'avenue des tombeaux: Les Aliscamps*[1] and several pictures called *L'Arlésienne*[2] painted in that month, the latter planned and patterned on the basis of Gauguin's *Arlésiennes se rendant à l'église* (Pl. 23A), show the influence of the Japanese prints for which both he and Gauguin had an equal admiration, and they are executed with relative calm and restraint; and in *La berceuse*[3] he captured something of Gauguin's rhythmic line. But after his first attack of madness at Christmas 1888 and Gauguin's departure Van Gogh soon reverted to type. In the months which followed he could and did paint many exciting pictures, but he no longer had a chance to advance in the field of controlled achievement. Van Gogh in a word must rank as a minor artist who made wonderful progress in a working career of six years broken into by attacks of madness. Beginning with no joy in colour and little feeling for form he advanced to *Le père Tanguy* which is enlivened by colour and is far less ragged in form than the pictures of the Neunen period; and thence he advanced, with Gauguin's assistance, to the relative grandeur of *La berceuse*. But he never arrived at the major grandeur of Gauguin's *La reine des Aréois* (Pl. 35) or to the simple serenity of Cézanne's monumental portraits; and it is hard to believe that, even if madness had not so soon destroyed him, he would ever have compassed the requisite control. He has had nevertheless a great influence on subsequent modern painting because he played a part in the liberation of colour from purely descriptive service and because at bottom he was romantically concerned (as Rembrandt was mainly and as Cézanne was partly concerned) with psychological values; and his work was thus, as we shall see, the ancestor both of the colour-aspect of the Fauve Movement at the beginning of the twentieth century and of twentieth-century Expressionism (developed by Rouault, Vlaminck, Segonzac and Soutine).

I have said above that the plan and pattern of Van Gogh's *L'Arlésienne* was evidently based on Gauguin's *Arlésiennes se rendant à l'église* (Pl. 23A) and I suggested earlier that Gauguin may have been influenced by The Douanier Rousseau in that

[1] Wassenaar, Holland. Kröller-Müller Foundation.

[2] New York. Adolph Lewisohn. Another version belongs or belonged recently to a German collector. A different composition *L'Arlésienne* belonging to Dr. and Mrs. Harry Bakwin (New York) was painted from a drawing (belonging to Dr. F. H. Hirschland, New York) which Gauguin made at Arles.

[3] Laren, Holland. V. W. Van Gogh. Other versions in Chicago: Art Institute (Birch-Bartlett Collection); in Wassenaar: Kröller-Müller Foundation; in Bâle: R. Stoechelin Collection; and elsewhere. This picture was painted at the beginning of 1889 after his recovery from his first fit of madness. It is clearly so influenced by Gauguin that I assume it to have been based on a drawing made by Van Gogh during Gauguin's stay if not indeed on a drawing by Gauguin.

21. CÉZANNE
Le verger, c. 1886
Paris. Durand-Ruel

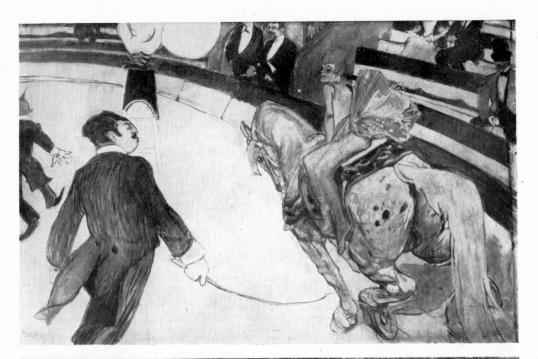

22A. LAUTREC
Au Cirque Fernando, 1888
Chicago. Art Institute (Winterbotham)
22B. GAUGUIN
Vision après le sermon : lutte de Jacob avec l'ange, 1888
Edinburgh. National Gallery of Scotland

picture.[1] We may possibly assume a direct as well as an indirect influence on Van Gogh from The Douanier whose early works he probably saw, as Gauguin probably saw them, in the *Salon des Indépendants* and whose remarkable contributions in this period I must now discuss.

The Douanier retired from the Customs about 1885 when he was just over forty; he exhibited regularly at the *Salon des Indépendants* from 1886 onwards. Completely untutored, unhampered by art school tricks, uninhibited by academic or revolutionary doctrines, he knew from the beginning what he wanted to do and calmly did it. From the first he combined the utmost directness of vision with a feeling for grandeur in design and an instinctive grasp of the principles of classical synthesis; and every picture he painted was wholly original and different from the last. The catalogues of the *Salon des Indépendants* show that his early exhibits were suburban views, portraits and subject pictures called *Un soir de carnaval* (1886), *Un pauvre diable* (1887) and *Un suicidé* (1889). In 1890 he exhibited *Moi-même: Portrait paysage* (Pl. 28A), and in 1891 the *Portrait de Monsieur L . . .* which I take to be the *Portrait de Pierre Loti* (Pl. 23B)), a composition titled *Surpris* and a river scene *Vue de la passerelle de Passy*.[2] In *Moi-même: Portrait paysage* (Pl. 28A), where the figure is just over half life-size, we see the artist himself on one of the quays of Paris; behind, a row of wine barrels outside an *octroi* shed recalls his former occupation; a sailing ship covered with real and imaginary flags of many nations (the British Red Ensign at the masthead) is moored beside the quay; behind the ship we see the Pont des Arts and the houses of Paris with chimneys silhouetted against the sky like the chimneys in Gentile Bellini's pictures of Venice; on the right a balloon rises against small clouds in an evening sky; the artist wears a Rembrandt artist's cap and in his coat he has the violet button of the *Palmes académiques* (awarded him as a teacher of drawing in a municipal school). In the composition *Surpris*,[3] a kind of modern 'Perseus and Andromeda', we see trees silhouetted against a lake and sky, a nude girl beneath a tree, and a bear, about to attack her, surprised by a shot from a *chasseur* behind a rock; Renoir was much impressed by *Surpris*; '*Quel joli ton, cette toile de Rousseau*', he said later referring to it in conversation with M. Vollard, '*et ce nu de femme faisant face au chasseur vêtu d'un complet de La Belle Jardinière! . . . Je suis sûr qu'Ingres lui-même n'aurait pas détesté ça!*' I can find no record that Loti sat for the amazing *Portrait de Pierre Loti* (Pl. 23B); and the picture may have been painted from a photograph or drawing in a newspaper. The *Vue du Parc Montsouris* (Pl. 27) seems to have been first exhibited in 1895 but it was painted I think in the early 'nineties if not earlier and I accordingly date it '*c.* 1892'; here The Douanier has recorded his sensation of the smallness of the doll-like promenaders contrasted with the towering trees; and the colour of the picture is predominantly green. Appearing thus, at the end of the 'eighties and at the beginning of the last decade of the nineteenth century, the early pictures by The Douanier seemed grotesque to dilettanti still obsessed with Realist and Impressionist standards; and the *Portrait de Pierre Loti* was in fact bought as a joke by a writer who had a collection of grotesque

---

[1] Cf. above, p. 78. [2] Paris. Mme Paul Guillaume.
[3] Merion: Barnes Foundation.

and humorous pictures[1]; but their bold patterning and fearless characterization would surely not have been lost upon Gauguin who was acquainted with The Douanier at an early date and played a trick upon him that I record elsewhere,[2] and who presumably saw them in the *Salon des Indépendants* in 1888 and 1891.

To understand and enjoy The Douanier's pictures we must of course approach them in the same way that we approach the early Italian paintings produced by men innocent of Renaissance and Baroque science; we must approach them with our eyes open to original classical convention and design, our minds open to The Douanier's simple imagination and ideas, and our hearts open to his simple personality. If we do this we realize that his pictures from the start were outstanding contributions in several ways and on several levels. As a classical designer, working quite instinctively, he arrived at much the same point that Seurat arrived at by intellectual processes—and there are indeed such amazing resemblances in the feeling for pattern and in stylization between *Moi-même: Portrait paysage* (Pl. 28A) and Seurat's *Chahut* (Pl. 28B), both exhibited in the 1890 *Salon des Indépendants*, that it is possible to suppose an influence even upon Seurat who is also known to have met him in connection with the organization of those *Salons*.[3] At the same time there is a directness in The Douanier's vision in the *Portrait de Pierre Loti* and the *Vue du Parc Montsouris* which is truly primitive; and if, from the realist standpoint his *Surpris* is ridiculous, it is no whit more ridiculous than Titian's *Perseus and Andromeda* and hundreds of other 'mythological' pictures by celebrated masters.

It remains to comment on the works by Toulouse-Lautrec between 1884 and 1897. I have said above that he made a contribution to the modern classical Renaissance in this period.[4] But in these years, as in the next decade, he was mainly an exponent of the old Realist and Impressionist procedures. He had painted pictures of sporting subjects from 1879 when he was a boy of fifteen until he began to paint studies of Montmartre women and pictures of the circus and Parisian dance halls about 1888 when he was twenty-four. I reproduce his *Au Cirque Fernando* (Pl. 22A) of 1888, and *La fille à l'accroche-cœur* (Pl. 31) and *Au bal du Moulin de la Galette* (Pl. 32B) both of 1889. When he painted *Au Cirque Fernando* he had just met Gauguin and become an enthusiast for Japanese prints. This is the first of his compositions (and almost the only one) where he employed the flowing rhythm that distinguishes Far Eastern drawing and Gauguin's pictures like *Vision après le sermon: Lutte de Jacob avec l'ange* (Pl. 22B) and *Mlle Loulou* (Pl. 30). After painting *Au Cirque Fernando* he reserved this aspect of his equipment for his admirable posters, which he began to design in 1891, and which, with this one picture, are the contributions to the Modern Classical Renaissance I referred to. In his paintings after 1888 he developed as a realist-Impressionist and social commentator, much influenced by Degas on the one hand and by Aristide Bruant on the other. Thus influenced he made studies of *pierreuses* and women of the Parisian underworld of which *La fille à l'accroche-cœur* (Pl. 31) is an early and vigorous example revealing, incidentally, his appreciation of *Le père Tanguy* (Pl. 24B) by Van Gogh

---

[1] Cf. p. 106. [2] Cf. p. 120. [3] Cf. pp. 107 and 120.
[4] Cf. p. 73.

23A. GAUGUIN
Arlésiennes se rendant à l'église, 1888
New York. James W. Barney, Esq.
23B. THE DOUANIER ROUSSEAU
Portrait de Pierre Loti, 1891
German collection

24A. CÉZANNE
Paysan assis, C. 1891

24B. VAN GOGH
Le père Tanguy, 1887

whom he had known since 1886. His first dance hall picture *Au bal du Moulin de la Galette* (Pl. 32B) gives us a very different impression of the establishment and its clientèle from that suggested by Renoir's *Le Moulin de la Galette* (Pl. 9B) of 1876: the place had probably 'gone down' in the interval, but even so Lautrec's picture makes us wonder if the habitués some thirteen years earlier were all as uniformly charming as Renoir has portrayed them. It is undeniable that Lautrec's *Au bal du Moulin de la Galette* is brilliantly clever and most original in observation, especially when we remember that he was only twenty-five when he painted it. The picture is arresting, intriguing and impressive as romantic-realist descriptive comment. But both the lyrical classicism of Renoir's *Le Moulin de la Galette* and the grand, monumental and architectural classicism of Cézanne's *Les joueurs de cartes* (Pl. 32A) are really finer and more of this period than Lautrec's picture which continues the drawings by Guys in the 'fifties and 'sixties and Degas' productions in the period covered by our Prologue.

ACT I: HOW IT HAPPENED

SCENE I: 1884-1886

From the *First Salon des Indépendants* and Seurat's *Baignade* to Seurat's *Un dimanche d'été à la Grande Jatte* at the *Eighth (and Last) Impressionist Exhibition* and Van Gogh's arrival in Paris

---

In May 1884 a number of artists who called themselves *Le groupe des Indépendants* arranged an exhibition of their works. The show was mismanaged and attracted no attention; but the exhibitors included Seurat aged twenty-five, Paul Signac aged twenty-one, Odilon Redon aged forty-four, Dubois-Pillet and Henry Edmund Cross. Seurat sent *Baignade*[1] which the *Salon* had rejected. He was congratulated on this picture by the artists I have named—unknown to him till then—and with them and some others he founded a new group, the *Société des Artistes Indépendants*, which was destined to render enormous service to contemporary creative art. The constitution of this *Société des Artistes Indépendants*, unchanged till the 1914 war, was based on the No Jury principle; any artist who paid a small fee could become a member with the right to exhibit; the committee was elected for two years by a general assembly of all members of three years' standing; Article 38 read: 'Political and religious discussions are absolutely forbidden both in the general assemblies and the meetings of the committee.'

The *First Salon des Indépendants* was held in December. The exhibitors included Seurat (who sent a sketch for *Un dimanche d'été à la Grande Jatte*), Odilon Redon, Signac, Dubois-Pillet, Cross, Eugène Valton (later President), Gauguin's friend Emile Schuffenecker, the Impressionist Guillaumin, Marie Bashkirtseff (who had died in October) and Bastien Lepage who died on the opening day. Violent snowstorms kept visitors from this exhibition, but the critic Felix Fénéon, then twenty-two, saw what Seurat was after and founded the *Revue Indépendante* to help the new Classical Renaissance.

Fénéon's discernment was quite exceptional in 1884 when the growing success of the Impressionists was increased by the *Manet Memorial Exhibition* and the *Manet Sale* at the Hôtel Drouot which both took place this year. The *Manet Memorial Exhibition* (held at the Ecole des Beaux-Arts despite the protests of some officials) contained a hundred and sixteen paintings and numerous pastels and drawings; Zola wrote the preface to the catalogue; the attendance was thirteen thousand.

[1] London. National Gallery, Millbank.

85

The *Manet Sale* contained a hundred and sixty-nine works (mainly belonging to Mme Manet) and the total realized was just over a hundred and sixteen thousand francs.[1] After this sale the exchange value of Manet's pictures in the international art trade began to rise; the singer Faure intimated that though he had twice refused twenty thousand francs for *Le bon bock*, he might be tempted by thirty, and as Manet, despite his abstention from the Impressionist Exhibitions, had been widely spoken of as an Impressionist, this rise in the prices of his pictures helped the Impressionist artists and the dealers who backed them.

In this year 1884 Amédée Modigliani was born at Livorno; Huysmans published *A rebours*, Joséphin Péladan published *Le vice suprême* and Alphonse Daudet published *Sapho*; Zola published *La joie de vivre* (twelfth in the Rougon-Macquart series), and *Germinal* appeared as a serial in *Gil Blas* and the London paper *The People*; the Swedish playwright, novelist and painter August Strindberg published *Marriages* and was prosecuted in Stockholm for 'writings injurious to morality and offensive to religion'; Lautrec, aged twenty, wrote, in a letter, of John Singer Sargent's pictures in the *Salon*: '*Chercheriez-vous à vendre, Monsieur Sargent? Certes la manière dont vous essuyez votre pinceau est merveilleuse, mais vraiment l'art international ne se régénera guère au contact emballé de votre brosse*'; Marcel Proust, aged thirteen, wrote in a Confession Book in answer to the question '*Quel est pour vous le comble de la misère?*'—'*Etre séparé de maman*'; André Antoine, aged twenty-six, back from military service in Tunis, resumed work as a clerk in the Gas Company; and the first dirigible airship *La France*, designed by Colonel Renard, made a successful flight from and back to its hangar at Chalais-Meudon.

In the next year 1885, André Lhote was born at Bordeaux, Roger de la Fresnaye was born at Le Mans and Robert Delaunay was born in Paris; Constantin Guys, aged eighty, was run over and crippled after selling some hundreds of his drawings at two francs apeice to the Musée de la Ville de Paris (Musée Carnavalet); André Gill died; Verlaine published *Jadis et naguère* and served a month's imprisonment for drunken assault; Sigmund Freud, aged twenty-nine, arrived in Paris to study psychiatry under Charcot; Karl Marx's *Das Kapital Vol. II.*, was posthumously published; Jules Laforgue published *Complaintes*, and Zola *Germinal* (in book form). André Antoine joined the amateur dramatic company *Le Cercle Gaulois*; Henri Becque's play *La Parisienne*, refused by the Comédie Française, was produced at the Renaissance and failed; and Alphonse Daudet's *Sapho*, produced as a play (with Jane Hading as Sapho), was a popular success. Whistler and Sickert spent the summer with Degas at Dieppe where Whistler read his *Ten o'Clock* to George Moore, Lady Archibald Campbell and a number of French artists; James Ensor (already referred to as a member of the Brussels Group Les XX) painted the Surrealist pictures *Meuble hanté* and *Cauchemar*; Odilon Redon drew the lithographs published as *Hommage à Goya*; Van Gogh at Neunen in Holland had just painted *Paysan Hollandais* (Pl. 17B); and Seurat's *Baignade* returned unsold to Paris from an exhibition, arranged by Durand-Ruel, in New York.

[1] The fluctuations in exchange make it of course impossible to estimate the equivalent in present money. But perhaps five hundred thousand francs may be somewhere near it if the franc is estimated at 25 to the pound sterling.

There was no *Salon des Indépendants* in 1885 as Seurat and his associates wanted time to organize their effort. These artists now foregathered in Signac's studio (as the Impressionists had foregathered twenty years earlier in Bazille's) and Signac took Seurat to the Normandy coast. Pissarro, hearing of the meetings in Signac's studio, called there one day to learn what this new movement was about. Seurat then took Pissarro to his own studio and showed him *Un dimanche d'été a la Grande Jatte* (Pl. 18). Pissarro, aged fifty-five, was dumbfounded at this achievement by a young man of twenty-six; he listened with attention while Seurat explained his attitude to Impressionist 'sketching', and his Divisionist system; and soon after he painted a series of pictures in Seurat's pointillist technique. Pissarro in his turn talked to Seurat and Signac of Cézanne, and he now persuaded Signac to buy Cézanne's landscape *Dans la vallée de l'Oise*[1] (painted about 1880); this purchase was made from Tanguy who had the keys of Cézanne's Paris studio with instructions to sell the large pictures for a hundred francs and the small ones for forty; Pissarro, Signac and Gauguin chose the picture together—Gauguin at this time being so short of money that he took a job at the end of the year as a billsticker at five francs a day. Meanwhile Cézanne himself was working at Aix and l'Estaque in the spring, visiting Renoir at La Roche-Guyon and Zola at Medan in July, and painting in the autumn at Gardanne.

On May 22 of this year 1885 Victor Hugo died at the age of eighty-three. He had written in his will: '*Je donne cinquante mille francs aux pauvres: je désire être porté au cimetière dans leur corbillard. Je refuse l'oraison de toutes les églises. Je crois en Dieu.*' His corpse was placed in the *corbillard des pauvres*; but the funeral was nevertheless made into a pageant which drew enormous crowds from all parts of France to Paris. De Goncourt wrote in his diary: '*Cette Kermesse me dégoûte*'; the British ambassador reported: 'There was nothing striking, splendid or appropriate either in the enormous catafalque erected under the Arc de Triomphe or in the trappings of the funeral. The studied avoidance of any recognition of religion did away with all solemnity. There was nothing mournful or solemn in the demeanour of the people. The impressive part of the scene consisted in the vast crowds. At some points attempts were made to raise anarchical or socialistic cries but met with no response. . . .' Renoir (at work on *Les grandes baigneuses*) (Pl. 19B) spluttered forth his detestation of Hugo and his works: '*Ce raseur—ce poseur—ce vaniteux. Je le déteste pour son horreur de la vie. Il ne sut jamais rien faire aux proportions de la réalité. Avec lui un cheval n'est plus un cheval mais un animal antédiluvien.*'

The next year 1886 was marked by the exhibition of Seurat's *Un dimanche d'été à la Grande Jatte* (Pl. 18) in the *Eighth (and Last) Impressionist Exhibition* and the *Second Salon des Indépendants*, and by Van Gogh's arrival in Paris.

The *Eighth (and Last) Impressionist Exhibition* took place in May in rooms above the restaurant *Maison Dorée* at the corner of the Boulevard des Italiens and the rue Laffitte. It was organized by Berthe Morisot and her husband Eugène Manet in consultation with Degas who insisted that the word 'Impressionist' should be dropped from the title and that the show be advertised simply as '*8ᵉ Exposition de Peinture*'. Renoir, Monet, Sisley, Caillebotte and Cézanne declined to take part in

[1] This picture was still in Signac's possession when he died in 1935.

it—Renoir because he was engrossed in *Les grandes baigneuses* (Pl. 19B), Monet because he had sent his best works to an exhibition in New York, Sisley because his works were now being accepted by the *Salon* and acquired by dealers, Caillebotte because he had quarrelled with Degas, and Cézanne (who had just married and was about to inherit a third of his father's large fortune) because he could not be bothered. Faced with these abstentions Degas invited his pupil Mary Cassatt, his friend Forain and some others; and he was persuaded by Pissarro to invite Seurat, Signac, Gauguin, Emile Schuffenecker and Odilon Redon. The Exhibition had a whole so-called 'Divisionist' (or 'Pointillist') gallery containing landscapes by Pissarro in Seurat's technique, pictures by Schuffenecker and Signac also influenced by Seurat, and some port scenes, as well as *Un dimanche d'été à la Grande Jatte*, by Seurat himself. The originality of Seurat's masterpiece enraged the academic painters, one of whom, Alfred Stevens (already encountered as a friend of Manet and Berthe Morisot), spent the opening day between the gallery and Tortoni's (the fashionable café) collecting friends whom he piloted in groups to Seurat's picture '*pour leur montrer à quel degré d'abjection était tombé son ami Degas en hospitalisant de telles horreurs*'; impatient to renew the attack he gave gold at the turnstile and forgot to wait for change. George Moore, back in Paris after some years' absence, heard Seurat's picture described as a vast canvas, all blue and violet, 'featuring' a monkey with a tail a yard long; he went to the exhibition and was completely bewildered; recording the experience he wrote a few years later: 'How well I remember being attracted towards an end of the room which was filled with a series of most singular pictures . . . executed in a series of minute touches, like mosaic . . . unrelieved by any attempt at atmospheric effect, all painted in a series of little dots! . . . My wonderment was tenfold increased on discovering that only five of these pictures were painted by the new man, Seurat, whose name was unknown to me; the other five were painted by my old friend Pissarro. My first thought went for the printer; my second for some *fumisterie* on the part of the hanging committee, the intention of which escaped me. . . . Owing to a long and intimate acquaintance with Pissarro and his work, I could distinguish between him and Seurat, but to the ordinary visitor their pictures were identical. . . . To say that these scientifically-painted pictures are strange, absurd, ridiculous, conveys no sensation of their extravagances; and I think that even an elaborate description would miss its mark. For in truth, the pictures merit no such attention.' George Moore was only thirty-four when he went to this Exhibition but his pictorial receptivity had already finally closed down. In these circumstances Félix Fénéon came forward with a counterblast—a brochure explaining the character of the new movement—as Duranty had done for Degas in 1876 and as Duret had done in 1878 for the Impressionists; this brochure was titled *Les Impressionistes en 1886* and its sub-title was *MM. Pissarro, Seurat et Signac innovent*.

In the *Second Salon des Indépendants* where Seurat again exhibited *Un dimanche d'été à la Grande Jatte* he also exhibited *La Seine à Courbevoie*,[1] *Le Bec du Hoc à Grandcamp*[2] and some port scenes. His associates there included Signac, Dubois-Pillet, Cross, and Lucien Pissarro (Pissarro's son). The Douanier Rousseau, who

[1] Paris. Mme Cachin-Signac.   [2] London. Sir Kenneth Clark.

had just retired from the Customs, made his début at this exhibition with four pictures which (as my knowledge goes) have since disappeared.

It was in February 1886 that Van Gogh, aged thirty-three, arrived on the Parisian scene. He shared lodgings with his brother Théo who was manager of a branch of the Goupil Gallery on the Boulevard Montmartre (where Van Gogh himself had worked in 1874). Théo, who dealt in pictures by the Impressionists, also admired the works by Seurat and his associates, and he made the place a rendezvous for these artists and their friends. In the Goupil Gallery at this time Van Gogh thus had valuable contacts and he rapidly developed in a way which he described in an important but little known letter to an Antwerp friend: 'In Antwerp I did not even know what the Impressionists were. Now I have seen them . . . and much admired nudes by Degas and landscapes by Monet . . . I have made a series of colour studies in painting—simply flowers, red poppies, blue cornflowers and myosotis, white and rose roses, yellow chrysanthemums, seeking oppositions of blue with orange, red and green, yellow and violet, and *les tons rompus et neutres* to harmonize brutal extremes. I am trying to render intense colour and not a grey harmony. . . . French air clears up the brain and does one a world of good. . . . Trade is slow here; the great dealers sell Millet, Delacroix, Corot, Daubigny, Dupré and a few other masters at exorbitant prices. They do little or nothing for young artists. . . . The second class dealers sell these but at very low prices. . . . I have found four dealers who have studies of mine . . . now the prices are 50 francs . . . one must sell cheap—even at cost price—to rise.' In the mornings at this time Van Gogh painted from the model in Cormon's Academy where he met Lautrec and Emile Bernard (then eighteen and all enthusiasm for some pictures by Cézanne which he had just discovered in Tanguy's shop). In the evenings Van Gogh frequented the Café Tambourin on the Avenue Clichy which had some dubious customers including a Peruvian named Prado, a swashbuckling adventurer, burglar, and seducer of women who had murdered a prostitute at the beginning of this year (and who will reappear in our story). The Café Tambourin was run by a former artists' model known as La Siccatore who took a fancy to Van Gogh and commissioned him to paint a series of panels for the main room.[1] Gauguin who had been working at Pont Aven in the summer met Van Gogh at the Goupil Gallery in the autumn. Van Gogh was captured at once by his personality and intellectual power; and we know from Gauguin's writings that he on his side was profoundly impressed by Van Gogh's personality and by the tales he told him of his life as a lay preacher in the Borinage. Between Van Gogh and Lautrec, on the other hand, there was not and could not of course be anything more than superficial contacts; for Van Gogh burned at all times with smouldering passion while Lautrec—as Tristan Bernard wrote of him years later—enjoyed life like a child let loose on a public square. Lautrec at this time was contributing drawings for the illustrated papers and one titled *Gin Cocktail*, published this year in the *Courrier Français*, was probably the first pictorial presentation of the subject by a major artist (though the word 'cocktail' and the brands known as 'stone

[1] Van Gogh's still-life titled *L'absinthe* (Laren: V. W. van Gogh) was probably painted in this café and La Siccatore was probably the model for his *L'artiste au restaurant* (same collection).

fence' and 'sherry cobbler' had appeared in literature—in Irving's *A History of New York from the Beginning of the World to the End of the Dutch Dynasty by Diedrich Knickerbocker*—as early as 1809). Lautrec, though he still looked in from time to time at Cormon's Academy, was already launched on his career and had already painted *Suzanne Valadon*[1] in a technique influenced by Boldini whose dexterity impressed him; in the evenings he was frequently at Aristide Bruant's cabaret *Le Mirliton* which had been opened, as I have chronicled, the year before. Bruant's cabaret was installed in premises vacated by Salis' *Chat Noir* cabaret which had moved elsewhere; the *Chat Noir* had been appointed in Louis XIII style and, in removing, Salis had accidentally left one Louis XIII chair behind; Bruant exploited this accident as *réclame* for his own cabaret by hanging the chair upside down from the ceiling and composing a ditty to the effect that the chair belonged to Salis but could only be seen Chez Bruant and only reached by high kickers of the 'Can-Can' Quadrille (which was then 'the rage'). As a result the 'Can-Can' Quadrille was known for a time as '*La Quadrille de la chaise Louis Treize*' and Lautrec painted a picture with this title[2] which he gave to Bruant who hung it in his cabaret and inscribed upon the frame;

> *Ah! Messieurs, qu'on est à l'aise*
> *Quand on est assis sur la chaise Louis XIII.*

In this year 1886 Liszt died at the age of seventy-five; Eric Satie, aged twenty, wrote *Ogives*, his first composition, for the piano. Lugné-Poë, aged seventeen, started an amateur dramatic company, *Le Cercle des Escoliers*, with the students of the Lycée Condorcet; and André Antoine made plans to produce two new plays with the amateurs of the *Cercle Gaulois*. Pierre Loti published *Pêcheur d'Islande*; and Verlaine after publishing Rimbaud's *Illuminations* passed long months in hospital where he was visited by, among others, Huysmans, Anatole France, Maurice Barrès (aged twenty-four) and André Gide (aged seventeen). Zola now published *L'œuvre*, in which the central figure, Claude Lantier, a neurotic painter tormented by his inability to achieve an impossible ideal, was constructed from Zola's contacts with Cézanne and the other artists whom he had known so intimately in his early days; Cézanne's friends were deeply incensed by this book; and Renoir said that it showed Zola's inability to do what he always pretended to do, i.e. transcribe the facts of a milieu experienced; Zola sent a copy to Cézanne who read it and thanked him for it 'in memory of bygone years', but declined thereafter to speak to him again.[3]

Political and social happenings of these years 1884–1886 include the expulsion of the Orléans and Bonaparte princes from France and the presentation by the Duc d'Aumâle of the Château de Chantilly with its art collection (the Musée Condé) to the nation. There were fierce disputes about divorce (which had been legalized by

---

[1] Copenhagen. Ny Carlsberg Museum.

[2] Paris. J. Dollfus. Another picture by Lautrec showing Bruant's cabaret and Bruant singing the ditty with the chair in the background, *Le refrain de la chaise Louis XIII*, belongs to MM. Durand-Ruel.

[3] Cf. below, pp. 114 and 115.

the Revolution, made illegal again in 1815, and was now relegalized by Jules Ferry); there were disputes also about the passing of another Education Law to secularise education. I must also mention the beginning of an anti-Semitic campaign, launched by the publication of a book called *La France juive* by Edouard Drumont (founder later of the anti-Semitic journal *La Libre Parole*); a wave of anglo-phobia[1]; and the first appearance of General Boulanger as a public figure.[2]

[1] This wave of anglophobia, which began in 1885, was caused by the disappearance in the Sudan of Olivier Pain (Rochefort's companion in the evasion from Noumea (cf. above, pp. 34, 46)), while General Gordon was besieged at Khartoum; Rochefort declared that Lord Wolseley had accused Pain of spying and offered £50 for his head, and that Major Kitchener, '*un sinistre gredin nourri de psaumes et abreuvé de whisky,*' had arranged for his murder by the Arabs; rumour then had it that Pain had been buried alive; and Rochefort urged the populace to avenge Pain's death on '*la vieille peau*' of Lord Lyons, the British Ambassador in Paris; but nothing happened as Lord Lyons was away. This wave of anglophobia reached Rimbaud who was at Harrar after exploring Ogaden; '*Leur Gordon*', Rimbaud wrote, '*est un idiot, leur Wolseley un âne, et toutes leurs entreprises une suite insensée d'absurdités et de déprédation.*'

[2] General Boulanger (for whom Gauguin was later mistaken, as I relate elsewhere (cf. p. 99)) became popular in 1886, when he was Minister for War, by issuing an order permitting all ranks in the army to wear the full beards then so greatly admired by the women. He owed his place in the Cabinet to Clémenceau (then leader of some sixty Radicals in the Chamber) who looked upon him as 'the only truly Republican General'. Handsome and dashing, he caught the popular fancy and his name was always applauded in the music halls where a song called *En revenant de la revue*, which had a verse about him, was a favourite at this time.

ACT I: HOW IT HAPPENED

SCENE II: 1887-1888

From Seurat's *Poseuses*, Renoir's *Les grandes baigneuses*, and the foundation of Antoine's *Théâtre Libre*, to Cézanne's *Mardi Gras*, Gauguin's *Vision après le sermon* and *Arlésiennes se rendant à l'église*, Van Gogh's madness, and General Boulanger's attempt to become Dictator

---

In 1887 Juan Gris was born in Madrid and Marc Chagall was born at Vitebsk in Russia; Georges Roualt, aged sixteen, began work in a stained glass factory in Paris, and Henri Matisse, aged eighteen, was in a lawyer's office at Saint Quentin. Debussy, aged twenty-five, went with Brahms, aged fifty-four, to a performance of *Carmen* in Vienna, and Borodine, composer of *Prince Igor*, died. Zola published *La terre*, de Maupassant *Le Horla*, Paul Bourget *André Cornélis*, Mallarmé *Poésies complètes*, and Pierre Loti *Mme Chrysanthème*. Jules Laforgue died at the age of twenty-seven—(his *Hamlet ou Les suites de la piété filiale*, *Salomé* and other fantasias being published soon after as *Moralités légendaires* by Félix Fénéon, the poet Gustave Kahn and other friends).

In this year also the *Théâtre Libre* was founded by André Antoine, who was introduced in January to a group of Montmartre artists and writers calling themselves *La Butte* because they foregathered in a block of studios in the rue Ravignan (where Picasso and his friends were to foregather some twenty years later). Through Paul Alexis who was a member, Antoine secured a one-act play by Zola, *Jacques Damour*, and also a short play *Mademoiselle Pomme* ('une espèce d'acte guignolesque') left by Duranty among his papers. These plays and two others formed the programme of his first production. The *première* was fixed for March 30, the earliest possible date (as Antoine required his month's salary from the Gas Company before he could pay the 100 francs rent of the hall hired for the occasion). The actors (amateurs of the 'Cercle Gaulois') rehearsed by night in a cellar below a public billiard room; for the scenery Antoine borrowed furniture from his mother's house, and he wheeled it to the theatre on a handcart. On March 28 Alexis brought Zola and the publisher Charpentier to a rehearsal; and Zola returned next day with Théodore Duret and Alphonse Daudet. The first performance was well received and for his next performance on May 31 Antoine secured a three-act play in verse by the poet Emile Bergerat, *La nuit bergamasque* (which the

Comédie Française had refused). Jean Richepin, François Coppée, Catulle Mendès, Jules Lemaître, Sarcey the all-powerful dramatic critic, Coquelin *cadet* the actor, Porel Director of the Odéon, and the musician Chabrier attended this second performance which was financed by Bergerat with the aid of small subscriptions from Antoine, the other actors and Antoine's friends. Catulle Mendès, with his flair for talented beginners and his desire to help them, invited Antoine to luncheon, kept him to dinner and then took him to the theatre and supper—finally dismissing him with the present of his play *La femme de Tabarin* for autumn production. Antoine then determined to ask Théodore de Banville for a play; he called on de Banville in the luncheon hour, ran, unfed, all the way back to the Gas Company to get there in time for his afternoon's work, and was able to tell his actors that de Banville had promised to write him a Pierrot play called *Le baiser*. In July he had circulars printed inviting subscriptions for the autumn; in the evenings he wrote one thousand three hundred long letters, '*différentes selon les destinataires*', covering the circulars which he delivered himself late at night; he delivered the last, addressed to Clémenceau, at 5 o'clock in the morning. All this inevitably affected his work at the Gas Company—(already in April he noted in his diary: '*Mon chef de bureau au Gaz me fait des yeux terribles et surveille mon travail de beaucoup plus près*')—and he now resigned. When he began his autumn season he had three thousand seven hundred francs in subscriptions and a thousand francs of debts. The plays included *Sœur Philomène* (adapted from the de Goncourts' novel), *L'évasion* by Villiers de l'Isle-Adam, Mendès' *La femme de Tabarin*, de Banville's *Le baiser* (with music by Paul Vidal), *La sérénade* by Jean Jullien, and *Tout pour l'honneur* adapted from Zola's *Le Capitaine Burle* by Henri Céard. At the end of this year he wrote in his diary: 'I understand that I am to be decorated on January 1 with the *palmes académiques* . . . I should prefer some money.'

While Antoine was thus launching, rather belatedly, a realist movement in the theatre, the reaction against realism in painting was being carried forward by Seurat who was working on *Poseuses* (Pl. 19A), by Cézanne who had just painted *Le verger* (Pl. 21) and was working on *Mardi Gras*,[1] by Renoir who had just completed *Les grandes baigneuses* (Pl. 19B) and by Gauguin who had gone from Brittany to Panama and thence to Martinique. At the same time Van Gogh painted *Le père Tanguy* (Pl. 24B) and more panels for La Siccatore's café, which Seurat went to the café to see. Lautrec also went to the café and drew Van Gogh seated at a table. In November the café went bankrupt and was closed (owing perhaps to La Siccatore's connection with the murderer Prado who was arrested at this time); and Van Gogh lost not only the payment for his pictures but the pictures as well. Van Gogh sent nothing to the *Third Salon des Indépendants*. But The Douanier Rousseau sent three pictures (which have since disappeared) and Seurat sent *Honfleur: hospice et le phare*,[2] *Honfleur: entrée du port*[3] and *Le pont de Courbevoie*[3] (loaned respectively by the poet Verhaeren, Félix Fénéon and the critic Arsène Alexandre). At the end of the year Seurat's *Un dimanche d'été à la Grande Jatte* returned unsold from Brussels where it had been invited by the society *Les XX*.

[1] Moscow. Museum of Modern Western Art.   [2] London. Mrs. Chester Beatty.
[3] London. Samuel Courtauld.

ACT I: HOW IT HAPPENED

In January of the next year 1888 both Gauguin and Van Gogh were in Paris, and Van Gogh made Seurat's acquaintance. In February Van Gogh went to Arles to work out his destiny far from the Goupil Gallery and its habitués whom he now thought of as 'Parisian rotters'. In March the *Fourth Salon des Indépendants* had Seurat's *Poseuses* (Pl. 19A) and *Parade*,[1] and five paintings (which, as my knowledge goes, have since disappeared) by The Douanier Rousseau who was already to some extent a figure in the Parisian art world, as his work had attracted the attention of Rémy de Gourmont and the critic Gustave Coquiot, and among the painters, that of Odilon Redon, Seurat and also probably Gauguin and Van Gogh.[2] In May the Goupil Gallery had an exhibition of Gauguin's Martinique pictures with some others painted in Brittany in 1886 and the spring of 1887; Gauguin made some money from this show and went back to Pont Aven where he was joined by a young student from the Académie Julian, Paul Sérusier, then aged twenty-three, and Emile Bernard. Sérusier was still a hesitant convert to the new ideas. But Bernard, as recorded, had become an admirer of Cézanne's work in 1885 and he shared Gauguin's enthusiasm for the aesthetic of stained glass workers. At Pont Aven Gauguin now painted *Vision après le sermon: La lutte de Jacob avec l'ange* (Pl. 22B) and *Trois chiens*[3] and discussed the 'Synthesis' and 'Symbolist' theories with Emile Bernard (who painted at this time and later some Brittany pictures resembling Gauguin's). At Pont Aven Gauguin stayed at the Pension Gloanec which was full of academic landscape painters, French and foreign; he took his meals with his friends in a separate room which the academic painters referred to as 'the asylum'; the rival groups quarrelled; Gauguin wrote to Van Gogh inviting him to join the fray; Van Gogh replied by inviting him to come to Arles; and on October 20 Gauguin accepted his invitation.

When Gauguin went to Arles he was forty and Van Gogh was thirty-five. The two friends lived together in Van Gogh's house. They were financed by Théo Van Gogh who had been making Van Gogh an allowance in exchange for his pictures and now made an arrangement of the same kind with Gauguin. They pooled the two allowances; Van Gogh did the marketing and Gauguin cooked. In the middle of December Van Gogh began to show signs of madness. On December 21 he threw a glass at Gauguin in a café; the next day he followed him in the street with an open razor in his hand; Gauguin, alarmed, slept that night in an hotel; in the morning Gauguin found the police and a crowd outside the yellow house; Van Gogh had cut off his ear; Gauguin telegraphed to Théo who arrived on Christmas Eve; and fearing that his presence might aggravate Van Gogh's illness Gauguin then left immediately for Paris, where three days later he saw the execution of the murderer Prado whom Van Gogh, unsuspecting, had so often sat next to at the Café Tambourin.[4]

---

[1] New York. Stephen C. Clark.　　　　[2] Cf. above, pp. 78, 81, and below, pp. 110 and 120
[3] Paris. Mme Sternheim.

[4] Gauguin has left us an account of this execution. '*La planchette bascula si bien qu'au lieu du cou ce fut le nez qui porta. De douleur l'homme fit des efforts et brutalement deux blouses bleues pesèrent sur ses épaules ramenant le cou à la place désignée. Ce fut une longue minute et enfin le couteau fit son devoir.*' The account of Prado's exploits revealed at the trial made sensational reading and the trial was reported by all the European press. We get an allusion to it in the circular letter which Nietzsche, who went mad at this moment, sent to all his friends including August Strindberg—for the letter which revealed his madness to them had '*Ich bin Prado*' as its opening phrase.

25A. SEURAT
Le Crotoy : Aval, 1889
Paris. J. Seligmann
25B. VAN GOGH
Champ de blé, 1888
Toledo (U.S.A.) Museum

26. GAUGUIN

Jésus au Jardin des Oliviers, 1889

While Gauguin and Van Gogh were at Arles, Antoine (who also witnessed Prado's execution and noted in his diary: '*Cette sinistre cérémonie me guérit pour toujours de ma curiosité malsaine*') had continued his efforts at the *Théâtre Libre*. He had rented the Théâtre des Menus-Plaisirs on the Boulevard de Strasbourg for his productions, and he amazed the public by putting the lights out in the auditorium during the performances—which had never been done before in Parisian theatres; and, when acting, he often turned his back to the audience—an innovation then considered so extraordinary that in music hall reviews he was always burlesqued in that attitude. Apart from Antoine himself, who now ranked as a professional, and Lugné-Poë, who was acting in his company at this time, all the actors of the *Théâtre Libre* were still amateurs who earned their livings in various ways in the daytime—some were employed in offices, one had an umbrella shop, another was a wine merchant, a third was an architect, and one of the leading ladies was a dressmaker. Antoine's new plays included *La puissance des ténèbres* by Tolstoy, *La fin de Lucie Pellegrin* by Paul Alexis, *Les bouchers* by Fernand Incres, *L'amante du Christ* by Rodolphe Darzens, and *La chance de Françoise* by Georges de Porto-Riche. In Tolstoy's play he used real Russian costumes borrowed from Russian political refugees in Paris; in *Les bouchers* he hung real joints of meat in the butcher's shop; *L'amante du Christ* was a religious play in verse which heralded the work of Paul Claudel. The year's takings did not cover the expenses but the budget was balanced by performances in Brussels which Catulle Mendès, who was consistently helpful, had arranged. In the summer Antoine decided that he would like to produce Ernest Renan's play *L'abbesse de Jouarre* (which Eleanora Duse had produced in Italy) and he called on Sarah Bernhardt to ask her to play La Duse's part. 'I found her', he tells us in his diary, 'reclining on a *chaise longue*, covered with furs. She knew nothing about the *Théâtre Libre* and I tried to make her feel how helpful her support would be as her public would follow her anywhere, and—as Catulle Mendès had pointed out in a recent article—she had not so far used her genius in any fighting cause. But she remained unmoved and just smiled graciously at my enthusiasm. . . . When I spoke of La Duse she asked an old lady in the next room if she had ever heard of this actress and the old lady answered "Yes, I've seen her but she's not much good".'

In this year 1888 Giorgio de Chirico was born of Italian parents in Greece; Alfred Jarry, aged fifteen, wrote a first version of *Ubu Roi* and produced it as a marionette show at his school in Laval; Marcel Proust, aged seventeen, took his baccalauréat and began to contribute to a literary paper *La Revue Lilas*; Yvette Guilbert made her début as a comedy actress at the *Nouveautés*; de Maupassant went mad; Péladan went to Bayreuth and began to call himself 'Sar' and conceived the plan of his *Amphithéâtre des sciences mortes*; the *Société des gens de lettres* commissioned Rodin, aged forty-eight, to make a public statue of Balzac; Mallarmé published his translation of Whistler's *Ten o'Clock*; George Moore, aged thirty-six, published *Confessions of a Young Man*; and Verlaine drew caricatures of General Boulanger and asked Félicien Rops to draw a frontispiece to *Parallèlement*, which he described as '*Un livre d'une extrême et pour ainsi dire ingénue sensualité*'.

In 1887–1888 French Liberalism was attacked by Royalists and Right Extremists who aimed at the installation of General Boulanger as dictator to prepare the way for a Royalist restoration. Boulanger's Liberalism, which had attracted Clémenceau,[1] had in fact been a pose to capture popular support and hide secret intrigues with the Royalists and the Right. In 1887 his intrigues were discovered or suspected by Rouvier, the Liberal Prime Minister, who removed him from his office as Minister of War, appointed him commander of an army corps in Clermont-Ferrand, and added a condition that he must not come to Paris without leave. Boulanger's supporters, enraged by this prohibition, demonstrated at the Gare de Lyon when his train was about to start and detached his coach to prevent his departure; Boulanger replied in fine theatrical fashion by mounting the engine and standing in top hat and frock coat with arms folded beside the driver, as the train, which was placarded with '*Il reviendra*', steamed dramatically away. The Royalists and Right Extremists then launched a propaganda campaign describing the martyred Boulanger as a simple soldier out for Order and Strong Honest Government, a patriot who would be supported by everyone except corrupt parliamentarians, red revolutionaries, and other subversive and degenerate persons. The Boulevards were placarded with posters, one of which showed Boulanger crucified, with France as the Mater Dolorosa and members of the Government as the mocking crowd. At the same time some sections of the press made violent attacks on Antoine's realist productions and in particular on *La fin de Lucie Pellegrin* by Zola's friend Paul Alexis; Anatole France, who was a Boulangist, attacked Zola's *La terre* in the *Temps*; and the *Figaro* published a famous manifesto (*Le manifeste des Cinq*) against Zola. In October 1887 events played into the hands of the Boulangists. For a deputy named Wilson, son-in-law of Jules Grévy, President of the Republic, was found to have trafficked in honours, and many officials were involved. Jules Grévy resigned; and in December, after street riots in which Déroulède's *Ligue des Patriotes*[2] took part, Sadi Carnot was elected President—the extreme Left and the extreme Right having worked together to exclude the Liberal Jules Ferry. In the first months of the next year 1888 Boulanger, disguised and pretending to be lame, paid three secret visits to Paris; relieved of his command for this contravention of orders he became a private citizen and thus eligible for the Chamber; he now appeared as leader of a political party who called themselves 'The Nationalists' and announced a political programme in which, concealing his connection with the Royalists, he declared parliamentary government effete and useless and proposed an alternative system with a Dictator-President (himself) governing directly with a Council of State, a Chamber where no discussion would be permitted, and plebiscite references from time to time; during the rest of the year he stood as candidate at every bye-election for the Chamber, and at the end he had been elected to six seats and he was standing at an election, which he was expected to win, in Paris.[3]

---

[1] Cf. above, p. 91.   [2] Cf. above, p. 50.

[3] This system of multiple election was possible because the elections to the Chamber were then conducted by the method known as *scrutin de liste* which was subsequently abolished as a result of the use which the Boulangists made of it.

27. THE DOUANIER ROUSSEAU
Vue du parc Montsouris, c. 1892
Paris. M. Pierre Wertheimer

28B. SEURAT

Chahut, 1889-90

Wassenaar Kröller-Müller Foundation

28A. THE DOUANIER ROUSSEAU

Moi-même: Portrait-paysage, 1889-90

Prague, Museum of Modern Art

ACT I: HOW IT HAPPENED

SCENE III: 1889

From the first 'Synthetist-Symbolist' exhibition in the Café Volpini at the *Exposition Universelle* and Lautrec's début at the *Salon des Indépendants*, to Gauguin's *Jésus au Jardin des Oliviers* and the collapse of Boulangism

On January 28, 1889, Antoine wrote in his Diary: '*Nous nous promenions hier soir sur les boulevards dans la foule tandis qu'on attendait les résultats de l'élection Boulanger à Paris. Nous sentions que la capitale était prête à toutes les folies.*' The next day it was known that Boulanger had won with a huge majority and he was urged by his party to seize dictatorship by a *coup d'état*. At this point Anatole France, who may have hoped to become Minister of Art or Education in the Boulanger Council of State, persuaded his friend Mme de Caillavet to invite the General to dinner. The General came and Mme de Caillavet summed him up: 'He makes me doubt history and wonder if all the great figures who seem to us so imposing from a distance were really nothing more than *concoctions d'un panache, d'un plumet ou de l'engouement populaire*; he is not a lion, he is only a fox.' [1] Events proved that Mme de Caillavet was right. Liberal opinion had been organized against dictatorship, and Boulanger, informed of the strength of this resistance, was afraid to proceed to the *coup d'état*. By March the Government felt strong enough to charge him with conspiracy and to issue a warrant for his arrest; and thus threatened he fled the country in April.

The *Exposition Universelle* which opened on May 1 had been announced as a centenary celebration of the French Revolution, and all the monarchist governments, with the exception of Persia, had agreed to boycott it. The French Royalists refused to beflag their houses on the opening day, smart Parisians mocked the hordes of provincials and foreigners who invaded the city, and the dilettanti railed angrily at the Eiffel Tower constructed at a cost of 15,000,000 francs for the occasion. But the *Exposition* was nevertheless a great success. Thousands were interested by the *Palais des Machines*; the Eiffel Tower delighted the populace; The Douanier Rousseau, aged forty-five, was moved to write a vaudeville: '*Un voyage à l'Exposition*; Antoine was thrilled by the Indo-Chinese actors; Toulouse-Lautrec, aged twenty-five, went round the side-shows in the 'rue du Caire' and drew *La belle Fathma*, *La danse du ventre*, *Danseuse Javanaise* and *Derviche tourneur*;

[1] J. M. Pouquet. *Le Salon de Mme Arman de Caillavet.*

Debussy, aged twenty-seven, was intrigued by the Javanese music; and Guillaume Apollinaire, aged nine, was spellbound by the *fontaines lumineuses*.

The *Salon* of the *Exposition* in the Palais des Beaux-Arts was reserved for the official artists and others approved by them. Works by Monet and Pissarro, now considered respectable, were admitted; Cézanne's *La maison du pendu*[1] (painted in 1872) was forced in by its owner, Choquet, who had been asked to lend some furniture and agreed on condition that Cézanne's picture was hung; and in the Retrospective Section fifteen pictures by Manet, including *Le guitarrero*[2] (1860), *Lola de Valence*[1] (1861), *Olympia*[1] (1863), *Le fifre*[1] (1866) and *Le bon bock*[3] (1873) were applauded by the dilettanti. During the exhibition an American collector approached Manet's widow with a view to buying the *Olympia*; when this became known Monet and John S. Sargent opened a subscription to secure it for the Louvre; they collected close on 20,000 francs and Mme Manet sold them the picture; the subscribers included Huysmans, Mallarmé, Mirbeau, Rodin, Antonin Proust, Duret, Gustave Geffroy, Durand-Ruel and about forty painters. The picture was refused for the Louvre but accepted for the Luxembourg.[4]

The new tendencies in French creative painting were only discoverable at the exhibition by the rare visitors who chanced to take refreshment in the exhibition branch of the *Café Volpini* where the proprietor had arranged a show of paintings and lithographs by Gauguin, Emile Bernard, Schuffenecker, Laval, Louis Anquetin (a newcomer who developed on academic lines) and Daniel de Monfreid (who was later to be Gauguin's closest friend and confidant). In the Café Volpini show the pictures were in white frames, an innovation due to Gauguin; the catalogue, which had a blue and white striped cover and facsimiles of two drawings by Gauguin, described the exhibitors as '*Le Groupe Symboliste et Synthétiste*'; Gauguin's paintings included *Les Mangos: Martinique*,[5] *Jeunes lutteurs*,[6] *Femme dans les vagues*,[7] *La ronde des Bretonnes*,[6] and a dozen others. This show, where the pictures were seen amid the clatter and smell of a cheap restaurant, had considerable effects in spite of the unfavourable conditions; it revealed Gauguin to Pierre Bonnard, Edouard Vuillard and other students from the Académie Julian; it converted Sérusier from a hesitant admirer to an ardent apostle; and it attracted the poet Charles Morice (later Gauguin's biographer) and the critic Albert Aurier from literary circles.

Gauguin went again to Pont Aven as soon as the Café Volpini exhibition was arranged. He was joined there by Sérusier, and in the summer he painted *La belle Angèle*.[1] In September, becoming weary of Pont Aven, which was now a crowded artists' colony, he moved along the coast to Le Pouldu where, in the autumn, he painted *Le Christ Jaune*,[8] *Le Calvaire*,[9] and *Jésus au Jardin des Oliviers* (Pl. 26) already referred to.[10] At Le Pouldu he lived in a primitive inn where at first he had no one with him except Sérusier who soon returned to the Académie Julian with a cigar-

[1] Paris. Louvre.
[2] New York. W. Church Osborn.
[3] Philadelphia. C. S. Tyson.
[4] Cf. below, p. 218.
[5] Perhaps the picture now belonging to Mr. Alexander Maitland (Edinburgh).
[6] Paris. Ambroise Vollard.
[7] Cleveland (Ohio). F. H. Ginn.
[8] Paris. Paul Rosenberg.
[9] Brussels. Musée Royal.
[10] Cf. above, pp. 78, 79.

box painted by Gauguin which he used to demonstrate Gauguin's theories of pattern and rhythm and expressive distortion to spellbound students who included Maurice Denis, Vuillard and Bonnard. Later in the autumn Gauguin was joined by a crippled Dutchman named Meyer de Haan who had admired his work at the Café Volpini and procured an introduction to him from Pissarro; de Haan had money and paid Gauguin's bills at Le Pouldu for about nine months. In the winter when Gauguin was working at a lonely spot he was accosted by a gendarme on patrol duty against a possible landing by General Boulanger who was believed to be in Jersey at the time; 'He began to question and re-question me', Gauguin tells us, 'and made me so nervous that I burst out with "Do you imagine that I am General Boulanger himself?" the gendarme answered "There are more unlikely things than that". "Have you a description of him?" Gauguin said. "A description?" said the gendarme. "I don't give a hang for that. It's quite clear that you are simply defying me. You are arrested. Come along with me." And Gauguin had to go to the police station at Quimperlé where he was told that as he was not General Boulanger he had no right to pretend to be a general and insult a gendarme in the exercise of his duty. When Gauguin protested "But I did not pretend to be a general", the reply was "You must have pretended to be a general because the gendarme mistook you for General Boulanger. . . ."' And it was some time before the police dismissed him with a caution.

Van Gogh, meanwhile, had recovered from his first attack of madness, and painted the famous *Portrait de l'artiste à l'oreille coupée*[1] with the bandaged head. He had returned to his yellow house; but he was now treated as the village idiot; and after some time, on petition from his neighbours to the Mayor, he was sent back to the local hospital. He was allowed out sometimes under supervision and painted some admirable and, for him, rather unusually controlled spring landscapes, which were admired by Signac who came to Arles to see them. After three months of this cat-and-mouse existence he asked the hospital authorities to transfer him to a recognized institution for the insane, and he went to an asylum at St. Rémy in May. His first pictures painted at Saint Rémy were relatively calm studies in the asylum garden; and he wrote to his brother: 'I have done well to come here; by seeing the actual truth about the life of the various madmen and lunatics in this menagerie I am losing the vague dread, the fear of the thing. . . .' In June and July he produced some impressions of cornfields and cypress trees, using flame-like swirls in his technique; and then he wrote: 'I am terribly distressed that the attacks have come back, when I was beginning to hope that it would not return. This new attack came on me in the fields when I was in the midst of painting on a windy day. I will send you the canvas. I went on and finished it in spite of the attack. . . .' At his request Théo now sent him prints after Rembrandt, Delacroix, Millet, Gustave Doré and others, and from them he improvised free copies at times when the doctors judged him well enough to paint but not well enough to venture out. In the autumn he painted among other things the landscapes known as *Effet de pluie*,[2] *Champ de pavots*,[3] *Forêt de sapins au déclin du jour*,[3] *Le ravin*[3] and

---

[1] London. Samuel Courtauld. Another version belongs to Paul Rosenberg, Paris.
[2] Paris. Paul Rosenberg.   [3] Wassenaar. Kröller-Müller Foundation.

Boulevard de Saint Rémy: les paveurs.[1] Against Gauguin (whom some of Van Gogh's biographers have tried to make responsible for his madness) he harboured no ill-will, and he wrote suggesting that he would like to join him in Brittany; but Gauguin answered that it was quite impossible to find a room.

The *Fifth Salon des Indépendants*, held in the autumn, had a hundred and twenty exhibitors. Seurat sent three port scenes; Van Gogh a landscape and a flower piece; The Douanier Rousseau three pictures (which seem to have disappeared); Lautrec made his début at this exhibition with *Au bal du Moulin de la Galette* (Pl. 32B), *M. Fourcade au bal de l'Opéra* and a study of a Montmartre woman—probably *La fille à l'accroche-cœur* (Pl. 31). Seurat's *Poseuses* (Pl. 19A) was shown this year in the exhibition of *Les XX* in Brussels. *Les XX* at this moment was recovering from the turmoil caused by the huge satirical work *L'entrée du Christ à Bruxelles en 1889*,[2] which James Ensor had painted the year before; most of the members wanted to expel Ensor for this picture but he retained his position by one vote.

The Impressionists were now all profiting by their established reputations. A joint exhibition by Monet and Rodin was an undisputed success; Octave Mirbeau and Gustave Geffroy, newcomers as art critics, wrote forewords to the catalogue—the first for Monet and the second for Rodin. Degas, who now worked less hard than formerly, installed himself in a triple apartment in the rue Victor Massé, delivered some pictures and pastels to fulfil his contract with Durand-Ruel and then went to the country, and, later, to Spain with Boldini. Renoir visited Cézanne at Aix and painted Cézanne's favourite motif in *La montagne Sainte-Victoire*;[3] Cézanne himself was almost forgotten by Parisians but his existence was recalled to them by Emile Bernard who now published in *Les hommes d'aujourdhui* the first panegyric on his work.

The theatres suffered from the competition of the *Exposition Universelle* which was open in the evenings. But Antoine contrived to get audiences for *La reine Fiammette*, a six-act drama in verse by Catulle Mendès, *La patrie en danger* which Jules and Edmond de Goncourt had written in 1866, *Le cœur révélateur* by Edgar Allan Poe, and *Madeleine* by Zola. During a rehearsal of *Madeleine* Antoine was visited by Zola who had just travelled forty miles on the engine of a train to gain experience for his railway novel *La bête humaine*. To help his finances Antoine took his company to London and while there he saw Irving and Ellen Terry in *Macbeth*; he thought little of their acting but was impressed by the production.

There was a craze this year for slimming exercises which one Schweiniger had made fashionable, and '*le sport*' was practised '*avec une quasi-frénésie*'; Zola, now forty-nine, did the Schweiniger exercises and bicycled with gusto; Odilon Redon, who was also forty-nine, and Mallarmé, who was two years younger, went sculling together at Samois; and the guests in the salons of Mme de Caillavet and Mme Straus (formerly the wife of the composer Bizet) played vigorously at '*le tennis*', refreshing themselves afterwards with cool drinks passed to them by Marcel Proust, who rolled his large eyes and doubtless asked them their opinion of the latest publications: d'Annunzio's *Il piacere*, Verlaine's *Parallèlement*, Huysmans' *Certains*, and Bergson's *Les données immédiates de la conscience*.

[1] Paris. M. Leclerc.   [2] Still in the artist's possession.
[3] Merion. Barnes Foundation.

29. DEGAS
Danseuses roses, c. 1890
Boston. Museum of Fine Arts

30. GAUGUIN
Mlle Loulou, 1890
New York. Chester Dale, Esq.

ACT I: HOW IT HAPPENED

SCENE IV: 1890-1891

From Seurat's *Chahut* and *Jeune femme se poudrant*, The Douanier's *Moi-même: Portrait paysage*, Lautrec's first Moulin Rouge pictures, the foundation of Paul Fort's *Théâtre d'Art* and the death of Van Gogh; to the first Gauguin Sale, Gauguin's first departure for Tahiti, The Douanier's *Surpris* and *Portrait de Pierre Loti*, the foundation of *Gil Blas Illustré* and the *Revue Blanche*, and the death of Seurat

In 1890 Van Gogh, Cézanne, Odilon Redon, Signac and Lautrec had pictures in the exhibition of *Les XX* in Brussels where Lautrec challenged a Belgian artist to a duel because he spoke offensively of Van Gogh's work; the *Sixth Salon des Indépendants* had Seurat's *Chahut* (Pl. 28B) and *Jeune femme se poudrant*,[1] ten pictures by Van Gogh, Lautrec's *Au Moulin Rouge: la danse*,[2] and six pictures by The Douanier Rousseau including *Moi-même: Portrait paysage* (Pl. 28A). Lautrec was on the Committee for this *Salon des Indépendants* and he defended The Douanier whom some of the members were anxious to expel because sections of the public had guffawed at his pictures. When the exhibition ended Zidler, the proprietor of the Moulin Rouge, acquired Lautrec's picture *Au Moulin Rouge: la danse* and hung it with Lautrec's *Au cirque Fernando* (Pl. 22A) in the foyer.[3] At the same time Yvette Guilbert, aged twenty-two, left the 'legitimate' stage where she was having no success and made her début—also without success—as a *diseuse* at the Eldorado and Eden Concert music halls; and Sarah Bernhardt aged fifty-five astonished the public with her '*éclat de jeunesse*' in *Cléopâtre*—('*une pièce habillement découpée dans le chef-d'œuvre de Shakespeare*'). The *Société Nationale des Beaux-Arts* (often called the *Salon du Champs de Mars* and hereinafter referred to as the *Salon de la Nationale*) was founded by Puvis de Chavannes aged sixty-six, Eugène Carrière aged forty-one, Rodin aged fifty, and others seceding from the *Salon des Artistes Français* (the old *Salon*). Alfred Vallette and his wife Madame Rachilde launched the *Mercure de France* that we know to-day; Maurice Maeterlinck aged twenty-eight published *Les aveugles*, *L'intruse* and *La princesse Maleine*; Anatole France published *Thaïs*; and Mme de Caillavet's son Gaston, and Robert de Flers who was later to write plays with him, became friends of Marcel Proust who was now nineteen and serving in the army.

[1] London. Courtauld Institute.   [2] Paris. Seligmann.
[3] The pictures remained there for the next three years.

Van Gogh sold one of his pictures at the Brussels exhibition to a Belgian woman painter, and the tide seemed turning in his favour. But it was now too late for any success to serve him. He had left the Saint Rémy asylum and gone north to Auvers to put himself in charge of Dr. Gachet whom he knew and liked and looked on as a fellow neurotic and a fellow enthusiast for art; at Auvers he painted the *Portrait du Dr. Gachet* (with the de Goncourts' *Germinie Lacerteux* (1865) and *Manette Salomon* (1867) on the table[1]) and a number of landscapes; and there he shot himself on July 27.

A few months after Van Gogh's death his brother Théo went mad. His place at the Boulevard Montmartre branch of the Goupil Gallery was offered to Maurice Joyant by Boussod the proprietor who said: 'Our late manager, a madman of sorts, like his brother the painter, is now in a sanatorium. He has accumulated appalling things by modern painters which have brought the firm to discredit. Do the best you can with these horrors which I leave in your hands. I also leave you some pictures by Claude Monet; we have a contract with him and we can sell his things in America, but he loads us up with landscapes which are undistinguishable one from another. Run the branch as you please. I shall close it if you bother me about it.' Joyant found that the 'horrors' included paintings by Van Gogh, Gauguin, Lautrec, Degas, Pissarro and Guillaumin, and lithographs by Odilon Redon; and he began his work by inviting more pictures from Lautrec (with whom he had been at school).

In November of this year 1890 Gauguin returned from Le Pouldu to Paris. Dressed in a fisherman's striped jersey, an enormous ulster, a fisherman's beret, and clogs which he had carved and polychromed, he installed himself once more with Schuffenecker who had taken a new house and was playing the part of the artist-collector with an artistic salon. Schuffenecker's collection then included *Le Christ jaune*[2] and other paintings by Gauguin; several pictures by Cézanne; drawings by Odilon Redon; and *Le facteur Roulin*,[3] *Oliviers en Provence*,[3] *Portrait de l'artiste à l'oreille coupée*,[4] *Le bon Samaritain*,[5] *L'Arlésienne*[5] and *Les tournesols*[6] by Van Gogh; his studio contained his own paintings and a frieze of prints by Hokusai and Utamaro which belonged to Gauguin; and there he entertained young artists including Sérusier and Emile Bernard and other followers and admirers of Gauguin. While Gauguin had been absent in Le Pouldu, Sérusier and Emile Bernard had been attracting some attention by their pictures; they were now spoken of as the 'Symbolists' and their names were linked with Gauguin's. When Gauguin realized the situation he was furious; he had advanced a long way since Sérusier and Bernard had first had contact with him at Pont Aven and though he had probably learned something from Bernard he looked on both as minor artists

[1] German collection. Another version without the books belongs to M. Paul Gachet, Auvers.
[2] Paris. Paul Rosenberg.
[3] Wassenaar. Kröller-Müller Foundation.
[4] The version now belonging to M. Paul Rosenberg, Paris.
[5] The version which belongs or belonged till recently to a German collector.
[6] German collection.

and he had no desire to link his reputation with theirs. Contemptuous of Schuffen-ecker who placed their works on a level with his, he treated him badly, finally broke with him before the year was out, and left the label 'Symbolist' to Sérusier, Bernard and his other followers and associates.[1] It was at this moment that the poet Paul Fort, aged eighteen, founded the 'Symbolist' *Théâtre d'Art* to compete with the realist drama of Antoine's *Théâtre Libre*. Paul Fort's *Théâtre d'Art* was supported from the outset by the poets Henri de Regnier, Jean Moréas, Mallarmé, Verhaeren and Verlaine; and these poets were soon joined by Maurice Maeter-linck. Fort also received help at the start from the 'Symbolist' painters; he induced Gauguin himself to design a programme cover and he employed Sérusier to design the scenery for Pierre Quillard's *La fille aux mains coupées*, one of his earliest productions.

Undismayed by this challenge Antoine continued his Realist productions at the *Théâtre Libre*. In January 1890 he notes in his Diary: 'I saw Zola this evening and he spoke to me of a Scandinavian author named Ibsen who is sixty-two and living in Munich. He urged me to produce a play called *Les Revenants*'; and Antoine in fact produced it in May, scoring one of his greatest successes as Oswald.[2] Other productions by Antoine this season were *Le pain d'autrui* (from Tourguenief), *Ménages d'artistes* by Eugène Brieux (then thirty-eight and still a journalist at Rouen), *La fille Elisa* (from Edmond de Goncourt's novel), a hospital play *La belle opération* by Julien Sermet, *Les chapons* (a play about the 1870 war) by Lucien Descaves who was an anti-militarist, and Auguste Linery's *Conte de Noël*—'une fusion de réalisme et du mysticisme' where a peasant woman has an illegitimate child which is disposed of by murder and then thrown to the farmyard pigs who devour it while Christmas bells ring out. On December 22 the *Théâtre Libre* was the subject of a debate in the Senate—a Senator asserting that the plays produced there were habitually obscene and anti-patriotic (the second accusation having special reference to *Les chapons*) but Léon Bourgeois, then Minister of Fine Arts, told the Senate bluntly that the Ministry was concerned to encourage Antoine because he had rendered enormous services to young authors.

In the next year 1891 Jean Cocteau was born; Lautrec's first poster *La Goulue au Moulin Rouge* appeared on the hoardings; Thadée Natanson founded *La Revue Blanche* which was to be helpful to many writers and artists in the 'nineties; and drawings of Parisian *mœurs* by Steinlen began to appear weekly in a new paper *Gil Blas Illustré* which printed poems by Verlaine, Mendès, Richepin and Xanroff, and stories by Zola and de Maupassant in early issues. Steinlen's drawings expressing the romantic-realist attitude to the Parisian underworld (which had appeared in Bruant's songs in 1885 and influenced as noted Toulouse-Lautrec[3]), became at once a factor encouraging the success of cabarets like Bruant's *Le Mirliton* which was now more crowded than ever; and Rodolphe de Salis at the old *Chat Noir* began his famous *Théâtre d'Ombres*—shadow plays designed by Henri Rivière

---

[1] Cf. above, pp. 77 and 78.

[2] 'Ghosts' had been performed in London in March and most of the English papers had de-scribed it as immoral and obscene.

[3] Cf. above, pp. 72 and 82.

with libretti by Maurice Donnay and music by Charles de Sivry.[1] Yvette Guilbert (who later included *Adolphe ou le jeune homme triste* and other poems by Donnay in her repertoire) found the right material for her talents at this moment by the chance purchase on the quays of Xanroff's *Chansons sans gêne* (which included *Pauvre enfant c'était pour sa mère* and *C'est le printemps*) and scored her first success with them in a trial performance at Liège; but she did not capture Paris till the period covered by our Act II.

In the first months of this year 1891 Gauguin was much in evidence at the Café Voltaire (Place de l'Odéon) where on Monday evenings he foregathered with Eugène Carrière, Redon, Daniel de Monfreid, Verlaine, Mallarmé, Albert Aurier, and his two subsequent biographers Jean de Rotonchamp and Charles Morice. But though in this world he was not of it; the time came when he could bear the talk of 'Symbolism' no longer; and he made up his mind to leave Paris for Tahiti. To finance this adventure he arranged a sale of his pictures at the Hôtel Drouot. Octave Mirbeau, instructed by Mallarmé, wrote *un article retentissant* in the *Echo de Paris* praising his work and stressing the romantic character of his imminent departure for the tropics. The sale offered thirty pictures which included *Le gardien de porcs*,[2] *La gardeuse de moutons*,[3] *La belle Angèle*,[4] *Vision après le sermon: La lutte de Jacob avec l'ange* (Pl. 22B), *Femme dans les vagues*,[5] and some pictures painted at Arles and Martinique. Degas bought *La belle Angèle*; and the sale provided Gauguin with ten thousand francs (of which it is difficult to estimate the equivalent in present money). Gauguin and his friends were well pleased with this result, as the outstanding Le Pouldu pictures had been excluded (*Le Christ jaune* had been acquired by Schuffenecker, *Le Calvaire* and *Jésus au Jardin des Oliviers* (Pl. 26) had been acquired by or deposited with, respectively, the Goupil Gallery and de Monfreid). On March 23 some thirty friends gave Gauguin a farewell banquet at the Café Voltaire; Mallarmé was ill and could not be present; but Redon, Carrière, Aurier, Morice, de Rotonchamp, Vallette and Mme Rachilde, and Gauguin's painter followers toasted him and recited Mallarmé's poems. Paul Fort also came forward with a gesture— a special 'Symbolist' programme of the *Théâtre d'Art* for the benefit of Gauguin and Verlaine; this performance took place at the Vaudeville Theatre which had paintings by Gauguin in the foyer for the occasion; the programme included first performances of Maeterlinck's *L'intruse* and Verlaine's *Les Uns et les Autres* with settings by Carrière and Redon, and the recitation of Mallarmé's translation of Poe's *The Raven* and of poems by Baudelaire, Hugo, Charles Morice and so forth; the profits—which came in the end to no more than a hundred francs—were paid to Verlaine, as Gauguin had already sailed for Tahiti. When Renoir heard of Gauguin's

---

[1] The two most celebrated of these shadow plays were *Phryné* and *Ailleurs*, the latter containing the witty life story of *Adolphe ou le jeune homme triste*—Adolphe who in art, in love and in politics was always 'quelque chose en "iste"' and always 'triste, triste, triste':

> *Quand il mourut d'un eczéma*
> *Il exigea qu'on le crémât*
> *Et sur son urne un Symboliste*
> *Ecrivit ces mots: 'Il fut triste'.*

[2] Paris. Georges Wildenstein et Cie.   [3] Paris. Paul Rosenberg.
[4] Paris. Louvre.   [5] Cleveland (Ohio). F. H. Ginn.

departure he made a smiling comment, '*on peut si bien peindre aux Batignolles*' (where he himself was then living).

After Gauguin's departure Sérusier and his other 'Symbolist' followers and associates continued to voice their theories and to show their pictures. They mixed an admiration for Gauguin with an admiration for Puvis de Chavannes (now sixty-seven) and launched a vogue for mediaevalism and pale 'aesthetic' colours, for twilight effects, 'musical' colours, 'coloured' music, and poetic atmosphere. This mode (which was later exploited also by the Rose-Croix group) was supported at this moment by Paul Fort's *Théâtre d'Art*, where Maurice Maeterlinck aged twenty-nine was *persona grata*, and it came to a climax in Fort's production of *La cantique des cantiques*, described as '*huit devises mystiques et trois paraphrases*' designed by Sérusier and accompanied by music and perfumes '*composés dans la tonalité correspondant aux différents versets*' with special reference to Rimbaud's *Voyelles*.[1]

The *Théâtre Libre* continued to resist the competition of the *Théâtre d'Art*. Antoine was now more famous than ever as a champion of realist drama—(Porto-Riche's *Amoureuse* performed for the first time this year by Réjane at the Odéon was labelled 'Antoinisme' by the critics)—and he was bombarded with scripts of plays. In one month he read five hundred plays and he picked out three—*L'envers d'une sainte*, *Les fossiles* and *La figurante*—signed by three names unknown to him—which all proved later to be the work of François de Curel who had thus tested the truth of Antoine's statement that he read all manuscripts submitted. In this season he produced *Le canard sauvage* by Ibsen; *Nell Horn* (with a Salvation Army scene in a London square) by Rosny; a play by the humorist Courteline, and a comedy, *Leurs filles*, by Pierre Wolff, a nephew of Albert Wolff the old enemy of the Impressionist painters and a long-standing enemy of Antoine himself.[2]

In January the Porte Saint-Martin theatre invited Antoine to give a public performance of de Goncourt's *La fille Elisa* (already played at the *Théâtre Libre* where the audience was nominally restricted to subscribers); the Censor forbade the public performance and the question was debated in the Chamber; the accusers described the play as subversive of public morals (as the novel had been described when it appeared amid the stormy politics of the Right Wing drive in 1877);[3] the defenders declared it a work of art unjustly penalized by authorities who permitted all sorts of indecencies in café-concert songs; and one defender said: '*La fille Elisa a été un scandale parce que de Goncourt a quitté la région du demi-monde où s'agitent les dames à camélias, les lorettes, et autres lionnes, pour jeter un coup*

---

[1] Cf. above, p. 31. Rimbaud had just died at the age of thirty-seven. After exploring Ogaden he had made money selling arms, etc., in Abyssinia and on August 10, 1890, he had written to his mother, 'I am coming home and should like to marry next spring . . . Do you think I could find anyone who would follow me on my travels?' He started home in February and then developed cancer of the knee which caused him agony on the journey and for some months after at Marseilles where he died.

[2] After the performance of *Leurs filles* Albert Wolff went to Antoine's dressing-room and said 'You're an intelligent man and I'm an old fool. You've taken a fine revenge. Permit me to thank you and shake hands.'

[3] Cf. above, pp. 38 and 39.

d'œil sur la fille pauvre.' The debate was inconclusive; but it brought into being a *Commission de la Censure* (with Dumas, Sardou, Zola, de Banville, Bergerat, de Goncourt and Antoine) to discuss the centre of the problem and report.

Meanwhile the Classical Renaissance in painting was upheld in the *Seventh Salon des Indépendants* which had Seurat's *Cirque*,[1] a *Van Gogh Memorial Exhibition*, and seven pictures by The Douanier Rousseau including *Surpris* and the *Portrait de Pierre Loti* (Pl. 23B) and three suburban landscapes. The humorist Courteline bought the *Portrait de Pierre Loti* as a joke and placed it in his collection of humorous and ridiculous pictures; but Renoir was greatly struck by *Surpris* as already recorded.[2] On the day before the opening of this *Salon des Indépendants* Puvis de Chavannes went round the exhibition, while Seurat watched him from a distance; he passed by *Cirque* without stopping even for a moment before it, and Seurat was bitterly chagrined. Seurat at this time was suffering from a quinsy in his throat; this became severely septic and he died ten days later at the age of thirty-two.

There were important political and social happenings in these last two years of our Act I. In 1890 the Comte de Paris (Royalist Pretender since the death of the Comte de Chambord in 1883) confessed his share in the Boulangist campaign; the Pope in an Encyclical declared the Republican form of government compatible with the Catholic Church; and May Day was celebrated in Paris for the first time as an International Labour Day. In 1891 Left Extremists rioted in Paris; the troops fired on the rioters and arrests were made; one Bulot acted as prosecutor of the arrested persons; the judge, one Benoit, inflicted heavy sentences; and both Bulot and Benoit were victimized by Anarchists next year (as I shall chronicle).[3] On September 20 General Boulanger, who had been condemned for treason in his absence, committed suicide in Brussels.

[1] Paris. Louvre.   [2] Cf. above, pp. 81 and 82.   [3] Cf. below p. 145.

Plate (C) SEURAT

Sketch for Chahut, 1889

London. Samuel Courtauld, Esq.

(cf. page xi)

ACT I: THE MASTERS' LIVES

GEORGES SEURAT (ii)[1]

From twenty-five to his death at thirty-two (1884–1891)

Seurat, it would seem, never made any personal contact with Cézanne—though artistically speaking they worked shoulder to shoulder in 1884–1891. But as I have shown in 'How it happened', he had contacts with most of the artists of our story. His immediate circle consisted of Signac, Cross and the other artists with whom he founded the *Salon des Indépendants* in 1884. He met Gauguin, Lautrec and Van Gogh in the Goupil Gallery under the auspices of Théo Van Gogh; he received Pissarro in his studio, as recorded, in 1885; he met The Douanier Rousseau in connection with the exhibitions of the *Salon des Indépendants*; and he may have met Degas, Berthe Morisot and Schuffenecker as fellow exhibitors in the *Last Impressionist Exhibition* in 1886. But seeing that he was known to so many artists of the period surprisingly little has been recorded of his life and habits. We are told that he worked incessantly; that, as he coloured on a scientific system, he could and did continue painting in his studio far into the night; and that, when away from his studio, he observed and meditated wherever he went and made written notes and sketches on little note-pads held in the palm of his left hand. He was fascinated by scenes where people congregated, by the circus and fairs, and after 1885 by ports and shipping. We are told that when he was in Paris it was his custom to take most of his meals in his mother's house; and it would appear that his mother financed him as he sold very few pictures in his lifetime. It is clear that he was very reserved in character and manner and very reticent about his personal affairs. He did not admit his friends or his mother to his full confidence; and no one knew, till after his death, of the existence in his life of Madeleine Knobloch, his model for *Jeune femme se poudrant*, who became the mother of his son in 1890. For the rest we have the exhibiting of his pictures, beginning with *Baignade* in 1884 and ending with *Cirque* in 1891, which I have chronicled in 'How it happened'. And we know that his port scenes were painted at Grandcamp in 1885, at Honfleur in 1886 and 1887, at Port-en-Bessin in 1888 and 1890, at Le Crotoy in 1889 and at Gravelines in 1891. He died of a septic quinsy on March 20, 1891, in his mother's house; his year-old son had caught the infection and died a few days later.

When Seurat died his mother owned *Baignade, Un dimanche d'été à la Grande*

[1] For the present distribution of the pictures mentioned, cf. my Bibliographical and Catalogue Notes in Appendix I.

Jatte and *Cirque*; Signac owned a sketch for *Chahut*; and *Poseuses* and *Chahut* belonged to the poet Gustave Kahn who had acquired them from the exhibitions of *Les XX* in Brussels. Regarding the price paid for *Poseuses* we have a letter from Seurat to the secretary of *Les XX*: 'I don't know exactly how to fix a price for this picture. I calculate that it cost me a year's work at seven francs a day. You see where that leads us. But the personality of the buyer might compensate me for a difference between his price and mine.' After his death, his mother, the critic Félix Fénéon (who had backed him, as recorded, from the time of *Baignade*) and Maximilien Luce (one of his artist followers) made an inventory of the pictures, *croquetons* and drawings in his studio; these included ten drawings and thirteen *croquetons* for *Baignade*, twenty-three drawings and thirty-eight *croquetons* for *Un dimanche d'été à la Grande Jatte*, five drawings and three *croquetons* for *Parade*, and some preliminary studies for *Le Chahut* and *Cirque*; the finished pictures included *Parade*, *Jeune femme se poudrant*, twenty-five early paintings and fifteen port scenes. These works were divided between his mother and two or three friends, and Madeleine Knobloch. Félix Fénéon has calculated that he produced at least seven hundred *croquetons* and drawings in his eight or nine working years—apart from the seven major paintings and the port scenes.

Among the papers found by Seurat's executors there were numerous extracts from books which had helped him to formulate his 'Divisionist' method. The books thus used included Chevreul's *De la loi du contraste simultané des couleurs* and Charles Blanc's *Grammaire des arts et du dessin* (which he had found in the library at the Ecole des Beaux-Arts) and *Le cercle chromatique* and other works by Charles Henry and *Les phénomènes de la vue* by M. D. Sutter (which he studied in his later years). His papers also included many notes of his observations, especially of shipping, revealing a painter's eye and a poet's spirit; one such note reads as follows: '*Les mâts sont si élancés, si fins, si gracieusement étagés dans les airs. Et ces vergues qui les coupent en croix de distance en distance, et qui montent de plus en plus minces et de plus en plus courtes, jusqu'à leurs grêles sommets; ces hunes à jour dont la blancheur se détache au milieu des haubans comme un bois de harpe sous ces cordes renversées; et ces milliers de manœuvres tendues dans tous les sens, de haut en bas, de tribord à bâbord, de l'avant à l'arrière, séparées, confondues, parallèles, obliques, perpendiculaires, croisées de cent façons, et toutes fixées, propres, bien peignées, vibrant au moindre souffle; tout cela si harmonieux, si complet, si admirablement assorti dans ses moindres détails, qu'une coquette ne mettrait pas plus d'art et de magie dans les dispositions voluptueuses de sa parure de bal!*'

31. LAUTREC
La fille à l'accroche cœur, 1889
London. Reid and Lefevre

32A. CÉZANNE
Les joueurs de cartes, c. 1891
Merion. Barnes Foundation
32B. LAUTREC
Au bal du Moulin de la Galette, 1889
Chicago. Art Institute (Coburn)

ACT I: THE MASTERS' LIVES

PAUL GAUGUIN (ii)[1]

From thirty-six to forty-three (1884–1891)

At the end of 1883 Gauguin went with his wife and children to Copenhagen as recorded. This expedition was a failure. The Danes showed no disposition to order sun blinds from this unusual *commis voyageur*; his wife's relations offered him no acceptable employment; and when he painted pictures nobody would buy them. He was moreover ill at ease in a very bourgeois entourage and he could not resist the temptation to shock the Lutheran prejudices of his wife's family and friends. After eighteen months neither he nor his wife could bear the situation any longer and they agreed that he should again try his luck as an artist in Paris, taking with him Clovis, his eldest son now aged eleven, while his wife remained in Copenhagen with the other children and tried to make money translating Zola's novels for Danish readers. Before leaving he sold most of his Impressionist pictures to his brother-in-law (keeping his two pictures by Cézanne, two or three by Pissarro and several others) and gave the proceeds to his wife.

He arrived in Paris in the summer of 1885. He now had very little left of his savings and he rented a simple room which the boy Clovis shared. He resumed contact with Schuffenecker and Pissarro, met Seurat and Signac, and painted in the environs of Paris. But once again no dealer would buy his pictures; when the winter came he found himself entirely without money and Clovis fell ill; a letter to his wife written before Christmas describes the weeks that followed: 'Distracted, I conceived the notion of asking a railway advertising company for work as a billposter. My bourgeois appearance made the manager laugh, but I told him earnestly that I had a sick child and that I was really in need of work. So I pasted advertisements for five francs a day. In the evenings I went home to look after Clovis still in bed with fever. This lasted for three weeks and to-day the director of the company has taken me on as an inspector and secretary at 200 francs a month.'

At the beginning of 1886 this crisis—the worst in Gauguin's career—was over. He had sold one or two of the remaining pictures in his collection and somehow collected some other funds. He was ill in hospital for a month but he was able to send Clovis to a boarding school and when he recovered he painted some pictures

[1] For the present distribution of the pictures mentioned and others cf. my Bibliographical and Catalogue Notes in Appendix I.

and produced some ceramics in Schuffenecker's studio and sent nineteen paintings and a carving to the *Eighth (and Last) Impressionist Exhibition*. When this exhibition closed, he went to Pont Aven in Brittany, not yet a crowded artists' colony but already a resort of a few landscape painters who foregathered in a modest inn, the Pension Gloanec, where board and lodging was obtainable for next to nothing. He painted at Pont Aven all the summer and made the acquaintance of Emile Bernard who knew Schuffenecker and came with an introduction from him. In the autumn he returned to Paris and made the acquaintance of Van Gogh.

At the beginning of 1887 he was attacked by nostalgia for his seaman days. A young painter, one Charles Laval, who had fallen under the spell of his personality, offered to go with him to the tropics and, probably, to provide the greater part of the expenses in return for the company of a man who knew the ropes. Gauguin heard that there was money to be made in Panama where there was much afoot in connection with the building of the Canal; and in April, after storing the remains of his collection with Schuffenecker, he took ship accompanied by Laval. Before he left he arranged with his wife to fetch Clovis from his boarding school and take him to Copenhagen. In Panama Gauguin and Laval found that, as the phrase goes, there was 'nothing doing' except digging as a labourer; but the digging was exceptionally well paid and both men therefore dug for a month or so and saved some money. On the way out the ship had stopped at Martinique which had greatly attracted Gauguin and they accordingly went there with the proceeds of the digging. In Martinique they took a hut in the centre of sugar and cocoa plantations peopled by Indians, Negroes and Chinese. Gauguin painted some twenty or thirty pictures. Laval went down with malaria and became so demoralised that he tried to kill himself. Then Gauguin was attacked by dysentery. When both recovered they had had enough of the tropics for the time being; and they were back in Paris by the beginning of 1888.

Gauguin went straight to Schuffenecker who now had a house and studio at Montrouge. There he was nursed back to health and allowed to conduct himself as master of the house; visitors tell us that he was rude and overbearing to his host; but Schuffenecker remained devoted, accounting the continuous company of genius an ample compensation for occasional insults or indignities. Gauguin remained for six weeks or two months with Schuffenecker, painting the group *Le peintre Schuffenecker et sa famille* (inscribed '*Je vote pour Boulanggg*' in allusion to General Boulanger's bid for dictatorship), and producing ceramics which were fired in the works of a noted ceramist named Chaplet, which happened to be at hand. He left Schuffenecker in March and rented a studio in the region of the Avenue de Montsouris for three months, and it was probably at this time that he first saw The Douanier Rousseau's pictures and made his acquaintance. In May he had an exhibition of his Brittany and Martinique pictures and some ceramics in the Goupil Gallery, arranged by Théo Van Gogh; some works were sold, and with the proceeds he went back in June to Pont Aven where he worked with Emile Bernard, Laval and Sérusier amid the quarrels at the Pension Gloanec till he left in October to join Van Gogh at Arles as recorded.[1] His stay at Arles, cul-

[1] Cf. above, p. 94.

minating in Van Gogh's madness, his return to Paris at Christmas and presence at Prado's execution, his exhibition with Bernard, Schuffenecker, Laval, Anquetin and a new friend Daniel de Monfreid at the Café Volpini in the *Exposition Universelle* of 1889, his summer at Pont Aven with Sérusier, the year which followed in Marie Henry's inn at Le Pouldu with Meyer de Haan, and the episode at the end of 1889 or early in 1890 when he was mistaken for General Boulanger, have all been chronicled.[1] He painted *La belle Angèle* at Pont Aven in the summer of 1889 and offered it as a present to the sitter a local bourgeoise, Madame Satre, who refused it on the advice of his enemies the academic painters of the Pension Gloanec. When he first went to Le Pouldu in September 1889 it was an unknown fishing village and Marie Henry's inn was simply furnished; when he left in November 1890 it had been made an artists' colony and the inn had been transformed; the windows and ceiling of the dining-room had been painted by Gauguin and his friends; the walls had a large portrait of Marie Henry by Meyer de Haan and landscapes by Gauguin; the mantelpiece had Gauguin's bust of Meyer de Haan; Gauguin's *Bonjour, Monsieur Gauguin* was nailed to the door; and two panels of a cupboard had portraits of Gauguin and Meyer de Haan by Gauguin. At Pont Aven and Le Pouldu in 1889–1890 Gauguin painted among other things *Jésus au Jardin des Oliviers* (Pl. 26), *Le calvaire*, *Le Christ jaune*, the child's portrait *Mlle Loulou* (Pl. 30), and the *Portrait de Marie Henry* with Cézanne's *Compotier, verre et pommes* in the background.

He returned to Paris in November 1890 and went again to Schuffenecker who was now established in a new and larger house in the Plaisance quarter behind Montparnasse, with the collection of pictures by Gauguin, Van Gogh, Redon and others already referred to. On this visit Gauguin, now undeniably the central figure of a group of artists, was more exigent than ever and Schuffenecker in his fine new house was less tolerant than before. There were quarrels; and at the end of the year Gauguin took a room at an hotel and accepted an offer made by Daniel de Monfreid to use his studio close by.[2]

At the beginning of 1891 Gauguin etched a portrait of Mallarmé and copied Manet's *Olvmpia* (then in the Luxembourg). He was now contemplating another expedition to the tropics and he is said to have chosen Tahiti after reading an account of it in a popular guide book (which may well have been the case since the island was always described as the most beautiful in the Pacific, and the natives as an exceptionally handsome race). The decision taken, he went to the Director of the Beaux-Arts, one Ary Renan, and obtained from him the right to describe himself as entrusted with a '*mission artistique*'; the mission was undefined (except that it was understood that he would accumulate data for pictures to be painted on his return) and no fee or salary was attached, but it was calculated to provide him with a status among the French officials in Tahiti; Renan moreover assured him that the Beaux-Arts would buy some of his pictures on his return—that being the custom in such cases. I have already chronicled Mirbeau's article which announced the departure in the *Echo de Paris* (February 16, 1891), the sale (in March) at the Hôtel Drouot, the farewell banquet at the Café Voltaire (March 23), and the

---

[1] Cf. above, pp. 94, 98 and 99.   [2] Cf. above, pp. 102 and 103.

benefit performance by the *Théâtre d'Art* at the Vaudeville Theatre which took place in May when Gauguin had already sailed with a photograph of Manet's *Olympia* in his luggage, and a note of encouragement from Mallarmé in his pocket. In a deserted café, a few days before he sailed, he had broken down in a private conversation with Charles Morice; there were tears in his eyes when he spoke of his failure to support his wife and children without denying the drive of his creative mind and spirit.

He arrived at Papeete, the port of Tahiti, on his forty-third birthday, June 8, 1891. The island had at this time some ten thousand inhabitants of whom about one-eighth were French and foreigners; Papeete itself had a population of about three thousand five hundred, half of whom were French or French half-castes and miscellaneous whites; there were also some hundreds of Chinese. The French and other whites had established sugar mills with distilleries attached, and also cotton and coco-fibre manufactories. The landscape included mountains, volcanic rocks, luxuriant vegetation and forests. The natives were a Polynesian race, presumed to be Maori, with a skin varying from light olive to a full dark brown, the women as a rule a good deal smaller than the men. The majority of the natives professed the Protestant religion. Tahiti and the adjoining islands were administered as a French protectorate by a governor-general at Papeete; before that the natives had kings of their own and a feudal system of government; the last nominal King of the Islands was still living when Gauguin arrived and presented his credentials to the French governor-general, a negro named Lacascade. Gauguin was at first very gravely disappointed. Having travelled to the centre of the Pacific he found himself in a small European society permeated with *snobisme colonial*—'a grotesque puerile imitation, an exaggerated caricature of European conditions'. But soon after his arrival he caught a glimpse of the old native culture he had hoped to find. The last nominal King of the Islands died suddenly and the natives from the interior and from neighbouring islands came to Papeete for the funeral. The King lay in state, in a chamber adorned with flowers and boldly patterned textiles, while the Queen and the Tahitians robed in black wailed traditional incantations. The actual funeral was an official ceremony with speeches by the negro governor, the Protestant pastor and so forth; but on the informal return to the city Gauguin saw the real Tahitians comporting themselves with uninhibited simplicity, and he determined to leave Papeete and 'go native' in a native village about twenty-five miles along the coast.

A month or so later he had acquired a hut and begun to make friends with the natives in the village. He had at first a half-caste mistress from Papeete; but he soon sent her back to the city. He then chose a young Tahitian girl called Tehoura to live with him as his *vahiné*—the native word for wife. 'Are you a good man?' her mother asked him before he took her, 'Will you make her happy?' He answered ('*non sans trouble*' he tells us) 'Yes'. 'Take her', said the mother. 'Send her back after a week; if she is not happy that will be the end.' Tehoura went home at the appointed time; in her absence Gauguin, who had been greatly charmed with her, was nervous and depressed, and he welcomed her gladly when after a few days she came back. Little by little, he now shed, or tried to shed, the acquired characteristics of French civilization and French culture. '*Je commence à penser simplement*', he wrote, '*à n'avoir que peu de haine pour mon prochain—mieux à l'aimer. J'ai toutes jouissances de la vie libre animale et humaine. J'échappe au factice, j'entre dans la nature.*' And before this year 1891 was out he had painted the first of his Tahitian pictures.

ACT I: THE MASTERS' LIVES

PAUL CÉZANNE (ii)[1]

From forty-five to fifty-two (1884–1891)

From 1884 to 1887 Cézanne lived mainly at Aix, Gardanne, and in the environs. He sent no pictures to the exhibitions in Paris, where he was quite forgotten except by Pissarro, Renoir, Monet, Zola and one or two other friends. Many of his earlier pictures were stored in his Paris studio of which Tanguy had the key.[2] Tanguy himself owned *Achille Emperaire*, which Cézanne had given him in payment for colours, and he would show it with the pictures in Cézanne's studio to anyone who wished to see them; the large pictures in the studio could then be bought for a hundred francs and the small ones for forty; and Théodore Duret bought some at these prices; but the only other purchaser would seem to have been Signac who was taken to Tanguy's by Pissarro and Gauguin as related.[3]

In 1885 Cézanne went north to Vernon where he was near Zola at Medan and Renoir at La Roche-Guyon. He stayed with Renoir and painted *La route tournante à La Roche-Guyon*, which he gave to him. In July he visited Zola at Medan. At this time he was harassed by a love affair of which the details appear to be unknown; letters exchanged between the lovers were addressed to Zola who sent them or handed them on; the affair ended, we are told, in August—'*dans l'amertume et le dégoût*'. Records of it may possibly exist in some portraits wrongly catalogued as '*Madame Cézanne*'.

In April 1886 he married Hortense Fiquet; and in October his father died leaving him a third of 1,200,000 francs and various property. He then painted at Aix and Gardanne, and went to Hattenville in Normandy where he stayed with Choquet. In this year Zola sent him *L'Œuvre*; and, as I have chronicled, Cézanne broke his friendship with Zola after reading it. But the book was probably not the sole cause of the estrangement; it was rather in the nature of a last straw; for in recent years Cézanne had found himself more and more a fish out of water in Zola's Medan castle filled with bric-a-brac and servants and the master's admirers; and he had less in common with the successful Zola than he had had with the struggling Zola of the early days. Moreover, like all neurotics, he had a horror of outside encroachments on his independence; physically he disliked being touched;

---

[1] For the present distribution of Cézanne's pictures painted in this period the student must consult Venturi's catalogue (cf. my Bibliographical and Catalogue Notes in Appendix I).

[2] Cf. above, p. 87.   [3] Cf. above, pp. 58 and 87.

and in the moral sphere his habitual phrase '*Je ne veux pas qu'on me mette le grappin dessus*' reveals this phobia; he was thus bound eventually to flee from anyone who had as it were impinged upon his integrity and placed a moral debt upon him by helping him when he required assistance. Zola (who had done this when he lent him money for Hortense in 1878) had done it again recently when he acted as intermediary in the mysterious love affair; in 1886 Cézanne, I fancy, had reached a point when he could only capture calm by forgetting this recent episode and everything connected with it; hence probably his marriage at this moment; hence also his use of *L'Œuvre* as an excuse to banish Zola from his mind.

In 1888 he was in Paris and he worked at Chantilly and on the banks of the Marne. In 1889 *La maison du pendu* was badly hung and attracted no attention in the official *Salon* of the *Exposition Universelle*.[1] Cézanne spent most of that year in Paris and Emile Bernard now wrote the first appreciation of his work in *Les hommes d'aujourd'hui*.[2] In 1890 he had three pictures in the exhibition of *Les XX* in Brussels. The invitation to the Brussels show had reached him in the autumn of 1889 and he had replied to the secretary: 'In acknowledgment of your flattering letter, I thank you and accept with pleasure your kind invitation. May I be allowed, however, to deny the accusation of disdain with which you charge me in connection with my refusal to take part in exhibitions of painting? I must explain that having achieved only negative results from the numerous studies to which I have devoted myself, and dreading criticisms that are only too well justified, I had resolved to work in silence until such time as I should feel myself capable of defending theoretically the result of my experiments. But in view of the pleasure of finding myself in such good company, I do not hesitate to modify my resolution and beg you to accept my thanks and fraternal greetings.'[3] His contributions were a bather composition and two landscapes which again attracted no attention.

He spent most of 1890 and 1891 in Paris. He had now begun to suffer from diabetes. And in the summer of 1891 he went to Switzerland, possibly on doctor's orders. This was his only recorded journey outside France. Unlike Degas, Renoir and Monet, he never went to England, Italy, Spain or Holland. Swiss landscape seems to have made no appeal to him, and no pictures painted on this journey appear to have survived. At Neuchâtel he is said to have left behind him two unfinished canvases which were afterwards found and painted over by another artist who visited the hotel. He was, as I have chronicled, an orthodox Catholic, and at Fribourg on this Swiss journey he is said to have been so distressed by an anti-Catholic demonstration that he left the town instantly without even waiting to inform his wife.[4]

In these seven years, when he was forgotten in Paris, he painted some hundreds of pictures—landscapes, still life studies, bather compositions, portraits of himself and his family, compositions of figures in harlequinade clothes, and studies of peasants grouped round a table playing cards. These pictures are now treasured in museums and collections all over the world. But there can, I think, be no shadow of doubt that they would not have been painted had Cézanne not had the good

[1] Cf. above, p. 98.
[2] Cf. above, p. 100.
[3] Translation from Mack: *Paul Cézanne.*
[4] Cf. pp. 39 and 178

fortune to be entirely free from financial cares. As Renoir said: '*Voyez-vous Cézanne, n'ayant de rentes, obligé pour vivre d'attendre le client? L'imaginez-vous se contraignant à sourire complaisamment à l'amateur qui se serait permis de dédaigner Delacroix?* Cézanne with his nervous temperament and passion for independence, and without his large private means, would have produced quite different pictures—or none at all —in this period of his life when he built on his earlier researches and laid the foundations of the works produced in the period to come.

ACT I: THE MASTERS' LIVES

AUGUSTE RENOIR (ii)[1]

From forty-three to fifty (1884–1891)

After the Durand-Ruel Exhibition of 1883 Renoir completely changed his manner of painting for some years; and from 1884–1887 he made the great contributions to the modern movement that I have already chronicled in the Introduction to this Act.

In the spring of 1884 he was in Genoa and on the Italian Riviera with Monet; and he probably went down to Pisa and Florence to add to his 1881–1882 experiences of Italian frescoes. On the way back he had contact with Cézanne at Aix and he was in touch with Cézanne all through the middle 'eighties—working with him at La Roche-Guyon in 1886 and at L'Estaque in 1887. In 1884 and 1886 he saw Seurat's *Baignade* and *Un dimanche d'été à la Grande Jatte* and had contact with Pissarro, then a convert to Seurat's theories; and his own pictures of this period, painted indoors, in a spirit of reaction against Impressionism, include *Mlle Chapuis au cerceau*, *Le parti de volant*, *Femme allaitant son enfant*, *L'enfant au chat*, *La femme à l'éventail*, *La natte* and the central composition *Les grandes baigneuses* (Pl. 19B) which he worked on from 1885 to 1887.

In thus changing his manner so completely for five years Renoir deliberately jeopardized the position he had won as a successful Impressionist painter. The dilettanti (including George Moore) were horrified at what they looked on as the intolerable coldness and dryness of his new classical procedures; and it was not in fact till the twentieth century, when Seurat's achievements became widely appreciated, that Renoir's contribution in this period was really understood. He was free thus to explore a new country in his art, because, like the other Impressionists, he had now passed through his years of financial stress; he had a comfortable studio in Montmartre and he often went for a holiday to Essoyes in Champagne where Mme Renoir's family owned a property. Moreover, while he was experimenting and making endless drawings for his new compositions he accepted a few lucrative commissions for portraits which brought him the current money he required. The portrait group of the Bérard children—*Les enfants à Wargemont*—painted in 1884 was a commission of this kind; and *Les trois filles de Catulle Mendès* was painted in 1888. After painting *Les trois filles de Catulle Mendès* he entered a

[1] For the present distribution of the pictures mentioned and some others cf. my Bibliographical and Catalogue Notes in Appendix I.

117

phase of hesitation and transition which continued for some fifteen years. Cézanne's influence is evident in *La montagne Sainte Victoire* painted in 1889; and also in *Les chapeaux d'été* which dates from 1890. In *La vendeuse de pommes* painted 1890–1891 he returned to the line of least resistance—his old Impressionist technique. In 1890 he went in the summer to Pont Aven where he met Emile Bernard and other followers of Gauguin and was intrigued by their experiments in patterned pictures. I have already referred to his comment in 1891 when Gauguin left for Tahiti (*'on peut si bien peindre aux Batignolles'*); and also to his admiration for The Douanier Rousseau's *Surpris* in the *Salon des Indépendants* of that year.[1]

A feature of his work from 1889 onwards is the employment of two little girls, one blonde and one brunette, as his favourite models. These girls first appear as children aged approximately twelve to fourteen in *Les chapeaux d'été* and *La vendeuse de pommes*; the blonde appears in the *Nu dans l'eau* painted presumably in 1890 or 1891; and they appear again year by year gradually changing from childhood to adolescence and thence to young womanhood in the pictures of the 'nineties that I shall refer to in Act III.[2]

[1] Cf. above, pp. 81 and 105.   [2] Cf. below, p. 190.

ACT I: THE MASTERS' LIVES

THE DOUANIER ROUSSEAU (i)[1]

To the age of forty-seven (1844–1891)

Henri Rousseau, who was forty when this period opens, was born at Laval in 1844.
Jules Tyrol has found in the Laval archives that he was the great-grandson of one
Colonel Jean Pierre Guyard, Chevalier of St. Louis, who died 'a faithful dog to the
Emperor in 1815'; the grandson of Captain Jean Baptiste Guyard, Chevalier of
the Legion of Honour, who died in the Algerian campaign of 1833; and the nephew
of a *juge de paix* (all on his mother's side).[2] His father was a tinker or ironmonger;
and Rousseau had the ordinary schooling of his class at Laval. At eighteen he did
his military service where he played some instrument in the regimental band; and
during this time he went to Mexico in the force sent by Napoleon III to impose the
Archduke Maximilian on the Mexicans.[3] His memories of Mexican forests lay
dormant in his mind for many years, and no records of them appear in his earlier
pictures; but in his old age he recalled the tropical flora, the gibbering monkeys
and the strange wild beasts seen or imagined in those parts; and these memories
produced the wonderful pictures that I refer to in Act III. He returned from
Mexico in 1866 and was demobilised next year; he then worked for a while as a
clerk for a lawyer; and after that he obtained a post in the octroi department of
the Customs and Excise. In 1870 he was in the army again with the rank of sergeant; and he told Apollinaire that he had saved the town of Dreux from '*les
horreurs de la guerre civile*' by his presence of mind in some crisis and that all the
townsfolk had acclaimed him with cries of '*Vive le sergent Rousseau*'. He was
demobilised again in 1871 and returned to his employment as a '*gabelou*' i.e. minor
octroi officer at a toll station on the outskirts of Paris. He was then twenty-seven
and there is no evidence that he had so far drawn or painted; but he had been a
musician since his youth, able to play the flute and the clarinet and perhaps also the
violin (his favourite instrument later); and may therefore have made some extra
money by his music even at this date. In any case it is clear that he was rather
peculiar as a *gabelou*. For he often told his comrades that he was harassed on night
duty by unpleasant ghosts; one of these ghosts, he said, tormented him regularly

[1] For the present distribution of the pictures mentioned and others cf. my Bibliographical
and Catalogue Notes in Appendix I.

[2] The Douanier seems never to have referred to these distinguished ancestors in conversation
with his friends Uhde and Apollinaire, his first biographers, who evidently knew nothing about
them (cf. my Appendix I). Perhaps the archivist is wrong.   [3] Cf. above, p. 21.

for over a year, making long noses at him and insulting h m with nauseating fumes; when The Douanier shot at or tried to grapple with this phantom it sank into the earth and reappeared elsewhere. His companions, sceptical about these stories, contrived a practical joke to test them; working one night in the *Halle aux vins* they fixed a skeleton between the casks and made it move by pulling strings; to their astonishment The Douanier bowed to the apparition and asked it politely if it had come there for a glass of wine.

At some point of this period The Douanier had an amorous experience with a Polish woman who became a sentimental memory. He always referred to her later as 'Yadwigha'. The name appears in a poem appended to his last picture *Le Rêve* (Pl. 63)[1]; and a 'Madame Yadwigha' is also a character in a play, *La vengeance d'une orpheline russe*, which he wrote and submitted unsuccessfully at a date unknown to the Comédie Française and of which I give an abstract in Appendix III.

When the 'Yadwigha' romance was ended The Douanier married and had a daughter; and about 1884–5 he began to paint pictures in his leisure hours. About 1885 he was entitled to retire from the Customs with some small pension and he did so. To supplement this pension he now devoted more time to painting and he persuaded the local tradesmen in the poor Plaisance quarter where he lived to sit to him for portraits at a few francs a piece; he also painted suburban views and subject pictures which he offered for sale in a small paper shop looked after by his wife. In this period he obtained a post as teacher of drawing in a municipal school and his services there were rewarded by the violet button of the *Palmes académiques* which appears in his button-hole in his self-portrait *Moi-même: Portrait paysage* (Pl. 28A) of 1890. In the 'eighties he also began to give music lessons to the sons and daughters of his neighbours. Sometimes (as we know from Rémy de Gourmont who saw him doing it) he would take his fiddle and play popular songs in the local streets to *petites ouvrières* who stood round in a circle and sang the refrains. At other times he played the flute or the clarinet or the violin in an orchestra in the Tuileries Gardens.

I have already referred to his exhibits in the *Salon des Indépendants* from 1886 to 1889, most or all of which would seem to have disappeared. Some of his works exhibited in the *Salon des Indépendants* in 1890 and 1891, including *Moi-même: Portrait paysage* (Pl. 28A), the *Portrait de Pierre Loti* (Pl. 23B), the composition *Surpris* and one or two suburban landscapes, have been preserved. Gauguin, who I suggest was influenced by him as early as 1888,[2] especially praised his handling of blacks, and at some date before his final departure for Tahiti in 1895 he played a trick upon him to mock his confident simplicity: he told him that the State had given him an official decorative commission, and sent him to the Ministry of the Beaux-Arts to find out the details—which were, naturally, not forthcoming when he got there. Others who knew him in this period were Rémy de Gourmont and Gustave Coquiot, the historian of the *Salon des Indépendants*, who tells us that by 1888 he and Odilon Redon were already extolling him as a painter who 'attained at times to a noble classic style'. Renoir, as recorded, admired his *Surpris*, Seurat met him in connection with the arrangements of the *Salon des Indépendants*, and Lautrec defended him on the Committee of the *Indépendants* in 1890.[3]

[1] Cf. pp. 206, 208.   [2] Cf. p. 78.   [3] Cf. above, pp. 81, 82, 101.

ACT I: THE MASTERS' LIVES

EDGAR DEGAS (ii)[1]

From fifty to fifty-seven (1884–1891)

In this period Degas was still more successful and prosperous. He had a contract with Durand-Ruel who took all the pictures and pastels he cared to produce and paid him a regular allowance and such extra sums as he cared to demand. His correspondence, however, again reveals him frequently despondent, always disinclined to work, and always out of Paris for many months each year. In 1884 he wrote to his friend the painter Henry Lerolle, 'If you were a bachelor passed fifty (by a month) you would have times when you would close your door on your friends—and others. At such times one eliminates everything and then one proceeds to eliminate oneself—to kill oneself—in disgust. I feel frustrated and impotent. . . . I kept all my plans and projects locked in a cupboard in my head—always expecting in spite of my feeble eyesight (*infirmité de vue*) to be able to execute the plans some day. Now I have lost the key of the cupboard; and I feel sunk for good and all in a comatose condition. Henceforward I shall just kill time as they say ('*je m'occuperai, comme disent les gens qui ne font rien, et voilà tout*'). And later in this year he writes, '*Ah, où est-il le temps où je me croyais fort, où j'étais plein de logique, plein de projets. Je vais descendre bien vite la pente et rouler je ne sais où, enveloppé dans beaucoup de mauvais pastels comme dans du papier d'emballage.*' In this frame of mind he paid visits to the Valpinçons at the Château de Menil-Hubert and to other friends in the country. At Menil-Hubert he made an effort to be sociable and composed some verses for amateur theatricals played by inmates of the Château. He also began a bust, with arms, of Hortense Valpinçon—(whom he had painted as a little girl when he stayed there at the time of the Commune)—work which was wasted, as the bust when finished was destroyed by an accident in casting. Back in Paris, after sending round to Durand-Ruel for cash to pay some bills, he produced for him *La chanteuse verte* and some other pastels ('*articles*' as he now always called them), and he then relapsed into gloom, signing himself in a letter to Bartholomé '*l'homme qui veut finir et mourir tout seul sans bonheur aucun*'. In 1885 '*bien embêté par les nécessités de fabrication*' he drew the pastels *La sortie du bain* and *Danseuses se baissant* and spent the summer at Dieppe with Sickert. At the beginning of 1886 he went to Naples to sell some property and wrote to Bartholomé: '*A part*

---

[1] For the present distribution of some works by Degas in this period cf. my Bibliographical and Catalogue Notes in Appendix I.

121

le cœur . . . il me semble que tout vieillit en moi, proportionnellement; et même ce cœur a de l'artificiel—les danseuses l'ont cousu dans un sac de satin rose, du satin rose un peu fané, comme leurs chaussons de danse'. When he returned to Paris he prepared his '*articles*' for the *Eighth (and Last) Impressionist Exhibition* which included, as the catalogue informs us, a '*suite de nus de femmes se baignant, se lavant, se séchant, s'essuyant, se peignant ou se faisant peigner*'.

At this period he dined very frequently with Henri Rouart for whom he painted a dinner service with ballet dancers recalling his pictures. In 1886 he wrote to Rouart: '*C'est le mouvement des choses et des gens qui distrait et qui console même, si l'on peut être consolé quand on est aussi malheureux. Si les feuilles des arbres ne remuaient pas, comme les arbres seraient tristes et nous aussi! Il y a une espèce d'arbre dans le jardin de la maison voisine qui remue par un souffle de vent. Eh bien! J'ai beau être à Paris, dans mon atelier, presque sale, je me dis que cet arbre est délicieux.*' And this reference to consolation in movement was significant. For like many neurasthenics Degas was impelled to continual *déplacements*; he rarely remained in one place for long and when he did so remain he was always intending to leave each day. From this time onward he acquired the habit of walking for hours in the Paris streets—a habit that became a mania in his old age. His delays in finishing commissioned pictures, already referred to, now continued and increased. In 1886 he was still corresponding with Faure about the pictures promised him in 1874 and assuring him, as he had done so frequently, that they would be sent to him 'in a few days' or 'at the beginning of next week', till in 1887 Faure brought an action for the pictures and Degas was compelled to deliver them. In the autumn of 1887 he went to Cauterets to take a cure for a real or imaginary attack of asthma, and enjoyed the Punch-and-Judy show in the public gardens. He now divided his time between visits to such health resorts and to his friends in the country, the fabrication of '*articles*' for Durand-Ruel, and collecting pictures, prints and drawings by his favourite French artists—Ingres, Delacroix, Daumier, Gavarni and the 'old masters'. And his collection from this date onwards was in fact the central passion of his life.

In 1889 he installed himself in an old-fashioned building in the rue Victor Massé in Montmartre, where he gradually became more difficult of access except to his particular friends. In this building he occupied the three top floors; on the third floor he had his living rooms where he hung selected examples from his collection; on the fourth he had his studios; and on the fifth he stored the bulk of his collection and his own pictures. In August 1889 he was again at Cauterets for a 'cure' and wrote gossipy letters about the fashionable ladies in the main hotel; and in September he went, as related, with Boldini to Madrid and thence down to Seville and on to Tangiers. In 1890 he produced some '*articles*' for Durand-Ruel, and then bought carpets and so forth for his new home, pottered in the workshop of the chromo-lithographer Manzi, and went with Mme Straus to her dressmaker's where he watched the gestures of the modistes, snipping and trimming and pinning her elaborate gowns (and when Mme Straus asked him why the procedure amused him he answered: '*J'adore les mains rouges de la petite qui tient les épingles*'). In the summer he went to Pau, to Lourdes, and again for a cure to Cauterets. Of his visit to Lourdes he wrote: '*Toutes sortes de choses émouvantes . . . miracles du corps ou de l'âme, réaction physique ou mystique—que de choses peintes sur les figures.'* At Cauterets he persuaded his old friend the bassoonist Dihau (who had posed to him for *L'orchestre*) and a young flautist to play parts of Gluck's *Orphée* to him in a rural setting, and was disappointed with the result because, as he explained to Bartholomé, *'elle m'eut touché cette flute, loin de la nature, sur une toile peinte, parce que la présence de la nature est insipide dans une œuvre d'un tel art et que, si l'idée du bonheur doit me faire pleurer—c'est quand je suis malheureux et au théâtre.'* In the middle of September he tired of Cauterets—('*il faut aimer la nature plus que moi, pour supporter une cure à Cauterets; mais sacré matin je l'aimerais, si elle ne me menaçait pas à tout instant de ses maux*'); he then stayed at Carpentras with a painter friend de Valernes, on whom he vented his ill humour. At the end of September he went on the driving tour through Burgundy in a tilbury with the sculptor Bartholomé. This tour restored him for a moment to good humour; he was delighted with the old white horse acquired for the occasion, and he sent his friends the menus of the excellent meals provided in small places; the tour lasted three weeks and ended at Melun where the travellers were met by Manzi and Forain, the latter on a tricycle '*dans une tenue de Garibaldien*'. Back in Paris he wrote a letter of apology to de Valernes: 'On many occasions I must have seemed very hard in my treatment of you. But I have always been hard on myself . . . and I have been or have appeared to be hard on everyone. In fact this is due to a kind of brutal rage (*entraînement à la brutalité*) arising from my disquiet and my bad temper. I have felt myself so ill-fitted, so ill-equipped, so feeble—while believing that my attitudes to art (*mes calculs d'art*) were the right ones; I have sulked with everyone and with myself; I ask your pardon if pretexting my confounded art (*sous le prétexte de ce damné art*) I have wounded your high spirit, your fine intelligence and perhaps even your heart'— (and to complete the gesture, the letter concludes with appreciations of paintings by de Valernes). A few months later he invited de Valernes to Paris: 'You can have a bed in your old friend's house and you will meet once more other old friends including Desboutin who is still young at seventy and still smoking his pipe at the café door.'

He now began to complain more repeatedly of the trouble with his eyesight which he had already complained of to de Goncourt seventeen years before. In 1891 he writes, 'All winter my sight has been worse than ever; I read no newspapers but make my servant Zoë read them to me while I eat my *déjeuner*. You in your solitude have at least the pleasure of your eyesight—*ah, la vue, la vue, la vue*'. But the trouble in fact was not severe enough to interfere with his production; he continued his pastels and lithographs of dancers and women bathing; and for the bathing pictures he now had a modern bath placed in the studio, and his models posed in that in place of the tin tub which figures in the earlier pictures.

In this period, as noted, Degas was influenced to some extent by the Classical Renaissance launched by Seurat and we see this influence in *Les danseuses roses* (Pl. 29) which dates from the late 'eighties or 1890.[1] Of the other artists of the new movement his favourite was Gauguin whose pictures he collected from the time of the first Gauguin sale in 1891 where he bought *La belle Angèle*.[2]

[1] Cf. above, pp. 73, 75.   [2] Paris. Louvre.

ACT I: THE MASTERS' LIVES

HENRI DE TOULOUSE-LAUTREC (i)[1]

To the age of twenty-seven (1864–1891)

Henri de Toulouse-Lautrec, who was twenty in 1884, was born at Albi on November 24, 1864. His father, Count Alphonse de Toulouse-Lautrec-Monfa, was a fantastic grand seigneur who combined a passionate love of animals and birds with devotion to the ritual of sport, a habit of solitary meditation, and a taste for modelling in clay. His mother, née Adèle Tapié de Celeyran, a first cousin of his father, was a quiet cultivated lady who looked after his early education. His parents owned the Hôtel du Bosc at Albi, the Château de Malromé (near Bordeaux), the Château de Celeyran (near Narbonne) and various sporting properties. The family mentor in matters pertaining to art was Lautrec's uncle Count Charles de Toulouse-Lautrec, an enthusiastic amateur painter. In 1872 when Lautrec was eight his parents took a house in Paris which had a studio where his father kept falcons and modelled animals and birds; and Lautrec was sent to the Lycée Condorcet where he met Maurice Joyant. On his twelfth birthday his father gave him a book on falconry inscribed as follows: '*Rappelle-toi, mon fils, que la vie au grand air et au grand jour est la seule saine; tout ce qui est privé de liberté se dénature et meurt rapidement. Ce petit livre de fauconnerie t'apprendra à apprécier la vie des champs spacieux, et si tu connais un jour les amertumes de la vie, le cheval en premier ligne, puis le chien et le faucon pourront t'être des compagnons précieux, faisant oubliant un peu.*' The inscription was ill-omened, for Lautrec was never to lead *la vie au grand air* of a sporting gentleman. He was a delicate boy whose bones were abnormally brittle; at the age of fourteen he slipped on a polished floor and broke one thigh, and a year later, in 1879, he stumbled into a shallow ditch and broke the other. He had already acquired the habit of drawing and painting, and in this he was encouraged by his parents, by his uncle Count Charles, and by a friend of his father's, one René Princeteau, a deaf and dumb painter of sporting pictures who happened to have a studio near the Lautrec's apartment in Paris, and thus made the family's acquaintance. While still a boy Lautrec impressed Princeteau by drawing a portrait of him which 'made him shudder', and the boy, whose entourage disposed him to take pleasure in sporting subjects, was naturally in his turn impressed by Princeteau's pictures; he also enjoyed the pictures by John Lewis Brown, another sporting

[1] For the present distribution of Lautrec's pictures painted in this period and earlier cf. my Bibliographical and Catalogue Notes in Appendix I.

painter also acquainted with his father. After his accidents he went each winter, for two or three years, to Nice and spent the rest of his time on the family estates. In these years he drew and made water colours and painted oil pictures of local subjects and equestrian scenes 'in the manner' of Princeteau and John Lewis Brown, using, I take it, photographs as Princeteau and Brown also doubtless used them.

In 1882, at eighteen, he returned to Paris. The bones of his legs had now grown firmer and he was reasonably robust. But his legs had remained unusually short and he thus appeared with a normal head and torso on the legs of a dwarf. He had a very red and large-lipped mouth surrounded by a black beard and moustache, a rather coarse nose and short-sighted eyes behind pince-nez glasses; and there seems no doubt that he was quite abnormally ugly. In Paris he renewed his inter-course with Princeteau; and the deaf-mute artist and the deformed youth went together to theatres, the music halls and the circus, where Lautrec profited as the youth Watteau had profited when Gillot took him to the Italian Comedy at the Paris Fairs; at this time Lautrec also had contact with Forain who included both Princeteau and Count Alphonse in his curiously varied acquaintance. It was now agreed that he should become a professional artist; his mother came to Paris and arranged living rooms and a studio for him in her Paris apartment; and he entered the art school of Léon Bonnat. He described his first experience at this art school in a letter to his uncle Charles; Bonnat said to him 'Votre peinture n'est pas mal: c'est du chic, mais enfin ça n'est pas mal. Mais votre dessin est bonnement atroce'. In 1883 Bonnat gave up his art school and Lautrec entered the school run by Fernand Cormon, a painter of historical and religious pictures much admired in the Salons. Of Cormon's instruction he wrote to his uncle: 'Cormon's criticisms are much kinder than Bonat's; he looks at everything shown to him and makes encouraging remarks. But though you may be surprised to hear it—I like this less than my old boss's scourging which used to ginger me up.' He worked regularly at Cormon's studio all the year round producing a large number of studies from the model. In addition to these studies he painted a series of sporting pictures, and portraits, and made many drawings in his Paris studio and, in the summer months, at Celeyran and Malromé. He gave most of these works to his parents who greatly admired and carefully preserved them.

In 1884 he painted at Cormon's art school in the mornings and worked at home in his mother's house in the afternoons. In 1885 when he was twenty-one he made arrangements with his father which secured his financial independence; and he then took a studio at Montmartre which he shared with an artist friend. In 1885–1887 he still sometimes looked in at Cormon's atelier to draw from the model in the mornings; and in the evenings he frequented the Elysée Montmartre and the Moulin de la Galette dance halls, the Fernando circus and Aristide Bruant's new cabaret. At the same time he went to all the art shows—to the Salon each year, to the Eighth (and Last) Impressionist Exhibition in 1886, and the minor exhibitions in dealers' galleries. His heroes were Degas, Forain, Boldini, and Renoir; he collected Goya's etchings (Les caprices) and Japanese prints; and he began to draw for the illustrated papers. After painting La quadrille de la chaise Louis XIII à l'Elysée

Montmartre in 1886 he produced another dance scene at the Elysée Montmartre; he then went to Malromé in 1887 and painted an Impressionist portrait of his mother in her drawing room. Back in Paris he painted *Valentin le Désossé et La Goulue au Moulin de la Galette* and *Au Cirque Fernando* (Pl. 22A) in 1888.

Meanwhile he had begun a series of studies of Montmartre girls and women painted sometimes in his studio and sometimes *en plein air* in the garden of a photographer named Forest where he worked from time to time in the next few years. A photograph of the period shows him at work on a picture known as *Berthe la sourde* (*à l'ombrelle*); the model sits against a background of shrubs: she wears a straw hat and has a parasol across her knees; Lautrec sits brush in hand beneath an umbrella and works at the picture where the face, the clothes and the attitude are all realistically recorded. Lautrec gave or lent a number of these studies to Aristide Bruant who hung them in his cabaret labelled with the titles of his songs—*A Montrouge, A Saint Lazare, A la Bastille, Aux Batignolles, Rosa la Rouge* and so on.[1]

In 1889 when he was twenty-five he left the friend with whom he shared his studio and took a studio of his own which remained his Montmartre headquarters for ten years; and there he painted *La fille à l'accroche-cœur* (Pl. 31) and *Au bal du Moulin de la Galette* (Pl. 32B) that year. His work was already attracting attention; he had met Van Gogh at Cormon's; through him he met Théo Van Gogh and thus acquired entrée to the artists' reunions at the Goupil Gallery; he was invited by Théo to leave some pictures in the gallery; and some of his works were shown soon after by Tanguy and by the dealer Le Barc de Boutteville. Through the meetings at the Goupil Gallery he had contact with Seurat, Signac and the other artists who were running the *Salon des Indépendants* and he made his début there with *Au bal du Moulin de la Galette* (Pl. 32A). He also met Catulle Mendès at this time and drew a head of him which the curious will find it intriguing to compare with Jean Cocteau's impression drawn twenty years later.[2]

In 1890 he began to go often to the *Moulin Rouge* lately launched by the impresario Zidler; and his first Moulin Rouge picture, *Au Moulin Rouge: La danse: Dressage des nouvelles*, painted that year, shows Valentin le Désossé putting a new floor dancer through her paces and teaching her to do 'the twist'. Zidler acquired this picture and also *Au Cirque Fernando* and hung them in the foyer of the Moulin Rouge, as I have chronicled.[3] Lautrec made friends at this time with the Dihau family of musicians—Désiré Dihau, bassoonist, who had sat to Degas for *L'orchestre* in 1868, his brother Henri, and his sister Mlle Dihau (whom Degas had painted seated at a piano); and he challenged Degas by painting another *Mlle Dihau au piano* and in portraits f both brothers. It was in 1890 also, as I have chronicled, that he attended the banquet of *Les XX* in Brussels and called out a member to a duel because he had denigrated Van Gogh's pictures—a quarrel adjusted by the other members; that he defended The Douanier Rousseau on the Committee of the *Salon*

---

[1] In some cases these titles have adhered to the pictures. In other cases the pictures are now known by other titles such as *La rousse, Pierreuse dans la rue, Gueule de bois* (cf. Appendix I).

[2] Lautrec's drawing is reproduced in Joyant: *Toulouse-Lautrec*, Vol. II, p. 15. Cocteau's is reproduced in his *Portraits-Souvenir*.   [3] Cf. above, p. 101.

des Indépendants; and that his friend Maurice Joyant succeeded Théo Van Gogh as manager at the Goupil Gallery and began to arrange exhibitions of his pictures.

Lautrec's cousin, Dr. Tapié de Celeyran, now arrived in Paris and became his inseparable companion. The strange pair—de Celeyran tall and lean with a long red nose, drooping moustache, affecting a fantastic old-fashioned dandyism, and Lautrec in a dark morning coat and 'sporting' top coat, his dwarf legs in light trousers, his satyr's face crowned by a bowler hat, went everywhere together; and they were soon familiar figures not only at the Moulin Rouge but also at theatres and at social gatherings when Lautrec felt inclined to pass an evening in Society—as he did from time to time. Tapié de Celeyran was attached to the Hôpital International; Lautrec thus obtained the entrée to the hospital where he was allowed to attend operations and make studies; he was especially intrigued with the flamboyant personality of the surgeon Péan; he made numerous drawings and caricatures of him—his first series of studies of one person observed in a number of circumstances both on the stage, as it were, and behind the scenes; and he painted him at work in *Une opération par le chirurgien Péan*. In return for these opportunities for study Lautrec delighted the students by taking La Goulue to an evening party at the hospital.

Meanwhile he continued his paintings of individual Montmartre girls and women, and his studies at the dance halls. He now produced a second *Moulin de la Galette* and some single studies of the habitués—*Pierreuse: Casque d'or* and *La fille à la fourrure*, and the second of his Moulin Rouge series, *Repos entre deux tours de valse*, where La Goulue strolls into the bar on the arm of her partner after finishing her dance, while in the background her rival dancer, Jane Avril, performs fantastic 'scissor' steps to amuse her friends at a table. At the same time he produced the sinister picture *A la mie* (a deliberate challenge to Degas' *L'absinthe*); a series of studies of women at their toilet (also of course a challenge to Degas), and his first poster *Le Moulin Rouge*, where La Goulue high kicks and Valentin le Désossé, in the foreground, is pretending to be shocked.

Accounts left by his friends prove that Lautrec at this period was a witty and agreeable companion who enjoyed life and knew how to make his friends share in his enjoyment. He was not wealthy, like Degas or Cézanne, but he had sufficient money to relieve him from any need to sell his pictures or to produce any work in order to make money; and though terribly handicapped by physical infirmity and a repellent appearance, he was naturally an extravert and thus able to conquer the handicaps by a lively interest in the world around him and more particularly in proletarian eccentrics, whom he treated with courtesy while keeping them firmly outside the circle of his intimates who were all men of intelligence and parts. There are those who describe him as a contemptible degenerate; and later, as I shall show, he went undeniably downhill. But from 1888–1891, when he had already arrived at his personal art, and for some years thereafter, he was above all essentially an exceptionally lively-minded and active artist who worked extremely hard and produced a large number of intensely characterized pictures which are a kind of climax of the Realist-Impressionist movement which our Prologue has recorded.[1]

[1] Cf. above, pp. 82 and 83.

ACT II

1892-1903

From Gauguin's *La reine des Areois* and *L'esprit veille*, The Douanier's *Le centenaire de l'Indépendance* and Lautrec's posters; to Cézanne's *Les grandes baigneuses*, the foundation of the *Salon d'Automne*, the first *Fauve* exhibition, Picasso's 'blue' pictures, the death of Pissarro and the death of Gauguin

ACT II

1892-1903

From Gauguin's *La reine des Areois* and *L'esprit veille*, The
Douanier's *Le centenaire de l'Indépendance* and Lautrec's
posters; to Cézanne's *Les grandes baigneuses*, the foundation
of the *Salon d'Automne*, the first *Fauve* exhibition, Picasso's
'blue' pictures, the death of Pissarro and the death of
Gauguin

INTRODUCTION

In the period 1892–1903, as before and after, the general public and the bourgeois
were given the art they desired by the painters who exhibited in the official *Salon*;
the dilettanti patronized the Impressionists, admired the Realist works by Lautrec
and were intrigued by the Symbolists, the Nabis and the Rose-Croix painters;
and a few exceptional personalities were also alive to the Modern Classical
Renaissance to which the chief contributors were Gauguin in Tahiti, Cézanne in
Provence, and, in Paris, The Douanier Rousseau and Lautrec (in his posters); in
the later years Henri Matisse and Pablo Picasso appear upon the scene.

Gauguin back from Tahiti arranged an exhibition of forty new pictures in 1893.
In the two years he had spent in Tahiti he had opened his mind and sensibilities to
the tropical world which surrounded him, rejoicing in the luxuriant form and
colour, and absorbing himself, as far as might be, in the primitive life. In his first
Tahitian pictures, *Rêverie*,[1] *Fatata ti miti (Près de la mer)*[2] and *Ia Orana Maria (Ave
Maria)*,[3] he continued the rhythmic patterning he had evolved in Brittany. But
after a few months his art became broader and more grandly simplified in drawing,
more resonant in colour, and more profound in spirit; and the pictures he brought
back with him were truly magnificent. I reproduce three pictures from this great
series, *La reine des Areois* (Pl. 35), *Manao Tupapau (L'esprit veille)* (Pl. 36) and
Hina Marouru (Fête à Hina) (Pl. 37A). The drawing of the nude native girl surrounded by tropical flora in *La reine des Areois* is superbly simple; like The Douanier
Rousseau, Gauguin was not hampered by art-school dexterity in drawing from the
figure, and he could use drawing for the direct pictorial expression of his vision or
ideas. The colour too in this picture is daring and original; the green mound the

[1] Paris. Georges Wildenstein et Cie. (formerly New York: Stransky).
[2] London. Marc Oliver.   [3] New York. Adolph Lewisohn.

131

figure sits on is covered with a night-blue patterned cloth, the ground is red, the flowering plants behind are purple and the trees against the mountains make golden notes repeated in golden and citron patches in the foreground. In *L'esprit veille* (Pl. 36), the most celebrated of all his pictures, we see his new powers as a painter combined with the 'Symbolic' factors that appeared in *Vision après le sermon: Lutte de Jacob avec l'ange* (Pl. 22B) and in *Jésus au Jardin des Oliviers* (Pl. 26) in 1888–9. *L'esprit veille* records Gauguin's discovery of the frightened soul of his little Tahitian mistress Tehoura; and he has himself described its genesis: 'One day I had to go into Papeete. I had promised to be back by evening but . . . I had to do part of the journey on foot and it was one o'clock in the morning when I returned. We were short of oil for the lamp and when I opened the door the lamp was out and the room was in darkness. I had a sudden feeling of apprehension and suspicion—a sudden fear that I should find an empty nest. I lit matches quickly and then I saw her—quite still and naked, lying on her stomach on the bed; and her eyes immensely large in fear looked at me without seeming to know me. I remained for some moments in a strange incertitude. Tehoura's terrors were contagious, I seemed to see a phosphorescence in the light from those fixed eyes. She had never seemed to me so lovely, so moving, so disturbing in her loveliness. I stood quite still, afraid that in the half darkness—inhabited, no doubt, by vague intimations and enemy forms—any movement on my part might drive the child to a crisis of terror. How did she see me in that moment? How did I appear to her? Did my anxious face seem one of those demons or spectres, those *tupapaus* of Tahitian legend who have their being in the sleepless night? How indeed could I know that what she feared might not in fact be real? The intensity of the feeling that possessed her, physically and morally enslaved by her superstitions, had transformed her into a being quite unknown to me, entirely different from everything that I had been able to see in her before. . . . At length she became herself again and I made efforts to set her mind at peace and to restore her confidence. She listened to me, sulking, and then in a voice where sobs trembled: "Don't leave me alone again without light".' That was the initial experience. Gauguin himself has also described the finished picture: 'The bedclothes are chrome yellow because this colour *suggests* night without *explaining* it, and the passage also serves as a transition from the orange yellow to the green, thus completing the musical accord. The flowers are both flowers and (as in her mind) phosphorescence; for the natives believe that the phosphor sparks which they see at night are spirits of the dead. It is also a fine piece of painting—although it is not "a painting from nature".' [1] Gauguin made a series of woodcuts of the subject of this picture and also of a number of his other works; he claimed later that he had renewed the art of woodcutting which had declined and perished when called on to compete with engraving in the fifteenth century; and one aspect of the modern revival of the woodcut, especially in England, is in fact directly due to his achievements in this field. The highly decorative painting *Hina Marouru* (*Fête à Hina*) (Pl. 37A) shows Gauguin's interest in the traditional Tahitian cults (largely supplanted by Christianity in his day) and

[1] Another account of this picture is given by Gauguin in a letter to his wife quoted in Rewald's *Gauguin* (cf. my Bibliographical and Catalogue Notes in Appendix I).

33. THE DOUANIER ROUSSEAU
Bonne fête, 1892
London. Charles Laughton, Esq.

34. THE DOUANIER ROUSSEAU
Le Centenaire de l'Indépendance, 1892

in primitive native carving which he admired and understood. '*L'art primitif*', he wrote, '*procède de l'esprit et emploie la nature. L'art soi-disant raffiné procède de la sensualité et sert la nature. La nature est la servante du premier et la maîtresse du second. Mais la servante ne peut oublier son origine, elle avilit l'artiste en se laissant adorer par lui.*' In his second Tahitian period 1895–1903 Gauguin never quite recaptured his former contact with the primitive world. The design in *Trois Tahitiens*[1] of 1897 is monumental; the colour in *Tahitiennes au mango* (Pl. 45A) of 1899 is rich and resonant; and the drawing in both is grand and simple; but both pictures are more European than the earlier pictures—closer to '*l'art soi-disant raffiné*'—than to his own definition of primitive art. In 1901 he left Tahiti for the Marquesas hoping there to find material to renew his spirit. But though some of his Marquesan pictures are decorative and pleasant, he was too exhausted by disease and persecution-mania to recapture the contact he had lost.

Cézanne in these years 1892–1903 reached the summit of his power and painted many of his finest works. I reproduce *La tour aux pigeons* (Pl. 48A), painted about 1892, the *Portrait de Gustave Geffroy* (Pl. 44A) of 1895, the water-colour *Nature morte au melon* (Pl. 48B) of about 1900, and the large picture known as *Les grandes baigneuses* (Pl. 49) which he worked on from approximately 1898 till he died in 1906. In *La tour aux pigeons* (Pl. 48A) his method is well seen; the brilliantly mastered blue-green verdure-forms encircle the yellow pigeon house and retire to encircle the building on the right—and the single structure thus created basks gently in the warm pervading light of the Southern sun against an intense blue sky. In the still life *Nature morte au melon* (Pl. 48B) the eye travels down from the handle of the pot to the contours of the melon supported by the related forms of the apples, jug, sugar bowl, white tablecloth and rug; the melon in this picture is green, the white cloth has blue and red shadows, the rug is red, green and blue, and the milk jug and sugar bowl are blue and white.

The very famous *Portrait de Gustave Geffroy* (Pl. 44A) shows the critic in his study as Degas has shown the critic Duranty in 1879. Geffroy wears an ultra-marine coat silhouetted with the chair against the yellow and light-blue paper books which line the shelves; there is a coloured map on the page of one of the books lying open on the table; all the forms and tones and colour spaces are miraculously dovetailed one with another in this admirable picture where the two elements in Cézanne's approach to portraiture are evenly balanced and combined. *Les grandes baigneuses* (Pl. 49) is the largest of the numerous compositions with nude figures that he made at all periods of his life—compositions executed without models, as he was wholly concerned to use the attitudes and gestures of the figures as constituents in a three-dimensional design. *Les grandes baigneuses* records his resolve to end this series with a final classical arrangement challenging the Renaissance and Baroque masters; and as I have pointed out in my earlier writings the structure of this picture is fundamentally the same as that of Raphael's *School of Athens*.[2] In this picture the constituents—the figures, the arched trees and the

[1] Scotland. Alexander Maitland, Esq.

[2] Cf. my *The Modern Movement in Art* (Faber) and *French Painting* (Medici) where the two pictures are reproduced on one page.

supporting horizontals—are planned not as units with meaning in themselves but once more, and more than ever, as fragments without other meaning than their part in the rhythmic music of the three-dimensional design; and the nude figures are deliberately distorted to that end. In general effect *Les grandes baigneuses* is a symphony in blue—though the figures are touched with pink and yellow and the tree trunks with brown. Though he laboured intermittently at this work for years Cézanne left it uncompleted, in the sense that many bars and bridge passages in the symphony are blank; but it is not an unfinished symphony because the essential structure is all there.

Cézanne has been called the primitive of modern art. But the phrase is misleading. He was in no sense a primitive at any stage of his career. As a man he was simple in the sense that he was not a metropolitan but a bourgeois provincial always ill at ease with sophisticated Paris. But as an artist he was not simple or in any sense a primitive. The truly primitive painter finds it perfectly easy to paint exactly as he wants to paint. He has vivid, mainly two-dimensional, impressions of formal phenomena and when he works without nature before him, the images in his mind's eye are simple and clear cut. Cézanne on the other hand saw, perceived and sensed three dimensions and infinite complexities in formal phenomena, and as the mastery of these complexities, in the way he attempted it, was more difficult than anything attempted by an artist before, he found every picture he began a tremendous problem which he worked out with infinite patience and which he rarely felt that he had solved in every detail. Compared with the confident primitive, or the man content to parade dexterity and tricks, he seemed even in his old age a fumbling and diffident artist—like Rembrandt in his old age. But in fact, in his old age, he was a virtuoso as great as Rembrandt, a post-Baroque master who had gathered immense experience and was able to record it, organized, with subtlety and power.

Meanwhile the true primitive of this period, The Douanier Rousseau, was calmly confident and painting original pictures without hesitation or mental conflict. I reproduce his *Bonne Fête* (Pl. 33) painted as a birthday greeting for his wife in 1892, the large composition *Le centenaire de l'Indépendance: Le peuple danse autour des deux républiques, celle de 1792 et celle de 1892, se donnant la main sur l'air de: Auprès de ma blonde qu'il fait bon, fait bon dormir* (Pl. 34), exhibited in 1892; the full-length portrait *La femme de l'artiste* (Pl. 39B) painted about 1895 and probably repainted later, *La bohémienne endormie* (Pl. 42) of 1897, *La carrière* (Pl. 43B) and *La banlieue* (Pl. 43A) dating from the late 'nineties, and *L'enfant au jouet* (Pl. 40B) exhibited in 1902. The general arrangement of *Bonne Fête* was probably taken from a Christmas card or 'valentine', but enlarged to a picture with the hand and flowers life-size and transformed by The Douanier's serene and classical technique, it comes to us as a gentle and personal poem. In *La femme de l'artiste* (Pl. 39B) the sitter wears the wide sleeves which also figure in Lautrec's *May Belfort* (Pl. 39A); and it is instructive to compare The Douanier's formal vision with Lautrec's realist approach. Compared thus with Lautrec's picture, *La femme de l'artiste* is seen to be primarily a two-dimensional design deliberately planned and grandly patterned; and the picture is humanized as it were by the engaging simplicity of The Douanier's mind. *Le centenaire de l'Indépendance* (Pl. 34) is an intricately composed, exquisitely coloured and most delicately painted picture to which no black and white reproduction can do justice; and when I first saw it the colour and the handling recalled to me the pictures by the elder Brueghel— *La danse villageoise*, for example, in Vienna. *La carrière* (Pl. 43B), again a most delicately handled picture, shows the quarry against the blue of an evening sky when one stands, as the little man in the picture stands, with one's back to the setting sun; the shrubs on the towering heath are green and russet. In *La banlieue* (Pl. 43A) the clouds over a green-blue sky are exquisite in colour. The large and strangely moving Surrealist picture *La bohémienne endormie* (Pl. 42) is surely the central masterpiece of The Douanier's production in these years. It belonged at one time to the American collector John Quinn; it returned in 1926 (after Quinn's death) to Paris and Jean Cocteau then described it in terms so perfectly in accord with the picture that I quote from them rather than attempt a new description of my own. '*Nous sommes dans le désert. Le rêve emporte si loin la bohémienne couchée au deuxième plan, ou bien le rêve l'apporte de si loin, comme le mirage apporte le fleuve du quatrième plan, qu'un lion, au troisième plan, la flaire sans pouvoir l'atteindre. Au fait, peut-être ce lion, ce fleuve, sont-ils le rêve de la dormeuse. Quelle paix! Le mystère se croit seul et se met tout nu. . . . La bohémienne dort, les yeux mal fermés. . . . Pourrai-je dépeindre cette figure immobile qui coule, ce fleuve d'oublie? Je pense à l'Egypte qui savait garder les yeux ouverts dans la mort comme les plongeurs dans la mer. . . . D'où tombe une chose pareille? De la lune. . . . Au reste, ce n'est peut-être pas sans motif que le peintre qui n'oubliait jamais un détail ne marque le sable d'aucune empreinte autour des pieds endormis. La bohémienne n'est pas venue là. Elle est là. Elle n'est pas là. Elle n'est en aucun lieu humain. Elle habite des miroirs. . . .*'[1] This great and amazingly original picture forestalls in its dream-atmosphere the Surrealism of Chirico's pre-war pictures—the *Rue Italienne: le cerceau* (Pl. 68B) for example and also Chirico's *Lion et gladiateurs* (Pl. 86A) of 1927[2]; in the choice and treatment of the still life it forestalls *motifs* that were universally used in later Cubist pictures; and in the classical generalizations of the drawing it forestalls the post-Purist works by Metzinger, Herbin and Severini in 1924–1926.[3] It is now in the New York Museum of Modern Art.

Lautrec, in the 'nineties, as artist and personality, was much more conspicuous in Paris than The Douanier, who was only appreciated by certain artists and writers. As stated, it was, however, chiefly in his posters and some bookcovers that Lautrec contributed to the contemporary revival of rhythmic drawing and design; in his paintings and drawings for the illustrated papers he continued to develop on the realist basis of his early pictures, *Au bal du Moulin de la Galette* (Pl. 32B) and *La fille à l'accroche-cœur* (Pl. 31). In 1892 he painted eight of his celebrated pictures of floor-dancers at the Moulin Rouge; and in the next few years he painted many portraits of his friends and of actors and actresses and music-hall singers. I reproduce his *May Belfort en rose* (Pl. 39A) and the drawing *Oscar Wilde* (Pl. 38). He drew this *Oscar Wilde* from memory after a short meeting with Wilde in London in 1895; he has tinted the hair yellow, the coat of the dress-suit blue, and suggested 'Big Ben' and the Houses of Parliament behind; as a portrait the drawing is more a

[1] Cf. below, p. 309.　　　　[2] Cf. below, p. 310.　　　　[3] Cf. below, p. 304.

'Symbolist' statement of the artist's impression of Wilde's face than a categoric record of his features; and the freedom of the calligraphy challenges the Japanese and Chinese masters. In *May Belfort en rose* Lautrec has yielded to the model's charm, and challenged Degas as a painter of footlight effects.

The Impressionists took no part in the artistic adventures of these years. Renoir, after his splendid contribution of *Les grandes baigneuses* (Pl. 19B) and his other classical pictures of the 'eighties, was now passing through a period of hesitation when he swung between the Impressionist and the Classical attitudes and produced a number of relatively speaking academic compromise pictures on the way to the final achievements of his marvellous old age that I refer to in Act III. Pissarro after his flirtation with Seurat's theories had reverted to Impressionism and in the later 'nineties he painted a series of bird's-eye views of Parisian street scenes—imitating Monet's *Boulevard des Capucines*[1] of 1873. Monet himself had just painted the *Meules* series and the *Peupliers* series recording the changing effects of sunlight on the same haystack and the same poplars at different hours of the day; and in this period he did the same thing with the façade of Rouen cathedral (which he portrayed as pink sugar icing in some lights and blue sugar icing in others) and with the lily pond in his garden at Giverny. Sisley continued to paint Impressionist pictures till he died in 1899. Degas, who now worked relatively little, produced mainly pastels, mostly unfinished, of women at their toilet and in or round a *baignoir* in his studio, which add little to his earlier achievements. But just because the Impressionists were now repeating their earlier gestures and standing aside from contemporary efforts they now had continuously more and more success. The dilettanti crowded to Durand-Ruel's to see large exhibitions by Renoir and Pissarro in 1892; and all the Impressionists became figures with world-wide reputations when their works were shown in a comprehensive manner in the *Exposition Centennale* in 1900. As I shall show in 'How it happened' the Parisian dilettanti in these years had many chances to learn to understand the post-Impressionist orientations in painting. There were large exhibitions of Seurat's works in 1892 and 1901, there were Gauguin exhibitions in 1893, 1894, 1898 and 1903; there were Cézanne exhibitions in 1895 and 1898; there were pictures by The Douanier Rousseau in the *Salon des Indépendants* every year; there was a Van Gogh exhibition in 1901, and there were *Fauve* demonstrations, which I shall refer to later, in 1903. Some exceptional collectors—led by Auguste Pellerin—began to buy Cézanne's earlier pictures in 1895. But in 1903 the main body of the dilettanti were still blind to the art of Seurat, of Gauguin, of Van Gogh, and even of Cézanne; they were hostile to the art of The Douanier Rousseau; they were shocked and indignant at the first *Fauve* pictures; and they were so imperceptive of Picasso's genius that despairing of success he rolled some scores of his 'Blue' pictures in a bundle, stored them with a friend, and left Paris, as he thought for ever, in the spring of 1903.

Apart from the Impressionists, the artists who found favour with the dilettanti in this period were Lautrec (as a Realist) and three interlocking groups—the Symbolists, the Nabis, and the Rose-Croix 'mystic' painters—concerned in their

[1] Moscow. Museum of Modern Western Art.

several ways to combat Realism. The dilettanti, familiar with Realist art in Courbet and Manet's pictures, in Zola's novels and in the plays at Antoine's theatre, and captured, as I show in 'How it happened', by Bruant, Steinlen, Forain and Yvette Guilbert, were intrigued and fascinated by Lautrec's night-life pictures—though they did not go so far as to buy them in this period partly because Lautrec, who had money, made no great efforts to sell and partly because they thought them unsuitable for rooms inhabited by ladies. They extended some favour to the Symbolists, the Nabis and the Rose-Croix painters because the subjects in many of their pictures were literary or 'mystic' ideas and because the colours in many of these pictures were the pale faded colours of Puvis de Chavannes' palette which were then regarded as 'aesthetic'.

The Symbolists, led by Sérusier, have appeared in our story in 1890–1891; in the 'nineties, as I shall show, they continued to work for Paul Fort's *Théâtre d'Art* (founded, as noted, in 1890) and for the new *Théâtre de l'Œuvre* now founded in 1893 by Lugné-Poë; and they had close contacts with Odilon Redon and the Rose-Croix mystic painters who were launched by Péladan. The work of a Rose-Croix painter, one Osbert, at this moment was thus described by the critic Coquiot: '*Il exprime la poésie de l'apaisement, des crépuscules, des solitudes qu'animent des êtres de rêve; des solitudes où les arbres mettent des entrecolonnements réguliers de temples, où les eaux stagnent; Edens violets, de très doux sites; des figures y glissent, au pas des canéphores, ou elles y méditent. . . .*' Octave Mirbeau impatient of these Symbolist and Rose-Croix painters referred to them contemptuously as '*tous ces jobards ou ces pauvres farceurs—les mystiques, les symbolistes, les larvistes, les occultistes, les néopédérastes, les peintres de l'âme. . . .*'; but it is clear from Coquiot's description that Osbert's picture was in fact a step on a path to be explored, twenty years later, with greater truth to the character of dream-images, by Chirico and the first Surrealists.[1] The French Symbolist and Rose-Croix movements of the 'nineties (which were parallel to the 'Aesthetic Movement' in England) were minor efforts at a time when Cézanne, Gauguin, and The Douanier Rousseau were regenerating painting, but they nevertheless produced some works of consequence—Redon's pastels, Maeterlinck's plays and music by Debussy.

The Nabis were a group formed in 1892 by other painters already encountered as followers of Gauguin in his Brittany days—Maurice Denis, Pierre Bonnard and Edouard Vuillard. This group was linked with the Symbolist group because Sérusier had also been a follower of Gauguin and because both Sérusier and Maurice Denis divided their allegiance at this period between Gauguin and Puvis de Chavannes. I give details of the Nabis' activities in 'How it happened'. Here we need only observe that Bonnard and Vuillard made contributions whic h had nothing to do with Symbolist or Rose-Croix art; in the middle 'nineties they sought and found patterns in their visual experience of the daily life around them. I reproduce Bonnard's *Devant l'omnibus* (Pl. 37B) where a pattern is made by a woman in a dress with leg-of-mutton sleeves against the yellow spokes of an omnibus wheel. Vuillard who sought his patterns mainly in interior scenes, ingeniously mingled the flower-patterns or stripe-patterns on the wall-papers with

[1] Cf. below, pp. 207, 208.

flower and striped patterns on women's clothes. Bonnard became more Impressionist as this period advanced; and his *L'après-midi bourgeoise: La famille Terrasse* of
1900–1903 is a wittily observed Impressionist picture with elements derived from
Manet, Whistler, Renoir, Lautrec and Puvis de Chavannes. Both contributed at this
time to the liberation of colour from representational service.[1]

In 1895 (while the Nabis were scoring their successes in Paris and Lautrec
was painting the *May Belfort en rose* and drawing the *Oscar Wilde*) Pablo Picasso aged
fourteen was painting *La fillette aux pieds nus* (Pl. 40A) in Corunna. In the later
'nineties Picasso worked in Madrid and Barcelona where there was much talk of
French art among the Spanish art students; and he went to Paris to see it for himself in 1900. As I chronicle later in more detail this first visit to Paris was a short
one; he paid a second visit of ten months the next year, and a third of three or
four months in the winter of 1902–1903. In the three years 1901–1903 he painted
over two hundred pictures—fifty in Paris in 1901 and most of the others in
Barcelona in 1902 and 1903. I reproduce *L'enfant au pigeon* (Pl. 45B) painted in
1901, the head of an old woman *Célestine* (Pl. 46) of 1903 and *Le vieux guitariste*
(Pl. 47) also of 1903. Everything drawn and painted by Picasso, in this as in the
later periods, is arresting; all his works grip the spectator by the force of the
personality that produced them. Picasso was twenty in 1901 and his pictures of
1901–1903 are alive with the fire of his own youth. To have contact with them
is to have our interest roused and our sympathy stirred by a young man eager to
make us share his passions and his discoveries. In the next decade he was to lead
the Cubist Renaissance; but at this period he was a Romantic-Realist, and more
romantic than realist—for all his pictures of 1901–1903 are records of his personal
experience of emotive fragments of life. On his visits to Paris he painted music-
hall scenes and café scenes influenced technically speaking by Steinlen, Lautrec,
the Nabis and Gauguin. We see Gauguin's simplified drawing in the charming
L'enfant au pigeon where the attitude is one which occurs very frequently in
Gauguin's paintings—in *Tahitiennes au mango* (Pl. 45A) for example. At this
moment Picasso also painted some crouching figures, and figures with raised
shoulders and hunched backs seated at café tables, which recall some figures in
certain works by Gauguin—the *Meyer de Haan*[2] for example and *D'où venons-nous?
Que sommes-nous? Où allons-nous?* (Pl. 41); and there is much of Gauguin also in the
Arlequin accoudé (aux allumettes)[3] also painted in 1901. But, though influences of
this kind are apparent in these early paintings, they are permeated and transformed
by the animating originality and drive of the new personality. In 1901–1903
Picasso was already a master who, rejecting the tricks of photographic painting
'by the tone values', is creating his own pictorial language for each work. Certain
motifs—the harlequin and circus figures, the mother and child, the bull fight—
which recur again and again later—are already to be seen in this series; and
Célestine (Pl. 46) proves that had he so chosen, he could have become the greatest,
the most relentless—and of course the most unpopular—portrait painter of our
epoch. When he returned to Barcelona, deeply discouraged, in 1903 he painted a

[1] Cf. pp. 77, 197–8, 201, 204, 209.   [2] New York. Private collection.
[3] Boston. Q. A. Shaw McKean.

series of emotive figures—beggars, women with their children and so forth—culminating in two profoundly moving Romantic-Realist pictures *L'étreinte* (sometimes titled *L'amour pur*)[1] and *Couple et femme avec enfant* (sometimes titled *La vie* or *Dans la vie*)[2]. In this series he portrayed a number of emaciated figures of which *Le vieux guitariste* (Pl. 47) and *Vieux juif et garçon*[3] are typical examples. In many of his pictures between the end of 1901 and the end of 1904 the colour blue predominates—and these years are known accordingly as his 'Blue' period—though the term is too categoric, as vermilion and dark colours appear in certain pictures of this time.

Henri Matisse first exhibited in the Salon de la Nationale in 1896 when he was twenty-seven. Born at St. Quentin in 1869, he had been trained as a lawyer and he had begun to paint in 1890. He worked first in the art school at St. Quentin and in 1892 he went to Paris where the academic Bouguereau was one of his first masters. In 1893 he became a pupil of Gustave Moreau then sixty-seven and one of the professors at the Ecole des Beaux-Arts. Moreau recognized his talents and treated him as a personal pupil; and he was still under Moreau in 1896. His first pictures were sober still life studies influenced by Chardin and grey landscapes and interiors influenced by Corot. In the next two years he was captured by Impressionist painting and more especially I fancy by Renoir's landscapes and Renoir's compositions with figures at a table set with crockery, glass and fruit; In this stage he painted *La desserte*,[4] a large and finely executed table composition which was shown in the *Salon de la Nationale* in 1898 and proved that had he wished he could have won success as a derivative performer in the Impressionist tradition. But the creative urge within him was too strong to make tolerable this easy progression on the line of least resistance. In 1899–1901 he discovered Gauguin, Seurat, Cézanne and Van Gogh and the secrets of their several aesthetics; and he resolved to play his part in the pictorial Renaissance those artists had begun. At first it was Cézanne chiefly who showed him a direction; and in *Carmelina* (Pl. 44B) of 1901 he tried the bold experiment of combining the realism of Courbet's *Enterrement à Ornans*, Manet's *Olympia* and Degas' *Femme à sa toilette* (Pl. 13) with the architectural art which culminated in Cézanne's *Portrait de Gustave Geffroy* (Pl. 44A). As a realist Matisse went beyond these masters in his *Carmelina*. For there is here no pretence of 'subject' to sugar the realist pill—no significant title as in Manet's *Olympia* and no suggestion that the naked girl depicted has been surprised at her toilet unawares as in Degas' composition. The model is frankly posed on a table—and that, as far as it goes, is that. But that is only the beginning, the jumping-off point of this remarkable picture—for in painting it Matisse crossed the Rubicon from the side where representation is looked on as an end to the side where it is looked on as a means. In painting *Carmelina* he discovered his personal aesthetic; the colour, it is true, is still sombre—mainly browns and ochres; but the patterning is already personal; and we observe here also a dualism that we shall encounter in much of Matisse's later painting—the same dualism that we found in Cézanne's portraits and groups. *Carmelina* is a fine, very pure and very fearless

[1] Paris. Mme Paul Guillaume.   [2] Paris. Etienne Bignou.
[3] Moscow. Museum of Modern Western Art.   [4] German collection.

picture; and it stands, with the Van Gogh Exhibition of 1901 and with some landscapes and still life compositions and other nudes by Matisse, at the source of the first phase of the Fauve movement which Matisse organized in 1901–1903. I give the history of the Fauve movement in 'How it happened'. Here I need only mention that Matisse's early associates included Marquet, Rouault, Vlaminck and Derain; that the group—not yet known as Fauve—made concerted demonstrations in the *Salon des Indépendants*, the first *Salon d'Automne* and in Mlle Weill's gallery in 1903; and that in these years Derain and Vlaminck were spurred to the use of violent colour by the Van Gogh Exhibition, while Matisse studied Byzantine mosaics, Near Eastern, Persian and Far Eastern painting, pottery and textiles before driving the darker colours from his palette and becoming the master of colour that we know.

35. GAUGUIN
La reine des Areois, 1892
Paris. Mme Desjardins

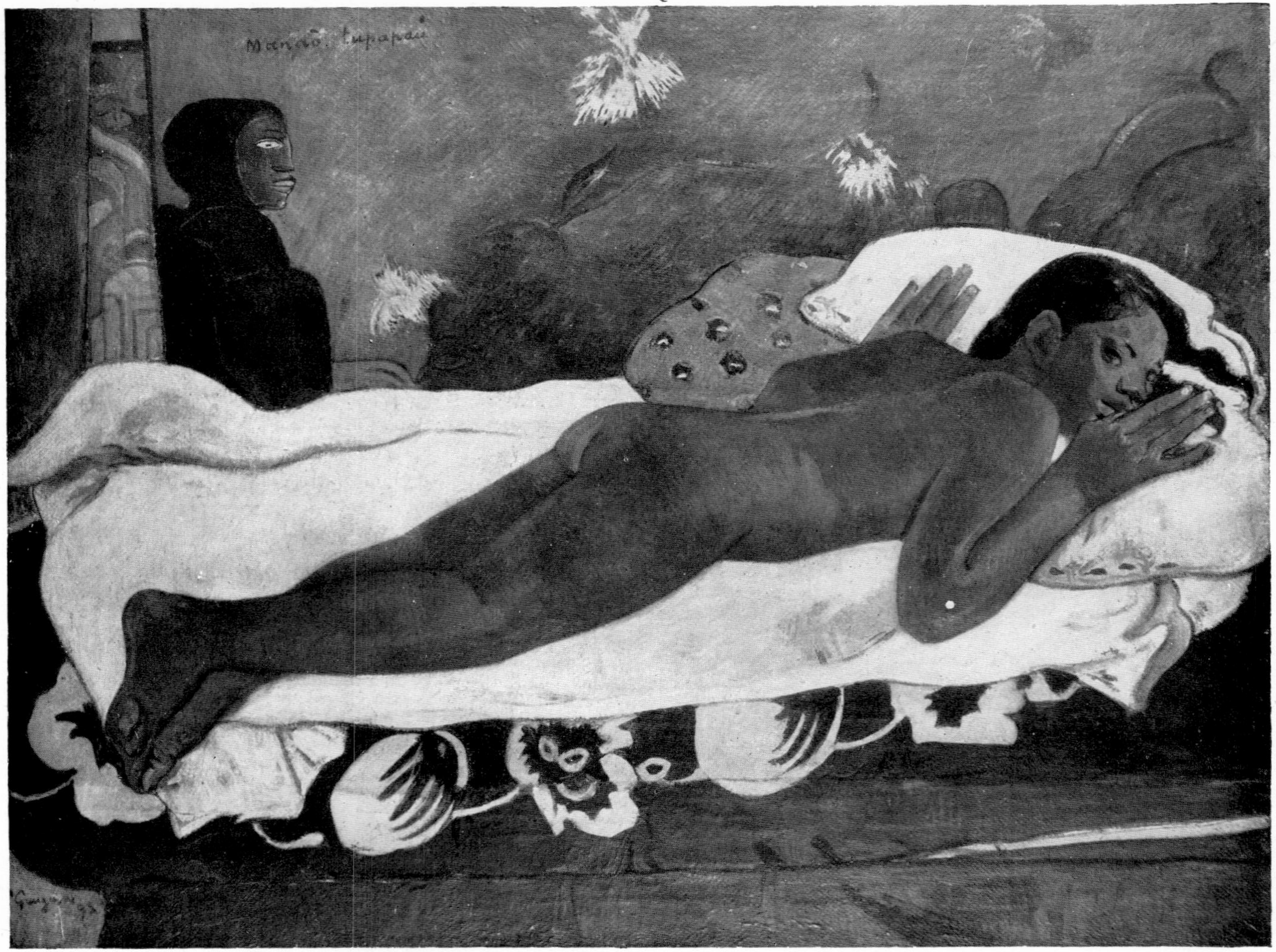

36. GAUGUIN
L'esprit veille, 1892

ACT II: HOW IT HAPPENED

SCENE I: 1892-1893

From the *Seurat Memorial Exhibition*, The Douanier's *Le centenaire de l'Indépendance*, Lautrec's *Bruant* posters, the first Rose-Croix and Nabi exhibitions and the first Anarchist outrages; to Gauguin's return from Tahiti, his first exhibition of Tahitian pictures, the foundation of Lugné-Poë's *Théâtre de l'Œuvre*, and the Panama Scandal

---

In 1892 Parisian night-life had the special character which we associate with the 'naughty nineties'. Yvette Guilbert sang every evening first at the Moulin Rouge (which had a music-hall show before the floor-dancing started) and then at a cabaret called the *Divan Japonais* whither Lautrec, who now discovered her, and Maurice Donnay, whose *Adolphe : ou le jeune homme triste*[1] was now in her repertoire, habitually went on with her. Lautrec had a table reserved for him every evening at the Moulin Rouge where he studied the floor dancers La Goulue, Jane Avril and the rubber-legged Valentin-le-Désossé. Bruant was paid large sums to come down from Montmartre and sing at the Ambassadeurs and the Eldorado music halls on the Boulevards where Lautrec's posters were displayed. Bruant also sang nightly at his own cabaret, now thronged with fashionable folk and dilettanti whom he turned out in a body on one occasion when he noticed Antoine, Carrière and the critic Gustave Geffroy and decided that he would sing for them alone. Steinlen's drawings illustrating the songs sung by Bruant and Yvette Guilbert appeared each week in *Gil Blas Illustré* and were eagerly collected. Forain drew daily in the *Figaro*. Loie Fuller, waving her skirts on sticks in changing limelight, was drawn as a fantastic butterfly by Lautrec. And Antoine still running his realist *Théâtre Libre* produced *Les fossiles* and *L'envers d'une sainte* by François de Curel and Brieux's *Blanchette*.

The Symbolist and Rose-Croix movements were active in anti-realist endeavours. Paul Fort, recently joined by Lugné-Poë at his *Théâtre d'Art*, employed Vuillard to design Laforgue's *Concile féerique*, Maurice Denis to design *Théodat* by Rémy de Gourmont, and *Le chevalier du passé* by Edouard Dujardin, and Sérusier and Bonnard to design other plays. 'Sar' Péladan arranged a *First Rose-Croix Salon* of 'mystic' paintings and a series of Rose-Croix concerts where he was assisted by Erik Satie who was now twenty-six and who had earned his living as a pianist in cafés since we met him as the composer of *Ogives* in 1886. At the same time

[1] Cf. above, p. 104.

141

Péladan published *Comment on devient Mage* and *Comment on devient Fée*; Debussy aged thirty bought Maeterlinck's *Pelléas et Melisande* on the quays and, encouraged by Satie, resolved to set it to music; Rémy de Gourmont published *Le latin mystique* and *Litanie de la rose*; and James Ensor painted the Surrealist *Masques scandalisées* and *Poissardes mélancoliques*. Whistler aged fifty-eight and now a Chevalier of the Legion of Honour (following the acquisition by the Luxembourg of his *Portrait of my Mother*) returned to Paris and was welcomed as the painter of 'mystic' nocturnes by Odilon Redon who had an artists' salon in the Avenue de Wagram and had just produced the lithographs *Songes*, *Les yeux clos* and *Entretien mystique*, and by Mallarmé who read his translation of Whistler's *Ten o'Clock* at one of his Tuesday evenings—*Les mardis de Mallarmé*—in the rue de Rome.

A caricature by Bonnard of this year records the foundation of the group called *The Nabis* to which I have referred in the Introduction to this Act. The drawing shows the Place Clichy, Montmartre, with the Nabis Bonnard, K. X. Roussel and Vuillard in the foreground, and Denis hurrying across the square on some business for the group; behind, in front of the Moulin Rouge, we see the lean long-nosed figure of Lautrec's cousin and inseparable companion Dr. Tapié de Celeyran and Lautrec himself (who though never a Nabi was associated with them). Aristide Maillol, not yet a sculptor but a painter and follower of Gauguin, was soon made a member of this group; other members were Paul Ranson and a Swiss called Félix Vallotton; there were no musician or writer members, but Debussy, like Lautrec, was, as the phrase goes, in the Nabi 'set'. The Nabis soon started a monthly dinner in imitation of the monthly dinners at the Café Riche where the old Impressionists now foregathered. And they held this year their *First Nabi Exhibition*, called *Exposition des peintres Impressionistes et Symbolistes* in the gallery of the dealer Le Barc de Boutteville who secured Lautrec's *Au lit: Le baiser*[1] as a sensational addition. The Nabi group was encouraged by the *Revue Blanche* (founded as noted in 1891 by Thadée Natanson); and Mme Natanson now started a literary and artistic *salon* to assist them. The Nabis were also encouraged as stated by Paul Fort and Lugné-Poë at the *Théâtre d'Art*; and their works were praised by the critics Gustave Geffroy and Félix Fénéon.

The most successful exhibitions in 1892 were a retrospective show of works by Renoir and a show of a hundred pictures by Pissarro, both arranged by Durand-Ruel. But Mirbeau's eulogy of Pissarro's exhibition contained the following sentence: '*On a dit de M. Camille Pissarro comme de M. Claude Monet, qu'ils ne rendaient que les aspects sommaires de la nature et que cela n'était vraiment pas suffisant*'—which makes it clear that the Impressionists had now reached the stage when their admirers felt the need to defend their procedures against new theories in the air. From the standpoint of our history the most important events of the year were the pictures painted by Gauguin in Tahiti and by Cézanne in Provence; the *Eighth Salon des Indépendants* which had The Douanier Rousseau's *Le centenaire de l'Indépendance* (Pl. 34) and a *Seurat Memorial Exhibition* with forty-six works (none of which were sold); the arrival from St. Quentin of Henri Matisse aged twenty-three to study painting under Bouguereau; and the discovery by a new dealer Ambroise Vollard of pictures by Cézanne in old Tanguy's shop.

[1] Le Vésinet. Mme Dortu.

In the next year 1893 Gauguin returned from Tahiti. As he now appeared he was a flamboyant figure. He no longer wore carved sabots and a Brittany fisherman's jersey; but walked the streets instead in a long blue coat fastened with mother-of-pearl clasps, a blue waistcoat with a yellow and green collar, putty-coloured trousers, an astrakhan cap (or sometimes a large felt hat trimmed with a blue ribbon) and white kid gloves; he carried a stick which he had ornamented with 'sculptures barbares' and a large pearl inserted at the top. He had brought with him forty pictures painted in Tahiti and these were exhibited at Durand-Ruel's gallery in November. Neither the public nor the press understood these Tahitian paintings; and the exhibition was a grandiose failure, though Gauguin sold eleven pictures, and some exceptional visitors expressed their admiration—Mallarmé exclaiming: 'C'est extraordinaire qu'on puisse mettre tant de mystère dans tant d'éclat'. Degas visited the exhibition and bought *Hina Tefatou*[1]; when some young people asked Degas to explain the exhibition he referred them to La Fontaine's fable of the well-fed house dog with a collar on his neck and the lean wolf who refused to exchange his freedom for home comforts; 'Voyez-vous?' he said, 'Gauguin c'est le loup.' As Degas was leaving the exhibition Gauguin said: 'Monsieur Degas, vous oubliez votre canne' and handed him a carved stick which was hanging on the wall as an exhibit.

Lautrec's poster *Jane Avril dansant au Jardin de Paris*—black twirling leg, white flounces, yellow petticoat, orange dress, scarlet mouth, orange hair—now appeared on the Boulevards hoardings; and his friend Maurice Joyant arranged a one-man show of his pictures in the Goupil Gallery on the Boulevard Montmartre. This show included *Au Moulin Rouge: Les deux valseuses*,[2] *Jane Avril sortant du Moulin Rouge*[3] and a lithograph *Sarah Bernhardt dans Phèdre*. This show was praised by the critics Gustave Geffroy and Roger Marx and attracted a good deal of attention; but Degas, who lived close to Lautrec at this time, said pointedly to him, 'Ah ça, Lautrec, on voit que vous êtes du bâtiment'. Lautrec also exhibited at the *Ninth Salon des Indépendants* this year where The Douanier Rousseau sent five works (since, apparently, lost) and where the Nabis also sent some pictures. Catalogue entries suggest that a Dane, one Willumsen, made contributions forestalling later developments, for three of them had subtitles which read:

'Ornamental form inspired by chestnut tree in all the force of its luxuriant verdure; ornamentation created by the rain drops on the lake; frame carved to carry on the ornamental form (the contour lines become parallel by degrees with the eternal straight lines of the frame).'

'Ornamental image designed to produce the sensation of pressure in nature—carried through the clouds and the trees on the mountain. The uniform green colour is designed to tie the leaves to the trees and the trees to the forest.'

'(Ceramic.) New-born baby still in its embryonic form.'

The Symbolist and the Rose-Croix movements were mainly conspicuous at the *Théâtre d'Art* where Paul Fort and Lugné-Poë mounted Maeterlinck's *Pelléas et Mélisande* with costumes copied from Memlinc's *St. Ursula*. After this production,

---

[1] New York. Museum of Modern Art (Bliss Collection).
[2] Prague. Museum of Modern Art. [3] London. Samuel Courtauld.

Paul Fort resolved to leave the theatre and devote himself to verse. But Lugné-Poë embarked at once on a new venture, the *Théâtre de l'Œuvre*; for this he recruited Maurice Denis, Vuillard, Bonnard and Ranson as designers; and he gave Ibsen's *Rosmersholm*, designed by Vuillard, as his opening play. 'Sar' Péladan's play *Babylon* was produced in the autumn at the Palais du Champ-de-Mars and Péladan organized a second *Rose-Croix Salon* which contained paintings by Seurat's friend Aman Jean and a portrait of Péladan by the engraver Marcellin Desboutins who had drawn Degas and sat to him for *L'absinthe* and was now seventy and still smoking his pipe at his favourite cafés.

Degas himself, meanwhile, was represented by an exhibition of pastel land-scapes at Durand-Ruel's—his only landscape exhibition and the last public ex-hibition of his works he permitted. His picture *L'absinthe*, just referred to, was on show at the same time in London (where Verlaine was lecturing and Wilde was scoring his first successes with *Lady Windermere's Fan* and *A Woman of No Importance*). *L'absinthe*, painted it will be recalled in 1876, was in the inaugural exhibition of the Grafton Galleries and raised a storm of discussion; Walter Crane described it as 'a study in human degradation, male and female', and Richmond, a Royal Academician, said the picture was 'not painting at all' but merely 'an expression in painting of the deplorable side of modern life'; D. S. Maccoll and George Moore replied in defence of Degas; and the President of the Academy, asked to settle the matter by his opinion, said gravely that to give it in his position 'would be unbecoming'.[1]

While London in 1893 was thus distressed by Degas' Realism of 1876, Antoine had come to the conclusion that Realism in the Paris theatre had run its course and had its day. 'I am beginning to think', he wrote in his diary, 'that artistically we are approaching the end of our tether and that our movement is coming to an end.' He went this year to Berlin to see Hauptmann's *L'Assomption d'Hannele Mattern* and he produced *A bas le progrès* by Edmond de Goncourt, *Le ménage Bresile* by Romain Coolus (then a professor of philosophy at Chartres), *Boubouroche* by Courteline, Björnson's *Une faillite* with programme designed by Lautrec, *Les amants éternels* a parody of Romeo and Juliet (with Lautrec's *La mère Capulet* as part of the scenery), *Les tisserands* by Gerhardt Hauptmann, and *Mlle Julie* by Strindberg who had just had an exhibition of his paintings in Stockholm and was now full of theories for the construction of new theatres with top lighting instead of footlights, and so forth. *Les tisserands*, in which the actor Gemier scored his first success, made a great impression on the socialist Jean Jaurès, who sent word to Antoine that the play *'faisait plus de besogne que toutes les campagnes et les discussions politiques'*. The year's productions, as always, cost more money than they brought in, and Antoine wrote: 'I have put into this work everything I had in me; and my authors and actors have done the same; but I can't get money from the air.'

In this year 1893 Hérédia published *Les trophées*; Anatole France published *La rôtisserie de la reine Pédauque* and Sigmund Freud published *Über den psychischen*

---

[1] *L'absinthe* was owned at this time by a Scottish collector who was so distressed at the idea of possessing 'a study of human degradation male and female' that he sold it to Count Camondo who eventually bequeathed it to the Louvre.

37B. BONNARD
Devant l'omnibus, c. 1894
Paris. M. Félix Fénéon

37A. GAUGUIN
Hina Marouru (Fête à Hina), 1893
Paris. Georges Wildenstein

38. LAUTREC
Oscar Wilde, 1895
Paris. J. Seligmann

Mechanismus hysterischer Phänomene. Joan Miro was born in Barcelona; Georges Rouault aged twenty-two and Henri Matisse aged twenty-four were personal pupils of Gustave Moreau at the Ecole des Beaux-Arts; and Léon Bakst aged twenty-seven came to Paris to paint the triumphal reception of the Russian admiral Avellan (who had just toured the French ports with his squadron as symbol of the Franco-Russian alliance). Bakst, though a Jew, had already succeeded as an artist in St. Petersburg and found a patron in Count Benckendorff who procured him a post as drawing master to the children of the Grand Duke Vladimir Alexandrovitch and then gave him this commission. It was in this year also that Théodore Duret presented El Greco's *Saint François et un novice* to the Louvre which up till then had owned no picture by that master.[1]

In politics the years 1892–1893 were marked by anarchist outrages and the beginning of an anti-Semitic campaign launched by Edouard Drumont who had published *La France juive* in 1886 and now founded a newspaper *La Libre Parole* mainly devoted to fomenting hatred of the Jews.[2] The anarchist outrages began on March 11, 1892, when a bomb exploded in the house of the judge Benoît; on March 14 another exploded at the Lobau barracks; on March 27 a third exploded in the house of the Public Prosecutor Bulot—these crimes being acts of vengeance for the bloodshed at the May Day demonstration of 1891.[3] An episode at the Restaurant Véry, Boulevard de Magenta, took place some weeks later; a waiter at that restaurant had given information to the police which led to the arrest of a journeyman dyer named Ravachol; the day before Ravachol's trial a bomb exploded at the restaurant; Ravachol, convicted for the explosions of March 11 and March 27 (and for three previous murders which came to light in the course of the proceedings), was condemned to death and executed in July; he went to the scaffold singing:

> *Pour être heureux, nom de Dieu,*
> *Il faut pendre les propriétaires.*
> *Pour être heureux, nom de Dieu,*
> *Il faut couper les curés en deux.*

The anarchist paper *L'En-dehors* applauded the outrages; and Ravachol was made into a political martyr—(though the death sentence was for the earlier non-political murders—the bombs having caused no loss of life).[4]

In 1893 there were students' riots in the Quartier Latin (in which a number of people were hurt and one man killed) because the police had arrested two girl

---

[1] The Louvre acquired a second picture by El Greco, *Saint Louis Roi de France accompagné d'un page* in 1903 and a third *Le Christ en croix adoré par les frères Diego et Antonio Covarrubias* in 1908.

[2] Cf. above, p. 91.　　　　　　　　　　　　　　　　[3] Cf. above, p. 106.

[4] After Ravachol's execution the working-class quarters were placarded with a new *Carmagnole* known as *La Ravachole* which began as follows:

> *Dans la grand' ville de Paris,*
> *Il y a des bourgeois bien nourris;*
> *Il y a aussi des miséreux*
> *Qui ont le ventre bien creux.*
> *Ceux-là ont les dents longues—*
> *Vive donc le son, vive le son,*

models at the 'Quatre Arts' ball on the ground that their costumes were indecorous or insufficient. Anarchists were said to have fomented these Quartier Latin riots, and there were anarchist outrages all the year. In April de Goncourt wrote in his journal: 'I have just found in my letter-box a circular on red paper headed *Manifeste des Dynamiteurs*; this clamours for a great work of liberation founded on quivering flesh (*chairs pantelantes*) and scattered brains (*cervelles éparses*); it predicts more explosions and declares that bourgeois society must disappear even if cities are reduced to ashes in the process.' In August an anarchist cabman named Charles Moore shot at an ex-minister because, he said, he had not answered the letters he had written him. In November there was *L'Affaire Leauthier* when a crazy shoe-maker dined sumptuously at Marguery's famous restaurant, refused to pay the bill on the ground that the '*sales bourgeois*' had taken all his money, and then walked to the Avenue de l'Opéra where he stabbed the Serbian Minister 'because', he said, 'he was well dressed and wore a decoration'. In December there was *L'Affaire Vaillant* when a harmless bomb exploded in the Chamber of Deputies; Vaillant, known to the police as a half-witted fanatic, had been approached by *agents-provocateurs* who had supplied him with the bomb; when this circumstance was discovered prominent men of all parties demanded a pardon, but Sadi Carnot, the President of the Republic, advised by Casimir-Perrier, the Prime Minister, refused it—a refusal which may have caused Carnot's death next year.[1]

The Panama Scandal began in 1892 and continued through 1893. Ferdinand de Lesseps, engineer of the canal (and formerly engineer of the Suez Canal), his son Charles de Lesseps, Gustave Eiffel the contractor, the financiers Baron Jacques de Reinach and Emile Arton, a journalist named Cornelius Herz, and others, were accused of maladministration and corruption. At the inquiry prominent statesmen were shown to have received large sums from the company's funds; and Clémen-ceau lost his seat as a Deputy and was reduced to selling his collection of pictures by Monet, Pissarro and other Impressionists, as the result of wild charges brought against him in this connection by Déroulède and others of the Extreme Right Wing.

> Ceux-là ont les dents longues,
> > Vive le son de l'explosion!
> Chorus
> Dansons la Ravachole,
> > Vive le son, vive le son,
> Dansons la Ravachole,
> > Vive le son de l'explosion!
> Ah, ça ira, ça ira, ça ira,
> > Tous les bourgeois gout'ront de la bombe!
> Ah, ça ira, ça ira, ça ira,
> > Tous les bourgeois on les sautera.

[1] Cf. below, p. 152.

ACT II: HOW IT HAPPENED

SCENE II: 1894-1895

From the reunions in Gauguin's studio, the end of the *Théâtre Libre*, the murder of President Carnot, the *Procès des Trente* and the beginning of the *Affaire Dreyfus*; to Gauguin's second sale and second departure for Tahiti, Cézanne's *Portrait de Gustave Geffroy* and first exhibition at Vollard's, and the dispute about the Caillebotte Bequest

In 1894 Gauguin had a studio in the rue Vercingétorix hard by the humble lodgings of The Douanier Rousseau; and it was possibly at this time that Gauguin played the trick already recorded in my notes on The Douanier's life.[1] In this studio Gauguin entertained among other friends—de Rotonchamp and Charles Morice, later his biographers, the devoted de Monfreid, Strindberg, Mallarmé (who retired this year with a pension after thirty years as a schoolmaster), Odilon Redon, Aristide Maillol (who was now designing tapestry) and Paco Durio a Spanish ceramist, later a friend of Picasso. We know the appearance of this studio from accounts written by several of these visitors. The walls, painted chrome yellow, were hung with knobkerries, boomerangs and hatchets in red, yellow and black woods; the windows and the panels of the door were painted with Tahitian subjects in imitation of stained glass, the doorway was inscribed *Te Faruru* (*Ici l'on aime*), the mantelpiece was laden with shells and crystals, and the furniture included an enormous camera on a stand; Gauguin's paintings were displayed on easels; a Javanese girl called Anna was installed as hostess; and a monkey sprang about the floor.

Quite other interiors could be visited by an artist or a dilettante at this moment. In the rue du Bac there was Whistler's apartment—blue front door leading to a blue and white panelled room with pale blue ceiling, shelves lined with blue and white china and dark blue matting on the floor; elsewhere the veteran de Goncourt was surrounded with eighteenth-century pictures, ormolu, and silver, and tapestries by Boucher; and elsewhere again, the veteran dramatist Henry Becque dined in a room with nothing but his bust by Rodin, a trestle table of white wood, and a few white wood chairs—a simplicity then regarded as eccentrically austere.

The Nabis—Maurice Denis, Vuillard, Bonnard, Maillol and the others—continued to attract attention by exhibitions of their paintings. All worked for the

[1] Cf. above, p. 120.

147

Théâtre de l'Œuvre where Lugné-Poë employed Vuillard to design Ibsen's *Le maître constructeur*, Lautrec to design an Oriental scene for *Le chariot de terre cuite* by Victor Barrucaud, and the English painter Burne-Jones then aged sixty-one to design the costumes for *La belle au bois dormant* by Robert d'Humières and Henri Bataille then aged twenty-two. The Nabis also made drawings and posters for the *Revue Blanche*, of which Tristan Bernard was now *directeur sportif* with Félix Fénéon as chief art critic and Léon Blum, Marcel Proust and Alfred Jarry among the literary contributors. Jarry (whom we have met in 1888 as a schoolboy writing a first version of *Ubu Roi* as a marionette play), was now twenty-one and mainly employed as a journalist with Rémy de Gourmont on *L'Imagier* and with Vallette and Mme Rachilde on the *Mercure de France*; Mme Rachilde, intrigued by his misogyny, his courage, his fantastic wit, his pockets stuffed with books, and his passion for bicycling, had been quick to perceive his talents and she had captured his respect on his first visit to her house by ignoring his rudeness and making him wind wool for her knitting. Jarry was painted this year by The Douanier Rousseau who portrayed him with a parrot and a chameleon in a picture that was later damaged and has since, I believe, disappeared.[1]

The season was disastrous for Antoine's *Théâtre Libre* and saw him temporarily defeated. He staged *L'Assomption de Hannele Mattern* by Gerhardt Hauptmann, *Le missionnaire* by Marcel Luguet and *Une journée parlementaire*, his first political play, by Maurice Barrès (which he had accepted against his inclination because he had been asked to do so by Mme de Loynes). *Le missionnaire* was his last production at the *Théâtre Libre*; in June he handed over to one Larochelle and then took his actors on a continental tour; at the end of the year he found himself and his actors, abandoned by his impresario, in Rome; and he wrote in his diary: 'Thus ends the odyssey of the *Théâtre Libre*. Seven years ago I left my attic in the rue de Dunkerque with forty sous in my pocket to rehearse our first show at the little wine shop in the rue des Abbesses. Now I am in Rome with about the same sum in my purse, with fifteen comrades in the same condition, and a hundred thousand francs of debts awaiting me in Paris. I have no idea what we shall do to-morrow.' [2]

In this year 1894 the Comédie Française produced *Les Romanesques* by the new poet Edmond Rostand aged twenty-six; Rouault and Matisse were joined by Henri Manguin aged twenty and Albert Marquet aged nineteen in Gustave Moreau's studio; Whistler was represented in the *Salon de la Nationale* by his portrait of Comte Robert de Montesquiou (already referred to in connection with Huysmans' *A Rebours*)[3]; and Marcel Proust studying de Montesquiou for certain aspects of what was later to be 'M. de Charlus' was so engrossed with him that he acquired unconsciously his tricks of gait and speech. The new books were Karl Marx's *Das Kapital*, Vol. III (posthumous), Zola's *Lourdes*, Anatole France's *Lys rouge*, Verlaine's *Dans les limbes*, Maeterlinck's *Trois petites drames pour Marionnettes* (*Alladines et Palomides*, *Intérieur*, *La mort de Tintagiles*), D'Annunzio's *Trionfo della*

---

[1] Cf. below, pp. 181, 215.

[2] Larochelle continued the *Théâtre Libre* with little success till it came to an end in 1896. For Antoine's subsequent action cf. below, pp. 156, 188, 215.

[3] Cf. above, p. 72.

39B. THE DOUANIER ROUSSEAU
La femme de l'artiste, c. 1895
Paris. Baron Napoléon Gourgaud

39A. LAUTREC
May Belfort en rose, 1895
New York. Museum of Modern Art (Bliss)

40B. THE DOUANIER ROUSSEAU

L'enfant au jouet, c. 1902

Switzerland, Private Collection

40A. PICASSO

La fillette aux pieds nus, 1895

morte, George Moore's *Esther Waters*, and Péladan's *Comment on devient artiste*. The humorous journal *Le Rire* began publication and printed Lautrec's drawing of a new music-hall performer Mlle Polaire in an early issue. Lautrec produced his album of lithographs of Yvette Guilbert with text by the critic Geffroy, and Clémenceau writing in *La Justice* described it as a social document; Tanguy died, and when his pictures were sold six landscapes by Cézanne brought a total of eight hundred francs, and a picture by Seurat was knocked down for fifty; and Caillebotte died and embarrassed the Beaux-Arts officials by the bequest of his Impressionist collection to the Luxembourg.

In the next year 1895 the Beaux-Arts officials wrangled with Caillebotte's executors for six months. Caillebotte's will made in 1876 contained the following clause: 'I bequeath to the State the pictures of which I die possessed; but as I want this gift to be accepted, and accepted in such a way that these pictures will be placed neither in a storehouse nor in a provincial museum, but directly in the Luxembourg, and later on in the Louvre, it is necessary that a certain time be allowed to elapse before this clause is executed; that is, until the public is ready— I do not say to understand—but to acknowledge this kind of painting. This period will be at most twenty years; in the interim my brother Martial, or in his default another of my heirs, will keep them. I beg Renoir to act as my testamentary executor and to accept a picture which he will choose himself; my heirs will insist that he select an important one.'[1] The collection consisted of sixty-five pictures, including three by Manet, sixteen by Monet, nine by Sisley, eighteen by Pissarro, eight by Renoir, two by Cézanne and seven (small pastels) by Degas. The officials of the Beaux-Arts, led by the director Roujon and Léonce Bénédite, wanted to decline the bequest; and they were determined—even if they accepted it—to keep the pictures from the Luxembourg and to disperse them in various less accessible museums outside Paris. In this attitude they were supported by the artists of the official *Salons*. Gérôme, for example, said in an interview published by the *Journal des artistes*: 'Only great moral depravity could bring the State to accept such rubbish. . . . These artists are all Anarchists and madmen.' In the end the Beaux-Arts accepted forty out of the sixty-five pictures for the Luxembourg; and rejected eight pictures by Monet, one by Manet, two by Renoir, three by Sisley and eleven by Pissarro.[2]

In the spring of this year 1895 Gauguin arranged a sale of his pictures at the Hôtel Drouot to raise funds for returning to Tahiti. At this sale Degas, who already

[1] Translation from Mack: *Paul Cézanne*.

[2] Cézanne's biographers habitually state that two or three pictures by Cézanne were rejected. G. Mack in his *Paul Cézanne* shows that two pictures by Cézanne were in fact accepted and none rejected. Mack adds: 'Between 1896 and 1908 Monsieur Martial Caillebotte, animated by a most commendable public spirit and an earnest desire to carry out the original provisions of his brother's testament, made repeated efforts to persuade the Luxembourg to admit the twenty-five rejected canvases. But his overtures met with an obstinate refusal, and after twelve years of futile struggle his patience was exhausted. He exacted a promise from his wife and daughter that after his death they would have no dealings with the State museums. That promise has been kept.' The Caillebotte Bequest pictures are now in a well-lit gallery in the Louvre where they were installed with the Moreau Nélaton Bequest in 1928. For an attack upon them when they were first exhibited in the Luxembourg, cf. p. 155.

owned *Hina Tejatou*[1] and *La belle Angèle*,[2] bought *Vahine no te vi*[3] (Femme au fruit) and Gauguin's copy of Manet's *Olympia*; and Schuffenecker bought two Tahitian pictures and the Brittany pictures *Bonjour, Monsieur Gauguin*.[4] The catalogue of the sale contained an exchange of letters between Strindberg and Gauguin which greatly puzzled the visitors; Strindberg's letter began: 'I cannot grasp your art and I cannot like it. I cannot get contact with it because in its present form it is exclusively Tahitian. . . . I have been pursued in my dreams at night by the sun-filled pictures that I saw in your studio—by the trees unknown to botanists, the humans of your own creation, the seas surely born of volcanoes, the skies in which no God could live. You have created a new earth and a new heaven. But I who love chiaroscuro am not happy in your sun-flooded world; and the Eve who inhabits your paradise is not my ideal. . . . I know that this confession will neither astonish nor wound you—for you seem to draw strength from the hatred of others. Your personality, jealous of its integrity, rejoices in the antipathy it excites. And perhaps rightly—because were you to be approved of and admired and followed by partisans, you would be classed and labelled, and within five years the young would use the label to denote an obsolete phase of art destined to be superseded by their own achievements.' Gauguin's rejoinder said: 'I conceived the idea of inviting you to write the preface to my catalogue when I watched your blue Northern eye examining my pictures while you played the guitar and sang in my studio. I asked you because I was conscious then of the clash between your civilization, which makes you suffer, and my barbarism which keeps me young. The Eve of your civilized conception makes you and makes most of us misogynists. . . . The ancient Eve who terrifies you in my studio, is the only Eve who can logically remain naked before our eyes. Your Eve cannot walk naked without immodesty—she is perhaps too beautiful. . . . ' The sale took place in February and excited relatively little interest (because it contained for the most part the pictures shown in 1893). In March Gauguin left Paris for ever.

A *Cézanne Exhibition* with pictures of all periods from 1868–1894 which took place in November roused heated controversy and discussions. Cézanne at this time was fifty-six; and his work, scarcely seen in Paris for eighteen years, was scarcely remembered by anyone except Renoir, Monet, Pissarro, Gauguin and the Nabis who had heard of it from Gauguin and from Emile Bernard (who had discovered it at Tanguy's in 1886). The exhibition was staged by the new dealer Ambroise Vollard in his shop in the rue Laffitte. It was partly a *succès de scandale* and partly a genuine success. *Salon* painters came and commented in contemptuous anger; Gérôme, who, as just recorded, still regarded even Impressionist painting as the work of 'anarchists and madmen', said in Vollard's hearing, 'Time will avenge those who try to paint without spending time upon their work.' Puvis de Chavannes walked round and treated Cézanne's pictures as he had treated Seurat's *Cirque*.[5] But Auguste Pellerin came and began his collection. Count Camondo bought several pictures and advised King Milan of Serbia to do the same; on leaving

[1] New York. Museum of Modern Art (Bliss Collection).
[2] Paris. Louvre.
[3] Paris. Paul Rosenberg.
[4] Prague. Museum of Modern Art.
[5] Cf. above, p. 106.

the gallery King Milan said to Vollard, '*Pourquoi ne conseillez-vous pas à votre Cézanne de peindre plutôt de jolies petites femmes?*' The more competent press critics wrote appreciations; Gustave Geffroy, of whom Cézanne had just painted the great portrait (Pl. 44A) wrote, as Zola had written of Manet's works in 1866, that the day would surely come when the Louvre would be happy to own and exhibit these pictures. But the *Journal des Artistes*, representing the artists of the official *Salon*, described the exhibition as a nightmare show of atrocities '*dépassant la mesure des fumisteries légalement autorisées*', and advised its female readers to keep away from it if they would avoid embarrassment.[1]

In this year 1895 the first cinema opened on the Boulevard des Capucines; Pablo Picasso aged fourteen painted *La fillette aux pieds nus* (Pl. 40A) at Corunna; Matisse, Rouault, Manguin and Marquet were joined by Charles Guerin and by Charles Camoin (later to be Cézanne's friend) in Gustave Moreau's studio; and Rouault's *Christ mort pleuré par les saintes femmes*[2] was submitted for and failed to win a Prix de Rome. Maurice de Vlaminck aged nineteen was now painting his first landscape under an academic painter at Chatou, staring at pictures by the Nabis in Le Barc de Boutteville's shop window on occasional visits to Paris, competing as a racing cyclist at the Vélodrome Buffalo, and earning his living by playing the fiddle in café orchestras; Tristan Bernard in bowler hat and knickerbockers was painted by Lautrec against a background of the Vélodrome Buffalo;[3] Whistler appeared as defendant in the French courts in the 'Baronet and the Butterfly' dispute; Burne-Jones exhibited *Love among the Ruins* at the *Salon de la Nationale* and Octave Mirbeau wrote in *Le Journal*: '*Il raconte à ses familiers: "Moi, je ne suis pas un Anglais, je suis un Italien du XVe siècle!" Pas Anglais, lui! Pauvre petit! C'est-à-dire qu'il résume à soi seul toute l'Angleterre burlesque! Pas Anglais! Mais ce n'est pas Burne-Jones qu'il devrait s'appeler, c'est Bull-John!*' Monet had a successful show of his Rouen Cathedral pictures; Berthe Morisot died at the age of fifty-four; Sisley aged fifty-five applied for naturalization as a Frenchman but remained in fact English, as the application was refused on technical grounds; Rodin's group *Les bourgeois de Calais* was formally installed in Calais on the Place d'Armes; Maurice Donnay's *Amants* was produced at the Renaissance; Verdi's *Falstaff* was performed at the Opéra Comique, with Verdi himself aged eighty present at the performance; Sarah Bernhardt, Lucien Guitry and de Max played together in Rostand's *La princesse lointaine*; Anatole France published *Le jardin d'Epicure*, Pierre Loti published *Jérusalem* and *Le désert* and Péladan *Les XI chapitres mystérieux du Septer Bereschit du Kaldéen Moscho*; and Verlaine—now fifty-two, lame, miserably diseased, and living with a plebeian woman in wretched rooms where he painted his furniture, pipes and bibelots with penny bottles of gold paint—was elected *Prince des Poètes* in succession to Lecomte de Lisle.

There were contacts at this time between certain English and French artists. Whistler moved to and fro between Chelsea and the rue du Bac. Sir William— then 'Will'—Rothenstein was often in Paris where he knew Degas, Lautrec,

---

[1] For the present distribution of some pictures shown in this exhibition cf. my Bibliographical and Catalogue Notes in Appendix I.

[2] Grenoble: Museum. [3] Paris. Tristan Bernard.

Verlaine, Mallarmé and many others as related in his 'Men and Memories'. Sickert and Beardsley were often with J. E. Blanche and Degas at Dieppe; and Burne-Jones, as chronicled, exhibited in Paris and designed a play for the *Théâtre de l'Œuvre*. Lautrec went in April 1895 to London, where he met Wilde, was impressed with his courage, and made from memory the drawing *Oscar Wilde* (Pl. 38); and Alphonse Daudet wrote from London to de Goncourt of Wilde's sufferings when he was released on bail before the final trial and driven from hotels and threatened with violence from roughs said to have been hired by the Marquis of Queensberry. Lugné-Poë now took his company to London where they played Ibsen's *Rosmersholm* and *Le maître constructeur* and Maeterlinck's *L'Intruse* and *Pelléas et Mélisande*, and Bernard Shaw wrote of these performances in the *Saturday Review* (then edited by Frank Harris), his notice of *Rosmersholm* beginning: 'The library of Pastor Rosmer got on my nerves a little. What on earth did he want, for instance, with *Sell's World Press*? That he should have provided himself with a volume of my own dramatic works I thought right and natural enough, though when he took that particular volume down and opened it, I began to speculate rather uneasily on the chances of his presently becoming so absorbed as to forget all about his part. . . .'

Anarchist outrages, the assassination of President Carnot, the *Procès des Trente* and the first phase of the *Affaire Dreyfus* were the political sensations of these two years. On February 12, 1894, a bomb was thrown at the Café Terminus, near the Gare St. Lazare, by one Emile Henry, a middle-class well-educated journalist who had worked with a clockmaker to study the mechanism of bombs. On February 19 there were bomb explosions in the Faubourg St. Martin and the rue St. Jacques presumed to be the work of a Belgian anarchist named Pauwels. On February 26 de Goncourt records a condition of panic: buildings in which magistrates had apartments were fitted, he tells us, with special interior front doors only opened by a porter. On March 13 there was an explosion in the Eglise de La Madeleine; when the police went in they found, de Goncourt tells us, the mutilated body of Pauwels—'*la figure exsangué pareille à une figure de cire, le bas du corps une bouillie sur laquelle se répandaient ses entrailles.*' On April 4 a bomb exploded at the Café Foyot injuring Laurent Tailhade who had said of a previous outrage, '*qu'importent les victimes si le geste est beau.*' On June 24 President Carnot was assassinated at Lyons; the assassin was an Italian youth of twenty—and his act was interpreted as revenge for the execution of Vaillant the year before.[1]

After the assassination of Carnot the Government passed an emergency law forbidding anarchist propaganda in any shape or form and started proceedings against thirty writers and propagandists, including the painter Maximilien Luce, one of Seurat's followers, Laurent Tailhade, and Félix Fénéon who had contributed to the anarchist papers *L'En dehors* and *Le Père Pennard*. At the trial, known as the *Procès des Trente*, the prisoners were charged with '*association de malfaiteurs*'; the judge said to Fénéon, '*On vous a vu causer avec an anarchiste derrière un bec de gaz*'; and Fénéon answered, '*Pouvez-vous me dire, mon Président, ce que c'est que le derrière d'un bec de gaz?*' In the end Fénéon and most of the others were acquitted. But

[1] Cf. above, p. 146.

Luce and Tailhade were condemned to imprisonment, the latter for an article against the Czar of Russia. This prosecution which roused great indignation in artistic and literary circles in Paris at the time was really the result of a good deal of muddleheaded flirtation with the anarchists by the more adventurous artists and critics. The anarchists declared themselves admirers of all 'advanced' forms of art, because they looked upon them as gestures of defiance against established dogmas—(the anarchist Emile Henry, for example, stated at his trial that he had intended to throw his bomb at the Café Américain, but perceiving Antoine and Catulle Mendès sitting at a table he had gone on and thrown it at the Café Terminus instead). The critics on their side drew parallels between the unfair treatment of adventurous art by the official art world and the Government's use of *agents-provocateurs* against anarchists like Vaillant; and they made it a form of snobbism to concoct excuses for the anarchists.

The *Affaire Dreyfus* began in October 1894. One Colonel Henry betrayed to Edouard Drumont (editor of the anti-Semitic *La Libre Parole*) the official secret that a Jew, Captain Dreyfus, was under arrest in a military prison on a charge of communicating secrets to a foreign power. Drumont published the information, adding the lie that Dreyfus had confessed. The Right Wing press joined *La Libre Parole* in calling for instant vengeance; General Mercier, the Minister of War, ordered a prosecution; on December 22 Captain Dreyfus was condemned to public degradation and imprisonment on the Ile du Diable for the remainder of his life; and he was publicly degraded on January 5, 1895.

ACT II: HOW IT HAPPENED

SCENE III: 1896-1897

From Matisse's début at the *Salon de la Nationale* and the production of Jarry's *Ubu Roi* to The Douanier's *Bohémienne endormie* and Gauguin's *D'où venons-nous? Que sommes-nous? Où allons-nous?*

In 1896 Henri Matisse aged twenty-seven sent four pictures—two titled *Nature morte*, an *Intérieur* and a picture called *Liseuse*—to the *Salon de la Nationale*. These works, influenced by Chardin and Corot, as I have chronicled, were well received by the artists of the Nationale and their public. Picasso now fifteen won a scholarship at the Fine Arts Academy in Madrid; Pierre Bonnard now twenty-nine exhibited *Du vent dans la rue*[1] and *Devant l'omnibus* (Pl. 37B) with other paintings and some lithographs in a one-man show arranged by Durand-Ruel; and a show of paintings by Van Gogh—the first since the Memorial Exhibition in the *Salon des Indépendants* of 1891—was arranged by Lugné-Poë at the *Théâtre de l'Œuvre*. Lugné-Poë produced Wilde's *Salome*—with Lautrec's drawing of Wilde (Pl. 38) as a cover to the programme—and Ibsen's *Peer Gynt*. The *Saturday Review* sent Bernard Shaw to Paris to report on the Ibsen production, and Shaw predicted in his notice that 'The witches in "Macbeth", the ghost in "Hamlet", the statue in "Don Juan", and Mephistopheles, will not be more familiar to the twentieth century than the Boyg, the Button Moulder, the Strange Passenger and the Lean Person.'

After *Peer Gynt* Lugné-Poë produced the terrific fantasia *Ubu Roi* by Alfred Jarry. Maurice Denis took a part in the staging of the play but Jarry himself planned the scenery, costumes and masks. The scenery was conventional; changes of scene were announced by cardboard notices; Ubu hung a cardboard horse's head around his neck to symbolize the mounting of his charger—*le cheval à phynances*; a single soldier symbolized his army, etc. etc. Jarry had made drawings for Ubu which resemble the monstrous figure in the foreground of Ensor's *L'entrée du Christ à Bruxelles en 1889*. The music was written by Claude Terrasse (Pierre Bonnard's brother-in-law). Before the first performance Jarry explained that the piece would be played by actors wearing masks and moving as marionettes, and that the scene was laid '*en Pologne, c'est-à-dire nulle part*'. The play began with what we should to-day call Dada or Neo-Surrealist shock tactics. The monster Ubu,

[1] Paris. Félix Fénéon.

154

symbol of all swollen-bellied idiotic bullies and humbugs, flung forth in a voice of thunder the distorted word '*M—drre*'. The boos, hisses and catcalls at this opening lasted, Mme Rachilde tells us, a quarter of an hour, but the play went on, with other interruptions, to the end. Next day the critics spoke of Ubu as a terrifying and unforgettable figure: '*Le Père Ubu existe*', Mendès wrote. '*Il deviendra une légende populaire des instincts vils, affamés et immondes. . . .*'

In this same year Octave Mirbeau bought a candlestick at the William Morris shop in London and had his money refused by Morris because he had written against Burne-Jones. Marcel Proust aged twenty-five published his first book *Les plaisirs et les jours* with a preface by Anatole France and illustrations by a fashionable flower painter called Madeleine Lemaire whose house, for some reason I have not discovered, had been wrecked by anarchists. Bergson published *Matière et mémoire*. Edmond de Goncourt died at seventy-four; Morris died at sixty-two; and Verlaine died at fifty-two.[1]

In the next year 1897 the *Thirteenth Salon des Indépendants* had The Douanier Rousseau's full length portrait *Mlle M. . . .* (later bought by Picasso) and his great picture *La bohémienne endormie* (Pl. 42); Pissarro went to London for Queen Victoria's Jubilee and painted *La fête du Jubilée à Bedford Park*;[2] and Rodin published a portfolio with reproductions of a hundred of his drawings; Matisse again exhibited at the *Salon de la Nationale* and was made an Associate at the instance of Puvis de Chavannes now seventy-three. At the same time Matisse's master Gustave Moreau died, and by his will his house and pictures were bequeathed to the nation as the Musée Moreau and his pupil Rouault was appointed the curator. In the spring the pictures finally accepted by the state from Caillebotte's collection were exhibited in the Luxembourg, and Senator Hervé de Soisy attacked them as a '*misérable collection*' representing '*sous les aspects les moins attractifs un art absolument en décadence et dans lequel nos jeunes élèves ne peuvent trouver aucune étincelle du feu sacré qui doit éclairer leur carrière*'. Pierre Bonnard and some of his group were now taken up by the dealer Vollard who made his gallery a rendez-vous for the artists whose works he dealt in, as Théo Van Gogh had made the Goupil Gallery a rendez-vous some ten years earlier. A caricature by Bonnard of this date shows Vollard's gallery full of unframed pictures stacked against the walls and scattered on the floor, Pissarro, Renoir and Degas examining them, Bonnard himself

---

[1] Verlaine, the doctors certified, had been destroyed by diabetes, syphilis, hypertrophy of the heart, cirrhosis of the liver and ankylosis of the knee. When he was lying dead the visitors included Comte Robert de Montesquiou and his secretary; on the mantelpiece Verlaine had left a row of gilded pipes and bibelots with oranges placed symmetrically between; the Count's secretary absentmindedly took one of the oranges from the mantelpiece, ate it, and threw the skin beneath the bed. The pall bearers at the funeral were François Coppée, Catulle Mendès, Edmond Lepelletier, Robert de Montesquiou, and Roujon representing the Beaux-Arts; halfway to the Batignolles cemetery Coppée gave up his place to Mallarmé, and de Montesquiou gave his to Maurice Barrès; when the procession reached the Avenue de Clichy it was held up for a moment and Mendès bought an evening paper which he read with attention—still holding the pall cordon with one hand—'*un menu fait, attribuable sans doute à une simple distraction, qui produisit l'impression la plus fâcheuse*'. Funeral orations were pronounced at the graveside by Coppée, Mendès, Mallarmé, Lepelletier, Barrès, Moréas and Gustave Kahn. (Cazals et Le Rouge, *Les derniers jours de Paul Verlaine*.)   [2] London. G. C. Bensusan-Butt.

arriving with his latest works, and Vollard in the centre with one of Cézanne's *Baigneurs* in his hand. Theatre goers had an entertaining year. Lugné-Poë started the *Théâtre des Pantins*, with marionettes made by Bonnard, as an adjunct to the *Théâtre de l'Œuvre*; Brieux's *Les trois filles de Monsieur Dupont* was produced at the Gymnase; the Grand Guignol theatre began its series of four thousand one-act 'thrillers'; Sarah Bernhardt played in Rostand's *La Samaritaine*; Coquelin played in Rostand's *Cyrano de Bergerac*; and Antoine started the second phase of his career with the *Théâtre Antoine* in the *Salle des Menus Plaisirs*. The new books included *Ramuntcho* by Pierre Loti, *Le mannequin d'osier* and *L'orme du mail* by Anatole France, and *Les chevaux de Diomède* by Rémy de Gourmont. Oscar Wilde, released from prison and living at Berneval near Dieppe as 'Sebastien Melmoth' was offered a contract by *Le Journal* to write literary articles, which he refused because he was unwilling to exploit the notoriety now attaching to his name; 'Will' Rothenstein tells us that in a letter to him Wilde said: 'There is no one in this little inn but myself . . . and the chef is an artist of great distinction; he walks in the evening by the sea to get ideas for the next day. Is it not sweet of him? . . . I hope to work again and write plays or something . . . I am not really ashamed of having been in prison; I often was in more shameful places; but I am really ashamed of having led a life unworthy of an artist. . . .' I must chronicle one other happening of this year—an episode related by Paul Leclercq the novelist, who was sitting to Lautrec for his portrait; after some hours' work one day Lautrec said to him, 'Petit gentleman, take your hat and coat and we will go and call on her'. 'Call on whom?' said Leclercq; '*Mystère*,' answered Lautrec and took him for a long drive to a house in a poor quarter on the outskirts of Paris where they went up to a room on the sixth floor and found a little old woman seated by a stove; and then Lautrec turned to Leclercq and said 'Allow me to introduce you to the original of *L'Olympia* by Manet'.

Gauguin meanwhile, forgotten in Tahiti, was ill, short of money, and chagrined that Degas did not trouble to reply to his letters. Charles Morice aware of these distresses called upon Roujon, still Director of the Beaux-Arts, and asked him to give Gauguin a commission for some decorative work; Roujon banged his fists on the arms of his chair and answered 'Never! While I am director M. Gauguin shall *never* have a state commission'; he was none the less persuaded to 'do something'; and after some delay he sent 200 francs *à titre d'encouragement* to Gauguin. When the money reached Gauguin he sent it back. 'I have struggled all my life outside the official world,' he wrote to de Monfreid. 'I have made continuous sacrifices to preserve my dignity. I have never begged from the state. All my efforts would lose their significance were I now to begin to beg.' Gauguin wrote this in 1896. At the end of 1897 he completed his largest painting *D'où venons-nous? Que sommes-nous? Où allons-nous?* (Pl. 41) while nerving himself for an attempt at suicide. Parisians knew nothing of this. But his existence was recalled to them by the publication at this moment, in the *Revue Blanche*, of parts of 'Noa Noa' (his account, written with Charles Morice, of his first expedition to Tahiti); Charles Morice, who arranged this publication, also projected a *Noa Noa* ballet and discussed it with Antoine; but nothing came of the idea.

41 · GAUGUIN

D'où venons-nous? Que sommes-nous? Où allons-nous? 1897

Boston. Museum of Fine Arts

42. THE DOUANIER ROUSSEAU
La bohémienne endormie, 1897
N. York M. 6 M. I. Art

In politics in these two years Extremists on both wings became increasingly embarrassing to the central Liberals Millerand and Bourgeois, who were working for progress by co-operation and reforms by constitutional procedures. On the left wing the Marxian Socialists adopted Eugène Pottier's *L'Internationale* as the official Worker's War Song in 1896, and on the right wing a new group calling themselves *Socialistes Chrétiens*, with the anti-Semite Drumont as their president, put forward a programme that we should now describe as Fascist. In this year also the Czar Nicholas of Russia paid a ceremonial visit to Paris; the first aeroplane *L'Avion* flew three hundred metres; and an Italian force was defeated and massacred at Adowa by the Abyssinians. The *Affaire Dreyfus* now assumed its second phase. Colonel Picquart, chief of the secret police, found a *petit-bleu* directed to one Major Esterhazy by the German attaché and letters by Esterhazy in writing identical with that of the *bordereau* on which Dreyfus had been condemned; when he brought these facts to the notice of the commander-in-chief he was transferred to Africa 'on a mission'; at the same time and quite independently a banker named Castro, examining a facsimile of the *bordereau* published in the press, recognized the handwriting as that of Esterhazy which he chanced to know; and Castro passed this information to Captain Dreyfus' brother Mathieu Dreyfus who began to work for a revision of the sentence. In 1897 Zola, who was in the confidence of Mathieu Dreyfus, published a series of articles called *La verité en marche* in the *Figaro*; and thereafter all France was divided into Revisionists and anti-Revisionists. The division cut across all groups and friendships. Its effect at the monthly dinners of the old Impressionists at the Café Riche was typical; Monet at once joined his old friend Zola as a Dreyfusard; Degas, who made his servant read *La Libre Parole* to him each day while he ate his luncheon, was furious with Zola (whom he had always disliked) and refused to speak to Monet; Cézanne was anti-Dreyfusard; Renoir contrived to be non-committal; Pissarro, now sixty-seven, a patriarchal Rabbinic figure with a long grey beard, took refuge in the thought that he was not only an old Jew but also an old artist: '*Toutes les tristesses*', he wrote to his son, '*toutes les amertumes, toutes les douleurs, je les oublie et même je les ignore dans la joie de travailler*'; and taking various rooms in Paris he worked on the series of bird's-eye views of street scenes on which I have commented in the Introduction to this Act.[1]

[1] Cf. above, p. 136.

ACT II: HOW IT HAPPENED

SCENE IV: 1898-1900

From Lautrec's London exhibition and Zola's *J'accuse*; to the
Exposition Universelle, the *Revue Blanche* Seurat exhibition, and
Picasso's first visit to Paris

In May 1898 Lautrec went to London to arrange an exhibition of his pictures at the Goupil Gallery. This show contained sixty paintings and some twenty drawings and lithographs—a representative collection of his life's work to that date. The catalogue (kindly lent me by Mrs. Marchant of the Goupil Gallery) records *Au bal du Moulin de la Galette* (Pl. 32B), most of the *Moulin Rouge* pictures, *May Belfort en rose* (Pl. 39A), *May Belfort chantant 'Daddy wouldn't buy me a Bow-Wow'*, *May Milton*, *Berthe Bady*, *La Clownesse Cha-u-Kao*, *Paul Leclercq*, *Désiré Dihau*, *Cipa Godebski*, *Henri Dihau*, *M. Boileau au Café*, *Jane Avril quittant le Moulin Rouge*, *Jane Avril dansant*, *Alfred la Guigne*, and others since equally famous.[1] The English dilettanti showed no desire to acquire these pictures and none were sold. The English art critics were more discerning. There were a few perfunctory condemnations; the *Daily Chronicle* wrote, 'M. de Toulouse-Lautrec has only one idea in his head—vulgarity'; and the *Lady's Pictorial*, which ignored the exhibition till it was replaced by a collection of works by Daubigny and Corot, said, 'The Lautrec exhibition is over, for which relief much thanks'; but the critics of the *Standard*, the *Morning Leader*, the *Star*, the *World*, the *Pall Mall Gazette* and the *Glasgow Herald* all treated the exhibition with respect and their editors gave them far more space for the purpose than they give to art commentators in our day. It is related that the Prince of Wales visiting the exhibition, found Lautrec asleep (and probably drunk) on a sofa, and that, touched by the pathetic aspect of the crippled figure, he refused to allow the attendant to disturb him.

In Paris, meanwhile, Whistler was recruiting members for a new group, '*The International Society of Sculptors, Painters and Gravers*'; as president of this society he rejected a proposal that Cézanne should be asked to join it and he made vain efforts to get Degas, saying '*Quant à la peinture il n'y a que Degas et moi*'. Whistler, at this time also, was teaching at an art school known as the *Académie Carmen* where he was idolized by crowds of English and American girl students, some of whom arrived in carriages accompanied by their maids. There was a fierce battle in the

[1] For the present distribution of these and other pictures in this exhibition, cf. my Bibliographical and Catalogue Notes in Appendix I.

Plate (D) THE DOUANIER ROUSSEAU

L'octroi, c. 1897

London. Samuel Courtauld, Esq.

(cf. page xi)

Salon de la Nationale this year over Rodin's *Balzac*, which was refused as grotesque by the *Société des gens de lettres* who had commissioned it in 1888 and waited ten years for its completion. Geffroy and Mirbeau defended Rodin in the papers; and Mirbeau described the *Salon* scenes: '*Ce sont des cris indécents, des colères folles, des rires insultants. Jamais une statue ne vit autour de son piédestal de plus laides figures, tordues par de plus hideuses grimaces. Chacun va jeter un peu de sa bave, un peu de sa boue sur ce monument, le plus impeccable peut-être que Rodin ait créé.*' This *Salon de la Nationale* also had Matisse's large picture *La desserte* already referred to[1]; but though Matisse was now an Associate the picture was badly hung. The *Fourteenth Salon des Indépendants* was a small show which does not appear to have attracted much attention. The same applies to an exhibition in de Monfreid's studio of a number of pictures including the large *D'où venons-nous? Que sommes-nous? Où allons-nous?* (Pl. 41) which Gauguin had just sent de Monfreid with a list of people to be invited to see them; the list included Degas, Renoir, Redon, Carrière, Rodin, Mirbeau, Arsène Alexandre, Geffroy, the actor Coquelin, Anatole France, the dealers Portier and Vollard, the *Mercure de France*, and the *Revue Blanche*; Gauguin's painter followers were expressly excluded; in the event Vollard bought eight of the pictures and re-exhibited *D'où venons-nous? Que sommes-nous? Où allons-nous?* in his own gallery.

In this year 1898 Ravel published his first work, the piano duet *Sites auriculaires*, and Verdi's last work *Quattro pezzi sacri* was performed in Turin with Toscanini as conductor; the Moscow Art Theatre was founded by Stanislavsky; and the art review *Mir Iskustva* (The World of Art) was founded by a group of writers, musicians and painters including Léon Bakst, Alexandre Benois and Serge Diaghileff. Bakst, who was now thirty-two, we have already met on his visit to Paris in 1893. Diaghileff, now twenty-six, was the son of a nobleman who had become a manufacturer in the Urals; he went to St. Petersburg in 1890 to study music and was soon made a member of an informal artists' club called 'The Pickwickians' in which Benois and Bakst were the leading figures. Benois who was twenty-eight in 1898 was the son of a successful architect, and grandson of a French émigré who had gone to Russia to escape the Revolution and obtained a place as *maître d'hôtel* at the Russian court. In this year also Mallarmé died at fifty-six, Boudin died at seventy-four, and Puvis de Chavannes died at seventy-four. A week before his death Puvis had sent for his doctor and said to him, 'I know I am dying. How long have I got to live? Speak the truth because I must divide my remaining days in the completion of my Panthéon pictures'; the doctor answered, 'Perhaps eight days'; Puvis thanked him and worked calmly eight hours a day for his remaining seven on the final cartoons of *Le ravitaillement de Paris* and *Geneviève veillant sur la ville endormie*. Publications of the year included *La Cathédrale* by Huysmans, *La terre du Christ* and *L'occulte Catholique* by 'Sar' Péladan; *La Citta Morta* by D'Annunzio, and *The Ballad of Reading Gaol* by Oscar Wilde who had moved from Berneval to Paris and was sometimes seen in the rue Royale at the Bar Achille (about to become the Café Weber) where Lautrec, Debussy, Marcel Proust and their associates now frequently foregathered.

In the next year 1899 Cézanne completed his *Portrait de Vollard*[2] which he

---

[1] Cf. above, p. 139.   [2] Paris. Ambroise Vollard.

had worked on intermittently since 1897. Vollard tells us that Cézanne perched him on a chair on a wooden case so small that the chair fell off if he made the slightest movement. After ninety sittings Cézanne still looked upon the picture as unfinished, and he was only satisfied, he said half seriously to Vollard, with the triangle of shirt above the waistcoat—a fitting answer to Gérôme's comment 'Time will avenge those who give no time to their pictures' (in Vollard's Cézanne exhibition of 1895). Vollard now arranged a *Second Cézanne Exhibition* in his gallery. This exhibition like the earlier one had a notable influence on the younger men, who also saw some thirty pictures by Cézanne—including *Le Verger* (Pl. 21), a number of Auvers and L'Estaque landscapes, *La maison du pendu*[1] and the *Mardi Gras*[2]—when the pictures inherited by Mme Choquet from her husband were sold at the Hôtel Drouot in July. Three pictures by Cézanne were also seen at the *Fifteenth Salon des Indépendants* where they had been invited by the committee at the instance of Signac, who, it will be recalled, had been persuaded by Pissarro and Gauguin to acquire a landscape by Cézanne in 1885. This *Fifteenth Salon des Indépendants* had only two hundred pictures. The Douanier Rousseau and the Nabis abstained. Lautrec sent nothing as he was in a sanatorium suffering from a mental breakdown. The Nabis and some others had an exhibition of their own called *Hommage à Odilon Redon* in Durand-Ruel's gallery where Emile Bernard, Sérusier, Daniel de Monfreid, Maurice Denis, Bonnard, Vuillard, as well as Redon—who had abandoned lithography and was producing pastel pictures—were represented. This show was a considerable success. When it ended Maurice Denis wrote to Gauguin in Tahiti inviting him to exhibit next year in a similar exhibition of 'Symbolist, Pointillist and Rose-Croix painters'; and Gauguin answered that it would be dangerous for him to appear 'among the numerous masters whose works he had so unworthily copied'.[3]

Meanwhile the artists whom Matisse was soon to lead in the *Fauve Movement* were making one another's acquaintance and beginning to exchange ideas. Maurice de Vlaminck, now twenty-three, had been doing military service since we last encountered him painting his first pictures, competing in cycle races and playing the violin in cafés in 1895. He had found life in barracks a soul-destroying experience: '*Au régiment*', he said, '*les âmes ont la sécheresse des arbres de la cour de la caserne, elles ont besoin de trompettes et de drapeaux pour ne pas désesperer.*' His service finished, he resumed his cycling and athletics, and also painting and violin playing in cafés at his native Chatou; and there this year when he was out painting landscape he met and made friends with André Derain, another young artist and athlete, who also lived at Chatou and chanced to be painting the same landscape. Derain, who was now nineteen, went frequently to Paris where he worked in the *Académie Carrière*—an art school to which Carrière (aged fifty) paid occasional visits but which was mainly a place where there was no tuition but always a model and where artists dropped in as they pleased to draw and paint from the figure—like the *Académie Suisse* where Pissarro first met Monet and Cézanne in the 'sixties. At the

---

[1] Paris. Louvre.   [2] Moscow. Museum of Modern Western Art.

[3] '*Je lui réponds que non; lui donnant pour raison que je ne puis exposer sans danger avec les nombreux maîtres que j'ai indignement copiés.*'

43A. THE DOUANIER ROUSSEAU

La banlieue (Petite maison au bord de l'eau), c. 1897

Paris. Mme Paul Guillaume

43B. THE DOUANIER ROUSSEAU

La carrière, c. 1897

Paris. M. O. Miestchaninoff

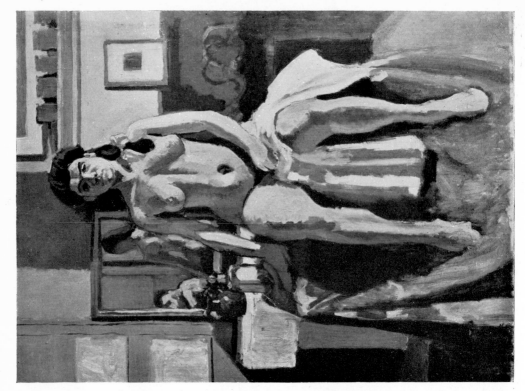

44A. CÉZANNE

44B. MATISSE

Académie Carrière Derain now met Jean Puy and Laprade and finally Matisse who had acquired the habit of drawing there after Gustave Moreau's death. Matisse himself, as related, was now evolving his personal approach and about this time he bought from Vollard a bust by Rodin, a painting of a boy's head by Gauguin, and a *Baigneuses* with three figures by Cézanne[1]; he was still in touch with his former colleagues in Gustave Moreau's atelier—Rouault, now twenty-eight, and curator as stated of the Musée Moreau, Manguin who was twenty-five, Marquet and Guérin who were twenty-four and Camoin who was twenty. And thus the *dramatis personae* of the next phase in art gradually assembled on the stage.

In this year 1899 Jean Cocteau aged seven was taken to the Nouveau Cirque to see Lautrec's favourite clowns Chocolat and Footit, while his parents, armed with the score, went *en grande tenue* to the Opera to hear *Les maîtres chanteurs*—after reading doubtless *L'œuvre Wagnérienne en France* which Catulle Mendès had just written. Jean Cocteau's parents also read, I presume, d'Annunzio's *La Gioconda*, Tristan Bernard's *Tel qu'on le parle*, and *La patrie* by Maurice Barrès, all published this year, and they surely went to the *première* of *Lys rouge* dramatized by Gaston de Caillavet from Anatole France's novel, with Réjane and Guitry in the leading parts—a *première* celebrated by a supper party which Mme de Caillavet and her son gave to guests including Anatole France, Réjane, Guitry, Clémenceau, Marcel Proust, Madeleine Lemaire (the illustrator of Proust's first book), Tristan Bernard and Robert de Flers.

In this year also Sisley died of cancer at the age of sixty. The day after his death Monet wrote to Gustave Geffroy: '*Le pauvre Sisley m'avait fait demander de venir le voir il y a huit jours, et j'avais bien vu ce jour-là que c'était un dernier adieu qu'il voulait faire.*' Sisley had sold his paintings for reasonable sums in the later period of his life—though he never became rich like the major Impressionists. Immediately after his death the exchange value of his work in the international art trade began to rise; twenty-seven pictures from his studio sold by his heirs brought 112,000 francs before the year was out.

In the next year 1900 thousands of visitors were attracted to Paris by the *Exposition Universelle*, for which the Grand Palais (where Matisse and Marquet stencilled a frieze), the Petit Palais, the Great Wheel, the Trottoir Roulant, and the Pont Alexandre III (symbol of the Franco-Russian alliance) had been constructed. The foreign powers made no attempt to boycott the Exhibition as they had done in 1889. They were all most anxious to take part in it. As many Frenchmen sympathized with the Boers in the Transvaal conflict, English visitors were rather unpopular; and the German Emperor improved the occasion with protestations of friendship which Delcassé the French Foreign Minister received with distrust. The official art show of the Exhibition—called the *Exposition Centennale*—was arranged in the new Grand Palais. Manet's pictures were again a feature of the Retrospective section; and the Impressionists were all represented—Monet by fourteen landscapes, Sisley and Pissarro each by eight, Degas by, among other things, *Le bureau de coton* (painted in 1873) and the pastel *Une répétition d'un ballet sur la scène*[2] (also painted in the 'seventies); Renoir by the early works *La petite*

<hr />

[1] Now Paris, Petit Palais, presented by M. Matisse.   [2] New York Metropolitan Museum.

danseuse,[1] *La tasse de thé*,[2] *La loge*,[3] *La couseuse*,[4] *La jeune fille au chat*,[5] and other pictures of all periods; and Berthe Morisot by *La servante*, *Femme au bal*[6] and *Femme étendue sur un divan*.[7] With this exhibition the present wide popular fame of the Impressionists began. Their art had been understood and admired by French culture in the 'seventies and by Parisian dilettanti in the 'eighties and 'nineties; Count Camondo now paid 43,000 francs for Sisley's *L'inondation*[8]; and Impressionist art was henceforth to be admired by all kinds and conditions of people in every country in the world. The *Exposition Centennale* also launched the world-wide fame of Rodin who was now sixty and had a one-man show of a hundred and sixty of his works in marble, bronze and plaster in a special pavilion which he himself erected with funds provided by some banker friends. When the Exposition ended Rodin transferred the pavilion and its contents to the grounds of the Villa des Brillants at Meudon which he had just acquired. At the same time he started an art school which was eagerly attended.

Of the art which had succeeded Impressionism—the Classical Renaissance of the 'eighties and the new movements which were now under way—the *Exposition Centennale* gave hardly a sign. There was nothing by Van Gogh or The Douanier Rousseau; and few visitors discovered the one picture, an early Brittany landscape, by Gauguin or the one picture, a port scene, by Seurat, or the two landscapes and a still life by Cézanne. In these conditions Félix Fénéon, now secretary general of the *Revue Blanche*, arranged a *Seurat Exhibition* financed by that journal in which the younger men and many of the general public saw for the first time *Un dimanche d'été à la Grande Jatte* (Pl. 18), *Baignade*[9], *Jeune femme se poudrant*,[10] *Cirque*[8] and a number of port scenes and croquetons—fifty works in all. All Seurat's pictures at this time were owned by people who had known him in his lifetime and none had been exhibited since the *Memorial Exhibition* in 1891.

In this year 1900 Pablo Picasso aged nineteen paid his first two months' visit to Paris and sold a picture to a new Montmartre dealer Mlle Weill, who was about to help and encourage creative talent and who earned eventually the sobriquet 'La Merveille' (*La mère Weill*). At the same time Aristide Maillol aged thirty-nine produced his first important sculpture *Femme accroupie: La pensée*, and while he was at work upon it at Banyuls, Matisse from Collioure hard by was a frequent visitor in his studio; Vollard began a series of illustrated books with Bonnard's lithographs to *Parallèlement* by Verlaine; Bergson published *Le rire*, and Freud published *Die Traumdenkung*; Isadora Duncan danced at parties given for her by Madame de Greffuhl and other Society hostesses; Sarah Bernhardt played in Rostand's *L'aiglon*; Henry Bernstein's first play, *Le marché*, was produced at the *Théâtre Antoine*; Rémy de Gourmont published *La culture des idées*; Péladan, *Les idées et les formes: La terre du Sphinx*, and D'Annunzio *Il Fuoco*; Nietzsche died mad at fifty-six; and Ruskin,

[1] Philadelphia. Widener Collection.
[2] Paris. Durand-Ruel.
[3] London. Samuel Courtauld.
[4] Paris. Etienne Bignou.
[5] Paris. B. E. Levy.
[6] Paris. Luxembourg.
[7] Paris. E. Rouart.
[8] Paris. Louvre.
[9] London. National Gallery, Millbank.
[10] London. Samuel Courtauld (on loan at National Gallery, Trafalgar Square).

almost continuously mad since 1889 died, in a lucid interval, of influenza, at eighty-one. After Ruskin's death Marcel Proust wrote an essay upon him which was later republished as the Introduction to his translation of the *Bible of Amiens*.

The political events of 1898–1900 roused passions in all classes. The *Affaire Dreyfus* was continuously in the limelight. At the funeral of Alphonse Daudet on January 6, 1898, Zola was hissed and insulted by 'storm troopers' of Déroulède's *Ligue des Patriotes*. On January 10 Esterhazy was tried for treasonable correspondence with a foreign power—and acquitted. On January 13 Zola wrote '*J'accuse: Une lettre au Président de la République*', charging the General Staff, the War Office, and the tribunal which tried Esterhazy, with concealing proofs of the innocence of Dreyfus and with acquitting Esterhazy though aware of his guilt. On February 7 Zola and Perreux, manager of *L'Aurore*, were tried for libel. Monet and Clemenceau went with Zola to the Court. Zola and Perreux were condemned to fines and four months' imprisonment; and both appealed. Between this date and the appeal ruling (which upheld the sentences) in July, there were riots and demonstrations all over France, and Zola fled to England. The anti-Dreyfusards and anti-Semites were jubilant. There were anti-Semitic riots as far afield as Algiers which returned Edouard Drumont, editor of *La Libre Parole*, as Deputy to the Chamber on an anti-Semite and anti-Red-Peril ticket. The tide turned on August 30 when Colonel Henry confessed that he had forged a letter which had been used against Dreyfus; Henry was committed to prison and found the next day with his throat cut. On October 4 the Cour de Cassation was formally instructed to consider the grounds for a new trial. All the anti-Dreyfusards were furious and Degas wrote: '*On ne parle pas des* affaires *pour ne pas en pleurer de colère*'.

In the next year 1899 there were still more sensational events. On January 30 Esterhazy fled to England; on February 16 the President Félix Faure died in mysterious circumstances after presenting a pearl necklace to a Madame Steinheil; and at the President's funeral Déroulède harangued the soldiers in the name of the *Ligue des Patriotes* and called on the general commanding to march on the Elysée and overthrow the Government. On June 4 the Cour de Cassation annulled the sentence of December 22, 1894, and summoned Dreyfus to appear before a second court martial at Rennes; Zola returned from England the next day with *Fécondité* written in England in his luggage; and he signalled his return with an article '*Justice*' in *L'Aurore*. A week later at the Auteuil races the new President Emile Loubet had his hat smashed in by a Royalist. On June 22 a new *Ministère de défense républicaine* with the Liberal Waldeck-Rousseau as Prime Minister, Delcassé as Minister for Foreign Affairs, and Millerand as Minister for Commerce, announced its intention to proceed against the Royalists and Right Extremists who now called themselves, as in the days of Macmahon and Boulanger, 'The Nationalists'. On July 10 Lepine, prefect of police, declared that Jules Guérin and Déroulède had been acting with the Duc d'Orléans and that Déroulède's harangue to the troops at Faure's funeral had been planned as the beginning of a Royalist *coup d'état*. On August 7 the Rennes court martial on Dreyfus began. On August 12 Déroulède was arrested and Jules Guérin, to avoid arrest, fortified himself in a so-called 'anti-masonic lodge', the '*Grand Occident de France, rite anti-juif*', in the rue Chabot and resisted a siege by police and troops for nearly six weeks—during which bands of hooligan supporters of the Right Extremists attempted to storm the street and rescue him. While the siege was in progress the Rennes court martial found Dreyfus guilty with extenuating circumstances and condemned him to degradation and ten years' detention; and Zola in protest wrote *Le cinquième acte*. On September 19 Waldeck-Rousseau's Government quashed the Rennes sentence and conferred a full pardon on Dreyfus, which enraged the anti-Dreyfusards and left the Dreyfusards almost equally indignant as nothing less than a proclamation of Dreyfus' innocence and his reinstatement in the army would content them. When Guérin and Déroulède were tried before the supreme court on November 9, the anti-Dreyfusards demonstrated with street riots in their favour; Déroulède was nevertheless condemned to ten years' banishment and Guérin to imprisonment for ten years.

In 1900 Waldeck-Rousseau's Government went forward with a Liberal programme of social construction all through the year. It established regional *Conseils de Travail*; opened the *Conseil supérieur de Travail* to trades union delegates; and declared a general amnesty for everyone connected with the *Affaire Dreyfus* (hoping vainly that the affair might thus be ended). In these measures Waldeck-Rousseau was supported by all the Liberals and also by Jaurès, leader of the moderate Opportunist Socialists who were working for the gradual construction of a socialist state by constitutional procedures. But he was harassed by extremists on both wings. On the Extreme Right, Charles Maurras and André Vaugeois (who had just founded the *Action française* group) appeared as new propagandists for the 'Nationalists'; Maurras preached anti-Semitism and salvation by a dictatorial monarchist régime to be imposed by force on all who were reluctant to accept it; '*Les métèques et les juifs*', he wrote, '*doivent être informés qu'ils ne sont pas Français. "Dehors les barbares!" c'est le nouveau cri national.*' On the Extreme Left the Marxist International Communists led by Jules Guesde proclaimed themselves opposed to all forms of co-operation with 'bourgeois' politicians; and an anarchist (encouraged by the murder of King Humbert of Italy) threw a bomb, unsuccessfully, at the Shah of Persia who was visiting the Exhibition.

45B. PICASSO
L'enfant au pigeon, 1901
London. Samuel Courtauld, Esq.

45A. GAUGUIN
Tahitiennes au mango, 1899
New York. W. Church Osborn, Esq.

46 . PICASSO
Célestine, 1903
Paris. Pablo Picasso

ACT II: HOW IT HAPPENED

SCENE V: 1901-1903

From the *Van Gogh Exhibition* in Bernheim's gallery, Maurice Denis' *Hommage à Cézanne*, the death of Lautrec and Picasso's return to Paris; to the *First Fauve Exhibition*, the *First Salon d'Automne*, Picasso's first 'blue' pictures, the death of Pissarro and the death of Gauguin

In 1901 Vollard arranged a first exhibition of '*Mystical and Decorative Pastels*' by Odilon Redon; and the Bernheim Gallery had a large *Van Gogh Exhibition* which was a main root of the Fauve movement, as I have mentioned in the Introduction. Derain and Vlaminck went to Bernheim's Gallery and were thrilled by Van Gogh's vigour: '*Ce jour-là*,' Vlaminck said later, '*j'aimais mieux Van Gogh que mon père*'; they went again and again and on one of their visits they met Matisse to whom Derain presented Vlaminck. Matisse has described the occurrence: 'I saw Derain accompanied by a young giant who was voicing his enthusiasm in authoritative tones and declaring that one must paint with pure vermilion, pure Veronese green and pure cobalt; Derain, I think, was a little afraid of him—while admiring his ardour and enthusiasm'. Vlaminck at this time was twenty-five, Derain was twenty-one and Matisse was thirty-two. The two younger men asked Matisse to come to Chatou and see their work, and in due course he went; 'I was happy to find', he tells us, 'that there were young men who had convictions similar to my own'; and thereafter he helped and encouraged them. As Derain's parents were obstructing their son's desire to be an artist Matisse called upon them with Mme Matisse and successfully explained to them that painting was really a respectable profession in which their son, as a serious student with talent, might have a reputable career.

The *Salon des Indépendants* was now more a centre of interest than ever and a thousand exhibits appeared there this year. The show was financed by one Comte Le Marcis who filled seven rooms with thirty-six immense pictures illustrating *Dante et Virgile aux enfers*; James Ensor sent ten Surrealist pictures including *Les masques scandalisées*; The Douanier Rousseau returned with six landscapes and a portrait; Bonnard sent a large triptych *La Seine*; Matisse, Vuillard and Marquet contributed for the first time; there were the usual works by Signac and the minor followers of Seurat; and Cézanne, once more specially invited, sent a landscape and a still life.

Cézanne was now venerated by all the artists who had formerly been follower or associates of Gauguin. Maurice Denis proclaimed the situation in his celebrated painting *Hommage à Cézanne*[1], showing Odilon Redon, Bonnard, Vuillard, Roussel, Sérusier, Denis and Vollard grouped round Cézanne's still life, *Compotier, verre et pommes*, which Gauguin had bought in his stockbroking days and inserted in the background of his *Portrait of Marie Henry*[2] in 1890. Denis sent this *Hommage à Cézanne* to the exhibition of *La libre esthétique* (which had succeeded *Les XX* as an advanced exhibiting society) in Brussels, and Cézanne's *Compotier, verre et pommes* was hung beside it; when *Hommage à Cézanne* returned from Brussels Denis sent it to the *Salon de la Nationale* where it was considered '*une audacieuse manifestation dirigée contre les maîtres de l'art officiel.*' When Gauguin, mortally ill in the Marquesas, heard of the growing interest in Cézanne's work, he wrote with bitterness: '*C'est toujours la même chose—maintenant que les tableaux sont chers, maintenant qu'il est de bon goût de comprendre Cézanne, maintenant que Cézanne est millionaire . . .*'

In this year 1901 Lautrec died of paralysis at the age of thirty-seven; Fernand Léger aged twenty became a student under Gérôme at the Ecole des Beaux-Arts; and Raoul Dufy aged twenty-four and Othon Friesz aged twenty-two, newly arrived from their native Le Havre, became pupils of Bonnat. Sigmund Freud published *Zur Psychopathologie des Alltagslebens*; Maeterlinck published *La vie des abeilles*; and Debussy became musical critic of the *Revue Blanche* to which Guillaume Apollinaire had now begun to contribute. Apollinaire's real name appears to have been Guillaume Apollinaire de Kostrowitzky; he was the grandson of a Polish general and he claimed to be the son of an Italian cardinal. Born in Rome in August 1880 he was brought up by his mother at Nice and other places on the Riviera; he went to school in Monaco and Nice, acquired a precocious passion for contemporary French poetry and letters, and wrote verses in Latin and French. When he left school he travelled in Germany before finally settling in Paris where he was now earning his living as a private secretary to the director of a bank. His earliest poem known to me, *La cueillette* (1900), begins:

> *Nous vînmes au jardin fleuri pour ta cueillette.*
> *Belle, sais-tu combien de fleurs, de roses-thé,*
> *Roses pâles d'amour qui couronnent ta tête*
> *S'effeuillent chaque été?*

Picasso meanwhile had arrived for a second time in Paris, taken a studio, pinned Lautrec's *May Milton* poster on the wall, and painted fifty pictures including *L'absinthe*,[3] *Le gourmand*[4] and *L'enfant au pigeon* (Pl. 45B). Vollard quick to perceive his genius gave him an exhibition in his gallery in June and the critic Coquiot wrote a preface to the catalogue. This exhibition brought him the friendship of the poet Max Jacob who had written art criticism in the 'nineties, and was now working as secretary to a lawyer. Max Jacob visited this exhibition and then called at Picasso's studio to make his acquaintance. Xervos, Picasso's biographer, has described the occurrence: Max Jacob passed the day looking at stacks of pictures,

[1] Paris. Luxembourg. [2] Chicago Art Institute (Winterbotham).
[3] New York. George Gershwin Estate.
[4] Chicago Art Institute (Lent Chester Dale.)

at intervals a number of Picasso's Spanish friends came and sat on the floor, when meal time arrived Jacob was pressed to remain, some one cooked beans which were eaten by the diners on the floor, the company drank from a Spanish pitcher and Jacob was instructed in the art of catching the drink from the side spout. The next evening Picasso and his Spanish friends paid a return visit to Max Jacob's lodgings; and Jacob read them his poems through the night. While Picasso was thus beginning his great career, Verdi died at eighty-eight and two hundred thousand people lined the streets of Milan to see the funeral procession, and Stravinsky aged nineteen was studying law at St. Petersbourg University.

In the next year 1902 Picasso was back again in Spain till the autumn painting more 'blue' pictures and portraits. In his absence there was an exhibition of fifteen of his 1901 paintings by the dealer Mlle Weill, who, as noted, had bought a picture from him on his visit to Paris in 1900. This exhibition seems however to have fallen flat. When he returned in the autumn he was so short of money that, unable to afford a studio, he shared a room with Max Jacob at the Hôtel Voltaire, sleeping by day when Jacob was out and painting by night when Jacob was asleep.

In 1902 the *Salon des Indépendants* had a *Lautrec Memorial Exhibition* with fifty works, and Maurice Joyant arranged a still larger show with two hundred paintings, lithographs and drawings in Durand-Ruel's galleries; Maurice Utrillo aged nineteen painted his first pictures of Parisian and suburban streets; Vollard published Mirbeau's *Le jardin des supplices* with drawings by Rodin and *Daphnis et Chloë* with lithographs by Bonnard; Maeterlinck published *Monna Vanna* and quarrelled with Debussy when their joint work *Pelléas et Mélisande* was produced at the Opéra Comique; Alfred Jarry published *Le Surmâle*—a Surrealist fantasia on the theme of mechanized man in conflict with sentient machines; Brieux published *Les avariés*, which the censor interdicted from public performance; and Cézanne aged sixty-three was refused the Legion of Honour by Roujon, still director of the Beaux-Arts.

In this year also Zola aged sixty-two was asphyxiated in his sleep from the fumes of a defective stove; when the news of his death reached the Boulevards, Right Extremists demonstrated in the streets and expressed their joy 'with such boisterous gestures'—the *Times* correspondent reported—as men indulge in on learning of a victory, many exclaiming savagely 'It was none too soon'. Dreyfus appeared at Zola's funeral where order was preserved by a huge force of police.

In the next year 1903, which ends our Act II, Gauguin died miserably in the Marquesas at the age of fifty-five; Whistler died in Chelsea at sixty-nine; and Pissarro died in Paris at seventy-three. Pissarro had been working most of the year in a room overlooking the quays at Le Havre whence he had written to his son: 'From my window I can see great steamers, transatlantics and others passing from morning till night; with the docks and the traffic it is truly magnificent. I think I can put out a new series that will be interesting.' Gauguin had said of him, '*Ce fut un de mes maîtres. Je ne le renie pas*'; Cézanne had said, '*Ce fut un père pour moi. C'est un homme à consulter et quelque chose comme le Bon Dieu*'; and even Degas broke through his anti-Semitism when he heard of his old friend's death: '*Le voici donc parti, le pauvre Juif errant. Il ne marchera plus et si on avait été prévenu on aurait bien marché un peu derrière lui. Que pensait-il depuis la sale Affaire, que pensait-il de la gêne qu'on avait malgré soi avec lui? . . . Avait-il l'idée seulement de se reporter au temps où nous ignorions à peu près sa terrible race'?* [1]

The *Nineteenth Salon des Indépendants* had works by Matisse, Derain, Vlaminck, Marquet, Manguin, and Camoin. At the same time Matisse organized the *First Fauve Exhibition* in Mlle Weill's gallery to which all these artists and also Dufy and Friesz were invited to contribute; but the word 'Fauve' was not used in the title of this exhibition as it had not yet been coined as a label for the group. In October 1903 the *Salon d'Automne* was founded by the new Fauve group and by certain artists from the *Salon de la Nationale*, including the portrait-painter Jacques-Emile Blanche and Frantz Jourdain who acted as president. Matisse, Rouault, Marquet and Bonnard were foundation members and all exhibited. This *First Salon d'Automne* included a *Gauguin Memorial Exhibition* which laid the foundation of Gauguin's reputation and had considerable influence on many of the younger men. Jacques-Emile Blanche and Frantz Jourdain, artists with wide social influence, made the opening of this new Salon, which took place in the evening, a fashionable event; and all the dilettanti, as the phrase goes, led by Comte Robert de Montesquiou and the Comtesse Anna de Noailles trooped round the galleries of the Petit Palais where the show was held. Neither Picasso nor The Douanier Rousseau sent works to this *First Salon d'Automne*. Picasso was still personally unknown to Matisse and his associates, and he was still so far from conquering Paris that, as already chronicled, he returned in despair to Barcelona where he now painted *Célestine* (Pl. 46), and *Le vieux guitariste* (Pl. 47). The new books of the year included Otto Weininger's *Geschlecht und Charakter*; and new plays included *Le retour de Jérusalem* by Maurice Donnay and *Maternité* by Brieux. The *Revue Blanche* now ceased publication after a twelve years' life in which it had printed drawings by Signac, Lautrec, Bonnard, Vuillard, and Maurice Denis, and literary contributions from, among others, Mallarmé, Paul Adam, Alphonse Allais, Maurice Barrès, Julien Benda, Tristan Bernard, Léon Blum, Clemenceau, Debussy, Duret, Félix Fénéon, André Gide, Alfred Jarry, Gustave Kahn, Octave Mirbeau, Marcel Proust, Charles-Louis Philippe, Jules Renard, and Guillaume Apollinaire.

The political events of these three years were dominated by the Church and State conflict. In 1901 Waldeck-Rousseau was still Prime Minister and the leader of a strong Liberal party which could count on support from the moderate Opportunist Socialists; and thus supported he carried through various laws for social services and a new *Law of Associations* against the Religious Congregations (monks, nuns, etc.)—as the existing legislation had failed of its effect. The execution of this *Law of Associations* caused disturbances in various places when a number of schools run by religious congregations were officially closed and their doors sealed up. In May 1903 Waldeck-Rousseau resigned and he was succeeded by a Government with Combes as Prime Minister, Delcassé as Foreign Minister, and Camille Pelletan (who had been painted in 1872 as a rising poet in *Un coin de*

[1] This passage comes from a letter by Degas to Henri Rouart printed in Guérin and Halévy's *Lettres de Degas*. The letter is not dated and the authors who print it next to letters written in 1903 say: '*Il s'agit d'un ami commun de Degas et des frères Rouart.*' I assume that it refers to Pissarro.

table[1] by Fantin-Latour) as Minister of Marine; the Socialist Jean Jaurès being Vice-President of the Chamber. This Combes Government continued Waldeck-Rousseau's Liberal programme of social services and introduced compulsory sanitary regulations, compulsory vaccination and compulsory declaration of infectious diseases. It also went forward with the Church and State conflict, claiming the right to nominate French bishops and making further enactments against the religious congregations including the Chartreux monks (whose liqueur was frequently referred to in the Chamber). Combes, like his Liberal predecessors, was continually harassed by extremists on both wings. On the Left, the Revolutionary Syndicalists became continually more vocal; and on the Right, Drumont and François Coppée founded a *Ligue pour le refus de l'impôt* whose members were to refuse to pay taxes until the Government resigned. France now enjoyed the friendship of both Russia and England. The Czar paid a second ceremonial visit to Paris in 1901. And the accession of Edward VII in that year was welcomed by everyone except some Right Extremists who called on the people to greet King Edward when he came to Paris in 1903 with cries of '*A bas les Anglais!*' and '*Vivent les Boers!*'

[1] Paris. Louvre. Cf. above, pp. 30 and 31.

ACT II: THE MASTERS' LIVES

PAUL GAUGUIN (iii)

From forty-four to his death at fifty-five (1892–1903)

Gauguin spent the whole of 1892 in Tahiti and produced within the year over sixty pictures and a number of carvings and drawings. He continued to live 'native' with Tehoura who was gentle—but unfaithful to him when he went out fishing. In the spring he was ill, vomiting blood so copiously and so often that the doctor in the hospital at Papeete feared for his life. He recovered and lived abstemiously, drinking no alcohol and eating very little. 'When I come back,' he wrote to de Monfreid, 'you will see me as slim as a young girl. I must have been disgusting with all the fat I had about me in Paris.' On the material side he was continually worried about money. The benefit performance at the *Théâtre d'Art* in 1891 had brought him nothing, such profits as there were being given, as I have chronicled, to Verlaine. He soon spent his small capital on initial installations and current expenses, hoping to make more by the sale of his pictures and also to receive various monies that were owed to him from Paris. But the debtors were in no hurry to send their money to the South Seas. There was now a market for his early Brittany pictures which his wife was selling for reasonable prices in Denmark, but as he allowed her to keep the money this put nothing in his pocket. He expected to sell his new work through relations with various dealers—including Maurice Joyant and Tanguy, and also through de Monfreid; and in the course of the year he sent them parcels of pictures. But his agents found it hard to sell these pictures because the dilettanti were not yet acclimatized to his Tahitian art; and they were only able to send him money for one or two Tahitian pictures in this first year. If he had remained in France and painted more Brittany pictures imitating his old ones he could doubtless have sold them easily, all through the 'nineties. But he declined to do this because he was fundamentally a creator with faith in his own powers: '*Je suis un homme fort*,' he wrote to de Monfreid, '*qui sais faire plier le sort à mes goûts*'; he was confident that if he were in Paris he could make a demonstration and work up interest in his Tahitian pictures; and in the spring of 1893 he decided to go back. A number of his Tahitian pictures had been sent to his wife for an exhibition in Denmark, and from this he hoped to find some money waiting for him by the time he reached Paris. There was moreover an uncle in Orleans who was dying; and if he died there would be an inheritance which it might be well to collect in person. By May his arrangements for departure were completed and he sailed for France—leaving a weeping Tehoura on the Tahitian shore.

He landed at Marseilles in the first week of August 1893. He then went to Orleans where his uncle, as he said, 'had had the good sense to die', and he collected an inheritance of some 13,000 francs, part of which he gave a little later to his wife. In September he went to Paris and arranged for the exhibition of forty of his Tahitian pictures at Durand-Ruel's, which took place, as I have chronicled, in November.[1]

Backed by his inheritance Gauguin now entered a period of defiance. He dressed fantastically, and entertained with Anna the Javanese girl as hostess in the flamboyant studio already described.[2] But beneath this bravura there was of course Gauguin the sturdy sailor—an imposing virile figure, Gauguin *le loup*,[3] Gauguin the highly intelligent theorist on art, and Gauguin the artist. To the writers and artists who spent long evenings with him in his studio he revealed himself strong, manly, sincere and relatively simple. But to casual visitors and to the public when he walked the streets in his arresting raiment he appeared a preposterous poser or, as we should say now, a blatant exhibitionist; and he thus gave his enemies material for attacks describing him as a vulgar charlatan. He went at this time to the Ministry of the Beaux-Arts to seek redemption of the promise that the state would buy some pictures on his return from Tahiti; he found that the director Renan, who had made the promise, was now replaced by the philistine Roujon who tried, as noted, to refuse the Caillebotte Bequest. Roujon inquired if his predecessor had put anything in writing; when he found that Gauguin had no documents he said: 'I decline to encourage your art. It is revolutionary; and it repulses me. I refuse to create a scandal at the Beaux-Arts by buying your pictures.'

At the beginning of 1894 he went to Belgium; he then went to Copenhagen to see his wife—his last interview with her; and after that he went with Anna, the Javanese girl, to Pont Aven where he painted a few pictures. In the summer when he was walking on the quay with Anna and a man friend, he became involved in a brawl with some drunken sailors who spoke offensively of the woman; he knocked down several of his assailants but one of them kicked him with his heavy sabot and broke his ankle. In great pain he was carried to his lodgings on a shutter, smoking a cigarette. The damage proved serious; he had to stay for weeks in bed. While he was thus crippled Anna left him, went to Paris, ransacked his studio, and vanished. In the autumn of 1894 he was still in Pont Aven, in pain and dispirited: 'I have suffered so much,' he writes to de Monfreid, 'especially at nights, when I never sleep at all, that I have lost my courage. And then, naturally, I have been unable to produce anything—four months wasted. And a great deal of expense. Anyway I've quite finally decided to go away and live the rest of my life in the South Seas. I shall come back to Paris in December and concern myself exclusively with selling up everything—at any price I can get. If that comes off I shall get away in February. Thus I shall end my days in freedom and peace without cares for the morrow,

[1] Cf. above, p. 143. For the present distribution of the pictures exhibited cf. my Bibliographical and Catalogue Notes in Appendix.
[2] Cf. above, p. 147.   [3] Cf. above, p. 143.

47. PICASSO
Le vieux guitariste, 1903
Chicago. Art Institute (Birch Bartlett)

48A. CÉZANNE
La tour aux pigeons, c. 1892
Cleveland. Museum of Art

48B. CÉZANNE
Nature morte au melon (Water colour), 1895–1900
Detroit. Edsel Ford, Esq.

delivered from the endless struggle against fools. . . . I shall say good-bye to painting—except for recreation; I shall carve the door-posts of my house. . . . Nothing induces me to stay in this disgusting Europe.' He returned to Paris according to this plan, limping from the damage to his ankle which remained and was to remain the rest of his life unsound. Putting on his blue coat and his embroidered waistcoat he went to the Colonial Office and applied for an administrative post in Tahiti or some other French colonial possession. His application was refused. But he was nevertheless determined to return to the tropics. A dealer offered him a contract with annual payments in return for his pictures, on condition that he stayed in Paris. His friends urged him to remain. But nothing would induce him to change his decision.

The sale of his pictures took place at the Hôtel Drouot in February 1895. The catalogue contained, in lieu of preface, the letter from August Strindberg and Gauguin's reply already referred to.[1] There were forty-nine 'lots' in the sale, two-thirds of which were Tahitian pictures unsold in the 1893 exhibition. Some of the pictures did not reach their reserves and Gauguin left them in de Monfreid's care. The total realised (impossible to estimate in present money) was approximately 23,640 francs.[2] In March Gauguin sailed for the second time to Tahiti. Before leaving he had contracted syphilis from casual intercourse with a street prostitute of Montparnasse.

By the autumn of 1895 he was again installed in Tahiti; he built himself a new and more comfortable hut; and there (we know from his letters to de Monfreid) he took, at first, the pleasures offered by the native '*gamines*' as a prelude to installing one of them as a regular '*vahine*'—(for Tehoura had remarried in his absence and she was only able to come for a stolen week to balance her infidelity in the old days when he went out fishing). In this mood he wrote to de Monfreid, 'You tell me that you are contemplating a divorce. . . . That idiotic institution marriage always lands one in bothers. . . . For my part I've now taken a firm line—I've just left. My family can stew in their own juice for all the help they will get from me. I expect to finish my existence here in perfect tranquillity—*Ah oui, je suis un grand criminel. Qu'importe? Michel-Ange aussi; et je ne suis pas Michel-Ange.*' Then he settled down to paint *Te Arii Vahine* (*Femme de race royale*)[3] which he describes in a letter to de Monfreid dated April 1896: 'I have just finished a picture which I think is the best thing I have done. . . . I don't think I have ever painted anything with such grand and grave sonority of colour.' In the same letter he offers to send this picture to Paris as security for a loan of 1,000 francs and he writes: 'I am at the end of my resources and the limit of my strength. . . . My health has broken up more and more every day since I came here. My broken foot gives me extreme pain. I have open sores which the doctor has failed up to now to heal. . . . You

[1] Cf. above, p. 150.

[2] In a letter to his wife (published in Pola Gauguin's '*My father*' (1937)) Gauguin says: 'Excepting 1370 frcs. of real sales everything was bought in by me under borrowed names,' and adds that as commissions and expenses amounted to 1834 frcs. he was 464 frcs. down on the sale. The sums for which the individual pictures were knocked down are given by Rotonchamp who attended the sale.

[3] Moscow. Museum of Modern Western Art.

must admit that life is hard on me. The last time I was here I made extraordinary efforts—you saw the results in my exhibition. And what became of them? Complete defeat. I only made myself enemies. Bad luck incessantly pursues me; I go down and down. It may be that I have no talent but (setting aside all vanity) I think nevertheless that a man cannot make an art movement, even a small one, without talent—or else there are more madmen about than one supposed. I have just borrowed 500 francs to ensure a few months' food; with 500 francs that I owe for my house that makes 1,000 francs of debt. And yet my demands are modest enough. I only require 100 francs a month for myself and my *vahine*, a girl of thirteen and a half. . . .'

As on his last visit, he was continually expecting money which did not arrive; on the strength of these expectations he had provided himself with a horse and trap and built a hangar to keep them in and thus involved himself in new liability before he had paid off the old; and he now tried in vain to arrange a '*combinaison*' whereby fifteen collectors, dealers and friends would provide him with 2,400 francs a year between them and take in exchange fifteen pictures which he would undertake to deliver in advance at the beginning of each year. In July 1896 he had to go to hospital and remain a month. He was actually there when Charles Morice made his *démarche* at the Beaux-Arts and Roujon behaved in the manner recorded.[1] When he came out of hospital he was only allowed to work an hour or two each day. He was able nevertheless to finish some pictures and send them to Paris. 'Such as they are I send them,' he writes, 'they are perhaps good: the intense anguish and suffering behind them may balance the clumsiness of execution due to my condition; with my type of temperament I have to paint my pictures straight off at fever heat, working an hour a day does not suit me.' In November he was better: 'I have been doing sculpture—a nude of a woman and a fine fantastic lion playing with its young. I have put my sculpture all about the field. The natives who have no knowledge of wild animals are *tout épatés*. The *curé* has done his utmost to make me remove the nude woman. But the authorities have laughed at him and I have told him to go to hell. If only I had the money owing to me my life here would be extraordinarily calm and happy. I shall shortly be the father of a half-caste. My atelier is splendid. I get a lot of work done between six in the morning and noon. Once one knows this Tahitian life one wants to live no other.' In December he writes that he owes 900 francs locally and has had to humiliate himself to borrow the last hundred.

In 1897 a series of disasters and sufferings wore down his will to work and live. In January he received some of the money owed to him from Paris. He paid his local debts and, as his illness was tormenting him, he decided to go for a while to hospital. But, in fact, he did not enter the hospital: 'The hospital officials', he wrote to Charles Morice, 'insulted me in every way; after a great to-do they gave me a ticket of admission at 5 francs a day inscribed "*Indigent*". As you will understand, although I was very ill I had to refuse to go in mixed up with soldiers and servants. The fact is that here as in France there are people who take me for a revolutionary (*un révolté*), and here as everywhere, and even more than elsewhere,

[1] Cf. above, p. 156.

the man who has money troubles is badly treated. This refers of course only to the Europeans in Papeete. Here in my own corner the natives are as always very kind and respectful.' In February and March he announces the completion and dispatch to Paris of *Nevermore*[1] and *Te Rerioa* (*Le rêve*).[1] Of *Nevermore* he wrote, 'I have tried to suggest a certain bygone barbaric luxury in a simple nude. . . . The whole picture is bathed in deliberately sombre colours. It is neither silk nor velvet nor batiste nor gold that creates this luxurious quality but simply a richness created by the hand of the artist. The title is *Nevermore*. Not 'The Raven' of Edgar Poe but the Bird of the Devil waiting its time.' Of *Te Rerioa* (*Le rêve*) he wrote, 'Everything is dream in this picture; the child, the mother, the rider on the road—are they real or are they the painter's dream? (*Est-ce l'enfant, est-ce la mère, est-ce le cavalier dans le sentier ou bien encore est-ce le rêve du peintre?*) All this, I shall be told, is beside the point in painting. Who knows? Perhaps not.' He urges de Monfreid not to exhibit his work; in particular he is to avoid exhibitions where Bernard, Denis, Sérusier, etc., show their things; exhibiting, he declares, will only give his enemies occasion to describe him as a follower of the artists who are really his followers; the proper procedure is to arrange with dealers to lend pictures to collectors, with an option of purchase, and allow them to keep them long enough to get attached to them; for the rest, de Monfreid is to store them against the day (*à esperer!*) when reasonable prices will be paid. In March 1897 he was feeling better and working with energy and confidence. Then disaster came. He had built his hut on leased land; the lease-holder died; the land was sold; and he had to find land elsewhere and build again—borrowing 1,000 francs from the *Caisse Agricole* of the *Banque de Tahiti* for the purpose. In July he writes to de Monfreid: 'I have a violent recurrence of my illness—fits of giddiness and attacks of fever, and my feet are so painful that they keep me in bed or sitting down.' In September: 'I owe 1,800 francs and I can get no more credit—though I am owed 2,500 francs from Paris. . . . To say nothing of my pictures. . . . *Je ne vois rien sinon la mort qui délivre de tout.* . . . *Folle mais triste et enchantée aventure que mon voyage à Tahiti.*' In October: 'This letter is about the last I shall send you. If nothing comes at the end of this month I shall have to take my decision. . . .' In November: 'My resolution to end things is changed in the sense that nature is doing the job for me though more slowly. . . . If anything should happen I beg you to keep in remembrance of me all the pictures now deposited with you: My family will anyway have too many.' And to Morice: 'My heart is much affected—I choke and I vomit blood every day. My carcass is still resisting but it is bound to break up—which is better than suicide to which I should have been driven. . . . I shall probably not see the book in print.'[2]

At the end of the year he had firmly decided to paint one more picture and then make an end. In continual suffering he worked with despairing energy on the large composition *D'où venons-nous? Que sommes-nous? Où allons-nous?* (Pl. 41). It was painted in a month—'*J'ai travaillé jour et nuit dans une fièvre inouïe*'—and com-

---

[1] London. Samuel Courtauld.

[2] The book here referred to was *Noa Noa* which Charles Morice was trying to get published in Paris. Some parts appeared in *La Revue Blanche* (cf. above, p. 156). No publisher would then undertake the whole text in book form and eventually Morice published it himself.

pleted at the end of December. In January 1898 he went to a deserted corner in the mountains and took arsenic hoping that his corpse would be devoured by ants. But the attempt miscarried; he vomited the poison and had to crawl back to his home where he was prostrated for a month from the effects.

When he recovered he was morally dejected and unable to work. In May he was unable to pay the instalment due on his debt to the *Caisse Agricole*, and to keep the wolf from the door he took a job as a clerk and inspector in the local office of Public Works at a salary of six francs a day. He worked thus, living in lodgings at Papeete—with a certain amount of free time for painting, a good deal of pain from his ankle and some visits to hospital—till the end of 1898.

Meanwhile he had sent the large picture *D'où venon-nous? Que sommes-nous? Où allons-nous?* with nine other pictures to de Monfreid in Paris suggesting a private exhibition, and Vollard, as I have chronicled, came to this exhibition and bought eight of the pictures and then exhibited the large picture in his own gallery. As a result Gauguin was able, early in 1899, to give up his hack employment and return to his hut and studio where he found the structure, his pictures and his drawings badly damaged by damp, rats and cockroaches, and various things missing. He repaired the damage and planted his garden with flowers sent to him by de Monfreid. He could count now on a small income from some cocoa trees on his new property and on money from Paris where speculation in his pictures had begun. But he was not to capture the tranquillity he had so long desired. His illness grew daily upon him. All through 1899 and 1900 it plagued him with skin rashes and sores; and there was always his damaged ankle as well. In December 1900 he writes: 'I go to hospital (twelve francs a day)'; in January 1901: 'I have received your letter in hospital'; in February 1901: 'I have just left hospital if not cured at any rate a little relieved.' The effect of the illness on his mind and morale was disastrous. He began to suffer with persecution mania and to quarrel with all and sundry over trifles. He publicly accused a former *vahine* of a paltry theft; and he publicly insulted a French official—who wisely ignored it. To relieve his spleen he wrote and manifolded several numbers of a satiric journal *Le Sourire* attacking his real or imagined enemies (ornamenting the publication with prints from his wood engravings). By March 1901 he had made himself unpopular all round. He even found it increasingly difficult to get native models. In April he decided to leave Tahiti and go to the Marquesas. 'I think,' he wrote to de Monfreid, 'that there with a new landscape and new and more barbaric elements and facility for models I shall do some fine things. Here my imagination has begun to cool. Moreover we have to consider the stupidity of the public. When they saw my Tahitian pictures they began to look upon my Brittany pictures as rose water; if I now show them some new and alarming Marquesas pictures they will begin to look upon my Tahitian work as eau de Cologne.' By August he had sold his Tahitian property, repaid what remained of his debt to the *Caisse Agricole* and sailed to the Marquesas.

In the Marquesas he established himself at Dominica (Atouana) in September 1901. He bought from the missionaries a bungalow surrounded by a small cocoa plantation; and a white horse. He set carved figures and paintings on the entrance verandah, and carvings in the garden. There by November he was comfortable, out of debt, and with a prospect of freedom from financial worries (as Vollard had contracted to send him a regular stipend in exchange for consignments of pictures) and he was also about to receive 1,500 francs from the sale of his large picture *D'où venons-nous? Que sommes-nous? Où allons-nous?* to a Bordeaux collector. The Marquesan women—taller than the Tahitians, with broad shoulders, narrow hips, long straight legs and a golden skin—delighted him; and he was also delighted with the Marquesan landscape and the remains of the traditional native art. 'You have no idea,' he writes, 'of the peace in which I live here, entirely alone, surrounded by verdure.' At the beginning of 1902 he was sufficiently settled to be able to start work in earnest. He painted a few pictures; but his fatal disease was there to destroy his peace and his plans; and he soon became irritable and paranoiac and began to quarrel with the local officials as he had done at Tahiti.

In the spring of 1903 he could only drag himself about painfully, his legs swathed in bandages, his mind in a state of half-demented irritation. In his calmer moments he wrote articles on art and frank autobiographical fragments for the *Mercure de France* which was afraid to publish them. A collection of these writings sent to the critic Fontainas were published years later as *Avant et Après*. At the same time he wrote defamatory reports of the local gendarmes whom he accused of ill-treating the natives and of connivance in smuggling. In March one of these gendarmes brought an action against him and he was condemned to three months' imprisonment and a fine of 1,000 francs for defamation. Appeal against the sentence meant the employment of lawyers and personal appearance at Papeete. Describing this disaster, he wrote to de Monfreid in April: '*Toutes ces préoccupations me tuent.*' And in fact on May 9, when he was fifty-five, he was found dead by his neighbour—a Protestant pastor. He was reverently buried by the Catholic missionaries whom he had frequently insulted.

ACT II: THE MASTERS' LIVES

PAUL CÉZANNE (iii)

From fifty-three to his death at sixty-seven (1892–1906)

Between 1892 and 1903 Cézanne worked steadily at perfecting his art and received the long delayed recognition. In the first three years he painted mainly in Provence, in the region of Fontainebleau and in Paris. The *Portrait de Gustave Geffroy* (Pl. 44A) of 1895 was painted in Geffroy's study at Belleville, one of the northern suburbs of Paris; after a great many sittings Cézanne suddenly packed up his materials and went to Aix, leaving the picture, as we know it, still unfinished according to his standards; he explained this sudden decision to Vollard: '*Comprenez: Geffroy est un brave homme et qui a beaucoup de talent; mais il parlait tout le temps de Clémenceau; alors je me suis sauvé à Aix*'; when Vollard asked why Clemenceau's name offended him, he said: '*Ecoutez un peu, Monsieur Vollard. Il a du tempérament: mais pour moi qui suis faible dans la vie il vaut mieux m'appuyer sur Rome.*'[1]

When Vollard opened the *Cézanne Exhibition* in his gallery in December 1895 Cézanne himself was at Aix, and he seems to have done nothing about the matter except give his son permission to send Vollard the paintings; and these are said to have arrived in Paris unframed and not even on stretchers, but just rolled up. I list some twenty-three of the pictures shown, with their present whereabouts, in Appendix I. This exhibition, as I have shown, was a *succès de scandale*, but it was also the beginning of Cézanne's later reputation and the beginning of the phase in his career when the younger men admired his pictures and some wealthy dilettanti began to collect them.

In 1896, at Aix, Cézanne met the critic Joachim Gasquet, son of an Aixois friend, a baker named Henri Gasquet, whose portrait he was painting. A genuine affection soon developed between Joachim Gasquet who was then twenty-three and Cézanne who was then fifty-seven. Gasquet admired Cézanne's pictures and said so simply. As an original creative artist Cézanne did not expect people to understand his efforts; but if he felt they really did so he was deeply pleased and moved. Jean Royère relates that Cézanne showed him a picture in 1894: '*Je lui exprimai mon enthousiasme,*' he writes, '*et aussitôt je le vis grave, ému, tremblant. Il me prit la main disant, "Je suis un simple. Il ne faut pas me faire de compliments et me mentir pour politesse"*' (which is Chantecler's '*J'ai l'âme encore ouverte: les rires entreraient*'). Similarly when young Gasquet convinced him of his enthusiasm he was so moved

[1] Cf. above, pp. 39 and 115.

that he gave him one of his cardinal paintings· *La montagne Sainte Victoire*.[1] In June of this year he was again much troubled with diabetes and he went for a cure to Vichy and later to Talloires on the Lake of Annecy in Haute Savoie. He painted *Le lac d'Annecy*[2] at Talloires; but no country excited him to the same degree as Provence and the Midi coast; 'The lake is all right with great hills round it,' he wrote from Talloires to an Aixois friend, 'but it does not compare with our own country. . . . When one has been born down there, nothing else is worth much.'

In the autumn of 1897 he was distressed by the death of his mother who had always been a good friend to him and to whom he was much attached. He could not bring himself to inhabit Le Jas de Bouffan and took rooms in the town. In 1899 he sold the property for 80,000 francs, retaining one-third of the sum, with one-third of his mother's fortune inherited from his father, as additions to his own large inheritance from his father. In 1899 he rented a house near Aix—the Château Noir—and lived there, with occasional visits to Paris and Fontainebleau, till 1902 when he finally established himself in a new house and studio he had built on the Chemin de Lauves—a hill looking down on Aix.

After the 1895 exhibition at Vollard's, his pictures could always be seen in Vollard's gallery and Vollard arranged a second formal exhibition in 1899, which I have chronicled; I have also chronicled the exhibition of his *Mardi Gras* and some thirty other works before the Choquet sale in 1899; his exhibits at the *Salon des Indépendants* in 1899 and 1901, and also in the *Exposition Centennale* of the 1900 *Exposition Universelle*; and the juxtaposition of his *Compotier, verre et pommes* (painted twenty years earlier) with Maurice Denis' *Hommage à Cézanne* in the Brussels *Libre Esthétique* exhibition in 1901.[3] He learned with pleasure from Vollard that French and foreign amateurs were now collecting his pictures; but the invitations to the *Salon des Indépendants* and the Brussels demonstration, evidences of growing appreciation among the younger artists, gave him profounder satisfaction. In 1901 Charles Camoin (who had been a colleague of Matisse and Rouault in Moreau's atelier in the 'nineties) was doing military service at Aix, and he called upon Cézanne to pay his respects and express his admiration; Cézanne was not pre-disposed to take an ex-student of Gustave Moreau's seriously because he detested Moreau's painting and looked upon him as an '*esprit philosophique*', who had been unable to shake himself free of academic standards—('*Le grand point, comprenez,*' he said to Vollard, '*c'est de sortir de l'Ecole et de toutes les Ecoles*'); he therefore received Camoin's advances with some suspicion; but once convinced of his sincerity he was simple and kind to him and gave him encouraging advice: '*Une ère d'art nouveau se prépare. Continuez de travailler sans défaillance. Dieu fera le reste,*' he wrote to him in January 1902—a sufficient answer to Cézanne's biographers who have been at pains to persuade us of his genius by stupid denigrations of the art since constructed on the basis of his achievements. In 1903 when he was sixty-four he accepted an invitation from Maurice Denis to exhibit at the *Salon d'Automne* next year—'*Il me semble,*' he said to Vollard, '*que je ne peux pas me séparer des jeunes gens qui se sont conduits avec moi d'une manière aussi sympathique.*' And, as I shall

---

[1] London. Samuel Courtauld. (On loan at the National Gallery, Trafalgar Square.)
[2] London. Samuel Courtauld.   [3] Cf. above, pp. 160, 162, 165, 166.

chronicle, his position as an animator of twentieth century painters was finally established by the success of this *Cézanne Exhibition* in the *Salon d'Automme* in 1904.

Visitors to Aix who knew him in his last years have described his simple method of living. On Sundays or when the mood took him he would dress in sober bourgeois clothes and take his coffee with his Aixois friends at the cafés beneath the trees in the Cours Mirabeau. On week-days when he went out to paint, he wore the clothes of a country farmer or artisan. As a rule he drove to the place where he wanted to paint—*le motif* as he called it—in a hired carriage, an old-fashioned affair, upholstered in faded red velvet, drawn by a pair of ancient white horses. But sometimes he would set out on foot with his easel and canvas on his back, a flask of wine at his girdle, and his paint box in his hand. And there were few days when he did not paint either indoors or out.

At the beginning of 1906 his diabetes became worse and he suffered from frequent headaches and other distresses. But he went out almost daily to paint landscapes as before. 'As a painter,' he wrote to his son in September, 'I am becoming more lucid in the presence of nature. But with me the realisation of my sensations is always very hard. I cannot reach the intensity which appears to my senses, I have not the magnificent richness of colour that animates nature.' A fortnight later he wrote to Emile Bernard: 'I am old and ill but I have sworn to die painting.' At the beginning of October the driver of his carriage, whom he had employed for many years, asked him to raise the price of the trip to and from *le motif* by three francs; Cézanne, who had always been mean with his money and remained mean in spite of his ever-increasing wealth, was indignant at this suggestion and refused it; 'I have sacked him,' he wrote to his son, 'I now go on foot with only my water-colour bag. I can't do oil painting until I find a place in which to store my equipment.' But such a place was difficult to find because rents had gone up and he was unwilling to pay more than 30 francs a year. A week later when he had trudged painfully to *le motif*, carrying his equipment, he was caught in a violent rainstorm at some distance from his home; he started to walk back, became thoroughly wet, and collapsed by the roadside where he was eventually picked up by a passing laundry cart. He died a week later, at sixty-seven, railing in the delirium of rheumatic fever against the director of the Aix Museum who had steadily refused to see any merits whatsoever in his pictures.

ACT II: THE MASTERS' LIVES

THE DOUANIER ROUSSEAU (ii)

From forty-eight to fifty-nine (1892–1903)

All through this period The Douanier lived in humble rooms above a plasterer's shop in the rue Perrel (behind Montparnasse), painting, as before, local portraits, suburban landscapes and compositions which he sent each year to the *Salon des Indépendants*. As before, he played the violin, the flute and the clarinette for recreation and he continued to give drawing lessons and music lessons to local youngsters to make ends meet. A prospectus for his drawing classes issued at the end of this period gives his name and titles (*Professeur des cours philo-techniques de la Ville de Paris; palmes académiques*) and announces 'Mixed Courses for Children and Adults' on Saturday afternoons from 2–5 o'clock; and a 'Drawing Class from the Nude for Adults only', on Thursday evenings from 8–10 o'clock; a footnote to this prospectus states: 'As the Professor is anxious that his students in all classes shall make rapid progress the number accepted will be limited. Parents may be present at both day and evening classes.' The fee for each student was 8 francs a month.

In 1892 or 1893 he met Alfred Jarry whose father he had known in Laval where both he and Jarry had been born. The meeting took place at the *Salon des Indépendants* where The Douanier was standing beside his pictures. Jarry, much intrigued by The Douanier and his pictures, sat to him for his portrait where he was shown with a parrot and a chameleon; this *Portrait d'Alfred Jarry* was exhibited in the *Salon des Indépendants* in 1894 and thereafter Jarry had it in his rooms till some years later it was so damaged by fire that nothing but the head remained.

In 1895 he was commissioned by *L'Imagier* (then edited by Rémy de Gourmont and Jarry) to draw a lithograph *Les horreurs de la guerre*. In that year also, hearing that a book was to be published with biographical accounts of leading contemporary artists, he went to the publishers and handed them an account of his career, with a self-portrait drawn in ink. This document, of which I have seen a facsimile, is in Rousseau's handwriting and the self-portrait shows a man in the prime of life with full beard parted in the middle. The text reads as follows:

HENRI ROUSSEAU
Painter

'Born at Laval in 1844. Compelled at first by his parents' lack of means to follow a career quite different from that to which his artistic tastes invited him.

It was accordingly not till 1885 that he made his *début* in Art after many disappoint-
ments. Has worked alone without any master but nature and some advice from
Gérôme and Clément. It is only after great hardships and struggles that he has
succeeded in making himself known to the numerous artists who now surround
him. He has perfected himself more and more in the original manner which he had
adopted and he is in process of becoming one of our best realist painters. He has
been a member of the *Indépendants* for many years, holding that complete freedom
of production should be given to any initiator whose mind aspires to the Beautiful
and the Good.

He will never forget the members of the press who have been able to understand him in his moments of discouragement and helped him to become what he
is to-day.'

Personal characteristics: Bushy beard.

Paris. July 10, 1895.[1]

The reference here to help received from journalist art critics was either window
dressing or ironic. For though one or two critics referred to him respectfully
as *le primitif moderne* the majority always made fun of his pictures, urging their
readers to go and see them because '*un moment d'hilarité est toujours bon à passer*' or
describing them as no better than the works of children or of imbeciles. He collected these press comments and stuck them in books; against one cutting he
wrote, '*Ecrit au journaliste pour article insolent. Excuses faites*'.

The Douanier as a truly simple person was often imposed upon. I have already
chronicled the trick played upon him by Gauguin, and other tricks.[2] His friends
further record that someone at some point in the 'nineties dressed up an old man
as Puvis de Chavannes and sent him to call; The Douanier told him that he had long
expected the visit and discussed painting with him without suspecting the impos-

---

[1] The French text (from which my translation omits the catalogue of pictures) reads as
follows:

'*Né à Laval en l'année 1844, vu le manque de fortune de ses parents, fut obligé de suivre tout d'abord
une autre carrière que celle où ses goûts artistiques l'appelaient.*

'*Ce ne fut donc qu'en l'année 1885 qu'il fit ses débuts dans l'Art, après bien des déboires, seul sans
autre maître que la nature, et quelques conseils reçus de Gérôme et de Clément. Ses deux premières créations
exposées furent envoyées au Salon des Champs-Elysées; elles avaient pour titre:* Une danse italienne *et* Un
coucher de soleil.

'*L'année suivante, il créa de nouveau:* Un soir de carnaval, Un coup de tonnerre, *puis ensuite,* Dans
l'attente, Un pauvre diable, Après le festin, Le départ, Dîner sur l'herbe, Suicidé, A mon père,
Moi-même (*portrait-paysage de l'auteur*); Tigre poursuivant des explorateurs, Centenaire de
l'Indépendance, La Liberté, Le dernier du 41ᵉ, La guerre, *portrait genre du littérateur A. J.*, plus
environ 200 dessins, plume et crayon, et un certain nombre de paysages parisiens et des environs.

'*C'est après de bien dures épreuves qu'il arriva à se faire connaître du nombre d'artistes qui l'environ-
nent. Il s'est perfectionné de plus en plus dans le genre original qu'il a adopté et est en passe de devenir l'un
de nos meilleurs peintres réalistes. Comme signe caractéristique, il porte la barbe broussaillante, et fait partie
des Indépendants depuis longtemps déjà, pensant que toute liberté de produire doit être laissée à l'initiateur
dont la pensée s'élève dans le beau et le bien. Il n'oubliera jamais les membres de la presse qui ont su le comprendre et qui l'ont soutenu dans ses moments de découragement, et qui l'auront aidé à devenir ce qu'il doit
être.*'—Soupault, *Henri Rousseau, 1927.*

[2] Cf. above, p. 120.

ture. On another occasion The Douanier received what purported to be an invitation from the President of the Republic to a soirée at the Elysée; he went on the appointed day, and, on his return, he covered his discomfiture by describing what happened (with additions) to his friends: 'I arrived at the main door, but as I had not brought the letter of invitation with me, I was told I could not be admitted. As I insisted, the President came out and put his hand on my shoulder: "What a pity, Rousseau," he said, "that you have come in your day clothes, because everyone to-night is in evening dress. Come another time instead." '

Rodin owned and was much attached to a picture by The Douanier; and artists of the calibre of Lautrec and Gauguin, men of letters like Rémy de Gourmont and Jarry and Gustave Coquiot among the critics, understood his work and enjoyed it in this period as we have seen; and in the last years of his life he was to win admiration among the intelligentsia of a younger generation, as I shall chronicle in Act III.[1]

[1] For the present distribution of some pictures painted by The Douanier in this period cf. my Bibliographical and Catalogue Notes in Appendix I.

ACT II: THE MASTERS' LIVES

TOULOUSE-LAUTREC[1] (ii)

From twenty-eight till his death at thirty-seven (1892–1901)

In 1892 Lautrec put out the posters *Yvette Guilbert au Divan Japonais*, *Aristide Bruant aux Ambassadeurs*, and *Aristide Bruant à l'Eldorado*. The *Divan Japonais* poster shows nothing of Yvette Guilbert except her characteristic costume—white satin dress and long black gloves; in the foreground we see the curling neck of a violoncello, and two members of the audience—Jane Avril and the yellow-haired, yellow-bearded, yellow-gloved, monocled and grey top-hatted playwright Edouard Dujardin. The Bruant posters, displayed in large format at the entrance to the theatres and on each side of the stage during Bruant's performances, were an immediate success; and they still provide us with our image of Bruant—the fine profile between the black sombrero and the scarlet muffler flung over the shoulder of his long black cloak.

Lautrec at this moment was a local hero at the Moulin Rouge. His pictures *Au Cirque Fernando* (Pl. 22A) and *Au Moulin Rouge: La danse* were in the foyer; his poster was outside; in the dance hall a table was regularly reserved for him, and he went there almost nightly with Tapié de Celeyran, the painter and scenic artist Maxime Dethomas, the critic Gustave Coquiot and other friends. As his connection with the establishment is widely known through the pictures that he painted of scenes there, it is sometimes assumed that the place and its habitués were the sole and central interest of his whole career. But in fact he only went there frequently in 1891 and 1892, and all his Moulin Rouge pictures—except two or three of the clownesse Cha-U-Kao which date from 1895—were produced between the end of 1890 and the end of 1892. I have already referred to several pictures in this series. Others painted this year were *Au Moulin Rouge: En place pour le Quadrille* where the quadrille dancers, with their raised skirts held at the hips, prepare to begin their high-kicking; *Au Moulin Rouge: Les deux valseuses* where Jane Avril waltzes with the clownesse Cha-U-Kao; two pictures representing visitors to the establishment *L'Anglais au Moulin Rouge* (showing the English painter Charles Conder) and *Au Moulin Rouge: La table*; and the studies of Jane Avril performing the 'twist' in a solo dance *Jane Avril dansant*, and leaving the establishment, tired, in cheap finery, pulling on her gloves *Jane Avril sortant du Moulin Rouge*. It was also

[1] For the present distribution of the pictures mentioned and others painted by Lautrec in this period cf. my Bibliographical and Catalogue Notes in Appendix I.

at the Moulin Rouge that he discovered Yvette Guilbert in 1892 as I have chronicled; and the numerous drawings and lithographs he made of her, on and off the stage, singing her various songs, taking her curtain call, drinking a glass of wine in the wings, and so forth, were all produced before 1895.

Lautrec was temperamentally disposed to enjoy life by observing it with an artist's eye, and in particular to observe it in places devoted to pleasure. From the Moulin Rouge he went on sometimes to *maisons closes* and in 1892–1894 he painted a series of *maison close* pictures and decorated the reception room of one house with medallion portraits of the girls. When producing these pictures he frequented the houses *en copain* in the day time, lunching with the girls, taking them out to dinner, and treating them as models. He portrayed the managers of one house in a study entitled *Monsieur et Madame*. These *maison close* studies were not made with any intention of creating a *succès de scandale*, and they were never publicly exhibited in his lifetime—though they are mostly quite unexceptionable apart from associated ideas. The culminating study is a large composition *Au Salon de la rue des Moulins* which he painted in 1894.

Lithography as a medium made a strong appeal to him and he produced a large number of lithographs at this time; it was his habit to begin with a sketch in oil, or rather in a mixture of oil and a lot of turpentine, on cardboard, and he then repeated and improved the composition on the stone. His first two lithographs *La Goulue et sa sœur* and *L'Anglais au Moulin Rouge* were published at 20 francs each by the Goupil Gallery in 1892. His lithographed cover for *L'Estampe originale* in 1893 shows Jane Avril examining a print just pulled by his pet printer, an old man called Cotelle.

In 1893 he had his first one-man show at the Goupil Gallery on the Boulevard Montmartre. This show, though praised by the critics Geffroy and Roger Marx as I have chronicled, was a great disappointment to Lautrec's father Count Alphonse, who looked upon it as a decline from the facile photographic pictures of sporting subjects of the earlier period; it also disappointed Lautrec's uncle Count Charles, who implored him 'for the honour of the family name' to paint no more pictures of Montmartre subjects. In 1894 Lautrec published his album of lithographs of Yvette Guilbert with text by Geffroy, and designed a poster for Yvette Guilbert which she refused; '*Pour l'amour du ciel*,' she wrote to him, '*ne me faites pas si atrocement laide! Un peu moins . . . ! Quantité de personnes venues chez moi poussaient des cris de sauvage en regardant le projet colorié. . . . Tout le monde ne voit pas exclusivement le côté artistique . . . et dame . . .*' A ceramic of Yvette Guilbert which he designed a year later bears the singer's autograph and '*Petit monstre! Mais vous avez fait une horreur!*'

In this period he continued to work for the illustrated papers; he also drew covers for songs sung by Yvette Guilbert and others; designed programme covers and scenery for Antoine and Lugné-Poë; and he drew illustrations for Geffroy's *Le Plaisir à Paris* (which appeared in the *Figaro Illustré*) and for various writings by Tristan Bernard (which appeared in the *Revue Blanche*). His drawing of Yvette Guilbert singing *Linger Longer, Lucy, Linger Longer, Loo* was first published in *Le Rire* in 1894. He never drew for *Gil Blas Illustré*—probably because he was jealous of Steinlen whom Bruant preferred above all others as an illustrator of his songs.

From 1894 onwards his chief pleasures were the music halls, theatres and the circus, and he produced a long series of lithographs and paintings of his favourite performers. With his eye for character he picked out Antoine, Lucien Guitry, Jeanne Granier, Berthe Bady, Brandès and Marcelle Lender in the theatre; Polaire, Cissy Loftus, Cléo de Mérode, May Belfort and May Milton at the music halls; and Footit and Chocolat at the circus. Of Marcelle Lender he produced a number of lithographs and two paintings—*Mlle Lender dansant le pas du Boléro dans l'opérette 'Chilpéric'* and *Mlle Lender en scène*. He drew posters for May Belfort and May Milton and painted *May Belfort en rose* (Pl. 39A) and May Belfort singing her successful ditty:

> 'Daddy wouldn't buy me a bow-wow,
> I've got a little cat
> And I'm very fond of that
> But I'd rather have a bow-wow-wow-wow-wow. . . .'

In 1895, when he went to London and made the drawing *Oscar Wilde* (Pl. 38), he frequented the Criterion Bar in Piccadilly and Sweeting's fish restaurant in Cheapside, and was ill at ease with '*Les Beardsley, les Symonds*' and *tutti quanti*, and said to Joyant, '*Ces gens-là me feront prendre Botticelli en horreur*'. Back in Paris he frequented Mme Natanson's salon, and contributed to the *Revue Blanche*; and he painted various portraits of the Natansons, a group showing Thadée Natanson, Mme Natanson, Vuillard and Vallotton at table, and a witty portrait of Tristan Bernard the *Revue Blanche*'s sporting editor.[1] His former favourite La Goulue had now left the Moulin Rouge and was running a booth known as '*La baraque de La Goulue*' where she danced '*en mauresque*' and appeared as a lion tamer; Lautrec painted two large panels for the exterior of this *baraque* and gave them to La Goulue as a mascot for her venture. The *baraque* soon failed; and the panels after various wanderings were eventually acquired by the Louvre.

In 1896 he travelled a good deal. He visited the Loire châteaux, and went by sea from Havre to Bordeaux; he stayed some time boating and swimming at Arcachon; and he visited Lisbon, Madrid, and Toledo. His Spanish visit is recorded in several drawings of Spanish types—*Gendarme espagnol en gare de Tolède, Deux profils d'espagnols*, etc.

He now began the set of lithographs called '*Elles*' which continued his earlier studies of women at their toilette. For these lithographs he made, as usual, a number of paintings as preliminary sketches and these include *La toilette, Femme se lavant*, and *Conquête de passage*—the last-named containing a portrait of Charles Conder. A number of his drawings appeared this year in *Le Rire*; one shows Ambroise Thomas at the rehearsal of *Françoise de Rimini*, another the negro clown Chocolat dancing at the Bar Achille (later the Café Weber). He also made drawings for de Goncourt's *La fille Elisa* (produced at the *Théâtre Libre* in 1890 and interdicted by the censor[2]), and he made character studies in court at the Procès Arton —an echo of the Panama Scandal.[3] At the music hall he was now attracted by a new dancer Ida Heath and he made drawings and lithographs which depict her dancing and, after the performance, drinking at the bar.

[1] Cf. p. 151.   [2] Cf. pp. 103, 105.   [3] Cf. p. 146.

In 1897 he again spent some time at the seaside swimming and boating with his friend Maxime Dethomas, and he went with Dethomas to Holland where the inhabitants mistook him for a performing dwarf with his manager. He also went to London, with one 'Spike' a trainer of racing cyclists, and made a drawing called *Les Horseguards*. He now fell to the charm of painting for painting's sake and produced a series of nudes in which his interest is more in form and colour than in the character of the model as heretofore. His portraits of this year include *Paul Leclercq* and *Berthe Bady*.

This was the peak moment of his career. He was thirty-three, happy and successful and making an effort to start a new and less illustrative approach to art. From Paul Leclercq the novelist, who was intimate with him at this time, we know that he was now more than ever an engaging companion, lively, witty, unpretentious, kind, enjoying life and anxious to amuse and enliven his friends. Dressed in a white barman's coat he would shake *les long drinks* and *les short drinks* at a bar erected in his studio; accompanied by Leclercq, whom he always addressed as *petit gentleman*, he would move about Paris on droll and whimsical expeditions— one of which (the call on the model for Manet's *Olympia*) I have chronicled.[1]

In 1898 when he went to London for his exhibition at the Goupil Gallery[2] he made the amusing chalk drawing *Barmaid au Criterion*, and painted *Soldat anglais fumant sa pipe*—a preliminary study for a tobacco poster never, I believe, carried out. Back in Paris he drew illustrations for Clémenceau's *Au pied du Sinaï* and for *Histoires naturelles* by Jules Renard.

He now began to indulge more recklessly in alcoholic habits, and to work less regularly and less hard. At the end of 1898 he drew the sinister lithograph *Di ti fellow*; and at the beginning of 1899 it was clear that he was losing his mental control. In February his friends had to arrange for doctors and attendants to trap him as he left his studio and take him to a sanatorium in the Madrid suburb at Neuilly. This incarceration was made the occasion of outbursts of malevolence in certain sections of the press. The *Journal* and the *Echo de Paris* were leaders in vilification. The latter described him as a wretched crippled degenerate who had wasted all his energies and talents: '*Chétif, rabougri, contrefait, plus semblable à un de ces nains grotesques qui grimaçaient derrière le fauteuil ducal dans les châteaux seigneuriaux qu'à un descendant de Raymond conduisant la Chrétienté à la délivrance du Saint Sépulchre, le malheureux dégénéré avait conscience du ridicule de sa double infirmité d'avorton et de noble sans le sou. . . .*' In point of fact, as the critic Arsène Alexandre pointed out in a rejoinder, Lautrec had always worked extremely hard and his mental breakdown only lasted a few weeks. As a result of a régime and abstinence from alcohol he was soon able to receive his friends in the sanatorium and by April he was at work on fifty pastel drawings of circus subjects (covering the whole equine, acrobatic and clown repertoire) which were afterwards lithographed and published as an album. In May the doctors pronounced him quite recovered and arranged for one of his friends Paul Viaud who lived at Bordeaux to look after him. He left early in June saying, '*J'ai acheté ma liberté avec mes dessins*' which was largely true. In July he went to Le Havre with Viaud and produced two celebrated studies of an English

[1] Cf. above, p. 156.   [2] Cf. above, p. 158.

barmaid, *L'Anglaise du 'Star' au Havre*. He then went to the coast near Bordeaux. At the end of the year he returned to Paris and painted the portrait *Romain Coolus*. '*Je te peindrai en Greco*,' he said to Coolus because his pointed beard and moustaches reminded him of El Greco's portraits which he had seen in Spain.

In May 1900 he sent out invitations for an exhibition in his studio of work produced since his release from the sanatorium; the card invited the visitors to drink a glass of milk with him and it was decorated with a caricature in which he is seated milking a cow. After the exhibition he went to Le Crotoy and other places on the coast. At Honfleur he met Lucien Guitry and drew for him a programme cover for the revival of Zola's *L'Assommoir* at the Porte St. Martin. In June he was again at Le Havre but he found the English barmaid flown; '*Old Chump*,' he wrote to Joyant, '*Les Stars et autres bars sont très surveillés par la police, rien à faire; il n'y a plus de barmaids. . . A toi H L and Co (tout ce qu'il y a de plus limited)*. From Le Havre he went to Arcachon where he painted the portrait *Maurice Joyant: En Baie du Somme*. In September he went to stay with his mother at Malromé and began the decorative panel *L'Amiral Viaud* which was left unfinished at his death. Later in the year he was with Viaud at Bordeaux where he produced pictures of the opera *Messaline* at the Bordeaux opera house, drawings of Mlle Cocyte in *La Belle Hélène*, some studies of *modistes*, projects for the portrait of a violinist, an impression of the *Bal des Etudiants à Bordeaux*, and a portrait of Paul Viaud. He also designed a poster this year for *La Gitane* by Richepin at the *Théâtre Antoine*.

In March 1901 he was still in Bordeaux, producing among other things some drawings of the local cardinals and a book cover for *Jouets de Paris* by Paul Leclercq. In April he returned to Paris, nominally to arrange an exhibition of his work. But in fact he knew that his end was near; for his legs were now attacked by paralysis. He was nevertheless able to paint a composition *Un examen à la faculté de médecine* and the portrait *André Rivoire*. For the rest he spent his time arranging, cataloguing and signing the numerous pictures, lithographs, drawings and so forth in his studio. In July he went to Arcachon and thence to Taussat where he collapsed with paralysis. His mother came there and took him to Malromé where he died on September 9.

On his death most of Lautrec's pictures, drawings and lithographs reverted to his parents as his next of kin. His father Count Alphonse, who had disapproved his productions since his adolescent period, refused to make money or glory from his reputation now that he was dead; he gave some of the pictures to Lautrec's friends, complete sets of the lithographs to the Luxembourg Museum and the Bibliothèque Nationale, and ceded all his *droits paternels artistiques* (rights relating to publication, photographs and so forth) to Maurice Joyant; 'I make no pretence to generosity in ceding all my paternal rights to you,' he wrote to Joyant, 'it is purely a matter of probity. . . . I have no intention of becoming converted to his art and publicly parading, now that he is dead, the work which I failed to understand in his lifetime and which I looked upon as nothing more than dashing daring studies properly kept in a studio portfolio. . . . You believed in his work more than I did and your judgment was right. . . . Your brotherly affection in his lifetime took the place of my feeble influence. . . . It is only logical that I should ask you to continue . . .'

TOULOUSE-LAUTREC, TO HIS DEATH AT THIRTY-SEVEN

In 1902 when the *Salon des Indépendants* had a *Lautrec Memorial Exhibition* and Maurice Joyant arranged the larger Memorial Exhibition in Durand-Ruel's galleries, Lautrec's family offered all or any of the paintings in the Durand-Ruel show to the Luxembourg Museum as a gift. After many hesitations the Luxembourg accepted one picture—*La femme au boa*—which was hung with the Caillebotte collection then exhibited in that Museum. The lithographs, already presented, were put into store and not exhibited.[1]

[1] For the installation of the Musée Lautrec at Albi cf. below, p. 299.

ACT II: THE MASTERS' LIVES

AUGUSTE RENOIR[1] (iii)

From fifty-one to sixty-two (1892–1903)

In the early 'nineties Renoir was living at Montmartre in an old house known as le Château des Brouillards, with his wife and children and two servants. His eldest son, Pierre, was seven in 1892; his second son, Jean, was born in 1893; Claude his last son was born in 1901. He worked in Paris in the winter months and in the summer he painted in the country or by the sea in Brittany—at Tréboul, Noirmoutier, or Pont Aven. Later he decided that the air of the northern coasts was too hard for him and he then went more frequently to Essoyes and to the south.

In the early part of this period he visited Holland and Spain. In Holland he found Rembrandt joyless, and sighed—(though he admired *The Jewish Bride*)—for *La Finette* by Watteau; of *The Night Watch* he said, 'If I owned that picture I should cut out the little figure with the chicken and scrap the rest.' In Spain he rejoiced in Goya's *Royal Family* where the variety of the coloured tones made him forget the apparent vulgarity of the personalities portrayed—the King with his 'air of a pork butcher' and the Queen who 'seems to have stepped out of a low café or worse'; and he discovered El Greco whom he spoke of to Vollard as *un très grand peintre*, though he was ill at ease with his 'studio lighting', and 'the long hands always the same' and 'the faked draperies'.

His paintings in the 'nineties include landscapes, genre figure studies, nudes, portraits and groups including *La famille de l'artiste* and *Berthe Morisot et sa fille*. In the genre studies we watch the continued growth of the two little girls, one brune, one blonde, who as already noted were favourite models from about 1890 onwards. In 1892 we see them as girls of fifteen or sixteen seated at the piano, and in 1894–1895 we see them outside in the meadows; at the same time we see them nude as bathers or asleep on the studio divan; and finally we see them as young ladies in their Sunday hats and dresses sitting awkwardly on little chairs at some local ceremony. Other pictures of this period show us the growth of Renoir's sons Pierre, Jean and the earliest years of 'Coco', i.e. Claude. Speaking generally, as I have noted in the Introduction to this Act, his work of this period is relatively hesitant, uninspired and academic—a transition from his splendid contribution of the 'eighties (*Les grandes baigneuses* (Pl. 19B)) to the equally and indeed still more

[1] For the present distribution of the pictures mentioned and others painted in this period cf. my Bibliographical and Catalogue Notes in Appendix I.

splendid contribution in the period covered by Act III, which was heralded by a charming little picture of Coco and his nurse, *Femme et enfant dans un parc*, painted in 1903.

As the 'nineties advanced he suffered more and more from rheumatoid arthritis and he spent more and more time in the south—in the country behind Nice, on the coast at Antibes, and in Provence, hoping to cure it. From 1898 to 1900 the trouble was so bad that he could hardly work at all; and in 1900 he made his headquarters in the Midi where he had various homes till in 1903 he installed himself at Le Cannet between Grasse and Cannes.

Apart from his illness he lived these years in a tranquillity which even the stupidities of Roujon and the official artists in the matter of the Caillebotte bequest[1] could scarcely disturb. His success of the 'eighties continued and grew in the 'nineties; he had arrangements with dealers which relieved him of financial worries; he could, and did, paint when and where and what he pleased; and he was served by a devoted family and servants who were willing to sit to him as models.

[1] Cf. above, pp. 149, 155.

ACT II: THE MASTERS' LIVES

EDGAR DEGAS (iii)

From fifty-eight to sixty-nine (1892–1903)

In these years Degas worked less than he had done before and took more holiday and 'cures' for his real and imaginary ailments. He lived alone all through the period in his triple apartment in the old house in the rue Victor Massé, and his neighbours met him on the stairs, continually pottering from one floor to the other, rattling his large old-fashioned keys. More hypochondriac than ever, he ate only the most simple foods cooked without seasoning for fear of indigestion. More miserly than ever, though he was now also wealthier than ever, he denied himself the most modest luxuries and comforts. His domestic staff was restricted to one old housekeeper who read aloud Drumont's attacks on the Jews in *La Libre Parole*, to give him an appetite for his tasteless food, and *Les Mille et Une Nuits* to send him to sleep. As chronicled he was a passionate anti-Dreyfusard and he declined to see Claude Monet for a number of years after Monet's appearance by Zola's side at Zola's trial in 1898.[1] He was now more and more engrossed in his collections, attending sales and searching Paris for bargains. In this period he bought works by Gauguin, already chronicled.[2] Another acquisition was Manet's *L'exécution de l'Empereur Maximilien* which he found in two pieces and had assembled.[3] He now had ten paintings and many drawings by Ingres, and a number of works by Delacroix; his letters of the 'nineties refer to purchases of prints by Gavarni and Dürer, a painting by Cuyp, and so forth. Most of these things were stacked, framed or unframed, untended and undusted, in his upper apartment; in his bedroom at one time he is said to have used a picture by El Greco to hang his trousers on at night.[4]

Vollard has decribed his studio and method of work in the later years of this period. He had numerous portfolios full of drawings and unfinished pastels. It was his habit to make tracing after tracing of his pastels, each tracing being larger than the last so that a study which was at first quite small eventually became a large picture. The majority of his pastels at this time are nude studies of models posing

[1] Cf. above p. 163.   [2] Cf. above, pp. 104, 143, 150.

[3] The original picture was damaged by damp; Manet's heirs removed the damaged portions and cut what remained into separate pieces which they sold to the dealers Portier and Vollard from whom Degas bought them. The London National Gallery bought them at the Degas sale in 1918. (For the circumstances connected with the painting of this picture and the ban on its exhibition in 1867 cf. above, p. 21.)

[4] E. de Gramont. *Mémoires* (Grasset, 1929).

in the modern bath introduced to the studio about 1890; and now, as before, he often used enlargements from photographs to assist him in his work. At the beginning of this period he produced some landscapes in pastel, and some in turpentine on cardboard, exhibited at Durand-Ruel's in 1893 as recorded.[1] Towards the end of the period he turned more and more to modelling which he found less strain on his eyes. He had modelled, on and off, since 1880 when he produced the wax figure *Petite danseuse de quatorze ans* in the real *toutou*.[2] He had made wax models of horses in action since the 'seventies. But from now onwards he mainly modelled nudes of dancers executing characteristic steps and of women in the attitudes of their toilet. Renoir referred to him at this period as 'the greatest living sculptor' and ranked him above Rodin.

It was his custom at this time to winter in Paris and divide the rest of the year between a 'cure' at some spa and visits to the Valpinçons at Menil-Hubert, to de Valernes at Carpentras, and to other friends in different parts of the country. In 1892 he went to Menil-Hubert with four shirts, saying, '*Quand elles seront finies ie m'en irai*'; but as the château's resources included laundry he stayed for two months. At Menil-Hubert he was with devoted friends, but he wrote gloomily to Bartholomé, '*Je ne sais plus me conduire. D'autres ont le bonheur d'être guidés par leurs passions. Des passions je n'en ai pas. . . .*' In 1893 he visited de Valernes who was in financial difficulties, and he bought back from him for 3,000 francs a portrait he had painted of him some twenty-five years earlier. In 1897 he took a cure at the Bains du Mont-Dore in the Puy de Dôme, where he was consoled for the presence of a Monsieur Levi at the hotel *table d'hôte* by the '*conversation antisémite*' provided by another guest. From Mont-Dore he went to Montauban where he examined the large collection of Ingres drawings, some of which he found to be studies for pictures in his own collection; he proposed as a bargain to the curator of the Musée Ingres to supply him with photographs of these pictures in exchange for photographs of the drawings; but nothing seems to have come of this proposal. As the years advanced he became less and less willing to make new acquaintances or to admit gushing admirers, journalists or collectors to his studio; and his reputation for misanthropy thus inevitably increased. But with his old chosen friends who humoured him and shared his prejudices he could on occasion be amiable and even gay.

His neurotic complaints about his eyesight became each year more frequent. In 1893 he wrote, 'My friends must no longer count much on me for letters. It is so difficult for me to reread what I have written, even with a magnifying glass, that I give up after the first lines.' But it was not till 1898, when he was sixty-four, that his friends observed any evidence of bad eyesight in his handwriting or spelling; and he was able to produce his pastels of dancers and women at their toilet when the spirit moved him and also to write letters all through this period; and the real failure of his eyesight which he had dreaded for so long had not yet happened at the end of this period when he was sixty-nine.[3]

[1] Cf. above, p. 144.   [2] Cf. above, pp. 45, 46, 54.
[3] For the present distribution of some works by Degas in this period cf. my Bibliographical and Catalogue Notes in Appendix I.

ACT III

1904—JULY 1914

From later Fauvism, Picasso's *Saltimbanques* and The Douanier's '*Le lion ayant faim* . . .'; to Negroism, Rhythmic Decoration, Cubism, Futurism and Surrealism

ACT III

1904–JULY 1914

From later Fauvism, Picasso's *Saltimbanques* and The Douanier's '*Le lion ayant faim . . .*'; to Negroism, Rhythmic Decoration, Cubism, Futurism and Surrealism

INTRODUCTION

The period 1904 to the German invasion saw the development of the *Fauve Movement*,[1] the influence of negro sculpture, then *Cubism* and *Futurism*, and then *Surrealism* launched by Chagall and Chirico; and each of these movements, and the personal achievements of Picasso and The Douanier Rousseau must be separately considered.

In 1904–1906 the Fauves, all grouped round Matisse, included among others Marquet, Vlaminck, Derain and Rouault and, as newcomers, Dufy, Friesz, Braque and eventually Van Dongen. Marquet, fundamentally an Impressionist, stood really closer to Manet than to Matisse and the Fauves. Vlaminck and Derain based their Fauvism on the excited handling and vivid colour in Van Gogh's pictures which they had seen, as noted, in the Van Gogh exhibition of 1901;[1] and in 1904–1907 they painted street scenes, river scenes, port scenes, landscapes, figures and still-life in vivid mosaics of pure vermilion, emerald, cobalt and cadmium—colours that must be visualized in the photograph of Derain's *Le port* (Pl. 50A) which I reproduce as a typical Fauve picture in the Van Gogh tradition at this moment. The colour in these Fauve works by Vlaminck and Derain was intense to the limits of the colourman's resources, and the handling was a violent symbol of the artists' exuberant excitement; but whereas Van Gogh's vivid colouring and excited handling recorded the contact of a disordered Northern personality with the warm South, Derain and Vlaminck's vivid colouring and excited handling at this period record the contact of perfectly healthy Frenchmen with Van Gogh's pictures, their pleasure in bright pigments squeezed from the colourman's tubes, and their sympathy with the movement to set colour free from representation. At bottom, the aesthetic of Derain and Vlaminck at this time, like the aesthetic of Marquet, was really Impressionist; and thus the colour in *Le port* and kindred pictures was only partially set free from representation; the colour sang—shouted even—of its

[1] Cf. above, pp. 140, 160 16c. 168.

197

freedom from descriptive drudgery, but all the time it was really describing ports and boats and masts and fishermen. These Fauve pictures by Vlaminck and Derain were nevertheless useful as a means of breaking in the dilettanti to the further stages in the liberation of colour about to be accomplished by others.

Rouault, who was not captured at this time by Van Gogh's vivid colour, continued and developed his personal Expressionism right up to the war. Selecting circus folk and the women in *maisons closes* as his subjects he set down his figures first, apparently, in red and black and then reinforced these statements with blue calligraphic lines. Fundamentally a romantic-realist and aiming above all at psychological affectivity and drama, Rouault thus brought the work of Degas and Lautrec to a climax and took rank as a descendant of Rembrandt through Daumier and Van Gogh. I reproduce his *Clown* (Pl. 59) of 1906–7 and the intensely affective *Christ* (Pl. 72) painted about 1914.

Matisse's contributions now became more adventurous each year. Gifted with an aesthetic which reacted above all to colour, and with a truly miraculous instinct for pattern and scale, he handled colour with daring originality and went farther than his colleagues in liberating it from representational service. He realized, as Gauguin had realized before him, that modern art would lose the double battle against academic pedagogy and the camera unless line, colour and pattern were used as aesthetic agents with the freedom of primitive art on the one hand and the formal science of Near and Far Eastern art on the other; and to acquire this freedom and this science he studied in museums and availed himself of the increased range of art experience which was now being made available by photographic reproductions and facilities for travel. In 1904–5 he was essentially Fauve in *Fleurs* (Pl. 50B) and *Nature morte au pot de fleurs*.[1] But he combined this with a more formal calligraphy in *La femme au chapeau*[2] of the same period and this tendency is still more apparent in *Marguerite lisant*,[3] *Nature morte au melon et tapis*[3] and *Le jeune marin*[4] all painted in 1906. In *Le jeune marin* the background is more or less flat pink, the folds in the ultramarine shirt and apple-green trousers are conventionally indicated with a few dark lines, and the features on the ochre face are drawn in a purely linear convention—green lines for the eyes, yellow-brown lines for the nose and cheek bone, and green and red lines for the mouth; and we realize here that the artist is not concerned to use line and colour to represent phenomena in effects of light and shade, and that he is also not concerned to describe phenomena in terms of their local colour; we do not believe that the boy's shirt was really that blue or his trousers really that green because we know that his mouth was not really one green lip and one red; we do not believe the local colours because we are not asked to believe them; we are left in ignorance of the starting-off point which produced the picture—the appearance of a particular boy in some particular clothes sitting in some particular light in a corner of the studio while the artist spreads lines and colours on a canvas—and what is revealed to us is only the result of the artist's action, i.e. the picture.

[1] Chicago. Frederick C. Bartlett.
[2] Vaucresson. Michael Stein (formerly Gertrude Stein, cf. below, p. 213).
[3] Grenoble. Museum.   [4] German collection.

49 . CEZANNE
Les grandes baigneuses 1898–1906
Philadelphia. Museum of Art

50A. DERAIN
Le port, 1906
Formerly Paris. Galerie Kahnweiler
50B. MATISSE
Tulipes et marguerites, 1905
Paris. M. Félix Fénéon

INTRODUCTION

Picasso in 1904 and 1905 pursued his own path uninfluenced by the Fauves and without influence himself on contemporary French painting. He returned to Paris from Barcelona aged twenty-three at the beginning of 1904 bringing with him his pictures of beggars and so forth, including *Le vieux guitariste* (Pl. 47). He then produced some more pictures with emotive emaciated figures including *La femme à la corneille*,[1] *La repasseuse*[2] and the wonderful large etching *L'aveugle* sometimes titled *Le repas frugal*; next came *La femme à la chemise* (Pl. 52) and some delicate coloured drawings of a youth contemplating a nude girl asleep (a motif to which he returned some thirty years later); and he then began a series of oil and gouache paintings, water colours and etchings depicting *saltimbanques*—circus performers, harlequins and so forth. In some of the oil and gouache paintings of 1904 and 1905, *La femme à la chemise* for example, the blue tints still predominate; in others such as *La toilette*[3] and *L'acrobate à la boule* (Pl. 53B) the colours are mainly blue and pink; in others again the dominant is pink; the year 1905 is accordingly known as his 'Pink period'—though here again the label is too categoric. The *saltimbanque* pictures, and the etchings (including *Salomé dansant devant Herod*) which go with them, were produced without models in the silence of his studio at night—for Picasso slept most of the day at this period and worked throughout the night; their aesthetic is Greek, in the sense that Tanagra terracottas are Greek; but this aesthetic is soaked through with the artist's romantic sensibility. All the works in the *saltimbanque* series are tender in feeling, most sensitively drawn, and given substance by the precision of the artist's visual memory and his imaginative powers. In these paintings, gouaches and etchings Picasso shows us not the public performances in the ring—which Degas had shown in *Miss Lola au cirque Fernando*[4] and Seurat had shown in *Cirque*[5] and Lautrec in *Au cirque Fernando* (Pl. 22A) and drawings—but the life of the *saltimbanques* before and after the performance either outside on the waste ground surrounding their tents where the juveniles are trained in their tricks and mounted on the horses, and the older children carry the youngsters pick-a-back or water the horses in a stream, or within the tents where the performers sleep and live and eat their meals from drum tops and care for their children as best they can. Picasso shows us charming child-tumblers and child-equestrians in contrast with the wistful grace of adolescent acrobats and harlequins; and these again are contrasted with herculean strong-men and the bulky flabbiness of older performers. But these pictures are in no sense a descriptive chronicle of circus conditions; they are records of aspects of life which moved the artist at this period cloaked, symbolized, disguised as it were in the familiar trappings of the acrobat's tights and the harlequin's check suit: and indeed as the series advances the trappings are left out, the harlequin's checks are forgotten, the acrobat's tights disappear, the horses are led without bridles and ridden to water by nude youths. I reproduce three examples of these engaging productions: *Femme à sa toilette et Arlequin avec enfant* (Pl. 53A), *La femme aux pains* (Pl. 54A) and *L'acrobate à la boule* (Pl. 53B). In all, as can be seen, the illustrative element

---

[1] Paris. Mme Paul Guillaume. [2] Formerly Paris. Ambroise Vollard.
[3] Buffalo. Albright Art Gallery. [4] Plate A.
[5] Paris. Louvre.

is more implicit than explicit; the spirit of the figures as humans, romantically observed, remembered or imagined, is the real subject of the pictures; and the language of record is entirely original, astonishingly simple and irresistibly expressive. The Tanagra aesthetic also dominates in a series of paintings with nude figures —*Le harem*,[1] *Nu au pichet*,[2] *Fillette, garçon et chèvre*[3] and *La fillette à la corbeille fleurie*[4] which date from 1905.

But the day came when the Tanagra aesthetic and romantic procedures no longer corresponded to Picasso's attitude; and indeed it was clearly impossible for the most fertile and virile creative artist of our century to plough for long in nineteenth-century fields or produce for ever the pictorial equivalents of Baudelaire's *Petits poèmes en prose*. We get a hint of this dissatisfaction in *Hollandaise à la coiffe*[5] where the form is monumental though the picture dates from 1905. In 1906 he reacted violently from the spirit behind his 'Blue' and 'Pink' pictures which he later referred to as 'all sentiment'; and he now sought an attitude nearer to Gauguin's description of primitive art, an attitude in which sensuous experience and sentiment would retire to the rank of servants and not dominate the artist in his creation of form. It was at this moment that he discovered negro sculpture and found it helpful. For here was an art vital not only with primitive gusto and primitive concern with magic, but also with formal characters unknown to Western art. And thus it came that *La femme aux pains* (Pl. 54A) was followed in 1906–7 by a series of pictures where the influence of negro sculpture is progressively apparent. This series began with pictures like the *Portrait de Gertrude Stein*[4] and the *Portrait de l'artiste* (Pl. 54B); it was continued in various compositions with nude figures including *Les demoiselles d'Avignon*[6] and it culminated in *Le corsage jaune*[7] and *Danseuse nègre* (Pl. 55A).

The years 1907–1912 were very important in the history of modern painting. For it was then that the idea of Abstract Art was systematically explored, first in Rhythmic Decoration on the one hand and then in Cubism on the other.

Speaking generally the type of Abstract Art that I call Rhythmic Decoration (or Rhythmic Fauvism) is concerned to create a rhythmic arabesque animated and coordinated in an organic way; its aim is to create an organic pictorial architecture which appears to have grown as a plant grows or to flow as a stream flows— and its aesthetic is the aesthetic that dominates in Far Eastern art. This type of art had been heralded by Gauguin in 1888–1890 in *Vision après le sermon: Lutte de Jacob avec l'ange* (Pl. 22B) and *Mlle Loulou* (Pl. 30); it had been carried farther in terms of three dimensions by Cézanne in *Les grandes baigneuses* (Pl. 49) of 1898–1905; and as I record in 'How it happened' a part in its development was played by the Cézanne Exhibitions in 1904 and 1907 and by the publication in 1907 of Cézanne's dictum '*Peindre ce n'est pas copier seulement l'objectif: c'est saisir une harmonie entre des rapports nombreux*'.

Of this Rhythmic Decoration Matisse from 1907 onwards was the chief ex-

---

[1] Cleveland. Museum of Art (L. C. Hanna). [2] Lausanne. Dr. Reber.
[3] Merion. Barnes Foundation. [4] Paris. Miss Gertrude Stein.
[5] Oslo. Stang Collection. [6] Paris. Mme Jacques Doucet.
[7] Paris. Mme Paul Guillaume.

Plate (E) PICASSO
Jeune homme et cheval, 1905
London. National Gallery, Millbank (Tate Gallery)
(cf. page xii)

ponent, and he developed it in various calligraphic ways. In 1907 he painted *Les oignons roses d'Espagne*[1] (where the pattern on the pot is set down with the calligraphic freedom of the painters of linear designs on Talavera ware), *Le chasseur de papillons* (Pl. 57A), *Le nu bleu*,[2] and *Bonheur de vivre* (Pl. 56). In *Chasseur de papillons* we find an intensification of the characters in the *Le jeune marin*; the boy wears a cream suit and a vermilion tie and he has chestnut hair; the background is dark ultramarine above and emerald green behind the figure; the ground is deep scarlet with emerald green at the corner. The *Bonheur de vivre*, a veritable landmark in modern painting, is a kind of climax to Gauguin's rhythmic ideals. In 1908 Matisse painted *La desserte*[3] (a decorative version in his new manner of *La desserte*[4] of 1898) and the arrestingly calligraphical *Mme Matisse au madras rouge*[5] which was followed by *La femme aux yeux verts*[6] in 1909 and *Marguerite au chat*;[7] and in 1909–1910 he painted the celebrated decorations *La danse*[3] and *La musique*.[3] In *La danse* where five nude figures calligraphically portrayed dance round in a circle against a flat bright-coloured background, everything is subordinated to the rhythmic flow of line; but the patterning is more static in *La musique* and in the pictures of 1911 and 1912—*Portrait de famille*[3] and a series painted in Morocco including *Fenêtre à Tanger*,[3] *Femme Marocaine*[3] and *Zorah sur la terrasse*.[3] In all these pictures Matisse entirely abjured the use of illusionist chiaroscuro and perspective. In *Portrait de famille*,[8] for example (an interior with two boys playing draughts and two young women), all spectroscopic and three-dimensional effects are avoided; the red suits of the boys, the black and white squares of the board, the black and ochre of the women's clothes, the red ochres of the carpet and the flowering pattern on the walls combine instead in a mosaic of colour spots that balance one another but do not fuse or merge. In these pictures line and colour are not yet quite set free from representational labours—that was to be accomplished by Picasso—but their doings one with another in their leisure hours, now much longer as it were than their working hours, are clearing the real subject of the picture. In 1913 Matisse entered a phase where his work was influenced by negro masks and by Cubism; we see the first influence in *La femme de l'artiste*[3] and the second in *La femme au tabouret*;[7] and this phase continued in the first years covered by my 'Interlude'.[9]

Matisse's associates and followers in this period did not keep pace with his development. Derain, who was still Fauve when he painted *La cathédrale de St Paul et la Tamise* (Pl. 58) in 1907, moved thereafter from Matisse's orbit to Picasso's, and his *La toilette* (Pl. 61) which marks the transition in 1908 combines the influences of a picture by Matisse of the same subject[10] painted in 1907, Gauguin's *La reine des Areois* (Pl. 35) and Picasso's *Portrait de l'artiste* (Pl. 54) of 1906; and Dufy and Van Dongen (Pl. 57B) rang the changes on Matisse's Fauvism in various witty and mondain ways till, in the later years of this period, Dufy learned to exploit his

[1] Copenhagen. Museum.   [2] Baltimore. Cone Collection.
[3] Moscow. Museum of Modern Western Art.   [4] German collection, cf. pp. 139, 159.
[5] Merion. Barnes Foundation.   [6] San Francisco. Miss Harriet Levy.
[7] Nice. Henri Matisse.   [8] Reproduced in my *The Modern Movement in Art*.
[9] Cf. below, pp. 258, 259.   [10] Oslo. Tryggve Sagen Collection.

talents in light and personal calligraphic paintings and charming designs for textiles, and Van Dongen adapted his Fauvism to the portraiture of beautiful *mondaines*.

Cubism, the other type of Abstract Art, which was developed in 1908–1912, became eventually a grand, austere and deliberate pictorial architecture constructed by Reason as a symbol of metaphysical order, a classical art fundamentally Western and preferring straight lines, circles and geometric forms to the free-flowing, organic lines and rhythms of Far Eastern art. This reasonable, classical, Cubist art (which did not reach its final stage of classical purity till Ozenfant transformed it to Purism in 1918–1926[1], after Picasso and Braque and others had made countless pioneer gestures of empirical and decorative kinds) had been heralded of course by Seurat's scientific study of linear and colour relations for his classical compositions in the 'eighties and by Cézanne's study of nature's architecture from the end of his so-called Impressionist period; and factors in its development were the Seurat Exhibition in 1905, the Cézanne Exhibitions of 1904 and 1907, and the publication in 1907 of Cézanne's dicta: '*Tout dans la nature se modèle selon la sphère, le cône et le cylindre. Il faut s'apprendre à peindre sur ces figures simples, on pourra ensuite faire tout ce qu'on voudra*' and '*Il faut traiter la nature par le cylindre, la sphère, le cône, le tout mis en perspective, soit que chaque côté d'un objet, d'un plan, se dirige vers un point central.*'

Picasso's 'negro' pictures of 1906–1907 were, as stated, his first move away from the sentiment of his 'Blue' and 'Pink' pictures towards a less sensuous and more formal art. And the day came, towards the end of 1907, when he realized that the emotive vitality and emotive distortions of these negro pictures were at bottom as romantic as the emotive emaciation in *Le vieux guitariste* (Pl. 47) and the emotive wistfulness of *La femme à la chemise* (Pl. 52), *La femme aux pains* (Pl. 54A) and *L'acrobate à la boule* (Pl. 53B), and that negro sculpture could not lead him in the field he was about to plough. And thus it came that at the end of 1907 after studying the Cézanne Exhibition and reading Cézanne's dicta already quoted, he painted *Les bols* (Pl. 55B) and embarked on Cubism.

The Cézannesque Cubism of *Les bols*, and of similar still-life compositions[2] painted by Picasso in 1907–8, was a forcing of Cézanne's architectural procedures in the direction of their logical conclusion; and in Picasso's hands these pictures were a stage in his effort to create a new abstract non-representational pictorial art. He advanced farther in this direction in 1909 and 1910 (as I shall chronicle) but while he was thus advancing a whole new school of painting was being founded on *Les bols*—a school which spread rapidly in all directions—east and west, and north and south. In the hands of Picasso's followers the Cézannesque Cubism of *Les bols* was not used as a stage in the creation of a new abstract non-representational art, but as a new stylistic formula in representational painting. These artists sought and found spheres and cones, cubes and cylinders and other geometric forms in the objects and in the component parts of the objects selected as material for their pictures, and they *represented* these objects, to some extent, in this new geometric language. The most dogmatic practitioners of this new formula in representational

---

[1] Cf. below, pp. 267–271.
[2] *Bol et compotier*, for example, in the New York University Museum of Living Art.

51. THE DOUANIER ROUSSEAU
Le lion ayant faim, 1905
Zurich. F. M. . . . collection

52 . PICASSO
Femme à la chemise, 1905
London. National Gallery, Millbank

painting gave us trees and human limbs recorded as cylinders and pipes; the less dogmatic used modifications of the new formula as a trick to give character to their otherwise characterless drawing, or as an aid to suggesting fashionable elegance, i.e. the distortions dictated by the sartorial fashions of the time. The most notable compromise was achieved by Derain who explored this type of Cubism from 1910–1912 and made the stylistic formula a vehicle for the expression of his sensibility; Derain went back in fact, through and by means of Picasso's *Les bols*, to the dualism in Cézanne's pictures from which Picasso had extracted only the architectural factor; and thus Derain's fine picture *Fenêtre sur le parc* (Pl. 66) of 1912 in fact stands closer to Cézanne's *Portrait de Gustave Geffroy* (Pl. 44A) of 1895 than to Picasso's *Les bols* of 1907 or to the later and more abstract forms of Cubism which I must now discuss.

Picasso's study of Cézanne's paintings did not cease when he had extracted the architectural factor for *Les bols*. As Ozenfant has pointed out in his lucid accounts of the Cubist movement in this period, there is a quality in certain paintings by Cézanne—notably in his *Gardanne* series and in many of his water colours—which remains unimpaired, becomes indeed intensified, when the pictures are turned upside down or sideways so that the representational element is destroyed;[1] thus seen, such pictures by Cézanne become an abstractly animated surface, the animation being a kind of music contained in the play of lines and angles and modulated tones and colours. In 1908–1909 Picasso and Braque (who was then working with him) extracted this quality from Cézanne's paintings and explored its possibilities as a factor in the new abstract pictorial art they were seeking to create. Cézanne had produced this music as a bye-product in the process of recording his perception of mutually related planes; he had produced it, that is to say, in the course of procedures which were still representational to a considerable extent. Picasso and Braque now sought to free this play of plane against plane from representation. And thus came the strange pictures known as *Facet-Cubism*, of which I reproduce *La femme au miroir* (Pl. 60) of 1909 where space as such, and the objects within it, are symbolized by advancing and receding planes, drawn and modulated in Cézanne's technique. But once again Picasso himself was the first to realize that he had not yet accomplished his real aim, that this art was still more representational than abstract, that the planes and facets in these pictures were really dancing in and on and round the objects seen, and that the veritable subject of the picture was his personal reaction to those objects. The day came, in fact, when Picasso realized that *La femme au miroir* was really as romantically personal and emotive as *La femme aux pains* (Pl. 54A). The next step was accordingly to make Facet-Cubism both more impersonal and more abstract by departing farther from representation and granting more freedom to the planes and facets, till in the end their dance became the veritable subject of the picture and the artist's task was completed when the choreography was done; and thus came the Facet-Cubist pictures of 1910–1911 where the planes which symbolize space, as such, cut through the figures and objects as they move to and fro and across the stage in criss-cross rhythm like the ballerinas in *Les Sylphides* or the archers in *Prince Igor*. At this point Picasso knew that

[1] Ozenfant: *Art* (Paris: Jean Budry).

Cézanne's contribution could no longer be of use to him because the next stage in abstraction was one which Cézanne had neither consciously nor unconsciously explored; that stage was the completely abstract architectural picture which Picasso and Braque sought to evolve in 1911–1912; and in that stage Cézanne could no longer serve them because Cézanne had laboured from first to last to organize his pictures as microcosms symbolizing his experiences of three-dimensional space, and the art which Picasso and Braque were now creating in Cubism was the organization of actual space—the animation of the actual two-dimensional surface of the canvas by formal arrangements of lines and shapes and colours frankly disposed upon it without any attempt to suggest recession into space behind the canvas. The basic principle of this art, which I christened 'Flat-pattern Cubism' in *The Modern Movement in Art*, was the acceptance of the canvas as a physical flat plane *on* to which other flat planes could be imposed or suggested; no illusion of recession *through* the canvas to imagined space behind was permitted; the canvas itself was always treated as the most distant plane, the visible backcloth as it were of the architectural structure; and upon that plane the structure rose in flat planes to the height of the actual pigments employed or, with the aid of illusion, to the height of two or three inches at the most. In other words the Dance of Facets had now become a Dance or a Tableau of Cards, the cards being all of different shapes and patterns. In the choreography of these Card-dances and Card-tableaux, Picasso and Braque displayed great powers of design and the most intriguing ingenuity in 1911–1914. They invented cards shaped in flat geometric forms, cards with contours obviously referring to familiar objects (fragments of violins and glasses, lettering and so forth) and cards of shapes that evoked no such associated ideas in the spectator's mind—(though all or most of the shapes in Picasso's pictures were in fact evolved from initial experiences of particular 'real' forms). To vary the surface or to suggest the different levels of the planes, they painted the cards in different colours and in different textures, alternating cards painted in oil paint with cards painted in Ripolin enamel or encrusted with sand; and they applied strips of newspaper, or wall paper or textiles, or grained wood—such application being known as Cubist *collage*—(which must not be confused with the Neo-Surrealist *collage* of the post-war period). Some of these Flat-pattern Cubist compositions were extremely simple—a nice balance of two or three shapes and a few lines, with the colour restricted to monochrome effects of black, grey, green, brown, cream and white. In others the designs were immensely complex; and Picasso used brighter colours after 1914. I reproduce Picasso's *Journaux et violon* (Pl. 64) of 1912 which is typical of these pictures. Here the most distant plane is the actual canvas—in parts left blank; the nearest plane is at the point where the U in the card *Journal* joins its neighbour; and from this point the planes recede, card behind card, till they reach the strips of newspaper adjacent to the canvas; the fruits seem at first glance to be representationally depicted; but they are not in fact portrayed as actual fruits in space but as pictures of fruits painted on flat cards and they thus remain behind the other flat cards shaped with violin contours and the others above those.

Braque worked shoulder to shoulder with Picasso in these years. Derain, however, stopped short at the point where Picasso and Braque left Cézanne, and he took no part in the Flat-pattern Cubist explorations. In his curiously emotive *Samedi* (Pl. 70) of 1914 we have some influence from negro sculpture and from both Cézannesque and Facet Cubism. The figures here are fixed points in a grave dance of planes and facets performed by the book, the napkins, the aprons, the fireplace and so forth; but the aesthetic of *Samedi* is not, at bottom, architectural but romantic; and the picture is emotive because the figures, which are points of focus, are romantically—not architecturally—distorted; the picture is very evidently eclectic, but it arrests and holds attention; and it rings true because Derain, fundamentally a romantic, has allowed his personality to dominate the several derived elements in the system of structure and the language of expression here employed.

As I relate in 'How it happened' the *First Futurist Exhibition* in Paris was held in 1912. The Futurist artists, all Italians, were not concerned to create an abstract non-representational architectural art. They were concerned in the first place to use painting and sculpture as agents in the social and political 'Dynamism' proclaimed in the *First Futurist Manifesto* of 1909.[1] Of Marinetti, who founded Futurism as a social and political gesture in 1909, Mussolini himself wrote: 'It is he who instilled in me the feeling of the ocean and the power of the machine'; and Marinetti likewise recently declared that he founded Futurism 'to renew, rejuvenate and quicken Italian pride' and that the movement 'created the aesthetic of machinery as the master of speed, synthesis, order and the art of living'. But in the *First Futurist Exhibition* this aesthetic only appeared in some pictures which attempted to symbolize the noise of a street clattering in through a window, the roar of a racing motor car, and so forth, and such pictures were in no sense a real contribution to an art extracting an aesthetic from machine order and functional reason which was developed later as Purism and Functionalism by Ozenfant, Léger and Jeanneret (Le Corbusier).[2] The other pictures in this Futurist exhibition were descriptive paintings disguised by a technique imitating cinema procedures on the one hand and the Dance of the Facets in Picasso's Cubist pictures of 1908–1909 on the other. The largest picture in the show—Severini's *La danse du 'Pan Pan' au Monico*[3]—described an erotic dance in a Montmartre cabaret by showing the successive movements of the dancers; the description however was anything but orderly or lucid because only fragments of each movement were shown and the fragments were superimposed one upon another as they might be in a film when the projector had suddenly gone wrong. Many people in 1912–1914 confused Futurism with Cubism. But the leading Cubists were well aware that the several types of Futurist painting were all very different from their own; and Futurism only influenced a few painters—Robert Delaunay for example—who was impressed by the 'Dynamism' of the Futurist Manifesto of 1909, and Marcel Duchamp, who mixed Futurism and Cubism in his *Nu descendant l'escalier*[4] in 1912.

Meanwhile between 1904 and his death in 1910 The Douanier Rousseau produced bold, classical, intriguing and original works which included a series of

---

[1] Cf. below, p. 223.   [2] Cf. below, pp. 269–271.
[3] German collection.   [4] Los Angeles. Walter C. Arensberg, cf. p. 238.

jungle pictures more intricate in composition than anything he had achieved before. The large jungle picture 'Le lion ayant faim. . . .' (Pl. 51) was shown in the Salon d'Automne in 1905, and Rousseau described it in the catalogue as follows: 'Le lion ayant faim se jette sur l'antilope, la dévore; la panthère attend avec anxiété le moment où elle aussi en aura sa part. Des oiseaux carnivores ont déchiqueté un morceau de chair de dessus le pauvre animal versant un pleur! Soleil couchant'; but, as my reproduction shows, the description gives only the illustrative constituents and not the composition and the emotive atmosphere of this amazing picture which records The Douanier's memories of the Mexican forests observed in his youth; the general colour scheme of Le lion ayant faim. . . . is blue-green and olive-green and brown, with rose tones in the background, and a deeper red for the antelope's blood. In another jungle picture of this period, Le repas du lion,[1] huge tropical flora surround the lion and his prey; in another, Combat d'Indien et singe,[2] a blood-red sun stands immobile above a blue haze which rises from a silent forest of huge blue-green blood-streaked leaves and orange flowers while a gorilla attacks a native whose brown and orange head-dress repeats the orange of the flowers; in another, Charmeuse de serpents,[3] a native snake charmer plays her pipe by the side of a pool or river while snakes creep from the undergrowth of the forest and hang down towards her from a tangle of boughs overhead; in yet another we see monkeys among green-blue trees gnawing orange fruits; and in the last picture of this series, Le rêve (Pl. 63), The Douanier has sought to join the qualities of the jungle pictures to the qualities of La Bohémienne endormie (Pl. 42). Le rêve was shown at the Salon des Indépendants of 1910 with the following légende in the catalogue:

> Yadwigha dans un beau rêve
> S'étant endormie doucement
> Entendait les sons d'une musette
> D'un charmeur bien pensant,
> Pendant que la lune reflète
> Sur les fleurs, les arbres verdoyants.

One of the critics described the presence of a nude woman on a couch in the middle of the jungle as intolerably naïf and Rousseau replied to him: 'The woman asleep on the couch is dreaming that she has been transported to this forest and that she can hear the enchanter's music. That is the explanation of the couch in the picture. . . . If I have preserved my naïveté it is because M. Gérôme who was professor at the Ecole des Beaux-Arts, and M. Clément, Director of the Ecole des Beaux-Arts at Lyons, urged me never to lose it. The time will come when you will no longer think this strange. I have been told that my work is not of this century. As you will understand, I cannot now change my manner which I have acquired as the result of obstinate toil. . . .' The grandly designed and fearless La muse inspirant le poète (Pl. 62) was painted in 1909 after Rousseau had met Guillaume Apollinaire, Marie Laurençin and Picasso as I relate in 'How it happened'. The muse has a lilac drapery and a wreath of darker pansies round her head, Apolli-

[1] New York. Lewisohn Collection.   [2] Paris. Georges Wildenstein.
[3] Paris. Louvre.

naire is dressed in black coat and trousers and brown waistcoat, the foliage is olive and dark emerald green and the sweet-williams in the foreground are scarlet and pink. Concurrently with the imaginative jungle pictures and this classical portrait group The Douanier painted a number of landscapes and flower pieces and also a number of pictures of contemporary life. In *La Liberté invitant les artistes à prendre part à la 22ᵉ Exposition des artistes indépendants*[1] of 1906 we see hundreds of artists approaching the exhibition galleries in procession, all carrying their pictures or wheeling them in handcarts, while above, floating through the air, a winged Liberty blows a welcome on a trumpet. And in *Joueurs de football*[2] of 1908 we have an exquisitely coloured picture where the game takes place in the clearing of an autumn wood against a pink-blue sky, and the players on one side have pink and blue striped jerseys and fair hair while the players on the other have dark hair and orange and brown striped jerseys repeating the golden foliage of the wood. And thus to the last The Douanier pursued his path—observing directly, imagining clearly, and painting without fear or doubt. His pictures are, inevitably, unequal; and his reputation has suffered because some of the works ascribed to him are fakes. But he was, I am convinced, a really great artist and appreciation of his pictures will certainly increase.

In 1912–1914 while Picasso was working out an abstract art in Flat-pattern Cubism, Odilon Redon was producing Surrealist pastels and Marc Chagall and Giorgio de Chirico were showing Surrealist pictures in the *Salon des Indépendants*. I have used the word *Surrealist* of James Ensor's *L'entrée de Christ à Bruxelles en 1889* and his fantastic pictures of masks and skeletons, of Odilon Redon's lithographs in the 'eighties, and of Osbert's pictures in the Rose-Croix exhibitions of the early 'nineties as described by Coquiot. I have also used it of The Douanier Rousseau's *La Bohémienne endormie* (Pl. 42); and I use it here of Marc Chagall's *Le marchand de bestiaux* (Pl. 67) and Chirico's *La conquête du philosophe: l'horloge* (Pl. 68A) and *Rue italienne: le cerceau* (Pl. 68B). As I chronicle in 'How it happened' the term *'Surnaturel'*, which became *'Surréaliste'*, was coined by Guillaume Apollinaire to describe Chagall's pictures of 1911–1912; but there was no concerted Surrealist movement before the war, and when the Neo-Surrealist movement appeared, as I shall chronicle, in 1924, Redon was dead and neither Chagall nor Chirico was officially connected with it. In this book I apply the term Surrealist (as distinguished from the term Neo-Surrealist) to works where the artist has consciously or unconsciously drawn upon some aspect of dream-experience; I apply it, that is, to works where the artist has consciously or unconsciously rendered his picture emotive by the use of images and 'unrealities' recalled from dreams or corresponding to dream-experience; and my use of the term will become, I hope, apparent when I add that I do not apply it to any pictures depicting a dreamer and his dream—Fuseli's *Nightmare*[3] for example or The Douanier's *Le rêve* (Pl. 63)—though, as stated, I apply it to The Douanier's *La Bohémienne endormie* (Pl. 42).

In Chagall's pictures of 1911–1914 the impossible mingles with the possible as in dream-experience; figures float in the air, a woman milking a cow is seen

[1] German collection. [2] Paris. Paul Rosenberg.
[3] Reproduced in my *English Painting* (Faber & Faber).

within or through the head of a cow (*Moi et le village*[1]), heads have profiles on both sides (*Paris par la fenêtre*[2]), bodies have their heads on upside down or sit headless while their heads appear elsewhere; and all this happens in conditions which are otherwise within the possible; and it all happens, I must add, in a world quite free from sadism or vice, for these headless figures have not been executed, they still live comfortably in one corner of the picture while their heads live comfortably in another; and the world they live in is a world influenced by Cubism and other aspects of painting in Paris at this time—for Chagall was then (as he has remained) a contributor to the aesthetic and classical renaissance which is the subject of this book. In *Le marchand de bestiaux* (Pl. 67), the finest of Chagall's pictures in these years, the impossible is restricted to one point—the transparency of the poor beast's belly; and the whole scene is made emotive by that incongruity—as whole scenes become emotive by one incongruity in dreams. Apart from this, *Le marchand de bestiaux* is aesthetically a moving picture, large in design and resonant with rich blues and reds.

Chirico's Surrealism at this period is different. Working like Chagall within the framework of the modern formal renaissance, he creates an emotive atmosphere by recalling the claustrophobia and the agoraphobia that we experience in dreams; he transports us to large silent deserted squares, where antique statues cast their shadows between long arcades; and in these empty places we encounter silent trains and large railway-station clocks, factory towers, giant *artichauts* plainly defined, unequivocal and near—the invasion of the possible by the impossible—as in dreams. These pictures, like Chagall's, are also aesthetically emotive; the patterning is simple and the colour is mainly Venetian red, grey, cream and olive green. In *Rue italienne: le cerceau* (Pl. 68B), which is typical, Venetian red is used for the shadowed arcade; and here we have a horse-box as a credible dream-incongruity and the sudden intrusion of the little girl who bowls her hoop, with careless innocence, in the disquieting stillness of this dream world. Chirico's Surrealism at this period is thus a new version of the 'pleasing horror' of Burke's 'Sublime'. But the 'pleasing horror' of Chirico's pre-war pictures, conveyed by a static dream-scene portrayed in classical architectural language, is fundamentally different from the 'pleasing horror' engendered by the contemplation of wild effects in landscape and their presentation by Salvator Rosa which Burke himself had in mind.

Cézanne died at sixty-three in 1906 leaving his large composition *Les grandes baigneuses* (Pl. 49) to some extent unfinished as already recorded. And it remains to consider the works produced in the pre-war period by the old Impressionists, especially Renoir, and by Bonnard and Utrillo.

Monet continued to paint Impressionist pictures all through this period; he worked in London in 1905, in Venice in 1908, and after 1908 he remained for the most part on his property at Giverny painting *Nymphéas* which became ever more amorphous—though the influence of the prevailing tendency towards abstract art is seen in his increasingly abstract use of colour; but since, in my judgment, Monet

---

[1] Brussels. Réné Gaffé. This picture was painted in 1911. (A watercolour version belongs to Baroness Hilla von Rebay.)

[2] New York. S. R. Guggenheim.

had minor gifts as a colourist, I assess his contributions to the Abstract movement as of relatively small account. Degas, increasingly neurasthenic and now genuinely troubled with his eyes, continued to draw occasional pastels till 1906 and to model wax figures of nude dancers and women at their toilet till he ceased work entirely in 1912; he lived for five years longer, a pathetic hermit, almost blind, till he died at eighty-three in 1917.

Renoir on the other hand began a new period of marvellous activity in 1904; more and more crippled by arthritic-rheumatism, and condemned in 1911 to paint in a wheeled chair with his brush strapped to the contracted fingers of his hand, he nevertheless produced a large number of his finest pictures between 1904 and 1916; and he continued to work occasionally almost up to his death at seventy-eight in 1919. In this last period Renoir abandoned his relatively speaking academic procedures of the 'nineties, and refashioned his art on the basis of Cézanne's attitude, as he had refashioned it on the basis of Seurat's attitude in the 'eighties. All his pictures of this period recall Cézanne's dictum: 'Peindre ce n'est pas copier seulement l'objectif: c'est saisir une harmonie entre des rapports nombreux'. Releasing and enlarging his personal aesthetic, which he had somehow damped down in the 'nineties, he now repainted his life's work in a series of new pictures, where the old motifs are perceived as material for three dimensional compositions. In these late works line and tone and colour escape more and more from representational duty. Renoir no longer asks his aesthetic to record phenomena but calls on phenomena to record his aesthetic. And in the result we have studies of women and children, flowers, nudes and half nudes, landscapes and landscapes with figures where, in the figure studies the form is as monumental as in Cézanne's pictures, and where, in the landscapes with figures, the figures and the landscape are architecturally dovetailed, while the colour—scarlet, blue, pink, emerald green and gold—challenges Rubens and Watteau, and the rhythm flows as freely as in pictures by Gauguin or Matisse. I reproduce the imposing group Les femmes au chapeaux (Pl. 65) of 1910 and the crowning pictures of his last years—Les grandes laveuses (Pl. 71A) which is Watteau's Grande fête dans un parc[1] set in Cézanne's Le verger (Pl. 21), and Le jugement de Paris (Pl. 71B) for which he summoned all his experience and resources for a great eclectic composition to rival Cézanne's Les grandes baigneuses (Pl. 49). In Le jugement de Paris, which the student will also compare with Renoir's own Les grandes baigneuses (Pl. 19B) of 1885–1887, there is something of Rubens, something of Botticelli and something of Cézanne, but there is more of Renoir, who thus closed his life of pictorial adventure by a final masterpiece.

Bonnard by 1904 had temporarily abandoned the influence of Gauguin and of Lautrec which had appeared in certain work of his Nabi days; and from 1904–1911 he painted some Impressionist studies of petites femmes nues in interiors; but at the same time he was developing a new eclectic manner in table compositions (in the tradition of Renoir's table compositions of the 'seventies) and a new personal interpretation of the Impressionist tradition in some sensitive landscapes and decorative panels.

Utrillo in 1904–1908 was still painting Impressionist townscapes at Pierre-

[1] London. Wallace Collection.

fitte-Montmagny (one of the northern suburbs of Paris) and his works of this series, some of which are very delicate in colour, are known as those of his 'Montmagny Period'. Thereafter from 1909–1914 the colour white predominates, and these years are accordingly known as his 'White Period'. In some of the paintings of his 'White Period' he imitated the surface of plaster buildings by plastering, as it were, his colours with a palette knife. After 1910 the influence of Cubism, personally interpreted, is discernible in certain of his works. In his best pictures of this period, like *L'église de Faouët* (Pl. 69), he achieved both intensity and grandeur; but his work is exceedingly unequal.

ACT III: HOW IT HAPPENED

SCENE I: 1904-1906

From Picasso's last 'Blue' pictures and the *Cézanne Exhibition* at the *Salon d'Automne*; to Picasso's 'Negro' period, the *Gauguin Exhibition*, the *Russian Exhibition* at the *Salon d'Automne*, the rehabilitation of Dreyfus and the Separation of Church and State

---

In 1904 the fame of the Place Clichy as a resort of artists had reached the world of tourists, who now went there not only for the Moulin Rouge and other entertainments but also in the hope of seeing artists and the '*vie de Bohème*'. But the Place Clichy was no longer what it had been when Bonnard drew it twelve years earlier. The restaurants and cafés now catered for the tourists, and prices had risen. The younger artists were therefore migrating to the Butte Montmartre and more especially to studios in the rue Ravignan known sometimes as the *Bateau-Lavoir* and sometimes as *La Maison du Trappeur*—(the same studios occupied twenty years earlier by the artists' colony *La Butte*, to which Antoine had been introduced by Paul Alexis in 1889). Here, or hard by, Picasso, Dufy, Friesz, Derain, Braque, Van Dongen and others installed themselves in 1904–1906 and eventually they all became acquainted.

Picasso went to the rue Ravignan in the spring of 1904; and there in a most uncomfortable studio, almost bare of furniture, he painted the final pictures of his 'Blue' period and etched the large plate *L'aveugle* already referred to. His friends were still for the most part Spanish artists resident in Paris—and Max Jacob. At this time he met Fernande Olivier who has thus described his appearance (in her book *Picasso et ses amis*): '*Petit, noir, trapu, inquiet, inquiétant, aux yeux sombres, profonds, perçants, étranges, presque fixes. Gestes gauches, mains de femme, mal vêtu, peu soigné. Une mèche épaisse, noire et brillante, balafrait le front intelligent et têtu. Mi-bohème, mi-ouvrier dans sa mise. . . .*' Matisse, who lived in another part of Paris and was not yet acquainted with Picasso, had his first one-man show in Vollard's gallery this year. Braque at this time knew neither Matisse nor Picasso as he had only recently arrived in Paris from Le Havre; the son of a colour merchant and decorator, he had been surrounded from childhood by the paraphernalia of house painting—sample boards of colours, 'grainings', 'marblings', lettering, and so forth, and he had attended an art school in Le Havre; in Paris he was soon allied with his fellow Havrois Dufy and Friesz, who had exhibited with Matisse in the first Fauve Exhibition at Mlle Weill's gallery in 1903, and thus he too was swept into the Fauve adventure.

ACT III: HOW IT HAPPENED

The *Twentieth Salon des Indépendants* had two thousand five hundred exhibits; Signac represented the 'old guard' of Seurat's day; Maurice Denis, Bonnard and Vuillard the Nabi tradition, and Matisse, Marquet, Manguin, Camoin, Friesz and Dufy were there as Fauves. The Douanier Rousseau sent *Eclaireurs attaqués par un tigre*,[1] two portraits of children and a flower piece. Van Dongen made his début with paintings still in the Impressionist tradition. The *Salon d'Automne* which took place in the Grand Palais (to the indignation of members of the old *Salon*) had works by Matisse and his associates, a roomful of pastels by Odilon Redon, a memorial exhibition of works by Puvis de Chavannes, and a large one-man exhibition by Cézanne. This *Cézanne Exhibition* in the *Salon d'Automne* (forty-two pictures) made a deep impression on the younger men. As Georges Rivière has put it: '*C'est surtout après l'exposition de 1904 que le pouvoir animateur de l'art de Cézanne apparut aux yeux de ceux qui avaient d'abord vu seulement en lui un puissant coloriste et un incomparable ouvrier.*' But the artists of the official *Salons* and their supporting critics were still uncomprehending and many were openly hostile. *Le Journal* described Cézanne's drawings as 'gauche' and his colour as heavy; the *Petit Parisien* in the Ruskin-on-Whistler tradition talked of paint thrown on a canvas and spread with a comb or a tooth brush; *La Lanterne* thought Cézanne was already dead and referred to him as '*un lamentable raté*' who had ignored the first elements of his *métier* and been unable to express any ideas he may have had; the *Eclair* considered the juxtaposition of shows by Cézanne and Puvis de Chavannes as an insult to Puvis; the *Univers* wrote: '*Les œuvres de Paul Cézanne sont ce qu'on peut rêver de plus abracadabrant; c'est faux, c'est brutal, c'est fou*'; the *Petit Temps* described Cézanne as '*un grand incomplet qu'une infirmité de vision a rendu depuis long-temps incapable de voir autrement que de guingois les lignes droites*'; and the *République Français* wrote: '*Il fallait être Goya pour peindre avec de la boue*'. Cézanne himself, meanwhile, had just met Emile Bernard (who had published the first appreciation of his work in 1889) and in April he had written to him the famous letter: '*Tout dans la nature se modèle selon la sphère, le cône et le cylindre. . . .*'[2]

In this year 1904 the Roumanian sculptor Brancusi arrived in Paris at the age of twenty-six; and Maurice Utrillo aged twenty-two began to attract attention by his pictures of Montmagny street scenes. Freud published *Der Witz und seine Beziehung zum Unbewusten* and *Bruchstück einer Hysterieanalyse*; Catulle Mendès wrote on Rouveyre's caricatures; Pierre Loti published *Vers Ispahan*; Bernstein produced *La rafale*; and Debussy's *Estampes*, Ravel's *Schéhérazade* and Vincent d'Indy's *Second Symphony* were performed for the first time in Paris. Puccini's *Madame Butterfly* was hissed off the stage at La Scala in Milan and was then made into three acts instead of two; Richard Strauss conducted the first performance of his *Sinfonia Domestica* in New York; Michel Fokine, in St. Petersburg, submitted notes on the reform of the Russian Ballet to the Director of the Maryinski Theatre, who ignored them; and Stravinsky aged twenty-two was advised by Rimsky-Korsakov

---

[1] Merion. Barnes Foundation.

[2] For the newspaper quotations in this paragraph cf. Vollard: *Paul Cézanne* (Paris, 1914). I list some of Cézanne's pictures in this exhibition, with their present whereabouts, in Appendix I.

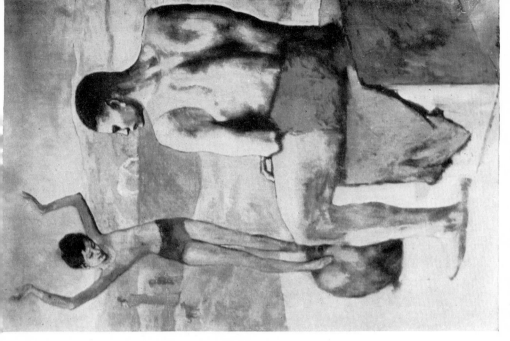

53B. PICASSO
L'acrobate à la boule, 1905
Moscow. Museum of Modern Western Art

53A. PICASSO
Femme à sa toilette et arlequin avec enfant, 1905
New York. Sam Lewisohn, Esq.

54B. PICASSO
Portrait de l'artiste, 1906
New York University. Museum of Living Art

54A. PICASSO
La femme aux pains, 1905
Philadelphia. Museum of Art

to abandon law and take up music as his profession. Jean Cocteau aged thirteen was taken this year by his parents to the *Nouveau Cirque*, where the clowns Footit and Chocolat had been displaced by Mr. and Mrs. Elks who danced the *Cake Walk*—'maigres, crochus, enrubannés, constellés d'étoiles, éclaboussés de lumière blanche, le chapeau sur l'œil et sur l'oreille, les genoux plus hauts que le visage renversé en arrière, les mains agitant une canne flexible, . . .' and behind them (as Cocteau has written in his *Portraits-Souvenir*) all Paris, all Europe, began to dance. At the same time the Americans Gertrude Stein and her brother Leo Stein arose on the horizon as collectors of modern pictures; and Fernande Olivier has thus described the Steins as they appeared to her: 'Leo—professorial, bald, gold spectacles, strange attitudes, short jerky gestures . . . the real type of American German Jew; Gertrude—stout, short, massive; fine strong head with noble, clear-cut, regular features; intelligent, clairvoyant witty eyes; clean-cut lucid brain; masculine in her voice and whole personality; both were dressed in chestnut corduroy and both wore sandals like Raymond Duncan who was a friend of theirs; Leo wanted to be a painter; Gertrude, who had a doctor's degree, was a writer; Wells had complimented her and of that she was no little proud.' The Steins lived in a little house and studio in the rue de Fleurus, where they already had Cézanne's *La dame à l'éventail*,[1] pictures by Daumier, Manet, Renoir, Gauguin and El Greco, and Chinese and Japanese paintings, bronzes and prints. When they turned their attention to paintings by the younger generation they began to entertain artists and writers and to introduce them one to another; and eventually Gertrude Stein kept open house on Saturday evenings to everyone interested in the modern movements in the arts.

In the next year 1905 the *Salon d'Automne* had a *Manet Exhibition*, a *Lautrec Exhibition*, three pictures (painted in the 'seventies) by Cézanne, a screen by Odilon Redon (who was now designing tapestries for the Gobelins factory), a whole gallery of Fauve pictures and The Douanier Rousseau's *Le lion ayant faim . . .* (Pl. 51). Braque made his début with the Fauves in this exhibition and it was at this moment that the term 'Fauve' was applied to these artists (by the critic Louis Vauxcelles who described the gallery with their pictures as a *Cage aux Fauves*). Camille Mauclair, writing in *La Grande Revue*, called the works by Rousseau and by Matisse and the other Fauves beyond words ridiculous and added of Cézanne—'son nom restera attaché à la plus mémorable plaisanterie d'art de ces dernières quinze années. Il a fallu "l'impudence des Cockneys" dont parlait Ruskin pour inventer le "génie" de cet honnête vieillard qui peint en province pour son plaisir et produit des œuvres lourdes, mal bâties. . . . M. Cézanne n'a jamais pu produire ce qu'on appelle une œuvre.' But *L'Illustration* published a supplement reproducing Rousseau's *Le lion ayant faim . . .* and a number of the Fauve pictures with appreciations by various critics; and Leo and Gertrude Stein went to the exhibition and bought *La femme au chapeau*[2] by Matisse.

The *Twenty-First Salon des Indépendants* was even more exciting than the *Salon d'Automne*; The Douanier Rousseau was represented by *Une noce à la campagne*[3]; all

---

[1] Miss Gertrude Stein still owns this picture.　　　　[2] Vaucresson. Michael Stein.
[3] Paris. Mme Paul Guillaume. (Formerly Paris: Serge Jastrebzoff.)

the Fauves sent pictures; and there were galleries given to a *Seurat Exhibition* and a *Van Gogh Exhibition*, each containing over forty works. The lenders in the *Seurat* show, which included *Baignade, Un dimanche d'été à la Grande Jatte, Cirque, La Seine à Courbevoie*, port scenes and minor works, were Félix Fénéon, Signac, the poet Verhaeren, the Belgian painter Van Rysellberghe, and Mme Cousturier (who later wrote the first book on Seurat). The lenders in the Van Gogh show, which included *Portrait de l'artiste à l'oreille coupée, La berceuse, Le père Tanguy* (Pl. 24B), *Le facteur* and *Les soleils*, were Dr. Gachet, Schuffenecker, Rodin, Matisse, Mirbeau, Signac and Comte Antoine de Rochefoucauld.

Picasso sent nothing to either of these exhibitions, and indeed he never sent works to any mixed exhibitions in this period. He preferred to work steadily— mainly, as stated, by night—and to sell his pictures, drawings and etchings for small sums to such dealers as would buy them. The first dealers to buy from him were Clovis Sagot (whom Fernande Olivier has described as *un vieux renard sans scrupules et sans pitié . . . le marchand le moins généreux de l'époque*) and a general bric-a-brac merchant, one Soulier, to whom Picasso sold drawings and so forth as a last resource for twenty francs (or less) apiece. In Sagot's shop this year Leo and Gertrude Stein bought Picasso's 'Pink' picture *La fillette à la corbeille fleurie*[1]; they then went to Picasso's studio, bought other works, and invited him to the rue de Fleurus. Picasso meanwhile had met Guillaume Apollinaire who has appeared in our story as a poet and contributor to the *Revue Blanche* in 1901; Apollinaire at this time was still earning his living as a private secretary in a bank and after work he habitually went to a small bar frequented, Xervos tells us, by '*filles et jockeys en retraite*'; Picasso heard of him from a mutual friend and went to the bar to meet him; Apollinaire entered '*escorté par un anglais et entouré de négresses*'; Picasso liked him and instantly made friends with him; and thereafter Apollinaire wrote an article on Picasso—the first written about him—in *La plume*, and became a driving animator and a central propagandist for contemporary creative art, attracting and attracted by all kinds of adventurous spirits, delighting in everything really vital and original—as well as in everything eccentric and bizarre—inciting, bewildering and charming his artist friends by what Vlaminck has described as a superlative '*adresse dans la fantaisie, une adresse d'équilibriste, une manière de professeur de tango qui inventerait des danses que lui seul pourrait danser*'—and serving, as his major contribution, the genius of Picasso.

In this year 1905 Durand-Ruel organized an *Exhibition of French Impressionist Pictures* at the Grafton Galleries in London. This exhibition contained nineteen works by Manet, fifty-nine by Renoir, forty by Pissarro, thirty-six by Sisley, thirteen by Berthe Morisot, thirty-eight by Boudin, and ten by Cézanne. The English critics received the exhibition as the 'latest thing' from Paris—though most of the works shown had been painted in the 'sixties, 'seventies and 'eighties. At the close some English dilettanti subscribed for the purchase of a landscape by Boudin, which the National Gallery (Trafalgar Square) was persuaded to receive.[2]

---

[1] Paris. Gertrude Stein. This is a mixed 'Pink' and 'Blue' picture, cf. above p. 199.

[2] I list some of the pictures seen in this exhibition, with their present distribution, in Appendix II.

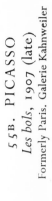

55B. PICASSO
Les bols, 1907 (late)
Formerly Paris. Galerie Kahnweiler

55A. PICASSO
Danseuse nègre, 1907 (early)
Paris. Mme Paul Guillaume

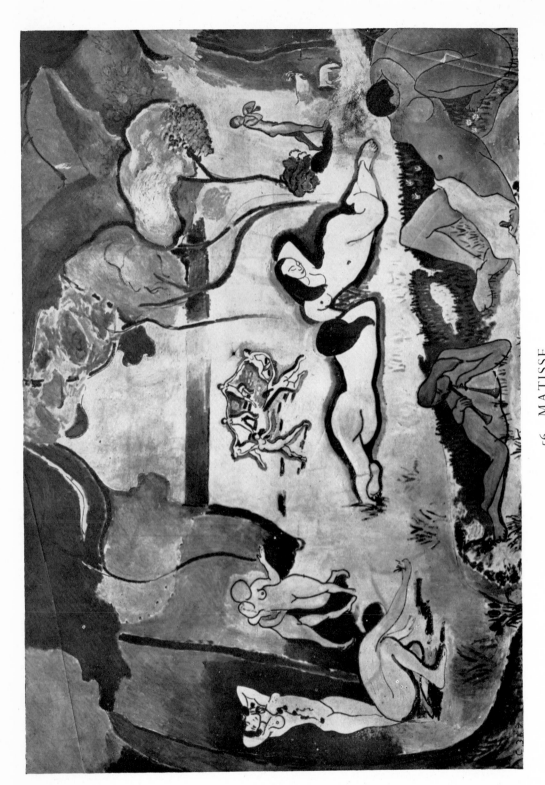

56. MATISSE
Bonheur de vivre, 1907
Merion Barnes Foundation

In the next year 1906 Amadeo Modigliani, aged twenty-two and Gino Severini aged twenty-three arrived in Paris from Italy, and Juan Gris aged nineteen arrived from Madrid; all three took modest studios on the Butte Montmartre where they became acquainted with one another and eventually with Picasso. Braque and Friesz meanwhile were painting Fauve pictures in Antwerp, Derain was painting Fauve pictures in London and Provence, Vlaminck was painting Fauve pictures at Chatou, and Dufy and Van Dongen were painting Fauve pictures in Paris and at Le Havre. Brancusi, who had been working under Rodin, had a first exhibition of his sculpture. Félix Fénéon became *directeur artistique* and organizer of exhibitions for the dealer Bernheim Jeune; and the Moreau Nélaton bequest (including *Le déjeuner sur l'herbe* and other pictures by Manet) was accepted by the Louvre. Marcel Proust published his translation of Ruskin's *Sesame and Lilies*; Ravel published the songs called *Histoires naturelles*, and Vincent d'Indy's *Jour d'été à la montagne* was performed. De Flers and de Caillavet produced their first success *Miquette et sa mère*, and Bernstein produced *Le voleur*. Antoine became director of the *Odéon*, and Gemier director of the *Théâtre Antoine*. Ibsen died. Eugène Carrière died. And Cézanne died on October 22 at sixty-seven.

The art journals which admired the *Salon* artists made hostile comments in announcing Cézanne's death. *L'Art et les Artistes* wrote: '*Homme de génie—d'aucuns vont jusqu'à le prétendre et des soucis mercantiles autorisent seuls une telle exagération.*' *La Revue des Beaux-Arts* wrote: '*J'oserais dire qu'il eut du génie comme une brute. . . .*'

Matisse meanwhile had a successful exhibition of fifty-five pictures in a gallery run by the photographer Druet; and a number of his admirers, French, English, American and Scandinavian, hired a studio and invited him to act as their professor; in this art school—which later developed to the famous '*Académie Matisse*'—Matisse refused to take fees for his tuition, '*ne voulant pas être pris par l'intérêt dès que je verrais quelques raisons pour cesser*'. It was at this time that Matisse, Derain and Vlaminck discovered negro sculpture and became impressed with its vitality and with the novelty of its aesthetic; Matisse passed on his enthusiasm to Picasso whom Gertrude Stein (now sitting to Picasso for her portrait) had just introduced to him. And thereafter Picasso began his 'negro period' with *Portrait de l'artiste* (Pl. 54B) as related.

Picasso's new friend Apollinaire now met Picasso's old friend the poet Max Jacob and another new friend of Picasso's, the critic André Salmon. Apollinaire also met Alfred Jarry who had been going downhill through excessive consumption of drink and drugs, and was indulging in fantastic exploits, insulting all and sundry, firing his revolver at café mirrors ('*pour casser la glace*') and so forth; Apollinaire found Jarry living in a room so low that a tall man was unable to stand up in it; and there he saw Jarry's portrait by The Douanier Rousseau, painted in the early 'nineties, or rather what remained of it—for the part containing the parrot and the chameleon had been destroyed by fire and only the head—(which has since, I believe, disappeared)—was undamaged.[1]

The *Twenty-Second Salon des Indépendants* in 1906 had no less than five thousand five hundred exhibits. The interest excited by the new movements in art had

[1] Cf. pp. 148, 181.

attracted large numbers of foreign art students to Paris; and pictures by foreign artists were a feature of the show to which The Douanier sent appropriately enough *La Liberté invitant les artistes à prendre part à la 22ᵉ Exposition des artistes indépendants*.[1] The Fauves were again conspicuous at this exhibition and Marie Laurençin, who had recently met Picasso and Apollinaire in the dealer Sagot's shop, appeared for the first time. The Fauves were also seen in force at the *Salon d'Automne* which had The Douanier Rousseau's jungle picture *Joyeux farceurs*,[2] and also a *Gauguin Exhibition* and a *Russian Art Exhibition*. This *Gauguin Exhibition*, which had two hundred and twenty-seven paintings and a number of carvings, ceramics, woodcuts and drawings, was a great success; and the dilettanti who had been blind to Gauguin's art in 1893 now endorsed Eugène Carrière's dictum (quoted by Charles Morice in the catalogue): 'We did not know how to profit by this genius whose passion for throbbing colour might have dowered stained glass windows with glorious flames and spread grand and inspiring harmonies upon our walls'. The *Russian Art Exhibition* occupied twelve galleries of the Grand Palais (where the *Salon d'Automne* was now regularly held) and it consisted for the most part of paintings by Russian artists of the past; but it also included works by some contemporary Russian painters and designers—notably Bakst and Alexandre Benois—and a formal garden, set with statues, in the grounds of the Grand Palais, designed by Bakst; the whole thing was arranged by Serge Diaghileff who thus made his début as an impresario in Paris; he had procured a guarantee for the expenses from the Imperial Russian Government which made good a deficit of 275,000 roubles at the end.

In 1904–1906 the Church and State conflict ended in a final victory for the State. In 1904 a number of congregations were disestablished and the State became owner of a number of convents and so forth. One building thus acquired was the Convent of the Sacred Heart on the Boulevard des Invalides—now better known as the Hôtel Biron—which was subsequently used as studios, as I shall chronicle, by Rodin and the Académie Matisse. The separation of the Church and State was promulgated in 1905. Full liberty of conscience was recognized for all religions; but henceforth there was to be no State religion: '*La République ne reconnaît, ne salarie, ni ne subventionne aucun culte*'.

France was now ruled by a Liberal party supported by the *Parti socialiste unifié* (Briand, Viviani and Jaurès); and the successive Prime Ministers in these years were Combes, Rouvier, Sarrieu and Clémenceau. Fallières succeeded Loubet as President of the Republic in 1906. The Sarrieu government made at last an end of the *Affaire Dreyfus* by final quashing of the Rennes trial verdict, a public proclamation of the complete innocence of Dreyfus, and his public reinstatement in the army; and Clémenceau who became Prime Minister for the first time in October 1906 formed a Cabinet with Picquart (exonerated with Dreyfus) as Minister for War, Viviani in the newly created office of Minister of Labour, and Caillaux (who had plans for a graduated income tax) as Minister of Finance. These Liberal-Socialist governments were harassed by Right Extremists who now organized the *Camelots du Roi* as 'storm troopers' for street demonstrations and began

---

[1] German collection.   [2] Los Angeles. Walter C. Arensberg.

a campaign against the Liberal teaching of history and politics at the Sorbonne and other universities. From the Left these governments' enemies included some anti-militarists who made demonstrations when conscripts were called up for service. There were two bomb outrages, without damage, by Anarchists in these years, both being gestures of protest against brutal treatment of Socialists and Republicans by foreign powers; the first bomb exploded outside the house of a Russian diplomat in Paris as a protest against the Russian shooting down and riding down of socialist petitioners in St. Petersburg in 1905—(when the dancer Nijinsky, then a boy, was wounded on the head by a Cossack's knout, and Isadora Duncan, then dancing in St. Petersburg, was moved to tears by the long procession of the victims' coffins); the second bomb was thrown without result at King Alphonso, when he visited Paris in 1905, as a protest against the Spanish treatment of Republicans, one of whom, Pedro Luis de Galvez, a poet and dramatist, had just been condemned to fourteen years' penal servitude for a Republican speech.[1]

[1] Pedro Luis de Galvez began his sentence in 1905. He fomented a riot in prison and he was then kept for two years with one leg closely chained to the wall of a rat-ridden dungeon. He wrote poems in these conditions; a friendly gaoler sent one, *El ciego de la flauta*, to a competition organized by the newspaper *El Liberal* and it won the prize. As a result King Alphonso granted a pardon. A detailed account of the poet's almost incredible sufferings in prison published by Guillaume Apollinaire in *Les Soirées de Paris*, March 1913, contains this statement: '*J'ai vu les jambes de Pedro Luis de Galvez. La gauche qui porta la chaîne est trois fois plus grosse que la droite.*' My readers will be inevitably reminded of the treatment of German political prisoners by the Nazi régime at the present time.

ACT III: HOW IT HAPPENED

SCENE II: 1907-1909

From Matisse's *Bonheur de vivre*, the *Cézanne Memorial Exhibition*, and the beginning of *Cubism*; to Picasso's *La femme au miroir*, The Douanier Rousseau's *La muse inspirant le poète*, the *First Futurist Manifesto* and the *First Russian Ballets*

In 1907 Clémenceau as Prime Minister, persuaded by his close friend Monet, agreed to the transference of Manet's *Olympia* (painted in 1863) from the Luxembourg to the Louvre, and the picture was escorted across Paris by cheering and capering art students. Publications of the year included Bergson's *L'évolution créatrice*, Maeterlinck's *L'intelligence des fleurs* and D'Annunzio's *Più che l'amore*. The Swiss Paul Klee aged twenty-eight now discovered the Anglo-Belgian James Ensor and painted the Surrealist *A table*[1] influenced by Ensor and Hieronymus Bosch; the Spaniard Juan Gris made weekly drawings influenced by Rouveyre and Van Dongen for a weekly paper called *Le Témoin*, and the Bulgarian Jules Pascin aged twenty-two contributed tragically satirical drawings of the underworld most delicately executed in nervous line to the Munich paper *Simplicissimus*. Richard Strauss's *Salomé* (to Wilde's text) was produced this year at the Metropolitan Opera, New York, and withdrawn as the result of protests; and Paul Dukas' *Ariane et Barbe Bleu* (to Maeterlinck's text) was produced at the Opéra Comique in Paris. Serge Diaghileff organized a series of Russian concerts at the Paris Opera, where Chaliapin sang, Rachmaninoff appeared at the piano, Nikisch conducted works by Rimsky-Korsakov, Scriabin and Moussorgsky, and some Right extremists made cat-calls as a protest against foreign music. Guitry and Simone played in Bernstein's *Samson* and Coquelin played in Sardou's *L'affaire des poisons*. The Japanese actress Madame Sada-Yacco—scarlet lips, jet black eyebrows and a milk-white make-up which made her teeth look yellow—amazed the Parisiennes by the prodigious range of her facial expression—particularly in *Le Dragon des Erables* where, as a demon-princess, she contracted her features to a mask of 'unspeakable horror'; and Jean Cocteau aged sixteen was captured by Sarah Bernhardt now over sixty—'Quel délire,' as he wrote later, 'lorsque le rideau aune s'écartait après la pièce, lorsque la tragédienne saluait. . . . Semblable à quelque palais de Venise, elle penchait sous la charge des colliers et de la fatigue, peinte, dorée, machinée, étayée, pavoisée, au milieu d'un pigeonnier d'applaudissements'—(an image

[1] Paris. Galerie Simon.

57B. VAN DONGEN
L'acrobate, C. 1909
Formerly Paris. M. K. Van Dongen

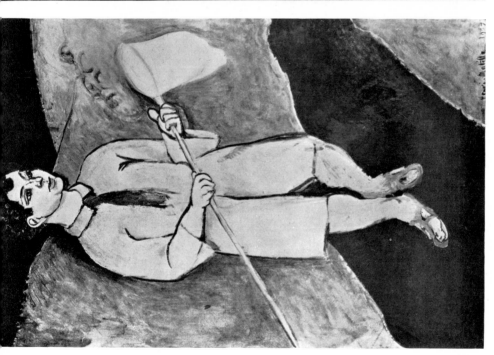

57A. MATISSE
Le chasseur de papillons, 1907
London. Reid and Lefevre

58. DERAIN
La cathédrale de St. Paul et la Tamise, 1906–7
London. Reid and Lefevre

as perfect as *Yvette Guilbert saluant* by Lautrec). Alfred Jarry died in November, 'saturated with drink and ether' at the age of thirty-four; his funeral was attended by Apollinaire, Octave Mirbeau, and Thadée Natanson with some fifty others from the *Mercure de France* and *Revue Blanche* groups; Apollinaire tells us that no one wept for '*Père Ubu*', conscious that '*pour de semblables funérailles, il faut que chacun montre un heureux orgueil d'avoir connu un homme qui n'ait jamais éprouvé le besoin de se préoccuper des misères qui l'accablaient, lui et autrui*'; after the funeral the mourners adjourned to a local café and mingled with a Sunday crowd who were singing, drinking and eating sausages—'*tableau truculent comme une description imaginée par celui que nous menions en terre*'.[1]

As I have recorded in the Introduction, Matisse now evolved a more decorative manner in *Bonheur de vivre* (Pl. 56) and Picasso painted *Les demoiselles d'Avignon*,[2] *Danseuse nègre* (Pl. 55A) influenced by negro sculpture, and finally *Les bols* (Pl. 55B) influenced by Cézanne. Gertrude Stein bought *Bonheur de vivre* from Matisse, and her own portrait from Picasso who had worked for months on the head in innumerable sittings and then entirely repainted it from memory. Vollard went to Picasso's studio and bought all his pictures of the 'Blue' and 'Pink' periods in one deal; a new dealer named Kahnweiler installed himself in Paris and decided that Picasso was the man; Braque and Derain moved from Matisse's orbit to Picasso's; and Derain made some carvings strongly influenced by negro sculpture.

The *Twenty-Third Salon des Indépendants* in 1907 had five thousand four hundred exhibits. Matisse and his circle were all represented. The Douanier Rousseau sent *Le présent et le passé (Pensée philosophique)*,[3] several landscapes and *Les représentants des puissances étrangères venant saluer la République en signe de paix*.[4] Picasso as usual abstained; but his orbit was represented by Braque, Derain and Marie Laurençin. Gertrude Stein's friend Alice B. Toklas sat down with a companion after touring this exhibition: 'Somebody behind us', we read in Gertrude Stein's *The Autobiography of Alice B. Toklas*, 'put a hand on our shoulders and burst out laughing. It was Gertrude Stein. You have seated yourselves admirably, she said. But why? we asked. Because right here in front of you is the whole story. We looked but we saw nothing except two big pictures that looked quite alike but not altogether alike. One is a Braque and one is a Derain, explained Gertrude Stein. They were strange pictures of strangely formed rather wooden blocked figures, one if I remember rightly a sort of man and woman, the other three women. . . .' Gertrude Stein and Miss Toklas then went to Picasso's studio; on the way home from the studio the following dialogue took place: 'What did you think of what you saw? asked Gertrude Stein. Well, I did see something. Sure, you did, she said, but did you see what it had to do with those two pictures you sat in front of so long at the vernissage? Only that Picasso's were rather awful and the others were not. Sure, she said, as Pablo once remarked, when you make a thing, it is so complicated making it that it is bound to be ugly, but those that do it after you they don't have to worry about making it and they can make it pretty, and so everybody can like it when the others make it.'

[1] Cf. Apollinaire. *Il y a* (Paris. Messein 1925.)   [2] Paris. Mme Jacques Doucet.
[3] Merion. Barnes Foundation.   [4] Paris. Pablo Picasso.

Picasso was now the centre of a circle which included Max Jacob, Salmon, and Apollinaire, Fernande Olivier, Gertrude Stein and Marie Laurençin—and as Gertrude Stein has characteristically put it in a roundabout: 'Everybody called Gertrude Stein Gertrude, or at most Mademoiselle Gertrude, everybody called Picasso Pablo and Fernande Fernande and everybody called Guillaume Apollinaire Guillaume and Max Jacob Max but everybody called Marie Laurençin Marie Laurençin.' Picasso had almost abandoned painting by night and he often went in the evenings to the circus, as Degas and Seurat and Lautrec had gone in earlier decades. 'Everybody went to the Cirque Medrano once a week, at least,' Gertrude Stein writes, 'and usually everybody went on the same evening. There the clowns had started dressing up in misfit clothes instead of the old classic costume and these clothes later so well known on Charlie Chaplin were the delight of Picasso and all his friends in Montmartre. There also were the english jockeys and their costumes made the mode that all Montmartre followed.' The performer Grock appeared about this time and delighted Picasso—'*Je n'ai jamais vu Picasso rire d'aussi bon cœur qu'à Medrano*' Fernande Olivier tells us. On Tuesday evenings Picasso and his entourage often crossed the river and passed the evening in the famous café called the *Closerie des lilas* (at the Bal Bullier end of the Boulevard Montparnasse). There Paul Fort and André Salmon carried on the Verlaine tradition and Gustave Kahn, Georges Duhamel, Charles Vildrac and Maurice Raynal were habitués. On other evenings Picasso and his friends went to the Montmartre café called the *Lapin agile* (more properly the *Lapin à Gill*, as the name came from the rabbit painted on the door at a time when the house belonged to the caricaturist André Gill who had been Rimbaud's unwilling host in 1871)[1]; the interior of the *Lapin agile* was now adorned with a full-size cast of the Apollo Citharoedus, a large plaster crucifix by Wasselet, an Indian Buddhist relief and a large harlequin painting by Picasso. Vlaminck, gigantic in some *costume sportif*, Derain and Braque discussing details of their boxing lessons, Van Dongen, Modigliani and Utrillo all frequented the *Lapin agile* at various times. Francis Carco (author subsequently of *La légende et la vie d'Utrillo*) was also a frequent visitor and sang Mayol's songs and Foreign Legion catches or recited his own poems and related incidents of his childhood in Noumea. Another habitué was Charles Dullin the actor, who had toured with a circus and recited poems by Baudelaire while a '*dompteuse*' danced in the lions' cage; and Dullin's career is said to have begun when a director of the *Théâtre des Arts* chanced to hear him reciting verse by Villon and Rimbaud in this café.

Guillaume Apollinaire, Marie Laurençin, Picasso and their friends now made the acquaintance of The Douanier Rousseau still in his humble lodgings in the rue Perrel, and still giving music and painting lessons to local youngsters for his living. At sixty-three The Douanier thus became a member of the most creative circle of the Parisian intelligentsia; he began to sell his pictures for modest sums to Joseph Brummer (who was later to become a dealer in New York), to the German Wilhelm Uhde and to one or two collectors; and he spent the money on little musical soirées where his pupils played as an orchestra and he himself performed on the violin for the pleasure of his new friends.[2]

[1] Cf. above, p. 28.   [2] Cf. below, pp. 243, 244.

59 . ROUAULT
Clown, c. 1907
New York. George Gershwin Estate

60. PICASSO

La femme au miroir, 1909

Exhibited London, Zwemmer Gallery, 1937

The Douanier's pictures influenced a number of the younger men including Fernand Léger who has recorded his admiration. But the chief influence in 1907 came, as I have stated, from the *Cézanne Memorial Exhibition* which was part of the *Salon d'Automne* this year and was supplemented by a show of Cézanne's watercolours arranged by Félix Fénéon in Bernheim Jeune's gallery.

This *Cézanne Memorial Exhibition* had forty-eight paintings lent for the most part by Auguste Pellerin, Paul Cézanne *fils*, and Maurice Gangnat (who was a friend of Renoir's and an eager collector of his later works). Emile Bernard and others who had known Cézanne in his old age, and received letters from him, now wrote accounts of their contacts and published some *dicta* from his letters including '*tout dans la nature se modèle selon la sphère, le cône et le cylindre . . .*' which started Cubism.[1] And from this time onward Cézanne's reputation, and with it the exchange value of his pictures in the international art trade, began rapidly to rise.

In the next year 1908 Derain destroyed most of his Fauve pictures of 1903–1907, sold the rest to Vollard in one deal, and then painted *La toilette* (Pl. 61) which was acquired by the new dealer Kahnweiler. Braque, working with Picasso towards Facet Cubism, sent Cubist landscapes to the *Salon d'Automne* which rejected them. Matisse was on the jury which rejected Braque's pictures, and speaking of them to the critic Louis Vauxcelles, he described them as 'entirely constructed in little cubes'; Braque then exhibited the pictures in Kahnweiler's gallery; Vauxcelles wrote of them as 'Cubiste', and thus the term Cubist was coined as a label for this form of art.

Matisse meanwhile was painting his second *La desserte*[2] and sending pictures to America for a one-man show in the Stieglitz Gallery in New York, and other pictures to an exhibition in Berlin, and signing a contract with the dealer Bernheim Jeune whom Félix Fénéon had persuaded to secure him. There was now a more or less open battle between the admirers of Picasso and Cubism and the admirers of Matisse and the remaining Fauve painters—Rouault, Vlaminck, Friesz, Dufy, and Van Dongen. The Matisse 'fans' had a headquarters in the *Académie Matisse* which had moved to large rooms in the Hôtel Biron (formerly the Convent of the Sacred Heart), and was crowded with students of all nationalities who read eagerly the exposition of his own art which Matisse published in *La Grande Revue* this year. In other sections of the Hôtel Biron, Rodin now had some studios. There too Jean Cocteau had a great room, with five windows overlooking what was formerly the convent garden, where he was visited by Catulle Mendès who had just met him and treated him as he had treated Antoine in 1887—i.e. invited him to lunch and kept him to dinner and then to supper while he looked him over and discovered his creative spirit and artistic gifts.[3]

The *Twenty-Fourth Salon des Indépendants* in 1908 had over six thousand exhibits, including Fauve and Cubist pictures, and *Combat de tigre et buffalo* and *Joueurs de football*[4] by The Douanier Rousseau, whose early work *Portrait de Mlle M.* had just been found by Picasso in Soulier's bric-a-brac shop and bought by him for five francs as old canvas. To celebrate this purchase Picasso gave a studio party in

[1] Cf. above, pp. 200, 202.   [2] Cf. above, p. 201.
[3] Cf. above, p. 93.   [4] Paris. Paul Rosenberg.

Rousseau's honour which is usually referred to as 'Le banquet Rousseau'. The company who assembled to do Rousseau honour included Braque, Apollinaire, Marie Laurençin, Fernande Olivier, Leo and Gertrude Stein, André Salmon, some Spanish painters, the critics André Warnod and Maurice Raynal; there was a dinner (for which most of the provisions arrived next day as Picasso had given the wrong date when ordering) and there were speeches, toasts, songs and so forth and Apollinaire recited his poem written for the occasion which began:

> 'Tu te souviens, Rousseau, du paysage aztèque,
> Des prés où poussaient dru la mangue et l'ananas,
> Des singes répandant tout le sang des pastèques
> Et du blond empereur qu'on fusilla là-bas.
>
> Les tableaux que tu peins, tu les vis au Mexique:
> Un soleil rouge ornait le front des bananiers.
> Et, valeureux soldat, tu troquas ta tunique
> Contre le dolman bleu des braves douaniers.
>
> Nous sommes réunis pour célébrer ta gloire.
> Ces vins qu'en ton honneur nous verse Picasso,
> Buvons-les donc, puisque c'est l'heure de les boire
> En criant tous en chœur : Vive! Vive Rousseau!'[1]

In this year 1908 Debussy completed Ibéria and conducted L'après-midi d'un faune and La mer in London; and Ravel's Rapsodie espagnole was performed in Paris. Diaghileff produced Rimsky-Korsakov's version of Moussorgsky's Boris Godounov and other Russian operas at the Paris Opera with Chaliapin in the leading roles; the Théâtre des Arts produced Candida by Bernard Shaw who was described by the critics as 'une sorte d'Ibsen anglais'; the Théâtre de l'Œuvre gave Hofmannsthal's Elektra and a series of plays acted by Grasso and his Sicilians; the Comédie Française gave Albert Samain's Polyphème and Pierre Loti's Ramuntcho; the Théâtre Antoine produced Sherlock Holmes; and elsewhere Parisians saw Le Roi by de Flers and de Caillavet, Bernstein's Israël, Bourget's Un divorce and Bataille's La femme nue. At the same time Anatole France published La vie de Jeanne d'Arc and L'Ile des pingouins (a satire on the Affaire Dreyfus); André Salmon became art critic on L'Intransigeant and Jacques Copeau, André Gide, Jean Schlumberger and Henri Ghéon founded La Nouvelle Revue Française. In this year also the Louvre acquired El Greco's Le Christ en croix adoré par les frères Diego et Antonio Covarrubias, their third picture by that artist.[2]

Meanwhile Isadora Duncan was dancing in London; Giorgio de Chirico aged twenty was studying pictures by Arnold Boecklin in Munich; Marc Chagall aged twenty-one was working in Léon Bakst's St. Petersburg art school with the dancer Nijinsky as a fellow student; and in Cardiff, Henri Gaudier aged eighteen was a clerk in the office of a coal contractor and drawing birds and sketching at the docks in his spare time. Gaudier (later known as the sculptor Gaudier-Brzeska) was the son

---

[1] Cf. my Bibliographical note on The Douanier Rousseau in Appendix I.
[2] Cf. above, p. 145.

of a French cabinetmaker; he had won a scholarship at Orleans which had taken him to University College, Bristol, to learn English, and thence he had gone to Cardiff.

In February of the next year 1909, Severini handed the *First Futurist Manifesto* to the *Figaro* which published it in full. The Manifesto was signed by F. T. Marinetti, the Italian leader of the Futurist movement. Its main declarations can be summarized as follows:

A Racing Motor-Car, its frame adorned with great pipes, like snakes with explosive breath—a Roaring Motor-Car which seems to be running on shrapnel—is more beautiful than the Victory of Samothrace. . . .

The Past is balsam for prisoners, invalids, and men on their deathbeds who see the Future closed to them.

We will none of it. We are young, strong, living—we are *FUTURISTS*.

Museums are cemeteries—public dormitories. We will permit flowers once a year before *La Gioconda*—but no more daily walking in these gloomy mausoleums, no more libations of living sensibility into cemetery urns.

We are out to glorify War—the only health-giver of the world—Militarism, Patriotism, the Destructive arm of the Anarchist, Ideas that kill, Contempt for Women. . . .

We are out to combat Moralism, Feminism and all Opportunist and Utilitarian meanness. . . .

We extol aggressive movement, feverish insomnia, the double-quick step, the somersault, the box on the ear. . . .

Poetry must be a violent onslaught. There is no masterpiece without aggressiveness. . . .

We shall sing of great crowds in the excitement of Labour, Pleasure, or Rebellion; of the nocturnal vibration of arsenals and workshops beneath their electric moons; of greedy stations swallowing smoking snakes; of factories suspended from the clouds by strings of smoke; of adventurous liners scenting the horizon; of broad-chested locomotives galloping on rails—giant steel horses bridled with long tubes; of aeroplanes with screws whose sound is like the flapping of flags and the cheers of a roaring crowd.

It is from Italy that we launch this Manifesto of Destructive Incendiary Violence.

Italy has been too long the market place of the Second-Hand Art Trade.

We must free our country from its canker of professors, archaeologists, cicerones, antiquaries and second-hand dealers.

On then, Good Incendiaries! Fire the libraries! . . . Turn the floods into museums! Let the famous pictures float! . . . We cast our Challenge to the Stars!

In the same month Isadora Duncan gave her first public performances in Paris. She appeared, with the children from her school, at Lugné-Poë's *Théâtre de L'Œuvre* with Colonne conducting his own orchestra; she danced in her Greek tunic before plain blue curtains to the Overture from Gluck's *Iphigénie en Aulide*; the critic Henri Bordeaux was delighted: '*Il faut à cette fille du Nord, chez qui se devine le sang bouillonnant d'une joueuse de tennis ou d'une écuyère, il faut le mouvement de la vie. . . . Libérée elle s'élance . . . et dans sa course dont aucune fougue ne brise la discipline, ce qu'elle distribue à chaque mouvement, c'est l'émotion chaste et sacrée de la Beauté'*; and on Cocteau she made a similar impression: *'Peu la dérange, notre danseuse, si la robe glisse et découvre des formes informes, si les chairs tremblent et si la sueur coule. Tout cela reste en arrière de l'élan'.*

In May 1909 Diaghileff produced the first Russian Ballets at the Châtelet Theatre which he had lavishly upholstered in scarlet cloth for the occasion. There were twelve performances of *Le Pavillon d'Armide* (music by Tcherepnin, decorations by Benois), *Prince Igor* (music by Borodin, decorations by Roerich), *Le Festin* (a Russian fantasia with mixed Russian music and costumes by Korovine), and *Le Lac des Cygnes* (music by Tchaikowsky, decorations by Benois). Fokine choreographed *Le Pavillon d'Armide* and *Prince Igor*. Nijinsky and Pavlova were the principal dancers. All fashionable Paris went to these performances; and the Russian Ballets were launched at once as the *dernier cri*. The designers employed by Diaghileff for these ballets were all Russian. He was not yet in contact with Picasso and the twentieth century Parisian artists. His friends were the dilettanti still led by Count Robert de Montesquiou, musicians including Debussy and Ravel, and among the artists Maurice Denis, Pierre Bonnard, Rodin and Lautrec's friend Maxime Dethomas, who had been employed as designer at the Opera.

Picasso and his circle, austerely occupied with Cubist experiments, were not attracted by the Russian Ballet which seemed to them suspiciously close to luxury art and suspiciously pleasing to the fashionable 'snob' world. In the creative studios the Russian name most frequently mentioned at this moment was not Diaghileff but Stchoukin—the rich collector who had just commissioned two panels *La danse*[1] and *La musique*[1] from Matisse, and whom Matisse had taken to Picasso's studio where he bought *La femme à l'éventail*[1] and other Cubist pictures. Both Matisse and Picasso were now past their periods of hardship. Matisse, weary of the adoration of his students, closed the *Académie Matisse* and concentrated on the pictures for Stchoukin. Picasso moved from the bare studio in the rue Ravignan to more comfortable quarters on the Boulevard de Clichy, where he painted the Facet-Cubist *La femme au miroir* (Pl. 60), *Portrait de Kahnweiler*,[2] *Portrait de Braque*[3] and *Portrait de Vollard*[4] and experimented with Facet sculpture. Picasso sold some of these Facet works to Kahnweiler who was also buying Facet pictures by Braque and Derain's new pictures, and who published Derain's woodcuts to Apollinaire's *L'enchanteur pourrissant* this year. The Cubist movement now acquired as new adherents Jean Metzinger, Albert Gleizes, Auguste Herbin, Francis Picabia, and Robert Delaunay who painted this year the Expressionist-Cubist *Saint Severin*[5] where the aisle in a Gothic interior takes on the semblance of a path through a leafless forest in winter. At the same time Apollinaire sat to The Douanier Rousseau for *La Muse inspirant le poète* (Pl. 62). The Douanier sent this picture to the *Twenty-Fifth Salon des Indépendants* where it attracted much attention; and he now began to sell his works to Robert Delaunay, to Vollard, to a Russian painter named Serge

---

[1] Moscow. Museum of Modern Western Art.   [2] Paris. Galerie Simon.
[3] New York. Frank Crowninshield.   [4] Paris. Ambroise Vollard.
[5] The New York Museum of Modern Art has a lithograph of this and a drawing for *La tour Eiffel* (cf. p. 228).

61. DERAIN

La toilette, 1908

Formerly Paris. Galerie Kahnweiler

62. THE DOUANIER ROUSSEAU
La Muse inspirant le poète, 1909
Moscow, Museum of Modern Western Art

Jastrebzoff and his sister the Baroness Oettingen, and some others. At the beginning of the year he had narrowly escaped imprisonment through entangling himself with a swindler who committed a financial fraud.[1]

In this year 1909 Modigliani made the acquaintance of Brancusi; Henri Gaudier aged nineteen arrived in Paris, where he worked by day as a translator in a bookshop and drew and carved in the evenings when and where he could; and the sculptor Ossip Zadkine, also nineteen, arrived at the same time. Monet, now sixty-nine, had a successful exhibition of new *Nymphéas* pictures; Odilon Redon, also sixty-nine, produced pastels in Paris and played tennis in his garden at Bièvres; and a gallery of works by Rodin, who was also sixty-nine, was opened in the Metropolitan Museum, New York. Marcel Proust aged thirty-eight now retired from society to write *A la recherche du temps perdu*; Jean Cocteau published *La lampe d'Aladin*, and Maeterlinck *L'oiseau bleu*; and Freud published *Über Psychoanalyse* (lectures delivered at Clark University, Massachusetts). Richard Strauss's *Electra* (to Hofmannsthal's text) was performed for the first time in Dresden; Lenormand's *Les possédés* was performed in Paris at the *Théâtre des Arts*, and Bataille's *Le scandale*, and Brieux's *Suzette*, at other theatres. Oscar Wilde's remains were removed to Père Lachaise cemetery and Jacob Epstein was commissioned by Wilde's executors to carve a monument. W. P. Frith, painter of *Derby Day*, died in London at the age of ninety; and Catulle Mendès aged sixty-eight, returning to his home at Saint Germain by the midnight train from Paris, mistook the lights at the entrance to a tunnel for the lights of the station, and stepped out of his compartment to the railroad where he was killed by another train.

In this period 1907–1909 Clémenceau's Liberal-Socialist government was embarrassed by strikes. On March 8, 1907, the *Times*' correspondent reported: 'Paris was plunged into partial darkness to-night in consequence of a strike among the electric workmen. The strike came as a surprise to the population. All the theatres and places of amusement are closed. The cafés and restaurants, few of which are fitted up with the alternative of gas, have recourse to candle-light. In many of the large restaurants bottles are used for candle-sticks. The outsides of the cafés are lit up with innumerable Chinese lanterns, which give them a picturesque appearance. The Boulevards are densely crowded with people apparently curious to see how Paris looks in the dark. Many of the newspapers will be unable to appear to-morrow.' A month later there was a waiters' strike; the waiters struck for the right to wear beards and moustaches and also, since they received no wages, for the right to keep their tips from which hitherto the proprietors had taken about half for wear-and-tear expenses and so forth; this strike lasted till May 3. In 1908 the Right Extremists were very provocative; their 'storm troopers', the *Camelots du Roi*, made noisy demonstrations when Zola's ashes were transferred to the Panthéon in June; a journalist tried to assassinate Captain Dreyfus at this ceremony; the *Action française* group now launched *L'Action française* as a daily paper with Henri Vaugeois as political director, Léon Daudet as editor in chief and Charles Maurras as chief collaborator; the historian Thalamis was insulted in the streets by *Camelots du Roi* for his lectures on Jeanne d'Arc at the Sorbonne; and

[1] Cf. below, p. 245 and Appendix IV.

ACT III: HOW IT HAPPENED

Georges Sorel in *Réflexions sur la violence* poured scorn on liberal democracy and social progress by reasonable arrangements, and prophesied that the middle classes would do the bidding of any one who used violence and spread sufficiently alarming propaganda about Red Peril: '*La bourgeoisie se laisse facilement dépouiller, pourvu qu'on la presse quelque peu et qu'on lui fasse peur de la révolution : le parti qui saura manœuvrer avec le plus d'audace le spectre révolutionnaire, aura l'avenir pour lui. . . .*' In 1909, Briand, who had succeeded Clémenceau with a new Liberal-Socialist government, had to deal with the first *apache* (hooligan) outrages in the suburbs of Paris; at Nanterre twelve people had been assaulted and robbed by these hooligans in one night, and one *apache*, named Liabeuf, who had killed a gendarme and wounded three others before he was overpowered, was found to be armed with a revolver, a knife, and leather wrist-bands studded with steel spikes.

63. THE DOUANIER ROUSSEAU
Le rêve, 1910
New York. Sidney Janis, Esq.

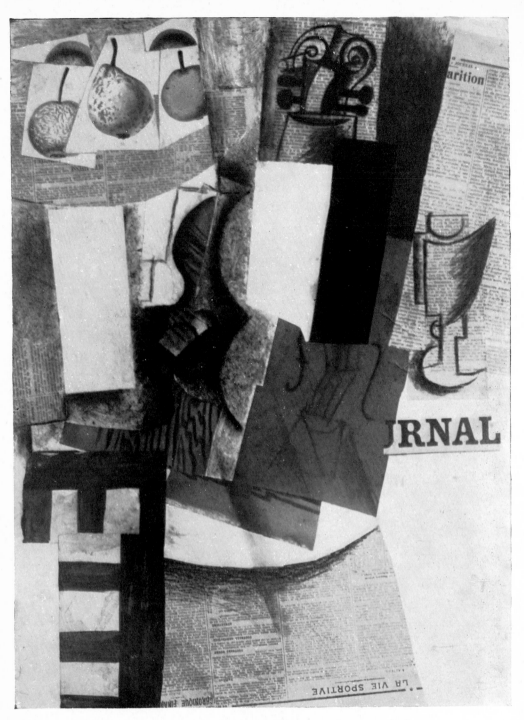

64. PICASSO
Journaux et violon, c. 1912
New York University. Museum of Living Art

ACT III: HOW IT HAPPENED

SCENE III: 1910-1912

From The Douanier Rousseau's last work *Le rêve*, Chirico's first Surrealist pictures, the first Bakst ballets, and the *First Post-Impressionist Exhibition* in London; to Picasso's Flat-pattern Cubist *Journaux et violon*, Matisse's Moroccan pictures, Chagall's Surrealist *Le marchand de bestiaux*, Nijinsky's ballet *L'Après-midi d'un faune*, the *First Futurist Exhibition* in Paris and the *Second Post-Impressionist Exhibition* in London

---

In January 1910 life in Paris was gravely disorganized by floods. In the early stages a tug called 'The Asquith' was swept off the river; later the four statues on the Pont de l'Alma were submerged to their armpits, and divers rescued the archives from the Palais de Justice; at the Jardins des Plantes the elephants groaned with rheumatism, a giraffe was drowned, and the polar bears were ecstatic with delight. When the floods and the emotions caused by them had subsided the dilettanti flocked to the *première* of Rostand's *Chantecler* (with Guitry as 'Chantecler', Simone as 'La faisane' and Galipaux as 'Le merle') and to Diaghileff's second series of Russian Ballets: *Schéhérazade* (music by Rimsky-Korsakov, choreography by Fokine, décor by Fokine and Bakst), *L'oiseau de jeu*, music by Stravinsky, décor by Golovin, choreography by Fokine), *Carnaval* (music by Schumann, orchestrated by Rimsky-Korsakov, choreography by Fokine, décor by Bakst), *Giselle* (music by Adam, choreography by Fokine, décor by Benois), *Cléopâtre* (music by Arensky, choreography by Fokine, décor by Bakst), and *Les Sylphides* (music by Chopin, selected by Diaghileff and orchestrated by Glazounov and Rimsky-Korsakov, choreography by Fokine, and décor by Benois). The decorative richness (largely influenced by Gauguin) and the luxuriant semi-oriental fantasy displayed by Bakst in these ballets were a great success with the dilettanti; Bakst turbans, patterns and *motifs* soon made their appearance in the ateliers of the milliners and modistes; and Jean Cocteau with Maurice Rostand (Edmond Rostand's son) produced a new literary review called *Schéhérazade*. During a performance of *Carnaval* Bakst received a visit from his former pupil Marc Chagall who had just arrived in Paris, aged twenty-three, financed by M. Vinaver, a Duma deputy: 'As soon as I arrived in the wings,' Chagall tells us, 'I caught sight of the red hair and the pink cheeks of Bakst; he smiled me a welcome; Nijinsky ran up and greeted me, hands on my shoulders; but Nijinsky was due on the stage—Karsavina was waiting for him—and Bakst adjusted the large cravat on his harlequin's suit. Hard by D'Annunzio was flirting sentimentally with Ida Rubinstein. . . .' Chagall asked Bakst to come and see his pictures; Bakst went to his studio and said to him, 'Maintenant, mon enfant, vos couleurs chantent'; but to Chagall's disappointment he did not invite him to work for the Russian Ballet.

In this year Freud published Über den Selbstmord, inbesondere der Schülerselbstmord and Eine Kindheitserinnerung des Leonardo da Vinci. Arnold Schoenberg, who had been attracting attention with 'atonal' music, had an exhibition of his paintings in Vienna; Elgar's Violin Concerto was played for the first time in London by Kreisler; Toscanini conducted the première of Puccini's The Girl of the Golden West at the Metropolitan Opera House, New York; and in New York also Max Weber arranged an exhibition of paintings by The Douanier Rousseau in the Stieglitz Gallery at 291 Fifth Avenue.

André Salmon now became art critic of Paris-Journal with four columns weekly at his disposition, and Apollinaire replaced him as art critic on L'Intransigeant. Jacques Rouché became director of the Théâtre des Arts; a new dealer, Paul Guillaume, began to concern himself with negro sculpture and the younger creative painters; and Paul Poiret became the leading couturier for all fashionable Parisiennes with artistic tastes. Bernheim Jeune had a Cézanne Exhibition, a Manet Exhibition (containing thirty-five paintings and pastels acquired by a syndicate of dealers from Auguste Pellerin who had formerly collected Manet's pictures but now collected exclusively Cézanne's) and a large exhibition of pictures by Matisse. Picasso and Braque were still painting Facet-Cubist pictures and moving steadily to more abstract ideals. Léger, who had met Picasso, had become a Cubist and the dealer Sagot was buying his pictures; Roger de la Fresnaye, Marcel Duchamp and Marcoussis (Louis Markous) were other new Cubist recruits; Robert Delaunay, influenced by Futurist propaganda, painted the Futurist-Cubist La tour Eiffel; André Lhote aged twenty-four had his first one-man show in Druet's gallery where Maurice Denis bought a picture and reproved him for 'dangerously Cubist leanings'; and Dunoyer de Segonzac aged twenty-six painted the Expressionist Les buveurs[1] much influenced by Cézanne's early work. Amédée Modigliani now twenty-six sent carvings influenced by negro sculpture to the Twenty-Sixth Salon des Indépendants, while his compatriot Giorgio de Chirico, in Florence, was painting his first Surrealist pictures of silent squares and streets, and the Futurists in Milan were following Marinetti's Manifesto of the previous year by a Manifesto of Futurist Painting (signed by Boccioni, Severini, Carro, Russolo and Balla) and Severini was making plans for a Futurist Exhibition in Paris. The Douanier Rousseau died at the age of sixty-six after showing his final masterpiece Le rêve (Pl. 63) in the Salon des Indépendants and selling it to Vollard.

The celebrated First Post-Impressionist Exhibition in London took place at the Grafton Galleries in the autumn of 1910–11. Officially titled Manet and the Post-Impressionists this show was sponsored by a committee of English dilettanti and the critic Roger Fry who wrote an essay as preface to the catalogue; it contained nine paintings by Manet (including Un bar aux Folies Bergère),[2] twenty-one by Cézanne,

[1] London. Lord Ivor Spencer Churchill.
[2] London. Samuel Courtauld (on loan at the National Gallery, Trafalgar Square).

65. RENOIR

Les femmes aux chapeaux, c. 1910

Paris. M. Philippe Gangnat

66. DERAIN
Fenêtre sur le parc, 1912
New York. Museum of Modern Art

forty-one by Gauguin (including *L'esprit veille* (Pl. 36) and *Jésus au Jardin des Oliviers* (Pl. 26)), twenty-two by Van Gogh, two port scenes by Seurat, five pictures by Signac, three by Odilon Redon, five by Maurice Denis, four sculptures by Maillol, and some pictures and sculpture by Matisse and the Fauves—Rouault, Manguin, Marquet, Friesz, Vlaminck and Derain; Picasso and the Cubists were not represented. The art critic of *The Times*, who evidently thought that Gauguin was still alive, was entirely at sea in this exhibition, and attacked it from the political angle: 'This art', he wrote, 'stops where a child would begin. . . . We have honestly tried and have failed to find any significance of gesture and movement in M. Gauguin's pictures. Where is the significance of gesture in the coffee-coloured Tahitian woman lying face downwards in a bed and in her strange arms and fingers? . . . Like Anarchism in politics, this art is the rejection of all that civilization has done, the good with the bad. M. Gauguin is not more eccentric than several of the other members of the school, if it is a school. There is the Dutch painter Van Gogh with his roughly modelled flower-pieces. . . . The artists' aim is to '*épater le bourgeois*' and this aim is most completely realized by the painter Henri Matisse. . . .' [1]

On August 22 of the next year, 1911, the *Times*' correspondent wrote: 'Paris has been startled this afternoon by the news of the disappearance of Leonardo da Vinci's masterpiece '*La Gioconda*' from the Louvre.' The theft of this picture, more generally known as *Monna Lisa*, had taken place early in the morning on the previous day, a Monday, when the Louvre (as always on that day) was closed to the public. The framed picture had been lifted from the wall, and the frame and glass had been left on a staircase. The removal from the wall had been quite easy because the Louvre authorities at this time would not screw the pictures to the walls as they wanted to be able to move them quickly in the case of fire. Great efforts were made to find the picture and the thief. The French police took fingerprints of all employés at the Louvre, from the Minister of Fine Arts downwards; the police of other countries co-operated; liners arriving in America were searched; but no clue was discovered. *L'Illustration* offered a reward of 10,000 francs for the recovery of the picture and a further 40,000 francs if it were brought to the office of the paper. *Le Matin* offered 5,000 francs to anyone who 'by somnambulation, spiritualism or other occult means' successfully indicated the identity of the thief or the whereabouts of the picture. The *Société des Amis du Louvre* offered 25,000 francs. But no information was produced. In the end the Louvre informed the public that love letters addressed to the picture were often received in the mails; and it was then widely assumed that the theft had been committed by a maniac or by someone in the service of a maniac. [2]

[1] This *First Post-Impressionist Exhibition* introduced Gauguin and the later artists to Londoners. But it had in fact been preceded by an *Exhibition of works by Modern French Artists* at Brighton in the summer. The Brighton show (organized by Bernheim Jeune, Maurice Gangnat, Théodore Duret, Octave Mirbeau and Alphonse Kann, with a London committee including the Russian mosaic worker Boris van Anrep, the journalist Robert Dell, Roger Fry, and Clive Bell) had works by all the Impressionists and also by Cézanne, Gauguin, Signac, Cross, Odilon Redon, Maurice Denis, Bonnard, Vuillard, Matisse, Rouault, Friesz, Vlaminck and Derain.

[2] It was apparently at this time that the grotesque distortion *Mona Lisa* first appeared as a title for this picture in certain sections of the press. The better informed papers wrote of course *Monna Lisa* (i.e. *Madonna Lisa*) or *La Gioconda* or *La Joconde*.

The *Monna Lisa* 'sensation' was followed by another in September when Dujardin-Beaumetz, secretary of the Beaux-Arts, stated that several small statues missing from the Louvre since 1906 had just been taken to the office of a newspaper by someone who declared that they had been stolen as an escapade to demonstrate the bad protection of the national art treasures. The newspaper was *Paris-Journal*, which 'featured the story', displayed the statues in its window, and then returned them to the Louvre. The thief was a former associate or secretary of Guillaume Apollinaire; the police made a detailed search in Apollinaire's apartment and arrested him for complicity; and wild rumours began to circulate—one being that Apollinaire had organized the thefts of these objects and also stolen the *Monna Lisa* as a joke. In the end the proceedings against Apollinaire were dropped, and the real thief, who had absconded, was never found.

In this year 1911 the *Théâtre Antoine* produced Dostoievsky's *L'éternel mari* dramatized by a young Pole, Alfred Posniansky, who called himself 'Alfred Savoir'; the *Théâtre des Arts* gave Dostoievsky's *Les frères Karamazov*, adapted by Jacques Copeau, with scenery and costumes by Maxime Dethomas, and a socialist play *Le pain* by Henri Ghéon; the Moscow Art Theatre played Maeterlinck's *L'oiseau bleu* at the *Théâtre Réjane*; the Odéon produced *L'armée dans la ville*, a 'collectivist' play in blank verse by Jules Romains, and *David Copperfield*, where the public was touched by '*ce Micawber qui, attaché à son élève, aide Miss Trotwood, sorte de bourrue bienfaisante, et tante de David, à arracher l'enfant aux bandits qui ont juré sa perte*'; Sacha Guitry made his début as a witty playwright and actor in *Un beau mariage*; Ida Rubinstein played *Le Martyre de Saint Sébastien*, a '*mystère en cinq actes*', written for her in French verse by D'Annunzio, with music by Debussy and scenery and costumes by Bakst; Ravel's *L'heure espagnole* was produced at the Opéra Comique and Strauss's *Rosenkavalier* was performed for the first time in Dresden. Diaghileff continued to triumph at the Paris Opera with a series of new Russian Ballets— *Sadko* (music by Rimsky-Korsakov, choreography by Fokine, décor by Anisfeld), *Narcisse* (music by Tcherepnine, choreography by Fokine, décor by Bakst), *Petroushka* (music by Stravinsky, choreography by Fokine and Benois, décor by Benois, with one scene, the negro's box, by Bakst), and *Le Spectre de la Rose* (music Weber's *Invitation à la valse*, choreography by Fokine, décor by Bakst). Nijinsky and Karsavina danced in the *Spectre de la Rose* which was based on Théophile Gautier's poem:

> *Je suis le spectre de la rose*
> *Que tu portais hier au bal . . .*

Nijinsky excelled himself in an unimaginable, soaring exit through the window. *Petroushka* was the combined invention of Stravinsky and Benois; Nijinsky danced Petroushka, Orlov the Negro, and Karsavina the Dancing Doll; the Fair scene was entirely devised by Benois. When Stravinsky's score was rehearsed at the Châtelet, the orchestra shrugged, laughed and made derisive comments; but when the music was played with the ballet, for which it had been written, the consonance was evident and made a great effect.

Picasso in 1911 had not yet met Stravinsky and he continued to frown on the Russian Ballet and the eclectic exuberance of Bakst. He spent the summer at

Ceret with Braque and together they worked out Flat-pattern Cubism with grain-ings, marblings, lettering and so forth as recorded in the Introduction. The Cubists now agreed to accept the term Cubist as a general group title and they made group demonstrations this year at the *Twenty-Seventh Salon des Indépendants*, at the *Salon d'Automne* (where Marcel Duchamp, aged twenty-four, and his brother the sculptor and architect Duchamp-Villon, aged thirty-five, made their débuts), and in a large *Cubist Exhibition* in Brussels, for which Guillaume Apollinaire wrote an essay in the catalogue. The *Rousseau Memorial Exhibition* was held appropriately in the *Salon des Indépendants* where so many of The Douanier's finest pictures had been shown; on the occasion of this show Apollinaire wrote of The Douanier with wit, elegance and understanding in *Les Soirées de Paris* of which he had become the editor, and Uhde published a charming monograph on his life and work.[1] At the same time Uhde, who was living at Senlis, discovered another proletarian artist in the person of his *femme de ménage*, Séraphine Louis, who painted fruits and other still-life pictures in her free moments in this period and who later painted some very interesting Surrealist pictures.[2] Dufy now illustrated Apollinaire's *Le bestiaire*; Vollard published Maurice Denis' drawings for Verlaine's *Sagesse*; Kahnweiler published Picasso's etchings for Max Jacob's *Saint Matorel*; Léger painted *Les nus dans la forêt* a blend of the Cubism of Picasso's *Les bols* with the jungle pictures of The Douanier; and Segonzac painted the Expressionist *Les deux nus couchés*[3] still influenced by Cézanne's early pictures. At the same time Apollinaire went to Chagall's studio where he saw *Moi et le village* and *Paris par la fenêtre* and coined the word '*Surnaturel*' which later became '*Surréaliste*' for his work; and Giorgio de Chirico arrived from Florence bringing with him his first Surrealist pictures, including *Nostalgie de l'infini*.[4] In the autumn Marinetti, Severini and Boccioni made propaganda for a Futurist exhibition to be held next year; Marinetti visited Picasso, harangued him for hours, but failed to convert him to Futurist ideas; Severini and Boccioni failed likewise with Apollinaire, who wrote in November: 'I have just met two Futurist painters MM. Boccioni and Severini. The first, who may be called the theoretician of the school, has a loyal intrepid air that predisposes one towards him. Both wear comfortable clothes of English cut. M. Severini, who is Tuscan, wears sandals and socks of different colours, on the day I met him one sock was raspberry red and the other bottle green; this Florentine coquetry is mistaken here for absentmindedness and café waiters point out the oversight to him in tactful whispers.'

In the next year 1912 the much heralded *First Futurist Exhibition* took place in February. Severini's *La danse du 'Pan Pan' au Monico*[5] and Boccioni's *La rue entre par la fenêtre*[5] were the outstanding pictures. These Futurist pictures, as I have stated in the Introduction, were a popularization of procedures invented for architectural purposes by the Cubists; and they had no lasting influence on con-temporary French painting. The public, however, found Futurism more compre-hensible than Cubism on the one hand or Fauvism on the other, because the notion

---

[1] Cf. my Bibliographical and Catalogue Notes in Appendix I.
[2] Cf. below, p. 284. [3] London. Lord Henry Bentinck.
[4] New York. Museum of Modern Art. [5] German collection.

of rapidly changing images had been made familiar by the cinema, and because at bottom the Futurist pictures were more illustrative than architectural or aesthetic.

Picasso now moved from the Boulevard de Clichy to the Boulevard Raspail and the centre of gravity of the Cubist movement was thus transferred from Montmartre to Montparnasse—a Montparnasse still innocent of night-bars and cabarets, a Montparnasse where most of the studios (except the new ones like Picasso's in the Boulevard Raspail) were ramshackle, where living was cheap, and where the *Café du Dôme* was a *bistro* with three small rooms (a bar which sold stamps and cigarettes and so forth, a billiard room just large enough to take the table, and a third room beyond with *banquettes* and half a dozen tables where the artists met for talk and drinks). At the same time the tourists heard about the Butte Montmartre and went there to see the artists who had once more evaded them.

In this year 1912 Picasso painted the Abstract Flat-pattern Cubist picture *Journaux et violon* (Pl. 64); a gallery called *La section d'or* was organized by Gleizes, Metzinger, the brothers Duchamp and Duchamp-Villon and a third brother Jacques Villon, as an exhibiting centre for the Cubist group; the dealer Sagot died and Kahnweiler made arrangements with Léger and took over Sagot's contract with Gris who had recently met Picasso and become a Flat-pattern Cubist. Gleizes and Metzinger published *Du Cubisme*—the first book on the movement; and there were Cubist Exhibitions in Barcelona and Amsterdam—the Amsterdam show being formally opened by the Burgomaster of the city. Meanwhile Matisse, after wintering in Morocco, had an exhibition of his Moroccan pictures including *Fenêtre à Tanger*,[1] *Femme marocaine*[1] and others eventually acquired by Stchoukin for his Moscow collection; Derain painted *La fenêtre sur le parc* (Pl. 66) and Kahnweiler published Derain's woodcuts for Max Jacob's *Les œuvres burlesques et mystiques du Frère Matorel*. The *Twenty-Eighth Salon des Indépendants* had Chagall's Surrealist *Le marchand de bestiaux* (Pl. 67), Gleizes' Cubist *Les grandes baigneuses*, Metzinger's Cubist *La femme au cheval*, Cubist pictures by Léger and Gris, Cubist sculpture by Zadkine, Delaunay's brightly coloured Cubist abstraction *Les fenêtres*[2] and his semi-Cubist football picture *L'Equipe de Cardiff*,[3] and de la Fresnaye's semi-Cubist *Joueurs de cartes*,[4] *Le cuirassier*[5] and *L'artillerie*.[6]

In this same year 1912 Jacob Epstein aged thirty-two completed the *Oscar Wilde Monument* for Père Lachaise cemetery; and Marcel Proust, now a neurasthenic asthmatic hermit in a cork-lined room, completed *Du côté de chez Swann* at the age of forty-one. Clémenceau aged seventy-one sat to Rodin aged seventy-two, and quarrelled with him because Rodin, he said, had caricatured him as a Japanese mask. Renoir, also seventy-one, painted *Les grandes laveuses* (Pl. 71A) and was working on *Le jugement de Paris* (Pl. 71B) and a large sculptured *Vénus*.[7] Degas aged seventy-eight, almost blind and unable to work, was compelled by *démolisseurs* to leave his old home in the rue Victor Massé and to seek a new one for himself and his collections; Anatole France aged sixty-eight published his last novel *Les dieux*

---

[1] Moscow. Museum of Modern Western Art.   [2] Paris. Léonce Rosenberg.
[3] Paris. Musée du Petit Palais.   [4] Brussels. René Gaffé.
[5] Paris. Jos. Hessel.   [6] Paris. M. Petiet.
[7] Paris. Ambroise Vollard.

ont soif; and Vuillard painted *Théodore Duret*[1] showing the sitter, aged seventy-four, with Whistler's portrait of him, painted in 1885, on the wall.

Theatre-goers in 1912 had a varied fare—Verhaeren's *Hélène de Sparte* with Ida Rubinstein, Paul Claudel's *moyen-âge* religious drama *L'annonce faite à Marie*, a play called *Nabuchodonozor* with costumes by Poiret and scenery by Dunoyer de Segonzac, Bernard Shaw's *La profession de Madame Warren* (which struck the French as '*La maison Tellier sans esprit*'), Knoblock's *Kismet* with Lucien Guitry, and *L'habit vert* (a skit on the *Académie Française*) by de Flers and de Caillavet. Diaghileff's new Russian Ballets were *Le Dieu Bleu*, *Thamar*, *Daphnis et Chloé* and *L'Après-midi d'un Faune*—all choreographed by Fokine and decorated by Bakst. *Le Dieu Bleu*, danced to music by Reynaldo Hahn, was planned by F. Madrego and Jean Cocteau; *Daphnis et Chloé* had music commissioned by Diaghileff from Ravel; *L'Après-midi d'un Faune* had Debussy's music and angular choreography and gestures devised by Nijinsky and Fokine who were inspired by Greek vase paintings and also, to some extent, by the classical temper of the Cubist Renaissance; the steps and gestures in this ballet were so much an innovation that a hundred and twenty rehearsals were required before the company was perfect. The dilettanti and all fashionable Paris were now completely fascinated by the Russian Ballets. Fortuni and Paul Poiret draped Greco-Persian-Russian-Ballet gowns and turbans on the ladies who appeared in the evenings with pink and purple wigs. Jean Cocteau calling on the aged Empress Eugénie at the Hôtel Continental (opposite the Tuileries Gardens) boldly asked her opinion of the purple wigs; she replied that she herself had worn more eccentric costumes—*la crinoline, les pantalons de linge qui depassent, les bottes à gland*—and called up images of half a century of social vagaries and fashions while Cocteau sat like a statue in fear of scattering the ghosts.[2]

Londoners, who had seen the Russian Ballets for the first time in 1911—(after Maud Allan had prepared the way with Mendelssohn's *Spring Song* and Pavlova with the *Bacchanale* and *La mort du Cygne*)—saw Diaghileff's new ballets in 1912; in that year they also saw Norman Wilkinson's designs for *Twelfth Night* and Albert Rutherston's for *A Winter's Tale* and for Shaw's *Androcles and the Lion* produced by Granville Barker; and they heard Schoenberg's *Five Orchestral Pieces* conducted by Henry Wood. In 1912 also there was a *Second Post-Impressionist Exhibition* at the Grafton Galleries which had eleven works by Cézanne, forty-one by Matisse, fifteen by Picasso, and works by Braque, Derain, Vlaminck, Bonnard, Marquet, Friesz, Van Dongen, Herbin, Lhote and one (a jungle scene) by The Douanier Rousseau. Cézanne's paintings were all landscapes of various periods; the Matisse display included *La coiffeuse*[3] of 1901, *Portrait de Marguerite*[4] of 1910, *Mme Matisse au Madras rouge*[5] of 1908, *Jeune marin*[6] of 1906, *Le luxe* of 1911, *Les capucines* of 1910, *Les poissons rouges*[7] of 1911, a version of *La danse*, six bronzes and a number of

[1] New York. Chester Dale.

[2] *Et je ne respire pas, je ne bronche pas, je tremble d'interrompre, par un geste malhabile, cette scène étonnante, de renfermer brusquement le tiroir de l'Impératrice, de faire entendre le chant du coq, de disperser les ombres.* (Cocteau: *Portraits-Souvenir*.)

[3] New York. Stephen C. Clark.   [4] Nice. Henri Matisse.

[5] Merion. Barnes Foundation.   [6] German collection.

[7] Moscow. Museum of Modern Western Art.

drawings and lithographs; Picasso's works included *La fillette à la corbeille fleurie*[1] and a number of Cubist works; Derain's central exhibit was *La fenêtre sur le parc* (Pl. 66); Vlaminck had landscapes and one still life—*Les figues*. The *Times*, which had been so lamentably at sea in the *First Post-Impressionist Exhibition* two years before, was now converted to the new school and treated the artists with respect: 'Most people', its critic wrote, 'look for beauty in a picture only in the objects represented which they expect to remind them of beautiful real things. They have no notion of beauty created, not imitated, in a work of art, and created by the effort of expression. One may say, if one likes, that M. Matisse is attempting things impossible to his art, that he is trying to turn painting into music. But one need not therefore fall into a rage and accuse him of incompetence or wilful perversity. . . . He is not incompetent but an artist of great powers. . . .'; in Picasso, whom he found more difficult to follow, he discerned an intellectual curiosity that reminded him of Paolo Uccello; he praised Lhote's *Port de Bordeaux*, and described Derain as concerned with 'an abstract grandeur of design while preserving the character of the objects represented'.[2] This *Second Post-Impressionist Exhibition* enraged some English academic artists who toured the galleries exclaiming 'imbeciles', 'impostors', and so forth; one shouted in my hearing: 'This is not Art but a dangerous and infectious disease.'

In this period the *apaches* continued to cause trouble in Paris. These hooligans, with the prostitutes who provided them with money and served them as decoys, were now openly installed in large numbers in the streets round the central markets; and tales of their exploits caused considerable panic; Rodin, for example, had revolvers in all his rooms at Meudon and a detective who slept in an armchair by his bed. Certain addle-pated intellectuals, influenced may be by memories of the romantic-realist concepts of *apaches* and *pierreuses* in Aristide Bruant's songs, made it a kind of snobbism to defend the *apaches* in the same way that others had defended the anarchists in 1894; thus when the bandit Liabeuf—already referred to as armed with knife, revolver and wrist-bands studded with steel spikes—was tried in 1910 for killing a gendarme, Gustave Hervé described him in his paper, the *Guerre Sociale*, as 'a professor of energy', whose fight with the police had 'a certain beauty and grandeur'—for which nonsense Hervé was condemned to a term of imprisonment and a fine. When Liabeuf was executed, bands of roughs, encouraged by the *Guerre Sociale*, howled '*Assassins! Assassins!*' at the police till the streets were cleared by troops. Briand's Liberal government was now faced with the rapid growth of Syndicalism and embarrassed by various strikes. In October 1910 there was a strike of railwaymen on the Nord line followed by a general strike on all the railways; the railwaymen were joined by the electricians and there was sabotage in various places; Briand replied by calling up all railway workers for military service; attacked by the Socialists for this use of mobilisation powers to suppress a strike, Briand replied that the action was in fact legal, and would have been justifiable even if illegal, since it is the duty of a government to remain master of the railways which are vital to the national defence. In 1911 a

[1] Paris. Gertrude Stein.
[2] The notices on the two exhibitions were presumably by different critics.

law limiting the use of the 'Champagne' label caused riots in the Aube to which the label was refused; the Aubois demonstrated with banners inscribed '*La Champagne ou la Mort*'; when concessions were offered to the Aube there were riots in the Marne; and at one moment ten thousand soldiers were drafted to these regions to keep order. In the summer of this year a detachment of French troops occupied Fez in Morocco to put an end to some local disorders; the German Emperor sent a gunboat to Agadir, and war was imminent; but Caillaux, who was now Prime Minister, declined the challenge and offered access to the Congo as appeasement; England intimated that she would stand by France; and the Germans decided to postpone the attack. In 1912 Caillaux resigned and Poincaré became Prime Minister with Léon Bourgeois, Millerand and Briand in the Cabinet; and the newspapers were full of exploits by a new type of hooligan—the motor bandits —who robbed post offices and so forth in various parts of France.

ACT III: HOW IT HAPPENED

SCENE IV: 1913–JULY 1914

From Chirico's Surrealist pictures in the *Salon des Indépendants*, Stravinsky's *Le sacre du printemps* and Copeau's foundation of *Le Vieux Colombier*; to Chirico's *Rue italienne: le cerceau*; Derain's *Samedi*, Rouault's *Christ*, the *Peau de l'ours* sale, the murder of Calmette, the murder of Jaurès and the German invasion

---

In April 1913 the Palais de Justice was heavily guarded with troops, and the public were excluded while a number of motor bandits were tried for robberies and murders. Several of the bandits were condemned to death and executed; one named Callemin spent his last hours reading the *Revue des Deux Mondes*; another named Monier composed a will leaving his revolver to the Musée de la Ville de Paris (with the request that 'Thou shalt not kill' be engraved upon it), his books (which included Darwin's *The Origin of Species* and Spencer's *The Data of Ethics*) to the Librairie Municipale de Paris, and 'to Society as a Whole his ardent wish that life may some day be ordered so as to give the individual more leisure for the study of Beauty and Knowledge'.

Later the Louvre announced that the *Monna Lisa* (stolen in 1911) had been found in Florence. The thief was a fanatic Italian painter and whitewasher who alleged that it had been his intention to transfer the picture to the Uffizi Gallery as an Italian masterpiece which properly belonged to Italy not France; he had been able to steal the picture without difficulty because he had worked in the Louvre and was known to the maintenance staff who let him pass out unchallenged with the picture (removed from its frame) wrapped up in his painter's smock; he was given a year's imprisonment and the picture was returned to Paris.

In this year Freud published *Totem und Tabu*; Marcel Proust published *Du côté de chez Swann* which had been refused by four publishers and was eventually printed at his own expense; Satie composed his *Descriptions automatiques*, *Croquis et Agaceries d'un gros bonhomme en bois* and *Peccadilles importunes*; Russolo published in Milan the *Manifesto of Futuristic Music*;[1] and Schoenberg completed the score of *Die Glueckliche Hand*, 'expressionist monodrama, to his own text, making use of colour dynamics,

[1] The full text of Russolo's Manifesto of Futurist Music is given (in English) in Slonimsky's *Music since 1900* (New York, 1937; London, Dent, 1938). The Manifesto said *inter alia*: 'We must break out of this narrow circle of pure musical sounds, and conquer the infinite variety of noise-

67. CHAGALL
Le marchand de bestiaux, 1911–12
Paris. Marc Chagall

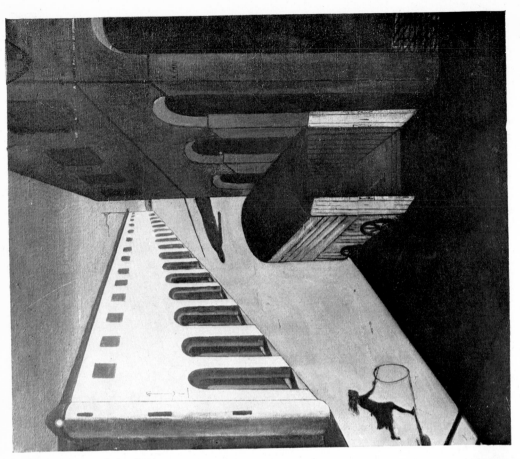

68B. CHIRICO

68A. CHIRICO

crescendo in the orchestra being accompanied by a *crescendo* of coiours—red—brown
—green—dark blue—purple'.[1]

Gordon Craig now founded a Theatre School in Florence (after producing
Hamlet for Stanislavsky's Art Theatre the year before in Moscow where Pitoëff had
just founded a rival Art Theatre); and Jacques Copeau founded his own theatre
Le Vieux Colombier in the Quartier Latin. At *Le Vieux Colombier* Copeau aimed at a
simplicity in the setting which was influenced by the Cubists, by Gordon Craig,
and by Granville Barker's artists; his leading actors were Dullin and Jouvet; his
first productions were Molière's *L'amour médecin* and a translation of Thomas
Heywood's *A Woman killed with Kindness* (first acted in 1603) and he followed these
with Paul Claudel's *L'échange*, Schlumberger's *Le fils Louverné* and Roger Martin du
Gard's *Le testament du Père Lelev*. Diaghileff, alternating opera and ballets, gave
Moussorgsky's *Khovatchina* with a Persian ballet choreographed by Bolm; Rimsky-
Korsakov's *Ivan le terrible*; and Borodin's *Prince Igor* with Chaliapin singing; and
three new ballets *Le sacre du printemps* with music by Stravinsky, scenery by Roerich,
choreography by Nijinsky; *Jeux* with music by Debussy, choreography by Nijinsky
and decorations by Bakst; and *La tragédie de Salomé* with music by Florent Schmitt,
decorations by Soudeikine and choreography by Romanov. At the première of
Le sacre du printemps there were whistles and catcalls all through the performance;
at the second performance the interruptions were fewer; and all was quiet at
the third. Later in the year Nijinsky went with the company to South America
and married Romola Pulsky who has faithfully written the tragic story of his later
life.

Picasso, still unacquainted with Stravinsky, did not attend a performance of
Le sacre du printemps and continued to hold aloof from the Russian Ballets. His new
Cubist pictures were less representational than ever, even such recognizable
references to experience outside the picture as occur in *Journaux et violon* (Pl. 64)
being eliminated in some cases. Matisse, as stated, was now influenced by Cubism[2];
the theory of Cubism was propounded by Apollinaire in *Peintres cubistes: méditations
esthétiques*; Delaunay produced a series of Flat-pattern pictures with brightly
coloured fragments of revolving discs—a type of Futurist-Dynamism which he

sounds. . . These are the futurist orchestra's six families of noises, which we shall soon produce
mechanically:

1	2	3	4	5	6
Booms Thunder-claps Explosions Crashes Splashes Roars	Whistles Hisses Snorts	Whispers Murmurs Mutterings Bustling noises Gurgles	Screams Screeches Rustlings Buzzes Cracklings Sounds obtained by friction	Noises obtained by percussion on metals, wood, stone, terra-cotta, etc.	Voices of animals and men: Shouts Shrieks Groans Howls Laughs Wheezes Sobs

[1] Slonimsky: *op. cit.*   [2] Cf. above, p. 201.

called *Simultanéisme* and which Apollinaire christened '*Orphism*'; de la Fresnaye painted the semi-Cubist *La vie conjugale*[1] and *La conquête de l'air*[2]; Lhote painted the semi-Cubist *L'escale*[3] and *Le jugement de Paris*[4]; Picasso and Braque sent Cubist pictures to the *Secession Exhibitions* in Berlin; Wyndham Lewis founded an English Cubist-Futurist movement in London which he christened *Vorticism*; and Fauvism, Cubism and Futurism were introduced by the American artists Arthur B. Davies and Walt Kuhn to New York, Chicago and Boston in the famous *Armory Exhibition*, where Matisse's pictures were a centre of storm, where the lawyer John Quinn and Miss Lillie P. Bliss began their collections of modern French art, where Henry McBride, Frank Crowninshield and Walter Pach appeared as its champions, and where Marcel Duchamp's Cubist-Futurist *Nu descendant l'escalier*[5] was more readily comprehended by the public than the purely Cubist pictures by Picasso and Braque. At the same time Haim Soutine aged nineteen arrived in Paris from Lithuania, financed by a Vilna doctor. The Surrealist approach was seen this year in the pictures sent to the *Salon des Indépendants* by Chagall and by Chirico, who now painted *La conquête du philosophe* (Pl. 68A), and *La place*[6]; Apollinaire sat to Chirico for his portrait; Paul Guillaume began to buy Chirico's pictures; and a German dealer, introduced to Chagall by Apollinaire, arranged to show his pictures in the gallery of *Der Sturm* in Berlin next year.

In the first half of 1914 the Paris season was more than usually spectacular and international. King George V and Queen Mary were received with fêtes and ceremonies, and other fêtes followed for the King and Queen of Denmark. Dufy designed textiles for Poiret to drape on fashionable ladies who wore them at parties given by Van Dongen in his new vast studio; all fashionable Paris continued the craze for costume balls which the Russian ballet had created; between these fêtes there was continual dancing in private houses, bars and restaurants to tango and negro rhythms; and Adolphe Sax's phone began to moan and wail. Poiret designed the scenery and costumes for *Aphrodite*—Pierre Loüys' novel of Alexandrian decadence arranged as a spectacle with a nude dance and the crucifixion of a girl as *pièces de résistance*. Diaghileff produced four new ballets all choreographed by Fokine—*La légende de Joseph* with music by Richard Strauss, costumes by Bakst and a Venetian setting by the Spanish decorator J. M. Sert (Massine replacing Nijinsky as chief dancer); *Coq d'or*, where the dancers mimed and a concealed choir sang to music by Rimsky-Korsakov, and the scenery and costumes were designed by a new Russian artist influenced by the Cubist movement—Natalie Gontcharova; *Papillons* arranged to Schumann's music with scenery by Doboujinsky and costumes by Bakst; and *Midas* with music by Maximilien Sternberg and decorations by Doboujinsky. Copeau produced *Twelfth Night* designed by Duncan Grant at *Le Vieux Colombier*, using curtains instead of painted scenery, and a formally constructed semi.permanent architectural set; and Eric Satie composed *Heures Séculaires et Instantanees* with the following text over the music: 'This vast part of the world is inhabited but by one man: a negro. He is bored to the point of dying of laughter.

[1] Paris. M. Petit.
[2] Brussels. René Gaffé.
[3] Paris. Musée du Petit Palais.
[4] Stockholm. Georges Pauli.
[5] Los Angeles. Walter C. Arensberg. Cf. p. 205.
[6] Paris. Paul Eluard.

69. UTRILLO
L'église du Faouët, 1912
Paris. Galerie d'art contemporain (Bing)

70. DERAIN

The shadow of millennial trees marks 9.17 o'clock. The toads call each other by name. For better thinking, the negro holds his cerebellum in his right hand, with outstretched fingers. From afar he looks like a distinguished physiologist. Four anonymous serpents hold him captive, suspended on the tails of his uniform, deformed by chagrin and solitude. On the bank of the river, an old mangrove-tree slowly laves its repugnantly filthy roots. It is not the shepherd's hour.'[1]

Paul Guillaume now opened his first Paris gallery with pictures by Chirico, Picasso and Derain who had just painted *Samedi* (Pl. 70) and *La cène*.[2] Chirico painted *Le cerveau de l'enfant*[3] and sent *Rue italienne: le cerceau* (Pl. 68B) to the *Salon des Indépendants* and Apollinaire wrote of him: '*C'est au moyen le plus moderne, la surprise, que ce peintre a recours pour dépeindre le caractère fatal des choses modernes*' (which explains why André Breton and the Neo-Surrealists of ten years later looked on Apollinaire as a forerunner[4]); and de la Fresnaye painted some serene semi-Cubist still-life compositions which anticipate to some extent Ozenfant's Purism of the first post-War years.[5] Meanwhile, in Berlin, Chagall's Surrealist Exhibition was a great success with the younger artists, and The Douanier's friend Wilhelm Uhde lectured on Picasso and Braque; and in London, where Paul Morand was an attaché at the Embassy, Wyndham Lewis and his Vorticist associates published *Blast* with Cubist-Futurist drawings by Lewis, Epstein, Gaudier, Wadsworth, Etchells, Roberts and other London artists, poems by Ezra Pound, short stories by Ford Madox Hueffer and Rebecca West, *The Enemy of the Stars* by Lewis, and a Manifesto composed by Lewis, Blasting among other things 'The Britannic Aesthete (cream of the snobbish earth)', 'Humour (quack English drug for stupidity and sleepiness)', Sport (humour's first cousin and accomplice), 'Paris (clap-trap Heaven of amative German professor)' and Blessing among other things ports, lighthouses 'cutting the storm like a cake', restless machines, the hairdresser who 'attacks Mother Nature for a small fee and makes systematic mercenary war on wildness', the British Grin, and France 'with its bushels of vitality to the square inch'.

It was at this time that the Louvre installed Count Camondo's collection formed in the 'seventies, 'eighties and 'nineties and bequeathed to the nation at his death. This collection (placed in a remote corner up several flights of stairs) includes Manet's *Lola de Valence* and *Le fifre*, Degas' *L'absinthe*, *Danseuse au bouquet saluant sur la scène*, *Les repasseuses* and *Le tub*, a number of pictures by Monet, Cézanne's *La maison du pendu* and *Les deux joueurs*, Renoir's *Jeune fille assise* and Lautrec's *La clownesse Cha-U-Kao*. As a collector of nineteenth century French pictures Camondo had been followed by, among others, the young Prince de Wagram who had bought thirty pictures by Courbet, twelve by Manet, fifty by Renoir, forty by Monet, eleven by Degas, twenty-six by Sisley, twenty by Pissarro, twenty-eight by Cézanne and forty-seven by Van Gogh, before he was twenty-five in 1908.[6] Collectors of twentieth-century pictures were also now on the increase. Thus a group of dilettanti who had formed themselves into an informal club called

[1] Slonimsky. *Op. cit.*
[2] Chicago. Mrs. F. R. Lillie.
[3] Paris. André Breton.
[4] Cf. below, pp. 255, 278.
[5] Cf. below, pp. 267–269.
[6] E. de Gramont. *Mémoires* (Paris: Grasset, 1929).

La Peau de l'Ours had been buying pictures by Matisse, Picasso, D
Friesz, Rouault, Vlaminck, Utrillo, Marie Laurençin and others for
and on March 2, 1914, they sold their collection at auction in the H
where the prices paid (which included fifteen thousand francs for
bateleurs,[1] the largest of his *saltimbanque* pictures of 1905) were very
to the artists and to other collectors of this school; the members (
l'Ours divided twenty per cent. of the sale proceeds between the art
the balance, which was still a handsome profit on the prices they had p
revealed that the whole collection had been bought from their winni
another at cards and from their winnings at the tables which they ha
pool for this purpose.

German preparations for war cast sinister shadows on French po.....s in these
eighteen months. In January 1913 Poincaré became President. In March Briand,
who had replaced him as Prime Minister, was succeeded by Barthou who passed a
Three Years' Military Service Law to meet the German rearmament. This law,
unpopular with the working classes, was opposed by Jaurès and the C.G.T. In
July Caillaux introduced a bill for progressive Income Tax which enraged the
financial magnates. In November eighteen anti-militarists were prosecuted for
pacifist propaganda in the army, there was a miners' strike, a bill for Women's
Suffrage was rejected in the Chamber, and the *Camelots du Roi* defaced the statue of
Waldeck-Rousseau. In December Barthou was succeeded by a more Radical
Cabinet with Doumergue as Prime Minister and Foreign Minister, and Caillaux as
Minister of Finance. On January 8, 1914, Gaston Calmette, editor of the *Figaro*,
began a series of attacks on Caillaux, charging him with corruption, political
pressure on behalf of dishonest financiers, and pro-Germanism; on February 25
Caillaux's Income Tax Bill was defeated in the Senate. Calmette continued his
attacks and on March 13 he published a private letter written by Caillaux to
Madame Caillaux (who was not then his wife); on March 16 Madame Caillaux,
learning that Calmette had photographs of a number of such letters and intended to
publish them, sent for her car, drove to a gunmaker where she bought a revolver,
then drove to her hairdresser where she had her nails manicured, and then drove
to the office of the *Figaro* where she shot Calmette dead. While Madame Caillaux
was in prison awaiting trial the Radical followers of Caillaux won a hundred and
thirty-six seats, the Socialists a hundred and two and other parties just over two
hundred together at the General Elections; Doumergue resigned and on June 14
Viviani became Prime Minister with a Radical-Socialist government pledged to
work for the Income Tax Bill and the maintenance of the Three Years' Service Law.
On July 18 President Poincaré paid an official visit to St. Petersburg where he
was received by the Czar. On July 20 Madame Caillaux's trial began; the witnesses
in the various matters raised included the novelist Paul Bourget, the playwright
Bernstein, the composer Isidore de Lara, Barthou, Caillaux himself and Caillaux's
first wife. On July 28 Madame Caillaux was acquitted and on the same day Jaurès
went to Brussels to confer with representatives of International Labour about ways
and means of preventing the imminent war. On July 31 Jaurès was assassinated in a

[1] Chicago Art Institute (lent Chester Dale).

71A. RENOIR
Les grandes laveuses, 1912
Paris. Paul Rosenberg
71B. RENOIR
Le jugement de Paris, c. 1914
Paris. Renou et Colle

72. ROUAULT
Christ, 1914
Exhibited London, St. George's Gallery, 1930

Paris café. On August 4 the Germans invaded Belgium and France and proclaimed the doctrine of *Furchtbarkeit* as they terrorized and shot the peasants.

Degas at this time was eighty, Monet was seventy-four and Renoir was seventy-three; Odilon Redon was seventy-four, Bonnard was forty-seven, Matisse was forty-five, Rouault was forty-three, Vlaminck was thirty-eight, Derain was thirty-four, Utrillo was thirty-one, Picasso and Braque were thirty-three, Chagall was twenty-seven and Chirico was twenty-six.

ACT III: THE MASTERS' LIVES

THE DOUANIER ROUSSEAU[1] (iii)

From sixty till his death at sixty-six (1904–1910)

In the first three years of this period The Douanier's position was much what it had been before. He still occupied his humble rooms in the Plaisance quarter behind Montparnasse, with *Cours de diction, musique, peinture et solfège* on the door; and he still made his living by painting local portraits and teaching drawing, painting and music to the local youngsters. In 1905 he began to attract the attention of the new generation of creative artists by his exhibits in the *Salon des Indépendants* and the *Salon d'Automne*; and in 1907, Guillaume Apollinaire, Marie Laurençin and Picasso made his acquaintance as related.

When Apollinaire met him The Douanier was sixty-three. A photograph of the period shows him in his room—a prematurely old, bowed figure, with drooping white moustache and shaved chin, sitting beside a table covered with a cheap cloth; a violin and an alarm clock are on the table; an umbrella and a broom lean against a chair; a tin basin lies under the chair; an oil lamp, a razor strop and a number of pictures are on the wall. In this room The Douanier now received the artists and writers in Picasso's circle, entertaining them at little musical parties which Apollinaire has charmingly described. He sent out manifolded invitations for these functions: "M. Rousseau requests you to honour him with your presence and participate at an informal *soirée artistique* which will take place on . . . at rue Perrel 2bis''; he took great pains with the musical entertainment provided by his pupils and himself; and he drew the programmes on gelatine and duplicated them in red and violet. The guests included local tradesmen and their wives (the proud parents of the performing pupils), some old cronies of the *octroi* days, and his new friends of the Parisian art world. The concert habitually began with the *Marseillaise* played by the full orchestra led by The Douanier as first violin; '*Cécilette*' (polka), *Eglantine* (valse), *Rêve d'un Ange* (mazurka) and the *Polka des Bébés* followed as solo pieces performed by the baker's daughter on the mandoline, the grocer's son on the flute, and so on; then The Douanier himself played pieces of his own composition on the violin and sang popular songs of his youth. At the end of the evening the guests were given a glass of wine, and everyone went home '*tout content*', as Apollinaire says, '*d'avoir passé quelques heures en compagnie d'un brave homme*'. Picasso, Marie

---

[1] For the present distribution of the pictures mentioned and others painted by The Douanier in these years cf. my Bibliographical and Catalogue Notes in Appendix I.

Laurençin, Braque, Robert Delaunay, Max Jacob, André Salmon, a Russian painter Serge Jastrebzoff and his sister Baroness Oettingen (early collectors of his pictures), Max Weber, an American painter (the first to introduce The Douanier's work to America),[1] the Italian painter Ardengo Soffici, Georges Duhamel, Jules Romains, Francis Carco and the critics André Warnod and Maurice Raynal were among those who went to these parties at various times. Max Weber was sometimes persuaded to display his tenor voice in arias by Handel. The Douanier liked to feel that he was keeping open house, and American ladies, '*belles étrangères*' as he called them, were always welcome. He took the homage of the *intelligentsia* quite simply as his due. To Picasso he said, '*Nous sommes les deux plus grands peintres de l'époque—toi dans le genre égyptien; moi dans le genre moderne*'.

The first dealers to concern themselves with The Douanier's pictures were Joseph Brummer and the German Wilhelm Uhde; and Vollard bought pictures from him after 1908. The Douanier became much attached to Uhde who subsequently wrote a delightful book about him.[2] Uhde was in his rooms one day when he was conducting a musical examination of his pupils; 'The parents', Uhde writes, 'were seated on chairs along the wall. Rousseau wore a black suit with the violet ribbon of the *palmes académiques* in his buttonhole. . . . The examination began; but it was soon over—because the pupils would not do what the professor told them; they played the wrong pieces and wrong notes on purpose to torture him.' On other occasions, Uhde tells us, the pupils played practical jokes on The Douanier— inviting people whom he did not know to a *soirée* for which he had not sent invitations—and so on.

In 1908 Picasso, having found The Douanier's large picture *Mlle M.* . . . (painted in 1897) in Soulier's bric-a-brac shop and bought it for five francs, gave a studio party (*le banquet Rousseau*) to celebrate the occasion, as I have chronicled.[3] And in 1908–1909 The Douanier painted Apollinaire's portrait in *La Muse inspirant le poète* (Pl. 62). He began this full-length portrait, Apollinaire tells us, by taking careful measurements of his head and face and features and also of his body—a procedure which only painters concerned to imitate appearances by photographic copying will think comic. While Apollinaire was posing The Douanier sang songs to entertain him, and his favourite, Apollinaire tells us, was a ditty which began:

> '*Moi je n'aim' pas les grands journaux*
> *Qui parl' de politique*
> *Qu'est c' que ça m'fait qu'les Esquimaux*
> *Aient ravagé l'Afrique . . . .?*'

Apollinaire also tells us that when The Douanier was painting his pictures with jungles, lions and so forth he was completely absorbed by the spirit of the work: '*Il avait un sentiment si fort de la réalité que quand il peignait un sujet fantastique il s'épouvantait parfois et, tremblant, il était obligé d'ouvrir la fenêtre*'—which reminds one of Mrs. Siddons' panic when she was studying the part of Lady Macbeth. On other occasions The Douanier appears to have believed that the spirit of his dead wife was in the room, inspiring and directing his brush.

[1] Cf. above, p. 228.   [2] Cf. below, p. 231 and Appendix I.   [3] Cf. above, pp. 221, 222.

At the beginning of 1909 the pleasant successes of the artist's old age were cut across by a distressing episode. For he became entangled at the age of sixty-five with a swindler who used him as a cat's-paw in an attempt to defraud the Banque de France. The facts of the matter were as follows: Towards the end of 1908 The Douanier was approached by one Gabriel Sauvaget, a former music pupil and now a clerk in the Meaux branch of the Banque de France. Sauvaget persuaded him to open an account in the name of 'Bailly' at the Mélun branch of the bank and thus to possess himself of a cheque book; Sauvaget then had duplicates printed of the special forms and envelopes used by the branches of the Banque de France when arranging local credits for their clients; on one of these forms he wrote an instruction for a credit of 21,000 francs to be drawn upon by 'M. Bailly' at the Meaux branch; he signed this instruction with forged signatures of the director and cashier of the Mélun branch and sent it to the Meaux branch in the special type of envelope; he then provided The Douanier with false identity papers in the name of 'Bailly' and suggested that he should go to the Meaux branch and draw and cash a cheque for 21,000 francs. The Douanier did this and handed the money to Sauvaget who gave him 1,000 francs for his trouble. The trick was discovered at the beginning of 1909 and both Rousseau and Sauvaget were charged with *'faux et usage de faux'*. Counsel defending The Douanier stated quite accurately that he was and always had been a simple-minded man of small means who had never had experience of cheques and credits and had no idea that these complicated proceedings were in the nature of forgery and fraud; he had, he pleaded, been duped and made use of by Sauvaget (who was also charged with stealing bank notes by a trick in 1903). The jury were suspicious until counsel read extracts from The Douanier's collection of press cuttings which described his paintings as childish, and produced one of his jungle pictures, *Singes dans la forêt*, to prove the pathetic naïveté of a man who painted in this manner and believed it to be art; the jury then decided that, as the phrase goes, a man who could believe that could believe anything, and in the end Sauvaget was given five years' imprisonment and The Douanier was condemned to two years' imprisonment with benefit of the Loi Bérenger—(First Offenders Act)—which quashed the sentence. The Douanier had sat crestfallen while his counsel ridiculed his picture and the jury giggled; when his counsel's speech was finished he rose and said, *'Dis-donc, maintenant que tu as fini est-ce que je peux m'en aller?'*—which caused much amusement in Court and perhaps contributed by its simplicity to what amounted to his acquittal; when he heard the final verdict he bowed to the judge and said, *'Je vous remercie bien, Monsieur le Président. Je ferai le portrait de votre dame'* (cf. Appendix IV).

In these last years The Douanier conceived a senile and pathetic passion for a woman who gave him some encouragement while secretly considering him a ridiculous old fool. The woman was a widow aged fifty-four employed as *vendeuse* in a draper's shop in a suburb of Paris. Her name was Mme Léonie . . . He took her on expeditions to the country, wrote her long love letters, and made her expensive presents—spending thus the money which at last was coming from his pictures. At the beginning of 1910 he prepared a deed of gift making her his heir with ownership of all his pictures and all subsidiary rights; and he made   formal proposal for marriage to her parents. The woman and her parents replied that his pictures were absurd and obviously of no value and that a respectable woman could not marry a man who had been condemned for fraud by a court of law. The Douanier then went to Guillaume Apollinaire and to Vollard and asked them for certificates to his personal probity and to the merits of his work; both provided the certificates—Vollard writing on stamped paper, at his request. But Madame Léonie and her parents were obdurate; there was no marriage; and the deed of gift, which still exists in draft, was never signed.

In March 1910 The Douanier exhibited his last picture *Le rêve* (Pl. 63) in the *Salon des Indépendants*. In August he somehow wounded his leg and omitted to disinfect it; the poison spread, and he had to go to hospital where he spent his time writing long letters of entreaty to Madame Léonie who ignored them. On September 2 he expressed a wish to see his friend Uhde who hastened to the hospital; 'I sat by his bedside,' Uhde tells us, 'and he held my hand. But I knew that there was no hope of his recovery.' He died on September 4 at the age of sixty-six. The hospital registers are said to have described him, on what grounds I know not, as 'alcoholic'. Only seven people were present at his funeral, as Apollinaire, Picasso and all his artist friends were away from Paris. When Apollinaire returned he arranged with Queval (The Douanier's landlord for many years) and the painter Delaunay for a decent tomb, and he wrote upon the tombstone:

> *Gentil Rousseau tu nous entends*
> *nous te saluons*
> *Delaunay, sa femme, Monsieur Queval et moi*
> *laisse passer nos bagages en franchise à la porte du ciel*
> *nous t'apporterons des pinceaux des couleurs des toiles*
> *afin que tes loisirs sacrés dans la lumière réelle*
> *tu les consacres à peindre comme tu tiras mon portrait*
> *la face des étoiles.*

And in 1914 Apollinaire wrote the charming poem *Souvenir du Douanier*, which begins:

> *Un tout petit oiseau*
> *Sur l'épaule d'un ange*
> *Ils chantent la louange*
> *Du gentil Rousseau.*

The Salon painters always looked on The Douanier's works with peculiar malevolence because their grandeur and poetry and arresting qualities were achieved without art school tricks or other aspects of the art education which academic theory presumes essential for an artist. These Salon painters and their circle put out all kinds of rumours to damage The Douanier's reputation. One such rumour represented Alfred Jarry as his evil genius who had persuaded him, as a satanic joke, to leave the Customs and take to art. A version of this ridiculous story was told at a banquet of the *Société de Psychothérapie* in 1925 when the speaker said:

'Alfred Jarry, after a night spent in the region of Les Halles, was returning to his lodgings in the small hours of the morning with a painter friend and his model. Crossing the Pont des Arts Jarry observed a figure walking up and down the quay and asked him what he was doing. 'I am a douanier', the man answered, 'and I am attending to my business.' Jarry looked at him intently and then said, 'I can see in your countenance that you were born to be an artist. Genius in the arts is often visible in the face. It is clear that you ought not to waste your time as a douanier. You ought to paint pictures like my friend whom you see before you with his model.' The Douanier protested that he had no competence; but Jarry made the painter instal his easel while the model removed her clothes and struck an attitude beneath a tree. 'Now take this palette and brushes,' said Jarry, 'and paint "Eve in the Earthly Paradise".' The Douanier was persuaded; and a semblance of a female appeared on the canvas beneath the semblance of a tree. 'Now', said Jarry, squeezing red upon the palette, 'you must add the apples, because Eve, you remember, used an apple to tempt the father of mankind.' The Douanier dipped his brush in vermilion and soon the tree was covered with little red balloons. Meanwhile the strange group had caught the eye of a patrolling policeman. And in due course the *Douanier* appeared in court to answer the charge of an affront to decency. The magistrate dismissed him with a caution; and The Douanier thanking him offered to paint a portrait of his lady as a New Year's gift.' [1]

Readers of my account of The Douanier's life will recognize the confusions on which this rigmarole is based.

[1] Jean Saltas: *Souvenirs sur Alfred Jarry: Comment le douanier Rousseau devint peintre*. Article in *Les Marges*, March 15, 1925. The police court anecdote is a confusion with an episode that occurred in 1909. Cf. above, p. 245 and below, pp. 361, 376, 377. For Jarry's real relations with The Douanier cf. above pp. 148, 181.

ACT III: THE MASTERS' LIVES

AUGUSTE RENOIR (iv)

From sixty-three to his death at seventy-eight (1904–1919)

Between 1904 and 1906 Renoir lived at various places in the Midi, chiefly at Magagnosc and Cagnes; and in 1907 he bought a house and property at Les Collettes near Cagnes which was his headquarters for his last twelve years. His rheumatoid arthritis became steadily worse each year. In 1904 he wrote: '*Je suis pincé, cela va lentement mais sûrement; l'année prochaine je serai un peu plus mal et ainsi de suite. C'est une habitude à prendre et voilà tout; n'en parlons plus.*' But he was able for some time to make expeditions to Essoyes, to Paris and, as late as 1910, to Munich. In Paris in these years he sometimes stayed in the house of Maurice Gangnat, the principal collector of his later works; Maurice Gangnat's son, M. Philippe Gangnat, still lives in this house, where the walls are covered with Renoir's work from 1904 onwards, and where we can still see the porcelain pots which figure in some of the pictures that he painted there. Up to 1911 Renoir was able to walk with the aid of crutches. But thereafter he had to take to a wheeled chair. In 1912 he had operations on his foot and knee. On the day preceding one of these operations he was in bed in a nursing home and to pass the time he called for his colours and painted a still life from flowers sent him by some friends. In his last years the fingers of his right hand were so contracted that his brush was strapped into position between the contorted thumb and finger.

In his old age he was free from financial worries. He was a world-famous master whose pictures were now collected everywhere and had a high exchange value in the international art trade. His portrait *Mme Charpentier et ses enfants*,[1] painted in 1879, was sold in 1907 for 94,000 francs. He posed in this period as an old-fashioned fellow suspicious of experiment; young artists came to Cagnes to pay him homage and he tried to persuade them that he had always been a humdrum 'traditional' artist—though in fact, except for a few years in the 'nineties, he had made some gesture of exploration every day of his long life and, as I have noted in the Introduction to this Act, he was more original than ever in those great productions of his wonderful old age which include *Les femmes aux chapeaux* (Pl. 65), *Les grandes laveuses* (Pl. 71A) and *Le jugement de Paris* (Pl. 71B). It seems clear that— allowance made for the humours of a genuine invalid—he was at bottom an exceptionally kind old man devoted to the root simplicities of real French life.

[1] New York. Metropolitan Museum.

Plate (F) RENOIR

Femme nouant son soulier, c. 1916

London. Samuel Courtauld, Esq.

(cf. page xii)

He was in no way malevolent and misanthropic like Degas. On one occasion a forgery was brought to him that he might denounce it and secure conviction of the forger; but learning that the forger was a poor and miserable wretch he painted over the picture and thus transformed it to a work that was properly signed 'Renoir'. An event of the last years that gave him satisfaction was a letter sent him by a group of English admirers when *Les parapluies* entered the National Gallery in 1917. 'When your picture was hung among the chefs-d'œuvre of the "old masters",' the letter said, "we had the delight to realize that one of our contemporaries had already taken his place among the great masters of the European tradition.' His friend and biographer Albert André tells us that Renoir when he read this letter *'trouva ce jour-là que la gloire était une bonne chose'*. On the other hand, the German invasion of 1914 brought him great mental anguish. His two elder sons were in the army and Pierre Renoir's forearm was shattered.

In this period 1904–1919 he painted, as recorded, several hundred genre figures indoors and outdoors, portraits, head studies, nudes, landscapes, and still-life studies of flowers and fruit. He worked sometimes from models who came to his retreat from Nice, but he preferred to paint the members of his family and his maid servants—especially a girl called Gabrielle who sat to him continuously for several years. He also modelled some sculpture, with the aid of assistants, in this period, the best known pieces being *Femme allaitant son enfant*[1] and the monumental *Vénus*.[2] In spite of his infirmity he painted almost daily to the end; and when he died at seventy-eight on December 17, 1919, his studio was full of recent pictures completing a life's labour of at least four thousand works.[3]

[1] One bronze of this is in the London National Gallery, Millbank.

[2] Paris. Ambroise Vollard.

[3] For the present distribution of some of his later pictures cf. my Bibliographical and Catalogue Notes in Appendix I.

ACT III: THE MASTERS' LIVES

EDGAR DEGAS (iv)

From seventy till his death at eighty-three (1904–1917)

In his last thirteen years Degas was a lonely and pathetic figure. He had opened his heart to few people in his long life, treating most people as intruders on his privacy and objects of his caustic wit; he had done few acts of kindness that could bring him consolatory fruit; and his few friends were now old and dying one by one. More hypochondriac than ever, he now complained hysterically of deafness and gastric troubles—just as before he had complained hysterically of asthma. In 1904 he complained to his doctor of *grippe gastro-intestinale*; the doctor recommended mountain air; so he went to the Jura; but he went in miserable spirits knowing well, as he confessed in a letter, that his *gastralgie* was *une maladie mentale*—a neurotic's excuse for self-pity, an hysteric's device to capture the sympathy of others. His fear of blindness was now more harassing than ever; and after 1905 his eyesight veritably declined—though he could see much better than he pretended even when he was seventy-eight in 1912, for in that year he found himself by the side of Monet at the auction sale of Rouart's collection and said to him: 'I can't see you but I recognize your voice,' and then a few minutes later he pointed out to him quite small details in a picture held up by the auctioneer. At this sale his *Danseuses à la barre* was sold for £19,000 the highest sum ever paid for a work by an artist in his lifetime; and all through this period he saw his pictures sold to galleries and collectors for considerable sums. But this gave him no satisfaction; he was only enraged that those who had bought his work earlier should now be selling at a profit; '*Je suis comme le cheval qui a gagné la course,*' he said on one occasion, '*cela n'augmente pas sa ration d'avoine'*—though he had never been short of fodder and he had led an easy and prosperous life. At another sale he observed with more engaging wit, '*Je crois que celui qui a fait ce tableau n'est pas un imbécile mais celui qui l'a payé ce prix-là en est sûrement un.*'

His restlessness became a mania in this period. He wandered aimlessly for hours almost daily in the streets, or travelled on omnibuses or tramways from one part of Paris to another. At home in his old quarters in the rue Victor Massé he lived a hermit existence, except on the rare occasions when some old friend was invited or admitted. Vollard tells us that he found him on a winter's night before a smoking fire with Ellen André, the actress who thirty years earlier had posed with Desboutin for *L'absinthe*.[1]

[1] Paris. Louvre. Cf. above pp. 37, 144.

EDGAR DEGAS, TO HIS DEATH AT EIGHTY-THREE

In 1912 his house in the rue Victor Massé was pulled down, and he felt as much at sea as Fragonard had felt in his old age when Napoleon expelled him from his studio in the Louvre. He searched deliberately for a house as old-fashioned and devoid of comforts as the one he had lived in for twenty-five years. Eventually he found one on the Boulevard de Clichy. There he lived through the war and there he died on September 26, 1917.

His last pastels would seem to have been produced in 1907; but he occasionally modelled nude figures in the dancing and toilet attitudes he knew so well, till he left the rue Victor Massé. After his death his collection was dispersed at auction; and hundreds of his own drawings, pastels and paintings, many unfinished, found in his studio, were also sold. The founder Hebrard cast in bronze the whole series of his wax and clay models which can now be seen in the Louvre.[1]

I list some of the pastels of his last period, with their present whereabouts, in Appendix I.

[1] Duplicate casts of some of these figures were made by Hebrard for sale to other museums and collectors.

INTERLUDE

The War Years: August 1914-1918

Picasso—Modigliani—Matisse—*Dada*

INTERLUDE

The War Years: August 1914-1918

Picasso—Modigliani—Matisse—Dada

Picasso and Gris, as Spaniards, were not called on for service in the war. Matisse was also free to continue his own work. Derain was a driver in the artillery and produced no paintings till he was demobilised in 1918. Braque, Léger, Metzinger and most of the Cubists saw military service; Segonzac worked in the camouflage section; Braque was wounded in 1915 and invalided out. Debussy in 1914 wrote *Berceuse héroïque* 'In token of homage to Albert I of Belgium and his soldiers', in 1915 he wrote two sonatas signed 'Claude Debussy, musicien français' to demonstrate that 'though there are thirty millions of Boches, French thought is indestructible'; and in 1917 he wrote an unfinished *Ode à la France* before he collapsed in his last illness and died in the spring of 1918 at the age of fifty-six. Ravel aged thirty-nine served for a period and then wrote *Le tombeau de Couperin* in 1917. The sculptor Henri Gaudier, living in England as Gaudier-Brzeska, returned to France without a summons, and was killed in a charge at Neuville St. Vaast in 1915. Guillaume Apollinaire, though a Polish subject, joined the French artillery, and was wounded in the head in 1916; his play *Les mamelles de Tirésias*, subtitled *Drame surréaliste*, was performed in Paris in 1917; he died partly from his wound and partly from influenza on the eve of the Armistice, terrified, as he lay half-conscious in high fever, by shouts of '*Mort à Guillaume*' in the street outside. Jean Cocteau served for some time and conceived the first idea of the ballet *Parade* while hearing Satie's *Morceaux en forme de poire* when home on leave; later he published *Le potomak* and *Les Eugènes de la guerre* with terribly mordant drawings symbolizing the German ravages in France. Chirico was in the Italian army from 1915–1918 and continued painting in his periods of leave. Chagall who had gone to Russia in June 1914 to see his family and get married (leaving two hundred of his pictures and drawings in his Berlin exhibition at the *Sturm* Gallery and the remainder in his studio in Paris) was mobilised for auxiliary service in the Russian army and employed on clerical work till the Revolution, and he then founded an art school in his native Vitebsk. Utrillo was pronounced unfit for military service. Camille Bombois, later to be known as a painter, fought in the ranks, was wounded and won the *Croix de Guerre* and the *Médaille militaire*—(Bombois was thirty-one in 1914 and he had hitherto earned his living first as a wrestler in a travelling circus and then as a labourer in the building trade in Paris). André Bauchant, who was later

255

to design a ballet for Diaghileff and paint *Le bon vin* (Pl. 91), served as a telemetric draughtsman first in Macedonia and later on the Marne—(Bauchant was forty-one in 1914 and he had hitherto earned his living as a horticulturist). Another newcomer to our story, Jean Lurçat, painter later of *Les pilotis* (Pl. 88A) was a pacifist by conviction but volunteered for service and salved his conscience by writing pacifist poems and articles—(born in Paris of Spanish ancestry, Lurcat was twenty-two in 1914 and he had studied medicine till 1911 and thereafter science and philosophy at Nancy; he had drawn occasionally, encouraged by his friends the poets Paul Fort, Vildrac and Duhamel and the art critic Elie Faure, and in the war years he was able to make some drawings including the charming *Femme, fillettes et fleurs* which dates from 1917). The dealer Kahnweiler, who had done so much to help the Cubists, was in Switzerland when the war began and did not return to Paris in these years. The Douanier's friend Uhde was also away from France. Kahnweiler's place was taken by a new French dealer Léonce Rosenberg, who was serving in the army and spent his leaves buying Cubist pictures and financing the artists until 1918 when he opened a gallery called *L'effort moderne*. Paul Guillaume, who opened a new and larger gallery in the Faubourg Saint Honoré in 1915, was the main supporter of Modigliani in these years and in 1916 he lectured on Chirico to a hostile audience at the Vieux Colombier. In 1916 Odilon Redon died at seventy-six. In 1917, as chronicled, Degas died at eighty-three and Rodin died at seventy-seven. In 1918 Paris was bombarded by the German long-range guns; Ansermet conducted Stravinsky's *Histoire du soldat* with text by C. F. Ramuz at Lausanne; and after the Armistice, Honegger's *Le Dit des Jeux du Monde* was performed at the Vieux Colombier and the first Jazz Band appeared at the Casino de Paris.[1] In that year also the Stchoukin and Morosoff collections of modern French paintings were nationalized by the Soviet Government as the Moscow Museum of Modern Western Art.[2]

Picasso was in Provence when the war began; he returned to Paris soon after and worked there through the greater part of 1915 and 1916. In the spring of 1917 he went to Italy visiting Rome, Florence, Naples, and other cities; in the summer he went to Spain and presented *L'arlequin au rideau rouge* to the Barcelona Museum. In 1918 he installed himself in a new studio in the rue de la Boétie which remained his headquarters for a number of years. His paintings in 1914–1916 were mainly Flat-pattern Cubist compositions. But at the same time he started a series of outline portraits. These portraits began with drawings of his old friends Max Jacob and Apollinaire, the next sitters included Léonce Rosenberg and Vollard, and later sitters were some new friends including Jean Cocteau, Stravinsky and Eric Satie. Picasso married in this period and a group drawing of 1919 shows full-length figures of Satie, Cocteau, the English critic Clive Bell and Mme Picasso. His contacts with the Russian Ballet began in 1917 when he worked with Stravinsky,

[1] Slonimsky: *Music since 1900.*

[2] Numerous additions have subsequently been made to this museum. At the present time it contains among other things forty pictures by Matisse, thirty-eight by Picasso, seventeen by Derain, twenty-two by Gauguin, nine by Van Gogh and many by the Impressionists, especially Monet and Renoir. For Stchoukin's relations with Matisse and Picasso cf. p. 224.

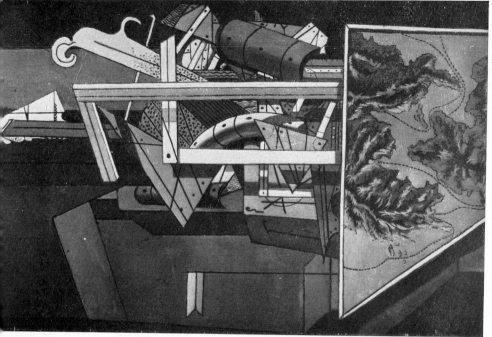

73B. CHIRICO
Mélancolie du départ, 1915
Exhibited London, Zwemmer Gallery, 1937

73A. CHIRICO
Jouets de prince, 1915
Paris. Mme Simone Breton

74. MATISSE

Intérieur: Quai St. Michel, 1916

London. Sir Kenneth Clark

Satie and Cocteau in Paris and in Rome, and helped them to convert Diaghileff from the baroque exuberance of his earlier standards to the Cubist way of thought. And thus it came that Diaghileff, whose last new ballet had been *Soleil de Minuit*, with choreography by Massine, music by Rimsky-Korsakov and scenery by Larionov in 1915, produced, in 1917, *Parade* by Cocteau, with music by Satie, choreography by Massine, and costumes and a drop-scene by Picasso.

In *Parade* Picasso and Cocteau set out to bring Flat-pattern Cubism, as it were, to life; the subject reflecting the modern artists' cult of the circus (which had continued as noted since the 'seventies) was that of Seurat's *Parade*—a group of performers on a platform outside a side-show at a fair, 'blowing their own trumpets' and doing fragments of their 'stunts' to attract the public to the show inside; the performers selected by Cocteau were two acrobats, a little American girl dancer, a Chinese juggler and—a complete innovation—three noisy, gesticulating Managers; Satie's music contained suggestions of typical modern noises—a battalion of typewriters being included among the instruments; in the ballet the little American girl did trick cycling, took Kodak snapshots, was shipwrecked, chased a thief with a revolver, and danced all aquiver like a cinema film; the Managers were encased in wooden constructions and one, an American, was shaped like a skyscraper; of these Managers Cocteau wrote later (in *Coq et Arlequin*): 'They were a sort of human scenery, animated pictures by Picasso . . . the problem was to take a series of natural gestures and to metamorphose them into a dance without depriving them of their realistic force, as a modern painter seeks his inspiration in natural objects in order to metamorphose them into pure painting; for reality alone, even when well concealed, has power to arouse emotion'.[1] The concept of the Managers was thus in line with Picasso's Cubism where all the forms (even those which in the final picture evoke no definable associated ideas) owe something of their vitality to the particular 'real' forms from which they were evolved. *Parade*, performed at the Châtelet in aid of war charities, was badly received by the critics, and Satie replied so vigorously to one critic that the matter was brought before the courts.[2]

When his work on *Parade* was finished Picasso painted a series of portraits and some pictures of figures in harlequin and pierrot clothes. This double series, which began with the *Arlequin au rideau rouge* and *Mme Picasso à l'éventail* of 1917 and continued with *Pierrot assis*[3] in 1918, was a kind of reversion to the human values of the 'Blue' period, disciplined by the experiences of Cubism, and a transition between the purely romantic approach in the *saltimbanque* series and the classical approach in pictures like *Le repos de l'acrobate* (Pl. 83), which I shall refer to later.[4] These transition pictures are characterized by a dualism—the classical elements being rendered humanly emotive by Picasso's romantic spirit and the romantic elements being generalized by classical style and controlled by classical restraints.

We get a similar dualism in many of the pictures by Amédée Modigliani in

[1] Translation. Rollo Myers: *Cock and Harlequin*.

[2] Satie sent the critic an insulting postcard and he was condemned to eight days in prison for 'public insults and defamation of character'; but the sentence was suspended or quashed.

[3] New York. Adolph Lewisohn.   [4] Cf. below, p. 300.

these war years. Modigliani, as chronicled, had come to Paris from his native Italy when he was twenty-two in 1906 and he had worked at first as a sculptor influenced by negro carvings and by Brancusi. By 1915 he had almost abandoned sculpture for painting, and nearly all his best pictures were produced between 1916 and the end of the war. These pictures include some sculpturesque monochrome paintings of figures in caryatid attitudes, and some recumbent nudes; but the majority are genre and portrait studies of single figures, which include portraits of the dealers Paul Guillaume and Zborowski who supported him and acquired his pictures (as they also supported Soutine who was now his friend). In his genre and portrait studies Modigliani expressed an extreme sensitiveness to the sitter's humanly emotive personality in a formal language invented for the purpose in each case. We see this in the *Portrait de Jean Cocteau* (Pl. 75B) and *La fillette à la collerette blanche* (Pl. 75A). All the influences of the ten years he had spent in Paris were pressed into service for these pictures, where the colour is rich and rather sombre and the pigment is opaque. There is much of Cézanne's *Achille Emperaire* as well as much that comes from Picasso and negro sculpture in the *Portrait de Jean Cocteau*; and there is much that comes from Gauguin's *Mlle Loulou* (Pl. 30) and from Matisse's pictures in *La fillette à la collerette blanche* and *La chocolatière* (Pl. 76); but Modigliani was in no sense a mere derivative eclectic artist; his pictures of this period are essentially original—the direct exteriorising of his personal experience by means expressly fashioned for that end. We see much the same characters in his studies of recumbent nudes painted at this time. In the largest, and one of the finest, of these nude studies, *Le grand nu* (1918),[1] the figure, very exquisite in carnations recalling the carnations in pictures by Giorgione and Titian—sings out in an elegant silhouette between the rich reds, greens, blacks and greys of the Indian shawl on the divan and the deep red of a curtain behind. Towards the end of 1918 Modigliani developed the formal language of *La fillette à la collerette blanche* into a rhythmic formula of oval forms, and he abandoned rich colouring and opaque pigment for pale sweet tints transparently applied. In this later method he produced a number of graceful and fascinating pictures; but eventually the method came perilously near to a stylistic trick derived from the veritable originality of his own earlier works.

Matisse worked in the first years of the war in Paris, where he had a studio on the Quai Saint Michel; he also worked at Clamart near Meudon where he had a country house, and in Nice where he went in the winter months. He painted several grey-green landscapes near Meudon (*Arbre près de l'étang de Trivaux*[2] and *Paysage de Trivaux* for example) in these years, and developed, in his studio pictures, the more austerely formal manner, influenced by Cubism, which had appeared in *La femme au tabouret*[3] in 1913. The most essentially Cubist of his works are a geometric abstraction titled *Tête blanche et rose*,[3] a large picture of a boy at a piano *La leçon de musique*,[4] and the pictures titled *Les coloquintes*,[5] *Les marocains*[3] and *Les femmes à la rivière*.[4] Cubist stiffening of rhythm is also evident in three interiors of this period, *Poissons rouges dans un intérieur*,[6] *La fenêtre*[7] and *Intérieur: Quai Saint Michel*

[1] Paris. J. Seligmann.
[2] Plate (G) facing p. 262.
[3] Nice. Henri Matisse.
[4] Paris. Mme Paul Guillaume.
[5] New York. Léonide Massine.
[6] Paris. Baron Gourgaud.
[7] Detroit. Institute of Art.

75B. MODIGLIANI
Portrait de Jean Cocteau, 1917
Paris. Mme Paul Guillaume

75A. MODIGLIANI
La fillette à la collerette blanche, 1918
Paris. M. J. Netter

76. MODIGLIANI
La chocolatière, 1917
London. D. M. Macdonald, Esq.

(Pl. 74). The colour in all these works and others of 1914–1916 is relatively sombre—the dominants in *Intérieur: Quai Saint Michel*, for example, being grey and Indian red. In the second half of 1916 and the first half of 1917 Matisse reverted to the freer more calligraphic drawing and the bold flat patterning of his pre-war painting and produced a number of studies of dark-haired girls where the hair is treated in the semi-Oriental manner that distinguished Gauguin's *Mlle Loulou* (Pl. 30). This series includes *La robe verte*,[1] *Les deux sœurs*,[2] *Les trois sœurs*,[3] *Jeune femme en vert au fauteuil rose* (1917),[4] *Jeune femme à l'accroche-cœur*[5] and the triptych, *Trois sœurs et sculpture nègre*, *Trois sœurs en costume Mauresque*, *Trois sœurs—à la table*.[6] With this series we must associate *La leçon de musique au piano Pleyel*[6] where the calligraphy has a still freer rhythm. In the colour schemes of these pictures green, brown, black and grey predominate with occasional notes of purple or magenta. In 1917 Matisse established himself at Nice and there he developed a colour-shape calligraphy which he combined with linear calligraphy in a very personal and original way. This method appears in *L'artiste et son modèle: Atelier Quai Saint Michel*[1] where colour-shapes of green and purple are the central *motif* of the picture. It also appears in the first pictures painted at Nice in 1917–1918—*La boîte au violon*,[3] *Intérieur à Nice*,[7] *Le balcon à Nice*,[8] *Deux jeunes filles dans une chambre à Nice (Le boudoir)*,[3] *Jeune femme en chemise: tapis rouge*.[6] In this series Matisse stands closer to the Impressionists and genre painters and closer to Bonnard and Vuillard than in any other works in his career; the pictures are more essentially visual impressions of interiors and interiors with figures, calligraphically recorded, than inventions in terms of pattern and colour; the touch too is more rapid and less deliberate than in the earlier pictures, and the colour, often dominated by pearl greys and by the pink of a carpet, is gentle and pretty. I stayed recently at Nice in a room appointed like the rooms portrayed in Matisse's pictures of these years—the white curtains were looped on either side of the slatted shutters, the dressing table was covered with white muslin over pink, the carpet was pink and criss-cross patterned, and a little patterned armchair sat waiting for a model; it was a pleasing experience to be thus transported to the centre of a Matisse picture; but I mention it not to record my pleasure but to point out that this type of pleasure would not have been possible in respect of the earlier pictures by Matisse because in all those pictures the jumping-off points—the initial visual impressions—were much more transfigured. In 1918 Matisse turned aside for a time from these genre interiors to paint the portrait known as *La toque de gouro*[3] (a girl in a plaid dress and a little hat with thin feathers twirling on each side) and several pictures from a beautiful girl whom he painted as a standing half-nude in a plumed hat, and whose portrait wearing the same hat—*Plumes blanches*[9]—is a striking pattern where lemon yellow, white and creamy pink form a light silhouette, and brown and black strike contrasting notes, against a middle-tone background of earth red.

[1] Nice. Henri Matisse.   [2] Paris. A. Kann.
[3] Paris. Mme Paul Guillaume.   [4] Winterthur. Dr. Hahnloser.
[5] New York. Adolphe Lewisohn. This picture is also known as *La femme accoudée*.
[6] Merion. Barnes Foundation.   [7] Philadelphia. R. Sturgis Ingersoll.
     Paris. Paul Rosenberg.   [9] New York. Stephen C. Clark.

The Van-Gogh-Fauve-Expressionist tradition was upheld in the war years by Rouault and Vlaminck. Rouault in 1916 made a passionately contemptuous chalk and water-colour drawing emblematic of the German Emperor—*Le Super-homme*[1] and in 1918 he drew in the same spirit *Le Père Ubu*[1] emblematic of the war profiteer. Vlaminck developed a personal expressionism in landscapes where platinum thunderclouds, vermilion roofs, inky tree-trunks, viridian leaves and yellow ochre earth combine in sultry dramas choreographed by Cézanne in the kingdom of Marieschi or some descendant of El Greco.

Surrealism hardly appeared in Parisian painting in the war years, because Chirico was in Italy and Chagall was in Russia as recorded. The pictures which Chirico painted in the intervals of military service in 1915–1918 were of two types; in the first he developed his Surrealist painting on the lines of the *Rue Italienne: le cerceau* (Pl. 68B) and in the second he pressed Flat-pattern Cubism into the service of this Surrealist art (which he himself called *Pittura metafisica*). Outstanding pictures of the first type are: *Jouets de prince* (Pl. 73A) where the dream disquietude is suggested by emotive perspective and recession and by a suggestion of animal vitality in mechanical forms (exploited later by Picasso in such works as *Dinard* (Pl. 89B)) and the profoundly disturbing picture *Les Muses inquiétantes*[2] where figures partly human, partly antique columns and partly dressmaker's stands, preside as terrifying idols on a terrace which recedes in long perspective to a city of factory chimneys and classical towers. In the pictures of the second type Chirico abandoned perspective and recession as emotive agents, working instead with the shallow depth and the forward movement of Flat-pattern Cubism,[3] and creating Surrealist disquiet by strange combination of inanimate objects with associated ideas—the geometrician's instruments of measurement, the geographer's relief map, the astronomer's charts, the jointed wooden lay figure of the artist's studio and so forth. The difference between Chirico's Surrealist Flat-pattern Cubism and Picasso's Flat-pattern Cubism can be seen if we compare Picasso's *Chien et poulet* (Pl. 79A) with Chirico's *Mélancolie du départ* (Pl. 73B). In Picasso's *Chien et poulet*, the material used as jumping-off point has been casually selected; Picasso happened to see his dog prowling in the kitchen about to steal the chicken from the table, or he came in and found the chicken stolen and the dog looking guilty, or he decided for some other fortuitous reason to paint a Flat-pattern Cubist *Chien et poulet*; the initial forms of the constituents—the attitudes of the dog and chicken, the intervening table and so forth—play parts in the final form of the picture, but they are in no sense descriptively defined or clearly evident, because they are largely transfigured by the processes producing the final result—in the way referred to by Jean Cocteau in his comments on *Parade*.[4] In Chirico's *Mélancolie du départ* the constituents are all fragments of objects and each fragment is precisely defined in descriptive technique and left clearly evident; and Chirico defined them thus and left them thus evident because he was out to use ideas associated with the fragments as factors in the creation of a Surrealist disquiet. Chirico's Surrealist, or as he called them 'metaphysical', pictures of the war years, including *Mélancolie du départ* (Pl.

---

[1] Formerly New York. John Quinn. Cf. p. 309.   [3] Cf. p. 204.
[2] Philadelphia. H. Clifford.   [4] Cf. pp. 257, 268, 285.

73B) and *Intérieur métaphysique*,[1] were exhibited in Rome in 1918 where they at once attracted the attention of some young artists who joined forces with him and helped him to found and direct a new review called *Valori Plastici*.

Chagall, the other pre-war Surrealist pioneer, painted a series of pictures at Vitebsk in 1914–1915 before he was enrolled for auxiliary service in the army, and another series when he was director of the Vitebsk art school in 1917–1918. The pictures of the first period, when he witnessed local pogroms, include some romantic-realist studies of Rabbis and some Surrealist pictures expressing his new-found happiness in his marriage—*La promenade*,[2] for example, where he walks with his beloved through the village and suddenly in exaltation the lovers fly into the air; and *L'anniversaire*[3] where his beloved floats to embrace him holding her birthday bouquet in her hand; and *Poète allongé* (where the poet, a kind of pierrot, lies dreaming in the verdure of a meadow with a horse and a sow and a farmhouse behind), a singularly beautiful picture recalling in spirit some of The Douanier Rousseau's most poetic productions[4]. In the second period Chagall was made commissar-director of his own art school at Vitebsk by Lounatcharsky the Soviet Minister of Education; but he neither knew nor cared anything for Communist theories or practice—'I knew nothing about Marx', he tells us in *Ma vie*, 'except that he was a Jew and had a long white beard.' His concern was to bring the gaiety and lyrical inconsequence of his personal art to the lives of the local peasants, and he set them to copy his pictures and use them as banners in the frequent fêtes and processions which the Soviet rulers, like other totalitarian dictatorships, imposed upon their flocks. There was trouble when the Soviet authorities asked him why the cows were blue and why men and women and cows flew across the sky in these singular banners; he was advised to put the peasants to work on busts of Marx and Lenin; and in the end there were intrigues against him and he left Vitebsk to become artistic director of a newly founded Jewish theatre in Moscow.

Chirico and Chagall were entirely responsible for the first two phases of Surrealism, 1911–1914 and 1914–1918. But, as already stated, they did not call themselves Surrealists (though the word had been invented by Apollinaire to describe Chagall's pictures); there was no nominal Surrealist movement in these years; and it is important not to confuse this original Surrealism, launched by Chirico and Chagall, with the 1924 movement which I shall refer to later as the Neo-Surrealist movement,[5] or with the 1916 Dada movement that I must now consider.

The *Dada movement* was launched not in or from Paris but in and from Zurich. Its founders were a Rumanian Tristan Tzara, an Alsatian Hans Arp, a German Hugo Ball and some others. Arp has thus described its genesis; 'I affirm that Tristan Tzara discovered the word *Dada* on the 8th of February 1916 at 6 o'clock in the evening. I was there with my twelve children when Tzara pronounced for the first time this word which aroused a legitimate enthusiasm in all of us. This took place at the Café de la Terrasse in Zurich and I had a roll of bread up my left nostril.' Tzara, in fact, discovered the word 'Dada' by opening a dictionary at random; and the dictionary was not an English dictionary where the word would

<hr>

[1] Connecticut. James Thrall Soby. [2] Moscow collection.
[3] German collection. [4] Plate (H) facing p. 278. [5] Cf. below, pp.275–284.

be defined as 'a childish term for father' but a French dictionary where it was defined as 'a hobby horse'—as in '*être sur son dada*' (to indulge in one's hobby). From this beginning the Dadaists launched a nihilist and anarchic movement calling for 'the negation of all systems, the destruction of all recognized values', and for 'creation for its own sake destroying itself in the act of creation'. The Dada doctrines were actively opposed to all forms of order, restraint and aesthetic in life, politics, literature and art; and they denounced with one and the same contempt not only all academic standards of technique in the arts but also the aesthetic-expressionist and abstract-architectural attitudes in contemporary painting. From the Dada standpoint all forms of personal aesthetic art, in a world where aggression with bombs, gas and machine-guns could only be countered by more bombs, more gas and more machine-guns, were merely butterflies destined to be crushed by contemporary wheels; and suicide by such art appeared more dignified than submission to destruction.

The Zurich Dadaists met first in a café run by Hugo Ball, and there at one soirée three Dadaist poets read gibberish poems simultaneously. The first Dada manifesto, written by Tzara and illustrated by another Rumanian Marcel Janko, was titled *La première aventure céleste de M. Antipyrine*; the second, called *Phantastische Gebete*, was written by a German Richard Huelsenbeck, and illustrated by Hans Arp. For their first review, called *Cabaret Voltaire*, the Dadaists secured help from Paris and elsewhere; the names of the contributors include, incongruously, Apollinaire, Picasso and Modigliani, and also the Italian Futurist Marinetti and the Russian abstract painter Kandinsky (a leader with Franz Marc of the German *Blaue Reiter* group). It was doubtless the element of acid despairing protest in Dada that appealed at this moment to Picasso and Apollinaire; and Apollinaire also contributed to a review called *Sic*, described as 'semi-Dadaist', which appeared in 1916 in Paris. The *Dada* attitude had, moreover, been anticipated in Paris by the Futurist-Cubist Marcel Duchamp (painter in 1912 of the *Nu descendant l'escalier*)[1] who in 1914 had begun to produce manufactured objects—bottle racks and so on— which he described as 'Ready-Mades' and signed as works of art. Duchamp went to New York in 1915 and found there the Futurist-Cubist Francis Picabia; and while Tzara and his friends were performing in Zurich in 1916, Duchamp, Picabia and the director of the Stieglitz Gallery launched a semi-Dada New York movement with a review called '291' (that being the street number of the Stieglitz Gallery on Fifth Avenue),[2] and Picabia painted a picture titled '*Objet qui ne fait pas l'éloge des temps passés ou c'est clair comme le jour (cette chose est faite pour perpétuer mon souvenir)*.[3] In 1917 Picabia painted *Parade amoureuse*[4] (where parts of a carburettor and similar forms are used to create a Dada version of Chirico's *Muses inquiétantes*) and he then went to Barcelona where he published a Dada review called '391' after which he joined Tzara in Zurich. In 1917 also, Dada gestures were made in New York by Marcel Duchamp with a review called *Wrong-Wrong* and with further 'Ready-Made' works of plastic art—including a porcelain plumbing fixture (which he titled 'Fontaine' and signed 'R. Mutt') and

[1] Cf. above, pp. 205, 238.   [2] Cf. above, pp. 221, 228.
[3] Paris. Mme Francis Picabia.   [4] Paris. Mme Simone Kahn.

Plate (G) MATISSE
Arbre près de l'étang de Trivaux, 1916
London. National Gallery, Millbank (Tate Gallery)
(cf. page xii)

by the Philadelphian Man Ray (later known as a photographer) who was now twenty-seven and a painter and influenced both by Cubism and Dada. In Paris in 1917 a semi-Dada review titled *Nord Sud* had contributions from Apollinaire and Max Jacob and also from three writers who were to establish seven years later (in 1924) the Neo-Surrealist movement—André Breton (a trained psychiater), Philippe Soupault and Louis Aragon.[1] In Berlin, to which the German Huelsenbeck had returned, there was now a Dada movement with the caricaturist George Grosz as the principal artist. Meanwhile the Zurich Dadaists were publishing reviews called *Dada I* and *Dada II* edited by Tzara and they had founded a Dada Gallery where they held picture exhibitions for which, enlisting outside help, as they had done for their first literary reviews, they procured works from the Swiss Paul Klee, from Kandinsky, and even, again incongruously, from Modigliani and Chirico. Paul Klee, whom we have encountered as the painter in 1907 of the Surrealist *A table* (influenced by Jerome Bosch and James Ensor), was now thirty-seven and developing an original personal art from which all established canons of accomplished technique were excluded, and in which the technical procedures commonly used by children aged about five were ingeniously exploited by a mature mind and passion. In 1918 a Cologne Dada group was formed by Hans Arp (who had gone there from Zurich) and Max Ernst (who, born near Cologne in 1891, had studied philosophy at Bonn from 1909–1914, served with the German artillery from 1915–1917, and had then become an artist, without any art school training, though he was acquainted with pre-war Parisian painting including the Surrealist pictures by Chirico and Chagall).

All through 1916–1918 the Dadaists indulged in provocative shock gestures and extravagant nonsensical demonstrations, using advertising tactics already employed by the Futurists—though never, we must note, by the Fauves or the Cubists or the pioneer Surrealists Chirico and Chagall. Some artists in the 'nineties had flirted with Anarchist doctrines as I have recorded,[2] but the Impressionists, Cézanne, Seurat, Gauguin, the Fauves and the Cubists had all resented attempts made to discredit them by connecting their art with political concepts with which in fact they had no concern; and all those artists had suffered when they were falsely described as 'Communards' or 'Anarchists' by the academic painters and their supporters and by political propagandists.[3] The Dada artists went farther than any artists of the 'nineties in courting the label 'Anarchist', for they proclaimed their artistic doctrines as aggressively anarchic, and the Berlin Dadaists were frankly concerned with politics. In the period next to be considered the Dada antics became in some cases purely ridiculous and in others too shamelessly offensive to be tolerable, and the Dada movement thus inevitably brought modern art to considerable discredit for a time. But this movement, symbol of the disillusions and disgusts engendered by the war, was of use to one highly original artist, the Swiss Paul Klee, and it also had its value as a satiric voice calling shrilly for the annihilation, as a bitter joke, of everything which the German crime of 1914 had not yet caused to be mutilated or destroyed.

[1] Cf. pp. 276–280.   [2] Cf. p. 153.   [3] Cf. pp. 13, 14, 38–41, 149, 229, 270, 271.

ACT IV

1919 to the Present Day

Purism — Functionalism — Associationism — Surrealism —
Neo-Surrealism—Ozenfant and Jeanneret (Le Corbusier)
—Chirico and Chagall—Matisse, Dufy, Rouault, Braque
—Bombois, Bauchant, Vivin—Picasso

ACT IV

1919 to the Present Day

Purism — Functionalism — Associationism — Surrealism —
Neo-Surrealism—Ozenfant and Jeanneret (Le Corbusier)
—Chirico and Chagall—Matisse, Dufy, Rouault, Braque
—Bombois, Bauchant, Vivin—Picasso

INTRODUCTION

The outstanding originalities in French painting in the first post-war decade were fruits of mental attitudes especially characteristic of the time. At the beginning of the decade, in 1919 and 1920, the world was more internationally-minded than at any moment in the period covered by this book. This happened because the world was then most veritably 'aware', as the psychologists say, of the havoc wrought by the German aggression of 1914. In 1919 and 1920 the conscience of mankind cried out for international action to create a new order for the safeguarding of peace; and as a result the League of Nations was conceived. As everyone knows, the stream of this active international idealism was dammed (and damned) by three cross-currents—(a) the fear that Germany would repeat the crime of 1914 unless she were rendered impotent until the League of Nations became strong enough to restrain her, (b) the fact that the word 'internationalism' had been brought to disrepute by the Russian Communists' propaganda for international action by one *class* everywhere against the others, and (c) the Monroe doctrine; and thus the Treaty of Versailles tried to make Germany impotent for thirty years; and the League of Nations started without Russia, Germany or the United States. But the impediments which thus blocked the construction of international order in world politics had no influence on the creative artists at this time; in art it was possible to pursue the ideals without regard to the fear of Germany, Soviet propaganda or the Monroe doctrine; and in that field at this moment there was a splendid effort to seek not only international but universal and constant principles of order.

This effort in the field of art was the *Purist Movement*, which was mainly the work of the French painter and theorist Amédée Ozenfant, who was thirty-three in 1919 and who had hitherto felt his way cautiously as a student of Cubism. To understand Ozenfant's achievement we must recall the development of Cubism and its derivatives. In 1911–1914 Picasso and Braque had built up their Flat-pattern

Cubist pictures with superimposed Cards, the shape of each card and the images upon it deriving habitually, in the first place, from the artist's experience of particular 'real' forms; the forms selected by Picasso had been mainly those of musical instruments, studio utensils and the bric-a-brac which he chanced to have about him—a Spanish jug in the form of a cock, a Spanish fan, an English pipe, playing cards, dice and so forth, and when Picasso introduced a card derived from the human figure it was usually a harlequin or clown *motif*; Braque's contribution to the material thus used had been the bric-a-brac of the house-decorator, the samples of grained wood, marbling, lettering, etc.; and Gris and Metzinger had brought other objects to this fortuitous material. In 1910–1912 the Italian Futurists had introduced disintegrated parts of speed-machines in their Futurist-Cubist pictures as part of the 'dynamism' of their political concept; in 1914 and 1915 the English Vorticists influenced by Futurism had used machine forms casually selected in their flat-pattern woodcuts reproduced in *Blast* No. 1 and *Blast* No. 2; in 1915–1918 the Dadaists had worked with 'Ready-Mades', i.e. the forms of casually selected everyday manufactured objects (the bottle rack, the porcelain plumbing fixture and so forth) and fragments of machine forms (carburettor parts, etc.) as symbols of their cynical onslaught on personal aesthetic art; and in 1919 Léger began to use forms derived casually from his war experience (portions of war-machines, traffic signals and so forth) in flat-pattern semi-Cubist pictures like *Le disque rouge* (Pl. 79B) where the ideas associated with the objects, together with the bold pattern and deliberately harsh colour combine in a certain severe grandeur which at bottom is decorative in kind. By 1919 Ozenfant had for long been critical of all these types of Cubist and semi-Cubist production because he was personally impatient both of decorative and of empirical procedures. In a review called *L'Elan*, published during the war, he had criticized Braque's Cubism as essentially decorative, and by 1918 he had come to the conclusion that Picasso's Cubism was essentially empirical because Picasso, fundamentally romantic, had always worked in empirical ways. As he saw things, the Cubist-Classical Renaissance, which had been at first an abstract architectural concept, had become in Picasso's hands an art more comparable with romantic empirical painting than with the classical architectural art of Seurat and Cézanne; and convinced that great art could never be achieved by casual selection of material he determined to do for Picasso's Cubism what Seurat and Cézanne had done for Impressionism—to convert it, that is, from an empirical art of personal expression to a new type of ordered reasonable classical art which he titled 'Purism'—and which he worked out himself in the next five years.

Thus Ozenfant's Purist pictures of 1918–1925 (of which I reproduce the central masterpiece *Accords* (Pl. 80)) embody a theoretic system as deliberate and considered as the system embodied by Seurat in *Un dimanche d'été à la Grande Jatte* (Pl. 18), *Chahut* (Pl. 28B) and his other compositions. This system was worked out in a book called *Après le Cubisme* which Ozenfant wrote with his friend and associate Jeanneret (later known as Le Corbusier) in 1918 and finally in a review called *L'esprit nouveau* which he edited with Jeanneret from 1920 to 1925. In my first book *The Modern Movement in Art* I wrote: 'The idea behind the modern movement in the arts is a return to the architectural or classical idea. . . . Romantic art assumes that the artist is more important than art, and that the artist's emotional personality should dominate his work. Classical art assumes that art is greater than the artist, and that the artist is merely a link between the spectator and some universal order, which man, as such, is always seeking to discover.' Ozenfant's contribution transformed Cubism from the one type of action to the other; and the principle behind that contribution can be briefly summarized as follows: The artist who is concerned to fashion classical architectural pictures must construct his architecture as far as possible with constant universal forms, and avoid as far as possible incidental and accidental forms and forms which are merely emotive to him personally for personal reasons; constant universal forms are of two kinds— *organic* and *mechanic*; organic constant universal forms are the type forms produced by nature for functional purposes—the egg, the shell and so forth: mechanic constant universal forms are the type-forms of man-made and machine-made things, the type being determined by the object's function in social life. Ozenfant thus carried the doctrine of the classical norm a stage farther than it had been carried in aesthetic philosophy before. Hitherto that doctrine had remained much as Reynolds had left it in his *Discourses*, where the artist was offered nothing to guide him in discovering the norm (which Reynolds described as 'Beauty') except the so-called 'Graeco-Roman' statues, which Reynolds thought of as Classical art, and the paintings by Italian artists of the High Renaissance in what Reynolds thought of as the 'Grand Manner'. Ozenfant proposed a principle to guide the artist in his search for the norm; and the dual nature of his principle corresponded to contemporary concepts in aesthetic which were disposed to regard machine-made (as well as man-made and natural) forms as aesthetic stimuli.[1]

What Ozenfant himself achieved by the application of this dual principle to painting can be seen by comparing his *Accords* (Pl. 80) with Picasso's *Journaux et violon* (Pl. 64) and *Chien et poulet* (Pl 79A) on the one hand and with Chirico's *Mélancolie du départ* (Pl. 73B) on the other. In *Accords* the forms of the objects used as material are clearly evident in the final picture and Ozenfant has left them evident because he had selected them, not as the result of casual experience or personal pleasure, but deliberately, by his Purist principle, as type norms; since he was not out, like Chirico, to create disquiet by the use of associated ideas, the spirit of the picture is serene and reasonable; and as nothing casual has occurred at any point in the picture's genesis, the formal architecture—the harmony of the related lines and forms—is more logical and classical than the architecture in the pictures by Picasso. In the hands of a dry artist, the Purism of *Accords* might easily, of course, have been mechanical and dead; but created by Ozenfant it is alive with a lyrical quality in the colour and a musical measure in the line.

With Ozenfant's *Accords* Flat-pattern Cubism came to a climax. Ozenfant had transformed it to a noble classical art and he had arrived himself at final perfection in the new form. But this does not mean that the Cubist-Classical Renaissance ceased with Ozenfant's Purist pictures, or that Purism was without important effects. It continued as we shall see to influence a number of painters for some years;

[1] For other aesthetic appreciations of machines cf. pp. 73, 205, 223.

and—what was of much greater consequence—it transferred Cubism from the private studio to the public square. For by transforming empirical Flat-pattern Cubism to a logical, albeit lyrical, architectural art, Ozenfant had equipped it for direct service in the field of architecture itself. Wyndham Lewis saw that the time was ripe for this when, in 1919, he wrote in *The Caliph's Design*: 'It has often been suggested of late that the Architect might become a branch of the Engineering industry. But why should he take all his bric-a-brac shop over to that clean, erect institution across the road? Rather let the Engineer and the Painter fix up a meeting . . . and produce what would be neither a world of boxes on the one hand, as it would be if the Engineer controlled house construction (*vide* skyscrapers), nor of silly antique fakes on the other, as happens when the Architect has his sweet and horrible way. . . . The Cubist painters of Paris . . . are the best fitted to fill this role of superseding, in a practical liaison with the Engineer, the virtually extinct architect. The energy at present pent up (and rather too congested) in the canvas painted in the studio and sold at the dealer's, and written of with a monstrous emphasis of horror or facetiousness in the Press, must be released and used in the general life of the community. . . . And you must put the Architect, as he drags out his miserable if well-paid life to-day, into the dustbin, and close the lid.' And that in fact is very much what happened. Jeanneret (Le Corbusier), who had been trained as an architect, painted Purist pictures while he worked with Ozenfant, and then went back to architecture, broom in hand, sweeping away the flummeries of 'ye olde' this and that, rejoicing in the new materials available, designing in terms of concrete, glass and chromium, planning for the needs and possibilities of contemporary living, creating a new Functional Architecture in Ozenfant's Purist-Cubist aesthetic. From 1924 onwards Purist-Functionalism became the guiding force in architecture, interior equipment, women's dress and so forth; and the dustmen carried to the incinerators pile after pile of obsolete ornaments and trimmings from the architects' studios, the cabinetmakers' workshops, and the sewing rooms of dressmakers and milliners; and thus Picasso's studio gestures when he painted *Les bols* (Pl. 55B) in 1907 and *Journaux et violon* (Pl. 64) in 1912, and Ozenfant's studio gestures in his Purist pictures which culminated in *Accords* (Pl. 80)—and, I must add, the austere and subtle architecture in Brancusi's sculpture—applied to daily life by Jeanneret (Le Corbusier), created the characteristic style of the first two post-war decades; and this style became known in the nineteen-twenties as *Le style mécanique* (and was popularized in vulgar imitations as '*Le style Jazz*').

As I have said, the creation of this new Purist order in art was not stopped by the cross-currents which prevented the organization of order in world affairs. But one of those cross-currents—the fear of Bolshevism—nevertheless delayed the appreciation of Cubist-Purist painting in France and other lands. For the French Cubist-Purist painters suffered discredit because in 1918–1920 some Russian Cubist-Purist painters (calling themselves 'Constructivists') were given commissions to design public ceremonies and so forth by the Russian Soviet government which looked upon their art as non-luxurious and so 'non-bourgeois' and a symbol of the new ascetic order which they were trying, theoretically at any rate, to

77 . MATISSE
Femme et fenêtre : Le peigne espagnol, 1919
Formerly Paris. Bernheim Jeune

24-5-20-

78. PICASSO
Stravinsky, 1920
Paris. M. I. Stravinsky

fashion; and the French Cubist-Purist painters, and others elsewhere, were accordingly described as 'Bolshevik artists' by academic painters who were glad of this rod with which to flog them. The Russian 'Constructivist' painters fell from favour in 1920 when Lenin put his taboo on all forms of aesthetic, expressionist and abstract architectural painting (as aspects of free original thought and incomprehensible by the masses) and ordered the 'discouragement' of painters practising such art and the encouragement of those willing to paint popular descriptive or narrative pictures which would be within the familiar experience of the masses and lead them by the subjects or by easy symbolism to eager appreciation of the Soviet régime. After Lenin's death in 1924 this taboo was endorsed by Stalin; but the French and other Cubist-Purist painters continued to be reviled with the reproach of 'Bolshevism' by their professional rivals and competitors. When the Cubist-Purist principles passed into French and other architecture, interior equipment and industrial art as Functionalism and the *style mécanique*, the architects and designers found themselves opposed from the beginning by practitioners in all the trades whose interests they threatened—the 'period' architects and 'period' interior decorators, the purveyors of miscellaneous otiose, obsolete and redundant flummeries, the dealers in real and spurious antiques and reproductions, the dealers in more or less old 'old masters', the academic sculptors of pseudo-Greek and pseudo-Renaissance nudes, the academic painters of life-size life-like portraits in gold frames, etc., etc.; and here again they were reproached with 'Bolshevism' by these professional rivals and competitors because the Functional style was soon accepted in Soviet Russia and endured there for about ten years. The style succeeded rapidly in Soviet Russia because the vested interests I have chronicled were all starved out there in the new penurious conditions and because the Soviet Government approved and encouraged it as a style concerned to use modern materials for modern needs; and it flourished there till early in the nineteen-thirties when Stalin, presumably to encourage Russian nationalism, pronounced against it in favour of a style said to be based on the architectures of Imperial Rome and eighteenth-century Russia. Looking back on the nineteen-twenties, the reproach of 'Bolshevism' levelled at Purist painting and Functionalism in architecture, interior equipment and industrial art, appears of course quite obviously ridiculous; and Purism and Functionalism are now clearly recognized as aspects of a single truly classical and most valuable Renaissance; but it was not so easy to see the high value of the service rendered by these pioneer artists and architects of these movements when they made their first gestures between 1919 and 1925.

Another characteristic feature of the first post-war years was a group of ideas which I must christen *Associationism* to make my meaning clear. Post-war Associationism was fundamentally the product of a concept which broke down barriers of place and time. This concept can be summarized in Friedrich Ratzel's dictum: 'A philosophy of the history of the human race, worthy of its name . . . must be charged with the conviction that all existence is one' which H. G. Wells set in 1920 at the head of his *Outline of History*, the most characteristic and important book of the period, in spite of its shortcomings, and one read by many millions of people, since two million copies were sold in the nineteen-twenties. Conditions enormously favoured the dissemination of the Associationist concept. In 1919–1923 communications were re-established after the restrictions of the war years and men again were free to travel; radio stations were being built on every hand (the British Broadcasting Company was founded in 1922); cars became cheap enough for Mr. Everyman to buy (with the help of moneylenders); and aeroplanes contributed to a rapidly increasing conquest of space. Wells' *Outline of History* expressed the post-war man's desire to conquer time as he was conquering space; and publishers began to realize that the labours of scholars who had filled libraries with books on human actions in all times and places could be used to slake the post-war thirst for universal knowledge and to appease the new impulses to capture contacts in all directions and compare things and find correspondences and associations across continents and ages. In the field of art there was now a vast and ever-growing mass of material available for these processes. Museums everywhere were full of miscellaneous objects of all times and places, which the directors began to rearrange so that East and West and North and South might be viewed together; carvings by savages were transferred from the ethnological sections in museums where nobody had seen them to the art sections where they were seen and compared with sophisticated sculpture; drawings by children and untutored men of the people were hung beside drawings by highly trained artists; and pictures painted a thousand years ago were hung beside paintings that were wet. At the same time more and more books with photographs and coloured reproductions of pictures of all periods and places became available; Etienne Houvet, sacristan of Chartres, took a thousand photographs of the cathedral's sculpture and glass and published them; and thousands of photographs of Egyptian, Mesopotamian, Assyrian, Indian, Chinese, Japanese, Javanese, Cingalese sculpture and paintings as well as thousands of photographs of European works of all times and regions began to appear in illustrated books. In these conditions artists and critics, captured by Associationist ideas, sought a common denominator in all these heterogeneous art activities now brought within their ken; and remembering that both the pre-war art of Matisse and the Fauves and pre-war Cubism were fundamentally aesthetic, they assumed that a common *aesthetic* denominator might be found to replace existing academic standards (based mainly on Greek and 'Graeco-Roman' sculpture and Italian Renaissance painting on the one hand and on Dutch seventeenth-century painting and nineteenth-century photographs and photographic painting on the other). Thus it came that in the first post-war decade the leading art critics told us *ad nauseam* that all Art is and always has been One, that its Oneness is and always has been its Aesthetic Character (meaning thereby, in most cases, a character analagous to the aesthetic in pictures by Matisse); and that no work in which this particular Aesthetic Character was not apparent, could be properly accepted as a work of art. There were however also those, myself for example, who sought a system of associations that would *explain* not only the works accepted as 'aesthetic' and therefore 'art' by those critics, but also, as far as might be, the works rejected by them as 'not aesthetic' and accordingly 'not art'—an attitude which led me to write *The Modern Movement in Art* in 1925–6 and which has now led me to the chronological cross-section treatment in this book. There were

79B. LÉGER
Le disque rouge, 1919
Formerly Paris. Léonce Rosenberg

79A. PICASSO
Chien et poulet, 1921
New York. Museum of Modern Art

80. OZENFANT

Accords, 1919—22

Boston. F. C. Bartlett, Esq.

others who were content to treat the Associationist concept as an entertaining pastime and to explore Associationism for Fun's Sake—i.e. to concoct surprising and amusing juxtapositions in the journalistic spirit, as in the review *Der Querschnitt* (The Cross Section) founded in Berlin by Alfred Flechtheim in 1921. There were others again who recalled the Surrealist dream pictures of the pre-war periods— The Douanier's *La bohémienne endormie* (Pl. 42), Chagall's *Le marchand de bestiaux* (Pl. 67) and Chirico's *Rue Italienne: le cerceau* (Pl. 68B) and conceived Association- ism as a breaking down of the barriers between the life of our sleeping and the life of our waking hours.

This last conception of Associationism, much in evidence in the post-war decades, has produced various developments of pre-war Surrealism which I shall hereinafter continue to call *Surrealist*, and also various developments with a different character which I shall refer to as *Neo-Surrealist* in order that the reader may keep them quite distinct. And I must now consider separately first *Post-war Surrealism* and then *Neo-Surrealism* in its several forms.

Contributions to *Post-war Surrealism*, which was a perfectly healthy develop- ment of pre-war Surrealism, were made in the nineteen-twenties by Jean Lurçat, Pierre Roy, Picabia and Joan Miro and also and pre-eminently in certain pictures by Picasso and in most of the pictures by Chirico and Chagall. In these Surrealist pictures all these artists were concerned to create pictorial equivalents for dream experience; they all give us juxtapositions and combinations of the 'real' and the 'unreal' conveying, in various degrees, new aspects of 'pleasing horror', i.e. new aspects of Burke's 'Sublime'. At the same time they all remained faithful to and worked within the framework of aesthetic, expressionist or abstract architectural art (the development of which is the central subject of this book); and in remaining thus faithful to those ideals they defied the new contempt for them launched by the Dada movement which was conspicuous in Paris from 1919 till its demise in 1923.[1]

Jean Lurçat, whom we have encountered in the war years,[2] contributed, about 1927, a series of architecturally designed and finely coloured Surrealist dream landscapes where the dream atmosphere is partly created by the use of a double horizon as in *Les pilotis* (Pl. 88A) which I reproduce as an excellent example. Pierre Roy, a newcomer to our story, had studied theology and architecture before turning to painting; in his first pictures he had taken Chirico's pre-war Surrealism with its dream-stillness, emotive perspective and clearly defined cast shadows, as a jumping-off point; about 1920 he evolved a manner of his own in which brightly coloured objects—shells, strings of birds' eggs, watches and chains, nautical instruments, magnets, twirls of twisted paper, blue prints, cart wheels and so forth—are wittily grouped, in some cases without regard to relative scale, and naturalistically depicted with a smooth precision recalling the works by Hoog- straaten and Vermeer; in one such picture a train passes the window of a room where a cart wheel leans against one wall and a string of gigantic birds' eggs hangs against the other; in another, two poles on a seashore rise against a sky, between them a number of giant birds' eggs are suspended on a string, a magnet tied to the string by a ribbon pulls it downward in the middle, and on the shore beneath, a

[1] Cf. pp. 261–263, 275–277, 296. [2] Cf. above, p. 256.

giant coil of paper threads its way through the spokes of a recumbent cart wheel. There is little or no 'pleasing horror' in Pierre Roy's compositions which at bottom are aesthetically motived and architecturally constructed; but I describe his art as Surrealist because its mixture of the familiar and the strange, the credible and the incredible, recalls the experience of dreams. Picabia, who seceded from moribund Dada in 1922, and devised the film-ballet *Relâche* in 1924, contributed to Surrealism between 1927 and 1929 when he achieved intriguing effects by superimposing transparent images; the finest of his Surrealist pictures known to me are a series painted for a bedroom in Léonce Rosenberg's apartment from which I reproduce *Myrtil* (Pl. 89A); in these pictures, where a transparent aquamarine is the dominant colour, the superimposed images create an affective dream-world where the pervading element appears to be not colourless air or spectrum light but blue water. Joan Miro, a Catalan, who began in Barcelona as a landscape painter with courage and an independent vision, arrived in Paris in 1919 and appears to have been then influenced successively by Van Gogh, the Fauves, Pierre Roy, Picasso, and finally about 1923 by the Russian Kandinsky whose abstract painting he transformed to an art where lines and colours refer us to the life of worms or insects which creep and squirm upon the earth or buzz and flutter in the air; in this transformation of Kandinsky's art Miro stands close to the Neo-Surrealists; his contributions to Surrealism proper were made about 1926 when he painted the strange pictures *Le chien et la lune* (Pl. 88B) and *Personnage, caillou et oiseau*;[1] since 1926 he has reverted to his Neo-Surrealist transformation of Kandinsky's art. Chagall, who returned from Russia in 1923, continued to explore the irrational and the inconsequent in a whimsical spirit controlled by a delicate aesthetic; and his pictures of this period, conceived more in fairy-tale than in dream images—*L'acrobate* (Pl. 90A), for example—evoked from Florent Fels the charming and apposite epigram:

> *Bonjour, Chagall, qui n'avez peur*
> *Ni de ne pas écrire en prose*
> *Ni de peindre votre bonheur.*

Chirico, who returned to Paris in 1925, was a dominant influence for the next five years. His *Les arbres dans la chambre* (Pl. 87) is a good example of the indoor-outdoor associationism (foreshadowed by Chagall with *Fleurs dans la rue* in 1925) which he explored in 1926–1928 in a series of pictures the genesis of which he himself described at the time: 'Have you ever noticed the singular effect of beds, wardrobes, armchairs, divans, tables, when one suddenly sees them in the street, in the midst of unaccustomed surroundings, as happens when one is moving, or in quarters of the town where dealers put part of their stock on the pavement? We then see the furniture grouped on the pavement in a new light, clothed in a strange solitude, linked piece to piece in a special intimacy in the midst of the city's ardent life and the hurried going and coming of the passers-by. . . . And we can well imagine that if a man, suddenly seized by panic, were to seek asylum in this comity of objects, if he were to sink down on one of these chairs, he might feel

[1] Brussels. René Gaffé.

81A. PICASSO
Les trois masques, 1921
Paris. Paul Rosenberg
81B. PICASSO
Femme et enfant au bord de la mer, 1921
New York. Mrs. Averill Harriman

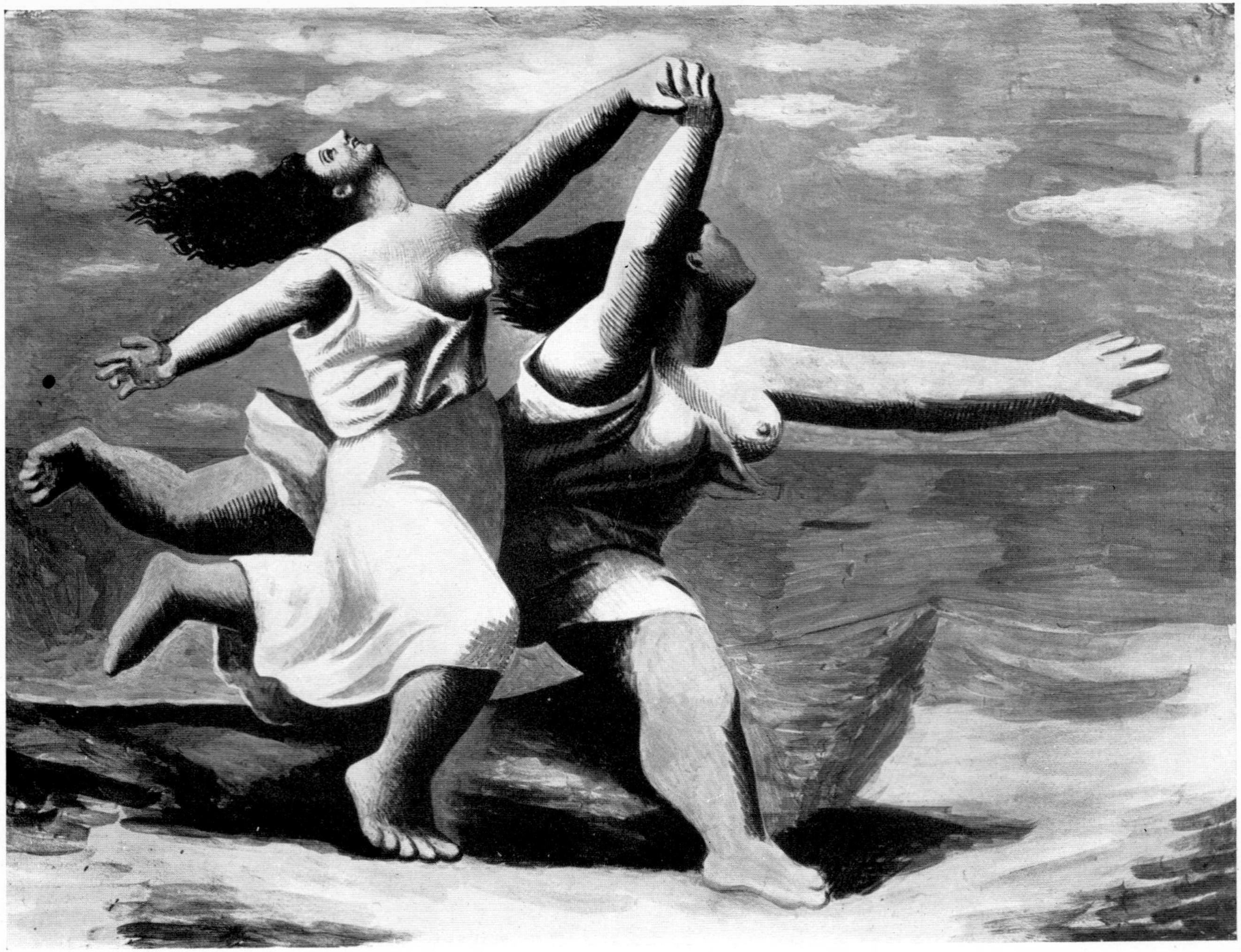

82. PICASSO

Femmes effrayées au bord de la mer, 1923

immune there from the persecutions of gods and men and wild crowds—as immune as the Sunday visitor to the Zoological Gardens who looks at the tiger vainly biting the bars of his cage. . . . And we must observe, too, that the presence of such objects, taken from our rooms and exposed in the open, can also awake in us an emotion which reveals the street itself in an unfamiliar aspect. Furthermore, furniture in empty spaces, in the midst of nature's infinity, can also profoundly move us; think of an armchair, a divan, and some small chairs grouped together in the solitude of a Grecian plain with antique ruins, or on the plains with no tradition in far America . . . furniture thus abandoned in the midst of nature takes on the pathetic characters of gentle innocence. . . . I have been haunted for some time by these strange characters in furniture removed from the shelter of houses, furniture on a shore by a roaring sea or in a deep valley surrounded by great mountains; and I have tried to express this emotion in some of my recent pictures. And then another thing. When you find yourself the only visitor in a museum of antique sculpture, the statues take on an unusual character. A statue in the open, on a palace against a Southern sky, has a kind of Homeric air and seems imbued with a stern aloof happiness in which melancholy also has a part; and on a public square a statue may surprise us (especially if its pedestal is low) by seeming to mingle with the daily life of the city and the agitations of living men. But in a museum the lines of the walls and the floor and ceiling come between the statue and the outside world; and the statue, no longer destined to mingle with life or with the beauty of a landscape or to complete the aesthetic harmony of an architectural construction, strikes us as a surprising ghostly apparition like the sudden appearance of people in a room that we thought empty. Nevertheless we have been long accustomed to statues in museums; and if we are to find new and more mysterious characters we must resort to other associations. A statue within a room, alone or in company of living persons, might give us for example a new emotion, especially if its feet are not on a pedestal but on the ground; and think of the effect of a statue seated in a *real armchair* or leaning at a *real window*.'[1] At the end of the nineteen-twenties Chirico wrote a number of poems and a Surrealist novel called *Hebdomeros* where a dream atmosphere is created by the abolition of barriers in time and space, the creation of credible-incredible dream images, and the transformation without warning of one image to another like superimpositions in cinema and television technique. But since 1930, as my knowledge goes, he has made no contributions to Surrealist art.

The Surrealist works by Lurçat, Pierre Roy, Picabia, Miro, Chirico and Chagall in this decade were thus highly interesting experiments. But the outstanding Surrealist picture of this period, in my judgment, is Picasso's terrific *Femmes effrayées au bord de la mer* (Pl. 82) which was painted as early as 1923.[2]

Neo-Surrealism, entirely a post-war product, was not a development of Surrealism (though it appropriated many tricks and elements from it). It was partly a development of Dada and partly an attempt to exploit the psychological concepts of Freudian psycho-analysts as material for literature and art. Pioneer

[1] Cf. pp. 308, 310, 367.
[2] Cf. below, pp. 300, 301, 308, 310.

Neo-Surrealist gestures were made by the Alsatian Dadaist Hans Arp, by the German Dadaist Max Ernst who invented the procedure known as Neo-Surrealist pictorial *collage* in 1919, and by the French Dadaist André Breton who, as noted, had been trained as a psychiater[1] and who invented Neo-Surrealist literary *collage* in 1921 and made experiments in that year with Philippe Soupault in 'automatic' writing; and each of these procedures must now be separately considered.

Neo-Surrealist pictorial collage was in the first place a technical device derived from the *collage* procedure invented by Braque and Picasso when, for the formal purposes of Cubism in 1910–1912 they had applied fragments of newspaper and wallpaper, textiles and so forth to their canvas as in *Journaux et violon* (Pl. 64).[2] Cubist *collage* as used by Braque and Picasso in those days was a means in the creation of a non-figurative art, and as their aims were architectural or decorative there was no question of selecting fragments with a view to combining them in an anecdotic way—(the strips of newspaper in *Journaux et violon* for example were cut at random without reference to the meaning of the words in the text which in some places is cut in half or in others is applied upside down). In Neo-Surrealist pictorial *collage* on the other hand we have fragments of engravings and so forth selected as *anecdotic* fragments and arranged in scrapbook fashion to create new anecdotic combinations of a disturbing and horrifying kind. Or, in other words, whereas Cubist *collage* was aesthetically or architecturally motived, Neo-Surrealist *collage*, which first appeared in a production called *Fatagaga* by the Dadaists Arp and Ernst in 1919, was motived, like Dada, by defiance of aesthetic and architectural standards, and aimed at a new kind of surprising and shocking anecdotic art. Thus Neo-Surrealist pictorial *collage*, as launched by these Cologne Dadaists, was (*a*) a technical device, (*b*) the continuation of Dada, (*c*) the exploitation of the dream-incongruities in Chirico's pre-war Surrealist pictures—*La Conquête du philosophe* (Pl. 68A), for example, and *Rue Italienne: le cerceau* (Pl. 68B) and (*d*) it was conditioned by Dada affection for shock tactics, and above all by Freudian concepts of the release of inhibitions. We know the extent of the Freudian influence from Ernst's account of his first experiments in the process:

'One day in 1919 I was struck by the way the pages of an illustrated catalogue obsessed my nervously excited gaze. It was a catalogue of objects of anthropological, microscopic, psychological, mineralogical and paleontological demonstration. I found here united elements such poles apart that the very incongruousness of the assembly started off a sudden intensification of my visionary faculties and a dream-like succession of contradictory images—double, triple and multiple images coming one on top of the other with the persistence and rapidity peculiar to memories of love and to the dreams that come between sleeping and waking. These images themselves suggested new ways for them to meet in a new unknown (the plane of unsuitability). All I had to do was to add, either by painting or drawing, to the pages of the catalogue . . . to transform what had been commonplaces of advertising into dramas revealing my most secret desires.'[3]

Neo-Surrealist literary collage was an analogous procedure in which 'poems' were composed by the *soi-disant* haphazard assembling (with occasional additions and

[1] Cf. p. 263. [2] Cf. p. 204. [3] Cf. Appendix I, p. 368.

alterations) of incongruous headlines, phrases, etc., cut from newspapers. This too was conditioned by the Dada affection for shock tactics and by Dada contempt for aesthetic literature and literary graces (which found expression between 1919 and 1922 in the printing of the alphabet and a page from the telephone directory as Dada 'poems' in a Dada review.[1] The following 'poem' by André Breton, with still more variations of type, is an example of this Neo-Surrealist literary *collage*:

MADAME,

une paire

de bas de soie

n'est pas

UN SAUT DANS LE VIDE

UN CERF

L'Amour d'abord

TOUT POURRAIT S'ARRANGER SI BIEN

PARIS EST UN GRAND VILLAGE

Surveillez

LE FEU QUI COUVE

La Prière

DU BEAU TEMPS

SACHEZ QUE

Les rayons ultra-violets

ont terminé leur tâche

COURTE ET BONNE

Neo-Surrealist 'automatic' writing was conditioned first and last by Freudian concepts of the release of inhibitions. The writers deliberately tried to exteriorize their subconscious; and they did this sometimes in solitude and sometimes by a system of collaboration in which two or more wrote alternate words or sentences or passages. André Breton has thus described the genesis of *Les champs magnétiques* produced as 'automatic' writing by himself and Philippe Soupault in 1921: 'Preoccupied with Freud and familiar with his methods of investigation which I had had some occasion to practise on the sick during the war, I determined to obtain from myself what I had sought to obtain from them—namely a monologue recited as rapidly as possible, unaffected by any critical judgement, unimpeded by reticence, and as accurately as possible *spoken thought.* . . . It was thus that Soupault and I set out to cover paper . . . with a laudable contempt for what the result might be.'[2]

Up to 1924 there was no organized Neo-Surrealist group or movement; the Neo-Surrealists were simply individual Dadaists who were experimenting with a view to converting Dada into something less purely nihilist. But in 1924, after the final demise of Dada, a Neo-Surrealist movement was formally founded and proclaimed.

This 1924 *Neo-Surrealist movement* was organized by André Breton, Philippe Soupault, Paul Eluard, Louis Aragon, Benjamin Péret, Pierre Naville, Roger Vitrac and some others most of whom had already appeared as Dadaists. Breton and his friends

[1] Cf. below, pp. 296, 297.   [2] André Breton. *Manifeste du Surréalisme.*

titled it 'Surréaliste', the term coined by Guillaume Apollinaire to describe Chagall's pictures in 1911–12 and used by him as subtitle to his play *Les mamelles de Tirésias* in 1917 as already recorded.[1] Breton tells us that they used the term '*en hommage à Guillaume Apollinaire qui venait de mourir*' (Apollinaire had died, as noted, in 1918) '*et qui à plusieurs reprises nous paraissait avoir obéi à un entraînement de ce genre*'. But as already explained I have rechristened this movement 'Neo-Surrealist' to distinguish it from the aesthetically motived Surrealist art developed from pre-war Surrealism in the nineteen-twenties by Picasso, Chagall, Chirico and other artists I have named.

The *Neo-Surrealist Creed* of 1924 was set forth in a manifesto written by Breton and titled *Manifeste du Surréalisme*. Neo-Surrealism is there defined as follows: 'It is pure psychic automatism by means of which one sets out to express, verbally, in writing or in any other manner, the real functioning of thought; it is dictation by thought without any control by reason or any aesthetic or moral preoccupation.' The Neo-Surrealists, Breton tells us, were to envisage the eventual merging in a new Oneness of conscious and subconscious, waking and sleeping, sane and mad, experience. 'Thanks to the discoveries made by Freud', he writes in the Manifesto, 'an aspect of mental life, with which we had affected no longer to concern ourselves (though I think it much the most important aspect), has recently been brought back to life. . . . It may be that the Imagination is on the point of reclaiming its rights; if the depths of our mind harbour strange forces capable of increasing those of the surface or of struggling successfully against them, then it is all to the good to make allies of those forces—to make allies of them first in order to subject them later, if need be, to the control of our reason. . . . Freud has very rightly concerned himself with dreams. For it is quite wrong that so little attention has been paid to this considerable part of our psychic activity. . . . I have always been amazed at the extreme difference in weight and importance which the ordinary observer attaches to the events of his waking and his sleeping life. I believe that in the future the two apparently contradictory states—the dream and reality—will resolve into a reality-absolute, a surreality. It is that which I am out to conquer.' But this conquest, Breton adds, can only be accomplished when man attains the power to recapture his dreams in their entirety, to realize them as a continuity and not merely as a series of partly remembered parentheses interrupting the continuity of his waking hours; this will take a long time and involve a memory-discipline of generations; and the first steps to be taken to achieve it are the dethronement of Logic as the ruling force in the mind and the enthronement of The Marvellous (*Le merveilleux*) in its place. The Marvellous, Breton tells us, is always Beautiful, and nothing but The Marvellous can be Beautiful. The Neo-Surrealists must surrender themselves to any and every aspect of The Marvellous, and do so in absolute freedom unshackled by logic, interest, or reason, or by aesthetic or moral considerations, and for so doing they have precedents, provided by, among others, Dante, Shakespeare '*dans ses meilleurs jours*', Young in his *Night Thoughts*, Swift in his malice, Hugo '*quand il n'est pas bête*', Poe in adventure, Baudelaire '*dans la morale*', Sade '*dans le sadisme*', and in a class by himself, Isidore Ducasse (Lautréamont).[2]

---

[1] Cf. pp. 207, 231, 255.
[2] Author of the *Chants de Maldoror* (1868), cf. pp. 22, 23.

Plate (H) CHAGALL
Poète allongé, 1915
London. National Gallery, Millbank (Tate Gallery)
(cf. page xii)

INTRODUCTION

The Neo-Surrealist creed was thus, in fact, a new Romantic Movement; and the mechanism was the search for the emotivity of unusually *juxtaposed* fragments, as distinguished from the mechanism of the old Romantic Movement of the nineteenth century which I defined in *The Modern Movement in Art* as the search for 'unusually emotive fragments' experienced as *isolated* fragments.

When I first read Breton's Manifesto I was reminded of a passage read elsewhere: 'If there is any permanent vitality in the Renascence of the Spirit of Wonder in Poetry and Art in modern Europe—if it is really the inevitable expression of the soul of man in a certain stage of civilization (when the sanctions which have made and moulded society are found to be not absolute and eternal but relative, mundane, ephemeral and subject to the higher sanctions of unseen powers that work behind "the shows of things") then perhaps one of the first questions to ask in regard to any imaginative painter . . . is "In what relation does he stand to the newly awakened spirit of romance? Has he a genuine independent sympathy with that temper of wonder and mystery which all over Europe preceded and has now followed the temper of imitation, prosaic acceptance, pseudo-classicism and domestic materialism? Has he reached the world which not all the pseudo-classicism that arose in the fifteenth century, ripened in the sixteenth and rotted in the eighteenth, could banish from the dreams of man?"' Breton's Manifesto reminded me, that is to say, of Watts-Dunton's essay on Rossetti written in 1883. But of course between the two pronouncements there had come (a) Freud's concepts of secret inhibitions and of complexes created by frustration, and (b) the vicious sadisms and despairing cynicisms engendered in the subconscious of three generations by the horrors of the German war. And thus the Neo-Surrealists of 1924 set out to surrender themselves to Watts-Dunton's 'temper of wonder and mystery' with a difference. Like Watts-Dunton they identified The Marvellous with Beauty; but they conceived The Marvellous as the secret significance of psychologically disturbing associations—which was much as Lautréamont had conceived it when he described as 'Beautiful' 'the chance meeting, on a dissecting table, of a sewing machine and an umbrella' and as Ernst had conceived it when he set out to reveal his 'most secret desires' in his *collages* inspired by the 'anthropological, microscopic, psychological, mineralogical and paleontological' catalogue in 1919. At bottom The Marvellous in Neo-Surrealist doctrine is any and everything conceived by completely unfettered imagination; and Breton did not shrink from the logical conclusion of this attitude; for we read in the Manifesto: 'Mad persons . . . exhibit so profound a detachment from the critical judgments passed upon them and from the various reproofs inflicted upon them, that it is permissible to suppose them so comforted by their imagination and so charmed by their delirious concepts that they can cherish the fact that those concepts are only valid for themselves; thus we see that hallucinations, delusions and so forth are not a negligible source of pleasure. . . . I could spend my life provoking the confidences of mad persons; for they are persons of scrupulous honesty whose innocence is only equalled by my own.' With this envy of the mental freedom of insane persons the Neo-Surrealists combined an envy of the mental freedom of normal men in their dreaming hours. The dream alone, the Manifesto says, leaves man his right to freedom; and if I read the Manifesto rightly it was chiefly as a new Romantic Movement with the slogan 'Wake up and Dream in Freedom' that Breton then desired the Neo-Surrealist movement to develop; at bottom the Neo-Surrealist creed as Breton conceived it in 1924 is expressed in the passage: '*Le seul mot de liberté est tout ce qui m'exalte encore. . . . Parmi tant de disgrâces dont nous héritons, il faut bien reconnaître que la plus grande liberté d'esprit nous est laissée. . . . Réduire l'imagination à l'esclavage, quand bien même il y irait de ce qu'on appelle grossièrement le bonheur, c'est se dérober à tout ce qu'on trouve, au fond de soi, de justice suprême.*'

Neo-Surrealism in 1924 was almost entirely a literary movement. There were no painter or sculptor signatories to the Manifesto though Breton there claimed the ex-Dadaist Picabia and Marcel Duchamp (who was also for a time a Dadaist) and beckoned to André Masson (who was then aged twenty-eight and still mainly influenced by Gris). At that time, as we have seen, the Cologne ex-Dadaist Max Ernst, who had arrived in Paris in 1922, was the only truly Neo-Surrealist artist and that only in his *collages* (for Ernst in his paintings, as distinguished from his *collages*, was concerned to some extent with aesthetic values and Breton accordingly described him in the Manifesto as only in part a servant of Neo-Surrealism and 'fettered by the pride of preconceived ideas'). After 1924 Ernst continued to produce Neo-Surrealist *collages* which are in no sense aesthetically motived; and these *collages* culminated in the, to my mind revolting, scrapbook *La femme 100 têtes* where fragments of banal popular nineteenth-century anecdotic engravings are reassembled in irrational and often gruesome ways.

In 1925 Ernst invented *Neo-Surrealist frottage* which like Neo-Surrealist *collage* was partly a technical device and partly a mechanism for aiding the artist's imagination and helping him to set his inhibitions free. Neo-Surrealist *frottage* was technically speaking like brass-rubbing, since in essence it was the obtaining of an image by rubbing paper with charcoal or some similar substance over an uneven surface; and Ernst himself has explained his attitude and motives in using this procedure:

'It all started on August 10, 1925, by my recalling an incident of my childhood when the sight of an imitation mahogany panel opposite my bed had induced one of those dreams between sleeping and waking. Happening to be at a seaside inn in wet weather I was struck by the way the floor, its grain accentuated by many scrubbings, obsessed my nervously excited gaze. So I decided to explore the symbolism of the obsession, and to encourage my powers of meditation and hallucination I took a series of drawings from the floorboards by dropping pieces of paper on them at random and then rubbing the paper with blacklead. As I looked carefully at the drawings that I got in this way—some dark, others smudgily dim—I was surprised by the sudden heightening of my visionary powers, and by the dream-like succession of contradictory images that came one on top of another with the persistence and rapidity peculiar to memories of love. Now my curiosity was roused and excited, and I began an impartial exploration, making use of every kind of material that happened to come into my field of vision: leaves and their veins, frayed edges of sacking, brush-strokes in a "modern painting", cotton unwound from a cotton-reel, etc., etc. Then I saw human heads, many different beasts, a battle ending in a kiss (the wind's sweetheart), rocks, sea and rain, earth-tremors . . .

the sphinx in its stable . . . a shawl covered with flowers of hoar frost, pampas, cuts of a whip, trickles of lava . . . vaccinated bread, conjugal diamonds . . . Eve, the only one remaining to us. . . . Thus the *frottage* process simply depends on intensifying the mind's capacity for nervous excitement, using the appropriate technical means, excluding all conscious directing of the mind (towards reason, taste, or morals) and reducing to a minimum the part played by him formerly known as the 'author' of the work. The process shows up as a true equivalent of what we now call 'automatic writing'. The author is present as a spectator, indifferent or impassioned, at the birth of his own work and observes the phases of his own development. In devoting myself to this activity (or passivity)—later we called it *paranoiac criticism*—and adapting *frottage* to the technical mediums of painting (for instance, scratching colours on a prepared coloured ground over an uneven surface) and in trying all the time to reduce my own active participation in the making of a picture, so as to widen the active field of the mind's capacity for hallucination, I succeeded in being present *as a spectator* at the birth of all my works after August 10, 1925, the memorable day of the discovery of *frottage*. Being a man of 'ordinary constitution'' (to use Rimbaud's terms) I have done my best to *make my soul monstrous*. A blind swimmer, I have made myself clairvoyant. I have *seen*. I have become the amazed lover of what I have seen, wanting to identify myself with it.'[1]

My comment on this statement by Ernst is simply that all this was bound up with Freudian ideas; and that as readers of 'How it happened' will not fail to notice it synchronized with Pirandello's plays and Joyce's *Ulysses*. I must add that it was not without precedent in the history of art; Alexander Cozens (1698–1786) made casual 'blots' of ink on paper, then crumpled the paper and accepted the result as a basis for a composition—a procedure which he christened 'Blot-drawing'; Leonardo da Vinci wrote: 'As our friend Botticelli remarks a sponge impregnated with various colours thrown against a wall leaves spots which may appear like a landscape; and a variety of images may be seen in such spots—heads of men, various animals, battles, rocky scenes, seas, clouds, woods and the like—according to the disposition of mind with which they are considered, just as the sound of bells may seem to say whatever we choose to imagine'; and earlier still Sung Ti, a Chinese artist who worked in the eleventh century, thus instructed his students: 'Take an old tumble-down wall and throw over it a piece of white silk, gaze at this until through the silk you can see the ruin with its prominences, levels, zigzags and cleavages, and when you have thoroughly absorbed all this, when you have stored it all in your mind and fixed it all in your eye, when you have got it all thoroughly into you, then you will see mountains and water, ravines and streams, plants and trees, and men and birds moving and flying, and if you then ply your brush at your fancy the result will be of heaven not of men.' And as a final comment I must quote from Ruskin's account of his first attack of madness (1878) (communicated to the *British Medical Journal* and published after his death in 1900):

'I lay for a fortnight in a state of wild delirium and when at last I began to regain consciousness . . . demons appeared to me constantly, coming out of the darkness and forming themselves gradually into corporeal shapes almost too horrible to

[1] Cf. Appendix I, p. 368.

think of. But even worse . . . were the fantastic, malignant and awful imps and devils and witches that formed themselves out of various articles in the room. The knob on one of the bedposts was continually turning into a leering gibbering witch . . . All ugly things assumed fearfully and horribly hideous forms and all beautiful objects appeared ten times more lovely . . . and this applied to the patterns in materials such as the borders on my window-curtains or the wall-paper. . . . I have sometimes wondered whether the peculiar habit of some persons who are for ever striving to find a resemblance, or fancy they do, between what they see and something quite different . . . can be a variation in a mild form of this disease. . . . Yet entirely healthy persons sometimes make a practice of it. Why, when I took my two little wards on a tour through Switzerland many years ago, there was nothing they saw—neither leaf, nor stone, nor pool nor mountain—but what in their eyes bore resemblance to some other thing which had no sort of connection with them. . . . So strong and continuous and unbearable did this habit become that I was obliged for my own comfort's sake to silence my little fairies and positively forbid them to make any more comparisons whatever. Under great and almost irresistible temptations (for them) they obeyed my order until our arrival at the Rhine Falls, at Schaffhausen, when they broke into a merry peal of laughter on instantly recognizing—as indeed we all three did at this moment —the extraordinary likeness of the centre rock to Mr. Punch; and as I had joined in their laughter they forced me to rescind my order.'

After 1929 a new contributor to Neo-Surrealism appeared in the person of the young Catalan Salvador Dali who joined the movement in that year and soon became conspicuous as a Neo-Surrealist propagandist, an inventor of Neo-Surrealist films and a painter of Neo-Surrealist pictures. Dali also invented a type of Neo-Surrealist sculpture which he describes as 'objects functioning symbolically'; these Neo-Surrealist 'objects' are either natural objects slightly altered or every-day manufactured objects doctored in some way to create in the spectator a psychological disquiet or a feeling of secret shame; and their ancestors are the anti-aesthetic Dada 'Ready-Mades' by Marcel Duchamp.[1] In my judgment it is an error to regard the concoction of these Neo-Surrealist 'objects'—a teacup lined with fur, a wheelbarrow upholstered in satin, a Louis XV shoe-heel trimmed with cutlet frills—as an art activity of importance; and it can I think be reasonably dismissed as a mildly amusing or mildly bawdy parlour game. Salvador Dali's films and paintings on the other hand are a more serious matter. His admirers' accounts of the film Le chien andalou which he devised with Luis Bunuel in 1929, and the Neo-Surrealists' own account of the film L'âge d'or which he devised with Bunuel in 1930, make it clear that both films exhibited fertility of imagination, that both contained obscenities, and that L'âge d'or was anti-clerical and sadistic. In some of his early pictures—Les plaisirs illuminés[2] (1929), La main (Le remords de conscience),[3] Le cheval,[3] La terrasse, and Le puits[4] (1930) for example—Dali did little more than rehash stale abracadabra with technical factors derived from Chirico, Ernst and Mantegna. But from 1930 onwards he transformed the collage procedures of Ernst

[1] Cf. p. 262; also p. 313. [2] New York. Sidney Janis.
[3] Exhibited Paris. Galerie Vignon, 1930. [4] New York. Edward Wasserman.

and the paintings by Pierre Roy, Viollier and Chirico, into a disturbing irrational anecdotic art which he describes as 'paranoiac criticism' meaning thereby the symbolical recording of *soi-disant* obsessions, fetishes and hallucinations. In his pictures of the nineteen-thirties he also gives us, with extreme ingenuity, an image or group of images with double meaning (i.e. a representation of an object or group of objects which can equally well be taken, like a pun, for another object or group of objects) and, as an aid to the rousing of psychological disturbance in the spectator by appealing to his sense of touch, he uses intensely vivid naturalistic (i.e. photographic) representation of the objects selected for emotive juxtaposition.

Technically speaking Dali's pictures have no place in this history of the development of modern painting; for thus considered his art is merely a reversion to popular nineteenth-century anecdotic painting executed with daguerreotypic illusionism oleographically coloured. But the character of the subject-matter in some of his pictures cannot be set aside as unimportant or irrelevant to our studies. It has been described by Mr. J. T. Soby in *After Picasso* (published in 1935) as follows: 'It comes direct from the dreams of Krafft-Ebing's case histories. Apart from the vast number of fetishes which appear in his pictures—slippers, hair, keys and phalli—the processes of paranoia are expressed by . . . the various phobias of abnormal psychology. . . . The inevitable implements of imagined persecution are here: knives and scissors; the devices of corruption, limp watches and swarming ants. . . . Dali himself has described the three great images of life as excrement, blood and putrefaction. All three images haunt his painting.' I find myself entirely out of sympathy with this concept of the art-activity as a kind of amateur psychopathology concerned to illustrate the secrets habitually reserved for confessionals and clinics; and I cannot resist the thought that the sadisms in this art are born of the sadisms which have disfigured life in the totalitarian countries of Europe in the nineteen-thirties, especially when I remember that the nearest parallels to Dali's paintings are Brueghel's *Triumph of Death*[1] and the paintings by Jerome Bosch engendered in the atmosphere of the burnings, hangings, pulling out of tongues and breakings on the wheel of Philip II's sadistic suppression of free thought in the Netherlands. It had been possible to look upon the Neo-Surrealism of 1924 (as defined in Breton's Manifesto) as a flight from the austere discipline of Ozenfant and Le Corbusier's objective Purist-Functionalism to the opposite ideal of subjective romantic freedom, as, in fact, a new romantic individualist movement and a symbolic protest against tyrannies supported by logical ideologies. But no such symbolism will explain the sadistic characters in the later productions of the movement; for these characters, unwittingly may be and against the movements' true principles, are more symbolic of the dominant vices in the international spirit of repression which set out in the nineteen-thirties to undo the Associationism launched by the international spirit of freedom in the nineteen-twenties. I say unwittingly may be and against its true principles, because Neo-Surrealism has never been characterized by clear thought; and it has indulged in addlepated contact with political Communism—with which it has no sort of affinity—from

[1] Madrid. Prado (up to the Franco invasion).

an early date. In 1925 Breton and his associates actually declared the adherence of their movement to Communism—Breton somehow reconciling his '*le seul mot de liberté est tout ce qui m'exalte encore*' with the collectivist concepts of political Communism; and since then, as I relate in 'How it happened', the Neo-Surrealists have been much chagrined by the refusal of the Russian Government to treat their books and pictures as valuable propaganda for the Communist cause.[1] In 1933 the Neo-Surrealists began to collaborate in a handsomely produced periodical entitled *Minotaure* published in Paris by A. Skira and edited by E. Teriade. *Minotaure* has frequently contained some objectionable features alternating with contributions of interest and value.

While the Neo-Surrealists were putting antic dispositions on, we have some genuine paranoiac paintings by Séraphine Louis, a sometime *femme de ménage* of The Douanier's friend Wilhelm Uhde.[2] When Uhde discovered Séraphine's untutored talent in 1912 she was painting simple still-life pictures at Senlis; when he returned to Senlis she was over sixty and earning her living by painting postcards sold in the local shops and by selling some of her pictures in local exhibitions; and the pictures we are here concerned with were painted from this time till shortly before her death in 1934. Séraphine Louis was obsessed with the mystic atmosphere of church interiors; she was also afflicted with persecution mania, perpetually suspecting plots against her by her neighbours, and barring her doors with numerous locks and chains lest they should steal her pictures (some of which were six feet high). The most strangely affective of her pictures—*L'arbre mystique*,[3] *L'arbre et l'oiseau*[4], *Feuilles d'automne*,[4] for example—burn with the coloured radiance of cathedral glass or flicker like candles on an altar. In some (where we have the unconscious creation of forms with the double and, as it were, punning significance that appears in certain works by Dali) the trees grow leaves that are also eyes or shells (*L'arbre mystique*[3]), the fruits become lamps or breasts (*Les fruits*[5]), and plants with snake-veins dispose themselves in the luminous filigree of rose windows or the jewelled patterns embroidered on priests' copes. These pictures are truly the release of secret inhibitions and a real exteriorizing of secret fears and exaltations; they are too painful to contemplate for long but more interesting than the Neo-Surrealists' pseudo-paranoiac concoctions.

The Neo-Surrealist painters might have had less success than they have had, if Chirico had not allowed his Surrealist pictures to be shown in their exhibitions and if Picasso had not gone even farther and allied himself, in all but name, with the movement since 1927. In 'How it Happened' I chronicle Picasso's post-war works and distinguish between his Surrealist pictures of 1923—*Femmes effrayées au bord de la mer* (Pl. 82) for example—and his later Neo-Surrealist productions of which I reproduce *Dinard* (Pl. 89B) of 1928 as a very mild example. And here I need only add some comments on his general output in this period.

[1] Accounts of the Neo-Surrealists' contacts with political Communism are given in David Gascoyne: *A Short Survey of Surrealism* (London, Cobden-Sanderson, 1935) and J. T. Soby: *After Picasso* (Hartford, E. V. Mitchell, and New York, Dodd, Mead, 1935). Cf. my Bibliographical and Catalogue Notes in Appendix I, p. 368. Cf. also pp. 307, 320, 321.

[2] Cf. above, p. 231.　　　　[3] Paris. Jeanne Bucher.　　　　[4] Paris. Wilhelm Uhde.
[5] Grenoble. Museum.

Picasso has been unquestionably the most arresting phenomenon in the art world from 1920 to the present day. Conspicuous, as we have seen, since 1901, he became still more conspicuous in the 'twenties and 'thirties. He has said with pardonable arrogance '*Je ne cherche pas, je trouve*'. And that is true. For though every one of his innumerable post-war productions is a pioneer opening of new ground he has never signed a work which is merely the statement of a problem left unsolved. We have his own analysis of his procedures: 'The artist absorbs and exteriorizes. That is the whole secret of art. . . . The artist is a receptacle for emotions coming to him from everywhere—from the sky and the earth, from a piece of paper, a passing figure, a cobweb. . . . Abstract art is not just painting, it is also drama. There is in fact no such thing as purely abstract art. One always begins with something. And so one can subsequently remove all appearance of reality without danger because the objective experience has left an indelible impression. It is wrong to speak of 'figurative' and 'non-figurative' art. Everything appears to us in the forms of figures. . . . A person, an object, a circle are figures affecting us more or less intensively; some being closer to our sensations produce emotions which touch our affective faculties; others address themselves more especially to the intellect; I have to accept them all because my mind has as much need of emotion as my senses have. . . . When I paint a picture I am not concerned with the fact that two people may be represented in it. Those two people once existed for me but they exist no longer. My vision of them gave me an initial emotion, then little by little their presence became blurred; they became for me a fiction, and then they disappeared altogether, or rather they were transformed into all kinds of problems, so that they became for me no longer two people but forms and colours—forms and colours which nevertheless resume an experience of two people, and preserve the vibration of their life.' [1] Here we have the secret of his multiple production in the post-war period when he painted the most heterogeneous pictures in the same year, the same month, the same week and indeed on the same day. It applies to his final Cubist pictures—represented here by *Chien et poulet* (Pl. 79A) and *Les trois masques* (Pl. 81A); to his 'Antique' and 'Classical' works—represented by *Mère et enfant au bord de la mer* (Pl. 81B) and *Le repos de l'acrobate* (Pl. 83); it also applies to the long series of semi-Cubist rhythmic pictures in 'stained glass' technique—represented here by *Femme assise tenant un livre* (Pl. 94); and to his Surrealist and Neo-Surrealist pictures which culminated in *Guernica* (Pl. 96). At bottom a passionate romantic, inspired in the first place by contacts with objects and organisms and phenomena, Picasso becomes more and more preoccupied as the picture grows with the new object, the new organism, the new phenomena which emerge at the dictates of his mind and hand. Fundamentally healthy, his art is sometimes calm and sometimes agitated, sometimes engaging and sometimes repellent, sometimes noble or tender and sometimes cruel or crass, sometimes detached and sometimes symbolically erotic. But it is always the expression of a proud, confident and conquering spirit, contemptuous of dogmas, indifferent to the effects of his work on other people, eager to absorb fresh sustenance for further efforts, firmly resolved that whatever happens he will never spare his

[1] Cf. my Bibliographical and Catalogue Notes in Appendix I, p. 364.

creative energy and repeat a success. '*On doit prendre son bien*', he has said, '*là où on le trouve—sauf dans ses propres œuvres. J'ai horreur de me copier. Mais je n'hésite pas, lorsqu'on me montre par exemple un carton de dessins anciens, à y prendre tout ce que je veux.*' Nor, I may add, has he ever hesitated to absorb an ambiance and convert it to his use. In these years in fact he has absorbed in his own being all the psychic conflicts of his environment and resolved them with unfaltering power and genius in his pictures. His *Femmes effrayées au bord de la mer* (Pl. 82) contains all Surrealism and carries it farther than any artist has carried it before or since. His Neo-Surrealist pictures put Neo-Surrealist doctrines into practice with a relentless power that no Neo-Surrealist painter has approached; for in these works he treats the 'real' and the 'unreal', waking and dream experience, cognition and sensation, logic and instinct, as all equally valid and all susceptible of record on a single plane. And when in his sensitiveness to life around him his spirit surged in anger at the recent crimes in Spain, he passed all other propagandists in the scathing etchings *Songe et mensonge de Franco* and the truly horrifying picture *Guernica* (Pl. 96)—a huge monochrome painted for the Spanish Pavilion of the *Exposition* in 1937. Picasso stands head and shoulders above the Neo-Surrealist artists not only because he is a dominant personality with staggering creative powers but also because he has never been seduced by Dada or Neo-Surrealist or Communist or Fascist contempt for aesthetic, expressionist and abstract architectural art. Some of his Surrealist and Neo-Surrealist pictures are undeniably repulsive; but they are all within the framework of the modern art movement which is the subject of this book; nothing yet produced by Picasso is really outside that movement—as Ernst's *collage* scrapbook *La femme 100 têtes* and Dali's daguerreotypic illusionism are outside it. For Picasso is always a formal artist, absorbing attitude after attitude from his environment, forcing it each time to a climax, and converting it to formal art.

As has appeared from the foregoing I look on Ozenfant's Purism developed to Functionalism by Jeanneret (Le Corbusier) as the central artistic happening in the first post-war decade; thereafter I rank the Surrealist contributions by Chagall, Chirico and Picasso and the whole of Picasso's output considered as a series of personal gestures. And I must now record a second contribution made by Ozenfant from 1929–1930 when he looked on his Purist-Functional achievements as a *fait accompli* and turned his attention to another task; and I must also record some pictures produced in the 'twenties and 'thirties by Rouault, Braque, Dufy and Matisse.

Ozenfant's second contribution was an intensely concentrated effort which culminated in an enormous picture called *La vie* (*biologique*) which he began in 1931 and completed in 1938 and which, as I write, has just been acquired by the Luxembourg Museum. His works in 1929–1933 were all in the nature of conscious preparations for that major effort. Stated briefly his aim in these years was to convert the architectural associationism of his Purist paintings to another type of associationism, another equivalent of Ratzel's 'a philosophy of the history of the human race, worthy of its name . . . must be charged with the conviction that all existence is one,' another type of ordered reasonable art, designed, this time, to symbolize the basic unity of man's body and spirit with the eternal elements— air, light, earth, and the waters of the sea and river. For the execution of this

83. PICASSO
Le repos de l'acrobate, 1923
Lausanne. Dr. Reber

84A. VIVIN

Nature morte aux huitres, 1923

Paris. Mme Gregory

84B. BRAQUE

Nature morte, 1925

Paris. Mme Pomaret

project he built up a theory and a system as he had done for his Purist art in the old days. He set himself to fashion fixed symbols for man in his several aspects and other fixed symbols for the elements which could be variously combined to symbolize various relations. His symbols for the elements are supporting lines for earth, and simple curves typifying the waves set up by man's contact with air and water. The symbols for man—based on the earliest known object in the history of art, the pre-historic Willendorf torso, are nude men, women and children, as single figures or in groups, each typifying some constant elemental aspect of man's being—love, loving-kindness, sensual delight, jealousy, melancholy, ardour, brutality, health, weakness, youth, maturity, maternity, old age, sleep, waking and so forth. In designing these groups and figures, which he regarded, as it were, as actors in a repertory theatre, he made each a silhouette modelled in thick paint within the contours, and when he arranged them in compositions they have the appearance of low-relief sculptures coloured in simple schemes of blue and white, earth brown, earth pink and ochre. In all there were some fifty of these 'actors' in Ozenfant's repertoire from 1929 to 1933 and some appear in numerous compositions as fixed symbols for the type ideas; and all appear with hundreds of other figures in the final composition *La vie (biologique)* where the figures are no longer modelled in thick paint but are given relief in the ordinary way by light and shade, and where the colour is much richer and the whole spirit is more dynamic than in any of Ozenfant's earlier works. *La vie (biologique)* is to be followed by a companion picture *La vie (mécanique)* in which man as a tool-using animal will be the theme.

Rouault, still curator of the Musée Moreau, has been less conspicuous than some of his contemporaries in the post-war period, because his pictures have been steadily acquired under contract by Vollard and relatively few of them have been seen in public exhibitions—though collectors have seen them in Vollard's private galleries and some were seen about 1930 by visitors to the Paris house of the Japanese Baron Fukushima who greatly admired and eagerly collected them. His Expressionist art was developed in the nineteen-twenties in passionately dramatic pictures for which now Christ as the Man of Sorrows, and now the flotsam and jetsam of contemporary conditions—circus folk, beggars, *filles de maisons*—provided the themes, and in which the drama, as in *Pierrot* (Pl. 93) is arrayed in notes of rich and concentrated colour that come towards us, as it were, through the confines of a sombre arabesque like the colour notes enclosed by masonry and leading in the Gothic windows which Rouault studied as a glass painter in his youth. As I write, Vollard has just published two superbly printed folio books illustrated with large coloured etchings and wood engravings by Rouault: *Passion* with text by André Suarès, and *Cirque de l'Etoile Filante* with text by Rouault himself. In these coloured etchings Rouault has attained to the maximum of Expressionist drama within the stained-glass technique, and the monumental character of the simple designs and the resonance of the colour are enhanced by their relation to the type.

Braque's pictures in the nineteen-twenties were among the outstanding decorative achievements of the period; abandoning the geometric technique of his Cubist manner, he evolved a personal curvilinear semi-Cubist semi-figurative two-dimensional art where oyster tints with notes of green and brown predominate in opulent patterns which are sometimes simple and sometimes, as in *Nature morte* (Pl. 84B), exceedingly complex. In his later pictures Braque appears to have been influenced by some of Picasso's Neo-Surrealist works; but his contributions in the nineteen-twenties have had much influence on recent developments in aesthetic which have shown a marked tendency to react from the geometric basis of the Purist-Functional architectural aesthetic in favour of a baroque luxuriance based on the free-flowing rhythm of organic, and especially of some vegetable, forms.[1]

Dufy in this period has attained to ever more brilliant dexterity, and the vital gaiety of his colour and the engaging lightness of his calligraphic drawing have become more irresistible each year. The subjects of his pictures are scenes of *mondain* life at the races, impressions of boating on the Seine and the Thames, impressions of London, Deauville and the Riviera, and studio studies. But these subjects are merely jumping-off points for an art that is wholly and delicately conventional, an art in which the azure radiance of the Midi or the glitter and sparkle of cold Northern light are wittily recorded in symbols invented for each case. No reproductions can convey the special attraction of Dufy's later pictures. But I include his *Nice* (Pl. 85A) of 1926 which is a transition work between his earlier and later manner.

Of Matisse it is habitual to say that all his pictures of this period are fundamentally the same. But this is an error as will be clearly demonstrated by the account of his pictures year by year which I shall give in 'How it Happened'. Matisse's nominal subject matter is admittedly in all cases very similar—young women clothed or nude or semi-nude with interiors as background, or interiors with incidental young women clothed or nude or semi-nude; and occasional landscapes and still life; admittedly also, the serenity of his detached objective attitude is invariably the same—for there are no records in his pictures of psychological changes, of passionate or intellectual crises, or of convulsions of the spirit; admittedly again his technical equipment, his sense of scale, his ingenuity as a patternist and his resource and daring as a colourist, are always as evident in his paintings as his courage and dexterity as a draughtsman are always evident in his innumerable drawings. But his immense production in this period is not a simple display of natural talent developing on the lines of least resistance and complacently repeating its own achievements. In the nineteen-twenties and thereafter, Matisse has been incessantly preoccupied with the problem of the nice balance of what the American critic Louis Danz adroitly differentiates as 'noun-painting' and 'verb-painting';[2] he has tipped the balance again and again, always deliberately, and always for a period of months or years, now on the side of thing-painting and now on the side of abstract art, now towards genre painting and now towards rhythms of one character or another. And thanks to this perpetual exploration, this continual originality, his art has retained its variety and life and his latest pictures are as compelling and animated as any painted at any moment in his long career. I repro-

---

[1] I say 'some vegetable forms' because, as Blossfeldt's photographs in *Art Forms in Nature* (London: Zwemmer) have shown, the vegetable world also provides bases for the geometric aesthetic.

[2] Louis Danz. *The Psychologist looks at Art* (London: Longmans, Green & Co.).

85A. DUFY
Nice, 1926
London. Reid and Lefevre
85B. BONNARD
La palme, 1926
Washington. Phillips Memorial Gallery

86A. CHIRICO
Lion et gladiateurs, 1927
Detroit. Institute of Arts
86B. CHIRICO
Chevaux au bord de la mer, 1927
Exhibited Paris, Galerie Bonjean, 1931

duce his *Femme et fenêtre: le peigne espagnol* (Pl. 77) of 1919, which is relatively speaking in the nature of genre painting and the *Odalisque bleue aux anémones* (Pl. 95) of 1936, which is miraculously three-dimensional though fundamentally decorative and abstract.

The post-war pictures by Dufy, Braque and Matisse are all types of luxury art, furniture pictures in the sense that the term can be applied to the pictures by Claude-le-Lorrain, Hubert Robert, Boucher and Fragonard; they are all, at bottom, luxurious wall furniture fitting naturally into the spirit of elegant drawing-rooms luxuriously appointed. Rouault's pictures and Chagall's are also at home in luxurious surroundings; but whereas the works by Matisse, Dufy and Braque must feel most comfortable when the rooms vibrate discreetly to the voices of cultured dilettanti and the twitter and sing-song of the ladies' contributions, Rouault's pictures and Chagall's must feel happiest in rooms reserved for solitude—because Rouault's speech is too passionate and Chagall's is too gentle for urbane intercourse in social life. Ozenfant's Purist pictures, such as *Accords* (Pl. 80) and his later elemental pictures with type figures, require a setting in the Purist-Functional style; his large picture *La vie (biologique)* could only appropriately be housed in a museum (and it has in fact been acquired by the Luxembourg as recorded). A museum also is the most appropriate habitat, I think, for Chirico's post-war Surrealist pictures. But even a museum is too domestic a setting for the multiple expressions of Picasso's spirit in post-war works. His production from 1920–1938 and indeed his whole production up to date could only appropriately be housed, like Poussin's life work, in some temple of philosophy and science, where students could explore and gradually unfold its complex character and manifold significance.

It remains to comment on the work of three unschooled sons of the people, Bombois, Bauchant and Vivin whose relation to sophisticated artists of the post-war period is the same as The Douanier's relation to the artists discussed in Acts II and III; and we may note at the outset that none of these artists is properly called a follower or imitator of The Douanier because all three have worked in isolation, unacquainted with one another, and unacquainted, until quite recently, with The Douanier's productions.

Camille Bombois, who began life as a wrestler in a travelling circus and then worked as a navvy, has appeared in our story in the war years.[1] He had painted as a hobby before he joined the army in 1914, and while he was away his wife sold some of his pictures for small sums; demobilised in 1919, with his wounds and his medals, he was so encouraged by these sales that he sought an occupation which might enable him to give more time to painting, and he found what he wanted in a newspaper printing works where he earned his living at night and painted in such hours of the day as were not required for sleep. A year or two later his pictures attracted attention, as I relate in 'How it Happened', and after 1923 when he was forty he was able to give all his time to painting. His art in its own way is almost as remarkable as The Douanier Rousseau's. Like Rousseau he has an amazing sense of space and scale and he looks at the life around him with a truly personal eye, recording his vision and reactions with absolute frankness and directness uninflu-

[1] Cf. above, p. 255.

enced by prevailing procedures in any type of contemporary art. His pictures fall into several groups, each recording some aspect of his typically peasant personality which is at once robust, poetical, humorous and naïvely erotic. In one group we have scenes in French villages and provincial towns where the women of the people lean from windows and gossip at street corners and trot to market across large squares like dolls beside the towering buildings; in another we have scenes in the neighbouring country where the men fish and the women wash the linen in the river and little girls in cotton frocks scale orchard walls or gather flowers in the meadows and the woods; in another we have circus scenes and impressions of fairs and caravans and roadside 'night clubs' for passing carmen; and in yet another we have female nudes. Every picture which Bombois paints is entirely original and different from the next. I should have to reproduce some dozens to do justice to the range and variety of his achievement. I have selected *Le marché à Honfleur* (Pl. 92) which reminds me, as his *Le Sacré-Cœur*[1] of 1932 still more vividly reminds me, of the scenes depicted in front of the Duc de Berri's castles by the brothers Limbourg in the famous calendar of *Les très riches heures du Duc de Berri*; for there are obvious formal resemblances in the actual pictures—the scale of the figures to the buildings and so forth—and also and still more there is a congruity in spirit between the Duke's artists who worked in the first decades of the fifteenth century and this artist working in the second and third decades of our own. Most of Bombois' paintings must be ranked as descriptive art—a type of art which has no reason for existence in these days of still and moving photographs unless it contains original comment. Bombois' descriptive paintings fulfil this condition; and when he turns to nudes and pictures like *La fillette au bouquet*[2] he also exhibits a natural feeling for grandeur of form.

André Bauchant, gardener and horticulturist, we have also encountered in the war years as a telemetric draughtsman in the army.[3] On demobilization he brought back with him some sketches of the country around Rheims where he had been stationed on his return from Macedonia; and he then began to paint pictures while reverting to his gardening for a living. In 1921 when he was forty-eight he exhibited *Panoramas de la Marne*, painted from these wartime sketches, at the *Salon d'Automne*; and from that time onwards he has steadily attracted more attention. I reproduce his genre picture *Le bon vin* (Pl. 91) where the red of the wine in the glasses and flowing from the barrel is the one deep note in a colour scheme of warm greys and greens; this picture which might be titled *L'été* could form a pendant to another titled *L'hiver*[4] where the artist's impression of some peasants in a winter landscape is charmingly set down. Less realist and descriptive than Bombois, Bauchant is primarily a poetic artist—lyrical in delicate and sometimes most exquisitely coloured flower pieces, naïvely epic in ambitious compositions in the 'historical' vein and tenderly observant in genre studies of contemporary life; and whereas Bombois composes in space and delights in deep recessions, Bauchant prefers a lateral composition where the centre of interest is in the foreground and the composition has to some extent the character of a coloured low relief.

[1] Switzerland. Mme Hostettler.   [2] Paris. Mme Gregory.
[3] Cf. above, pp. 255, 256.   [4] Exhibited London. Tooth's Galleries, 1938.

INTRODUCTION

Louis Vivin, a Post Office employé till he retired in 1922 with an inspector's pension at the age of sixty-one, had always painted for his amusement on Sundays and in leisure hours. His pictures attracted attention in 1923 (as I relate in 'How it Happened') and thereafter he painted regularly till he died at seventy-five in 1936. He painted still life, views of Paris with little figures, suburban, public park, river and seaside scenes, and some compositions with boars or stags pursued by hounds through woods. His pictures, which are both simpler and more formal than those by Bombois and Bauchant, record his naïf observation and quiet natural wit and they appeal by the extraordinary charm of their colour, the conventional language of representation, and a compositional balance depending partly on the colour and partly on a few bold curves contrasted with straight lines. In one river scene *Les rameurs*[1] we see a suburban regatta with the spectators at little tables drinking their coffee before a saffron-walled café; another, *La plage*,[1] shows a beach scene with bathing huts and motors on the road behind; in a third *Le casino*,[1] an orchestra, disposed in a semi-circle, performs upon a terrace; in others we have Parisian buildings conventionally represented brick by brick in conventional blue colour, and cars, and people promenading, on a *pavé* conventionally represented stone by stone, and fruit-stalls with every apple and orange conventionally portrayed in coloured circles. I reproduce his *Nature morte aux huitres* (Pl. 84A) an exquisitely coloured classical composition which is as formal, abstract and decorative as Braque's baroque, luxurious and sophisticated *Nature morte* (Pl. 84B).

As I record in 'How it Happened' these three unschooled men of the people, Bombois, Bauchant and Vivin, emerged from obscurity because their work chanced to catch the eye of some discerning dealers and collectors who felt confident that those who had been already captured by the art of The Douanier Rousseau would also eventually, if not immediately, be captured by the art of these artists who described and commented, like Rousseau, with original simplicity and frankness and painted delightfully without the aid of the tricks taught in art schools which are habitually referred to as 'good drawing' or 'technique'. Bombois, Bauchant and Vivin are clearly in their several ways exceptionally gifted men (though none in my judgment has the compelling powers of The Douanier); but they cannot be alone in their powers of observation and their ability to record their vision, thoughts and sensations; there are surely other unschooled sons of the people now painting in France, and elsewhere, with the gifts and powers to charm and interest if they were similarly discovered. For my own part I hope that more such artists will emerge in one way or another; for in these days of brutal tyrannies on the one hand and neurotic protests on the other, it is a relief and a refreshment to receive the message of such artists who record with confident tranquillity the direct experiences of their hearts and minds and eyes.[2]

[1] Exhibited London. Tooth's Galleries, 1938.

[2] Some works by English unschooled artists were shown in the *Young Artists' Exhibition* which I organized for the London *Daily Express* in 1927. Some works by American unschooled artists were shown in the *Masters of Popular Painting Exhibition* at the New York Museum of Modern Art in 1938 (cf. below, p. 325).

ACT IV: HOW IT HAPPENED

SCENE I: 1919-1923

From Ozenfant's Purism, Picasso's 'Antique' pictures and
Les trois masques, Derain's *Arlequin et Pierrot*, Matisse's first
'*Odalisque*' pictures and the Dada demonstrations in Paris; to
Picasso's *Le repos de l'acrobate* and *Femmes effrayées au bord de
la mer*

In 1919 Picasso designed the curtain, scenery and costumes for the Spanish ballet
Le tricorne produced by Diaghileff with music by de Falla and choreography by
Massine. Picasso's designs in this case were not Cubist like his designs for
Cocteau's *Parade*, but rather the ingenious exploitation of Cubist 'properties' in
decorative terms with reminiscences of Goya's tapestries. His other works this
year were numerous; he made drawings for Salmon's *Le manuscrit trouvé dans un
chapeau* and continued the series of line portrait drawings begun in the war years;
and he painted some landscapes and some Flat-pattern Cubist pictures with
harlequin or still-life *motifs*, notably a *Guitare et table* where the initial material—
the guitar, the table, the music and so on—is more recognizable than in the earlier
Cubist works, and the patterning is larger, bolder and more dynamic; one of his
drawings of the year shows a young Mediterranean goatherd and his girl posing as it
were for a photographer in their Sunday clothes beside a studio pillar; in others
the initial theme is a peasant and a girl reclining in a field.

Matisse now painted *Les plumes blanches*[1] and he continued the series of Nice
interiors which I have described as nearer Impressionism and genre painting than
his earlier pictures; suggestions of the clear light and vibrant heat of the Midi occur
as by-products in this series which includes *Femme et fenêtre: le peigne espagnol* (Pl.
77) and *La porte-fenêtre à Nice*[2] where a girl, with an oval face, sits in Turkish
trousers before a lofty shuttered window with one panel of the shutters fixed open
on a strut; after this he began to return to a more decorative manner, leaving the
genre aspect of his art to be developed on Impressionist lines with personal sensibility by Bonnard.

Derain, demobilised in 1918, had returned to work by 1919 and already produced some drawings and paintings, and some masks in copper very different in
their sensitive modelling from his stone carvings of 1907 and 1908 which had been
influenced by primitive and negro sculpture. In 1919 he designed the curtain,

[1] New York. Stephen C. Clark.   [2] Merion. Barnes Foundation.

scenery and costumes for *La boutique fantasque* produced by Diaghileff with music by Rossini arranged by Respighi and choreography by Massine (and Massine and Lydia Lopokova as chief dancers); in these designs, which wittily evoked a hundred memories of Manet's period, Derain used spots of rich black with the elegance of Manet himself, and his patterning throughout was admirably planned. In this year also he painted *Paul Guillaume*[1] (the sitter being now a most helpful supporter), *Tête de femme*,[2] and the three-quarter-length *La femme grecque* where the face is romantically expressive and the design is grand and classical. No trace of his earlier Fauve manner appears in Derain's 1919 work; and from this time onward—though the Cubist discipline still stiffens his art and Cézanne's influence still appears in his landscapes—he developed as a dexterous eclectic romantic realist, with Delacroix, Courbet, Manet, and Corot as his masters and concerned above all to record his personal reactions to emotive fragments of life and to translate with a full brush the ochres, blacks and whites on his palette to aesthetic drama on his canvas.

Surrealism, hardly seen in Paris in 1919, was being carried forward to some extent by Chagall's work in the Jewish theatre in Moscow and by Chirico and his associates in the *Valori Plastici* group in Rome (though Chirico himself was about to enter a period of technical research when his pictures were relatively speaking academic—a period heralded by the double portrait *L'artiste et sa mère*[3] painted this year). Dada in Cologne was continued by Arp and Ernst (who now invented Neo-Surrealist *collage*, as recorded, and produced the first series of such *collages* titled *Fatagaga*), and by one Baargeld who somehow contrived to subscribe both to Dada anarchism and political Communism and who founded a Dada newspaper called *Der Ventilator* which the British Army of Occupation found it necessary to suppress. In Berlin, where a Dada night club was opened, Dada was fundamentally political; in Zurich Tzara published Dada poems (illustrated by Arp) and an *Anthologie Dada*; Picabia published further numbers of *391*, and a Dada soirée caused a local uproar. In Paris Dada appealed to André Breton, Philippe Soupault, Louis Aragon and Paul Eluard who all contributed to a semi-Dada review called *Littérature*.

In this year 1919 Ozenfant launched the Purist movement which I have discussed in the Introduction. Modigliani, supported mainly by Zborowski and Paul Guillaume, painted his last pictures; Soutine began to attract attention by passionately expressionist works; Braque, still producing Flat-pattern Cubist compositions in mainly rectangular lines, had a successful exhibition at Léonce Rosenberg's gallery *L'Effort Moderne*—now a recognized centre for Cubist and Purist pictures; Brancusi, Laurens, Zadkine and Archipenko were conspicuous among the original sculptors; Gris painted *Pierrot* where a table recedes in perspective in defiance of Flat-pattern Cubist principles; Léger painted *Le disque rouge* (Pl. 79B) and *La flèche*[4] and made coloured illustrations for Cendrars' *La fin du monde*; Laboureur and Galanis attracted attention as engravers, the first by a witty and delicate rococo-ising of Cubism in the cause of social comment and the second by skilful exploita-

---

[1] Paris. Mme Paul Guillaume.   [2] New York. Museum of Modern Art (Bliss).
[3] Exhibited London. Zwemmer Gallery, 1938.
[4] Chicago. Mrs. John Alden Carpenter.

tion of the resources of wood engraving for decorative ends; and Bombois painted *L'écuyère au mouchoir*,[1] *Joueurs de boules*,[1] *Joueurs de cartes*,[2] *Femme nue au peigne*[2] and *Lavandières au bord de l'eau*[1] which all herald the characters of his subsequent achievements. The new books included Proust's *A l'ombre des jeune filles en fleurs*, and a war satire in dramatic form *Liluli* (with woodcuts by Masereel) by Romain Rolland (who had written *Au-dessus de la mêlée* in the war years). In the world of the theatre Jacques Copeau, who had worked in New York in the war years, returned to start a new *Vieux Colombier* where plays were produced in 'constructed' sets, with light effects on geometric solids (footlights and painted backcloths and wings being entirely abolished); and Rodolphe Darzens introduced Lenormand's psychological drama with *Le temps est un songe* at the *Théâtre des Arts*.

In this year 1919 Renoir died at seventy-eight; and Claude Monet aged seventy-nine was still painting iridescent pictures of his lily pond.

In the next year 1920 Picasso began to exhibit a series of large nude and draped *baigneuses*, in a style recalling to some extent antique sculpture, which he had begun at the end of 1919 and was to continue till the end of 1923—the years 1920–1923 being known accordingly as his 'Antique' period; his first 'Antique' paintings and drawings include several compositions with two large-limbed heavy-handed female nudes (one seated in a small armchair covered with drapery, the other standing or kneeling by her side) which are at once calm with a monumental grandeur and vibrant with mysterious disquiet. In 1920 he also designed the scenery and costumes for the ballet *Pulcinella* produced by Diaghileff with music by Stravinsky after Pergolesi and choreography by Massine; and he continued his cubist compositions and his outline drawings. In one of his Cubist compositions of this time, *Table, guitare, fenêtre ouverte*,[3] we observe a mixture of Flat-pattern Cubism with a naturalistic sky and perspective, the legs of the table standing evidently on a receding floor—an affront to Cubism already committed by Gris in the previous year; the line drawings include *Sylphides* and *Stravinsky* (Pl. 78) where he has used the camera's perspective, enlarging the hands, which are nearer to the spectator than the heads, to create a rhythmic linear arabesque in the spirit of the ballet in the one case and to achieve an emotive tactile quality in the other. Another of his works this year is a composition with three nude figures and a horse, generally referred to as *L'abduction*.[4]

Matisse in 1920 continued the transformation of his genre manner to more decorative terms with *La jeune fille en robe turque* (a girl in a Near-Eastern bolero and short white skirt seated by a table with a still-life of anemones against a large patterned background). He now began the long series of pictures titled *Odalisque*, one of the first of which shows a girl in Turkish trousers with a striped scarf on her head reclining on a red sofa;[5] and he enlarged his repertoire of subjects by a visit to Etretat where he painted several coast scenes;[6] at the same time he designed the

[1] Paris. Mme Gregory.
[2] Paris. Dr. F. Meyer.
[3] New York University Museum of Living Art.
[4] New York. Philip Goodwin.
[5] Merion. Barnes Foundation. A similar picture of the same year is in the Chicago Art Institute (Birch-Bartlett).
[6] Examples are in the collections of Lord Berners and Lord Ivor Spencer Churchill and in the Barnes Foundation.

curtain scenery and costumes for the ballet *Le chant du rossignol* produced by Diaghileff with music by Stravinsky and choreography by Massine.

In this year 1920 Modigliani died at the age of thirty-six. Proust published *Le côté de Guermantes I.* Ozenfant started, with Jeanneret, the Purist review *L'esprit nouveau.* Léonce Rosenberg published *Cubisme et tradition.* Léger painted *Deux femmes à la toilette*[1] and *Le petit déjeuner*[2]; Lhote made coloured drawings for Cocteau's *Escales* and developed his personal style—(naturalistic painting discreetly Cubised in lively or handsome patterns); Forain, aged sixty-eight, made drawings for Coquiot's *Les pantins de Paris* and continued the series of oil paintings of law-court scenes which he had begun before the war; and Bombois painted the charming *Fillettes cueillant des fleurs*[3] and some naïvely erotic pictures. The review *L'amour de l'art* appeared with the critic Waldemar George in charge of the sections dealing with contemporary art, and myself as London correspondent. Vlaminck cut woodblocks for Vanderpyl's *Voyages* and continued his personal Fauve expressionism; Derain painted *La polonaise* and made wood engravings for Salmon's *Le Calumet*; and Dufy drew lithographs for Mallarmé's *Madrigaux*, designed charming textiles with wittily drawn bird cages, girls in summer frocks, bathers, toy ships and toy waves, and designed the scenery for Cocteau's mime-ballet *Le bœuf sur le toit.* In *Le bœuf sur le toit* (the Nothing-doing-Bar) performed at the *Comédie des Champs Elysées,* Cocteau transferred early Surrealism to the footlights, as he had transferred Cubism in *Parade*; the performers were a barman, a gentleman in evening dress, a negro boxer, a jockey, a gendarme and a red-haired young female, all wearing huge head-masks which reduced their bodies to the scale of dwarfs; these little figures with huge heads and fixed expressions, moved slowly with the terrifying deliberation of a slow-motion film—the barman very slowly shook the cocktails, the gentleman played billiards and slowly, very slowly moved his cue, while the young female slowly, very slowly made amorous advances; and this deliberation was intensified by the contrast of rippling music by Darius Milhaud (who with Auric, Poulenc, Honegger, Louis Durey and Germaine Tailleferre now formed a group of musicians christened *Les Six* by the critic Henri Collet in *Comœdia*). Other events of 1920 were the foundation of the *Théâtre de l'Atelier* by Charles Dullin, the production of Vincent d'Indy's *La légende de St. Christophe,* the production by Copeau at the *Vieux Colombier* of Vildrac's *Le paquebot Tenacity* and of Jules Romains' *Cromedeyre-le-Vieil,* and the production by Darzens at the *Théâtre des Arts* of Lenormand's *Les ratés* and of François de Curel's *L'âme en folie*—the latter proving a considerable success though de Curel's earlier plays, produced by Antoine, had all failed.[4]

Meanwhile Tzara and the Zurich Dadaists, with Dadaists from Germany and elsewhere, had invaded Paris and begun to advertise themselves by provocative demonstrations. Picabia put out a review called *Cannibale*; Cocteau (though never a Dadaist) began to issue *Le Coq,* a series of witty broadsheets influenced by Dada methods; there were countless Dada manifestoes; and Dada literature reached its climax when the alphabet was signed as a poem in one review and a page of the

---

[1] Formerly Paris. Léonce Rosenberg.   [2] New York. Museum of Modern Art.
[3] Paris. Mme Gregory.   [4] Cf. above, pp. 105, 141.

telephone directory was signed as a poem in another.[1] At the same time Picabia, Man Ray, Ernst and Duchamp contributed to Dada art shows—(Duchamp exhibiting a copy of the *Monna Lisa* with a large moustache); and at a Dada demonstration in the Salle Gaveau the performers and the audience pelted one another with tomatoes and raw meat. The Parisian Cubists and Purists much resented these Dada antics as likely to bring modern art generally to discredit and when news reached them of a Dada Exhibition in Cologne so obscene and blasphemous that the police had to close it, they vented their resentment on any Dadaists who put in an appearance at the historic artists' café La Closerie des Lilas.[2]

In the next year 1921 Picasso continued his 'Antique' pictures which include *La source* and *Trois femmes à la fontaine*, some monumental studies of young women in hats, and a series of *Mère et enfant* compositions including the majestic *Femme et enfant au bord de la mer* (Pl. 81B). At the same time he painted the Cubist *Chien et poulet* (Pl. 79A)—already discussed and contrasted with Chirico's *Mélancolie du départ* (Pl. 73B) of 1916 and with Ozenfant's *Accords* (Pl. 80) of 1922—and *Les trois masques* (Pl. 81A) a superb pattern in ultramarine, brown and light grey, with lemon, ochre and vermilion notes, where the cardboard figures treated in the Flat-pattern Cubist manner and the recumbent dog beneath them are placed on a floor indicated by perspective (like the table in the still-life *Table, guitare, fenêtre ouverte* of the year before). Some delicately classical and at the same time animated drawings with nude figures *Au bord de la mer* also date from this year.

Matisse continued his genre manner but was moving gradually still farther away from it and concentrating more on decorative problems, using Moorish screens, textiles and furniture among his studio properties and dressing his models in Near-Eastern costumes; and with these properties he painted *La dame en vert*[3] (a girl in a green dress leaning on a table covered with a Moorish cloth before a window); he also painted more Etretat shore scenes and more 'Odalisque' compositions.[4] Dufy was conspicuous this year at the *Salon des Artistes Décorateurs*. At the *Salon des Indépendants*, works by Marcel Gromaire and the Japanese Foujita attracted attention. The *Salon d'Automne* had *La plage* by Friesz, *Fenêtre à Nice* by Dufy, Zadkine's carving *Mère et enfant* and Bauchant's *Panoramas de la Marne*.[5] Derain now painted *Portrait du peintre Kisling*,[6] *L'Italienne* and landscapes at Bandol; Braque made coloured wood engravings for Satie's lyric comedy *Le piège de Méduse*, Gris drew lithographs for Max Jacob's *Ne coupez pas, Mademoiselle*, De la Fresnaye drew lithographs for Gide's *Palludes*, Marie Laurencin made water colours for Gide's *La tentative amoureuse*, Segonzac illustrated Dorgeles' *Les croix de bois* and Vlaminck illustrated Duhamel's *Trois journées de la tribu*. Léonce Rosenberg upheld Cubism

---

[1] Cf. above, pp. 261–263, 277.

[2] Mr. David Gascoyne in his *Short Survey of Surrealism* (London, Cobden-Sanderson, 1935) thus describes the 1920 exhibition by the Cologne Dadaists: 'In order to enter the gallery one had to pass through a public lavatory. Inside the public was provided with hatchets with which, if they wanted to, they could attack the objects and paintings exhibited. At the end of the gallery a young girl, dressed in white for her first communion, stood reciting obscene poems.'

[3] New York. Museum of Modern Art (Bliss).

[4] One dating from this year is in the Luxembourg Museum.

[5] Cf. above, p. 290.   [6] New York. George Gershwin estate

and Cubist-Purism in a pamphlet titled *Cubisme et Empirisme*, and Paul Klee satirized this movement in a drawing titled *La ville froide*. Ernst still in Cologne exhibited a number of his *collages* in Paris at the Sans Pareil and Van Leer galleries; Breton tried his hand at literary *collages* and produced with Soupault *Les champs magnétiques* as 'team automatic' writing.[1] Proust published *Le côté de Guermantes II*, *Sodome et Gomorrhe I*; and James Joyce completed *Ulysses*. Cocteau's *Les mariées de la Tour Eiffel* was produced by Rolf de Maré's *Ballets Suédois* with masks and costumes by Jean Victor Hugo, décor by Irène Lagut, and music by all the members of *Les Six* (except Louis Durey). Diaghileff staged a Spanish gypsy ballet *Cuadro Flamenco* with traditional music arranged by De Falla and scenery and costumes by Picasso, and *Chout* (*Le bouffon*) with decorations by Larionov and music by Prokofieff. Gide's *Saul*, Schlumberger's *La mort de Sparte* and Ghéon's *Le pauvre sous l'escalier* were produced by Copeau at the *Vieux Colombier*; René Benjamin's *La pie borgne* (a satire on chattering women) and Paul Fort's *Louis XI* were produced at the Odéon; Jean Sarment's *Le pêcheur d'ombres* was played at the *Théâtre de l'Œuvre*; while Colette's *Chéri* and Alfred Savoir's *La huitième femme de Barbe Bleue* were popular successes at the *Théâtre Michel*. Paul Poiret organized a *Bal rouge et violet* at the Opera; and '*tout Paris*' flocked to evening parties in Van Dongen's studio.

Meanwhile, in Rome, Chirico was immersed in the study of 'old master' techniques (glazing, tempera, etc.) and producing romantic paintings showing Italian villas in cypress groves and so 'forth, some of which *Paysage romain*,[2] for example, recall the *Toteninsel* by the Swiss Romantic Boecklin (who had already inspired him in his youth); at this time Chirico also painted *Le retour de l'enfant prodigue* where the prodigal—a figure emblematic of the artist's *pittura metaphysica*[3] has returned penitent and is embraced by a figure in a frockcoat emblematic of the Romantic tradition. Chagall, still in Moscow, was designing scenery for Stanislavsky's Art Theatre; and Jean Lurçat who had spent the last two years in Germany (in contact with Rainer Maria Rilke) returned to France to decorate the Château de Villeflix (Noisy-le-Grand).

In the next year 1922 Picasso was still engrossed in the monumental concepts of his 'Antique' period which again include a number of *Mère et enfant* compositions, and also some very majestic single half-nude and draped seated figures portrayed with broad chiaroscuro and grandly simple drawing which recall Masaccio's paintings in the Brancacci chapel. And Italian art of the cinquecento is also recalled by his half-length of a peasant woman against a cloud-flecked sky, titled *Italienne assise*, painted at this time.

Matisse's pictures of 1922 include *Le concert*[4] (two girls playing instruments before a Moorish screen—where two discordant blues are miraculously mated), *Les jeunes filles au paravent mauresque*[5] (another interior where the pattern on a Moorish screen and the patterns on rugs and carpets enclose two figures), a number of nude and semi-nude *Odalisque* studies against patterned backgrounds, one or two repetitions of the old Nice interior *motif* where the genre character is now dom-

[1] Cf. above, p. 277.   [2] Florence. G. Castelfranco.   [3] Cf. p. 260.
[4] Paris. Georges Wildenstein. (Formerly New York, Stransky.)
[5] Boston. Robert Treat Paine 2nd.

inated by the picture's pattern as a whole, some Impressionist bird's-eye views of Carnival at Nice, one or two studies of women's heads seen across a table with books and flowers, and the first of several half-length paintings of a little girl in a Spanish mantilla.

Derain now completed one of his outstanding post-war works, his romantic-realist *Pierrot et Arlequin*[1], and developed a characteristic style in woodland landscapes where Cézanne's device of an arch of boughs enclosing the space from foreground to background is frequently employed. Braque abandoned straight line Cubism for his personal curvilinear Flat-pattern decorative semi-Cubist manner, which he applied not only to still life but also to figures—as in *Femme au fruit*.[2] Ozenfant completed his cardinal Purist picture *Accords* (Pl. 80) already discussed;[3] Léger painted the large composition *Le déjeuner*[4] where Flat-pattern Cubism, illusionist perspective and Purism are mingled; and Purist principles began to influence Gris and the former Futurist Severini who now began a series of classically conceived decorations with clown and harlequin *motifs* for Sir George Sitwell's Italian villa. At the same time a Neuilly bookshop, *Au sans pareil*, painted its walls in a strong-colour-square-triangle-and-circle formula extracted from Léger's manner in *Le disque rouge* (Pl. 79B), and thereafter such hideous and senseless vulgarizations of Flat-pattern Cubist and Purist-Functional formulae became a recognized type of popular decoration christened by the newspapers '*le style Jazz*'.

At the *Salon d'Automne* in 1922 Bauchant attracted attention with two ambitious compositions titled *La bataille de Palerme (guerres puniques-romaines) avec éléphants*[5] and *Adam et Eve chassés du paradis terrestre*; and his other pictures of the year include a *Portrait de l'artiste*[5] where he is seen in his gardener's hat behind a bed of multicoloured dahlias of his own growing. At the same time Louis Vivin retired with his Post Office pension and resolved to paint regularly as distraction in his old age. Bombois' pictures of this moment include *Au bras d'acier*[6]—a circus 'parade' scene in which the subject of Seurat's *Parade* and the Cocteau-Picasso-Stravinsky ballet is recorded as perceived by a simpler mind and eye.

In this same year 1922 the *Musée Lautrec*, containing six hundred works (paintings, lithographs, sketch books, etc.), presented by Lautrec's family to the town of Albi, was installed in the episcopal palace and formally opened by the Ministre de l'Instruction Publique et des Beaux-Arts; Marcel Proust died at the age of fifty-one after publishing *Sodome et Gomorrhe II*; Cocteau published *Le secret professionel* with his portrait drawn by Picasso as a frontispiece; Gaston Baty founded the *Baraque de la Chimère* where *Martine* by J. J. Bernard, *La farce du Papa Ghenorghé* by Adolphe Orna and *Le voyageur* by Denys Amiel were played; and Dullin produced Pirandello's *La volupté de l'honneur*, Achard's *Celui qui vivait sa mort* and Cocteau's *Antigone* with masks and scenery by Picasso at the *Théâtre de l'Atelier*. François de Curel's *La terre inhumaine* was played at the *Théâtre des Arts*. Léger designed *Skating Rink* for Rolf de Maré's Swedish Ballet; and Diaghileff produced *La belle au bois dormant*, *Le mariage d'Aurore* and *Renard* with decorations by Bakst

[1] Paris. Mme Paul Guillaume.   [2] Paris. Baron Napoléon de Gourgaud.
[3] Cf. above, pp. 267–269.   [4] Paris. Paul Rosenberg.
[5] Paris. Mme Jeanne Bucher.   [6] Paris. Mme Gregory.

in the first case, by Benois and Gontcharova in the second and by Larionov in the third. The illustrated books included Reverdy's *Cravates de chanvre* with etchings by Picasso, and Bernard's *Le tableau de la boxe* with etchings by Segonzac; and Vollard published a set of war lithographs *Miserere et Guerre*, including an affective *Crucifixion*, by Rouault.

In this year also the London British Broadcasting Association began to broadcast music, Arthur Bliss's *Colour Symphony* was performed at Gloucester, Eugène Goossens' incidental music to Somerset Maugham's *East of Suez* was performed in London, and the Salzburg International Musical Festivals began.

Dada was now dead, and from, as it were, its ashes Klee drew *La dame au voile* and *La machine à gazouiller*, and Tzara (with whom Breton and Picabia had quarrelled) wrote a play called *Le cœur à barbe*. Breton and his associates, preparing Neo-Surrealism, continued the review called *Littérature*, made more experiments in 'automatic' writing and literary *collage* and welcomed Ernst who arrived in Paris from Cologne.

In the next year 1923 Picasso, aged forty-two, was at the height of his amazing powers and his numerous great pictures of the year can be considered in five groups. In a first group we have the continuation of the 'Antique' series with *La flûte de Pan*[1] and *La femme en blanc: bras croisés*[2] which again recall Masaccio's works, and *Jeune femme et enfant*[3] which recalls Pompeian paintings; in a second group we have pictures, with delicately drawn and tinted figures, in a very pure and Classical style, including *Le repos de l'acrobate* (Pl. 83); *La femme de l'artiste: bras levé*; *La femme de l'artiste: mains jointes*;[6] *La femme de l'artiste écrivant une lettre*; *L'Italienne aux bras croisés*; *Les amoureux*,[4] a number of Harlequin figures, the noble and at the same time tender group of nudes called *Jeux familiales*, and some further *Mère et enfant* studies;[5] in a third group we have Spanish bull-fight scenes including the romantic *Cheval mourant* and *Cheval mourant et spectateurs*, and the *Taureau vainqueur* where horse and man are conquered and the man is stretched across the back of the charging bull; in a fourth group we have pictures with distorted figures including *Femmes effrayées au bord de la mer* (Pl. 82), *Deux baigneuses nues* and *Trois femmes au bord de la mer*; and a fifth group is made up of Cubist or semi-Cubist still-life compositions where curved lines are more used than in his earlier Cubist pictures. The second group of which I reproduce *Le repos de l'acrobate* (Pl. 83) is Picasso's most Hellenic achievement to this date; and we see what he had gained from the discipline of his Cubist and 'Antique' researches if we compare this picture with the Romantic *saltimbanques* of the 'Blue' and 'Pink' periods—the *Bateleur à la nature morte*[6] or *Comédien et enfant*[7] for example, or *Femme à sa toilette et Arlequin avec enfant* (Pl. 53A). The *Femmes effrayées au bord de la mer* (Pl. 82), which I reproduce from the pictures with distorted figures of this year, is one of the most tremendous of Picasso's works; the distortions here—(very different from Cézanne's architectural distortions in *Les grandes baigneuses* (Pl. 49) or Gauguin's religious distortions in *Vision après le sermon: Lutte*

---

[1] Paris. Pablo Picasso.   [2] New York. Museum of Modern Art (Bliss).
[3] New York. Pierre Matisse.   [4] Chicago Art Institute (Chester Dale) Cf. p. 302.
[5] Several of these are owned by Baron Fukushima, Paris.
[6] New York. Chester Dale.   [7] New York. Stephen C. Clark.

de Jacob avec l'ange (Pl. 22B) and *Jesus au Jardin des Oliviers* (Pl. 26))—are, technically speaking, distortions seen by a camera *facing* the figures and recorded by an
artist looking at the camera's vision as it were from the side; but this technical
tour de force is incidental; the central function of the distortions in this truly
Surrealist work is the creation of dream-terror, the transformation of the disquieting stillness in The Douanier Rousseau's *La bohémienne endormie* (Pl. 42) or
1897 and in Chirico's *Rue Italienne: le cerceau* (Pl. 68B) of 1914 to terrifying movement—another aspect of dream experience; these imposing figures, with their
huge pink limbs thrusting from cream draperies, career like panic-stricken horses
on the grey of a sea-shore, against the vivid blue of sea and sky, and cast dark
shadows on the earth and—impossibly but credibly because we are in the land of
nightmare—they also cast light shadows on the sea behind; when Chirico painted
later Surrealist pictures of horses careering by strange sea-shores he was merely
echoing this picture; and in my judgment nothing yet produced by the Neo-
Surrealists has even approached it as a work of art.[1]

Matisse's works of 1923 include *Odalisque, pose orientale*,[2] some Odalisque
pictures of a half-nude model standing or disposed in an armchair,[3] more half-
length studies of a little girl in a Spanish mantilla seated at a table, a number of
other half-lengths of girls at a table, some woodland landscapes, a still-life with
view through a window on the right (*Bouquet de fleurs et raisins devant les ponchettes*)
and an interior with two boys in striped jackets and a girl playing the piano against
a Moorish screen (*Autour du piano*). In some of these paintings he has treated the
figures, or parts of them, more naturalistically than the accessories, but in *Autour
du piano*[4] and *Petite espagnole aux fleurs*[5] everything is miraculously homogeneous and
decorative.

In this year 1923 Ozenfant with Jeanneret (now known as Le Corbusier),
continued to direct the Purist review *L'esprit nouveau*; Léonce Rosenberg had an
exhibition by a Dutch group of Purist architects (who called themselves *De stijl*) in
his gallery *L'Effort Moderne*; the Russian Soutine painted Expressionist landscapes at
Céret; and Marc Chagall returned to Paris from Russia. Pavel Tchelitchew[1]
another Russian (but not Jewish like Soutine and Chagall) arrived in Paris at the
age of twenty-five and at once attracted notice at the *Salon d'Automne*. There too
Pedro Pruna, a talented young Spaniard who had been in Paris for some time,

[1] Cf. above, pp. 273–275. Picasso's technical exploitation of the camera's distortions in this
picture (and in another picture called *Au bord de la mer* (New York: Valentine, Dudensing) of
this year and in the *Sylphides* and *Stravinsky* (Pl. 78) of 1920) was in its turn exploited ten years
later by Tchelitchew (cf. pp. 308, 313, 314, 315), who painted pictures with double and triple
perspective (i.e. with two or three points of view applied to various objects in the same picture)
from 1934 onwards. These experiments by Tchelitchew culminated in a huge picture titled
Phénomènes (exhibited at Tooth's Galleries in London in 1938) where all kinds of freaks and
abortions in nature and all kinds of man-made monstrosities are thus depicted in exaggerated
triple perspective.

[2] New York. Stephen C. Clark. This picture is sometimes titled *La pose de Buddha*, but the
attitude is not in fact one of the attitudes of Buddha. It is also sometimes catalogued as *Hindu pose*.

[3] Several of these are owned by Mme Paul Guillaume (Paris).

[4] Dundee. Royan Middleton.

[5] Paris. Gaston Bernheim de Villers.

attracted attention with *L'heureux ménage*, *Les deux sœurs*[1] and *Marin américain et fille* inspired by Picasso's works of the character of *Les amoureux* and *Le repos de l'acrobate* (Pl. 83). Bauchant now painted *Les gardeuses de chèvres*[2] and *La promenade dans le parc*[3] where the trees are treated with a delicacy rivalling The Douanier's handling in *Dame en brun dans la forêt*[4] painted twenty years earlier; Bombois painted *Deux fillettes aux bouquets*[5] and *La Cathédrale d'Albi*[6]; and Vivin painted the exquisitely coloured and classically formalized *Nature morte aux huitres* (Pl. 84A). Both Bombois and Vivin exhibited their work this year in the Montmartre street market *La Foire aux Croûtes* and thereafter Bombois' talents were discovered by the dealer Henri Bing and the collector Madame Gregory who enabled him to abandon his job in the newspaper office and give all his time to painting. The year's works by the group who were to launch the Neo-Surrealist movement next year included a film titled *Le retour de la raison* by Man Ray (who had been experimenting with photography for some time and had devised the 'rayograph' technique) and books titled *Les malheurs des immortels* and *Répétitions* by Paul Eluard and Max Ernst in collaboration. Proust's *Sodome et Gomorrhe II* was now posthumously published; and Cocteau wrote his essay on Picasso which contains the dictum: '*Ce n'est pas en pensant à la vie de l'ensemble vers quoi s'organisent les lignes que le dessinateur fera œuvre vivante, mais en sentant sa ligne en danger de mort d'un bout à l'autre du parcours—un danger d'acrobate. A ce seul prix l'ensemble vivra d'une vie propre . . . de toute autre maîtrise ne résultera qu'une singerie*'. Diaghileff's chief production was *Les Noces*, a choral ballet with four pianos and percussion as an orchestra, music by Stravinsky, choreography by Nijinska and curtain, costumes and scenery by Gontcharova. Léger designed *La création du monde* which was danced to Milhaud's music by the Swedish Ballet. Jules Romains' *Knock* and *M. le Trouhadec saisi par le Débauche*, Georges Duhamel's *La journée des aveugles* and Vildrac's *L'indigent* were played at the *Comédie des Champs Elysées*; Copeau produced his own play *La maison natale* and René Benjamin's *Il faut que chacun soit à sa place* at the *Vieux Colombier*; Orna's *Mlle le Feu*, Jean Sarment's *Facilité*, Colette's *La vagabonde*, and Achard's *Voulez-vous jouer avec moâ* were played at other theatres; and Georges Pitoëff, who had made himself a brilliant actor and producer by five years' work in Geneva, established himself in Paris with his wife Ludmilla Pitoëff as his leading lady, and Lenormand's *Le mangeur de rêves*, Shaw's *Androcles et le lion*, Andreiev's remarkable circus play *Celui qui reçoit les gifles* and plays by Pirandello in his repertoire.

In this same year 1923 Sarah Bernhardt died at seventy-eight and Pierre Loti died at seventy-three.

[1] London. Rollo Myers.   [2] Paris. Dr. F. Meyer.
[3] Paris. O. Mietschaninoff.   [4] Paris. A. Villard.
[5] Paris. Mme Gregory.   [6] Paris. Florent Fels.

ACT IV: HOW IT HAPPENED

SCENE II: 1924 to the present day

From Purist-Functional architecture and the *style mécanique*,
Matisse's *La séance de trois heures*, the Neo-Surrealist demonstrations and Chirico's return to Paris; to Picasso's *Guernica*
and the Paris 1937 Exposition

In 1924 the Neo-Surrealists began operations by a vulgar demonstration when
Anatole France died in October. They staged a mock funeral procession and distributed a pamphlet titled *Un Cadavre* expressing their hostility to the deceased's
attitudes and works: 'This day', the pamphlet said, 'should be regarded as a fête
day on which cunning, traditionalism, patriotism, opportunism, scepticism, realism and heartlessness are buried.'[1] Breton's *Manifeste du Surréalisme*, with his *Poisson
soluble* attached, was published some weeks later, and the first number of the Neo-
Surrealist review *La Révolution Surréaliste* reproducing works by Picasso, Chirico,
Ernst, Man Ray and André Masson, was published in December.

Picasso's 1924 pictures can again be divided into groups. In a first group we
have *Le tapis rouge*[2] and other semi-Cubist Flat-pattern still-life compositions in
which a fruit basket, a compotier with a slice of melon, a plaster head of a young
man, and a patterned rug disposed on a table, are used as *motifs* auxiliary to the old
repertoire of guitars, pages of music, etc., and free-flowing curves and baroque
patterning appear. In a second group Picasso seems influenced by Paul Klee's exploitation of very young children's graffiti—the objects being suggested by very
simple linear symbols; and this character also appears in some landscapes, painted
at Juan-les-Pins. In a third group which includes the charming portrait of his little
son *Le petit arlequin* he continues his classical manner with an added feeling for
silhouette patterning. In a fourth group we have some pictures with nude figures
which appear to be reflections in a distorting mirror, in some cases of the 1920
type of 'Antique' *Baigneuses*, in other cases of the Surrealist *Femmes effrayées au bord
de la mer* (Pl. 82) of 1923; and in these pictures he has evidently sought to increase
the dream-terror conveyed by *Femmes effrayées au bord de la mer*. In this year also he
designed the drop curtain for the ballet *Le train bleu* produced by Diaghileff with
music by Milhaud, costumes by Chanel and choreography by Nijinska, and the
scenery and costumes for the ballet *Mercure* produced by Diaghileff as '*poses plas-*

[1] David Gascoyne. *A Short Survey of Surrealism*. (London: Cobden-Sanderson, 1935.)
[2] Paris. Paul Rosenberg. Cf. p. 311.

303

tiques' with music by Satie and choreography by Massine. After the first performance of *Mercure* the Neo-Surrealists issued a Declaration titled *Hommage à Picasso* and
signed by, among others, Breton, Aragon, Soupault, Peret, Naville, Ernst and the
composer Poulenc, which said: '*Nous tenons à témoigner de notre profonde et totale
admiration pour Picasso qui au mépris des consécrations n'a jamais cessé de créer l'in-
quiétude moderne et d'en fournir toujours l'expression la plus haute. Voici qu'avec* Mercure
*il provoque à nouveau l'incompréhension générale, en donnant toute la mesure de son audace
et son génie. A la lueur de cet événement qui revêt un caractère exceptionnel, Picasso, bien
au delà de tous ceux qui l'entourent, apparaît aujourdhui la personnification éternelle
de la jeunesse et le maître incontestable de la situation.*' But Picasso was not sufficiently
captured by this flattery to ally himself formally with this group.

Matisse in 1924 had a much admired exhibition at Bernheim's gallery. His
pictures of the year include some interiors with a looped curtain above a doorway and a vista through the door (*Intérieur, rideau relevé, nature morte à l'ananas*;[1]
and *Intérieur, rideau relevé, nature morte et cage d'oiseau*),[2] some still-life studies,
including *Histoires juives*;[3] a very fine studio scene with a girl in a blue and white
spotted dress painting at an easel and a model standing on the throne covered with
a large-patterned Turkish rug (*La séance de trois heures*),[4] an almost naturalistically
modelled recumbent half-nude (*L'odalisque au magnolia*)[5] and a half-length portrait where the face and arms are also to some extent naturalistically modelled (*La
blouse rose*).[6]

The influence of the Purist and Functionalist doctrines expounded in *L'esprit
nouveau* by Ozenfant and Jeanneret (Le Corbusier) and in a review called *L'effort
moderne* started this year by Léonce Rosenberg, was now evident in many quarters.
In architecture and interior equipment this influence produced a style which Ozenfant described as 'the style of the typewriter, the Eversharp pencil and the Innovation trunk' and which was more generally known at the time as the *Style mécanique*.
In painting, the effects of the Purist-Classical Renaissance launched by Ozenfant in
pictures like *Accords* (Pl. 80) were seen in the 1924 works by Herbin and Severini,
in Léger's *Le Syphon, Athlète, disque et maison*, and *Femme au bouquet* and in classically formalized landscapes and figure subjects by Metzinger—*La partie de cartes,
L'écuyère, Baigneuse* and *Le bal masqué*.[7] Léger now designed a laboratory scene with
machine forms for a film by Marcel L'Herbier called *L'inhumaine* and (in collaboration with the American photographer Dudley Murphy) an 'abstract' film with geometric forms called *Ballet mécanique*; Picabia designed the Film-Ballet *Relâche* with
a décor of giant gramophone discs, produced by René Clair with music by Satie,
for the Swedish Ballets; and the *Style mécanique* was defended in the Chamber of
Deputies by M. Vaillant-Couturier with the argument that art is '*la discipline des
dons*' and not academic tradition or romantic anarchy. At the same time the vulgari-
zation of the style—(*le style Jazz*)—with silly half circles, right angles and sharp zig-

[1] Formerly Paris. Bernheim Jeune.   [2] Baltimore. Miss Etta Cove.
[3] Philadelphia. S. S. White 3rd.
[4] New York. Stephen C. Clarke. This picture is sometimes catalogued as *Atelier à Nice*.
[5] Paris. Gaston Bernheim de Villers.
[6] New York. Mrs. Walter Hochschild.
[7] Paris. Léonce Rosenberg, Galerie de l'Effort Moderne.

87. CHIRICO

Les arbres dans la chambre, 1927–28

Exhibited Paris, Galerie Bonjean, 1931

88A. LURÇAT
Les pilotis, 1928
Paris. Etienne Bignou
88B. MIRO
Le chien et la lune, 1926
New York University. Museum of Living Art

zags in bright colours—made rapid headway and now appeared in French domestic textiles and on women's scarfs and dresses.

In this year 1924 André Masson made drypoint etchings for Limbour's *Soleils Bas* and had his first exhibition of pictures (mainly influenced by Gris) at the Galerie Simon run by the dealer Kahnweiler who had returned to Paris; Jean Lurçat having finished his decorations at Noisy-le-Grand was travelling in Spain and painting *Paysage espagnol* in a style that was already personal, though influenced to a large extent by Braque. The Spanish sculptor Gargallo attracted attention with ingenious masks and figures in thin metal calligraphically handled, the third dimension being mainly suggested by concavities and hollows (as in Zadkine's sculpture also at this time). Bauchant painted the compositions *Ganymède* and *Le retour de l'enfant prodigue*; the aged Vivin painted the exquisitely coloured snow scene *Place du Tertre en hiver*;[1] and Bombois painted *La marchande de frites*,[2] *La fillette au bouquet*,[2] and *Le tambourin crevé*.[3]

Many of our artists were employed this year on designs for ballets. Picabia, as just noted, designed *Relâche* for Rolf de Maré's Swedish Ballets; de Maré also employed Foujita (whose half-European half-Japanese art now had numerous admirers) for *Le tournoi singulier*, and Chirico (who was still in Rome and painting the last of his 'old master' series, *Portrait de l'artiste: profile à la fenêtre*, and the first of his 'Antique' pictures, *Souvenir de l'Iliade*) for Casella's *La Giara*. Diaghileff employed Braque, Marie Laurençin, Gris and the Spaniard Sert. Braque's ballet was *Les fâcheux* which had music by Auric and choreography by Nijinska; Marie Laurençin (who had now developed her characteristic style in decorative pictures with frail flat figures in 'pastel' tints and notes of black) designed *Les biches* which had music by Poulenc and choreography by Nijinska; Gris designed *La tentation de la bergère* which was danced to seventeenth-century music by Monteclair with choreography by Nijinska; and Sert designed the Spanish ballet *Las Meninas* which had music by Gabriel Fauré and choreography by Massine. Léon Bakst died this year and the *Vieux Colombier* closed down. The new plays included Pirandello's *Chacun sa vérité* at the *Théâtre de l'Atelier* and his *Les six personnages en quête d'auteur* produced by the Pitoëffs at the *Théâtre des Arts*; Paul Demasy's *Jésus de Nazareth* (written in a German prison camp) produced by Baty at the Odéon; Simon Gantillou's *Maya*, Lenormand's *L'homme et ses fantômes* and *A l'ombre du mal*, Jean Sarment's *Les six grimaces de Don Juan*, Orna's *L'égoïste*, J. J. Bernard's *Le printemps des autres* and *L'invitation au voyage*, and Raynal's *Le tombeau sous l'arc de triomphe*. In this year also Honegger's *Pacific 231*, Milhaud's *Salade* and Prokofieff's *They are Seven* were performed in Paris, George Gershwin's *Rhapsody in Blue* was performed in New York, and Respighi's *Pines of Rome* was performed in Rome.[4]

In the next year 1925 Matisse painted a series of engaging decorative pictures —*La robe jaune*[5] (a full-length figure, in yellow dress, a scroll of music in her hand, a rug with Indian red pattern at her feet, a guitar by her side, and screens patterned with yellow, blues and greens as a background); *Jeune femme au piano*[6] (with

---

[1] Paris. F. Girtanner.   [2] Paris. Mme Gregory.   [3] Switzerland. Mme Hostettler.
[4] Slonimsky. *Music since 1900* (London: Dent, 1938).
[5] Baron Fukushima.   [6] New York. Stephen C. Clark.

Moorish screen background), *Jeune fille à une table près d'une fenêtre à Nice*, *Nappe rose et ananas*[1] and *Le jardin de Renoir à Cagnes*[2] (a landscape with the *Vénus* which Renoir sculpted in his last years). Braque whose pictures, like Picasso's, were now seen regularly at Paul Rosenberg's gallery, designed the scenery and costumes for the ballet *Zéphyr et Flore* produced by Diaghileff with music by Vladimir Dukelsky and masks and symbols by Oliver Messel, and painted *Nature morte* (Pl. 84B) and other still-life compositions with complex patterning, and also some compositions where his methods were again applied to the human form. Utrillo, who had followed his 'White' period by more richly coloured Montmartre and other townscapes with figures, was employed by Diaghileff for the scenery and costumes in the ballet *Barabau* which had music by Rieti and choreography by Balanchine. Diaghileff also employed the young Spaniard Pruna, who designed the scenery and costumes for two ballets *Les Matelots* and *Pastorale*, both danced to music by Auric. Gertrude Stein now discovered Pavel Tchelitchew and Christian Bérard, who was then twenty-three and influenced like Tchelitchew (who was four years older) by Picasso's non-Cubist works; and Madame Gregory bought Bombois' *Femme portant du bois dans la forêt* and Vivin's *Le Sacré-Cœur*.

Picasso's 1925 works include the pastel *La dame en bleu*,[3] a soft echo of his 'Antique' period; the quasi-Whistlerian portrait of his son *Le petit Pierrot au masque*, where the little boy stands as a white silhouette on a wine-coloured carpet against a background of flat blue-grey sky and balcony railings and an almost flat black curtain; *La statuaire*,[4] in which he developed the Paul-Klee-naïf linear conventions, seen in certain of his 1924 pictures, to a more sophisticated linear treatment recalling certain drawings on Greek vases; *L'atelier du peintre*,[5] *La table du sculpteur*,[5] and *La leçon de dessin*[6], in which disintegrated forms and formalized cast shadows are exploited in massive patterning; *La danseuse au tambourin*,[7] where the characters of *La statuaire* are combined with a hint of Neo-Surrealism in the head, which is profile and three-quarter at one and the same time; and—one of the most astonishing of his works—the large picture called *La danse*[8]—which I take to be a first (and perhaps a semi-serious) exploration of Neo-Surrealist doctrines.

Surrealism proper was carried on this year by Chagall and Chirico both now re-established in Paris. Chagall's 1925 pictures include *Fleurs dans la rue* (a giant still life of flowers in a pot surrounded by small figures in a village street), *Femme sur l'âne*[9] (where a young woman in a flowered frock is galloped through a topsy-turvy village), *La vache*[10] and *Le breuvage*.[11] In *Le breuvage* Chagall's technique resembles that of his pre-war and Vitebsk productions; but in the other pictures named and in his work henceforward the technique is softer, and blue and violet with accents of red are the dominating colours. Chirico's Romantic pictures painted in Italy (influenced by Boecklin and 'old master' procedures) had all been acquired by Italian collectors. His first works painted on his return to Paris were

[1] New York. Sam Lewisohn.
[2] Algiers. Museum.
[3] Paris. Etienne Bignou.
[4] New York. Stephen C. Clark.
[5] Exhibited Paris. Galeries Georges Petit, 1932.
[6] Exhibited London. Reid & Lefevre, 1931.
[7] Paris. Mme Paul Guillaume.
[8] Paris. Paul Rosenberg.
[9] Switzerland. Hoffmann Collection.
[10] Paris. Luxembourg.
[11] Paris. Vicomte Charles de Noailles.

 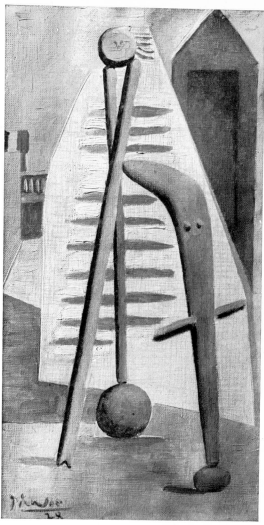

89A. PICABIA

Myrtil, 1929

Paris. Léonce Rosenberg

89B. PICASSO

Dinard, 1928

Paris. Paul Rosenberg

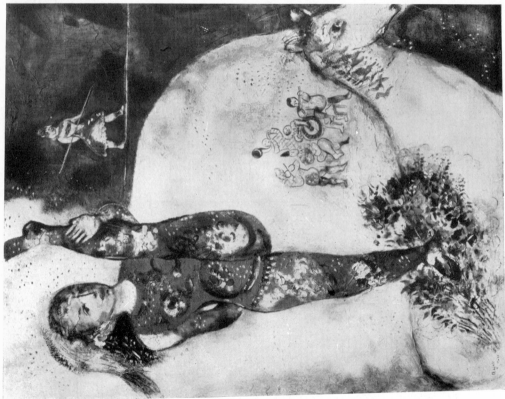

90B. TCHELICHEW
L'avocat, 1929

90A. CHAGALL
L'acrobate, 1926-27

shown in Léonce Rosenberg's gallery *L'Effort Moderne* this year; and here were seen the first of his Surrealist *Philosophes* series where semi-human semi-marble figures, in 'Antique' draperies, with faceless football heads, bear cardboard citadels on their marble knees while emerald seas surround the platforms which support them.[1]

The Neo-Surrealists were all considerably in the limelight. Péret and Paul Eluard published *Cent cinquante deux Proverbes* where they distorted well-known proverbs and aphorisms and invented new ones in the Neo-Surrealist shock spirit. The second number of the Neo-Surrealist review *La Révolution Surréaliste*, violently anti-militarist, anti-nationalist and anti-clerical, contained a declaration headed '*Open the Prisons: Disband the Army*'; and the cover had a figure of a scarecrow with the legend *L'art français au début du XXième siècle* in token of their antagonism to aesthetic and formal art. Ernst made his first *frottage* experiments;[2] an exhibition at the *Galerie Pierre* contained works by Ernst, Klee, Picasso, Chirico, Man Ray, Masson, Pierre Roy and Miro; and in the autumn the Neo-Surrealists as a group announced the adherence of their movement to political Communism.[3]

Ozenfant and Jeanneret (Le Corbusier) now stopped publication of *L'esprit nouveau* and Jeanneret published *Vers une architecture* signed 'Le Corbusier-Saugniet' (Saugniet standing for Ozenfant to whom this book, which has had great influence on modern architecture, was dedicated). The Purist-Functional style was much in evidence at the *Exposition des Arts Décoratifs*; and outside France it was now also manifest—notably in the designs by Gropius for the Bauhaus at Dessau. In painting, the Purist style was chiefly seen in severe and imposing flat-pattern compositions by Léger (*Le miroir, L'escalier, Contraste de formes*) and in pictures by Ozenfant, who had now begun to subject his norm forms to three-dimensional treatment and to group them architecturally in space so that they appear as symbols of model cities with great buildings in the new style.

Pirandello's *Henri IV* was produced this year by the Pitoëffs at the *Théâtre des Arts*, and his *Vêtir ceux qui sont nus* at the *Renaissance*; Bernard Shaw's *Saint-Jeanne* was played by the Pitoëffs at the *Théâtre des Arts*; Crommelynk's *Tripes d'or* was produced by Jouvet at the *Comédie des Champs Elysées*; Proust's *Albertine disparue* was posthumously published; Ravel's ballet-opera, to Colette's tale, *L'enfant et les sortilèges* was performed at Monte Carlo; Alban Berg's *Wozzeck* was performed in Berlin; and Erik Satie died at the age of fifty-nine, leaving several unpublished scores including a *Paul et Virginie* with libretto by Radiguet and Cocteau.

In the next year 1926 Surrealism was carried forward by Chirico in a series of highly original and poetically disquieting pictures which were shown in an exhibition organized by Paul Guillaume (who had just returned from a long tour in America where he had lectured on contemporary French painting and negro sculpture). These pictures by Chirico can be considered in five groups. In the first we have *Le repos du philosophe, Le consolateur*, and other works continuing the 'philosopher' series of the year before; in the second we have compositions with miscellaneous 'antique' emblems stacked to a pyramid called *Trophées*; in a third we have

[1] A triptych in this series is in the Whitworth Gallery, Manchester.
[2] Cf. above, p. 280.   [3] Cf. pp. 283, 284, 320, 321.

the characters of these two series amalgamated in pictures of the type of the singularly moving *Les Marathoniens* where Chirico has arrayed his faceless *philosophes* in Greek helmets and armour and set them back to the wall—(a wall composed of flimsy studio screens)—on a temple terrace lapped at by a turquoise sea; in a fourth group we have the first of his pictures with indoor-outdoor Associationism—a series which was continued the next year; and in a fifth we have the beginning of a series with semi-animal semi-antique-marble horses on strange seashores which was also continued the next year. In some of the pictures with horses the rhythm is slow and the effect is almost static; in others, where the horses gallop in panic, the more animated rhythm recalls Picasso's *Femmes effrayées au bord de la mer* (Pl. 82). Other contributors to Surrealism proper at this moment were Jean Lurçat, who was travelling in the Near East and painting *La sieste*[1] (influenced by Picasso's *La danseuse au tambourin*[2] of 1925) and his first Surrealist landscape *Smyrne*[3] (influenced by Chirico's pre-war pictures with emotive perspective); and Chagall who produced *L'acrobate* (Pl. 90A) and other gay circus pictures and a number of still-life-landscape associationist compositions including *Lys*, where a vase of lilies is embraced as it were by a calm sea, and *Fleurs et paysage* where a bowl of roses mingles in spirit with a Russian village landscape beyond. At this time also Chagall illustrated Gogol's *Les âmes mortes* with etchings commissioned by Vollard.

Picasso now made experiments with Neo-Surrealist *collages*, continuing, for the rest, on the lines of his production in 1925; and his recent pictures were shown at Paul Rosenberg's gallery. Matisse painted a number of standing and recumbent *Odalisque* pictures concentrating more than he had hitherto done on the graceful attitudes of an attractive sitter (*L'odalisque au tambourin*,[4] *Odalisque bleue*, *Nu assis: pantalon rouge*), modelling on occasion almost naturalistically (*Nu étendu*)[5] and beginning a series of paintings and lithographs from a sitter in a ballet-dancer's dress—a series known as his *Ballerinas*. Braque now arrived at more mastery in applying his methods in pictures with the human figure; Dufy lithographed illustrations to Apollinaire's *Le poète assassiné*, Vlaminck made lithographs for Radiguet's *Le diable au corps* and Reuillard's *Grasse Normandie*, Gromaire made etchings illustrating Baudelaire's *Petits poèmes en prose*, and Masson made etchings for *C'est les Bottes de Sept Lieues* by Desnos; Jean Victor Hugo designed scenery and costumes for Ben Jonson's *La femme silencieuse* (performed with music by Auric at Dullin's *Théâtre de l'Atelier*) and made coloured drawings for Cocteau's *Roméo et Juliette*; and Alfred Savoir produced *Le dompteur; ou l'anglais tel qu'on le mange*. Olga Sacharoff, a Russian living in Barcelona, attracted attention at the *Salon d'Automne* with *Sardanas* and other engaging pictures inspired by The Douanier Rousseau; Osbert, Sacheverell and Edith Sitwell became interested in the work of Tchelitchew; and Edith Sitwell's *Façade* (poems) with music by William Walton was performed at the Chenil Galleries in London.

Diaghileff's 1926 productions were *Jack-in-the-Box* with scenery and costumes by Derain, music from an unpublished score by Satie orchestrated by Milhaud and

[1] Paris. J. Bernheim.
[2] Paris. Mme Paul Guillaume (cf. above, p. 306).
[3] Antwerp. A. de Ridder.
[4] U.S.A. Paley Collection.
[5] Paris. Mme Paul Guillaume.

91. BAUCHANT
Le bon vin, 1929
Paris. M. Roger Dutilleul

92. BOMBOIS
Le marché à Honfleur, c. 1929
Paris. M. André Paz

choreography by Balanchin; *The Triumph of Neptune* by Sacheverell Sitwell with music by Lord Berners, choreography by Balanchin and scenery and costumes adapted by Prince Schervachidze from traditional settings in Pollock's Toy Theatre; and *Roméo et Juliette* danced in rehearsal clothes without scenery with music by Constant Lambert, paintings by Ernst and Miro, and choreography by Nijinska. *The Triumph of Neptune* was danced for the first time in London (where a hundred thousand people went this year to thirty performances of the various ballets in Diaghileff's repertoire); *Roméo et Juliette* was produced in Paris, and at the first performance the Neo-Surrealists (who resented the fact that Ernst and Miro had collaborated) made a hostile demonstration, showering hundreds of leaflets from the gallery and setting up, as the *Times* correspondent reported, 'a deafening blowing of whistles' and 'howling terribly' till the police were called in to remove them.

The Neo-Surrealists now opened their own art gallery, *La galerie Surréaliste*, where they exhibited works by the same artists who had contributed to the 1925 exhibition in the Galerie Pierre. Miro's *Le Chien et la lune* (Pl. 88B) was painted this year; Ernst published a collection of *frottage* drawings called *Histoire Naturelle*; Breton published more numbers of *La Révolution Surréaliste*; and a new painter Jean Viollier began to attract attention with pictures which heralded the macabre productions of a few years later by Salvador Dali.

In this year 1926 The Douanier Rousseau's *La bohémienne endormie* (Pl. 42) of 1897 was seen in Paris at the sale of pictures from the American John Quinn's collection, which also included Matisse's *Le nu bleu* of 1907 and other early pictures by the Fauves, water-colours by Rouault dating from 1914–1918, and *L'étable* by Segonzac. The Surrealism of *La bohémienne endormie*, exquisitely expounded in Jean Cocteau's Introduction to the catalogue of this sale,[1] made a deep impression on many artists who had not previously seen this wonderful picture. There was also at this time a large Retrospective Exhibition of the *Salon des Indépendants* in the Grand Palais, where The Douanier's *Une noce à la campagne*[2] and *La carriole de M. Juniet*,[2] Seurat's *Parade*,[3] works by Cézanne and Signac and Van Gogh, and Lautrec's *Au Moulin Rouge: La table*,[4] were shown with pre-war pictures by the Fauves, the Cubists and Chagall. And this year also saw the beginning of the splendid art review, *Cahiers d'art*, directed by Christian Xervos, and the death of Claude Monet at the age of eighty-seven.

In the next year 1927 Chirico painted *Le peintre de chevaux*—a faceless figure, emblematic of himself, seated at an easel and painting a horse's head, and by his side a marble head of a horse upon the floor; and he also painted *Chevaux au bord de la mer* (Pl. 86B) and other pictures with the horse *motif*. At the same time he began a series of pictures showing groups of nude gladiators, bareheaded or helmeted at the end of combats in the Roman arena—thus reviving, as Waldemar George observed, 'un thème académique qu'aucun peintre n'a osé aborder depuis la mort de Sir Alma-Tadema de sinistre mémoire'. These 'gladiator' pictures fall into two groups, the first painted early in the year and the second later. In one of the pictures of the first group, *Lion et gladiateurs* (86A), an armed gladiator thrusts his spear into a lion crouched

[1] Cf. above, p. 135.
[2] Paris. Mme Paul Guillaume.
[3] New York. Stephen C. Clark.
[4] Chicago. Art Institute (Birch Bartlett).

above a fallen unarmed man; but though we have thus a dramatic incident the action seems petrified, because the classically conceived figures are half humans and half statues; and the dream-atmosphere of the picture recalls The Douanier's *La bohémienne endormie* (Pl. 42) and Chirico's own early *La conquête du philosophe* (Pl. 68A) and *Rue Italienne: le cerceau* (Pl. 68B). In *Lion et gladiateurs* and other pictures of this first 'gladiator' series the scene is illuminated by sunlight; but there is nothing here of Impressionist flicker of sunlight and shade; the still Southern sun burns pitilessly down on the fighters and casts hard shadows round them in the sand. In the second series of 'gladiator' pictures the handling is more baroque and the spirit is more romantic; here the light, depicted by broken Impressionist touches, is less fierce and the semi-human semi-statue figures have been transformed to wholly human athletes with emotive muscles; and we find these same baroque and romantic characters and the broken Impressionist touch in pictures with the horse *motif* painted in the later part of this year—the oil *Chevaux et ruines*[1] and the gouache here reproduced (Pl. 86B), for example—as distinguished from the more classical characters in the earlier horse pictures. The Neo-Surrealist Roger Vitrac's monograph on Chirico's Surrealism appeared at this time; but as it recorded no pictures later than 1926 it did not refer to Chirico's chief concern in 1927—his exploration of indoor-outdoor Associationism (begun as noted in the previous year). I have quoted in the Introduction from Chirico's own account of his preoccupation with this problem[2], and Chirico's words explain the most intriguing of his 1927 pictures—the *Statues dans une chambre*—where semi-human semi-antique marble figures are seated in an ordinary room, *Meubles dans une vallée*, where we see a bed, an armchair and a chest of drawers in a landscape with antique ruins, *Intérieur dans une vallée*, where a man and woman with some pieces of furniture and a door and doorpost find themselves on a small space of wooden flooring in the centre of an uninhabited plain (now Chicago Art Institute (lent Chester Dale)) and the picture painted at the end of this series, *Les arbres dans la chambre* (Pl. 87), where emerald waves and tall trees appear in a room with pink walls.

Chagall, Lurçat and Picabia were other contributors to Surrealism in 1927. Chagall's pictures include a still life of flowers rising miraculously from the heads of embracing lovers (*Les amoureux aux roses et lys*), a giant basket of fruit wafted by a winged Eros to the window of the poet's beloved (*La fenêtre*), the poet riding through the twilight on a giant farmyard cock (*Promenade*), and similar conceits poetically, albeit sometimes rather sentimentally, conceived, and charmingly coloured. Lurçat painted a number of figure compositions, still influenced by Picasso's 1925 productions (*La Turquie*,[3] for example), and a series of original dream-landscapes where emerald seas divide strips of land inhabited by lonely walls and buildings and dwarf trees with giant leaves (*La grève*,[4] *Le château d'eau*[5] and *L'orage*,[6] for example). And Picabia began to create disquieting effects by superimposing transparent images.[7]

The Neo-Surrealist Ernst now used his *frottage* method in experiments with oil

---

[1] Cleveland. Paul Lamb.   [2] Cf. above, pp. 274, 275.
[3] Merion. Barnes Foundation.   [4] Moscow. Museum of Modern Western Art.
[5] Glasgow. A. Reid.   [6] Paris. Bomsel.   [7] Cf. p. 313.

paint; Masson (allied for a time only with the Neo-Surrealists) produced graffiti pictures (*Poissons dessinés sur le sable, Combat de poissons,*[1] *La poursuite*) where wiry lines drawn apparently 'blind' (as one draws a pig with one's eyes shut in the parlour game) intersect and overlap in an animated rhythm which somehow contrives to symbolize the characters of some low forms of organic life; a newcomer to the Neo-Surrealist camp, Yves Tanguy, aged twenty-seven, attracted attention at the Galerie Surréaliste with pictures (like *Maman, papa est blessé*[2]) transforming Chirico's pre-war Surrealist town spaces to desolate receding plains inhabited only by bone-like forms standing, singly, as solitary sentinels or, in rows, like troops of death; Miro (who was claimed by the Neo-Surrealists though he was not officially associated with the group) painted *Personnage, caillou et oiseau,*[3] which is similar in character to *Le chien et la lune* (Pl. 88B) of 1926; and Picasso himself began to develop seriously what I have described as his semi-serious Neo-Surrealist gesture in *La danse* of 1925.

In Picasso's 1927 Neo-Surrealist pictures we have ghastly arabesques in organic free-flowing outlines (drawn apparently 'blind') contouring disintegrated portions of human, animal, vegetable and machine forms—a foot continuing as a breast or as a nose or as a leaf or table leg; and these arabesques are imposed as transparencies on flat silhouettes—profile faces and so forth—quite logically portrayed. And here, as I have stated in the Introduction, Picasso puts Neo-Surrealist associationist theories into practice more powerfully and lustily than any Neo-Surrealist artist had yet done. But these Neo-Surrealist pictures were only one aspect of his work this year. At the same time he had, as usual, a number of other irons in the fire. For he was now continuing the boldly designed Flat-pattern semi-Cubist pictures with strong colours and free-flowing organic lines begun with *Le tapis rouge,*[4] and combining this manner to some extent in certain pictures—such as *Femme assise en rouge*[5] (originally I suspect a mother and child *motif*)—with his Neo-Surrealist procedures. His 1927 works also included a series of representational pen drawings titled *Le peintre et son modèle*—a *motif* which he was to treat in all mediums and in a score of different manners in the next few years.

The free-flowing organic curves which had appeared in Picasso's semi-Cubist compositions since 1924, and which now characterized his first Neo-Surrealist pictures, can also be observed from this time onwards in works by certain painters who had formerly been influenced by Cubism and then by Purism and the Functional *style mécanique*. Léger's compositions for example, formerly built up in static architectural structure with geometric lines and curves on Cubist-Purist principles, now show us objects which appear to float on invisible waves in space, and the objects now selected include large leaves with twining stalks; and Herbin's abstract 1927 compositions are constructed with organic vegetable curves. Matisse on the other hand now stiffened his art with semi-geometric drawing in *La femme à la voilette,*[6] *Nu de dos,*[6] *Odalisque couchée: (culotte grise),*[7] and above all in *Nu assis*[8] where

[1] Paris. Mme Jeanne Bucher.
[2] New York. Museum of Modern Art.
[3] Brussels. René Gaffé.
[4] Cf. above, p. 303.
[5] Connecticut. James Thrall Soby.
[6] Nice. Henri Matisse.
[7] Paris. Mme Paul Guillaume.
[8] Paris. Luxembourg.

before a background patterned with a huge design the back and thigh of the seated nude are contoured by rectangular straight lines. Matisse may have done this in reaction against the now prevalent use of the free-flowing organic line of his own earlier works—(*Bonheur de vivre* (Pl. 56), for example, of 1907 and *La danse*[1] of 1910)—or he may himself have been captured, at this moment, by the classical dignity of Purism just as in 1913–1916 he had been captured to some extent, and for a time, by Cubism. For the Purist-Functional *style mécanique* was more than ever in evidence this year when André Lurçat, Jean Lurçat's brother, designed some charming modern houses; when the audience in the foyer at the Théâtre Pigalle moved through a forest of glittering steel and copper tubing as within the bonnet of a Rolls-Royce car; when A. F. Maile designed a bedstead in chromium-steel and fibro-cement with bookcase attachments, and the Printemps store dressed its windows with wine glasses, plates, tennis balls and racquets in geometric lines and circles. The influence of the *style mécanique* was also seen in the Russian Ballet; for Diaghileff's new productions were *La Chatte* which had music by Sauget and geometric scenery in transparent celluloid designed by the Russian Purist-Constructivists Gabo and Pevsner, and *Le pas d'acier* which had music by Prokofieff and costumes and constructions by Jacouloff. In this year also Stravinsky's opera-oratorio *Œdipus Rex* to a text by Cocteau, translated into Latin, was produced by Diaghileff; the University of New York founded the Museum of Living Art for the purpose of collecting paintings by 'living creative and progressive artists'; I discussed the theory of 'architectural' painting in *The Modern Movement in Art*; Juan Gris died at the age of forty; and Theodore Duret died at eighty-nine.

In the next year 1928 Picasso's pictures can once more be divided in groups. In a first group we have a series of pictures painted at Dinard where *plage* objects come Neo-Surrealistically to life and perform a paradoxical ballet—as in *Dinard* (Pl. 89B) and *Figures sur la plage*[2] and *Dinard: la plage*;[3] in a second group we have some pictures in Dada child-technique including *Arbre et oiseau* and a Neo-Surrealist version of the *Peintre et son modèle* motif where the artist schematically symboled draws a naturalistic profile of the model who is also schematically symboled; and in a third group we have Neo-Surrealist sculpture where disintegrated human, animal and machine forms coalesce with vital rhythm to single forms suggesting some unknown and repulsive low life organism. Matisse, in 1928, continued his recent semi-geometric manner in *Le buffet vert*[4] and *Torse antique et bouquet d'œillets blancs*,[5] and began the pictures and outline pen drawings known as his *Odalisques aux échecs* series, where one or two recumbent girls in Turkish costume have a chessboard beside them against the large patterned background (which had appeared in 1927 in *Nu assis*) *Nature morte et odalisque aux échecs*[6] and *Odalisque, chaise et échecs*[7] for example. Chagall, commissioned by Vollard, now drew lithographs for La Fontaine's *Fables*. Jean Lurçat painted the finest of his Surrealist dream landscapes which include *L'île enchantée*,[8] *L'île enchantée et*

[1] Moscow Museum of Modern Western Art.
[2] New York. George L. K. Morris.
[3] New York University Museum of Living Art.
[4] Paris. Luxembourg.
[5] New York. Mrs. J. D. Rockefeller.
[6] Nice. Henri Matisse.
[7] Paris. Petit Palais.
[8] Philadelphia. Bernard Davis.

personnage,[1] *L'île enchantée: temps d'orage*[2] and *Les pilotis* (Pl. 88B). Chirico began a series of baroque panels with gladiator and chariot-racing subjects (*Combat de gladiateurs*, *Gladiateurs au repos*, *Le quadriga renversé*, and so on) for a marble-floored dining-room in Léonce Rosenberg's private house; and Picabia began the series of Surrealist transparencies including *Myrtil* (Pl. 89A) for a bedroom in the same house. Cocteau (whose *Orphée* was performed this year) published *Le mystère laic: essai d'étude indirecte*, an attempt to find verbal equivalents for Chirico's earlier Surrealist pictures; Waldemar George published a monograph on Chirico containing two prose pieces *Le fils de l'ingénieur* and *Le survivant de Navarin* and a poem by the artist. André Breton published *Le Surréalisme et la peinture* and a Neo-Surrealist romance called *Nadja* illustrated with reproductions of pictures by Ernst and Chirico, a photograph of a bronze glove (herald of the Neo-Surrealist 'objects'[10]) and *soi-disant* 'automatic' drawings by 'Nadja' the heroine who, eventually, was certified insane. The Neo-Surrealists arranged an art show for which they secured works by Arp, Masson, Miro, Picabia, Pierre Roy, Tanguy and Chirico. Max Ernst, who now painted *Le monument des oiseaux*,[3] and Miro had one-man shows at the Galerie Georges Bernheim. Paul Klee drew, as a child draws, the Dada masterpiece *Chat et oiseau*[4] (where the bird is seen in the mind of a cat crouching motionless with still fixed eyes) and made experiments with automatic graffiti which became in the end *Petit fou en transe*[5] (a satire I suspect on the Neo-Surrealists). Man Ray produced the film called *L'étoile de mer*. And Séraphine Louis at Senlis painted some of the last of the strange true paranoiac pictures which I have discussed in the Introduction.[6]

In this same year 1928 Ozenfant published *Art*, a highly interesting book with illustrations selected on the associationist principle, and began work on his series of elemental pictures already discussed.[7] Ravel's *Boléro*, Honegger's *Rugby* and Stravinsky's *Le baiser de la fée* were performed in Paris. Diaghileff produced three new ballets: *Les dieux mendiants* with music by Handel arranged by Beecham, choreography by Balanchine and scenery and costumes from designs left by Bakst and Gris; *Ode* with music by Nabokoff, choreography by Massine and scenery and costumes by Tchelitchew; and *Apollo Musagetes* with music by Stravinsky, choreography by Balanchine and scenery and costumes by Bauchant (who painted this year *Le cabaret du père Lathuile*, some delicately poetical flower pieces and the ambitious compositions with numerous figures *Vercingétorix*[1] and *La bataille de Marathon*).[8] Paul Guillaume began to collect pictures by two Expressionist newcomers Fautrier and Goerg. And Christian Bérard attracted more attention with pictures still influenced by Picasso's 'Blue' and 'Pink' periods but imbued in some cases with a personal tang—*La rencontre*[9] for example, where a little girl and a one-legged boy on a crutch confront one another in some deep conflict of the spirit.

[1] Paris. Mme Jeanne Bucher.
[2] Paris. Etienne Bignou.
[3] Paris. Vicomte Charles de Noailles.
[4] Washington. Phillips Memorial Gallery.
[5] German collection.
[6] Cf. above, p. 284.
[7] Cf. above, pp. 271-273, 286, 287.
[8] Paris. Jean Lurçat.
[9] Paris. M. Benoit-Méchin.
[10] Cf. p. 282.

In the next year 1929 Picasso's works include a pretty Whistlerian portrait of his little son known as *Le petit pierrot aux fleurs* and, in violent contrast, a number of pictures in the nature of projects for Neo-Surrealist sculpture. Some of these pictures—titled generically *Métamorphoses*—show repulsive pinkish fungi-growths of animal-vegetable form silhouetted against a delicate light blue cloud-flecked evening sky; others are a transition towards the concepts of the next year when, in pictures and sculptures, the fungi were transmogrified to bone organisms made cruel with metallic teeth. Apart from Picasso's paintings the most conspicuous Neo-Surrealist gestures of this year were the *collage* scrap-book *La femme 100 têtes* by Ernst, and the film called *Le chien Andalou*, by Louis Bunuel and Salvador Dali.[1]

Ozenfant now produced the first series of his elemental low-relief pictures with type figures including *Clair de lune*,[2] *Baigneuses aux oiseaux*[3] and *Belle vie au ciel blanc*.[4] Braque painted a series of relatively representational sombre dramatic coast scenes with inky skies, while continuing his abstract semi-Cubist baroque compositions. Matisse's productions, varied and unequal, included the calligraphic half-length known as *Le chapeau jaune*,[5] the vigorous *Le nu tatoué*, some impressions of pretty nude models including *Odalisque au feuillage vert*,[6] and the bronze titled *Nu assis: bras levé*.[7] Bauchant painted *Le bon vin* (Pl. 91), *Le charretier indolent*, *Les braconniers* and flower pieces; Vivin painted *Le sanglier traqué*;[8] and Bombois painted *Le marché à Honfleur* (Pl. 92) where wittily observed figures move in brightly coloured clothes across a square bordered by high buildings.[9]

As recorded in the Introduction some of Rouault's Expressionist paintings of the nineteen-twenties in the 'stained glass' technique of his later manner—*Pierrot* (Pl. 93), for example—were seen about this time by visitors to the Paris house of the Japanese collector Baron Fukushima. And Rouault was employed this year by Diaghileff to design the scenery and costumes for *Le fils prodigue*, which had music by Prokofieff and choreography by Balanchine. Diaghileff's other productions included *Le bal*, which had music by Rieti and scenery and costumes designed by Chirico. In his designs for *Le bal* Chirico introduced *motifs* from all his Surrealist pictures, and we thus saw, within a room with frieze and ceiling, trees and fragments of columns leaning against a sea which lapped around a temple on a rock, a rearing horse which looked in at one window and a mannequin in classic draperies with football head who was seated at another; the costumes were modern clothes transformed—the men's top hats being fluted like the Parthenon pillars, and the girls' skirts being curled like Doric capitals over fluted petticoats; the prevailing colours were blue and rose and grey. At the same time Chirico published his Surrealist novel *Hebdomeros* already referred to,[10] and the influence of his *philosophes* pictures was seen in the work of Tchelitchew whose 1929 paintings include *L'avocat* (Pl. 90B) where a cloak thrown over a screen, a plaster head, and a plaster foot on a base are combined as a semi-human semi-material figure, and *Jeune marin*

[1] Cf. above, pp. 276, 278, 282
[2] Paris. Léonce Rosenberg.
[3] Paris. Marcel Laloë.
[4] New York. Amedée Ozenfant.
[5] Nice. Henri Matisse.
[6] New York. Mrs. J. D. Rockefeller.
[7] Baltimore. Miss Etta Cone.
[8] Paris. Dr. François Meyer.
[9] Cf. above, pp. 289, 290.
[10] Cf. above, p. 275.

where similar elements, enveloped in a fishing net, are draped to a semblance of a legless figure on a chair.[1]

An indication of the artists favoured by the dilettanti in 1929 was provided by an exhibition this year of portraits of Mme Maria Lani, who had indulged in the interesting experiment of sitting for her portrait to fifty painters and sculptors. Mme Lani does not seem to have sat to Picasso, Maillol, Vuillard, Vlaminck, Segonzac or Miro, but her choice included Bonnard, Marquet, Rouault, Matisse, Dufy, Friesz, Derain and Van Dongen; Max Jacob, Braque, Delaunay, Lhote, Laboureur, Marcoussis, Foujita, Pascin, Cocteau, Kisling and Paul Poiret; Suzanne Valadon, Chirico, Chagall, Ozenfant, Léger, Lurçat, Picabia and Man Ray; Despiau, Bourdelle and Zadkine; and the young Expressionists Goerg, Gromaire and Soutine.

In June of this year Sisley's son, Pierre Sisley, aged sixty-two, was found dead in a humble room with a number of his father's pictures on the walls; the police doctor diagnosed the cause of death as starvation. 'It seems' wrote the London *Morning Post* on the occurrence 'that the poor man's misery partly at least arose from pronounced hypochondria . . . the last time he was seen he had changed a hundred-franc note.'[2]

The period 1924–1929, and indeed the whole first post-war decade 1919–1929, brought steadily increasing renown and prosperity to the leading artists of the modern schools—both the Frenchmen and the foreigners resident in Paris who were now known as the *Ecole de Paris*. The period also brought continually increasing prosperity to the dealers who had backed or were backing these artists and still more to the dealers who had backed their predecessors. One factor contributing to this prosperity was the knowledge that, as Germany was unarmed and democratic, no fresh German aggression need be feared at the moment; as the readiness of men to become fodder for German cannon was no longer, for a space, the dominant criterion of their merit, men felt free to court the quickening of the spirit which original art provides. Another factor was a general prosperity in America, Great Britain and France. And there were yet other factors more specifically responsible. For world-wide appreciation of pictures by the nineteenth-century French masters—the Impressionists and Cézanne, Seurat, Lautrec, Gauguin and Van Gogh—had been and was continually growing. Museums, collectors, and dilettanti had come to realize that these pictures were as admirable in their several ways as most pictures by the 'Old Masters', that in buying them they were buying pedigree objects without doubt or question by the artists named and not restored or repainted objects ascribed to this painter or that by guesswork pretending to be science; and that, as the exchange value of these pictures in the international art trade was continuously rising, they were evidently a sound investment for public or private funds. For one or all of these reasons museums and rich collectors everywhere were now competing to buy these pictures. In 1924 the London National Gallery acquired Renoir's *La première sortie* of c. 1880 and Seurat's *Baignade* of 1883–4 as first purchases from a fund of £50,000 provided by Mr.

---

[1] For Tchelitchew's subsequent productions with double and triple perspective and his *Phénomènes* of 1935–1938, cf. my footnote on p. 301.   [2] Cf. above, p. 161.

Samuel Courtauld, who bought for his own collection in this decade Seurat's *Jeune femme se poudrant* (1890), Manet's *Le bar aux Folies Bergères* (1881), Cézanne's *Le lac d'Annecy* (1897) and pictures by Renoir, Gauguin and Lautrec. Works by these artists were now sold to Scandinavia, Holland, Switzerland, Germany, Japan, and also of course to museums and collections in France; and—most important of all—scores were sold to museums and collectors in America, so that in 1929, when the New York Museum of Modern Art was founded, the director, Mr. A. H. Barr, was able to arrange an exhibition of a hundred works by Cézanne, Gauguin, Seurat and Van Gogh, nearly all loaned by American collections. This state of affairs also brought about demand for pictures by the living original artists of the twentieth century; for all buyers of works by the original nineteenth-century masters knew quite well that they were paying thousands of pounds or dollars for pictures which French dealers, who had backed those artists in their lifetime, had acquired for nominal sums; and all knew also that a fresh generation of French dealers had since backed a fresh generation of artists who had also proved to be 'winners'. American interest in twentieth-century French artists had been first aroused, as recorded, by the *Armory Exhibition*[1] in 1913; and in the first post-war decade the demand by American and other museums and collectors for pictures by these new 'winners' very rapidly increased. A symptom of the times was the foundation in 1927, as recorded, of the New York University Museum of Living Art for the purpose of collecting paintings by 'living creative and progressive artists'; and other symptoms were the production by French and German publishers of large colour-prints of pictures by nineteenth and twentieth-century French masters, the publication of illustrated monographs on individual artists, and the advent of the art reviews— *L'amour de l'art* and *Cahiers d'art*[2], *Formes* (which began in 1929) and others; for these publications contained appreciations by critics and admirable reproductions which travelled throughout the world. The result was a steady rise in the exchange value of our artists' pictures in the international art trade; and in the nineteen-twenties this exchange value in certain cases rose with such sensational rapidity that many people who had no interest in pictures as works of art began to buy and sell them or take part in such transactions purely as speculations. In cases where the artists were already dead—Modigliani for example—these conditions were, of course, of service only to the dealers and others who possessed the works. But in other cases, where the artists were alive, the artists themselves received much benefit; for firstly, they saw their fame so greatly extended that everyone everywhere, who cared at all for painting, became acquainted with their names and saw reproductions of their pictures; secondly, as they had for the most part fair arrangements with dealers who provided them with annual stipends or acted as their agents, they all made sufficient money for their needs and comforts, while some (the best business men) made considerable fortunes; and thirdly, as these conditions engendered an atmosphere of excitement in artistic circles, the artists were stimulated to continual production and in the case of the best of them to more and more original creative efforts.

Artistic production in Paris in the first post-war decade thus took place in an

---

[1] Cf. above, p. 238.   [2] Cf. above, pp. 296, 309.

93. ROUAULT
Pierrot, c. 1929
New York. C. de Hauke

94. PICASSO
Femme assise tenant un livre, 1932
Paris. Paul Rosenberg

atmosphere of active interest in original art. It also took place in an atmosphere of fête and gaiety. The Montparnasse cafés *Le Dôme* and *La Rotonde* became larger and larger and more and more crowded with cosmopolitan students. Tourists and pleasure seekers had discovered Montparnasse as the centre of artistic Paris and they went there in thousands to find the artists and *la vie de Bohème* as they had formerly gone to Montmartre; rents rose and luxurious studios were constructed; restaurants and 'Dancings', bars and cabarets sprang up; and the Boulevard de Montparnasse at nightfall assumed the appearance of a perpetual Fair illumined in scarlet with neon strips. But as artists soon tire of public gaiety, one by one the creative spirits began to vanish from their sometime haunts; most of the 'arrived' artists moved their homes to the centre of Paris or the country; and the new generation found quiet quarters and other cafés at Montrouge.

Philistines and political enemies of original art have tried (and are still trying) to discredit the 1919–1929 production in Paris by declaring that the artists owed their world-wide fame to a 'boom' in the international art trade. The 'boom' was there as I have just categorically stated. But the artists were there too, creating with amazing fertility and courage. And the first post-war decade must be set down as one of the most productive and significant periods of the seventy-five years which are roughly covered by this book.

But these conditions were about to change; and before 1929 was out our artists entered a period of dark days. Diaghileff died in Venice in the summer of that year and the Parisian artists thus lost a central animator and co-ordinator with real artistic feeling, a genius for discovering creative talent, unbounded courage of his convictions, and great powers as an impresario and showman. And a few months later the artists began to suffer from the 1930–1932 'slump' which the French still refer to with a shudder as '*la crise*'. There were, it is true, redeeming factors in these 'slump' years. The French art reviews continued publication, and the French art dealers continued to organize their exhibitions in order that the artists whose works they were concerned with might remain in the limelight. The Galeries Georges Petit had a large show of works by Dufy in 1930 and a magnificent retrospective *Exposition Picasso* in 1932. Other exhibitions elsewhere kept the artists' fame alive; in 1930 the New York Museum of Modern Art had an exhibition called '*Painting in Paris from American Collections*' where Matisse, Bonnard, Vuillard, Friesz, Dufy, Rouault, Utrillo, Vlaminck, Segonzac and Soutine, Picasso, Braque, Léger, Derain and Marie Laurençin, Chirico, Chagall, Lurçat and Miro were represented; in 1931 the Wadsworth Athenaeum, Hartford, exhibited works by Surrealist and Neo-Surrealist painters, there was an exhibition called '*Abstractions by Picasso*' in the New York Valentine gallery, and the New York Museum of Modern Art had, in February, a large show of works by Lautrec and Odilon Redon, and, in December, a Matisse show with seventy-eight paintings, some sculpture and many drawings and etchings (mainly lent by American collectors); in 1931 also there were other shows in American cities. In London there were exhibitions of works by Picasso and most of the other masters and by Bombois, Bauchant and Vivin in 1931; there was, in 1932, a large historical exhibition of French art (1200–1900) at the Royal Academy which was sponsored by the French Government and contained a number of works by Manet and the Impressionists, and also some by Seurat, Cézanne, Van Gogh, Gauguin and Lautrec. But though the artists' reputations thus grew still further in the 'slump' years the living artists were now deprived, for a period, of material rewards. American museums and rich collectors had ceased to buy pictures by living men and to compete among themselves for expensive works by dead ones; and as results the exchange value of all works of art (including pictures by the 'Old Masters' and by the nineteenth-century French masters) soon became so low that only impoverished owners were disposed to sell; many of the French dealers cancelled as far as might be existing contracts and arrangements with artists and declined to enter into new ones; and artists who had not yet made their fortunes, or had no private incomes, were harassed by financial difficulties bordering in certain cases on distress. But in spite of these conditions the creative figures we are concerned with continued to produce with originality and courage[1].

Thus in 1930 Picasso continued his Neo-Surrealist *Metamorphoses* paintings, with bone organisms and metallic teeth, of the previous year; and in 1931 he made thirty etchings in illustration of Ovid's *Metamorphoses* published by Skira at Lausanne. The etchings, very different in spirit from the *Metamorphoses* paintings, show groups of nude figures drawn in delicate outline recalling certain drawings on Greek vases; some of the figures are drawn in double action, the top part of the body being shown in one attitude and the lower half in another; this procedure can be interpreted as a Neo-Surrealist release of inhibitions, as a variation of Cubist procedure, or as a species of Classical regularizing of a Futurist trick designed to convey a sensation of movement, as when a marble group is slowly rotated on a stand. We find the same device of double action in a series of small loosely painted colourful pictures of recumbent nudes produced by Picasso in this period; but in these paintings he becomes progressively more concerned with formal ends, disintegrating the human forms and then recombining them, synthesized, as related shapes in a design. In some of these paintings with the recumbent nude *motif*, the component parts are locked in a dark outline recalling the leading in stained glass; and Picasso's paintings of 1931 and 1932 also include a number of large compositions designed as flowing patterns in more or less flat and very resonant colours—scarlets, emeralds and cadmium yellows—and contained by 'leaded' outlines of this kind. Picasso as already noted had begun to concern himself with the aesthetic of stained glass windows—(which had inspired Gauguin forty years earlier and had more recently inspired Rouault)—in *Le tapis rouge* of 1924[2]; and in his 1931–1932 pictures which continue this concern he uses sometimes still-life *motifs*, as in *Cruche et compotier*[3] and *Pichet et compotier*[3] of 1931, sometimes a reclining nude *motif* as in a series culminating in the *Nu au fauteuil noir*[4] of 1932 and sometimes other *motifs* as in the *Jeune fille au miroir*[5] and *Femme assise tenant un livre* (Pl. 94) of 1932. In his pictures of these years huge emerald

---

[1] Some exceptional English collectors, Sir Michael Sadler, for example, continued to buy works by original living artists, both French and English, for the sake of the artists, in the 'slump' years; and it may be that some exceptional French and American collectors did the same.

[2] Cf. above, pp. 303, 311.   [3] Paris. Paul Rosenberg.
[4] Paris. Pablo Picasso.   [5] Exhibited London. Paul Rosenberg Gallery, 1937.

95. MATISSE
Odalisque bleue aux anémones, 1936
Exhibited London, Paul Rosenberg Gallery, 1937

96. PICASSO
Guernica 1937

leaves repeatedly appear as important elements in the design. The prolific variety of Picasso's production since 1901 was shown in the London exhibition at the Reid & Lefevre Galleries, called 'Thirty Years of Pablo Picasso', in 1931, and in the retrospective Exposition Picasso at the Galeries Georges Petit in Paris in 1932. The London exhibition contained the Couple et femme et enfant (more generally known as La vie[1]) of 1903 and some thirty-five other pictures typical of the various periods; the Galeries Georges Petit exhibition, a staggering display, contained over two hundred large paintings of all periods, including eighty painted since 1924; it also included a number of etchings and illustrations beginning with the Saltimbanques series of 1903–4 and ending with drawings for Balzac's Le chef d'œuvre inconnu, published by Vollard in 1932.

In 1930 Ozenfant painted his last Purist picture Musique et arts plastiques for the hall of the Berlin house of the Purist-Functional architect Eric Mendelsohn; and he then continued his elemental paintings with fixed symbolic figures, variously disposed, in low relief—La grotte aux baigneuses,[2] Sur la terre comme au ciel and Maternités[2] being the outstanding pictures in this series from 1930–1932. Matisse's works of 1930–1932 include La jeune fille en jaune[3] (a girl seated in a large straw hat and yellow dress against a shuttered window at Nice), a bronze Tête et tiara[3] (recalling Chinese or Japanese Buddhist sculpture in its conventions) and a series of outline etchings for an edition of Mallarmé's poems published by Skira at Lausanne. In 1930 Matisse was invited to act as judge for the Carnegie Exhibition at Pittsburg and he went to the United States after staying for three months at Tahiti on the way. At Merion, Pennsylvania, he visited the Barnes Foundation with its great collection of works by nineteenth and twentieth-century French masters, including scores of paintings by Renoir and over fifty of his own, and he accepted a commission from Dr. Barnes to paint some mural panels for the Foundation. Returning to Nice in 1931 he set to work on these decorations, the subject of which is La danse (like the panel painted for Stchoukin twenty years earlier). In the new La danse, designed to fill three connected round-topped panels, nude dancing figures, approximately nine feet high, in pearl grey monochrome against a rose and black background, are treated in a linear convention recalling paintings on Greek vases. The first version of this decoration, completed in 1931–2, has since been acquired for the Musée d'Art Moderne, quai de Tokio (constructed for the 1937 Exposition). At the end of 1932 Matisse returned to Merion to paint the final version of his decoration on the spot.

Dufy, now in my judgment at the height of his powers, was especially active in these 'slump' years. His 1930 pictures include the Portrait de Mme R. D. (a half-length figure seated at a table against a brilliant blue ground), a number of Normandy landscapes, some river scenes including Le pilote des régates, a set of reclining nudes showing a coloured girl against a flowered background, and a set of pictures painted on an English visit including Hyde Park, Houses of Parliament and Epsom: Le défilé du Derby.[4] In 1931 he worked at Deauville producing among other things a

---

[1] Paris. Etienne Bignou.   [2] New York. Amedée Ozenfant.   [3] Baltimore. Miss Etta Cone.
[4] Dufy's outstanding works from 1930–1936 were exhibited at the Reid & Lefevre Galleries in London in 1936.

number of witty paintings of the race-course; and in 1932 he painted a series of Côte d'Azur scenes more intricate in pattern and resonant in colour than the *Nice* (Pl. 85A) of 1926.

The 'naif' painters Bombois, Bauchant and Vivin also continued their engaging art in 1930–1932. Bombois painted *La rue Saint Vincent* and *Dans le village*[1] in 1930; his London exhibition in 1931 already mentioned contained twenty-three pictures (including *Le pont de chemin de fer, Le lapin agile, Jeunes filles jouant cache-cache,* and *Jeunes filles à la maraude de roses*); his *Sacré-Cœur*[2] was painted in 1932. Bauchant's London exhibition in 1931 had thirty pictures including a number of flower pieces, *L'orage sur la campagne, La rivière, La petite ferme, Le pêcheur* and *Village Charentais,* all painted in 1930. Vivin's London exhibition the same year had twenty-four pictures including *Rameurs, Chasse printanière* and some still-life pieces resembling *Nature morte aux huitres* (Pl. 84A).

The last link with the artists discussed in the earlier sections of this book was broken in this period by the death of Forain at the age of seventy-nine in 1931; the friend of Gilles, Verlaine, Rimbaud, Cézanne, Degas and countless others, he had witnessed all the artistic adventures here recounted; in his last years he had painted mainly court scenes and Bible subjects; and he was influenced to the end by Daumier, Courbet, Manet and Degas.

The Neo-Surrealists were active and continuously in the limelight in these years. In 1930 Breton and Eluard published *L'Immaculée Conception* containing what Mr. Gascoyne describes in *A Short Survey of Surrealism* as 'simulations of various types of mental disease—mental debility, acute mania, general paralysis, delirium of interpretation and dementia praecox'; Salvador Dali wrote and illustrated *La femme visible*; and the title of the Neo-Surrealist review *La Révolution Surréaliste* was changed to *Le Surréalisme au Service de la Révolution,* Breton remaining the editor. Masson and Soupault had now seceded from the movement; Picasso and Miro remained as hitherto independent and detached. The Neo-Surrealists at this period were increasingly preoccupied with a vague addle-pated and vain hope that their activities as writers, painters and amateur psychopaths would be regarded as helpful political gestures by the Russian Communists; they had declared the adherence of their movement to Communism in 1925 as noted,[3] and in 1930 they had communications with the Moscow International Bureau of Revolutionary Literature, and Aragon attended a Kharkov Congress of Revolutionary writers.[4] Meanwhile Dali and Luis Bunuel had devised the second Neo-Surrealist film titled *L'âge d'or* already referred to.[5] This film which is said to have cost 1,200,000 francs was financed by a private gentleman and shown privately at his house in July; it was publicly shown from November 28 to December 3 at the *Studio 28,* where there was also an exhibition of pictures by Dali, Ernst, Ray, Miro, Tanguy and others; on December 3 'commissaires' of the *Ligue des Patriotes* and *La Ligue anti-Juive* interrupted the performance, threw ink at the screen, invaded the exhibition room, cut up the pictures, smashed the furniture and tore up or purloined the reviews

---

[1] Paris. Mme Gregory.   [2] Switzerland. Mme Hostettler.
[3] Cf. above, pp. 283, 284, 307.   [4] Cf. David Gascoyne: *op. cit.,* and J. T. Soby: *After Picasso.*
[5] Cf. above, p. 282.

and books; and a few days later the Censor banned the film amd the police seques-
trated all available copies for destruction. In 1931 Aragon back from Russia published a poem called *Le front rouge* and found himself indicted for 'incitement to
murder' and 'the provoking of insubordination in the army'; Breton and his
associates published protests defending Aragon's right as a poet to write what he
pleased; the prosecution was dropped; and Aragon then seceded from Breton and
his associates who should, he thought, have defended him as a political propagandist and not only on the general principle of free speech.[1] In this year Dali
painted *La persistance de la mémoire*[2] (better known as *The limp watches*) and began the
concoction of the Neo-Surrealist 'objects' which I have discussed in the Introduction;[3] and a Belgian René Magritte began to attract attention as a Neo-Surrealist
painter.[4]

In 1933 *la crise* began to abate and a gradual return to prosperity began. This
process has since been set back, repeatedly, in Europe and America by events and
conditions that are known to everyone. But, nevertheless, from 1933 to 1937
American and other museums and collectors gradually returned as buyers of our
artists' pictures, the exchange values of these pictures gradually recovered in the
international art trade, and the artists again enjoyed more material recompenses
for their labours.

Picasso in these years is once again the outstanding figure; and his works from
1933–1937 are as varied and astonishing and more compelling than ever. His 1933
productions must once more be divided into groups. In one group we have a
number of fantastic real-unreal Neo-Surrealist compositions of various types; one
type develops the Surrealist *plage* motifs of the 1928 *Dinard* series (Pl. 89B), incor-
porating as new material the large rubber animals and parti-coloured balls that
bathers play with; and in one picture of this type these objects come fantastically
to semi-human semi-animal life and fly through the air above a *plage* with cliff and
bathers' cabins representationally depicted; another type shows us flame forms
with human faces turning somersaults or performing tight-rope dances like circus
acrobats and clowns, or twisting and fluttering through the air like bats. In another
group we are given Neo-Surrealist sculpture in viscera forms which assault us with
punning significance. In a third group—in striking contrast to the others—we have
attractive pen-and-wash drawings in a baroque representational style where the
artist has returned to the motif of a youth contemplating a nude sleeping girl—a
motif which had inspired him to romantic watercolours in 1904.[5] And in yet another
group we have a return to the bull-fight motif which had inspired him at intervals
since his earliest youth. This new bull-fight series begins at the point reached in the
1923 *Taureau vainqueur* where the bull was shown with a matador upon his back
and charging a fallen horse.[6] In the first of the new series the bull charges madly into

---

[1] Cf. David Gascoyne: *op. cit.*
[2] New York. Museum of Modern Art.
[3] Cf. above, p. 282.
[4] Magritte's Neo-Surrealistic pictures exhibited since that date include a humorously obscene
and disquieting work titled *The Rape* (a female torso which is also a hideous face), a picture
showing a slice of ham with a human eye in the centre, another showing a pair of feet that grow
upwards into laced-up boots, etc. etc.   [5] Cf. p. 199.   [6] Cf. p. 300.

space and bears upon his back the horse and the matador, who is now half-male and half-female, while other matadors (distorted like the 1923 *Baigneuses* and *Femmes effrayées au bord de la mer* (Pl. 82) flee panic-stricken round the ring. In 1934 we have again a multiple production: Neo-Surrealist sculpture recalling prehistoric carvings where the artist appears to have worked as far as possible in the spirit of primitive prehistoric man; some fantastic Neo-Surrealist 'objects'; a set of classical line etchings and drawings for a translation of Aristophanes' *Lysistrata* (published by the Limited Editions Club, New York); a large etching titled *Minotaur*; a series of large paintings in his 'stained glass' manner with the *Artiste et son modèle* motif and a new motif of a woman or two children writing or drawing at a table; and a long series of new bull-fight paintings and chalk drawings. In the large *Minotaur* etching (which I take to be a symbolic statement of the new orientation of his spirit) we have figures recalling his earlier motifs (the emaciated beggars, the gentle figures of the 'Blue' and 'Pink' period and the serene figures of the 'classical' pictures) confronted by a gigantic Minotaur (the fabulous half-bull half-human monster which fed on human flesh) and a horse bearing a half-male half-female matador. In the 1934 bull-fight pictures we have one group of oil paintings (starting as it were from the point reached by the *Cheval mourant* and *Cheval mourant et spectateurs* of 1923) where dying horses, matadors and bulls are portrayed with progressively affective distortions; another group of paintings where the bull has become the Minotaur; and a third group consisting of drawings in brightly coloured children's chalks, where bull-fight scenes are portrayed in childlike graffiti. In 1935 Picasso applied his 'stained glass' and Neo-Surrealist procedures to a combination of the *Artiste et son modèle* motif with the motif of a woman or two children writing or drawing at a table and the motif of a woman seated on the ground and drawing in front of a picture or a mirror. One group of these 1935 pictures consists of small freely painted oil pictures with the motif of a girl asleep with arms crossed on a table top; others—which are very large—appear to be the classical *La femme de l'artiste écrivant une lettre* of 1923 transformed by the terrible disquietude of his new moods and vibrating with his later use of brilliant colours; and in all these pictures he passes continually, as is now his habit, from abstract to representational passages, from the credible to the incredible, from the 'real' to the 'unreal'. In 1936 Picasso was deeply indignant at General Franco's proceedings in Spain. This indignation was given form in January 1937 when he produced a series of terrific symbolical etchings called *Songe et Mensonge de Franco* accompanied by a burning text; some of these etchings are in the tradition of Goya's *Desastres de la guerra*; others show the bull as the Spirit of Spain snorting fiery defiance at the invader typified by obscene beasts, half-slugs and half-wasps, arrayed in armour and crowned with mitres, making ramshackle gestures of warfare and hollow pretensions to piety. In this mood too Picasso painted *Guernica* (Pl. 96), a passionate protest against Franco's savage bombing of Spanish towns and villages; this huge picture—entirely black and white—occupied one whole wall of the Spanish Government's Pavilion at the Paris 1937 Exposition; and no one who saw it will ever possibly forget it.

Other notable contributors in these years 1933–1937 were Ozenfant, Dufy and

Matisse. In 1931 Ozenfant had started his vast elemental picture *La Vie: (biologique)* which, as already noted, was completed in 1938 and acquired for the Luxembourg Museum.[1] Dufy, continuing his gay and attractive pictures, painted *Le bassin de Deauville, La jetée de Deauville, Deauville: le séchage des voiles, Langres*, and *Portrait de Michel B.* in 1933; *Le Manoir du Vallon: Nogent-sur-Marne, Deauville: le départ des huit metres*, and *Deauville: le bassin des yachts à la tombée du jour* in 1934; further pictures at Deauville, *Baigneuse à Saint-Adresse, L'atelier de l'artiste*, another *Nogent-sur-Marne*, another *Manoir du Vallon* and scenes at Epsom and Ascot in 1935; and *St. James Palace: le relève de la garde* and another series of impressions at Deauville in 1936.[2] Matisse, after completing his decoration at Merion in the summer of 1933, returned to Nice and produced a series of nudes schematically treated in a manner recalling those decorations; but before 1936 was out he had returned to free calligraphic painting with bold patterning. In 1937 some of his pictures, such as *Grande robe bleue, fond noir*, and *Tête ochre* are relatively schematic, and others such as *Odalisque jaune aux anémones, Odalisque bleue aux anémones* (Pl. 95), *Femme aux renoncules* and *Femme à la robe violette et anémones* are as free in calligraphy, as handsomely coloured and audaciously patterned as any painted in his whole career.[3] In these years also Matisse produced a number of large outline pen-and-ink drawings and made etchings and drawings in illustration of Joyce's *Ulysses* published (in 1935) by the Limited Edition Club, New York.

Appreciation of Realist, Impressionist, Aesthetic, Expressionist and Abstract Architectural painting and also of Surrealist (as distinguished from Neo-Surrealist) experiments has steadily grown in the Western democratic countries; and this growth has not been impeded by the well-known fact that when Adolph Hitler became Dictator of Germany in 1933 he imitated Lenin and Stalin and put his taboo on all these forms of art (as aspects of free original thought and incomprehensible by the masses) and ordered the 'discouragement' of all painters practising such art (together with the 'discouragement' of all painters of any kind who were Jews or Liberals or Communists or anti-militarists) and the encouragement of those willing to paint popular descriptive or narrative or nationalist-historical pictures, or popular academic pastiches of fifth-century Greek and Graeco-Roman statues of handsome boys and girls, which would be within the familiar experience of the masses and lead them by the subjects or by easy symbolism to eager appreciation of the Nazi régime.[4]

The established reputations were upheld and new reputations were made in these years by notable exhibitions in Paris, London and the American cities. In 1933 there was a *Renoir Exhibition* with a hundred and twenty-six pictures of all periods in the Musée de l'Orangerie in Paris. In 1934 the New York Museum of

[1] Cf. above, pp. 286, 287 and below, p. 368.

[2] Exhibited as noted (cf. above, p. 319) in London in 1936.

[3] Matisse's outstanding pictures of 1936 to June 1937 were exhibited in Paul Rosenberg's gallery, London, in 1937.

[4] Cf. above, p. 271, cf. also my *French Painting* (Medici, 1931), p. 194, where I have discussed the Napoleonic nationalist propaganda pictures, and the *style troubadour* (later known as the *style moyen-âge*) imposed by the Bourbons in 1816 to stress the idea that the new régime had restored the continuity of French history allegedly interrupted by the Revolution and Napoleon.

Modern Art exhibited the *Bliss Collection*, i.e. the collection of French nineteenth-century pictures and drawings, with paintings by Picasso, Matisse and Modigliani (and the Americans A. B. Davies and Walt Kuhn) bequeathed to the museum by Miss Lillie P. Bliss, a keen supporter of modern French painting since the Armory Exhibition in 1913; and at the end of the year the same museum had a *Fifth Anniversary Exhibition* where pictures lent by American collectors included works by many of our artists. In 1935 the same museum had a *Van Gogh Exhibition*, with sixty-six paintings and as many drawings, which was visited by many thousands of people attracted to it by the works themselves and by the artist's life story, in the form of extracts from his letters, printed in the introduction to the catalogue. In 1936 there was a *Gauguin Exhibition* at the Wildenstein Galleries in New York with fifty pictures (mainly lent from American collections), and the New York Museum of Modern Art had two large exhibitions, *Cubism and Abstract Art* and *Fantastic Art, Dada, and Surrealism*, and also an exhibition titled *Modern painters and sculptors as illustrators*. The Cubist exhibition at the Museum of Modern Art gave an admirable historical conspectus of that movement. The Surrealist exhibition began with an historical section showing various types of fantastic art from Arcimboldo's pictures with double punning meaning and the goblins concocted by Jerome Bosch and Peter Huys to Goya's *Los Caprichos* and drawings by Victor Hugo; it then displayed work by the artists described in this book as Surrealist, Dada and Neo-Surrealist, from Ensor to Chagall and Chirico, and from Klee to Ernst, Miro, Picasso and Dali; and it ended with photographs of fantastic architecture including the Paris Underground Railway stations designed in the 1900 *Art Nouveau* vegetable swirls by Guimard and the famous seaweed balconies by Gaudi in Barcelona. In Paris in 1936 there was a *Cézanne Exhibition* with a hundred and twelve paintings and as many drawings and water-colours in the Musée de l'Orangerie. In London in 1936 there was a large *Exhibition of French Nineteenth Century Painting* arranged by Paul Rosenberg and Alfred Flechtheim under the auspices of the Anglo-French Art and Travel Society, and a *Neo-Surrealist Exhibition* organized by Breton, Eluard, George Hugnet, Man Ray and an English Committee which included Rupert Lee and Herbert Read.

The countless visitors to Paris for the *1937 Exposition* saw the whole story I have told in this book magnificently displayed in a series of exhibitions, some within the actual Exposition, others in galleries hard by. A Retrospective Exhibition (*Chefs d'œuvre de l'art français*) at the Musée d'Art Moderne (quai de Tokio) together with a large *Degas Exhibition* at the Musée de l'Orangerie, and a *Van Gogh Exhibition*, told the story from the 'sixties through Cézanne and Seurat to Gauguin and Toulouse-Lautrec; the Petit Palais in a superbly arranged exhibition titled *Les maîtres de l'art indépendant 1895–1937* continued the story with the twentieth-century adventures from Bonnard and Vuillard and Seurat's followers through Matisse (represented by sixty pictures) and Picasso (inadequately represented by thirty) to Chagall and Chirico in painting, and from Rodin through Maillol to Gargallo and Zadkine in sculpture; the Musée du Jeu de Paume in an exhibition called *Origines et développement de l'art international indépendant* showed more precisely the parts played by the French artists and the Ecole de Paris in the development of non-figurative art, Purism and Functionalism, and some aspects of Dada, Surrealism and Neo-Surrealism; and the Musée de Grenoble arranged in the rue Royale in Paris an exhibition called *Les maîtres populaires de la réalité* with *Le Centenaire de l'Indépendance* (Pl. 34), *Le lion ayant faim* (Pl. 51), and a dozen other pictures by The Douanier Rousseau, and groups of pictures by Bombois, Bauchant, Vivin, and some other unschooled artists (with whom the organizers incongruously grouped Utrillo).[1] Many of our artists also appeared with large mural compositions commissioned from them for the various *palais* of the Exposition. Picasso, as related, painted *Guernica* (Pl. 96) for the Spanish Pavilion; Dufy designed a huge panel *L'histoire de l'électricité* for the Palais de la Lumière; Léger, Lhote and Gromaire produced panels for the Palais de la Découverte and Delaunay panels for the Palais des Chemins de Fer; Zadkine designed a faïence decoration for the Pavillon de la Céramique, and the adventurer of the early 'nineties, Maurice Denis, painted panels for the Théâtre du Trocadéro. A feature of the great exhibition at the Petit Palais was a set of tapestries from designs by Picasso, Matisse, Rouault, Jean Lurçat and others; and there can be no doubt that the freedoms achieved by the Fauve movement and the disciplines imposed by Cubism and Purism have made new achievements possible in this field—and also in the field of stained-glass windows; but it seems unlikely that social conditions in the immediate future will call upon artists for extended service in either of these fields.

As I write in 1938 Bonnard and Vuillard are seventy-one, Matisse is sixty-nine, Rouault is sixty-seven, Vlaminck is sixty-three, Dufy, Picabia and Friesz are fifty-nine, Derain is fifty-eight, Picasso and Léger are fifty-seven, Braque is fifty-six, Utrillo, Metzinger and Severini are fifty-five, Segonzac is fifty-four, Ozenfant is fifty-two, Chagall is fifty-one, Chirico is fifty, Ernst is forty-seven, Lurçat is forty-six, Miro is forty-five, Masson is forty-three, Tchelitchew is forty and Dali is thirty-four. Bauchant is sixty-five, Bombois is fifty-five and Vivin died in 1936 at the age of seventy-seven.

[1] In 1938 a number of the pictures shown in this exhibition and some others were exhibited at Tooth's Galleries in London; and the New York Museum of Modern Art organized with the Musée de Grenoble an exhibition titled *Masters of Popular Painting: Modern Primitives of Europe and America* (cf. above, p. 291).

APPENDICES

APPENDIX I: BIBLIOGRAPHICAL AND CATALOGUE NOTES[1]

EDOUARD MANET (1832-1883)

Manet's life and work are both historically recorded in Paul Jamot et Georges Wildenstein: *Manet*, 2 vols (Paris: Beaux Arts. Van Oest 1932). This splendid book—the only completely satisfactory work on any of our artists—provides a chronology of Manet's life (with references to sources of information), a complete and completely illustrated catalogue of all his paintings and pastels with their history and present distribution, and a bibliography and general index.

For Manet's personality the student should consult Théodore Duret: *Histoire d'Edouard Manet et son œuvre* (Paris, Floury 1902 and later editions) and Moreau-Nélaton: *Manet raconté par lui-même* (Paris, Laurens 1926).

I list some pictures by Manet in the 1905 *Durand-Ruel Impressionist Exhibition at the London Grafton Galleries* in Appendix II.

EDGAR DEGAS (1834-1917)

For information about Degas' work the student should consult the *Illustrated Catalogue of the Degas Exhibition at the Musée de l'Orangerie*, Paris 1937, which contains a bibliography; for his life and work generally—P. A. Lemoisne: *Degas* (Paris, Librairie Centrale 1912); P. Lafond: *Degas*, 2 vols. (Paris, Floury 1918–1919); P. Jamot: *Degas* (Paris Ed.: de la Gazette des Beaux Arts 1924); J. B. Manson: *The life and work of Degas* (London, The Studio 1927), and Robert Rey: *La renaissance du sentiment classique* (Paris, Beaux Arts 1931). For his personality he should consult G. Rivière: *Degas: Bourgeois de Paris* (Paris, Floury 1935), Halévy and Guérin's *Lettres de Degas* (Paris, Grasset 1931), A. Vollard: *Degas* (Paris, Crès 1924), and the articles titled *Degas et ses amis Valpinçon* in *Beaux Arts*, September 1936. For contemporary comments on his works he should read Duranty: *La nouvelle peinture* (Paris, Dentu 1876) which is said to have been largely inspired by Degas himself; and J. K. Huysmans: *L'art moderne* (Paris, Charpentier 1883 and Stock 1902).

There is as yet no complete and completely illustrated catalogue of Degas' numerous paintings and still more numerous pastels and drawings. But I understand that P. A. Lemoisne is now compiling one as a companion volume to Jamot and Wildenstein's

[1] The publications here recommended are selected for their informative content. I have not aimed at recording the innumerable books and articles which are wholly or mainly appreciative comment or art criticism. The pictures chronicled are restricted to those which I have seen or of which I had photographs before me at the time of writing. I have omitted pictures of which the present or recent ownership is unknown to me.

Manet. Degas' etchings and lithographs are listed and reproduced in Delteil: *Le peintre graveur illustré*, Vol. IX (Paris 1919). His exhibits in the Impressionist Exhibitions are listed in Jamot's *Degas*. The wax statue with the real ballet skirt (*Petite danseuse de quatorze ans*) of 1880 and bronze casts of wax and clay figures modelled in the last period are in the Louvre. M. Vollard owns many pastels of the last period.

The following is the present or recent distribution of some paintings and pastels by Degas directly or implicitly referred to in this book:

1855–1871[1]

René de Gas	Northampton, Mass.	Smith College Museum
Portrait de Degas (1855)	Paris	Louvre
Mme Edmond Morbilli (1855)	Paris	Louvre
Mendiante Romaine (1857)	London	Mrs. Chester Beatty
Jeunes Spartiates s'exerçant à la lutte	London	National Gallery, Millbank
Portrait de famille	Paris	Louvre
Tête de jeune femme	Paris	Louvre
La fille de Jephté	Northampton, Mass.	Smith College Museum
Sémiramis élevant les murs de Babylone	Paris	Luxembourg
Les malheurs de la ville d'Orléans	Paris	Luxembourg
Cours de gentlemen: avant le départ	Paris	Louvre
Les courses à Longchamps	Bâle	Baron von Hirsch
Albert Melida (1864)	Bayonne	Musée Bonnat
Léon Bonnat (1863)	Bayonne	Musée Bonnat
Oncle et nièce	Chicago	Mrs. Coburn
Amazone	Paris	Louvre
Portrait de Degas au chapeau à haute forme	Paris	Mlle Fèvre
La femme aux chrysanthèmes (Mme Hertel) (1865)	New York	Metropolitan Museum
Duc et Duchesse de Morbilli	Boston	Museum of Fine Arts
La femme aux mains jointes (Mme Gaujelin)	Boston	Mrs. Gardner
Achille de Gas	New York	Chester Dale
Les deux sœurs (Deux jeunes filles)	Paris	J. Laroche
L'amateur d'estampes	New York	Metropolitan Museum
Joseph Altès, musicien	New York	Metropolitan Museum
Mlle Fiocre dans le ballet de La Source	New York	Metropolitan Museum
L'Orchestre (1868)	Paris	Louvre
Mlle Dihau au piano	Paris	Louvre
Le violoncelliste Pillet	Paris	Louvre
Portrait de De Valernes	Paris	Dr. Viau
Baron Jules Finot	New York	Adolph Lewisohn
Plage (pastel)	Scotland	Private collection
Dunes au bord de la mer	Paris	C. Comiot
Mme Camus en noir	Saint-Germain-en-Laye	Alphonse Kann
Mme Camus en rose	London	H. Coleman

[1] As Degas rarely dated his paintings and pastels the dating of his works is in most cases approximate.

EDGAR DEGAS (1834–1917)

Henri Valpinçon enfant (1870)	Paris	H. Valpinçon
Mlle Valpinçon enfant (1870)	Paris	Georges Wildenstein
Trois Camarades	Paris	M. Jeantaud
Le Grand Rabbin Astruc et le Général Mellinet	Paris	M. Reinach
Mélancolie	Scotland	D. W. T. Cargill

1872–c. 1883

Portraits and Genre Groups

Le guitariste Pagans et le père de l'artiste	Paris	Louvre
Ditto (variant)	Boston	John T. Spaulding
Le bureau de coton (1873)	Pau	Museum
Jeune femme arrangeant un bouquet (1873)	Blouay-Vevey	Dr. Oppenheim
La femme à la potiche (1873)	Paris	Louvre
Bouderie	New York	Metropolitan Museum, (Havemeyer)
Bouderie	Paris	Dr. Viau
A la bourse (c. 1873)	Paris	Louvre
Place de la Concorde : Le Vicomte Lepic et ses enfants (1873–1874)	German	Collection
Portrait de femme	London	National Gallery, Millbank
La dame au miroir (*Mme Jeantaud*)	Paris	Mme Doucet
Femme à la fenêtre	London	Samuel Courtauld
Double portrait	Washington	Robert Woods Bliss
L'homme et le pantin	Paris	M. Gulbenkian
Intérieur (*Le viol*)	Philadelphia	H. P. MacIlhenny
Marcellin Desboutin et le Vicomte Lepic	Paris	Louvre
L'absinthe (1876–7)	Paris	Louvre
Sur la plage	London	National Gallery, Millbank
Un café Boulevard Montmartre (pastel)	Paris	Louvre
Portraits d'amis sur la scène (pastel)	Rhode Island	School of Design
Portrait de famille	Paris	David Weill
Femme assise	London	National Gallery, Millbank
Portraits dans une baignoire à l'Opéra	Washington	Corcoran Gallery of Art (Clark)
Diego Martelli	Edinburgh	National Gallery of Scotland
Duranty (1879)	Scotland	Sir William Burrell
Duranty (pastel)	New York	Adolph Lewisohn
Miss Cassatt au Louvre (pastel)	Paris	M. Exsteens
Miss Cassatt au Louvre	Chicago	W. S. Brewster
Miss Cassatt	Philadelphia	H. P. MacIlhenny
Conversation (pastel)	London	Mrs. Chester Beatty
Conversation (pastel)	German	Collection

Theatre Scenes

Le ballet de Robert le Diable (1872)	London	Victoria and Albert Museum
Ditto (variant)	New York	Metropolitan Museum
Musiciens à l'orchestre	German	Collection

Les figurants	Paris	Louvre
Scène de ballet	New York	Adolph Lewisohn
Aux Ambassadeurs (pastel)	Lyons	Museum
Café Chantant : Les Sisters (pastel)	Washington	Corcoran Gallery of Art (Clark)
Thérésa : 'La chanson du chien'	New York	Horace Havemayer
Danseuse sur la scène (pastel)	Paris	Louvre
Miss Lola au Cirque Fernando	London	National Gallery, Millbank
Deux danseuses sur la scène	London	Samuel Courtauld
Deux danseuses sur la scène	Paris	Mme Olivier Sainsère
Le baisser du rideau (pastel)	Boston	Robert Treat Paine 2nd
Danseuse sur la scène (pastel)	New York	Adolph Lewisohn
La pointe	Formerly London	Mrs. Workman
Danseuse au bouquet saluant sur la scène (pastel)	Paris	Louvre
Danseuse au bouquet (Fin d'arabesque) (pastel)	Paris	Louvre
La loge (pastel)	New York	P. H. Nitze
Danseuses derrière un portant	New York	Mrs. E. Jonas
Danseuse dans sa loge	Winterthur	O. Reinhart
Danseuse dans sa loge	New York	Adolph Lewisohn
Danseuse dans sa loge	New York	Peter B. Frelinghuysen
Chanteuse dans les coulisses	Paris	E. Rouart
Coulisses (pastel)	Washington	Corcoran Gallery of Art (W. A. Clark)
Le ballet de l'Africaine	Paris	Durand-Ruel

Dancers in Training

Le foyer de la danse rue Le Peletier	Paris	Louvre
Classe de danse	Boston	Robert Treat Paine 2nd
Classe de danse	Paris	Louvre
Répétition d'un ballet sur la scène	Paris	Louvre
Ditto (variant in pastel)	New York	Metropolitan Museum
Etude pour L'école de danse	New York	Mrs. C. H. Tweed
Danseuses à la barre	New York	Metropolitan Museum
Danseuses à la barre	New York	C. de Hauke
Le foyer	New York	Metropolitan Museum
Ecole de danse	Washington	Corcoran Gallery of Art (Clark)
La répétition au foyer de la danse	Scotland	Sir William Burrell
Trois danseuses dans une salle d'exercice	Paris	Comtesse de Béhague
Danseuses au foyer (pastel)	Formerly London	Reid and Lefevre
L'attente (pastel)	New York	Metropolitan Museum
Foyer de la danse : Danseuses et leurs mères (pastel)	Scotland	Sir William Burrell
La leçon de danse	California	Mrs. E. Fiske Hammond
Répétition de ballet	Washington	Phillips Memorial Gallery
Répétition	Philadelphia	Joseph Widener
Pendant la leçon de danse (Salle de danse)	New York	Cassatt

EDGAR DEGAS (1834–1917)

Toilet Scenes

La pédicure	Paris	Louvre
Femmes se peignant sur la plage	Formerly Paris	M. Lerolle
Femme nue (vue de dos) assise se coiffant)	Paris	Durand-Ruel
Femme à sa toilette (pastel)	Paris	Georges Wildenstein
Femme au tub	New York	Brooklyn Museum
Femme mettant son corset (pastel)	Paris	C. Comiot
Apres le bain : nu couché (pastel)	Paris	Durand-Ruel

Milliners

Chez la modiste (pastel)	Paris	M. Rouart
Chez la modiste (pastel	New York	Metropolitan Museum
L'essai du chapeau (pastel)	Paris	J. Durand-Ruel
L'essayage chez la modiste (pastel)	Paris	R. G. Gompel
Modiste travaillant (pastel)	New York	Metropolitan Museum
Modistes	New York	Peter B. Frelinghuysen

Laundresses

Repasseuse	New York	Metropolitan Museum
Repasseuses	Paris	Georges Wildenstein
Repasseuses	Paris	Louvre
Ditto (variant)	Paris	Durand-Ruel
Repasseuses	England	Mrs. Pleydell-Bouverie
Les blanchisseuses portant du linge	New York	Howard J. Sachs[1]

Racecourse Scenes

Avant la course (La descente de main)	Paris	M. Lerolle
Avant les courses	New York	Mrs. M. S. Danforth
Chevaux de courses	Boston	Museum of Fine Arts
Voiture aux courses	Boston	Museum of Fine Arts
Devant les tribunes	Paris	Louvre
Aux courses : jockeys amateurs	Paris	Louvre
Aux courses : avant le départ	London	Mrs. Chester Beatty
Jockeys avant la course (gouache)	Scotland	D. W. T. Cargill
Chevaux de courses	Cleveland	Mrs. Ralph King
Le Jockey	Pennsylvania	Museum of Art
Aux courses : le départ	Cambridge, Mass.	Fogg Art Museum
Le départ	New York	J. Hay Whitney

c. 1884—c. 1891

Portraits and Genre Groups

La femme au chien	Oslo	National Gallery
Femme au café	Paris	F. Salabert
Mlle Hélène Rouart	Paris	Mme René Gimpel

[1] This picture, or a variant, was originally owned by M. Coquelin (cadet).

APPENDIX I: BIBLIOGRAPHICAL NOTES

Theatre Scenes

Scène de ballet	Glasgow	Private Collection
La chanteuse verte	New York	Stephen C. Clark
Avant le ballet : danseuses roses	Copenhagen	Ny Carlsberg Museum
Quatre danseuses en bleu	Paris	Dr. A. Charpentier
Pendant le ballet : coin de scène (pastel)	Paris	Dr. Viau
Arlequin (pastel)	Paris	A. S. Henraux
Arlequin : Scène de ballet	Paris	Raymond Fourchy
Pierrot et Colombine	Paris	Dr. E. Mollard
Danseuses se baissant	Paris	M. Cognacq
Danseuses roses (pastel)	Boston	Museum of Fine Arts
Deux danseuses : corsages jaunes (pastel)	London	S. Courtauld

Dancers in Training

Cours de danse : Trois danseuses et violoniste	New York	Frick Collection
Leçon au foyer de la danse à l'opéra (pastel)	Scotland	D. W. T. Cargill
Le foyer de la danse (Green Room) (pastel)	Detroit	Institute of Arts
Répétition au foyer	Paris	Mathieu Goudchaux
Répétition au foyer	Paris	Georges Wildenstein (Formerly New York: Stransky)
Au foyer de la danse (pastel)	Paris	Durand-Ruel
Au foyer de la danse (pastel)	Paris	Dr. Viau
Danseuse tirant son maillot (pastel)	Paris	Mme Olivier Sainsère
Deux danseuses	Paris	Marcel Guérin
Danseuse assise se massant le pied gauche (pastel)	Paris	Louvre
Danseuse aux bas rouges (pastel)	Paris	M. Exsteens
Danseuses aux bas rouges (pastel)	London	Lord Ivor Spencer Churchill
Danseuse debout (pastel)	Paris	M. Exsteens
Danseuse se chaussant (pastel)	Paris	M. Exsteens
Le foyer de la danse	Philadelphia	J. Widener
Danseuses sur une banquette (pastel)	Paris	Dr. Viau
Danseuse rajustant son chausson (pastel)	Paris	R. G. Gompel
Danseuses s'exerçant au foyer	London	National Gallery, Millbank

Toilet Scenes

Après le bain : Nu debout s'épongeant le genou	Paris	Dr. Viau
Femme nue couchée près du tub (pastel)	Paris	M. Lerolle
Femme s'essuyant le cou (pastel)	Paris	Louvre
Femme s'essuyant le cou (pastel)	Paris	Olivier Senn
Femme accroupie dans son tub (pastel)	Paris	Louvre
La sortie de bain (pastel)	New York	Museum of Modern Art (Bliss)
La toilette	New York	Metropolitan Museum
Après le bain : femme s'essuyant les pieds (pastel)	Paris	Louvre

EDGAR DEGAS (1834–1917)

Femme nue accroupie, de dos (pastel)	Paris	Louvre
Femme nue allongée (pastel)	Paris	Dr. E. Mollard
Femme nue se coiffant	Paris	J. Hessel
Servante, et femme sortant du bain (pastel)	Paris	Louvre
Le coucher à la lampe (pastel)	?	?
Femme rousse s'essuyant les reins	Paris	Dr. Viau
Femme nue couchée	London	National Gallery, Millbank
Le bain	Chicago	Art Institute (Potter Palmer)
Femme nue s'épongeant (pastel)	London	Sir Kenneth Clark
Femme dans sa baignoire (pastel)	Paris	Dr. E. Mollard
Femme nue à la baignoire (*peignoir bleu*) (pastel)	Paris	M. Exsteens

Milliners

Vendeuse et chapeaux	Chicago	Art Institute (Coburn)

Racecourse Scenes

Chevaux de courses	New York	Museum of Modern Art (Bliss)

C. 1892—C. 1903

Landscapes

Paysage au champ roux (pastel)	Paris	Durand-Ruel
Paysage à la montagne jaune (pastel)	Paris	Durand-Ruel
Côtes rocheuses (pastel)	Vienna	Musée de Belvédère

Portraits

Portrait d'Henri Rouart (charcoal and pastel)	Paris	E. Rouart

Dancers

Deux danseuses (pastel)	Stockholm	National Museum
Danseuses dans les coulisses	St. Louis	City Art Museum
Danseuses (pastel)	Paris	Etienne Bignou
Danseuses au foyer (pastel)	London	National Gallery, Millbank
Danseuses au foyer	Paris	M. Goudchaux
Danseuse assise (pastel)	Paris	Georges Bernheim
Trois danseuses faisant des pointes (pastel)	Porto Rocco	E. M. Remarque
Classe de danse : six danseuses	Paris	A. Vollard
Deux danseuses entrant en scène (pastel)	Haarlem	F. Koenigs
Danseuses à mi-corps (charcoal and pastel)	Manchester	Whitworth Art Gallery
Deux danseuses à mi-corps rajustant leurs épaulettes (pastel)	Paris	Mme Olivier Sainsère
Deux danseuses à mi-corps (pastel)	Paris	Mme Friedmann
Danseuse à mi-corps rajustant son épaulette (pastel)	Paris	Mme Olivier Sainsère

Trois danseuses à mi-corps dans les coulisses	Cleveland	Museum of Art
Trois danseuses à mi-corps	Toledo	Museum of Art
Quatre danseuses à mi-corps en bleue rajustant leurs épaulettes	Moscow	Museum of Modern Western Art
Danseuses russes (pastel)	Stockholm	National Museum
Danseuses russes (pastel)	Paris	A. Vollard

Toilet Scenes

Nu à la baignoire	Paris	Mme Friedmann
Femme nue s'essuyant	Saint-Germain-en-Laye	Alphonse Kann
Femme sortant du bain	Paris	A. Vollard
Femme se contorsionnant près d'une baignoire	Paris	A. Vollard
Femme s'essuyant (pastel)	London	Lord Ivor Spencer Churchill
Après le tub (pastel)	London	P. M. Turner
Le repos (pastel)	New York	Adolph Lewisohn
Le bain	New York	Metropolitan Museum
Femme s'essuyant le bras (charcoal and pastel)	Paris	Mme Friedmann
Après le bain (pastel)	Paris	R. G. Gompel
La coiffure (pastel)	Paris	M. Nepveu-Degas
La sortie de bain	Paris	Victor Lyon
La sortie de bain	Cambridge, Mass.	Fogg Art Museum
Après le bain : Femme étendue sur un sopha (pastel)	Paris	Dr. Viau
Femme se peignant	Paris	Dr. Viau
Après le bain : Femme nue s'essuyant le cou (pastel)	Paris	Olivier Senn
Après le bain : Femme s'essuyant la jambe (pastel)	Stockholm	National Museum
Femme se coiffant (pastel)	Paris	Paul Rosenberg
Femme nue en se coiffant (charcoal)	Paris	M. Nepveu-Degas
Femme assise par terre se peignant (charcoal and pastel)	Paris	A. S. Hevraux
Femme s'essuyant (*vue de dos*)	Paris	Paul Rosenberg
Femme nue s'essuyant (charcoal and pastel)	Paris	A. Vollard
La toilette (charcoal)	Paris	Louvre
Femme s'essuyant la tête (charcoal)	Paris	Paul Rosenberg
Femme nue s'essuyant (pastel)	Saint-Germain-en-Laye	Alphonse Kann
Femme nue renversée sur le dossier d'une chaise longue (charcoal and pastel)	Paris	C. Comiot
La tasse de chocolat	Paris	M. Nepveu-Degas
La toilette	London	National Gallery, Millbank
La toilette	New York	Pierre Matisse

AUGUSTE RENOIR (1841-1919)

For Renoir's life and personality I recommend A. Vollard: *La vie et l'œuvre de Pierre-Auguste Renoir* (Paris, Vollard, 1919); G. Rivière: *Renoir et ses amis* (Paris, 1921. Bibliothèque d'art et d'archéologie 169.d.4); Albert André: *Renoir* (Paris, Crès, 1919, 1923 and 1928), and Georges Besson: *Renoir* (Paris, Crès, 1932).

There is as yet no complete and completely illustrated catalogue of his very numerous paintings with their history and distribution. The voluminous literature about them is mainly appreciative. Information about many is contained in the *Illustrated Catalogue* (2 vols.) *of the Renoir Exhibition at the Musée de l'Orangerie, Paris, 1933*, which has a bibliography; Meier Graefe: *Renoir* (Leipzig, Klinkhardt and Biermann, 1929); the list of works appended to Barnes and de Mazia: *The Art of Renoir* (New York, Minton Balch, 1935); and, in regard to the later paintings, the *Catalogue of the Maurice Gangnat Sale* (*Paris, Hôtel Drouot, 1925*) and Albert André: *L'atelier de Renoir* (Paris, Bernheim Jeune, 1931).

The following is the present or recent distribution of some pictures by Renoir directly or implicitly referred to in this book.[1]

1863—1883

Genre Figures (indoors)

La femme d'Algers (L'orientale) (1870)	New York	Chester Dale
Parisiennes habillées en Algériennes (1872)	Tokio	Matsukata
La petite danseuse (1874)	Philadelphia	J. Widener
La loge (Sketch) (1874)	Boston	W. Treat Paine 2nd
La loge (1874)	London	Samuel Courtauld
La songeuse (c. 1875)	Paris	Mme G. Menier
Une servante de chez Duval (c. 1875)	New York	Stephen C. Clark
La jeune fille au chat (c. 1876)	Paris	B. E. Levy
La liseuse (c. 1876)	Paris	Louvre
Femme cousant, au bouquet (c. 1876)	Chicago	Mrs. L. Coburn
La couseuse (c. 1876)	Paris	Etienne Bignou
Femme à la robe rayée (1876)	Formerly Paris	Paul Rosenberg
Chez la modiste (c. 1876)	Harvard	Fogg Art Museum
Au théâtre. La première sortie (1876)	London	National Gallery, Millbank
La pensée (1877)	Formerly Paris	Straus
La tasse de chocolat (1877)	Detroit	Edsel B. Ford
La sortie du conservatoire (c. 1877)	Merion	Barnes Foundation
Au cirque (c. 1879)	Chicago	Art Institute
Confidences (1878)	Winterthur	O. Reinhart
Au piano (c. 1879)	Chicago	Mrs. M. A. Ryerson
La fillette au faucon (1880)	Paris	Durand-Ruel

[1] The largest and most representative collection of Renoir's paintings of all periods is that in the Barnes Foundation, Merion; but as most of the works in that collection are listed and illustrated in Barnes and de Mazia's book referred to above, I have only included such Barnes Foundation pictures as appear to me of special significance.

Au concert (dans la loge) (1880)	U.S.A.	Private Collection
Jeune fille lisant (1880)	Paris	Dr. Viau
Femme à l'éventail (c. 1881)	Paris	J. Laroche
Mère et enfant (1881)	Merion	Barnes Foundation
Enfant en blanc (1883)	Chicago	Art Institute
La danse à la campagne (1883)	Boston	Museum of Fine Arts
La danse à la ville (1883)	Paris	Durand-Ruel

Genre Figures (outdoors)

Soirée d'été (half length) (c. 1868)	German	Collection
L'hiver au bois de Boulogne (1868)	Bâle	Baron R. von Hirsch
La barque (c. 1867)	Paris	E. Esmond
Lise (1867)	German	Collection
La Grenouillère (c. 1869)	Moscow	Museum of Modern Western Art
La Grenouillère (c. 1869)	Winterthur	O. Reinhart
Femme cueillant des fleurs (1872)	U.S.A.	Collection
L'amazone (1873)	Paris	Baron Gourgaud
L'allée cavalière au Bois de Boulogne (1873)	German	Collection
Les canotiers à Chatou (1872)	New York	Adolph Lewisohn
La serre (c. 1874)	Scotland	D. W. T. Cargill
La promenade (1874)	Paris	Paul Rosenberg
La source (c. 1875)	Merion	Barnes Foundation
Le Moulin de la Galette (1876)	Paris	Louvre
Le Moulin de la Galette (1876)	New York	J. H. Whitley
La balançoire (1876)	Paris	Louvre
Petite fille à l'arrosoir (1876)	New York	Chester Dale
La dame à la voilette (c. 1877)	Paris	Louvre
Le printemps au jardin (c. 1878)	Formerly Paris	Bernheim Jeune
La fin du déjeuner (1879)	German	Collection
Jeune femme à la Grenouillère (1879)	Paris	David Weill
La bûcheronne (1879)	Paris	Bernheim Jeune
Dejeuner des canotiers (three figures) (c. 1879)	Chicago	Art Institute
Cueillant des fleurs (c. 1879)	Chicago	Art Institute (Coburn)
La fête de Pan (1879)	Paris	Mme Alfred Bérard
La provende des poules (1879)	Paris	Baron R. de Rothschild
Pêcheuses de moules a Berneval (1879)	Paris	Durand-Ruel
Les vendangeurs (1879)	New York	Adolph Lewisohn
Les Grands Boulevards (c. 1880)	Formerly Paris	Bernheim Jeune
La Place Pigalle (c. 1880)	London	S. Courtauld
Les parapluies (c. 1880)	London	National Gallery
Sur la terrasse (1881)	Chicago	Art Institute (Ryerson)
Déjeuner des canotiers (1881)	Washington	Phillips Memorial Collection
Jeunes filles en noir (c. 1882)	Moscow	Museum of Modern Western Art
La promenade (c. 1882)	Formerly London	H. Coleman
Femme assise au jardin (1882)	Formerly Paris	Bernheim Jeune

AUGUSTE RENOIR (1841–1919)

Landscapes

Paysage de neige (c. 1868)	Orrouy	Count Doria
Chalands sur la Seine (1869)	Paris	Louvre
Le poirier d' Angleterre (c. 1869)	Paris	M. Fauchier-Delavigne
Le pont neuf (1872)	Cleveland	Ralph M. Coe
Chemin montant dans les hautes herbes (c. 1875)	Paris	Louvre
Le coup de vent (c. 1877)	Seaford	F. Hindley Smith
La barque à Argenteuil (1877)	Paris	J. Laroche
Paysages de printemps (1877)	Paris	Durand-Ruel
Pourville (1878)	Merion	Barnes Foundation
Les rosiers à Wargemont (1879)	Paris	Baron R. de Rothschild
Paysage à Wargemont (1879)	Oslo	W. Halvorsen
Capodimonte-Sorrento (1881)	Paris	Durand-Ruel
Naples (1881)	Paris	E. Bérard
Venise. Gondole sur le Grand Canal (1881)	Boston	Museum of Fine Arts
Le pont de chemin de fer à Chatou (1881)	Paris	Louvre
Brouillard à Guernesey (c. 1882)	New York	Museum of Modern Art
Guernesey (c. 1882)	Washington	Private Collection
Guernesey (c. 1882)	Winterthur	Dr. Hahnloser
Scène de plage à Guernesey (c. 1882)	Merion	Barnes Foundation

Portraits

Petite fille (Mlle Romaine Lancaux) (1864)	Paris	Mme Barret-Decap
Portrait de Bazille (c. 1866)	Paris	Louvre
Le cabaret de la mère Anthony (c. 1866)	Stockholm	National Museum
Portrait de Sisley (1868)	Paris	Mme C. Pomaret
Le ménage Sisley (1868)	German	Collection
Le capitaine Darras (1871)	German	Collection
Mme Darras (1871)	New York	Adolph Lewisohn
Mme Maître (1871)	Paris	M. Lecomte
Mme Maître (1871)	Northampton, Mass.	Smith College
La famille Henriot (1871)	Paris	Etienne Bignou
M. Lecœur (c. 1872)	Paris	A. Dorville
Mme Lecœur (c. 1872)	Paris	A. Dorville
Claude Monet (1872)	New York	A. Sachs
Mme Monet étendue sur un sofa (c. 1872)	Giverny	Michel Monet
Portrait de l' artiste (1872)	Paris	Wildenstein
Nini au jardin	London	Captain Molyneux
Mme Hartmann (1874)	Paris	Louvre
La fillette attentive (Mlle Legrand) (1875)	Paris	Bernheim Jeune
Claude Monet (à la palette) (1875)	Paris	Louvre
Mme Monet et son fils au jardin (1874)	Giverny	Michel Monet
Claude Monet peignant au jardin (c. 1874)	New York	Charles Corliss
Portrait de l' artiste (c. 1875)	Paris	H. Bernstein
Mme Choquet devant un tableau de Delacroix (1875)	Oslo	W. Halvorsen
Portrait de Choquet (1875)	Winterthur	O. Reinhart
Mme Henriot en travesti (1875)	New York	Stephen C. Clark

Mme Choquet lisant à la fenêtre (c. 1876)	New York	Mrs. E. Jonas
Mlle Jeanne Durand-Ruel (1876)	Paris	Mme A. F. Aude
Le baron Barbier (1877)	Paris	J. Seligmann
Mme Charpentier et ses enfants (1878)	New York	Metropolitan Museum
Mlle Jeanne Samary (c. 1877)	Moscow	Museum of Modern Western Art
Mlle Jeanne Samary (1877)	Paris	Comédie Française
Mme Charpentier (c. 1878)	Paris	Louvre
Mlle Charpentier assise (c. 1878)	Paris	M. E. Tournon
Mlle Thérèse Bérard (1879)	New York	Stephen C. Clark
Mlle Irène Cahen d'Anvers (1880)	Paris	L. Reinach
Mlle Grimpel au ruban bleu (1880)	Paris	H. J. Laroche
Mlle Grimpel au ruban rouge (1880)	Paris	H. J. Laroche
Paul Cézanne (pastel) (c. 1880)	Chicago	Art Institute
M. Fournaise (1880–1881)	Paris	M. Fournaise
Portrait de Wagner (1882)	Paris	Alfred Cortot
Portrait de Wagner (c. 1883)	Paris	Musée de l'Opéra
Mme Caillebotte et son chien (1883)	Paris	Georges Wildenstein
Au bord de la mer, femme assise (1883)	New York	Metropolitan Museum of Art
Mme Clapisson (1883)	Chicago	Art Institute (Ryerson)

Nudes

Diane chasseresse (c. 1866)	New York	Private Collection
Le garçon au chat (1868)	German	Collection
Baigneuse au griffon (1870)	German	Collection
La rose (half-nude) (c. 1872)	Paris	Louvre
Torse (c. 1875)	Merion	Barnes Foundation
Anna : la boucle d'oreille (1876)	Moscow	Museum of Modern Western Art
Femme nue assise (c. 1880)	Paris	Musée Rodin
La baigneuse blonde (1881–2)	London	Sir Kenneth Clark
La baigneuse blonde (1881–2)	U.S.A.	Private collection

1884–1891

Genre Figures (indoors)

Buste de jeune fille (fond bleu) (1884)	Paris	H. Bernstein
La natte (1887)	Baden, Switzerland	Sydney Brown
L'enfant au chat (Mlle Manet) (1888)	Paris	Mme E. Rouart
La coiffure (1888)	Paris	Durand-Ruel
Jeune fille lisant (c. 1890)	Paris	G. Viau

Genre Figures (outdoors)

Vendange : le repos (c. 1884)	Merion	Barnes Foundation
Le retour des champs (c. 1885)	London	Reid & Lefevre
Le parti de volant (1886)	Minneapolis	Institute of Art
Femme allaitant son enfant (c. 1886)	London	Mrs. Chester Beatty

AUGUSTE RENOIR (1841–1919)

Femme allaitant son enfant (c. 1886)	New Orleans	Hunt Henderson
Femme allaitant son enfant (c. 1886)	Paris	Philippe Gangnat
Blanchisseuse et enfant (c. 1886)	Merion	Barnes Foundation
Blanchisseuse et enfant (c. 1886)	Cleveland	F. H. Ginn
Les deux sœurs (c. 1890)	Cleveland	F. H. Ginn
Les chapeaux d'été (c. 1890)	Chicago	Art Institute (Ryerson)
La vendeuse de poissons (c. 1890)	Merion	Barnes Foundation
La vendeuse d'oranges (c. 1890)	Merion	Barnes Foundation
La femme au chapeau blanc (c. 1890)	Paris	Mme Jacques Balsan
La vendeuse de pommes (c. 1891)	Merion	Barnes Foundation
La vendeuse de pommes (c. 1891)	Paris	J. Seligmann

Landscapes

Paysage : Le pont (c. 1885)	Paris	G. Wildenstein (formerly New York, Stransky)
Le jardin de l'artiste (1887)	Paris	Durand-Ruel
Bougival (1888)	Paris	Durand-Ruel
Argenteuil : le bateau rouge (1888)	Merion	Barnes Foundation
Paysage : Le moissonneur (1888)	Merion	Barnes Foundation
La montagne Sainte Victoire (1889)	Merion	Barnes Foundation

Portraits

Les enfants à Wargemont (1884)	German	Collection
Mlle Lucie Bérard (1884)	Paris	Maurice Bérard
Mlle Chapuis au cerceau (1885)	New York	Private Collection
La dame à l'éventail (1886)	Merion	Barnes Foundation
Les filles de Catulle Mendès (1888)	Paris	Georges Wildenstein

Nudes

Baigneuse se coiffant (de dos) (1885)	Paris	Durand-Ruel
Baigneuse assise (1885)	Paris	Mme Balsan
Les grandes baigneuses (1885–7)	Philadelphia	C. S. Tyson
Nue assise dans un paysage (1890)	Baden, Switzerland	Sydney Brown
Caryatides (panneaux décoratifs) (1890)	Paris	A. Vollard
Le bain (c. 1890)	Paris	Mme Boivin
Femme à sa toilette, assise sur un fauteuil rouge (c. 1890)	Paris	Durand-Ruel
Nu dans l'eau (c. 1891)	London	National Gallery, Millbank
Nu dans l'eau (c. 1891)	Cleveland	Ralph M. Coe
Baigneuse au bracelet assise près d'une rivière (1891)	Paris	Durand-Ruel
Baigneuse endormie (c. 1891)	Winterthur	O. Reinhart

1892—1903

Genre Figures (indoors)

Deux jeunes filles au piano (c. 1892)	Paris	Louvre

Deux jeunes filles au piano (c. 1892)	Paris	Durand-Ruel
Deux jeunes filles au piano (c. 1892)	Paris	Mme Paul Guillaume
Deux jeunes filles au piano (c. 1892)	New York	Adolph Lewisohn
Le journal et le dejeuner (*Bonne, enfant et jeune homme*) (c. 1892)	Paris	Etienne Bignou
La bergère (*La Bohémienne*) (c. 1902)	Paris	Bernheim Jeune

Genre Figures (outdoors)

Le guitariste (c. 1896)	London	Reid & Lefevre
Deux jeunes filles au pré (c. 1894)	New York	Adolph Lewisohn
Paysage de Cagnes avec personnages (1895)	Paris	A. Bellier
Femme assise dans l'herbe (c. 1895)	Formerly Paris	Maurice Gangnat
Femme et enfant au parc (1903)	Paris	Philippe Gangnat

Portraits

Mme Renoir au peignoir (1892)	Philadelphia	Mullen Collection
Les deux sœurs (c. 1892)	Paris	Josse Hessel
La famille de l'artiste (1896)	Merion	Barnes Foundation
Berthe Morisot et sa fille	Paris	E. Rouart

Landscapes

Près de Pont Aven (c. 1892)	London	Reid & Lefevre
Noirmoutiers (1892)	Merion	Barnes Foundation
La ferme de Magagnosc (1893)	Paris	G. Bernheim de Villers
Le picnic (c. 1893)	Merion	Barnes Foundation
Village d'Essoyes (c. 1894)	London	Reid & Lefevre
Le bois de la Chaise à Noirmoutiers (1897)	Formerly Paris	Maurice Gangnat
Paysage à Antibes (1900)	London	Mrs. Chester Beatty
Le Cannet (1901)	Formerly Paris	Maurice Gangnat
Le jardin à Cagnes (c. 1902)	Paris	Josse Hessel
Le pont (c. 1902)	Formerly Paris	Maurice Gangnat

Nudes

Baigneuse assise (*rochers*) (c. 1892)	Paris	Durand-Ruel
Jeune fille nue sur un canapé (c. 1897)	Paris	Josse Hessel
Baigneuses au crabe (c. 1897)	Paris	Josse Hessel
Baigneuse assise lisant (1900)	Paris	Dr. Viau
Nu couché dans un paysage (1900)	Formerly Paris	Maurice Gangnat
Baigneuse debout se coiffant (c. 1895)	London	Reid & Lefevre
La toilette de la baigneuse (c. 1896)	Paris	Bernheim Jeune
Baigneuse couchée (c. 1897)	Merion	Barnes Foundation
Sept baigneuses dans un forêt (c. 1897)	Merion	Barnes Foundation
Femme nue endormie (*torse*) (1897)	Winterthur	O. Reinhart
Nu couché dans un paysage (1900)	Formerly Paris	Maurice Gangnat
La baigneuse brune (*Gabrielle s'essuyant*) (c. 1903)	London	Reid & Lefevre

AUGUSTE RENOIR (1841–1919)

1904–1919

Genre Figures (indoors)

Le bébé à la cuillère (c. 1904)	Paris	Philippe Gangnat
Tête de Coco en bleu (1904)	Paris	Philippe Gangnat
L'enfant au chapeau de paille (c. 1904)	Paris	Louvre
L'enfant jouant (Coco et les briques) (1904)	Formerly Paris	Maurice Gangnat
Le pierrot blanc (1905)	Paris	Mme Paul Guillaume
Femme au chapeau fleuri (c. 1905)	London	Reid & Lefevre
Coco (c. 1905)	Cambridge	Lord Rothschild
Coco dessinant (c. 1905)	New York	Stephen C. Clark
Coco écrivant (1905)	Paris	Philippe Gangnat
Garçon écrivant (1905)	Manchester	Sir Thomas Barlow
La frivolité (1906)	Formerly Paris	Maurice Gangnat
Tête de Gabrielle en blanc (1907)	Formerly Paris	Maurice Gangnat
Jeune fille assise (c. 1909)	Paris	Louvre
Femme lisant (1909)	Formerly Paris	Maurice Gangnat
La liseuse rouge (1909)	Formerly Paris	Maurice Gangnat
Femme en bleu (1909)	Formerly Paris	Maurice Gangnat
La danseuse au tambourin (1909)	Paris	Philippe Gangnat
La danseuse aux castagnettes (1909)	Paris	Philippe Gangnat
Femme se coiffant (1909)	Formerly Paris	Maurice Gangnat
Maria au repos (c. 1910)	Formerly Paris	Maurice Gangnat
Coco dessinant (1910)	Paris	Philippe Gangnat
Les femmes aux chapeaux (1910)	Paris	Philippe Gangnat
Gabrielle à la rose (c. 1910)	Paris	Louvre
Gabrielle au miroir (1910)	Paris	Bernheim Jeune
Gabrielle au chapeau (vase bleu) (1911)	Paris	Pierre Wertheimer
Gabrielle aux bijoux (c. 1912)	Paris	Mme Paul Guillaume
Tête de Gabrielle (1913)	Paris	Mme Paul Guillaume
Femme au corsage rouge (1914)	Formerly Paris	Maurice Gangnat
Jeune fille en bleu (1914)	Formerly Paris	Maurice Gangnat
La femme en bleu (1914)	Paris	Philippe Gangnat
Femme au corsage rose (1915)	Formerly Paris	Maurice Gangnat
La liseuse rose (1915)	Paris	Philippe Gangnat
Tête de jeune fille en mauve (1915)	Paris	Philippe Gangnat
Buste de Madeleine en chemise (1915)	Formerly Paris	Maurice Gangnat
Tête de jeune fille en rose (1916)	Paris	Philippe Gangnat
Odalisque assise (c. 1916)	Merion	Barnes Foundation
La liseuse blanche (1916)	Paris	Philippe Gangnat
Femme nouant son soulier (c. 1916 pl. (F))	London	S. Courtauld
Gabrielle au mains croisées (c. 1917)	Paris	Mme Paul Guillaume
La femme au bouquet (1917)	Paris	Philippe Gangnat
Odalisque couchée (c. 1917)	Merion	Barnes Foundation
Jeune fille à la rose (c. 1917)	London	Reid & Lefevre
Odalisque debout (c. 1918)	Merion	Barnes Foundation
Le concert (1919)	Paris	Claude Renoir

Genre Figures (outdoors)

Paysans (homme et femme) au repos (1907)	London	Miss G. Davies

Deux jeunes filles aux chapeaux (c. 1910)	Merion	Barnes Foundation
L'heure du thé (1911)	Merion	Barnes Foundation
Femme couchée (1912)	Paris	Philippe Gangnat
Femme au jupon rayé s'essuyant les pieds (1913)	Formerly Paris	Maurice Gangnat
Femme accroupie (1913)	Paris	Philippe Gangnat
Les grandes laveuses (1913)	Paris	Paul Rosenberg
Deux laveuses (1913)	Paris	Philippe Gangnat
Femme marchant dans l'herbe (c. 1913)	Paris	Philippe Gangnat
Jeune fille assise dans un paysage (c. 1914)	Merion	Barnes Foundation
La faneuse (1915)	Paris	Philippe Gangnat
Glaneuses (c. 1916)	Merion	Barnes Foundation
Paysage avec figures (c. 1917)	London	Paul Maze
Femme et chien dans un paysage (1917)	Formerly Paris	Maurice Gangnat
Femme allaitant son enfant (c. 1918)	Paris	Georges Keller

Portraits

Jacques Fray, enfant (1904)	Paris	Mme Val
Ambroise Vollard avec statuette (1908)	London	S. Courtauld
Portrait de l'artiste au chapeau blanc (1910)	Paris	Durand-Ruel
Mlle Colonna Romano (1913)	Paris	Louvre
Mme Tilla Durieux (1914)	New York	Stephen C. Clark
Maurice Gangnat (1916)	Paris	Philippe Gangnat
Ambroise Vollard en toreador (1917)	Paris	A. Vollard

Nudes

La grande baigneuse aux jambes croisées (1903–6)	Paris	Josse Hessel
La grande baigneuse aux jambes croisées (1903–6)	Paris	J. Laroche
Baigneuses au crabe (1904)	Cleveland, Ohio	Ralph M. Coe
Baigneuses au crabe (1905)	Paris	Josse Hessel
Nu sur un fauteuil (1905)	Formerly Paris	Maurice Gangnat
Baigneuse assise (1905)	Formerly Paris	Maurice Gangnat
Ode aux fleurs d'Anacréon (1908)	Paris	Théophile Bader
Le lever de Gabrielle (c. 1909)	Merion	Barnes Foundation
Baigneuse blessée (1909)	Paris	Mlle D. de la Meurthe
Buste de nu (c. 1909)	Merion	Barnes Foundation
Femme nue couchée (de dos) (c. 1909)	Paris	M. Charpentier
Après le bain (1910)	Merion	Barnes Foundation
Caryatides (c. 1910)	Merion	Barnes Foundation
La source (c. 1910)	Paris	Renou et Colle
Psyche (c. 1911)	Merion	Barnes Foundation
Nu : (de dos) (c. 1911)	Merion	Barnes Foundation
Baigneuse s'essuyant (1912)	Formerly Paris	Maurice Gangnat
Nu assis (de dos) (c. 1914)	Formerly Paris	Elie Faure
Le jugement de Paris (1914)	Paris	Renou et Colle
Nu à la méridienne (c. 1916)	London	Reid & Lefevre
Sept baigneuses (1916)	Merion	Barnes Foundation
Baigneuse s'essuyant (c. 1916)	Paris	Mme Paul Guillaume

La tasse de thé (1918)	Saint-Germain-en-Laye	Alphonse Kann
Six baigneuses (1918)	Merion	Barnes Foundation
Cinq baigneuses (1918)	Merion	Barnes Foundation
Baigneuses (*Les Nymphes*) (c. 1918)	Paris	Louvre

Landscapes

Antibes (1904)	Formerly Paris	Maurice Gangnat
L'église à Cagnes (1904)	Paris	Durand-Ruel
Vue de la poste à Cagnes (1906)	Formerly Paris	Maurice Gangnat
Vue de la poste (1907)	Paris	Philippe Gangnat
Le jardin de roses (1907)	Formerly Paris	Maurice Gangnat
L'arbousier (1908)	Formerly Paris	Maurice Gangnat
Les néfliers (1908)	Formerly Paris	Maurice Gangnat
Les néfliers (1908)	Paris	Philippe Gangnat
La terrasse (1908)	Formerly Paris	Maurice Gangnat
Les vignes (1908)	Formerly Paris	Maurice Gangnat
Jardin du peintre à Essoyes (1909)	Formerly Paris	Maurice Gangnat
Jardin des Collettes (1909)	Paris	Philippe Gangnat
Les oliviers de Cagnes (1909)	Formerly Paris	Maurice Gangnat
L'aloès (1910)	Formerly Paris	Maurice Gangnat
La mer à Cagnes (1910)	Formerly Paris	Maurice Gangnat
Les orangers (1910)	Formerly Paris	Maurice Gangnat
La ferme des Collettes (1910)	Paris	Philippe Gangnat
Les Collettes (1910)	Paris	Renou et Colle
Femme et enfant assis dans un paysage (c. 1911)	Merion	Barnes Foundation
L'arbre près de la ferme (1912)	Paris	Philippe Gangnat
Paysage bleu (1915)	Paris	Philippe Gangnat
Antibes (c. 1916)	Merion	Barnes Foundation
Vue aux environs d'Antibes (c. 1916)	London	Reid & Lefevre
Le grand arbre (1916)	Paris	Philippe Gangnat
Femme et chien dans un paysage (1917)	Merion	Barnes Foundation
Au jardin (c. 1918)	Merion	Barnes Foundation

N.B.—Renoir painted still-life studies of flowers and fruit all through his career. In his later years these studies are especially numerous—roses and anemones being the favourite flowers and strawberries among the favourite fruits. M. Philippe Gangnat has some good examples inherited from his father's collection.

PAUL CÉZANNE (1839-1906)

For Cézanne's life and personality the most informative book is Gerstle Mack: *Paul Cézanne* (London, Cape, 1936). But the student should also read A. Vollard: *Paul Cézanne* (Paris, Vollard, 1914), Georges Rivière: *Le maître Paul Cézanne* (Paris, Floury, 1923), Emile Bernard's articles in *L'Occident* (Paris, July 1904) and *Le Mercure de France* (Paris, December 1908, March 1920, June 1921), Emile Bernard: *Sur Paul Cézanne* (Paris, Michel 1925), Leo Larguier: *Le dimanche avec Paul Cézanne* (Paris, L'édition 1925 or 1926) which incorporates Charles Camoin's article published in *L'Amour de l'Art* (Paris, January 1921); Joachim Gasquet's article *Cézanne à l'atelier* in *L'Amour de l'art* (Paris, January 1921); and Gasquet: *Paul Cézanne* (Paris, Bernheim Jeune, 1921).

For information about Cézanne's works the most useful book is Lionello Venturi: *Cézanne*, 2 vols. (Paris, Paul Rosenberg, 1936). This is an almost complete catalogue listing and reproducing over a thousand paintings and over five hundred water colours, etc., with their history and distribution.

The literature on Cézanne, mainly appreciative comment and art criticism, is very voluminous. The bibliography in Venturi's book records about a thousand books, articles and exhibition catalogues. The student will find an abridged bibliography, chronologically arranged, in the *Catalogue of the Cézanne Exhibition in the Musée de l'Orangerie*, Paris, 1936. There is also a short bibliography in Mack's book.

The present or recent distribution of all the pictures by Cézanne referred to in my text is recorded in Venturi's catalogue; and I have followed Venturi's dating, though as Cézanne rarely dated his pictures, Venturi's dating is in most cases only approximate and in many cases purely conjectural.

I have compiled the following lists to show the present or recent distribution of some pictures by Cézanne exhibited in his lifetime.

Present distribution of some pictures by Cézanne in Vollard's 1895 Exhibition:

L'Orgie (1868)	Paris	M. Lecomte
Mme Cézanne. Buste en robe rayée (1877)	New York	Mrs. Sullivan
Portrait de l'artiste (1880)	Moscow	Museum of Modern Western Art
La campagne d'Auvers (1880)	Paris	M. Laroche
Louis Guillaume (1880)	New York	Chester Dale
Saint Henri, L'Estaque (1883)	Philadelphia	C. S. Tyson
Baigneuses devant la tente (1885)	Oslo	W. Halvorsen
La lutte (1885)	New York	Marie Harriman Gallery
Léda au cygne (1886)	Paris	J. V. Pellerin
Gardanne (1886)	New York	Dr. Hirschland
Baigneuses (1887)	New York	Mrs. F. Jonas
La maison abandonnée (1887 or 1892)	Cleveland	Ralph C. Coe
Le pont sur la Marne (1888)	Moscow	Museum of Modern Western Art
Allée à Chantilly (1888)	German	Collection[1]
Le Jas de Bouffon (1887)	German	Collection
Mme Cézanne dans la serre (1890)	New York	Stephen C. Clark
Cézanne au chapeau mou (1892)	Paris	J. V. Pellerin
Le grand pin (1892–4)	German	Collection
La corbeille de pommes	Chicago	Art Institute (Birch Bartlett)
Le garçon au gilet rouge (1890–1895)	Lausanne	Dr. Reber
Jeune fille à la poupée (1892–1896)	Saint-Germain-en-Laye	Alphonse Kann
Sous bois (1882 or 1894)	New York	Dr. Bakwin
Mme Cézanne (1894–95)	Merion	Barnes Foundation

Present or recent distribution of some pictures by Cézanne in the *Salon d'Automne* Exhibition in 1904.

Paysage: Pontoise (1873–75)	Baden	Sidney Brown
Maison à Auvers (1873–75)	Paris	Lecomte

1 Another version of this picture now belongs to Mrs. Chester Beatty, London.

PAUL CÉZANNE (1839–1906)

Petites maisons à Auvers (1873–74)	Cambridge, Mass.	Fogg Art Museum
Portrait de Cézanne (c. 1877)	Washington	Phillips Memorial Gallery
Portrait de Cézanne (c. 1879–82)	London	Lord Ivor Spencer Churchill
Portrait de Choquet (1879–82)	New York	Museum of Modern Art (Bliss)
La dame à l'éventail (1879–82)	Paris	Gertrude Stein
Plateau de la montagne Sainte Victoire (1882–85)	Moscow	Museum of Modern Western Art
L'aqueduc (1885–87)	Moscow	Museum of Modern Western Art
Mardi Gras (1888)	Moscow	Museum of Modern Western Art
Trois baigneuses (1879–82)	Nice	Henri Matisse
Baigneurs (1879–1882)	Paris	M. Lecomte
Le vase bleu (1883–87)	Paris	Louvre
Mme Cézanne (1885–87)	Detroit	Tannahill
Baigneurs (1883–87)	London	Lord Ivor Spencer Churchill
Baigneurs (1892–94)	Paris	Baron Gourgaud
L'Estaque et le Golfe de Marseille (1882–85)	German	Collection
Vase de tulipes (1890–94)	London	Mrs. Chester Beatty
Le pilon du roi (1890–1894)	Winterthur	O. Reinhart
La maison abandonnée (1890–94)	Cleveland	Ralph M. Coe
Fumeur accoudée (1895–1900)	Moscow	Museum of Modern Western Art
L'homme aux bras croisés (1895–1900)	German	Collection

The following pictures were in the *Salon d'Automne* in 1905:

Le vase rococo (1875–77)	New York	Chester Dale
Baigneurs au repos (1875)	Merion	Barnes Foundation
La moisson (1875–76)	Paris	G. Bernheim de Villers

N.B.—I give in Appendix II the present distribution of some pictures by Cézanne in the Durand-Ruel *Exhibition of French Impressionist Pictures* in London in 1905

The following were among the pictures in the Cézanne Memorial Exhibition at the *Salon d'Automne* in 1907:

La pendule noire (1869–71)	Hollywood	Edward G. Robinson (Formerly Emile Zola)
L'avocat (L'oncle Dominique (1865–67)	Paris	M. Lecomte
Achille Emperaire (1867–70)	Paris	M. Lecomte
La promenade (c. 1870)	Paris	P. Cézanne, fils
Une lecture chez Zola (1869–70)	Paris	J. V. Pellerin
L'éternel féminin (1875–77)	Paris	J. V. Pellerin
Tentation de St. Antoine (1873–75)	Paris	J. V. Pellerin
Portrait de l'artiste (1873–76)	Paris	M. Lecomte
Jeune paysanne (1873–77)	Paris	M. Laroche (originally Pissarro ; then Mirbeau)
Femme à la fourrure (Souvenir du Greco) (1879–82)	Paris	J. V. Pellerin

Le grand pin et les terres rouges (1885–87)	Paris	M. Lecomte
Léda au cygne (1886-90)	Paris	J. V. Pellerin
Arlequin (1888–90)	London	Lord Rothschild
Les joueurs de cartes (1890–92)	Paris	J. V. Pellerin
Mme Cézanne au fauteuil jaune (1890–94)	Paris	J. V. Pellerin
Nature morte (fruits, faïence, nappe, rideau jaune) (1890–91)	Merion	Barnes Foundation
La table de cuisine (1888–90)	Paris	Louvre
La bouteille de peppermint (1890–94)	New York	Chester Dale
La rivière (1888–94)	Paris	Philippe Gangnat
La vieille au chapelet (1900-04)	Paris	Mme Doucet
Gustave Geffroy (1895)	Paris	M. Lecomte
Grandes baigneuses (1898-1905)	Paris	J. V. Pellerin
Baigneuses (1900–05)	Paris	M. Lecomte
Nature morte (1895–1900)	New York	Museum of Modern Art (Bliss)
Portrait de Vallier (1904–05)	Paris	M. Lecomte

For the present distribution of the pictures given by Cézanne to Zola (dispersed in the first place at the Zola sale in 1903) cf. above, p. 57.

GEORGES SEURAT (1859-1891)

For Seurat's life and personality the authorities are Lucie Cousturier: *Seurat* (Paris, Editions de Cahiers d'Aujourd'hui. Crès. Second and revised edition, 1926), Gustave Coquiot: *Seurat* (Paris, Albin Michel, 1924) and Robert Rey: *La renaissance du sentiment classique* (Paris, Beaux Arts, 1931). Gustave Kahn published two volumes of facsimiles of a hundred and fifty of Seurat's drawings in 1928.

A complete and completely illustrated catalogue of all Seurat's paintings, *croquetons*, and drawings with their history and present distribution is now being compiled by M. Félix Fénéon.

The following notes on the present distribution of his works may be of service pending the appearance of M. Fénéon's definitive work:

Seurat's six large figure compositions are now distributed as follows:

Baignade (1883–84)	London	National Gallery, Millbank
Un dimanche d'été à la Grande Jatte (1884–86)	Chicago	Art Institute
Poseuses (1887–88)	Merion	Barnes Foundation
Parade (1887–88)	New York	Stephen C. Clark
Chahut (1889–90)	Wassenaar	Kröller-Müller Foundation
Cirque (1890–91)	Paris	Louvre (Bequeathed by John Quinn)

The picture titled *La Seine à Courbevoie* (1885) (a river scene with a woman in a bustled dress walking with a dog in the foreground) is owned by Mme Cachin-Signac (Paris). The river scene *Le pont de Courbevoie* (1886–87) and *Jeune femme se poudrant* (1890–91) belong to Mr. Samuel Courtauld (London), the latter being at present on loan to the London National Gallery, Trafalgar Square. Landscapes and port scenes are owned by, among others, Mrs. Chester Beatty, Sir Kenneth Clark and Mr. Samuel Courtauld in London, by M. Appert, M. Félix Fénéon and M. de Maré in Paris, by the New

York Museum of Modern Art (Bliss Collection) and the Saint Louis City Art Museum. Sketches for *Un dimanche d'été à la Grande Jatte* are owned by Mrs. Chester Beatty (London), Mr. Adolph Lewisohn (New York), and the Smith College Museum, Northampton, Mass. The New York Museum of Modern Art (Bliss Collection) owns *La brodeuse, Au Concert Européen* and other charcoal drawings; M. Appert, M. Fénéon, and M. François Cousturier (Paris) are among the other owners of drawings.

VINCENT VAN GOGH (1853-1890)

For Van Gogh's life and personality the cardinal sources are his letters: *The Letters of Vincent Van Gogh to his brother 1872–1886* with a memoir by his sister-in-law J. Van Gogh-Bonger, 2 vols. (London, Constable; and New York and Boston, Houghton Mifflin & Co. 1927); *Further Letters of Vincent Van Gogh to his Brother 1886–1889* (London, Constable; and New York and Boston, Houghton Mifflin & Co. 1929) and *Lettres de Vincent van Gogh à Emile Bernard* (Paris, Vollard, 1911). There is an account of the tragic dénouement at Arles in Gauguin's *Avant et Après*.

For Van Gogh's work the central book is J. B. de la Faille: *L'œuvre de Vincent Van Gogh: catalogue raisonné*, 5 vols. (Paris and Brussels, Van Oest, 1928), which contains a complete and completely illustrated catalogue of all Van Gogh's paintings and drawings with their distribution at the date of publication and information regarding certain forgeries. Other useful books are the later single volume edition of de la Faille's book; the *Catalogue of the 1935 Van Gogh Exhibition* at the New York Museum of Modern Art which contains a selected bibliography and quotes extracts from Van Gogh's letters; the *Catalogue of the Van Gogh Exhibition in the Paris 1937 Exposition* (Paris, L'Amour de l'Art); W. Scherjon and Jos de Gruyten's *Vincent Van Gogh's Great Period* (Amsterdam, De Spiegel (Nijhoff), 1937) which collates the letters with all the Arles pictures; and the volume of reproductions published internationally by the *Phaidon Press* in 1936.

PAUL GAUGUIN (1848-1903)

For Gauguin's life and personality the student should consult the following books in the following order: De Rotonchamp: *Paul Gauguin* (Paris, Druet, 1906) and enlarged edition, Paris, Crès, 1925); Charles Morice: *Paul Gauguin* (Paris, 1919, and new edition without the colour plates, Paris, Floury, 1920); Gauguin et Morice: *Noa Noa* (Paris: La Plume, 1900 and 1908 and 'édition définitive' Paris, Crès, 1925); Gauguin: *Lettres à Daniel de Monfreid* (Paris, Crès, 1919); Gauguin: *Le Sourire* (Tahiti 1899); Gauguin: *Avant et Après* (Paris, Crès, 1923); Chassé: *Gauguin et le Groupe de Pont Aven* (Paris, Floury, 1921); Robert Burnett: *The Life of Paul Gauguin* (London, Cobden-Sanderson, 1936); Pola Gauguin: *My Father* (London, Cassell, 1937); John Rewald: *Gauguin* (London: Heinemann, 1938) which contains a bibliography, sixteen colour plates and over a hundred other large reproductions; and the bibliography in Robert Rey's *La Renaissance du sentiment classique* (cf. below under 'Symbolism, Synthetism and the Modern Classical Renaissance' (p. 367),

There is no complete and completely illustrated catalogue of Gauguin's works with their history and present distribution (though I understand that M. Raymond Cogniat is preparing one). Some information about some of the pictures will be found in the *Catalogue of the 1936 Gauguin Exhibition* at the Wildenstein Gallery, New York; some information about his sculpture and ceramics will be found in the *Catalogue of the Gauguin Sculpture Exhibition* at the Musée du Luxembourg (1927), and photographs of some sculptures are reproduced in Charles Terrasse: *Paul Gauguin* (Paris. Albert Morancé, 1927) and in Charles

Morice's book referred to above. Gauguin's woodcuts are catalogued and reproduced in Guérin: *L'œuvre gravé de Gauguin* (Paris 1927).

The following is the present or recent distribution of some of Gauguin's paintings referred to directly or implicitly in this book:

1875–1883

Neige au bord de la Seine (Pont d'Iéna) (1875)	Paris	Paul Jamot
Village (1879)	Paris	A. Vollard
Etude de nu : femme raccommodant sa chemise (1880–81)	Copenhagen	Ny Carlsberg Museum
La voiture d'enfants (c. 1881)	Copenhagen	Ny Carlsberg Museum
Jardin sous la neige (c. 1881)	Copenhagen	Ny Carlsberg Museum
Intérieur d'atelier (c. 1881)	Oslo	National Gallery
L'église de Vaugirard (c. 1883)	London	Reid & Lefevre
Rouen : les toits (c. 1883)	German	Collection
Portrait de l'artiste peignant (1883–84)	Paris	Mme de Monfreid
Paysage de Bretagne (1884)	Chicago	C. H. Worcester
Tête de femme (pastel) (1884)	Worcester, Mass.	Museum of Art
Paysage de Bretagne en hiver (1885)	Formerly Paris	G. Brandès
Nature morte avec profile (1885–86)	Paris	Baron A. Herzog
Martinique : Paysage exotique (1887)	Edinburgh	Alexander Maitland
Martinique : paysage (1887)	Moscow	Museum of Modern Western Art
Martinique (1887)	Chicago	C. H. Worcester
Le gardien de porcs (1888)	Paris	Georges Wildenstein
Paysage de Bretagne (1888)	Paris	A. Vollard
Paysage de Bretagne (1888)	Tokio	Baron Matsukata
La ronde des Bretonnes (1888)	Paris	A. Vollard
En Bretagne (1888)	Paris	A. Vollard
La gardeuse de moutons (c. 1888)	Paris	Paul Rosenberg
Portrait de l'artiste (1888)	Moscow	Museum of Modern Western Art
Pont Aven : l'été (1888)	Copenhagen	Ny Carlsberg Museum
Ravine sur la côte (1888)	Paris	Musée des Arts Décoratifs
Paysage Breton (1888)	Paris	Emile Labeyrie
Paysage aux canards (1888)	Paris	Olivier Senn
Les trois chiens (1888)	Paris	Mme Sternheim
Paysanne dans les foins (1888)	Paris	H. de Monfreid
Jeunes lutteurs (1888)	Paris	A. Vollard
Arlésiennes se rendant à l'église (1888)	New York	J. W. Barney
Paysage d'Arles (1888)	Paris	Musée des Arts Décoratifs
Café à Arles (1888)	Moscow	Museum of Modern Western Art
L'Arlésienne (drawing)[1] (1888)	New York	Dr. F. H. Hirschland
Portrait de Van Gogh peignant (1888)	Amsterdam	V. W. Van Gogh.
Vision après le sermon : Lutte de Jacob avec l'ange (1888–89)	Edinburgh	National Gallery of Scotland

[1] Van Gogh based a picture on this drawing.

Le peintre Schuffenecker et sa famille (inscribed '*Je vote pour Boulangg*') (1888–89)	?	?
Le peintre Schuffenecker et sa famille (inscribed *Souvenir : à Schuffenecker*) (1888–89)	Formerly Paris	Schuffenecker
Mlle Schuffenecker (or Mlle Vaite Goupil) (1889–91)	Paris	Paul Rosenberg
Paysage de Bretagne (1889)	New York	W. Church Osborn
Scène Bretonne (1889)	Paris	Dr. Viau
Paysage à la falaise (1889)	Paris	Dr. Viau
Eve et le serpent (1889)	Paris	Georges Wildenstein
Femme dans les vagues (1889)	Cleveland	F. H. Ginn
Les moissonneurs (1889)	London	S. Courtauld
Garçon de Bretagne et oie (1889)	Paris	Paul Rosenberg
Paysage de Bretagne (c. 1889)	Paris	Etienne Bignou
Le saule : Paysage de Bretagne (c. 1889)	Paris	Dr. L. Ménard
La barrière (1889)	Paris	H. de Monfreid
Les meules (1889)	Paris	H. de Monfreid
Paysage de Bretagne au chien noir (1889)	Bâle	Rudolph Stoechelin
Jésus au Jardin des Oliviers (1889)	Headington	Sir Michael Sadler
La belle Angèle (1889)	Paris	Louvre
Paysage décoratif (1889)	Marly-le-Roi	Aristide Maillol
Portrait de l'artiste en style 'symboliste' (1889)	Exhibited London	Reid & Lefevre
Portrait de l'artiste au luth (c. 1889)	Pittsburgh	W. S. Stimmel
Bonjour, M. Gauguin (c. 1889)	Prague	Museum of Modern Art
Le Calvaire (1889)	Brussels	Musée Royal
Le Christ jaune (1889)	Paris	Paul Rosenberg
Meyer de Haan (1889)	Boston	Q. A. Shaw McKean
Côte de Belle-Angenay (c. 1889)	Paris	F. Norgelet
Nature morte aux fruits (c. 1889)	Baden, Switzerland	Sidney Brown
Marie Henry (1889–90)	Chicago	Art Institute (Winterbotham)
Tête de Marie Henry (c. 1889)	New York	Chester Dale
Le Pouldu : paysage au chien rouge (1890)	London	Maresco Pearce
Le champ de pommes de terre (1890)	New York	Gerald Brooks
Portrait de femme (c. 1890)	Grenoble	Museum
Ferme au Pouldu avec chien (1890)	Paris	A. Vollard
La mère de l'artiste (c. 1890)	Paris	M. W. Geiser
Mlle Loulou (1890)	New York	Chester Dale
Portrait de Mallarmé (etching) (1890)		About ten prints
Portrait de l'artiste au 'Christ jaune' (c. 1890)	Paris	Maurice Denis
Deux enfants (1890)	Paris	Paul Rosenberg

Tahitian Pictures (1891-1893)

Fatata ti miti (*Près de la mer*) (1891)	London	Marc Oliver
Rêverie (*Mélancolique*) (1891)	Paris	Georges Wildenstein (Formerly New York, Stransky)

Mlle Cambridge (1891)	Brussels	Musée Royal
Te Faatourama (La boudeuse) (1891)	Worcester, Mass.	Museum
Tahitiennes au bord de la mer (c. 1891)	Honolulu	Academy of Arts
Irarote oviri (sous les pandanus) (1891)	Boston	Gilbert E. Fuller
Ia Orana Maria (Ave Maria) (1891)	New York	Adolph Lewisohn
Tahitiennes assises au bord de la mer (1891)	Paris	Louvre
Le cheval blanc (1891)	Holland	Baron von der Heydt
Te Raau Rahi (Femme et Enfant : Paysage Tahitien) (1891)	Chicago	Walter S. Brewster
Femmes sous les palmiers (1891)	Cleveland	Ralph M. Coe
Te Teiare Farani (Le bouquet) (1891)	Moscow	Museum of Modern Western Art
Trois enfants à table (Scène d'intérieur à Tahiti) (1891)	Paris	Mme Georges Menier
Vahine no te tiare (Femme de la fleur) (1891)	Copenhagen	Ny Carlsberg Museum
Les parao-parao (1891)	Moscow	Museum of Modern Western Art
Vahine no te vi (Femme au fruit) (1892)	Paris	Paul Rosenberg
Manao Tupapau (L'esprit veille) (1892)	New York	H. Conger Goodyear
Mata moua (Autrefois) (1892)	Boston	Gilbert E. Fuller
Te Burao (1892)	Chicago	Art Institute
Te poipoi (Le matin) (1892)	Scotland	D. Cargill
Aa no Areois (La reine des Areois) (1892)	Paris	Mme Desjardins
Arii Matemoi (La fin royale) (1892)	Paris	G. Lerolle
Parau no varua ino (Paroles du diable) (1892)	Exhibited	New York, Wildenstein Gallery 1936
Noa Noa (Odorant) (1892)	Brussels	Devillez
Arearea (La joie) (1892)	Paris	Paul Rosenberg
Nave-Nave Moe (1892–93)	Moscow	Museum of Modern Western Art
Nafea fai-poipo (Quand te maries-tu?) (1892–93)	Bâle	Rudolf Stoechelin
Ah oe feii (Eh quoi, tu es jalouse?) (1892–93)	Moscow	Museum of Modern Western Art
Vairumatati (1892–93)	Moscow	Museum of Modern Western Art
Paysage aux paons (1892–93)	Moscow	Museum of Modern Western Art
A Tahiti (1892–93?)	London	National Gallery, Millbank
Pastorale Tahitienne (1893)	Moscow	Museum of Modern Western Art
Hina Tefatou (La lune et la terre) (1893)	New York	Museum of Modern Art (Bliss)
Hina Marourou (Fête à Hina) (1893)	Paris	Georges Wildenstein
Vahine no te vi (Femme au fruit) Inscribed *Ea haete ia oe* (1893)	Moscow	Museum of Modern Western Art
Metoua rahi no Tehamana (Les aïeux de Tehamana) (1893)	Paris	H. de Monfreid
Fleurs et fruits (1893)	Boston	J. T. Spaulding
Fruits (c. 1893)	Paris	Georges Wildenstein

PAUL GAUGUIN (1848–1903)

Rupe Tahiti (Glass painting) (1893)	Greenwich, Connecticut	Stephen Haweis
Otahi (Tahitienne accroupie) (1893)	Paris	Mme Olivier Sainsère
Portrait de l'artiste à l'idole (c. 1893)	Paris	Georges Wildenstein (Formerly New York: Stransky)

Most of the above were in Gauguin's Paris Exhibition in 1893.

1894–1903

Mahana No Atua (Jour du dieu) (1894)	Chicago	Art Institute (Birch Bartlett)
Anna la Javanaise (c. 1894)	Zurich	Kunsthalle
Portrait de l'artiste (à 'L'esprit veille') (c. 1894)	Paris	William Molard
Portrait d'homme (Painted on reverse of above)		
Portrait de l'artiste à la palette (inscribed 'à Ch : Morice') (1893–94)	Formerly Paris	Charles Morice
Paysage de Bretagne (1894)	Paris	Hugo Perls
Fillette de Bretagne en prière (1894–95)	Formerly German	Collection
Enfants de Bretagne (1894–95)	Paris	A. Vollard
Les lavandières (c. 1894)	U.S.A.	Robert McKay
Le vieillard à la canne (c. 1894)	Paris	Musée des Beaux-Arts de la Ville de Paris
Te Arii Vahine (Femme de race royale) (1896)	Moscow	Museum of Modern Western Art
Portrait de l'artiste (en blouse) (1896)	Paris	Ambroise Vollard
Portrait de l'artiste (inscribed 'à l'ami Carrière') (1896)	England	H. J. P. Bomford
Portrait de l'artiste (inscribed 'à l'ami Daniel') (c. 1896)	Paris	Mme Huc
Nave Nave Mahana (Jours délicieux) (1896)	Lyons	Museum
No Te Aha Oe Riri (Pourquoi es-tu faché?) (1896)	Chicago	Art Institute (Ryerson)
Poèmes barbares (1896)	New York	A. Conger Goodyear
Fleurs (1896)	London	Tate Gallery
Maternité (c. 1896)	New York	Adolph Lewisohn
Nevermore (1897)	London	S. Courtauld
Te Rerioa (Le Rêve. Sometimes called La Case) (1897)	London	S. Courtauld
Baigneuses à Tahiti (1897)	Paris	Georges Wildenstein et Cie. (Formerly J. Stransky, New York)
Te Fare Hymenée (Noce à Tahiti) (1897)	New York	L. W. Lowman
Trois Tahitiens (1897)	Edinburgh	Alexander Maitland
La Barque	Paris	H. de Monfreid
Portrait de l'artiste	Paris	H. de Monfreid
D'où venons-nous? Que sommes-nous? Où allons-nous? (1897)	Boston	Museum of Fine Arts
Faa Iheihe (Groupe Tahitienne)	London	National Gallery, Millbank
Baigneuses (1898)	New York	Adolph Lewisohn

z

W.M.F.P.

Laveuses à Tahiti (1898)	Paris	M. Kapferer
Le Cheval blanc (1898)	Paris	Louvre
Rave Tahiti aamu (L'idole) (1898)	Moscow	Museum of Modern Western Art
Tahitiennes au mango (1899)	New York	William Church Osborn
Nature Morte (Soleils) (1901)	Paris	Georges Wildenstein (Formerly New York: Stransky)
Nature Morte	Oslo	National Gallery
Te Mini na ve ite rata (Paysage Tahitien avec femme, navire et oie) (c. 1901)	New York	Private Collection
Et l'or de leurs corps (1901)	Paris	Mme Olivier Sainsère
Tahitienne et deux enfants (1901)	Chicago	Art Institute (Birch Bartlett)
Le Gué (The ford) (1901)	Moscow	Museum of Modern Western Art
Fleurs de Tahiti (c. 1801)	U.S.A.	Edward G. Robinson
Les soleils (c. 1901)	Chicago	R. McCormick
Nature morte (Oiseaux des Îles) (c. 1902)	Moscow	Museum of Modern Western Art
Chevaliers au bord de la mer (1902)	German	Collection
L'Appel (1902)	Paris	Georges Wildenstein
Contes barbares (avec Meyer de Haan) (1902)	German	Collection
Deux fillettes (1902)	Paris	Paul Rosenberg
Femmes et cheval blanc (1903)	Boston	John T. Spaulding

HENRI DE TOULOUSE-LAUTREC (1864-1901)

For Lautrec's life and personality the student must read Maurice Joyant: *Henri de Toulouse-Lautrec, Peintre* (Paris, Floury, 1926), and the same author's *Henri de Toulouse-Lautrec: Dessins: Estampes: Affiches* (Paris, Floury, 1927); Coquiot: *Toulouse-Lautrec* (Paris, Blaizot, 1913 and 1921) which contains some interesting photographs of Lautrec in his studio and elsewhere; and Paul Leclercq: *Autour de Toulouse-Lautrec* (Paris, Floury, 1921) which contains illuminating anecdotes of the author's friendship with the painter. All the subsequent books on Lautrec have been largely based on these. Joyant's books contain numerous illustrations and full catalogues; but the catalogue of the paintings is now to some extent out of date as many of the pictures have changed hands since 1927. The student should also consult the *Catalogue of the Exposition Henri de Toulouse-Lautrec* at the Pavillon de Marsan, Louvre (1931), the *Catalogue of the Toulouse-Lautrec Exhibition* at the Museum of Modern Art, New York (1931), and the *Catalogue of the Musée Toulouse-Lautrec* in the Palais de la Berbie at Albi. For reproductions of and information about Lautrec's posters and lithographs he should consult Delteil: *Le peintre-graveur illustré*, vol. x (Paris 1920).[1]

[1] Lautrec designed thirty posters: 1891 *Moulin Rouge* (La Goulue); 1892 *Le Pendu, Divan Japonais, Reine de Joie, Ambassadeurs: Aristide Bruant, Eldorado: Aristide Bruant*; 1893 *Jane Avril au Jardin de Paris, Caudieux, Au pied de l'Echafaud* ('Le Matin'), *Aristide Bruant dans son Cabaret*; 1894 *Aristide Bruant au Mirliton, L'artisan moderne, Babylone d'Allemagne, Confetti, Le Photographe Sescau*; 1895 *May Belfort, La Revue Blanche, May Milton, La Châtelaine ou le Tocsin Napoléon;* 1896 *Cycle Mickael, La Chaîne Simpson, La Troupe de Mlle Eglantine, Irish and American Bar: Rue Royale, L'aube* (revue illustrée), *La Vache Enragée* (journal mensuel illustré Willette and Roedel), *Au Concert, La Passagère du 54 ou Promenade en yacht*; 1899 *Jane Avril*; 1900 *La Gitane* (Théâtre Antoine).

HENRI DE TOULOUSE-LAUTREC (1864–1901)

The following list gives the present or recent distribution of some of the pictures by Lautrec directly or implicitly referred to in my text; and I have marked with an asterisk some pictures included in Lautrec's 1898 London Exhibition at the Goupil Gallery.

1879–1883

Cuirassiers à cheval (1879)	Paris	M. Exsteens
Artilleur sellant son cheval (1879)	Albi	Musée Lautrec
Un coupé attelé vu d'arrière (1879)	Albi	Musée Lautrec

1880

Un Dog-Cart (1880)	Albi	Musée Lautrec
Charrette anglaise (1880)	Paris	R. Ellissen
Le viaduc de Castel-Vieil à Albi (1880)	Albi	Musée Lautrec
Celeyran: Au bord de l'eau (1886)	Albi	Musée Lautrec
Celeyran: Vue de la plaine (1880)	Albi	Musée Lautrec
Vendanges à Celeyran (1880)	Albi	Musée Lautrec
Vendanges: Rentrée au Chai (1880)	Albi	Musée Lautrec
Cheval de chasse (1880)	Paris	R. Ellissen
Piqueur de chasse (1880)	Paris	R. Ellissen
Le Comte Alphonse de Toulouse-Lautrec con-duisant son mail-coach à Nice (1881)	Paris	Petit Palais
Le Comte Alphonse de Toulouse-Lautrec en fauconnier (1881)	Albi	Musée Lautrec
Faucon Pèlerin (1881)	Paris	M. Tapié de Celeyran
Cheval blanc: 'Gazelle' (1881)	Paris	M. Exsteens
La Comtesse de Toulouse-Lautrec à Malromé (1881)	Albi	Musée Lautrec
Raymond de Toulouse-Lautrec à 15 ans (1881)	Paris	Comte Robert de Toulouse-Lautrec
Attelage devant une grille (1881)	Albi	Musée Lautrec
Champ de courses (1881)	Albi	Musée Lautrec
Le jeune Routy à Celeyran (1882)	Albi	Musée Lautrec
Le jeune Routy, à Celeyran (1882)	Paris	Comte d'Anselme
La Comtesse de Toulouse-Lautrec dans son jardin (1882)	Paris	M. Séré de Rivières
La femme en prière (1882)	Paris	M. André Corneau
Vieille femme à Celeyran (1882)	Albi	Musée Lautrec
Un travailleur à Celeyran (1882)	Albi	Musée Lautrec
Celeyran: une avenue (1882)	Albi	Musée Lautrec
Celeyran. Cheval à l'écurie (1882)	Albi	Musée Lautrec
Deux chevaux au galop (1882)	Albi	Musée Lautrec
Bouquet de violettes (1882)	Paris	Dr. Viau
Portrait équestre du Comte de Toulouse-Lautrec (1883)	Paris	M. Séré de Rivières
Le labour dans les vignes (1883)	Paris	M. Rachou
Deux chevaux effrayés par un locomotive (1883)	Paris	Baron Reille

1884–1891

Parodie du Bois Sacré (Puvis de Chavannes) (1884)	Paris	M. Marseille
La grosse Maria (1884)	Stockholm	Museum

1885

Carmen (1885)	Albi	Musée Lautrec
Carmen (1885)	Paris	A. Huc
La robe à traîne	Paris	M. Chapelier
Danseuse assise sur un divan rose (1885)	Paris	Comte Robert de Toulouse-Lautrec
Emile Bernard (1885)	Paris	A. Vollard
Suzanne Valadon (1885)	Copenhagen	Ny Carlsberg Museum
Mme Grenier (1885)	Chicago	Carter H. Harrison

1886

La Quadrille de la Chaise Louis XIII à l'Elysée Montmartre (1886)	Paris	J. Dollfus
Le refrain de la Chaise Louis XIII chez Bruant (1886)	Paris	Durand-Ruel
Scène de ballet (1886)		Chicago Art Institute (Birch Bartlett)
Gin Cocktail (drawing) (1886)		Published in *Courrier Français*
Bar : rue de Rome (drawing) (1886)	Chicago	Carter H. Harrison
Au Café (drawing) (1886)	Providence, Rhode Island	J. Nicholas Brown
* *La Comtesse A. de Toulouse-Lautrec* (1887)	Albi	Musée Lautrec
Mme Aline Gibert (1887)	Cleveland	Ralph M. Coe
François Gauzi (1887)	Paris	François Gauzi
A l'Elysée Montmartre (1887)	New York	Knoedler
Au Cirque Fernando (1888)	Chicago	Art Institute (Winterbotham)
Valentin le Désossé et La Goulue au Moulin de la Galette (1888)	Albi	Musée Lautrec
La rousse au caraco blanc (1888)	Boston	J. T. Spaulding
Le peintre Grenier (1888)	Paris	M. Pierre Sanchez-Abreu
Au bois de Boulogne (1888)	New York	Adolph Lewisohn
Petit chien (1888)	Los Angeles	W. Preston Harrison
Le côtier de la Compagnie des Omnibus, Place Clichy (1888)	Paris	M. Exsteens
* *Bal au Moulin de la Galette* (1889)	Chicago	Art Institute (Coburn)
Fille à l'accroche-cœur (1889)	London	Reid & Lefevre
Gueule de bois (drawing) (1889)	Albi	Musée Lautrec
Femme rousse dans le jardin de M. Forest (1889)	Buffalo	Albright Art Gallery

Blanchisseuse (1889)	Le Vésinet	Mme Dortu
M. Samary en scène 1889)	Paris	M. Laroche
M. Fourcade au bal masqué (1889)	American	Collection
Femme à sa toilette (1889)	Paris	Sacha Guitry
Blaco. Fox-terrier de M. Forest (1889)	Paris	M. Gobin
Au Moulin Rouge : La Danse. Dressage des nouvelles (1890)	Paris	A. Seligmann
Trapéziste du Cirque Fernando (1890)	Paris	Mme Olivier Sainsère
Danseuse assise (1890)	Paris	Mme Olivier Sainsère
Berthe la Sourde à l'ombrelle (1890)	American	Collection
Berthe la Sourde (1890)	American	Collection
Femme se frisant (1890)	Toulouse	Musée des Augustins
En Meuble (La lettre) (1890)	Paris	Josse Bernheim Jeune
Femme à la cigarette (1890)	Brooklyn	Museum of Fine Arts
Mlle Dihau au piano (1890)	Albi	Musée Lautrec
Ecuyère (1890)	Paris	Jean Dollfus
Follette, chienne (1890)	Paris	Paul Rosenberg
Au Moulin Rouge : Repos entre deux tours de valse (1891)	Paris	Josse Bernheim Jeune
*La Goulue (Profile) (1891)	Paris	Mme Dortu
Fille à la fourrure (1891)	Paris	Gaston Bernheim de Villers
*Au Moulin de la Galette (1891)	German	Collection
Une opération par le chirurgien Péan (1891)	Paris	M. Tapié de Celeyran
Femme aux gants noirs assise dans un jardin (1891)	Paris	Mme Olivier Sainsère
Femme au chien dans un jardin (1891)	New York	Gerald Brooks
Femme à la voilette (1891)	Paris	Georges Wildenstein
Femme au jardin (1891)	New York	Cornelius J. Sullivan
Gabrielle : Femme assise au jardin (1891)	London	Tate Gallery
Femme se faisant les ongles (1891)	London	Mrs. Chester Beatty
Femme se coiffant : vue de dos (1891)	London	F. Hindley Smith
La lecture (1891)	New York	Adolph Lewisohn
A la mie (1891)	Scotland	D. W. T. Cargill
*Henri Dihau dans son jardin	Albi	Musée Lautrec
Désiré Dihau (1891)	Albi	Musée Lautrec
*Paul Sescau, photographe (1891)	Brooklyn	Museum of Fine Art
Celle qui se peigne (1891)	Winterthur	O. Reinhart

1892—1901

Au Moulin Rouge : Les deux valseuses (1892)	Prague	Gallery of Modern Art
Au Moulin Rouge : Le départ du Quadrille (1892)	New York	Chester Dale
*Au Moulin Rouge : En place pour la Quadrille (1892)	Paris	Josse Bernheim Jeune
Au Moulin Rouge : La Table (1892)	Chicago	Art Institute (Birch Bartlett)
*Au Moulin Rouge : Entrée de la Goulue (1892)	Paris	M. Gaston Bernheim de Villers

L'Anglais au Moulin Rouge (sketch for lithograph) (1892)	Albi	Musée Lautrec
**Jane Avril dansant* (1892)	Paris	M. A. Personnaz
Jane Avril sortant du Moulin Rouge (1892)	London	S. Courtauld
Au Hanneton (L'Assommoir) (1892)	German	Collection
Au Music Hall : Loie Fuller (1892)	Paris	M. Gobin
La femme au boa noir (1892)	Paris	Luxembourg
Au lit (1892)	Paris	M. Exsteens
Au lit : le baiser (1892)	Le Vésinet	Mme Dortu
Dans le lit (1892)	Paris	M. A. Personnaz
Médaillons du salon de la maison rue d'Amboise (1892)	Paris	Mme Ch: Pomaret
**M. Boileau au café* (1893)	Cleveland	Museum of Art
Aristide Bruant à bicyclette (1893)	Albi	Musée Lautrec
**Louis Pascal* (1893)	Albi	Musée Lautrec
Mme Gortsikoff (1893)	Paris	Georges Wildenstein
Monsieur et Madame (1893)	Albi	Musée Lautrec
Femme de maison (1893)	Paris	Mlle J. Renouardt
Femme accroupie (1893)	Paris	M. H. Nocq
Au canapé (Le divan) (1893)	Paris	Georges Wildenstein
Femme à sa fenêtre (1893)	Albi	Musée Lautrec
La Macarona en Jockey (1893)	Le Vésinet	Mme Dortu
Jane Avril au Jardin de Paris (sketch for poster) (1893)	Paris	Georges Wildenstein
La mère Capulet (1893)	Paris	A. Corneau
Femme de maison (1894)	Paris	Mme Dortu
Femme de maison (1894)	Paris	F. Duché
Femme de maison (1894)	Paris	J. Laroche
Le sopha (1894)	Paris	A. S. Henraux
Les deux amies (1894)	London	Reid & Lefevre
Femme assise, nue (1894)	Albi	Musée Lautrec
Deux femmes marchant en chemise (1894)	Albi	Musée Lautrec
Femme nue qui tire son bas (1894)	Albi	Musée Lautrec
L'escalier (1894)	Albi	Musée Lautrec
Au salon de la rue des Moulins (1894)	Albi	Musée Lautrec
Le blanchisseur (1894)	Albi	Musée Lautrec
**Alfred La Guigne* (1894)	New York	Chester Dale
Yvette Guilbert saluant (1894)	Albi	Musée Lautrec
Yvette Guilbert (Project for a poster) (1894)	Albi	Musée Lautrec
**La clownesse assise* (1895)	Paris	Louvre
**La clownesse : jambes écartées* (1895)	Paris	Mme Olivier Sainsère
**La clownesse Cha-u-Kao* (1895)	Cleveland	Frank H. Ginn
Au Moulin Rouge : La Clownesse	Winterthur	O. Reinhart
**May Milton* (1895)	Chicago	Walter S. Brewster
**May Belfort en rose* (1895)	New York	Museum of Modern Art (Bliss)
**May Belfort en jaune avec chat* (1895)	Paris	Gaston Bernheim de Villers
May Belfort en jaune avec chat au Café Concert 'Les Décadents' (1895)	Le Vésinet	Mme Dortu
May Belfort en rouge avec chat (sketch for poster) (1895)	Paris	M. Guérin

May Belfort (Head) (1895)	Paris	A. Peytel
La danse mauresque (Décoration de la Baraque de La Goulue) (1895)	Paris	Luxembourg
La Goulue dans la danse de l'Almée (1895)	Le Vésinet	Mme Dortu
La Goulue et Valentin le Désossé (Décoration de la Baraque de La Goulue) (1895)	Paris	Luxembourg
Tristan Bernard au Vélodrome Buffalo (1895)	Paris	Tristan Bernard
Oscar Wilde (1895)	Paris	Jacques Seligmann
Mme Pascal au piano (1895)	Albi	Musée Lautrec
Mme Natanson (1895)	Paris	M. Guérin
A table: Vuillard, Mme Natanson, Valloton, Thadée Natanson (1895)	Paris	Josse Hessel
Tête de lad (1895)	Albi	Musée Lautrec
Un cocher de bonne maison (1895)	Albi	Musée Lautrec
Mlle Lender dansant le pas du Boléro dans l'opérette Chilpéric (1896)	Le Vésinet	Mme Dortu
Mlle Lender en scène (1896)	Paris	Georges Wildenstein
Figurante aux Folies Bergères (1896)	Albi	Musée Lautrec
Aux Folies Bergères (1896)	Albi	Musée Lautrec
Conquête de passage (1896)	Toulouse	Musée des Augustins
La toilette (1896)	Paris	Luxembourg
Femme se lavant (Elles) (1896)	Le Vésinet	Mme Dortu
Le repos du modèle (La toilette) (1896)	Paris	Gaston Bernheim de Villers
Femme qui se peigne (1896)	Albi	Musée Lautrec
Dame au piano (1896)	Paris	Georges Wildenstein (Formerly New York: Stransky)
* Maxime Dethomas au bal de l'Opéra (1896)	New York	Chester Dale
*Cipa Godebski (1896)	Paris	M. Kelekian
* Mlle Béatrice Tapié de Céleyran (1896)	Buenos Aires	A. Santa Marina
Lucie Bellanger (1896)	Albi	Musée Lautrec
*Chocolat dansant dans la Bar Achille (1896)	Albi	Musée Lautrec
Carnaval du Moulin Rouge. Entrée de Cha-u-Kao (1896)	Albi	Musée Lautrec
Femme nue devant la glace (1897)	Le Vésinet	Mme Dortu
Femme rousse nue accroupie (1897)	Paris	M. Exsteens
Femme nue assise sur un divan (1897)	Paris	M. Exsteens
Femme nue étendue sur un divan (1897)	Paris	M. Exsteens
*Paul Leclercq (1897)	Paris	Louvre
*Berthe Bady (1897)	Albi	Musée Lautrec
M. de Lauradour (1897)	Paris	J. Goldsmidt
Mme Missia Natanson au jardin (1897)	London	Reid & Lefevre
*Henry Nocq (1897)	Paris	H. Nocq
Femme nue debout de face (1898)	Albi	Musée Lautrec
A la toilette (Mme Poupoule)	Albi	Musée Lautrec
La Sphvnge (1898)	Paris	E. Blot
Barmaid au Criterion, Londres	Le Vésinet	Mme Dortu
Soldat anglais fumant sa pipe (1898)	Albi	Musée Lautrec

Mlle Andrée Ciriac: (Commère aux Ambassadeurs et l'Eldorado) (1898)	Le Vésinet	Mme Dortu
* *Romain Coolus (1898)*	Albi	Musée Lautrec
Manzi (c. 1898)	Paris	Mme Manzi
Au Cirque: La Clownesse (1899)	Paris	Petit Palais
Au Cirque (fifty pastels) (1899)	Le Vésinet	Mme Dortu
Le gardien: Maison de Santé Madrid-Neuilly (1899)	Albi	Musée Lautrec
L'Anglaise du 'Star' au Havre (1899)	Albi	Musée Lautrec
L'Anglaise du 'Star' au Havre (profile) (1899)	New York	Cornelius J. Sullivan
Mlle Nys (1899)	Paris	M. Sacha Guitry
Deux bœufs (1899)	Paris	Comte d'Anselme
Messaline à l'Opéra de Bordeaux (1900)	Chicago	Art Institute (C. H. Worcester)
Messaline à l'Opéra de Bordeaux (1900)	New York	Adolph Lewisohn
La modiste (Mlle Margouin) (1900)	Albi	Musée Lautrec
La toilette (Mme Poupoule) (1900)	Le Vésinet	Mme Dortu
Maurice Joyant: en baie de Somme (1900)	Albi	Musée Lautrec
Paul Viaud: en matelot, Arcachon (1900)	Paris	M. Guérin
Un examen à la Faculté de Médecine	Albi	Musée Lautrec
L'amiral Viaud (1901)	Malromé	La Comtesse de Toulouse-Lautrec
André Rivoire (1901)	Paris	Petit Palais

THE DOUANIER ROUSSEAU (1844-1910)

The first book on The Douanier's life, personality and work was Wilhelm Uhde's *Henri Rousseau* (Paris, Figuière, 1911); and about the same time Guillaume Apollinaire described his personality in *Les Soirées de Paris*—a text later reprinted in a collection of Apollinaire's writings titled *Il y a* edited by Ramón Gomez de la Serna (Paris, Messein, 1925). These two texts are the basis of all subsequent accounts of The Douanier's life. Uhde's book, now out of print, contains twenty-five plates; a German edition with fewer and different plates and some additional text was published by Kaemmerer, Dresden, in 1921. Reproductions of twelve pictures by The Douanier were published as *Dodici opere di Rousseau* by the Libreria della Voce (Florence 1914). Philippe Soupault published some letters by The Douanier and The Douanier's own biographical note in his *Henri Rousseau, Le Douanier* (Paris, Edition des Quatre Chemins, 1927). Reproductions of about ninety of The Douanier's surviving pictures are given in Xervos: *Rousseau* (Paris, Cahiers d'Art, 1927), and there are also illustrations in André Salmon: *Henri Rousseau: dit Le Douanier* (Paris, Crès, 1927), and in books on The Douanier by Adolph Basler, and 'Roch Grey' (Baroness Oettingen). Accounts of the 'Rousseau Banquet' in Picasso's studio in 1908 will be found in Fernande Olivier: *Picasso et ses amis* (Paris, Stock, 1933), André Warnod: *Les berceaux de la jeune peinture* (Paris, Albin Michel, 1925), Gertrude Stein: *The Autobiography of Alice B. Toklas* (London, John Lane, 1933) and a pamphlet called *Testimony against Gertrude Stein* (Service Press, The Hague, 1936); the student will find it entertaining to collate them.

Extracts from The Douanier's play *La vengeance d'une orpheline russe* were first published, I believe, by Robert Delaunay in *Les arts plastiques*; extracts were also published in the catalogue of a Rousseau exhibition in the Galerie Flechtheim in Berlin in 1926; the summary which I give in Appendix III is based on the text in Flechtheim's catalogue which the late Mr. Flechtheim kindly supplied to me for the purpose.

The Douanier's biographers have not given the facts of his trial for *faux et usage de faux* in his old age in 1909. All refer vaguely to a 'complicated matter of a cheque of which he understood nothing'—and then record what amounted to his acquittal under the *Loi Béranger* (First Offenders Act). My account of the matter is based on reports of the trial in *Le Temps*, Jan. 10th and 11th, 1909, which I print in Appendix IV. The detail of The Douanier's remark to his counsel[1] is not in *Le Temps* but in an article by Charles Chassé, *Les fausses gloires: D'Ubu-Roi au Douanier Rousseau* in *La Grande Revue*, 1923. The production of his book of press cuttings and his picture and their effects are recorded in a malicious account of the trial by Jules Claretie in the *Figaro*, January 10th, 1909. The Douanier's thanks to the judge on this occasion were of course the origin of the entirely false episode concocted by the speaker at the *Société de Psychothérapie*.[2]

No complete and completely illustrated catalogue of The Douanier's surviving paintings with their history and present distribution has yet been compiled.

The student will find a list of his pictures exhibited at the *Salons des Indépendants* and the *Salons d'Automne* in Uhde's book.

The following list, arranged in what I believe to be roughly the chronological order, shows the present or recent whereabouts of some of The Douanier's pictures referred to directly or implicitly in my text. Dates in brackets after the pictures indicate the year of exhibition in the *Salon des Indépendants*; dates with an asterisk in brackets indicate the year of exhibition in the *Salon d'Automne*; dates without brackets indicate a picture of which the date is recorded; dates prefaced by *circa* are my ascriptions.

Portraits and Genre Figures

Moi-même: portrait paysage (1890)	Prague	Museum of Modern Art
Pierre Loti (1891)[3]	German	Collection
La femme de l'artiste (dans un jardin) c. 1895[4]	Paris	Baron Gourgaud
Portrait de Mlle M. (1897)[5]	Paris	Pablo Picasso
Portrait de l'artiste à la lampe	Paris	Robert Delaunay
Portrait de la femme de l'artiste à la lampe	Paris	Robert Delaunay
L'enfant à la poupée	Paris	Mme Paul Guillaume
L'enfant au jouet, c. 1902	Switzerland	Private Collection
Jeune fille à l'agneau dans une forêt	Penlynn (Pa.)	R. Sturgis Ingersoll
Une noce à la campagne (1905)	Paris	Mme Paul Guillaume
Femme assise dans un jardin	Merion	Barnes Foundation
Dame en brun dans la forêt	Paris	A. Villard
Le présent et le passé (Pensée philosophique) (1907)	Merion	Barnes Foundation
La carriole du père Juniet 1908	Paris	Mme Paul Guillaume
Portrait de M. Brummer 1909	Paris	O. Mietschaninoff
Femme dans une forêt exotique	Merion	Barnes Foundation
La Muse inspirant le poète (1909) (first version)	Moscow	Museum of Modern Western Art
La Muse inspirant le poète (second version)	Germany	Private Collection

[1] Cf. above, p. 245.   [2] Cf. above, p. 247.
[3] I assume this to be the *Portrait de M. L.* in the *Salon des Indépendants* in 1891.
[4] Probably worked on after 1900.
[5] I assume this to be the *Portrait de Mlle M.* in the *Salon des Indépendants* in 1897.

APPENDIX I: BIBLIOGRAPHICAL NOTES

Landscapes, Townscapes and Suburban Scenes generally with Figures[1]

Vue de la passerelle de Passy[2] (1891)	Paris	Mme Paul Guillaume
Vue du Parc Montsouris (Promenade sous l'allée), c. 1892 (1895)	Paris	Pierre Wertheimer
La promenade (Parc Montsouris)	Paris	A. Villard
Promeneurs au Parc Montsouris	Merion	Barnes Foundation
Vue de Saint Cloud	Formerly Paris	M. Uhde
L'octroi (pl. (D) p. 158)	London	Samuel Courtauld
Paysage aux gensdarmes	New York	Marie Harriman Gallery
L'ombrelle	New York	Mrs. Charles S. Payson
Coin de rue : banlieue de Paris : fils télégraphiques	Merion	Barnes Foundation
Les poteaux télégraphiques 1903	Paris	M. G. Renand
Banlieue de Paris	Cleveland	Museum of Art
Banlieue (sketch)	Wiversfield	W. Rees Jeffreys
Paysage au bétail	Formerly Paris	Druet
La tour Eiffel	Germany	Private Collection
Vue du pont de Sèvres	Moscow	Museum of Modern Western Art
La Seine à Alfortville	Paris	Pierre Wertheimer
La Seine à Charenton	Paris	Pierre Wertheimer
Paysage aux poules blanches	Paris	W. Kandinsky
La banlieue (Grand paysage) c. 1898	Paris	Mme Paul Guillaume
La banlieue (Petite maison au bord de l'eau[3]) c. 1898	Paris	Mme Paul Guillaume
Le kiosque	Paris	G. Renand
Le verger	Paris	G. Renand
La carrière	Paris	O. Mietschaninoff
La fabrique de chaises	Paris	Mme Paul Guillaume
Le printemps : Vue d'Alfortville	Paris	Mme Flachfeld
L'été : Le pâturage	Paris	Mme Flachfeld
L'automne : Vue de Damery-Boursault, bords de la Marne	Paris	Mme Flachfeld
L'hiver : Effet de neige	Paris	Mme Flachfeld
Banlieue : (pêcheurs à la ligne et avion)	Paris	Mme Paul Guillaume
Vue des bords de l'Oise (1905*)	Moscow	Museum of Modern Western Art
Vue des environs de Paris : Bagneux	Paris	A. Lefevre

Jungle Pictures

Eclaireurs attaqués par un tigre	Merion	Barnes Foundation
Nègre attaqué par un léopard dans la forêt	Germany	Private Collection
Le lion ayant faim . . . (1905)	Zurich	F. M . . . .

[1] Many of the following were probably exhibited at the *Salon des Indépendants* as pictures with similar titles figure in the catalogues.

[2] This picture is sometimes known as *Vue du pont de Grenelle*. Rousseau exhibited pictures called *Vue de la passerelle de Passy* in 1891 and 1895 and one called *Vue du pont de Grenelle* in 1892.

[3] This picture reproduced as Pl. 43A is a smaller version of *La banlieue (Grand paysage)*.

Le répas du lion	New York	Adolph Lewisohn
Forêt exotique avec lion	New York	Museum of Modern Art
		(Bliss Collection)
Joyeux farceurs	Los Angeles	Walter C. Arensberg
Indien attaqué par une guérilla	Paris	Georges Wildenstein
La récolte des bananes	Germany	Private Collection
Les flamants	Germany	Private Collection
La forêt équatoriale 1909	New York	Chester Dale
Paysage exotique avec singes	Germany	Private Collection
Paysage exotique avec singes	Chicago	Mrs. Robert McCormick
Singes aux oranges dans la forêt	New York	Miss A. Milton de Groot
Singes aux oranges	Paris	Pierre Wertheimer
La cascade 1910	Chicago	Art Institute
		(Birch Bartlett)
Le rêve 1910 (1910)	New York	Sidney Janis

Compositions other than Jungle Pictures

Surpris (1891)[1]	Merion	Barnes Foundation
Le centenaire de l'Indépendance 1892[2]	Germany	Private Collection
Bonne Fête 1892	London	Charles Laughton
Les artilleurs	London	Exhibited, Tooth's
		Galleries, 1938
La bohémienne endormie 1897	New York	Museum of Modern Art
Heureux quatuor (1902)	Germany	Private Collection
La Liberté invitant les artistes à prendre part à la 22e Exposition des artistes indépendants (1906)	Germany	Private Collection
Les représentants des puissances étrangères venant saluer la République en signe de paix (1907)	Paris	Pablo Picasso
Charmeuse de serpents 1907	Paris	Louvre
Les joueurs de football 1908	Paris	Paul Rosenberg
Le repas du lapin 1908	Paris	A. Villard

Flower Pieces and Still Life

La chandelle rose	Washington	Phillips Memorial Gallery
Fleurs	Paris	Dr. Charpentier
Vase de fleurs	Cleveland	Mr. and Mrs. R. C. Coe
Vase de fleurs	New York	William S. Paley
Panier de fleurs (Fleurs du poète)	New York	William S. Paley
Nature morte	Great Neck	Max Weber
Bouquet de fleurs	London	National Gallery, Millbank
Fleurs 1910	Formerly Paris	Galerie Georges Petit

[1] The Barnes Foundation picture (to which Renoir referred in the passage quoted in my text) is presumably either the picture *Surpris* in the *Salon des Indépendants* in 1891 or the picture called *Mauvaise surprise* in that Salon in 1901.

[2] The painter Robert Delaunay owns or owned a smaller oblong version of this picture entitled *La Carmagnole*.

HENRI MATISSE (Born 1869)

The literature on the life and work of Matisse is mainly appreciative; and there is as yet no complete and completely illustrated catalogue with the dates and distribution of his pictures up to date.

The student will find informative: Marcel Sembat: *Henri Matisse* (Paris, Edition de la Nouvelle Revue Française, 1920); the *Illustrated Catalogue of the Matisse Exhibition* at the Museum of Modern Art, New York (1931) which contains a bibliography to that date; the reproductions in Roger Fry: *Henri-Matisse* (Paris, Chroniques du Jour, New York, E. Weyhe, and London, Zwemmer, 1930); the biographical note, the reproductions and the dated list in Barnes and de Mazia: *The Art of Henri Matisse* (New York, Scribners, 1933); Pierre Courthion: *Henri-Matisse* (Paris, Editions Rieder, 1934); R. Escholier: *Henri-Matisse* (Paris, Floury, 1937); the catalogue of the *Maîtres de l'Art Indépendant* Exhibition at the Petit Palais in 1937; and for recent pictures, the catalogue of the *Matisse Exhibition* at the Paul Rosenberg Gallery, London, in 1937

The account of Matisse's personality given in Gertrude Stein: *The Autobiography of Alice B. Toklas* (London, John Lane, 1933) should be read in conjunction with Matisse's comments upon it in the pamphlet titled *Testimony against Gertrude Stein* (Service Press, The Hague, 1936) already referred to (p. 360).

About forty of Matisse's works of 1907–1913, formerly in the Stchoukin and Morosoff Collections, are now in the Moscow Museum of Modern Western Art. Representative collections of Matisse's work of all periods are owned by the Barnes Foundation, Merion, and by Mr. Stephen C. Clark, New York. Other American owners of his pictures include Dr. Harry Bakwin, Mr. Ralph M. Coe, Mr. Chester Dale, Miss Etta Cone, Mr. Frank Crowninshield, Mr. A. Conger Goodyear, Mr. Earl Horter, Mr. Preston Harrison, Dr. Hirschland, Mrs. E. Jonas, Mr. Adolph Lewisohn, Mr. Sam Lewisohn, Mr. Robert Treat Paine, Mr. J. T. Soby, Mr. S. S. White, Mr. Joseph Winterbotham, the Phillips Memorial Gallery, Washington, the Chicago Art Institute, the Detroit Institute of Arts, the Boston Museum of Fine Arts, the Worcester Art Museum, the Fogg Art Museum, and the New York Museum of Modern Art. English owners of works by Matisse include the London National Gallery, Millbank, Lord Berners, Lord Ivor Spencer Churchill, Mrs. Chester Beatty, Mr. William Boyd, Mr. Samuel Courtauld, Mr. R. J. T. Griffin, Mr. St. John Hutchinson, Mr. W. Rees Jeffreys, Mr. William McInnes, Mr. R. Middleton, Sir George Sutton and Sir Kenneth Clark. In Paris his work can be seen in the Musée du Luxembourg, the Petit Palais, and the Musée de l'art moderne (quai du Tokio).

PABLO PICASSO (Born 1881)

For the life and personality of Picasso up to the war the student should consult Fernande Olivier: *Picasso et ses amis* (Paris, Stock, 1933), Gertrude Stein: *The Autobiography of Alice B. Toklas,* and Christian Xervos: *Pablo Picasso Vol. I. Œuvres de 1895–1906* (Paris, Editions des Cahiers d'Art, 1932). Some information relating to the pre-war period and the nineteen-twenties is contained in André Level: *Picasso* (Paris, Crès, 1928); and sidelights on Picasso's personality in the nineteen-thirties are revealed in *Picasso 1930–1935* (Paris, Cahiers d'Art, 7–10, 1935) which contains some of his writings in that period and a statement by him from which I have translated the passages quoted in the Introduction to Act IV.[1] Photographs of Picasso are contained in Gertrude Stein's and André Level's

[1] Cf. above, p. 285.

books, in the Catalogue of the New York University Museum of Living Art and in the issue of *Cahiers d'Art* just referred to.

No complete and completely illustrated catalogue of Picasso's very numerous paintings, gouaches and drawings up to date with their history and distribution has yet been compiled. But Christian Xervos has begun the task in *Pablo Picasso. Œuvres de 1895–1906* (referred to above) which lists, reproduces and gives the present or recent distribution of three hundred and eighty-four pictures produced before the end of 1906. Information about the present distribution of Picasso's works after 1906 is very hard to come by because no such information is provided in the voluminous literature about them. For reproductions of and some information about them the student should consult the *Catalogue of the Exposition Picasso* at the Galerie Georges Petit (Paris 1932); Xervos: *Pablo Picasso. Œuvres de 1920–1926* (Paris, Editions des Cahiers d'Art, 1926); Waldemar George: *Picasso et la crise actuelle de la conscience artistique* (Paris, Chroniques du Jour, 1929); Eugenio D'ors: *Picasso* (Paris, Editions des Chroniques du Jour, New York, E. Weyhe, and London, Zwemmer, 1930); Maud Dale: *Modern Art: Picasso* (New York, Knopf, 1930); Henri Mahaut: *Picasso* (Paris, Crès, 1930); the review called *Documents* (Paris 1930); the catalogue of the Exhibition called *Abstractions by Picasso* (New York, Valentine Gallery, 1931); Jacques Maritain: *Picasso* (Paris, Cahiers d'Art 3–5, 1932); Xervos: *Pablo Picasso* (Milan, Hoepli, Arte Moderna Straniera, 1932) which has a bibliography with some three hundred entries; the *Catalogue of the New York Museum of Modern Art's Cubism and Abstract Art Exhibition* (1936) which contains a selected bibliography; the number of *Cahiers d'Art* (Nos. 7–10, 1935) titled *Picasso 1930–1935* already referred to; the reproductions in Cassou's *Picasso* (Paris, Braun, Collection des Maîtres, 1937); and *Cahiers d'Art* 1–3, 1937, which reproduces the *Songe et Mensonge de Franco* etchings (without Picasso's text); the Catalogue of the *Maîtres de l'Art Indépendant* Exhibition at the Petit Palais in 1937 and the Catalogue of the *Recent Works by Picasso* Exhibition at Paul Rosenberg's London Gallery in 1937. A complete catalogue of Picasso's etchings and lithographs up to 1931 is contained in Bernhard Geiser: *Picasso peintre-graveur* (Berne, Geiser, 1933). A list of most of the books illustrated by Picasso is contained in the *Catalogue of the 1936 New York Museum of Modern Art's Exhibition, Modern Painters and Sculptors as Illustrators*.

About forty of Picasso's pre-war pictures formerly in the Stchoukin and Morosoff collections are now in the Moscow Museum of Modern Western Art. American owners of his pictures include Mrs. J. A. Carpenter, Mr. Stephen C. Clark, Mr. Frank Crowninshield, Mr. Chester Dale, the late Mr. George Gershwin's Estate, Mr. Philip Goodwin, Mr. Preston Harrison, Mrs. Patrick Hill, Mr. Earl Horter, Mr. Sidney Janis, Mr. Chester Johnson, Mrs. E. A. Jordan, Mr. Adolph Lewisohn, Mr. Sam Lewisohn, Mr. H. P. McIlhenny, Mr. G. L. K. Morris, Mr. J. Pulitzer, Mr. J. T. Soby, Mr. A. Stieglitz, Mr. Edward Warburg, Miss M. H. Wiborg, the New York University Museum of Living Art (which has a small but very representative collection of works between 1906–1928), the New York Museum of Modern Art, the Barnes Foundation, Merion, the Albright Art Gallery Buffalo, the Chicago Art Institute, the Phillips Memorial Gallery Washington, the Cleveland Museum of Art, the Philadelphia Museum of Art, the Rhode Island School of Design, the Fogg Art Museum, and the Smith College Museum of Art Northampton. British owners of works by Picasso include the London National Gallery (Millbank), the Courtauld Institute of Art London University, the Whitworth Art Gallery Manchester, Mrs. Chester Beatty, Mr. Francis Cooke, Lady Cunard, Mr. Samuel Courtauld, Mr. O. T. Falk, Mr. W. Rees Jeffreys, Mr. Edward James, Mr. William McInnes, Mr. Y. Ito, Mr. J. M. Keynes, Miss Norah MacCaw, Mr. E. L. T. Mesens, Mr. Roland Penrose, Mr. Herbert Read, Sir Michael Sadler, Mr. F. Hindly Smith, Mr. Stephen Spender, Mr. S. W. Sykes, Mrs. Dorothea Vestris, Mr. Edward Wadsworth and Mr. Peter Watson.

AMEDÉE MODIGLIANI (1884-1920)

The very voluminous literature about Modigliani is mainly appreciative and non-informative; and there has been a tendency to over-dramatize his life. The student will find a short bibliography in Adolphe Basler: *Modigliani* (Paris, Crès, 1931), and a bibliography with three hundred entries in Lamberto Vitali: *Disegni di Modigliani* (Milan, Hoepli, 1936).

No complete and completely illustrated catalogue of Modigliani's paintings and drawings with their history and present distribution has yet been compiled.

Examples of his work are owned by the Moscow Museum of Modern Western Art, the New York Museum of Modern Art, the Chicago Art Institute, the Detroit Institute of Arts, the Los Angeles Museum, the Phillips Memorial Gallery Washington, and by Mr. A. Conger Goodyear, Mr. Chester Dale, Mr. Ralph M. Coe, Mr. Paul Lamb and other private collectors in America. In Paris a number of his works are owned by Mme Paul Guillaume and M. J. Netter.

MARC CHAGALL (Born 1887)

For Chagall's life and personality the student should consult his own book *Ma Vie* (Paris, Stock, 1931) and André Salmon: *Chagall* (Paris, Chroniques du Jour, 1928).

No complete and completely illustrated catalogue of his paintings and gouaches up to date with their history and present distribution has yet been compiled. Salmon's book contains forty-five reproductions and there are reproductions and bibliographical references in Waldemar George: *Marc Chagall* (Paris, Editions de la Nouvelle Revue Française (Gallimard) 1928), and in the Chagall number of *Selection* (Selection, Antwerp, 1929). The student will also find information in the catalogues of the *Chagall Exhibition* at the Leicester Galleries, London (1935), the *Peintres instinctifs* exhibition at the Wildenstein Gallery, Paris (1935), the *Fantastic Art, Dada and Surrealism Exhibition* at the New York Museum of Modern Art (1936), the *Maîtres de l'Art Indépendant* exhibition at the Petit Palais (1937) and the *Origines et développement de l'art international indépendant* exhibition at the Musée du Jeu de Paume (1937).

Pictures by Chagall are in the Luxembourg Museum, Paris, the Barnes Foundation, Merion, the Los Angeles Museum (Preston Harrison Collection), the New York University Museum of Living Art and in many American and other private collections.

Chagall has illustrated Gogol: *Les âmes mortes*, La Fontaine: *Fables* and the Old Testament *Les prophètes*. These illustrations were all commissioned by Vollard who published the first book in 1926; the other two books, I believe, have not yet been published.

GIORGIO DE CHIRICO (Born 1888)

No complete and completely illustrated catalogue of Chirico's paintings and gouaches up to date with their history and present distribution has yet been compiled.

The student should consult Boris Ternovetz: *Giorgio de Chirico* (Milan, Hoepli, 1927), Roger Vitrac: *Georges de Chirico* (Paris, Editions de la Nouvelle Revue Française (Gallimard) 1927) which contains fifty reproductions of pictures up to 1926; Waldemar George: *Chirico* (Paris, Chroniques du Jour, 1928), which contains some writings (prose and verse) by Chirico himself and thirty reproductions of his paintings in 1925–1927, and the Chirico number of *Selection* (Selection, Antwerp, 1929) which contains fifty reproductions and biographical and bibliographical information to the end of the nineteen-twenties, and a photograph of the artist. Chirico's 'Gladiator' paintings for M. Léonce Rosenberg's house are reproduced in *Formes* (Paris, Editions de Quatre Chemins, January, 1930). Chirico's own statement *Statues, meubles et généraux* from which I have translated passages in my text was published in '*L'effort moderne*' (Paris, Léonce Rosenberg, October, 1927).[1] His Surrealist novel *Hebdomeros* was published by Editions du carrefour, Paris, in 1929.[2]

Pictures by Chirico are owned by the Moscow Museum of Modern Western Art, the New York University Museum of Living Art, The New York Museum of Modern Art, the Barnes Foundation, Merion, the Detroit Institute of Arts, and by Mr. Cornelius N. Bliss, Mr. Henry Clifford, Mr. Sidney Janis, Mr. Earl Horter, Mr. Paul Lamb, Mr. J. T. Soby, Mr. M. Speiser, Miss M. H. Wiborg and other American Collectors. English owners include the Whitworth Art Gallery, Manchester, Mr. Osbert Sitwell, Mr. Peter Watson and Mr. Roland Penrose. M. René Gaffé of Brussels owns some pictures of the 1912–1916 period. In Italy M. Mario Broglio, Cuneo, owns some pictures of 1917–1919. M. André Breton, M. Paul Eluard and Mme Paul Guillaume are among the Parisian owners.

REALISM AND IMPRESSIONISM

Zola: *Mon Salon* 1866 (Reprinted in *Mes haines*, Paris, Charpentier); Duranty: *La nouvelle peinture* (Paris, Dentu, 1876); Théodore Duret: *Les peintres impressionistes* (Paris, Librairie Parisienne, 1878) reprinted in *Les peintres impressionistes* (Paris, Floury, 1923); J. K. Huysmans: *L'art moderne* (Paris, Stock, 1883) and Gustave Geffroy: *Histoire de l'Impressionisme* (Paris, Dentu, 1894).

SYMBOLISM, SYNTHETISM AND MODERN CLASSICAL RENAISSANCE

Félix Fénéon: *Les Impressionistes en 1886* (Paris, Bibliothèque d'art et d'archéologie, Brochure 9403); Albert Aurier: *Les peintres symbolistes* (Paris, Mercure de France, 1891); Maurice Denis: *Théories du Symbolisme et de Gauguin vers un nouvel ordre classique* (Paris, Roualt, 1912); Maurice Denis: Introduction to *Catalogue of the exhibition called Gauguin et ses amis* organized by *Beaux-Arts*, and *La gazette des Beaux-Arts* (Paris 1934); R. H. Wilenski: *The Modern Movement in Art* (London, Faber, and New York, Stokes, 1927, and subsequent editions); R. H. Wilenski: *French Painting* (London, Medici, and Boston, Hale, Cushman & Flint, 1931, and subsequent editions); and Robert Rey: *La Renaissance du sentiment classique* (Paris, Beaux-Arts (van Oest), 1931) which contains a copious bibliography of French art criticism relating to nineteenth century French painting.

SALONS DES INDÉPENDANTS

Coquiot: *Les Indépendants 1884–1920* (Paris 1921).

FAUVISM

No informative book on this subject exists.

[1] Cf. above, p. 275.   [2] Cf. above, p. 275.

CUBISM, PURISM, FUNCTIONALISM AND STYLE MÉCANIQUE

For these movements historically considered the student should consult Gleizes et Metzinger: *Du Cubisme* (Paris, Figuière, 1912); Léonce Rosenberg: *Cubisme et Tradition* (Paris, L'effort moderne, 1920) and *Cubisme et Empirisme* (Paris, L'effort moderne, 1921) and the whole series of *L'effort moderne* (Paris, Léonce Rosenberg, 1925–1927); Ozenfant: *Après le Cubisme* (Paris, 1918) and the whole series of *L'esprit nouveau* edited by Ozenfant and Jeanneret (Paris 1919–1925); Ozenfant and Jeanneret: *La peinture moderne* (Paris, Crès, 1924); Jeanneret (Le Corbusier): *Vers une architecture* (Paris, Crès, 1925); Ozenfant: *Art* (Paris, Budry, 1928); R. H. Wilenski: *The Modern Movement in Art* (London, Faber, and New York, Stokes, 1927, and subsequent editions); and the catalogue of the New York University Museum of Living Art.

The *Catalogue of the Exhibition called Les créateurs de Cubisme*, organized by Beaux-Arts and La Gazette de Beaux-Arts (Paris 1935) contains a useful chronology by Raymond Cogniat. Mr. Alfred Barr's *Catalogue of the New York Museum of Modern Art Exhibition called Cubism and Abstract Art* (New York 1936) contains a very detailed historical account of these movements (with numerous subdivisions), over two hundred illustrations and copious bibliographical information.

An interesting account of the genesis of Ozenfant's large picture *La Vie* (biologique) is included in Ozenfant: *Journey through Life* (London, Gollancz, 1939).

FUTURISM

All the Futurist manifestoes have been reprinted at Milan by the Istituto editoriale italiano. The student should also consult Marinetti: *Le futurisme* (Paris, Sansot, 1911) and Boccione: *Pittura, scultura futuristi; Dinamismo plastico* (Milan, Poesia, 1914).

SURREALISM, DADA AND NEO-SURREALISM

For these movements historically considered the student should consult the *Catalogue of the New York Museum of Modern Art's Exhibition called Fantastic Art, Dada, Surrealism* (New York 1936) which contains a detailed historical account of these movements, numerous illustrations (including some of historical precedents) and bibliographical material.

For Neo-Surrealism (as distinguished by me from Dada and Surrealism) the student should consult André Breton: *Manifeste du Surréalisme* (Paris, Kra, 1924); the statement titled *L'affaire de L'âge d'or* and other documents issued from the Hours Press, Paris (1930–1931) in connection with the film *L'âge d'or* by Louis Bunuel and Salvador Dali; the periodicals *La Révolution Surréaliste* (Paris 1924–1929); *Le Surréalisme au service de la révolution* (Paris 1930–1933); *Minotaure* (Paris, Skira, 1933–1939); David Gascoyne: *A Short Survey of Surrealism* (London, Cobden-Sanderson, 1935); J. T. Soby: *After Picasso* (Hartford, E. V. Mitchell, and New York, Dodd, Mead & Co., 1935); and H. Read: *Surrealism* (London, Faber, 1936).

The passages from statements by Max Ernst which I have quoted in the Introduction to Act IV[1] are extracts from the translation printed in the symposium titled *The Painter's Object* (London, Gerald Howe, 1937).

[1] Cf. above, pp. 276, 280, 281.

MODERN FRENCH PAINTERS AS ILLUSTRATORS

Information on this subject is contained in the *Catalogue of the New York Museum of Modern Art Exhibition called Modern Painters and Sculptors as Illustrators* (New York 1936).

POSTSCRIPTA

In collecting dates for the sections titled '*How it happened*' I have used the French and English press, the books referred to in the text, and also, for the literature, Hugo P. Thième: *Bibliographie de la littérature française 1800–1930* (Paris, Druz, 1933); and for the theatre, Henry Bordeaux *La vie au théâtre 1910–1919*, 5 vols. (Paris, Plon-Nourrit, 1910–1919); Louise Delpit: *Scènes d'avant-garde depuis trente ans* (Northampton, Mass.: Smith College Studies in Modern Languages 1924–1925); Edmond Sée: *Le théâtre français contemporain* (Paris, Colin, 1928) and Clifford H. Bissell: *Les conventions du théâtre bourgeois contemporain en France 1887–1914* (Paris, Les presses universitaires de France, 1930). For the music I have used the standard books of reference and Slonimsky's admirable chronology *Music since 1900* (London, Dent, 1938) which was published in time for me to extract from it a few additional dates and one or two curious facts which I have acknowledged by footnotes in the text.

Since my notes were made the Kröller-Müller Foundation (formerly a private collection in The Hague) has been transferred from Wassenaar to Hoenderlo.

APPENDIX II: LONDON GRAFTON
GALLERIES EXHIBITION, 1905

The following pictures, now distributed as stated, were included in the *Durand-Ruel Exhibition of French Impressionist Pictures* at the London Grafton Galleries in 1905.

MANET

Musique aux Tuileries (1860)	London	National Gallery, Millbank
Le ballet espagnol (1862)	Washington	Phillips Memorial Gallery
Musiciens ambulants (1862)	New York	Chester Dale
Un philosophe (1865)	Chicago	Art Institute
Combat de taureaux (1866)	Chicago	M. A. Ryerson
Eva Gonzalez peignant (1869)	London	National Gallery, Millbank
Jetée de Boulogne (1869)	Paris	Durand-Ruel
Courses à Longchamps (1872)	Chicago	Art Institute
La famille Monet au jardin (1874)	German	Collection
Enfant dans les fleurs (1875)	Paris	Durand-Ruel
Pertuiset chasseur de lions (1881)	German	Collection
Le banc : Jardin de Manet (1881)	Paris	Durand-Ruel
Bar aux Folies Bergères (1881)	London	Samuel Courtauld (on loan at the National Gallery)

RENOIR

La loge (1874)	London	S. Courtauld
Petite danseuse (1874)	Philadelphia	J. E. Widener
Jeanne Durand-Ruel (1876)	Paris	A. F. Aude
La tasse de chocolat (1877)	Paris	Durand-Ruel
Pêcheurs de moules à Berneval (1879)	Paris	Durand-Ruel
A la Grenouillère (1879)	Paris	David Weill
La loge (Au concert) (1880)	U.S.A.	Collection
Capodimonte-Sorrento (1881)	Paris	Durand-Ruel
Guernesey : Baigneurs sur la plage (1882)	Merion	Barnes Foundation
La femme à l'éventail (1886)	Merion	Barnes Foundation

CLAUDE MONET

Examples of the *Rouen*, *Meules*, *Peupliers* and *Vétheuil* pictures; cliff scenes at Dieppe and Pourville; and landscapes painted at Bordighera and Juan-les-Pins.

DEGAS

Voitures aux courses (1873)	Boston	Museum of Fine Arts
Miss Lola au cirque Fernando (1879)	London	National Gallery, Millbank

And numerous pastels from the *Ecole de danse* and *Toilette* series.

CÉZANNE

Les petites maisons à Auvers (c. 1873)	Cambridge, Mass.	Fogg Art Museum
La côte des bœufs (Pontoise) (c. 1875)	New Orleans	Hunt Henderson
Un dessert (c. 1875)	Philadelphia	C. S. Tyson
Le plat de pommes (c. 1875)	Paris	Durand-Ruel
Pommes et gâteaux (c. 1875)	Paris	Durand-Ruel
Vase de fleurs (c. 1875)	Paris	Durand-Ruel
Le mur d'enceinte (c. 1875)	Paris	Durand-Ruel
Portrait de Choquet (c. 1879)	New York	Museum of Modern Art (Bliss)
Le verger (c. 1885)	Paris	Durand-Ruel
Vase de tulipes (c. 1890)	Chicago	Art Institute (Coburn)

APPENDIX III: SUMMARY OF A PLAY BY THE DOUANIER ROUSSEAU SUBMITTED TO THE COMÉDIE FRANÇAISE

La Vengeance d'une Orpheline Russe

*Drame en 5 Actes et 19 Tableaux par Mme Barkowsky
et M. Henri Rousseau*[1]

ACT I

SCENE I

Scene: St. Petersburg; garden of the house of MME YADWIGHA *who is discovered reading. Her niece* SOPHIE *aged 18 is doing embroidery. Russian costumes 1855.* SERVANT *enters.*]

THE SERVANT. Oh! Mesdames, mes bonnes maîtresses, un malheur nous est arrivé. Not' joli canari n'est plus dans sa cage, il s'est envolé, j'n'savons point où, ma fé. A moins qu'il n'ait été dévoré par un chat, c'te pauvre p'tite bête.

[*Elle essuie un pleur.*]

MME YADWIGHA. En effet, ceci est bien contrariant, ce canari, dont j'aimais tant entendre le gai gazouillement, qui dès l'aube du jour charmait mes oreilles ainsi que mes vieux ans, est perdu. . . .

SOPHIE. Je vous en prie, Anna, dépêchez-vous de le chercher. Mort ou vivant, apportez-le.

ANNA. Laissez-moi faire, je pars de suite à sa recherche, j'y courons!

SCENE II

[*House of Henri, a neighbour, twenty-seven, fair.*]

THE SERVANT. Pardon, mon bon m'sieur, si j'venons vous déranger ainsi, mais voyez-vous, j'avons tant d'chagrin à la maison . . . pour le petit canari.

HENRI. Soyez rassurée. Je l'ai aperçu ce matin sur le bord de ma fenêtre: ne sachant à qui il appartenait, j'ai donné l'hospitalité à ce gai voyageur. Dites à vos maîtresses que je le reporterai moi-même et de suite.

[*Exit* SERVANT. HENRI *met le canari dans son chapeau, le recouvre de son mouchoir, refait un peu sa toilette.*]

HENRI. Oh! bonheur, je vais donc pouvoir lui adresser la parole à cette jeune fille qui fait l'objet de mes rêves. . . .

---

[1] Nothing seems to be known of Mme Barkowsky. She may have been the mysterious 'Yadwigha', cf. above, pp. 120, 206, 208, also pp. 360–361.

SCENE III

SERVANT [*annonce*]. M. Henri Schumann.

MME YADWIGHA. Quel bonheur, le voici retrouvé ce petit coureur qui s'échappe ainsi de sa cage. Comme tous, il était avide de liberté et voulait en profiter, ceci avec raison, car qu'est-ce qui n'aime pas la liberté?

SOPHIE. Que faire pour vous remercier, monsieur, de la complaisance que vous avez eue de nous rapporter notre petit déserteur. C'est bien à vous d'avoir agi ainsi, nous vous en récompenserons certainement.

HENRI. Mademoiselle, j'en suis déjà récompensé par le bonheur inespéré pour moi de vous voir de plus près, d'admirer le sourire gracieux de votre visage, de vous parler pour la première fois. Car je vous aime, mademoiselle, je vous aime. . . .

SOPHIE. Vous m'aimez, que voulez-vous dire?

ACT II

[*The intrigue has developed by means of 'une correspondance fort savoureuse'; and the 'tourtereaux' have eloped together.*]

SCENE I

[*A room in a hotel at Brussels. Table 'copieusement servie'.*]

HENRI. Enfin, nous voici seuls, chère Sophie, oui, bien seuls! Je vais pouvoir te contempler à mon aise, t'admirer, toi, si belle, si jolie. Oh! oui, tu es jolie, tes joues sont colorées d'une douce rougeur, tes yeux si grands et si beaux paraissent animés d'une flamme étincelante, ta poitrine frémit sous les battements précipités de ton cœur. Un désir ardent s'empare de moi, oui, celui de poser un baiser sur tes joues roses respirant la vie, la jeunesse, la beauté, laisse-moi.

[*Il s'approche de Sophie et cherche à la prendre par la taille.*]

SOPHIE [*se lève de son siège et dit*]. Monsieur, que faites-vous? Vous manquez à tous vos devoirs de convenance, il me semble. Je trouve même que vous êtes très insolent et maladroit dans votre manière d'agir avec moi. Si vous m'aimez comme vous le dites, vous devez me respecter. Tâchez de ne pas vous laisser aller de nouveau à une telle exubération d'esprit.

HENRI [*se levant aussi*]. Insolent! moi quand je brûle d'amour pour vous. J'ai pu me laisser aller à un sentiment d'excitation, je souffre, ma tête se perd. Oh! ma Sophie, bien-aimée, ne soyez pas si cruelle envers moi. [*Il se met à ses pieds.*] Vous me voyez à vos pieds. Pardonnez-moi, chère Sophie, laissez-moi déposer un doux baiser sur vos mains si jolies, si blanches.

[SOPHIE *avance sa main droite sur laquelle il pose un baiser.*]

Oh! merci, chère Sophie, merci. Ce doux baiser que vous avez permis est bien peu, il est vrai, mais il me rend le plus heureux des hommes.

[SOPHIE *dit à* HENRI *de se relever, il se rassied de nouveau à ses côtés.*]

Oh! chère Sophie, laissez-moi déposer un baiser sur cette bouche qui m'a dit: 'Je vous aime' et qui ne mentait pas. Laissez-moi vous presser sur mon cœur qui palpite. Mon cerveau est en feu, je frissonne. Je ne puis supporter plus longtemps cette fièvre qui m'accable, ce désir brûlant qui s'empare de tout mon être. [*Il se rapproche d'elle, l'embrasse tendrement, et lui dit.*] Sophie, ma chère Sophie, soyez à moi, je suis à vous. [*Tous deux se lèvent,* SOPHIE *laisse tomber sa tête sur l'évaule d'*HENRI, *puis ils se retirent, marchant doucement.*

APPENDIX III

SCENE II

Café de l'Hôtel de France

HENRI [*seul*]. Enfin, elle m'a cédé, et ce n'est pas sans peine; cette enfant, elle croyait réellement que j'allais l'épouser! fi donc, une fille sans dot, sans avenir! Moi, son mari! [*Il fait un rire moqueur.*] Moi, qui suis si bien noté comme employé de banque, c'est quelque chose cela! Je ne dis pas qu'elle ne soit jolie, mais voilà tout. La beauté n'est pas l'argent. Oh! argent, Dieu du monde entier devant qui tout le monde se courbe, qui est si souvent cause de tant de bassesses et de crimes, je ne t'adorerai jamais assez, je te cajolerai. Oh! argent, bel argent, ne me quitte jamais, tu vaux mieux que toutes les femmes de la terre. Mais, je réfléchis, ma présence ici est désormais inutile, pendant que cette insensée de Sophie repose, je vais jouer la fille de l'air, et comme un oiseau léger, je me sylphiderai bien vite.

ACT III

[HENRI *has led* SOPHIE *to believe that he has committed suicide.* SOPHIE *has met* LE GÉNÉRAL BOSQUET *on the* Place de l'Hôtel de Ville *in Brussels and been taken under his fatherly protection.*]

SCENE I

The General's apartment

LE GÉNÉRAL. . . . Maintenant, je te prierai de ne jamais prononcer devant moi ce mot de peur et prends pour principe de ne jamais trembler d'avance. Si j'n'avais pas été ainsi, cent mille tonnerres, mes cheveux et moustaches n'auraient pas blanchi sur les champs de bataille à la lueur des flammes du canon et de l'odeur de la poudre. Ce petit ruban rouge que je porte à ma boutonnière, je l'ai bien gagné en risquant ma vie maintes et maintes fois pour ma patrie la France, la première nation du monde! Oh, France, ma patrie, ma chère patrie, où sont-ils nos aînés, tes grands défenseurs patriotes tels que Hoche, Marceau, Kléber, Carnot, Masséna, Augereau, qui ont fait des prodiges et qui pour de l'argent, ce vil métal, n'auraient pas vendu leur courage, leur honneur, en un mot, tout ce qui fait l'homme. Oh, France, chère France, sois toujours la nation des fiers guerriers, les Gaulois, y compris le grand Vercingétorix et les Francs ne te laisseront jamais tomber. Salut! oh, France! Salut!

SOPHIE [*émue*]. C'est bien beau et grand, mon père, ce que vous dites là. Que je suis donc fière de ce que vous m'ayez adoptée comme votre fille. Permettez-moi de vous embrasser. Il serait à souhaiter que tout soldat ait les mêmes sentiments que vous à l'égard de sa patrie.[1]

SCENE II

The same. (The General has fallen mortally ill)

LE GÉNÉRAL [*d'une voix faible*]. Chère enfant, je ne sais ce que j'ai, je ne me sens pas bien du tout. Mes membres, quoique nous soyons en été, sont comme dans un bain de glace. Mon cœur est serré dans un étau, je me meurs, je me . . . meurs!

SOPHIE. Oh! mon père, mon bon père! [*Elle sonne une domestique et lui dit*] Allez vite, chercher un médecin, le plus près d'ici.

[*Un médecin arrive.*]

[1] The date when Rousseau wrote this play is unknown. But this passage suggests a reference to the Affaire Dreyfus.

LE MÉDECIN. Mon Général, ce n'est rien, vous en avez vu bien d'autres ; prenez un bon verre que vous avez près de vous. [*Se retournant vers* SOPHIE, *il lui dit bien bas.*] Votre père est très mal, tout lui remonte au cœur, c'est fini ! Du courage, du courage.

THE GENERAL [*tenant dans les siennes les mains de* SOPHIE *et celle du médecin*]. Adieu, mes enfants, adieu !

[*Le* GÉNÉRAL *meurt.*]

CURTAIN

375

APPENDIX IV: TRIAL OF THE DOUANIER ROUSSEAU

From *Le Temps* January 10, 1909

TRIBUNAUX

Les faux d'un employé de banque

Un homme de trente ans, Gabriel Sauvaget, commis de la Banque de France à la succursale de Meaux, et un vieil artiste peintre, Henri Rousseau, laissé en liberté provisoire en raison de son âge—il a soixante-quatre ans—et peut-être aussi parce qu'il n'a été complice que par excès de complaisance, étaient poursuivis hier devant la cour d'assises de la Seine pour faux et usage de faux.

Le nom du peintre Henri Rousseau est très bien connu de tous les Parisiens. Ancien soldat, ancien douanier—il a déclaré hier à la cour d'assises qu'il avait pris sa retraite après trente-deux ans de service—il ne devait trouver sa voie que parvenu à l'âge de raison: on sait comment! Ses tableaux, depuis quelque vingt ans, sont la joie du public à toutes les expositions des Artistes Indépendants. Soit comme portraitiste, soit comme paysagiste, soit comme peintre allégorique et symbolique, Henri Rousseau y traite tous les genres avec une ferveur sans égale. Du reste, ses tendances ne sont nullement révolutionnaires; bien au contraire. C'est avec une candeur digne d'un meilleur succès qu'il s'attache, comme il peut et comme il sait, aux traditions de l'école.

On se rappelle qu'il y a deux ans l'ancien douanier désireux de célébrer lui aussi après tant d'autres, le rétablissement de la paix entre le tsar et le mikado, les représentait tout nus, debout, et se serrant la main. La police voulut y voir une offense à ces deux souverains, et un commissaire de police fit retirer la toile.[1]

Comment cet artiste pacifique se trouve-t-il aujourd'hui sur les bancs de la cour d'assises? Voici les faits.

Sur les conseils de Sauvaget, Henri Rousseau s'était fait ouvrir dans le nom de Bailly, propriétaire à Lieusaint, et s'était fait remettre un carnet de chèques. Puis, toujours sur les mêmes conseils, il avait fait imprimer à Paris des 'bordereaux du disposition', identiques à ceux dont se servent les succursales de la Banque de France pour aviser les autres agences des versements préalablement effectués en faveur de tel ou tel client. Il avait commandé, en outre, des enveloppes à en-tête de la Banque de France, et de tous points

---

[1] I have not been able to find any other reference to this episode which is not mentioned by The Douanier's biographers. The story, I presume, is a *canard* in some way connected with the picture *Les représentants des puissances étrangères venant saluer la République en signe de paix* exhibited in the *Salon des Indépendants* in 1907. This picture represents a number of European sovereigns—but they are not nude (cf. pp. 219, 363).

semblables à celles dont elle fait usage quand elle correspond avec des directeurs. On devine la suite: Sauvaget établit un 'bordereau de disposition' avertissant la banque de Meaux qu'elle aurait à payer à M. Bailly une somme de 21,000 francs; ce bordereau était revêtu des fausses signatures du directeur et du caissier de la succursale de Melun, et quelques jours plus tard, en produisant les pièces d'identité fabriquées encore par Sauvaget au nom de Bailly, Henri Rousseau présentait à l'agence de Meaux un chèque de 21,000 francs qui lui fut payé sans la moindre difficulté. Il garda 1000 francs et remis le urplus à Sauvaget.

Celui-ci (Sauvaget) a, d'autre part, à répondre d'un détournement de 15,000 francs commis au préjudice de la succursale de la Banque de France de Périgueux, alors qu'il y était employé en 1903. Une lettre contenant 15 billets de 1000 francs destinés à un banquier de Montignac lui avait été remise par un employé de la comptabilité, M. Brousse, pour être pesée. La lettre parvint bien à son destinataire, mais elle contenait, au lieu des billets annoncés, des formules télégraphiques. M. Brousse, poursuivi devant les assises, fut heureusement acquitté. Sauvaget était le coupable. Il a avoué ce détournement et les faux. Henri Rousseau reconnaît de son côté le rôle qu'il a joué dans le nom de Bailly. Ils sont défendus par Mes Charles Lebreton et Guilhermet. Me Ulrich se présente pour la Banque de France.

L'arrêt sera rendu aujourd'hui.

From *Le Temps*, 11 Janvier 1909

TRIBUNAUX

Les faux d'un employé de banque

Sous ce titre, nous avons conté hier les exploits de ce commis de la Banque de France, Gabriel Sauvaget, et M. son malheureux complice, Henri Rousseau, l'ancien douanier devenu peintre, et dont les envois aux Salons des Artistes Indépendants firent la joie du public, accusés de faux et usage de faux.

Après plaidoiries de Me Ulrich pour la Banque de France, et Mes Lebreton et Guilhermet, Sauvaget a été condamné à cinq ans de reclusion, et Henri Rousseau à deux ans de prison avec sursis et aussi à une amende de 100 francs. Ils sont, en outre, condamnés solidairement à 21,000 fr. de restitution.

'Je vous remercie bien,' a dit au président en se retirant le vieux 'peintre' Rousseau. 'Je ferai le portrait de votre dame.[1]'

[1] For references to the trial in my text, cf. pp. 225, 245, 246, 247, 361.

GENERAL INDEX

INDEX

INDEX

INDEX

Eiffel, Gustave, 146
    Tower, The, 97
Elgar, Sir Edward, 228
El Greco, 78, 188, 190, 213, 260
    acquisition by Louvre of pictures by, 145 and n
    Degas and a picture by, 192
Elks, Mr. and Mrs. (dancers), 213
Eluard, Paul, 238, 277, 294, 302, 307, 324
Elysée Montmartre, The, 125, 126
Emperaire, Achille, portrait of, 10 and n, 58
    alluded to, 57
Ensor, James, surrealism of, 23, 207
    foundation member of *Les XX* society, 48
    Masques Scandalisées, 48, 142
    Meuble hanté, 86
    Cauchemar, 86
    his satirical *L'entrée du Christ à Bruxelles en 1889*,
      100, 154, 207
    Poissardes mélancoliques, 142
    and the 1901 *Salon des Indépendants*, 165
    alluded to, 263, 324
Epstein, Jacob, 255, 239
    his monument to Wilde, 232
Ernst, Max, alluded to, 263, 276, 297, 300, 302,
      303, 304, 313, 320, 325
    and Neo-Surrealist *collage*, 276, 280, 282, 286,
      294, 298, 368
    and Neo-Surrealist *frottage*, 280, 281, 307,
      310, 368
    and Russian Ballet, 309
    Histoire naturelle, 309
    Fatagaga, 276
    La femme 100 têtes, 314
Esterhazy, Major, 157
    tried for treason, 163
    flees to England, 163
Etchells, F., 239
Eugénie, Empress, 13, 24, 25, 233
Esprit Nouveau (see *L'esprit Nouveau*)
Exposition Centennale, The, 136, 161, 162, 179
Exposition des Arts Décoratifs, 307
Exposition des peintres Impressionistes et Symbolistes, The,
    142 (see Nabis)
Exposition Universelle of 1867, 21
    1878, 41
    1889, 97 (the Salon of), 98
    1900, 161, 179
    1937, 286, 324, 325
Expressionism, 80, 198, 273
    Cubist, 224
    Segonzac's, 228, 231
    Van Gogh and, 260
    Vlaminck's, 260
    Rouault's, 287, 314
    Fauve, 296
    Soutine's, 301

Fallières, 216
Fantin-Latour, alluded to, 18, 49
    Hommage à Delacroix, 18

Fantin-Latour
    Un coin de table, 30, 168, 169
    and First Impressionist Exhibition, 33
    L'atelier des Batignolles, 61
Fascism, 157, 226, 286
Faure, Elie, 256
Fauré, Gabriel, 305
Faure, Félix, 163
    (singer), 34, 40, 53, 54, 55, 122
Fauve movement, The, 80, 136, 138, 140, 160,
    165, 197, 213, 238, 263, 272, 274, 309,
    325, App. 367
    its character discussed, 140, 165, 197–8
    origin of the term 'Fauve', 213
    First Exhibition of, 168, 211
    artists of, 140, 168, 197, 198, 201, 215, 221
    Rhythmic Fauvism, 200–1
    Derain and, 201, 221, 294
    and the *Salon des Indépendants*, 212, 214, 216,
      221
    and the *Salon d'Automne*, 140, 168, 212, 216
    Braque's début with, 213
    the dilettanti and, 136
    the public and, 231
    the Van-Gogh-Fauve-Expressionist tradition,
      260
Favre, Jules, 26
Fédération des Artistes, founded by the Commune
    (1871), 29
    rules and members of, 29
Fels, Florent, 274, 302
Fénéon, Félix, alluded to, xxvii, 214 (Pl. 37B),
    (Pl. 50B), 348, 349
    founds *Revue Indépendante*, 85
    Les Impressionistes en 1886, 88
    defends the Divisionists, 88
    publishes Laforgue's *Moralités légendaires*, 92
    one of Seurat's executors, 108
    praises the Nabis, 142
    art critic of *La Revue Blanche*, 148
    Secretary-General of *La Revue Blanche*, 162
    arranges a Seurat Exhibition, 162
    and the anarchist outrages, 152
    in *Le procès des Trente*, 152
    directeur artistique for Bernheim Jeune, 215,
      221
    and Matisse, 221
Ferry, Jules, 23, 32, 42, 50, 91, 96
Fête Nationale, Le, 50
Fiquet, Hortense, 30, 41, 57–9, 114, 115
Flaubert, *Madame Bovary*, 4, 45
    alluded to, 34, 36
    on Manet, 43
Flechtheim, Alfred, 273, 361
Fokine, Michel, 212, 224, 227, 230, 233, 238
Fontainas, 177
Forain, alluded to, 28, 30, 36, 42, 45, 47, 58, 88,
    123, 125, 137, 141, 296, 320
    Cabinet particulier, 43
    Coulisses de l'Opéra, 43

INDEX

INDEX

INDEX

INDEX

INDEX

INDEX

Renoir, Pierre Auguste
  Manet on, 61
  makes money by portraits, 61, 62, 117
  marriage of, 62
  travels of, 62, 117, 190
  Wagner sits to, 62
  his illness, 62–3, 191, 248–9
  and the Classical Renaissance, 73, 117
  abandons Realist-Impressionism, 75
  on Rousseau, 81, 120
  his detestation of Hugo, 87
  and Eighth Impressionist Exhibition, 87, 88
  and Zola's *L'œuvre*, 90
  models of, 118, 190, 191
  Lautrec and, 125
  'compromising' period of, 136
  influences Matisse, 139
  and Caillebotte, 149
  and l'Affaire Dreyfus, 157
  the sons of, 190
  on Goya, 190
  on Rembrandt and Watteau, 190
  on El Greco, 190
  work in the 'nineties' of, 190
  growing success of, 191, 248
  on Degas as sculptor, 193
  death of, 209, 249, 295
  his sculptured *Vénus*, 232, 249
  and the German invasion (1914), 249
  later work of, 249
  works by, in London (Grafton Galleries) Exhibition, 370
  Barnes Foundation's collection of works by, 319, 337
  the 1933 exhibition of works by, 323, 337
  Bibliographical note on, App. 337
Works by:
  Canotiers à Chatou (Pl. 6A), 5, 6, 22, 31, 74
  Le Moulin de la Galette (Pl. 9B), xix, 5, 7, 8, 39, 40, 49, 63, 74, 75, 83
  La balançoire, 8, 39
  Sur la terrasse (Pl. 12), 8
  Esmeralda, 18 and n, 60, 61
  Soirée d'été, 18, 60
  Diane chasseresse, 18
  Le cabaret de la mère Anthony, 19, 20 and n
  Lise, 22, 60
  Baigneuse au griffon, 22, 61
  La femme d'Algers (Pl. 6B), 22, 61
  Le capitaine Darras, 30, 61
  Parisiennes habillées en Algériennes, 31
  L'allée cavalière du Bois de Boulogne, 31
  La loge, 33, 34, 63, 162
  La petite danseuse, 33, 62, 161
  La promenade, 34
  La source, 34
  La serre, 34
  La fillette attentive, 37
  Mme Charpentier et ses enfants, 42, 43, 62, 248
  Mlle Samary, 43, 62

Renoir, Pierre Auguste
  Works by:
    Mlle Irène Cahan, 46, 63
    Le déjeuner des canotiers, 47, 63
    La femme à l'éventail, 47, 117
    Portrait de Wagner (Pl. 14), 47, 49, 62 and n, **63**
    La baigneuse blonde (Pl. 16), 8, 49, 62, 63
    La danse à la campagne, 49, 63
    La danse à la ville, 49, 63
    Le poirier d'Angleterre, 61
    Mme Darras, 61
    Mme Maitre, 61
    La famille Henriot, 61
    La jeune fille au chat, 62, 162
    Femme cousant au bouquet, 62
    La tasse de chocolat, 62
    Paysage à Wargemont, 62
    La fête de Pan, 62
    Pêcheuses de moules, 62
    Gondole sur le Grand Canal, 62
    La liseuse, 63
    La bucheronne, 63
    La fillette au faucon, 63
    Les rosiers à Wargemont, 63
    Venise, 63
    Claude Monet, 63
    Les grandes baigneuses (Pl. 19B), 75, 87, 88, 93, 117, 136, 190, 209
    Les parapluies, 75, 249
    La montagne Sainte-Victoire, 100, 118
    Mlle Chapuis au cerceau, 117
    Le parti de volant, 117
    Femme allaitant son enfant, 117, 249
    L'enfant au chat, 117
    La natte, 117
    Les trois filles de Catulle Mendès, 117
    Les chapeaux d'été, 118
    La vendeuse de pommes, 118
    Nu dans l'eau, 118
    La tasse de thé, 162
    La couseuse, 162
    La famille de l'artiste, 190
    Berthe Morisot et sa fille, 190
    Femme et enfant dans un parc, 191
    Les femmes aux chapeaux (Pl. 65), 209, 248
    Les grandes laveuses (Pl. 71A), 209, 232
    Le jugement de Paris (Pl. 71B), 232, 248
    Jeune fille assise, 239
    La première sortie, 315
  Other works by, App. 337–45
Republic, The Third, first years of, 26 et seq., 32, 38
Republicanism, 23, 25, 28, 38, 40, 50
  Mme Charpentier's *Salon*, 34, 39
  the Pope and, 106
Respighi, 294, 305
Reuillard, 308
Reverdy, 300
Revue Blanche, The, 162, 186, 214
  ceases publication, 168
  literary contributors to, 168

414

INDEX

Reynolds, Sir Joshua, 269
Rhode Island (School of Design), 42, 76
Rhythm, in dancing, 75
    in Gauguin's art, 78, 79, 99, 131
    in Matisse's art, 79, 200, 258, 259. 288
    in Lautrec's art, 135
    in Renoir's art, 209
    in Braque's art, 288
    in Chirico's art, 308
Rhythmic decoration, in Abstract Art, 200, 201
Ribera, 4 and n
Richepin, Jean, 93, 103, 188
Richmond, Sir W. B., 144
Rieti, 314
Right Extremists, Political, artists suffer from, 12,
    13, 14, 38–41, 96, 105, 270, 271, 323
    in the Third Republic, 32
    La Ligue des Patriotes, 50, 96, 163
    and Boulanger, 95, 96
    and the Panama scandal, 146
    and l'Affaire Dreyfus, 153
    and the Liberal Government, 164
    and Zola's death, 167
    anglophobia of, 169
    organize the *Camelots du Roi*, 216, 225, 240
    (*See also* Déroulede, Drumont, *Spectre Rouge* and
    Anti-Semitism)
Rimbaud, alluded to, 25, 27, 28, 30, 281, 320
    and André Gill, 28, 220
    and Verlaine, 30, 31, 32, 47
    the *Voyelles* sonnet quoted, 31, 105
    Illuminations, 31, 90
    in Stuttgart, 35
    at Aden, 47
    in Abyssinia, 91 n
    on General Gordon and Lord Wolseley, 91 n
    return from Abyssinia, 105 n
    death of, 105 n
Rimsky-Korsakov, 212, 218, 222, 227, 230, 237,
    238, 257
Rivière (critic), Georges, 34
    L'Impressioniste review, 40
    Cézanne and, 58, 212
Rivière, Henri, shadow plays by, 103, 140 and n
Rivoire, André, 188
Robert, Hubert, 289
Roberts, W., 239
Robinson, Edward G., 30
Rochefort, Henri, alluded to, 23, 24, 32, 36, 91 n
    deported, 32
    escapes from Noumea, 34
    Manet's portrait of, 46
    (*See* Pain)
Rockefeller, Mrs. J. D., 312, 314
Rodin, Auguste, and the Franco-Prussian war, 24
    first *Salon* exhibit, *L'homme au nez cassé*, 35
    Victor Hugo and, 36
    his bust of Clémenceau, 45 n, 232
    alluded to, 98, 101, 167, 215, 224, 225, 324
    his statue of Balzac, 95, 159

Rodin, Auguste
    show with Monet (1899), 100
    his bust of Becque, 147
    Les bourgeois de Calais, 151
    drawings by, 155
    one-man show in *Exposition Centennale* (1900)
    162
    moves to Meudon, 162
    art school of, 162
    and Rousseau, 183
    and the twenty-first *Salon des Indépendants*, 214
    his studios in Hotel Biron, 221
    and *apaches*, 234
    death of, 256
Roerich, 224, 237
Rolland, Romain, 295
Romains, Jules, 230, 244, 296, 302
Romanov, 237
Romantic Movement, The, discussed, 3
    Romantic-realism (*see* Realism)
    Cézanne influenced by, 10
    alluded to, 67, 268
    distortions, 78
    Romantic Expressionism (*see* Expressionism)
    Van Gogh and, 80, 260
    Picasso as Romantic, 138, 199–201
    Derain as Romantic-Realist, 294
    Chirico as Romantic, 298, 306
    Neo-Surrealism as a new Romantic movement,
    279–80, 283
Rops, Félicien, 45, 95
Rosa, Salvator, 208
Rose-Croix movement (and group), The, alluded
    to, 72, 79, 105, 131, 136, 137, 143, 160
    Rose-Croix Salon, 141
    Rose-Croix concerts, 141
    second *Rose-Croix Salon*, 144
    surrealism and, 207
    (*See* Péladan and Satie)
Rosenberg, Léonce, 232, 256, 274, 275, 294, 296,
    297, 301, 304, 307, 313, 314
    Cubisme et Tradition, 296, 368
    Cubisme et Empirisme, 297–8, 368
    L'effort Moderne (*see*)
    Picasso's drawing of, 256
Rosenberg, Paul, xxvii, 34, 79, 98, 99, 102, 104,
    150, 207, 221, 299, 300, 303, 306, 308,
    318, 323
    his *Exhibition of French Nineteenth Century Paint-
    ing* (London), 324
Rosny, 105
Rossetti, quoted, on the French School, 18
    alluded to, 279
Rossini, Cocteau on, 16 and n
    La boutique fantasque ballet, 294
Rostand, Edmond, *Les Romanesques*, 148
    Cyrano de Bergerac, 156
    La Samaritaine, 156
    L'aiglon, 162
    Chantecler, 227

415

INDEX